ARTIFICIAL INTELLIGENCE APPLICATIONS AND INNOVATIONS III

IFIP – The International Federation for Information Processing

IFIP was founded in 1960 under the auspices of UNESCO, following the First World Computer Congress held in Paris the previous year. An umbrella organization for societies working in information processing, IFIP's aim is two-fold: to support information processing within its member countries and to encourage technology transfer to developing nations. As its mission statement clearly states,

> *IFIP's mission is to be the leading, truly international, apolitical organization which encourages and assists in the development, exploitation and application of information technology for the benefit of all people.*

IFIP is a non-profitmaking organization, run almost solely by 2500 volunteers. It operates through a number of technical committees, which organize events and publications. IFIP's events range from an international congress to local seminars, but the most important are:

- The IFIP World Computer Congress, held every second year;
- Open conferences;
- Working conferences.

The flagship event is the IFIP World Computer Congress, at which both invited and contributed papers are presented. Contributed papers are rigorously refereed and the rejection rate is high.

As with the Congress, participation in the open conferences is open to all and papers may be invited or submitted. Again, submitted papers are stringently refereed.

The working conferences are structured differently. They are usually run by a working group and attendance is small and by invitation only. Their purpose is to create an atmosphere conducive to innovation and development. Refereeing is less rigorous and papers are subjected to extensive group discussion.

Publications arising from IFIP events vary. The papers presented at the IFIP World Computer Congress and at open conferences are published as conference proceedings, while the results of the working conferences are often published as collections of selected and edited papers.

Any national society whose primary activity is in information may apply to become a full member of IFIP, although full membership is restricted to one society per country. Full members are entitled to vote at the annual General Assembly, National societies preferring a less committed involvement may apply for associate or corresponding membership. Associate members enjoy the same benefits as full members, but without voting rights. Corresponding members are not represented in IFIP bodies. Affiliated membership is open to non-national societies, and individual and honorary membership schemes are also offered.

ARTIFICIAL INTELLIGENCE APPLICATIONS AND INNOVATIONS III

Proceedings of the 5TH IFIP Conference on Artificial Intelligence Applications and Innovations (AIAI'2009), April 23-25, 2009, Thessaloniki, Greece

Edited by

Iliadis
Democritus University of Thrace
Greece

Maglogiannis
University of Central
Greece

Tsoumakas
Aristotle University of Thessaloniki
Greece

Vlahavas
Aristotle University of Thessaloniki
Greece

Bramer
University of Portsmouth
United Kingdom

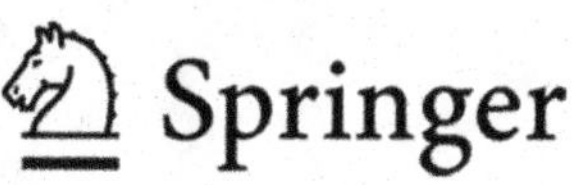

Artificial Intelligence Applications and Innovations III

Edited by Lazaros Iliadis, Ioannis Vlahavas and Max Bramer

p. cm. (IFIP International Federation for Information Processing, a Springer Series in Computer Science)

ISSN: 1571-5736 / 1861-2288 (Internet)
ISBN: 978-1-4419-5497-8
eISBN: 978-1-4419-0221-4

Printed on acid-free paper

9 8 7 6 5 4 3 2 1

springer.com

Preface

The ever expanding abundance of information and computing power enables researchers and users to tackle highly interesting issues, such as applications providing personalized access and interactivity to multimodal information based on user preferences and semantic concepts or human-machine interface systems utilizing information on the affective state of the user. The general focus of the AIAI conference is to provide insights on how AI can be implemented in real world applications.

This volume contains papers selected for presentation at the 5th IFIP Conference on Artificial Intelligence Applications & Innovations (AIAI 2009) being held from 23rd till 25th of April, in Thessaloniki, Greece. The IFIP AIAI 2009 conference is co-organized by the Aristotle University of Thessaloniki, by the University of Macedonia Thessaloniki and by the Democritus University of Thrace. AIAI 2009 is the official conference of the WG12.5 "Artificial Intelligence Applications" working group of IFIP TC12 the International Federation for Information Processing Technical Committee on Artificial Intelligence (AI).

It is a conference growing and maintaining high standards of quality. The purpose of the 5th IFIP AIAI Conference is to bring together researchers, engineers and practitioners interested in the technical advances and business / industrial applications of intelligent systems. AIAI 2009 is not only focused in providing insights on how AI can be implemented in real world applications, but it also covers innovative methods, tools and ideas of AI on architectural and algorithmic level.

The response to the 'Call for Papers' was overwhelming resulting in the submission of 113 high quality full papers. All contributions were reviewed by two independent academic referees. A third referee was consulted in some cases with conflicting reviews after the submission of the reviews was officially over. Finally, 30 full papers and 32 short papers were accepted. This amounts to an acceptance rate of 27% for full papers and 28% for short ones. The authors of the accepted papers come from 19 countries from all over the world. The collection of papers that were included in the proceedings offer stimulating insights into emerging applications of AI and describe advanced prototypes, systems, tools and techniques. The 2009 AIAI Proceedings will interest not only academics and researchers, but also IT professionals and consultants by examining technologies and applications of demonstrable value.

Two Keynote speakers are invited to make interesting presentations on innovative and state of the art aspects of AI:

1. Professor Nikolaos Bourbakis, Associate Dean for Engineering Research, Distinguished Professor of Information Technology and Director of the ATR Center at Wright State University will talk about "*Synergies of AI Methods for Robotic Planning & Grabbing, Facial Expressions Recognition, and Blind's Navigation*".

2. Professor Dominic Palmer-Brown, Dean, Metropolitan University London, UK, will talk about "*Neural Networks for Modal and Virtual Learning*".

We would like to express our thanks to the Program Committee chair, Associate Professor L. Iliadis, to the Workshop chair, Assistant Professor N. Bassiliades, and to the Organizing Committee chair Professor Yannis Manolopoulos, for their crucial help in organizing this event. Special thanks are also due to the co-editors of the proceedings, Assistant Professor Ilias Maglogiannis and Lecturer Gregory Tsoumakas.

The AIAI 2009 conference comprises of the following seven (7) main thematic Sessions:

- *Machine Learning and Classification*
- *Knowledge Engineering and Decision Support Systems*
- *Ontologies and Knowledge Representation*
- *AI in Medical Informatics & Biomedical Engineering*
- *Signal and Image Processing for Knowledge Extraction*
- *Artificial Intelligence Applications*
- *Intelligent Environments and HCI*

Also Workshops on various specific AI application areas, such as Software Engineering, Bioinformatics and Medicine, Learning, Environment, have been scheduled.

The wide range of topics and high level of contributions will surely guarantee a very successful conference. We express our special thanks to all who have contributed to the organization and scientific contents of this conference, first to the authors and reviewers of the papers, as well as the members of the Program and Organization Committees.

Ioannis Vlahavas
Max Bramer

Organization of the AIAI'2009 Conference

General Conference Chairs

Ioannis Vlahavas, Aristotle University of Thessaloniki, Greece
Max Bramer, University of Portsmouth, UK

Program Committee Chair

Lazaros Iliadis, Democritus University of Thrace, Greece

Workshop Chair

Nick Bassiliades, Aristotle University of Thessaloniki, Greece

Proceedings co-Editors

I. Maglogiannis, University of Central Greece
G. Tsoumakas, Aristotle University of Thessaloniki, Greece

Organizing Committee

Y. Manolopoulos, Aristotle University of Thessaloniki, chair
N. Dimokas, Aristotle University of Thessaloniki
A. Gounaris, Aristotle University of Thessaloniki
M. Kontaki, Aristotle University of Thessaloniki
A. Papadopoulos, Aristotle University of Thessaloniki
D. Rafailidis, Aristotle University of Thessaloniki
S. Stavroulakis, Aristotle University of Thessaloniki

Program Committee Members

P. Agelov, Lancaster University, UK
C. Badica, University of Craiova, Romania
J. Debenham, University of Technology, Sydney, Australia
Y. Demazeau, CNRS, LIG Laboratory, France
A. Fanni, University of Cagliari, Italy

C. Georgiadis, University of Macedonia, Thessaloniki, Greece
I. Hatzilygeroudis, University of Patras, Greece
M. Hilario, CUI - University of Geneva, Switzerland
A. Kameas, Hellenic Open University, Greece
V. Karkaletsis, NCSR Demokritos, Greece
C. Karpouzis, National Technical University of Athens, Greece
P. Kefalas, City College, Thessaloniki, Greece
D. Kosmopoulos, NCSR Demokritos, Greece
K. Kotropoulos, Aristotle University of Thessaloniki, Greece
M. Koumbarakis, University of Athens, Greece
S. Lecoeuche, Ecole des Mines de Douai, France
G. Leonardi, University of Pavia, Italy
A. Likas, University of Ioannina, Greece
I. Maglogiannis, University of Central Greece
F. Makedon, University of Texas Arlington, USA
S. Montani, University del Piemonte Orientale, Italy
E. Onaindia, Technical University of Valencia, Spain
D. Palmer-Brown, Metropolitan University, UK
H. Papadopoulos, Frederick University of Cyprus
C. Pattichis, University of Cyprus
W. Pedrycz, University of Alberta, Canada
E. Pimenidis University of East London, UK
G. Potamias, FORTH, Greece
I. Refanidis, University of Macedonia, Thessaloniki, Greece
H. Reichgelt, Georgia Southern University, USA
I. Sakellariou, University of Macedonia, Thessaloniki, Greece
P. Y. Schobbens, Institut d'Informatique, Belgium
T. Sellis, National Technical University of Athens, Greece
S. Senatore, University of Salerno, Italy
S. Spartalis, Democritus University of Thrace, Greece
C. Spyropoulos, NCSR Demokritos, Greece
A. Stafylopatis, National Technical University of Athens, Greece
V. Terziyan, University of Jyvaskyla, Finland
A. Tsadiras, TEI of Thessaloniki, Greece
D. Tsaptsinos, Kingston University, UK
G. Tsoumakas, Aristotle University of Thessaloniki, Greece
V. Verykios, University of Thessaly, Greece
G. Vouros, Aegean University, Greece
D. Vrakas, Aristotle University of Thessaloniki, Greece

Table of Contents

Ontologies and Knowledge Representation

Full papers

Short papers

Signal and Image Processing for Knowledge Extraction

Full papers

Short papers

Artificial Intelligence Applications

Full papers

Synergies of AI methods for Robotic Planning and Grabbing, Facial Expressions Recognition and Blind's Navigation

Nikolaos G. Bourbakis

Information Technology Research Institute &

Department of Computer Science and Engineering

Wright State University

3640 Colonel Glenn Highway

Dayton, Ohio 45435-0001

USA, bourbaki@cs.wright.edu

Abstract Artificial Intelligent (AI) techniques have reached an acceptable level of maturity as single entities and their application to small and simple problems have offered impressive results. For large scale and complex problems, however, these AI methods individually are not always capable to offer satisfactory results. Thus, synergies of AI methods are used to overcome difficulties and provide solutions to large scale complex problems. This talk presents several synergies of AI methods for solving different complex problems. In particular, the first synergy combines AI planning, stochastic Petri-nets and neural nets for coordinating two robotic hands for boxes placement, and neuro-fuzzy nets for robotic hand grabbing. The second synergy is based on neural color constancy for skin detection and enriched with fuzzy image segmentation & regions synthesis and local global (LG) graphs method for biometrics application by detecting faces and recognizing facial expressions. The third synergy uses several image processing and computer vision techniques in combination with formal modeling of vibrations to offer to the blind 3D sensations of the surrounding space for safe navigation. Examples from other synergistic methodologies, such as, body motion-tracking and robotic 3D brain surgery are also presented.

Please use the following format when citing this chapter:

Bourbakis, N.G., 2009, in IFIP International Federation for Information Processing, Volume 296; *Artificial Intelligence Applications and Innovations III*; Eds. Iliadis, L., Vlahavas, I., Bramer, M.; (Boston: Springer), pp. 1–1.

Neural Networks for Modal and Virtual Learning

Dominic Palmer-Brown

Dean of Computing Faculty

London Metropolitan University

166-220 Holoway Road,

London N7 8DB

UK, d.palmer-brown@londonmet.ac.uk

Abstract This talk will explore the integration of learning modes into a single neural network structure in order to overcome the inherent limitations of any given mode (for example some modes memorize specific features, others average across features and both approaches may be relevant according to the circumstances). Inspiration comes from neuroscience, cognitive science and human learning, where it is impossible to build a serious model of learning without consideration of multiple modes; and motivation also comes from non-stationary input data, or time variant learning oblectives, where the optimal mode is a function of time. Several modal learning ideas will be presented, including the Snap-Drift Neural Network which toggles its learning (across the network or on a neuron-by-neuron basis) between two modes, either unsupervised or guided by performance feedback (reinforcement) and an adaptive function Neural Network (ADFUNN) in which adaption applies simultaneously to both the weights and the individual neuron activation functions. The talk will also focus on a virtual learning environment example that involves the modal learning Neural Network, identifying patterns of student learning that can be used to target diagnostic feedback that guides the learner towards increased states of knowledge.

Please use the following format when citing this chapter:

Palmer-Brown, D., 2009, in IFIP International Federation for Information Processing, Volume 296; *Artificial Intelligence Applications and Innovations III*; Eds. Iliadis, L., Vlahavas, I., Bramer, M.; (Boston: Springer), pp. 2–2.

A Hybrid Technology for Operational Decision Support in Pervasive Environments

Alexander Smirnov, Tatiana Levashova, Nikolay Shilov, Alexey Kashevnik

St.Petersburg Institute for Informatics and Automation of the Russian Academy of Sciences (SPIIRAS), 39, 14th line, St.Petersburg, 199178, Russia
{smir, oleg, nick, alexey}@iias.spb.su

Abstract The paper addresses the issue of development of a technology for operational decision support in a pervasive environment. The technology is built around the idea of using Web-services for self-organization of heterogeneous resources of the environment for decision support purposes. The approach focuses on three types of resources to be organized: information, problem-solving, and acting. The final purpose of the resource self-organization is to form an ad-hoc collaborative environment, members of which cooperate with the aim to serve the current needs according to the decision situation. The hybrid technology proposed in the paper integrates technologies of ontology management, context management, constraint satisfaction, Web-services, and intelligent agents. The application of the technology is illustrated by response to a traffic accident.

1 Introduction

Pervasive environment consists of increasing number of heterogeneous resources communicating through interconnected network. These resources produce large volumes of information and provide different services. The goal of pervasive computing is to enable computing anywhere at anytime. This goal can be achieved through spontaneous organization of the surrounding resources in a context aware manner to meet the real-time needs.

The paper proposes a hybrid technology intended for operational decision support in a pervasive environment. It combines technologies of ontology management, context management, constraint satisfaction, Web-services, and intelligent agents. The technology sustains context-sensitive self-organization of the surrounding resources according to a decision situation (a situation in which decisions are to be made). The purpose of the resource self-organization is to form an ad-hoc resource collaborative environment, members of which cooperate with the aim to serve the current needs of the operational decision support.

Please use the following format when citing this chapter:

Smirnov, A., Levashova, T., Shilov, N. and Kashevnik, A., 2009, in IFIP International Federation for Information Processing, Volume 296; *Artificial Intelligence Applications and Innovations III*; Eds. Iliadis, L., Vlahavas, I., Bramer, M.; (Boston: Springer), pp. 3–12.

The idea behind is to use Web-services as mediators between the pervasive environment and the surrounding resources. It is proposed to represent the resources by sets of Web-services. The set of Web-services representing each resource implements the functionality of this resource. This makes it possible to replace the self-organization of resources with that between the Web-services. In terms of this replacement the resource collaborative environment is correspond to an ad-hoc service network.

The decision situation is modeled at two levels: abstract and operational. At the abstract level the decision situation is represented by the *abstract context* that is an ontology-based model of this situation expressed by constraints. At the operational level the decision situation is represented by the *operational context* that is an instantiated abstract context. The operational context is produced by the self-organized service network representing resources to be collaborated.

The decision support system (DSS) built upon the hybrid technology is based on service-oriented architecture. The architecture enables interaction with the heterogeneous resources using the ad-hoc Web-service network and Web-service communications using an agent-based service model [1].

2 Hybrid Technology

The hybrid technology sustaining operational decision support in pervasive environments is based on ontology engineering, ontology management, context management, constraint satisfaction, profiling, Web Services, and intelligent agents. These technologies are applied depending on the objectives the DSS meets at the particular moment (Table 1).

Effects and advantages of exploiting ontology in DSSs are universally recognized now [2]. The approach offered here uses application ontology (AO) for representation of the knowledge of the application domain. The AO is created by subject experts, knowledge and ontology engineers. It either can be created from scratch or through integration of existing ontologies. In the former case *ontology engineering* technology is used. In the latter case ontology engineering technology is integrated with *ontology management*. The AO is specified by means of the formalism of object-oriented constraint networks (OOCN) [3] in order that tasks specified in this ontology can be solved as constraint satisfaction problem (CSP).

Resources are represented by sets of *Web-services*. To provide the Web-services with semantics [4] the Web-service descriptions are aligned against the AO. Alignment is an objective of *ontology engineering* and *ontology management*.

The technologies mentioned up to this point are involved at a preliminary stage preceded to the stage of decision support. The stage of decision support starts with introducing the decision situation to the DSS through the user (decision maker) request. The request specifies the type of the situation to be modeled.

Table 1. Technological framework

Objectives	Techniques	Technology	Result in terms of OOCN
AO building	Integration of existing ontologies, knowledge formalisation	Ontology engineering, ontology management	OOCN without variable values
Representation of resource functionalities	Alignment of the AO and Web-service descriptions	Ontology engineering, ontology management, Web-services	OOCN without variable values
Extraction and integration of relevant knowledge	Abstract context composition	Ontology management	General problem model
Self-organization of Web-services	Agent interactions	Intelligent agents	Instantiated problem model
Gathering and processing of relevant information	Operational context producing	Context management, Web-services	Instantiated problem model
Search for a solution	Problem solving	Constraint satisfaction, Web-services	A set of feasible solutions
User preferences revealing	Context-based accumulation of made decisions	Profiling	A set of user constraints

Based on the type of the situation the DSS extracts knowledge relevant to this type from the AO and integrates it in the *abstract context* that is an ontology-based model of the situation. The knowledge is extracted along with Web-services, descriptions of which are aligned against this knowledge. To operate on the extraction of knowledge and its integration *ontology management* methods are applied.

The abstract context is the base for self-organization of Web-services that have been included in the abstract context, into a service network. The purpose of the service network is the organization of a resource collaborative environment for producing an *operational context* and for taking joint actions required in the situation. The operational context is the instantiated abstract context or an instantiated model of the decision situation. The operational context is interpreted as CSP by the service network using the *constraint satisfaction technology*.

Self-organization of the Web-services is carried out through negotiation of their needs and possibilities. To make the Web-services active components capable to self-organize an agent-based service model is used. *Intelligent agents* negotiate services' needs and possibilities in terms of the AO negotiating input (service needs) and output (service possibilities) arguments of the functions that the Web-services implement. To operate on the producing the operational context technologies of *context management, Web-services*, and *intelligent agents* are involved.

The decision situation (the operational context) and a set of solutions for tasks represented in this context are presented to the decision maker. The solution chosen by the decision maker is considered to be the decision. The abstract and operational contexts, the set of solutions, and the decision are saved. The DSS uses them for revealing user preferences. This is the focus of the *profiling* technology.

3 Service-Oriented Architecture

In the architecture (Fig. 1) of the DSS intended for functioning in a pervasive environment two types of Web-services are distinguished: *core Web-services* and *operational Web-services*.

The core Web-services are intended to support the DSS users and the abstract context creation. These Web-services comprise:

- **UserProfileService** creates, modifies, and updates the user profile; provides access to this profile; collects information about the user; accumulates information about the made decisions in a context-based way; reveals user preferences;
- **UserInteractionsService** is responsible for interactions of the DSS with its users. It communicates between the DSS and its users providing DSS messages, context-sensitive help, pictures of decision situations, results of problem solving, and delivering information from the users to the DSS;
- **AOAccessService** provides access to the AO;
- **AbstractContextService** creates, stores, and reuses abstract contexts;
- **ManagementService** manages Web-services to create the abstract context. It operates with the service registry where the core services are registered.

The operational Web-services self-organize a Web-service network. In the ar-

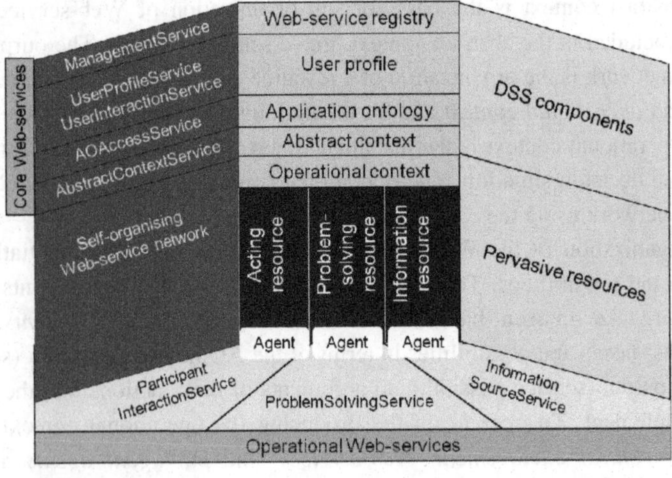

Fig. 1. Service-oriented architecture

chitecture the information, problem-solving, and acting resources are distinguished. The information resources are resources providing information to the abstract context from the information sources. The problem-solving resources are computational modules, applications, services, *etc.* that can be used to solve problems formalized in the abstract context. The acting resources are organizations and persons acting in decision situations according to their roles.

The set of operational Web-services comprises:

- **InformationSourceService** – a set of Web-services responsible for interactions with information sources of different types and for processing information provided by these sources. The following main types of information sources are distinguished: *sensors*, *databases*, *Web-sites*, and *humans*;
- **ProblemSolvingService** – a set of Web-services in charge of problem solving.
- **ParticipantInteractionService** that is a set of Web-services responsible for support of and interactions with acting resources. They provide communication between the DSS and human representatives of the acting resources.

4 Case Study: Traffic Accident

The hybrid technology is illustrated by decision support to response to a traffic accident that was caused by the ignition in the car petrol tank. The AO used for this purpose represents knowledge of the emergency management domain.

As soon as the DSS receives the information that a traffic accident had happened, the DSS creates or reuses the abstract context characterizing the accident situation. An exemplified piece of the abstract context (the taxonomy) for the traffic accident is shown in Fig. 2. Because of the petrol tank ignition the context combines knowledge required to response to both traffic accident and fire event.

Within the abstract context the acting resources fall into classes *Actor* and *Job Role*. The *emergency medical service organisation* is responsible for providing emergency teams (*emergency medical technicians* in Fig. 2), *ambulances*, and *rescue helicopters* for emergency medical care of injured people and / or for transportation them to *hospitals*. The *fire department* is responsible for providing firefighter brigades (*firefighters* in Fig. 2), *fire trucks*, and *fire helicopters* for fire extinguishing. *Local police organisation* is responsible for providing *police officers* and *police trucks* to investigate the accident and to go through formalities. Two types of transportation are possible: *Air transportation* used by fire and rescue helicopters and *Automobile transportation* used by ambulances, fire trucks, and police trucks.

Problem solving knowledge is collapsed in the class *Emergency Response*. This class formalizes tasks to be solved to respond to the traffic accident. They are as follows.

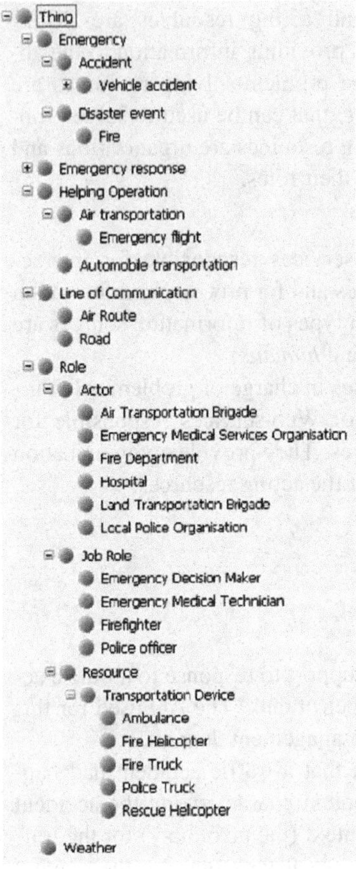

Fig. 2. Abstract context: taxonomy

- The task *Quantity of emergency teams and firefighter brigades* calculates the required quantity of these kinds of groups.
- The task *Brigade availability* determines the availability of emergency and traffic police teams, and firefighter brigades.
- The task *Brigade location* determines the current location of emergency and traffic police teams, and firefighter brigades.
- The task *Hospital availability* returns a list of hospitals of the region, hospital addresses, free capacities, and hospital availabilities.
- The *Route availability* task determines availability of a particular route depending on its type (road, air route, etc.) taking into account (i) the types of vehicles used by the emergency and police teams, and firefighter brigades; (ii) the closed roads; (iii) the traffic jams; and (iv) the weather conditions.
- The *Shortest routes* task calculates the shortest routes for the appropriate acting resources.
- Joint solution for the tasks *Firefighter brigade selection*, *Emergency team selection*, *Hospital selection, Police team selection*, and *Route selection* produces a set of feasible plans of actions for the acting resources.

The network of Web-services organized to solve the tasks described above is shown in Fig. 3. Arrows in the figure depict execution sequences of the Web-services. The tasks implemented by Web-services organizing parallel paths can be solved simultaneously.

Web-services implementing tasks concerned with supplying the DSS with the data from the information sources use the following kinds of information resources. The current weather conditions are taken from the *sensors* and *Web-sites*. Information about the locations of the roads of the region is taken from the *GIS*. Information about emergency teams, firefighter brigades, and police teams available in the region is read from a *database*. Information about the locations of these teams and brigades is provided by the *GPS-based devices* installed on the vehicles of these teams and brigades. Information about the accident location, its type (traffic accident with fire), and the approximate number of victims is provided by the car *smart sensor*. Information about hospitals available in the region and their lo-

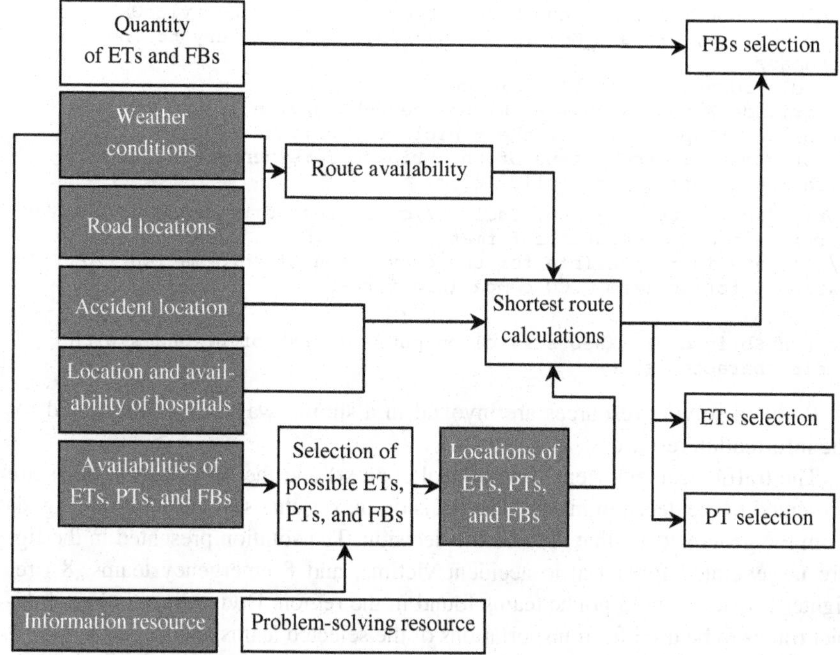

ET – Emergency Team; PT – Police Team; FB – Firefighter Brigade

Fig. 3. Network of information and problem-solving Web-services

cations is read from the healthcare infrastructure *database*, hospital free capacities are provided by *hospital administration systems*.

The common model of a Web-service implementing information resource functions is illustrated by the example of Web-service responsible for receiving information about emergency and police teams, and firefighter brigades available in the region. This Web-service requests the database storing information about the emergency and police teams, and firefighter brigades and returns a list of such teams and brigades. The list contains identifiers of the teams and brigades, URIs of their Web-services (this Web-services are used to receive additional information about the teams and brigades, e.g. current brigade location), and types of vehicles used by these teams and brigades. The Web-service being illustrated is implemented in PHP [5]. Key steps of the service are as follows:

```
...
$conn = odbc_connect ("brigades"); //connection to the database storing information about the emergency and police teams, and firefighter brigades
```

```
$sql = "SELECT id, brigade_Description, brigade_WebserviceURI,
brigade_Type, brigade_WorkType FROM brigades"; //query to the
database
// id - identifier of the brigade
// brigade_WebserviceURI - URI of the Web service of the brigade
// brigade_Type - type of the vehicle the brigade uses
// brigade_WorkType - type of the brigade (emergency team or
firefighter brigade or police team)
$brigades = GetData($conn, $sql); //query result returned to the Web
service in OOCN compatible format
// GetData is responsible for the conversion of information from
database format into OOCN compatible format
...
return $brigades; //Web service output - a list of brigades with
their characteristics
```

Problem solving resources are invoked in a similar way as it is illustrated for the information resources.

The traffic accident scene (operational context) and the set of action plans are presented to the decision maker. The decision maker chooses one solution (Fig. 4) from the generated set that is to be the decision. The solution presented in the figure is generated for 4 traffic accident victims, and 8 emergency teams, 8 firefighter brigades, and 3 police teams found in the region. Dotted lines in Fig. 4 depict routes to be used for transportations of the selected teams and brigades.

The decision is delivered to the leaders of the emergency teams, firefighter brigades, police teams, and to the hospital administrations. They have access to the operational context through any Internet browsers (a browser supported by a notebook, PDA, mobile phone, *etc.*).

The DSS has been implemented as a distributed system for operational decision support. The interface of the system is Web-based, i.e. regular Web browsers can be used for working with the system.

5 Related Research

The field of pervasive computing is a focus of many up-to-date research efforts. Research in this area aims at management of sensor networks, industry of context-aware services including self-adaptable, self-configurable, self-optimized services, development of resource-aware services, building smart spaces, etc.

Organization of collaborative environments from autonomous entities is a focus of approaches to building context aware DSSs [e.g., 5, 7], self-optimization and self-configuration in wireless networks [8], organization of context-aware co-operative networks [9] and collaborative context-aware service platforms [10], *etc.* Issues close to the subjects investigated in the research presented in this paper are considered in the framework of PLASTIC (Providing Lightweight & Adaptable Service Technology for Pervasive Information & Communication) [11] project sponsored by the EC FP6. Among other issues in this project a service oriented

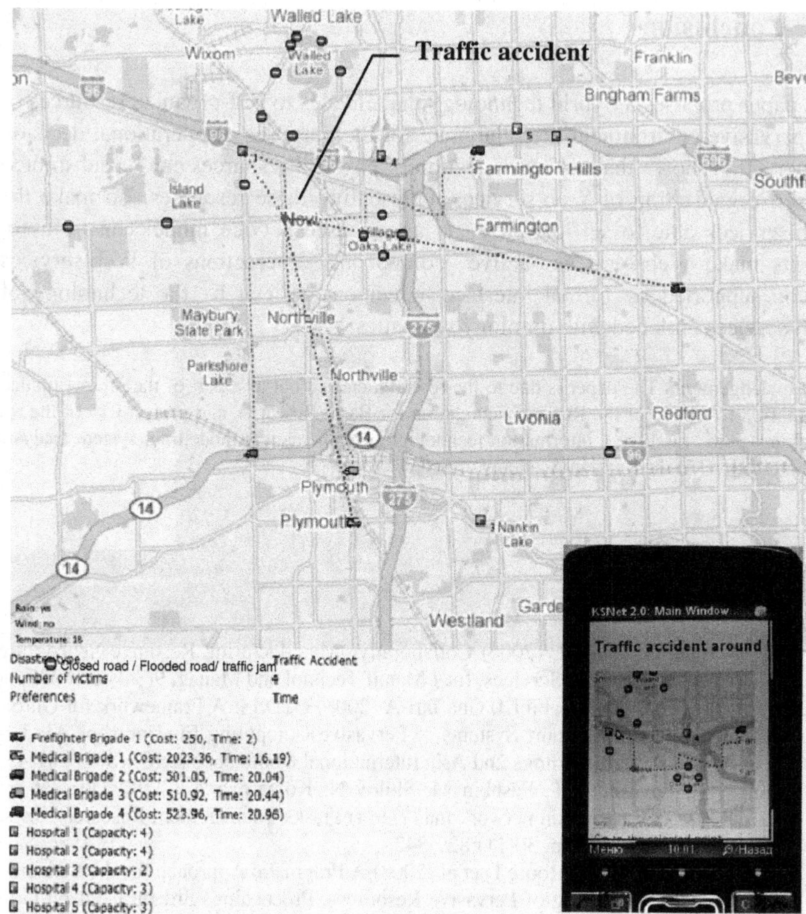

Fig. 4. Operational context: plan for actions

approach allowing for ad hoc context awareness in pervasive environments has been developed. In the PLASTIC-approach context-related entities – all taking the form of contextual services – are purposed to dynamically self-organize and self-adapt to optimally exploit available, possibly heterogeneous, contextual resources at the specific time and place.

The approach described in this paper combines the ideas of context aware decision support with the ideas of self-contextualization and self-organization. Distinguishing features of the proposed approach comparatively to the related ones are using Web-services to ensure interoperability between heterogeneous devices of pervasive environment, involving problem-solving resources in customization of the environment functionality, and organization of a collaborative environment comprising not only physical devices and software services but organizations and persons.

6 Conclusion

The paper proposes a hybrid technology that enables to self-organize resources of the pervasive environment to collaborate for the purposes of operational decision support. It is shown that self-organization of physical resources can be substituted for self-organization of Web-services representing these resources. To make the Web-services able to self-organize, an agent-based service model can be used. Agents make Web-services "active" components. Interactions of Web-services can be supported by formal interface agreement defined by the technology of Web-services enriched with ontology semantics.

Acknowledgements The paper is due to the research carried out as a part of the project funded by grant 08-07-00264 of the Russian Foundation for Basic Research, and project 213 of the research program "Intelligent information technologies, mathematical modelling, system analysis and automation" of the Russian Academy of Sciences.

References

1. Hao Q, Shen W, Wang L (2006) Collaborative Manufacturing Resource Scheduling Using Agent-Based Web Services, Int J Manuf Technol and Manag, 9(3/4):309-327.
2. Saremi A, Esmaeili M, Habibi J, Ghaffari A (2008) O2DSS: A Framework for Ontology-Based Decision Support Systems in Pervasive Computing Environment. Modeling & Simulation, Proceedings 2nd Asia International Conference (AICMS 08), 41-45.
3. Smirnov A, Levashova T, Pashkin M, Shilov N, Komarova A (2007) Disaster response based on production network management tasks. Management Research News, Emerald Publishing Group. 30(11):829-842.
4. Bandara A, Payne T, De Roure D et al (2008) A Pragmatic Approach for the Semantic Description and Matching of Pervasive Resources. Proceedings 3rd Int Conf on Grid and Pervasive Computing (GPC 2008). 434-446.
5. The PHP Group: "PHP" (2009). http://www.php.net. Accessed 15 January 2009
6. Kwon O, Yoo K, Suh E (2005) UbiDSS: a Proactive Intelligent Decision Support System as an Expert System Deploying Ubiquitous Computing Technologies. Expert Syst Appl 28(1):149-161.
7. Burstein F, Zaslavsky A, Arora N (2005) Context-aware mobile agents for decision-making support in healthcare emergency applications. In: Bui T, Gachet A (eds). Proceedings Workshop on Contextual Modelling and Decision Support, Paris, France. CEUR Workshop Proceedings, 144: http://ftp.informatik.rwth-aachen.de/Publications/CEUR-WS/Vol-144/07_burstein.pdf. Accessed 15 January 2009.
8. Self-optimisation and self-configuration in wireless networks (SOCRATES) (2008). ICT-2007.1.1 The network of the future. http://cordis.europa.eu/. Accessed 14 January 2009.
9. Ambient Networks Project (2006). IST-2004-2.4.5 Mobile and Wireless Systems and Platforms Beyond 3G. http://www.ambient-networks.org/. Accessed 14 January 2009.
10. Ejigu D, Scuturici M, Brunie L (2008) Hybrid Approach to Collaborative Context-Aware Service Platform for Pervasive Computing. J Computers. 16(1):40-50.
11. PLASTIC. http://www.ist-plastic.org/ (2008). Accessed 11 January 2009.

An Expert System Based on Parametric Net to Support Motor Pump Multi-Failure Diagnostic

Flavia Cristina Bernardini and Ana Cristina Bicharra Garcia and Inhaúma Neves Ferraz

ADDLabs – Active Documentation Design Laboratory,
UFF – Universidade Federal Fluminense
Av. Gal. Milton Tavares de Souza, s/nº – Campus da Praia Vermelha, Boa Viagem, Niterói, RJ, Brazil. E-mail: flavia @addlabs.uff.br

ADDLabs – Active Documentation Design Laboratory
IC – Instituto de Computação
UFF – Universidade Federal Fluminense
Av. Gal. Milton Tavares de Souza, s/nº – Campus da Praia Vermelha, Boa Viagem, Niterói, RJ, Brazil. E-mail: bicharra@ic.uff.br

ADDLabs – Active Documentation Design Laboratory
IC – Instituto de Computação
UFF – Universidade Federal Fluminense
Av. Gal. Milton Tavares de Souza, s/nº – Campus da Praia Vermelha, Boa Viagem, Niterói, RJ, Brazil. E-mail: ferraz@ic.uff.br

Abstract Early failure detection in motor pumps is an important issue in prediction maintenance. An efficient condition-monitoring scheme is capable of providing warning and predicting the faults at early stages. Usually, this task is executed by humans. The logical progression of the condition-monitoring technologies is the automation of the diagnostic process. To automate the diagnostic process, intelligent diagnostic systems are used. Many researchers have explored artificial intelligence techniques to diagnose failures in general. However, all papers found in literature are related to a specific problem that can appear in many different machines. In real applications, when the expert analyzes a machine, not only one problem appears, but more than one problem may appear together. So, it is necessary to propose new methods to assist diagnosis looking for a set of occurring fails. For some failures, there are not sufficient instances that can ensure good classifiers induced by available machine learning algorithms. In this work, we propose a method to assist fault diagnoses in motor pumps, based on vibration signal analysis, using expert systems. To attend the problems related to motor pump analyses, we propose a parametric net model for multi-label problems. We also show a case study in this work, showing the applicability of our proposed method.

Please use the following format when citing this chapter:

Bernardini, F.C., Garcia, A.C.B. and Ferraz, I.N., 2009, in IFIP International Federation for Information Processing, Volume 296; *Artificial Intelligence Applications and Innovations III*; Eds. Iliadis, L., Vlahavas, I., Bramer, M.; (Boston: Springer), pp.13–20.

1 Introduction

Motor pump fails detection is an important issue in prediction maintenance. Traditional maintenance procedures in industry have taken two routes. The first is to perform fixed time interval maintenance, and the second is to simply react to the plant failure as and when it happens. However, predictive maintenance through condition monitoring has become a new route to maintenance management. Researchers have studied a variety of machine faults, such as, unbalanced stator and rotor parameters, broken rotor bars, eccentricity and bearing faults, and different methods for fault identification have been developed [10]. These different methods are used effectively to detect the machine faults at different stages using different machine variables, such as current, temperature and vibrations. An efficient condition-monitoring scheme is capable of providing warning and predicting the faults at early stages. Monitoring systems obtain information about the machine in the form of primary data. Through the use of modern signal processing and analysis techniques, it is possible to give vital diagnostic information to equipment operator before it catastrophically fails. The problem with this approach is that the results require constant human interpretation. The logical progression of the condition-monitoring technologies is developing methods and tools to guide and, as a next stage of validation and improvement of the classification models, automate the diagnosis process. To this end, intelligent systems are used.

Recent artificial intelligent techniques, such as neural networks, fuzzy logic, expert system and genetic algorithm, have been employed to assist the diagnostic task to correctly interpret the fault data. Many researchers have explored these techniques to diagnose faults in induction motors, motor rolling bearings, and so on [4,5,13,6]. These papers describe diagnosis methods based on characteristics extraction and neural networks models induction for each separated fail. However, all papers found in literature are related to a specific problem that can appear in many different machines. In real applications, when the expert analyses a machine, not only one problem appears, but more than one problem may also appear. Another important characteristic of this problem is that different features of the collected signals are analyzed for each problem [7]. For this reason, it is necessary to propose new methods to assist diagnosis looking for many possible fails that can appear together.

There are many peculiar characteristics in machinery diagnostic problems that turns it an interesting research problem from machine learning and pattern recognition perspective. First, there are many signals captured from a machine that should be analyzed, which means that the method to be proposed to treat all the problems together should (a) be able to treat a large number of features, or (b) preprocess the data to predict the fails. Second, problems which an instance can be labeled with more than one class are called multi-label problems, and the development of methods in artificial intelligence to treat this kind of problem is still in research [12,9,11,2]. Third, to apply machine learning algorithms, such as artificial neural networks, support vector machines, and so on, it is necessary to have labeled instances of the domain to extract the model and predict future labels. In machinery failures, there are some fails that real instances can easily be obtained, e.g. unbalance and misalignment; but there are some that cannot and can seriously damage the machine, e.g. cavitation and bearing problems. Unbalance problems turns difficult to induce good classifiers [1]. All these reasons let us put a lot of effort to try to solve early diagnostic of motor pump failures problem.

In this work, we propose a method to assist fault diagnoses in motor pumps using expert systems, based on vibration signal analysis. Since the number of signals to be analyzed is large and, for some fails, there are not instances available to use machine learning algorithms, we decided to investigate a method to construct a parametric net model, based on expert knowledge. The main advantage of this method is that the model can explain its decisions by showing what was the reason followed by the parametric net to fails (labels) suggestion. To show the usability of our proposal, we describe a case study where we show the expert analyses and the results obtained by our proposed method in a specific type of motor pump.

This paper is organized as follows. Section 2 briefly describes how failures appear in vibration signals. Section 3 proposes a parametric net model to multi-label problems. Section 4 describes the parametric net model proposed for motor pump failure diagnosis. Finally, Section 5 concludes this work.

2 Vibration Signal Analysis

Motor pumps, due to the rotating nature of their internal pieces, produce vibrations. Accelerometers strategically placed in points next to the motor and the pump allows acceleration of the machine over time to be measured, thus generating a signal of the vibration level. Fig. 1 shows a typical positioning configuration of accelerometers on the equipment. In general, the orientations of the sensors follow the three main axes of the machine, *e.g.* vertical, horizontal and axial.

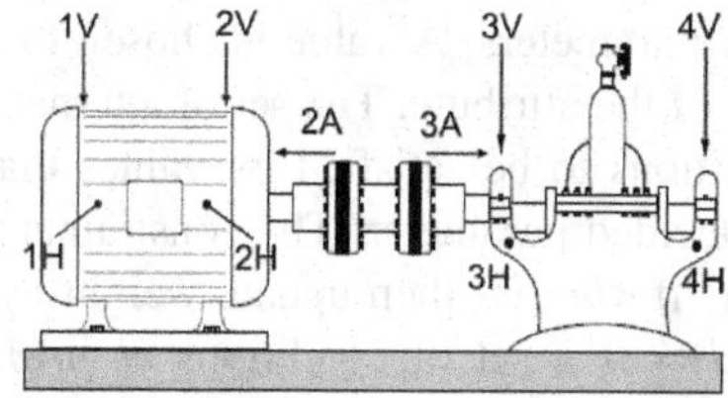

Fig. 1 . Motor pump with extended coupling between motor and pump. The accelerometers are placed along the main directions to capture specific vibrations of the main axes. (H=horizontal, A=axial, V=vertical)

The presence of any type of machine faults causes change in mechanical and electrical forces that are acting in the machine [10]. The degree of change depends upon the nature and intensity of the fault. The change in machine vibration is the excitation of some of the vibration harmonics. Some of machine faults can be directly related to the vibration harmonic. Table 6.0, "Illustrated Vibration Diagnostic Chart", in [7], shows how to analyze signals, searching for mechanical and electrical faults. In what follows, electrical and mechanical faults are briefly described.

3 A Parametric Net Model Proposed for Multi-label Problems

Until the late '80s the most popular approach to classification problems was a knowledge engineering one, consisting in manually defining a set of rules encoding expert knowledge on how to classify documents under the given categories. In the '90s, this approach has increasingly lost popularity in favor of the machine learning paradigm, according to with a general inductive process automatically builds a general hypothesis to classify new instances, based on instances previously labeled by some domain expert [9,8]. However, there are some problems that label attributed to the instances are not 100% guaranteed that are true, or there are unbalanced classes, which difficult the induction model process [1]. In these cases, it is interesting to construct an expert system, which contains the knowledge of the expert domain, represented in a parametric net, to (a) classify new instances with a set of labels; and (b) validate the available instances.

Parametric nets are used to inference logical facts, supporting decision making. In a parametric net, the parameters represent the problem features, domain properties, or decisions that must have made during the reasoning process. The various parameters of a knowledge base are inter-connected. These are directed connections, because they represent the dependency between parameters and define the logic precedence of the parameters instantiation. The parameter values represent the actual state of the problem being solved.

In its basic version, proposed in [3] to Active Document Design (ADD), and illustrated in Fig. 2, the parameters belong to one of three categories: primitive, derived or decision. Primitive parameters normally are the representation of the problem requisites. In general, these values are informed by the user during the reasoning process. Values of derived parameters are calculated based on values of other parameters. A value is chosen to a decided parameter from a set of alternatives of the attribute. The set of alternatives is filtered by constraints that represent conditions to be satisfied by values that come from the parameters connected to the decided parameter. The constraints are represented by rules. The rules has the form "if *<body>* then update weight w_k with (positive or negative) *value*", where *<body>* is a set of conditions as *primitive <operator> value*, and *<operator>* may be $>$, $<$, $\leq$, $\geq$ and $=$. At the end of the reasoning process, all the alternatives are compared, and one alternative is chosen as an answer to the problem being solved. One common way to decide what is the best alternative is weighting each alternative. An evaluated criterion represents the value to be added to an alternative. The alternative with the maximum weight at the end of the evaluation criteria is selected as the best alternative.

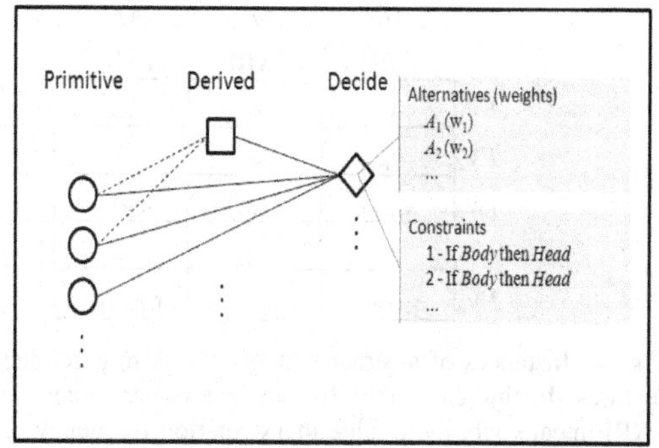

Fig. 2 . Sample of a parametric net. Dot lines represent link between primitives and derived parameters; regular lines represent link between one primitive or derided parameter and another decided parameter. Derived parameters are optional. Values are set into primitives.

In domains where the features can be seen as different instantiations of a set of abstract features, each instance may increment or decrement the weight of an alternative. For example, in machine analyses using vibration signal, each signal captured in one different position of the machine is an instantiation of the possible vibration harmonics used to analyze the machine, and the intensity of each vibration harmonic value in each signal may reinforce or weaken an alternative. Fig. 3 illustrates how the signals are instances of abstract features. So, to adapt the model to offer more than one alternative, each abstract feature set instantiation is shown to the model, which may influence positively or negatively the alternatives. Again, in vibration analyses, each signal in frequency domain is pre-processed, and values related to each important vibration harmonic are extracted. Then, each set of vibration harmonic values, extracted from each signal, is shown to the model, and each alternative weight may be updated if the values obey the set of constraints. At the end of the process, all alternatives with positive weights are considered as possible classes, offering multi-label classification. The positive weights of each class can be normalized to the interval 0 to 1, and values from 0 to 1 are related to each alternative, which can be used to help the expert to decide what the best class (alternative) is.

4 A Parametric Net Model Constructed to Assist Motor Pumps Failure Diagnostic

Model Construction: The type of motor pump considered in our study has the following characteristics: horizontal centrifuge with one stage (one rotor), direct coupling without gear box, and actuated by AC induction squirrel cage motor. The faults considered in our study are unbalance, misalignment, electric, hydraulic, cavitation, turbulence, bearing faults, looseness and resonance. Fig. 1 shows the points on motor pump where specific vibrations are captured. On each point, a time signal is captured by an accelerometer, and signal operators are applied to obtain acceleration, velocity and envelope signals. Each signal is important to detect groups of faults, or specific faults. These pieces of information about motor pump

	AF_1 (1XRF)	AF_2 (1XRF)	AF_3 (1XRF)	...	AF_M (...)	
FV_1	x_1	x_2	x_3	...	x_M	(1H-VxF)
FV_2	x_{M+1}	x_{M+2}	x_{M+3}	...	x_{2M}	(1V-AxF)
FV_3	x_{2M+1}	x_{2M+2}	x_{2M+3}	...	x_{3M}	(1A-ExF)
...	...	...	...	...	...	...
FV_T	$x_{(T-1)M+1}$	$x_{(T-1)M+2}$	$x_{(T-1)M+3}$	...	x_{TM}	...

Fig. 3 . Instances of abstract features. Texts in parentheses comprehend an example of abstract features. In this case, the abstract features are vibration values in harmonic frequencies, e.g. 1XRF means vibration value in 1x rotation frequency, 2XRF means vibration value in 2x rotation frequency, and so on. The feature instances are signals (VxF – velocity per frequency signal; AxF –acceleration per frequency signal; ExF – envelope per frequency value) captured on motor pump points (1, 2, 3 and 4) at different directions (H – horizontal, V – vertical or A – axial).

diagnoses vibration are extracted from Table 6.0, "Illustrated Vibration Diagnostic Chart", in [7], and were explained and detailed by domain experts. All of this knowledge was used to construct constraints of the failure decision parameter. The parametric net model that aims to classify signal sets into a set of classes has one decision and many primitive parameters. Each fault is an alternative of the failure decision parameter of the parametric net.

Since vibration harmonics are what influence each alternative, each one is a primitive parameter. The primitives considered are vibration values in harmonic (1X, 2X,...) and inter-harmonic (0.5X, 1.5X,...) of the rotational frequency in r.p.s; RMS calculated in harmonic and inter-harmonic frequencies; BPFO, BPFI, BSF and RHF frequencies; electrical frequency; and pole frequency. Also, there are primitives that give to the model characteristics of the capturing position: velocity, acceleration, envelope, radial, axial, motor and pump, and they are set to true or false depending on the signal. E.g., if the signal is captured in position 1V and is the velocity signal which is being analyzed, then velocity is set to true, where as acceleration and envelope are set to false; radial is set to true[1] where as axial is set to false; and motor is set to true where as pump is set to false.

Model Application: To analyze a motor pump, ten acceleration signals in frequency domain are captured (one signal per point). Applying the mentioned operators, 30 signals are obtained. The model has all alternative weights initialize with 0. Each velocity, acceleration and envelope signal of each point is shown to the model, which may increment the weight of each alternative. At the end of this process, all alternatives that have positive weights (greater than zero) are normalized to the range 0-1, which are shown to the analyst.

A Case Study: We implemented a computational system, called ADDRPD, to help the analyst in all of the analysis process. Time signals of a specific motor pump are imported to the system. All transformations are applied and the resulting signals are shown to the user. One instance was labeled by the expert having only

[1] Signals read in H (horizontal) position are also considered radial.

one problem: unbalance. However, when the parametric net was applied to the instance, three faults were diagnosed: unbalance (0.46), misalignment (0.44) and looseness (0.10). When showed to the expert domain, he explained that it is true that the three problems appears in the machine, however unbalance is the most problematic fault in that case. The expert analysis was basically based on Fig. 4.

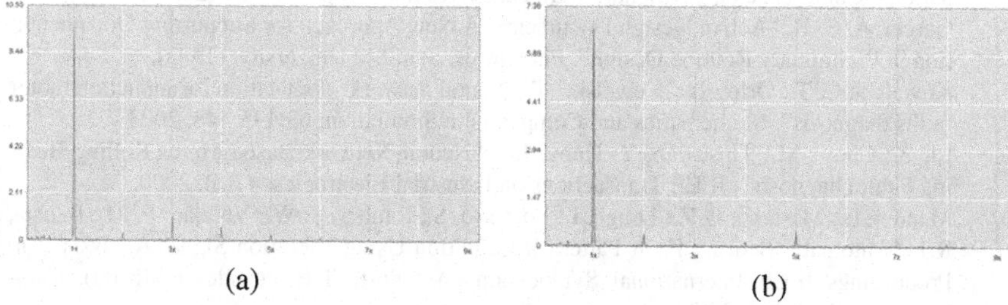

(a) (b)

Fig. 4 . Velocity (RMS/s) per rotational frequency harmonics signals, showing high vibration and lower peaks in rotational frequency harmonics (a) captured at 1H and (b) captured at 2A.

Both signals showed in Fig. 4 are velocity per frequency signals, however Fig. 4 (a) was captured at radial direction, where as Fig. 4 (b) was captured at axial direction. So, since both has high peak vibration at 1X, this represents that unbalance is the most representative failure in the motor pump. But the signal Fig. 4 (b) is from axial direction, which highly indicates misalignment failure, and the lower peaks at harmonic frequencies weakly indicate looseness. The analysis shows that the parametric net join to visual tools are efficient ways of analyzing motor pumps to diagnostic their failures.

5 Conclusions and Future Work

We propose in this work a method to assist fault diagnosis using parametric nets to represent the expert knowledge, based on vibration analysis. To this end, we propose a parametric net to multi-label problems. We present a model we developed for a special type of motor pump – horizontal centrifuge with one stage (one rotor), direct coupling without gear box, and actuated by AC induction squirrel cage motor. To preliminary evaluate the proposed model, we present a case study, using signals captured from a motor pump in use in real world. We could notice that the model could assist the expert interpretation of the signals.

Our method was implemented in a computational system called ADDRPD. The system will help to classify new instances, which we intend to improve our method. Ongoing work includes evaluating our method using recall and precision measure for each class, as a multi-label problem [12]. After validating (part of) the dataset, the parametric model will be updated and machine learning algorithms will be used to induce models and compare to the method proposed in this work.

References

1. Batista, G.; Prati, R. C.; Monard, M. C. A study of the behavior of several methods for balancing machine learning training data. SIGKDD Explorations, 6(1):20-29, 2004.
2. Brinkler, K; Hullermeier, E. "Case-Based Multilabel Ranking". In: Proceedings 20th International Conference on Artificial Intelligence (IJCAI '07), pp. 702-707 (2007).
3. Garcia, A. C. B. "Active Design Documents: A New Approach for Supporting Documentation in Preliminary Routine Design", PhD thesis, Stanford University, (1992).
4. Kowalski, C. T.; Orlowska-Kowalska, T. "Neural networks application for induction motor faults diagnosis". Mathematics and Computers in Simulation, 63:435-448, 2003.
5. Li, B.; Chow, M.; Tipsuwan, Y; Hung, J.C. "Neural-Network-Based Motor Rolling Bearing Fault Diagnosis". IEEE Transactions on Industrial Electronics, 47(5), 2000.
6. Mendel, E.; Mariano, L. Z.; Drago, I.; Loureiro, S.; Rauber, T. W.; Varejão, F. M.; Batista, R.J. "Automatic Bearing Fault Pattern Recognition Using Vibration Signal Analysis". In: Proceedings IEEE International Symposium on Industrial Electronics (ISIE'08), Cambridge, pp. 955-960 (2008).
7. Mitchell, J. S. Introduction to Machinery Analysis and Monitoring, PenWel Books, Tulsa (1993).
8. Mitchell, T. Machine Learning. McGraw Hill (1997).
9. Sebastiani, F. "Machine learning in automated text categorization". ACM Computing Surveys. 34(1):1-47, 2002.
10. Singh, G.K.; Kazzaz, S. A. S. A. "Induction machine drive condition monitoring and diagnostic research – a survey". Electric Power Systems Research, 64:145-158, 2003.
11. Schapire, R. E.; Singer, Y.. "BoosTexter: A boosting-based system for text categorization". Machine Learning, 39(2/3):135-168, 2000.
12. X. Shen, M. Boutell, J. Luo, and C. Brown "Multi label Machine learning and its application to semantic scene classification". In: Proceedings of the 2004 International Symposium on Electronic Imaging (EI 2004), pp. 18-22 (2004).
13. Zhang, S.; Ganesan, R.; Xistris, G. D. "Self-Organizing Neural Networks for Automated Machinery Monitoring Systems". Mechanical Systems and Signal Processing, 10(5):517-532, 1996.

Providing Assistance during Decision-making Problems Solving in an Educational Modelling Environment

Panagiotis Politis[1], Ioannis Partsakoulakis[2], George Vouros[2], Christos Fidas[3]

1 Dept. of Primary Education, University of Thessaly,

38221 Volos, Greece

ppol@uth.gr

2 Dept. of Information and Communication Systems Engineering, University of the Aegean, 83200 Samos, Greece

{jpar, georgev}@aegean.gr

3 Dept. of Electrical and Computer Engineering, University of Patras,

26500 Rio Patras, Greece

fidas@ece.upatras.gr

Abstract In this paper we present the model-checking module of decision-making models in the frame of ModelsCreator, an educational modelling environment. The model-checking module aims to assist young students to construct qualitative models for decision-making problems solving. We specify the decision-making models that may be built and we explain the model checking mechanism. The model-checking mechanism compares the student model with the reference model constructed by the teacher and provides immediate advice to the student to help him create a valid model. So, the model-checking module of a decision-making model aims to facilitate student to structure convincing decisions in the proper situations.

1 Introduction

Modelling is a procedure of describing physical or simulated systems that provides an important means for individuals to examine and understand all the aspects, constraints, characteristics, entities, relations and processes that support the behaviour of every such system. Thus, modelling can be a very strong tool to help young students to appreciate the world and to discover new forms of expression (Becker & Boohan, 1995), (Teodoro, 1994). ModelsCreator is a modelling learn-

---

Please use the following format when citing this chapter:

Politis, P., Partsakoulakis, I., Vouros, G. and Fidas, C., 2009, in IFIP International Federation for Information Processing, Volume 296; *Artificial Intelligence Applications and Innovations III*; Eds. Iliadis, L., Vlahavas, I., Bramer, M.; (Boston: Springer), pp. 21–29.

ing environment that supports expression of different kinds of models (semi-quantitative models, quantitative models, and decision making models) mostly for students 11-16 years old. In this paper we present the ModelsCreator (Dimitracopoulou et. al., 1997), (Dimitracopoulou et. al, 1999) decision making module (Partsakoulakis & Vouros, 2002).

ModelsCreator decision-making module offers support to students to be able to construct models with or without doubts (expressed by probabilities). The module provides generic techniques for models' validation to successfully assist students discover mistaken features in their models and attain an accord with the instructor. The models meet the requirements of many curriculum subject matters, permitting interdisciplinary use of the modelling process. ModelsCreator puts great emphasis on visualization of the modelling entities, their properties and their relations. Visualization is crucial in supporting the reasoning development of young students and favours the transition from reasoning over objects to reasoning with abstract concepts (Teodoro 1997). This feature is extended also to the simulation of executable models allowing their validation through representation of the phenomenon itself in a visual way and not in an abstract one, as it is usually the case.

2 Architecture of the Environment

If M is a model then it can be represent verbal as follow:

$M = \{ E_i, i=1, \ldots, k, R_j, j=1, \ldots, l, A_m, m=1, \ldots, n \}$

where E represent the node entities of the solution, R the relationships connecting them and A the attributes of the entities that participate in the solution.

The decision making models consist basically of entities and relations which connects their attributes. Seven supported types of relations make the environment a very powerful tool for creating and testing decision models. The supported types of relations are the AND, THEN, OR, AND, ELSE and NOT types whereas two types of object notes are supported.

2.1 Structure of Entities

A major concern in the designing phase of the ModelsCreator environment was to provide the ability to end- users to define and manage their own libraries of entities. A component of MC that contributes to its open character is the editor of entities. The end users can define entities and insert them in their object libraries. Properties are assigned to these entities and iconic representations that correspond to the defined properties states, thus providing it with behaviour.

These educational entities provide furthermore interfaces to the COM standard and support the XML semantics thus enabling their integration to the MC environment and increasing their manageability, reusability and maintenance. The DTD and the XML structure of an entity are given in the appendixes A and B.

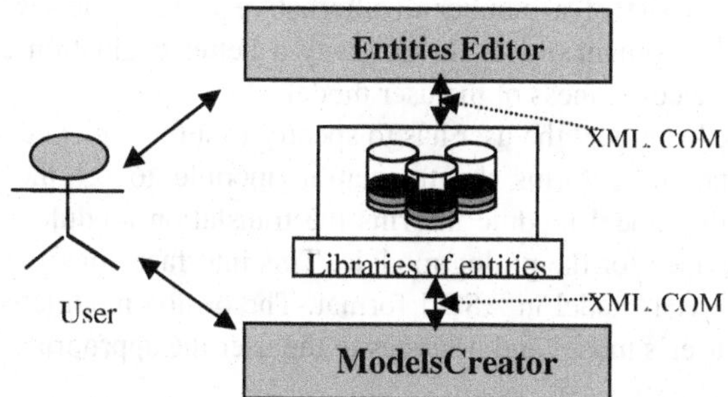

Fig. 1 The entities follow the COM standard and the XML specification

2.1 Constructing Decision-making Models

Models for decision-making are typically qualitative models. Each decision making model has precisely one hypothesis part, precisely one decision part and at most one counter decision part. The student selects certain properties/attributes, sets the desired values and relates them with the appropriate logical connective. For instance, the IF connective applies to an AND expression, while the AND connective, applies to an OR expression and to a property of an entity.

Using such an environment, one may construct fully parenthesised expressions of arbitrary complexity that are according to the following formal grammar:

```
Expression = if Construct then Construct
           | if Construct then Construct else Con-
struct
Construct = (Construct and Construct)
          | (Construct or Construct)
          | not(Construct)
          | Entity_Property_or_Attribute
```

3 Testing a Model

Testing a model means to find out its correctness. But some times a solution to a decision making problem might not be totally true or false. Furthermore there are alternative correct solutions to a decision problem. The model-checking mechanism of the decision-making module aims to facilitate the cooperative process between students and instructors to make an agreement about the situations in which a decision is valid.

To overcome this problem a reference model has been specified for each logical domain (any curriculum subject). This way exist for each logical a reference model which consist of a number of alternative right models which have been specified by the domain owner. In this way a better evaluation can be achieved while testing the correctness of the user model.

To evaluate his model the user has to specify first the logical domain. The logical domain module informs the translation module to set the right reference model. Then the model module informs the translation module which starts preparing the interface for the prolog module. This interface consists of the reference model and the user model in ASCII format. The prolog module checks the reference with the user's model and provides to the user the appropriate feedback.

3.1 The Prolog Model-checking Module

The model-checking module consists of four major steps. First, the two models (student and reference model) are converted using model-preserving formulas in equivalent Conjunctive Normal Forms (CNF). After that, the two models are compared and the results of the comparison are raised intermediately and can be visualized in the form of a comparison table. Mistaken aspects of student's model may be diagnosed by inspecting the comparison table. Finally, the mechanism decides on the appropriate feedback message that should be given to the student

3.1.1 Converting the model

To sustain the fundamental relation between the hypothesis and the decision part of the model, the student-model and reference-model are recorded independently. Each part is then converted using tautologies in CNF. A sentence in CNF is a conjunction of a set of disjunctive formulas (figure 5). Each disjunctive formula consists only of atomic formulas.

$$\underbrace{(a_1\ \ddot{I}\ a_2\ \ddot{I}\ \ldots\ \ddot{I}\ a_{n_a})}_{(A)}\ \Omega \ldots \Omega\ \underbrace{(z_1\ \ddot{I}\ z_2\ \ddot{I}\ \ldots\ \ddot{I}\ z_{n_z})}_{(Z)}$$

Fig 2: The Conjunctive Normal Form

Before comparing the two models the mechanism simplifies the sentences by removing redundant elements (atomic formulas present more than once in the same disjunctive sentence, disjunctive formulas that form part of the whole formula and that imply the whole formula).

3.1.2 Comparing student model and reference model

The two models are equivalent in the case that each disjunctive formula of one of the models is implied by the other one. So, each disjunctive formula is converted to a set of atomic formulas to compare the two models in CNF. For example the formula a Ï b Ï c Ï d is converted to the set $\{a, b, c, d\}$. In other words, each model is converted to a set of sets, where each inner set corresponds to a disjunctive formula and contains atomic formulas.

The comparison process achieved by the model-checking mechanism results the recording of the atomic formulas that are missing or that are surplus in each disjunctive formula in both models. The comparison table reflects the result of the comparison process. Entries of this table correspond to pairs of disjunctive formulas. Each entry (i,j) contains a sub-table with the missing and surplus elements of the i-th disjunctive formula of the student model compared with the j-th disjunctive formula of the reference model.

3.1.3 Judging the student model

If in each row and column of the comparison table there is a sub-table with no missing or surplus atomic formulas, that means that for each disjunctive formula of student's model exists a matching formula in the reference model, so the student model and the reference model are equivalents. If the two models are not equivalents, then the model-checking mechanism can diagnose different situations by inspecting the comparison table.

If the student has over-specified the situations where a decision can be formed, or the student has specified the right properties/attributes for the right entities, but has not assigned the proper values for (at least) one of these properties/attributes that means that the student has missed at least one atomic formula. This formula may correspond to an entity participating to the model, to a property, to an attribute or to a value assigned to a property/attribute of a participating entity.

If the student has under-specified the situations where a decision can be formed that means that at least one atomic formula in student model is surplus. This formula may correspond to an entity participating to the model, to a property, to an attribute or to a value assigned to a property/attribute of a participating entity.

If the student has related two entities with a wrong logical connective, the diagnosis is also based on atomic formulas that are missing and surplus.

All the mentioned cases are not measured the same. A total score is computed that specifies the providing feedback to the student. So, the student model is assigned a score value that is a number between 0 and 100 (Table 1).

Table 1. Situation and score assigned during student model's judgment

Score	Situation
0	Non recognizable error
10	Surplus entity
20	Entity missing
30	Surplus property
40	Property missing
50	Wrong value in property
60	Wrong probability value
70	Connective misuse
100	Equivalent to reference model

3.1.4 Providing feedback to the student

The score assigned during the student model's judgment specifies the feedback message provided by the environment. To each score level one or more messages are assigned with a preference. Messages with lower preference are more or equally detailed.

The purpose of the system is to facilitate the student to assemble his model equivalent to the reference model. The feedback messages should give the suitable assistance students construct their valid models. To attain this aim, the system creates and displays messages of increasing factor.

If the system has diagnosed that the student over-specified the situations for making a decision, e.g. by specifying a surplus entity, it is proposing to the student to confirm the entities in the model. In case that the student does not improve his score, the checking mechanism provides suggestion by prompting the student to ensure if there are any surplus entities in the student model. After that, if the student insists in the same invalid situation, the checking mechanism provides a more detailed assistance by saying that the specific entity is not related to the situation being modelled.

4 Conclusions

The ModelsCreator decision-making module aims to help young students to build qualitative models during decision-making problems solving. Decision making models comprise entities and theirs properties that participate in a decision making state, represented by the student model, to another, correct model, the reference model. The model-checking mechanism compares the student model with the reference model and provides active comment to the student to help him create a suitable model. The model-checking mechanism of the decision-making module aims to assist the communication between students and teachers to reach an accord about the circumstances in which a choice is convincing.

References

1. Beckett, L., Boohan, R.: Computer Modelling for the Young - and not so Young – Scientist, Microcomputer Based Labs: educational research and Standards, R. Thinker (ed), Springer Verlag, ASI series, Vol 156, (1995) 227-238
2. Dimitracopoulou, A., Vosniadou, S., Ioannides, C.: Exploring and modelling the real world through designed environments for young children. In Proceedings 7th European Conference for Research on Learning and Instruction EARLI, Athens, Greece (1997)
3. Dimitracopoulou, A., Komis, V., Apostolopoulos P., Politis, P.: Design Principles of a New Modelling Environment Supporting Various Types of Reasoning and Interdisciplinary Approaches. In Proceedings 9th International Conference of Artificial Intelligence in Education, IOS Press, Ohmsha, (1999) 109-120
4. Fidas, C., Komis, V., Avouris, N., Dimitracopoulou, A.: Collaborative Problem Solving using an Open Modelling Environment. In G. Stahl (edited by), Computer Support For Collaborative Learning: Foundations For A CSCL Community, Proceedings of CSCL 2002, Boulder, Colorado, Lawrence Erlbaum Associates, Inc., (2002) 654-655
5. Partsakoulakis, I., Vouros, G.: Helping Young Students Reach Valid Decision through Model Checking. In Proceedings 3rd Hellenic Conference on Technology of Information and Communication in Education, Rhodes, Greece (2002) 669-678
6. Teodoro, V. D.: Learning with Computer-Based Exploratory Environments in Science and Mathematics. In S. Vosniadou, E. De Corte, H. Mandl (Eds.*),* Technology -Based Learning Environments: Psychological and Educational Foundations, NATO ASI Series, Vol. 137, Berlin: Springer Verlag. (1994) 179-186
7. Teodoro V.D. Modellus: Using a Computational Tool to Change the Teaching and Learning of Mathematics and Science, in "New Technologies and the Role of the Teacher" Open University, Milton Keynes, UK (1997)

Appendix A

```
<!ELEMENT Entity(NAME,TYPE,COMMENT,GUID, ICON,
ATTRIBUTE+,ENTITYSTATE+)>
          <!ELEMENT NAME(#PCDATA)>
          <!ELEMENT TYPE(#PCDATA)>
          <!ELEMENT COMMENT(#PCDATA)>
          <!ELEMENT GUID(#PCDATA)>
          <!ELEMENT ICON(#PCDATA)>
          <!ELEMENT ATTRIBUTE
(ID,NAME,TYPE,COMMENT,VALUES, ATTRIBUTESTATE+)>
```

```
            <!ELEMENT ID(#PCDATA)>
            <!ELEMENT NAME(#PCDATA)>
            <!ELEMENT TYPE(#PCDATA)>
            <!ELEMENT COMMENT(#PCDATA)>
            <!ELEMENT VALUES(MIN,MAX,DEFAULT)>
              <!ELEMENT MIN (#PCDATA)>
              <!ELEMENT MAX (#PCDATA)>
              <!ELEMENT DEFAULT (#PCDATA)>
            <!ELEMENT ATTRIBUTESTATE(VALUES+)>
              <!ELEMENT VALUES(ATTRSTATEID,MIN,MAX)>
              <!ELEMENT ATTRSTATEID (#PCDATA)>
              <!ELEMENT MIN (#PCDATA)>
              <!ELEMENT MAX (#PCDATA)>
          <!ELEMENT ENTITYSTATE (ID, ICON
FILENAME,ATRIBUTE+)>
            <!ELEMENT ID(#PCDATA)>
            <!ELEMENT ICON(#PCDATA)>
            <!ELEMENT ATRIBUTE(ATTRSTATELIST+)>
            <!ELEMENT ATTRSTATELIST(ID,ATTRSTATEID)>
              <!ELEMENT ID(#PCDATA)>
              <!ELEMENT ATTRSTATEID (#PCDATA)>
```

Appendix B

```
<?xml version="1.0" encoding="UTF-8"?>
< ---!DOCTYPE Sustem SYSTEM
"../ModellerLibraryElement.dtd">
<Entity Name="ENTITY_NAME" Type="ENTITY_TYPE" Com-
ment="xxx">
          <GUID value="xxxx-xxxx-xxxx-xxxx"/>
          <Icon path="xxx" />
          <Attribute id="xx" Name="ATTR_NAME"
Type="ATTR_TYPE" Comment="xxx">
          <Values max="xxx" min="xxx" default="xxxx">

          <AttributeState >
          <Values AttributeStateID ="xx" max="xxx"
min="xxx" default="xxxx">
</ AttributeState>
          <AttributeState >
          <Values AttributeStateID ="xx" max="xxx"
min="xxx" default="xxxx">
</ AttributeState>
```

```
            <AttributeState >..........
            </Attribute>
            <Attribute ..............
            <EntityState id="xxx">
              <Icon Filename="xxx" />
              <Attribute ID="xxx" AttributeStateID ="xx"
  />
              <Attribute ID="xxx" AttributeStateID ="xx"
  />
              <Attribute.....
            </EntityState>
            <EntityState >..............
  </Entity>
```

Alternative Strategies for Conflict Resolution in Multi-Context Systems

Antonis Bikakis[1], Grigoris Antoniou[2], and Panayiotis Hassapis[3]

[1]Institute of Computer Science, FO.R.T.H., Greece, bikakis@ics.forth.gr

[2]Institute of Computer Science, FO.R.T.H., Greece, antoniou@ics.forth.gr

[3]Department of Computer Science, Athens University of Ecomomics and Business, chasapis@aueb.gr

Abstract Multi-Context Systems are logical formalizations of distributed context theories connected through mapping rules, which enable information flow between different contexts. Reasoning in Multi-Context Systems introduces many challenges that arise from the heterogeneity of contexts with regard to the language and inference system that they use, and from the potential conflicts that may arise from the interaction of context theories through the mappings. The current paper proposes four alternative strategies for using context and preference information to resolve conflicts in a Multi-Context Framework, in which contexts are modeled as rule theories, mappings as defeasible rules, and global inconsistency is handled using methods of distributed defeasible reasoning.

1 Motivation and Background

A Multi-Context System consists of a set of contexts and a set of inference rules (known as mapping or bridge rules) that enable information flow between different contexts. A context can be thought of as a logical theory - a set of axioms and inference rules - that models local context knowledge. Different contexts are expected to use different languages and inference systems, and although each context may be locally consistent, global consistency cannot be required or guaranteed. Reasoning with multiple contexts requires performing two types of reasoning; (a) local reasoning, based on the individual context theories; and (b) distributed reasoning, which combines the consequences of local theories using the mappings. The most critical issues of contextual reasoning are the heterogeneity of local context theories, and the potential conflicts that may arise from the interaction of different contexts through the mappings.

The notions of context and contextual reasoning were first introduced in AI by McCarthy in [10], as an approach for the problem of generality. In the same paper,

---

Please use the following format when citing this chapter:

Bikakis, A., Antoniou, G. and Hassapis, P., 2009, in IFIP International Federation for Information Processing, Volume 296; *Artificial Intelligence Applications and Innovations III*; Eds. Iliadis, L., Vlahavas, I., Bramer, M.; (Boston: Springer), pp. 31–40.

he argued that the combination of non-monotonic reasoning and contextual reasoning would constitute an adequate solution to this problem. Since then, two main formalizations have been proposed to formalize context: the propositional logic of context (PLC [7], [11]), and the Multi-Context Systems introduced in [9], which later became associated with the Local Model Semantics proposed in [8]. MCS have been argued to be most adequate with respect to the three dimensions of contextual reasoning, as these were formulated in [5] (*partiality*, *approximation*, and *proximity*), and have been shown to be technically more general than PLC [13]. Multi-Context Systems have also been the basis of two recent studies that were the first to deploy non-monotonic reasoning methods in MCS: (a) the non-monotonic rule-based MCS framework of [12], which supports default negation in the mapping rules allowing to reason based on the absence of context information; and (b) the multi-context variant of Default Logic proposed in [6], which models bridge relations between different contexts as default rules, handling cases of inconsistency in the imported knowledge. However, none of these approaches includes the notion of priority or preference, which could be potentially used for conflict resolution.

This paper focuses on the problem of global conflicts in Multi-Context Systems; namely the inconsistencies that may arise when importing conflicting information from two or more different contexts. Even if all context theories are locally consistent, we cannot assume consistency in the global knowledge base. The unification of local theories may result in inconsistencies caused by the mappings. For example, a context theory A may import context knowledge from two different contexts B and C, through two competing mapping rules. In this case, even if the three different contexts are locally consistent, their unification through the mappings defined by A may contain inconsistencies. In previous work [3], we proposed a reasoning model that represents contexts as local rule theories and mappings as defeasible rules, and a distributed algorithm for query evaluation, which exploits context and preference information from the system contexts to resolve such conflicts. In this paper, we describe three alternative strategies for conflict resolution, which differ in the extent of context knowledge that system contexts exchange in order to be able to resolve the potential conflicts.

The rest of the paper is organized as follows. Section 2 describes the proposed representation model. Section 3 describes the four alternative strategies for global conflict resolution, and how they are implemented in four different versions of a distributed algorithm for query evaluation. Section 4 presents the results of simulation-based experiments that we conducted on the four strategies using a prototypical implementation of the algorithms in a Java-based P2P system. Finally, the last section summarizes and discusses the plans of our future work.

2 Representation Model

Our approach models a Multi-Context System P as a collection of distributed local rule theories P_i:

$$P = \{P_i\}, i = 1,...,n$$

Each context (local theory) P_i has a proper distinct vocabulary V_i and a unique identifier i. It is defined as a tuple (V_i, R_i, T_i), where V_i is the vocabulary used by P_i, R_i is a set of rules, and T_i is a preference order on P.

R_i consists of two sets of rules: the set of local rules (R_i^l), and the set of mapping rules (R_i^m). Local rules contain only local literals (literals from the local vocabulary, V_i) in their heads and bodies. They are of the form:

$$r_i^l : a_i^1, a_i^2, ..., a_i^{n-1} \rightarrow a_i^n$$

Local rules express local context knowledge. Local rules with empty body are used to express factual knowledge.

Mapping rules associate literals from V_i (*local literals*) with literals from the vocabulary of other contexts (*foreign literals*). A mapping rule may contain both local and foreign literals in its body, and a local literal in its head. Mapping rules are modelled as defeasible rules; namely they cannot be applied to support their conclusion if there is adequate contrary evidence. They have the following form:

$$r_i^m : a_i^1, a_j^2, ..., a_k^{n-1} \Rightarrow a_i^n$$

The above mapping rule is defined by P_i, and associates some of its own local literals (e.g. a_i^1) with some of the local literals of P_j (a_j^2), P_k (a_k^{n-1}) and other system contexts. The head of the rule (a_i^n) contains a local literal of the theory that has defined the rule (P_i).

Finally, each context P_i defines a (total/partial) preference order T_i on P to express its confidence on the knowledge it imports from other contexts. This is of the form:

$$T_i = [P_k, P_l, ..., P_n]$$

A context P_k is preferred by P_i to context P_l if P_k precedes P_l in this order. A total preference order enables resolving all potential conflicts that may arise from the interaction of contexts through their mapping rules. Partial ordering enables resolving only conflicts caused by the interaction of certain contexts. However, it is closer to the needs of real-world distributed applications, where distributed entities cannot always be aware of the quality of information imported by any available information source. In case of partial ordering, the contexts that are not included in T_i are equally preferred by P_i and less preferred than the contexts that are contained in T_i.

3 Four Alternative Strategies for Conflict Resolution

In this section, we describe four versions of a distributed algorithm, *P2P_DR*, for query evaluation in MCS. Each version implements a different strategy for conflict resolution and handles the following problem: *Given a MCS P, and a query about literal x_i issued to context P_i, find the truth value of x_i considering P_i's local theory, its mappings and the rule theories of the other system contexts.*

A common characteristic of the four strategies is that they all use context knowledge and preference information from the system contexts to resolve potential conflicts that may arise when importing information from two or more different sources. Their main difference is in the type and extent of information that the system contexts exchange to evaluate the quality of imported context information. To demonstrate their differences, we describe how each strategy is applied to the scenario depicted in Fig. 1.

P_1	P_2	P_3
$r^l_{11} : a_1 \rightarrow x_1$	$r^l_{21} : c_2 \rightarrow a_2$	$r^l_{31} : \rightarrow a_3$
$r^m_{12} : a_2 \Rightarrow a_1$	$r^l_{22} : b_2 \rightarrow a_2$	
$r^m_{13} : a_3, a_4 \Rightarrow \neg a_1$	$r^m_{23} : b_5 \Rightarrow b_2$	
	$r^m_{24} : b_6 \Rightarrow b_2$	

P_4	P_5	P_6
$r^l_{41} : \rightarrow a_4$	$r^l_{51} : \rightarrow b_5$	$r^l_{61} : \rightarrow b_6$

Figure 1: A MCS of 6 context theories

In this system, there are six context theories and a query about literal x_1 is issued to context P_1. To compute the truth value of x_1, P_1 has to import knowledge from P_2, P_3 and P_4. In case the three system contexts return positive truth values for a_2, a_3 and a_4 respectively, there will be a conflict about the truth value of a_1 caused by the two conflicting mapping rules r_{12} and r_{13}.

3.1 Single Answers

Single Answers requires each context to return only the truth value of the queried literal. When a context receives conflicting answers from two different contexts, it resolves the conflict using its preference order. The version of the distributed algorithm that implements this strategy (*P2P_DR$_{SA}$*) is called by a context P_i when it receives a query about one of its local literals (say x_i) and proceeds as follows:

1. In the first step, it determines whether the queried literal, x_i or its negation $\neg x_i$ derive from P_i's local rules, returning a positive or a negative truth value respectively.
2. If Step 1 fails, the algorithm collects, in the second step, the local and mapping rules that support x_i (as their conclusion). For each such rule, it checks the truth value of the literals in its body, by issuing similar queries (recursive calls of the algorithm) to P_i or to the appropriate contexts. To avoid cycles, before each new query, it checks if the same query has been issued before, during the same algorithm call. If the algorithm receives positive answers for all literals in the body of a rule, it determines that this rule is applicable and builds its Supportive Set SS_{r_i}. This derives from the union of the set of the foreign literals contained in the body of r_i, with the Supportive Sets of the local literals in the body of r_i. In the end, in case there is no applicable supportive rule, the algorithm returns a negative answer for x_i and terminates. Otherwise, it computes the Supportive Set of x_i, SS_{x_i}, as the *strongest* of the Supportive Sets of the applicable rules that support x_i, and proceeds to the next step. To compute the strength of a set of literals, *P2P_DR*$_{SA}$ uses the preference order T_i. A literal a_k is considered stronger than literal b_l if P_k precedes P_l in T_i. The strength of a set is determined by the weakest element in the set.
3. In the third step, the algorithm collects and checks the applicability of the rules that contradict x_i (rules with conclusion $\neg x_i$). If there is no such applicable rule, it terminates by returning a positive answer for x_i. Otherwise, it computes the Conflicting Set of x_i, CS_{x_i}, as the strongest of the Supportive Sets of the applicable rules that contradict x_i.
4. In its last step, *P2P_DR*$_{SA}$ compares the strength of SS_{x_i} and CS_{x_i} using T_i to determine the truth value of x_i. If SS_{x_i} is stronger, the algorithm returns a positive truth value. Otherwise, it returns a negative one.

In the system of Fig. 1, *P2P_DR*$_{SA}$ fails to produce a local answer for x_1. In the second step, it attempts to use P_1's mapping rules. The algorithm eventually receives positive answers for a_2, a_3 and a_4, and resolves the conflict for a_1 by comparing the strength of the Supportive Sets of the two conflicting rules, r_{12} and r_{13}. Assuming that $T_1=[P_4,P_2,P_6,P_3,P_5]$, it determines that $SS_{r_{12}}=\{a_2\}$ is stronger than $SS_{r_{13}}=\{a_3, a_4\}$ and returns positive answer for a_1 and eventually for x_1.

An analytical description of *P2P_DR*$_{SA}$ is available in [3]. The same paper presents some formal properties of the algorithm regarding (a) its termination; (b) required number of messages ($O(n^2l)$, where n stands for the total number of contexts, whereas l stands for the number of literals a local vocabulary may contain); (c) computational complexity ($O(n^2l^2r)$, where r stands for the number of rules a context theory may contain); and (d) the existence of a unified defeasible theory that produces the same results with the distributed algorithm under the proof theory of Defeasible Logic [1].

3.2 Strength of Answers

The Strength of Answers strategy requires the queried context to return, along with the truth value of the queried literal, information about whether this value derives from its local theory or from the combination of the local theory and its mappings. To support this feature, the second version of the algorithm, $P2P\_DR_{SWA}$, supports two types of positive answers: (a) a *strict* answer indicates that a positive truth value derives from local rules only; (b) a *weak* answer indicates that a positive truth value derives from a combination of local and mapping rules. The querying context evaluates the answer based not only on the context that returns it but also on the type of the answer. This version follows the four main steps of $P2P\_DR_{SA}$ but with the following modifications:

a) A Supportive/Conflicting Set (of a rule or of a literal) is not a set of literals, but a set of the answers returned for these literals.
b) The strength of an element in a Supportive/Conflicting Set is determined primarily by the type of answer computed by the algorithm (strict answers are considered stronger than weak ones); and secondly by the rank of the queried context in the preference order of the querying context.

Given these differences, the execution of $P2P\_DR_{SWA}$ in the system depicted in Figure 1, produces the following results: The Supportive Sets of rules r_{12} and r_{13} are respectively: $SS_{r_{12}} = \{weak_{a_2}\}$, $SS_{r_{13}} = \{strict_{a_3}, strict_{a_4}\}$ (the truth values of a_3 and a_4 derive from the local theories of P_3 and P_4 respectively, while P_2 has to use its mappings to compute the truth value of a_2) and $SS_{r_{13}}$ is computed to be stronger than $SS_{r_{12}}$. Eventually, the algorithm computes negative truth values for a_1 and x_1.

3.3 Propagating Supportive Sets

The main feature of *Propagating Supportive Sets* is that along with the truth value of the queried literal, the queried context returns also its Supportive Set. The algorithm that implements this strategy, $P2P\_DR_{PS}$, differs from $P2P\_DR_{SA}$ only in the construction of a Supportive Set; in this case, the Supportive Set of a rule derives from the union of the Supportive Sets of all (local and foreign) literals in its body.

In the MCS depicted in Figure 1, $P2P\_DR_{PS}$ when called by P_2 to compute the truth value of a_2, and assuming that $T_2=[P_5,P_6]$, returns a positive value and its Supportive Set $SS_{a_2} = \{b_5\}$. The answers returned for literals a_3 and a_4 are both positive values and empty Supportive Sets (they are locally proved), and $P2P\_DR_{PS}$ called by P_1 computes $SS_{r_{12}} = \{a_2,b_5\}$ and $SS_{r_{13}} = \{a_3,a_4\}$. Using $T_1=[P_4,P_2,P_6,P_3,P_5]$, $P2P\_DR_{PS}$ determines that $SS_{r_{13}}$ is *stronger* than $SS_{r_{12}}$ (as both P_3 and P_4 precede P_5 in T_1), and eventually computes negative values for a_1 and x_1.

3.4 Complex Supportive Sets

Complex Supportive Sets, similarly with *Propagating Supportive Sets*, requires the queried context to return the Supportive Set of the queried literal along with its truth value. In the case of *Propagating Supportive Sets*, the Supportive Set is a set of literals that describe the most *preferred* (by the queried context) chain of reasoning that leads to the derived truth value. In the case of *Complex Supportive Sets*, the Supportive Set is actually a set of sets of literals; each different set describes a different chain of reasoning that leads to the computed truth value. The context that resolves the conflict determines the most *preferred* chain of reasoning using its own preference order. $P2P\_DR_{CS}$, differs from $P2P\_DR_{SA}$ as follows:

a) The Supportive Set of a rule derives from the product of the Supportive Sets of the literals in the body of the rule.
b) The Supportive Set of a literal derives from the union of the Supportive Sets of the applicable rules that support it.
c) Comparing the Supportive Set and the Conflicting Set of a literal requires comparing the *strongest* sets of literals contained in the two sets.

In the system of Figure 1, $P2P\_DR_{CS}$ called by P_2 computes a positive truth value for a_2 and $SS_{a_2} = \{\{b_5\},\{b_6\}\}$. When called by P_3 and P_4, $P2P\_DR_{CS}$ returns positive truth values and empty Supportive Sets for a_3 and a_4 respectively, while when called by P_1, it computes $SS_{r_{12}}=\{\{a_2,b_5\},\{a_2,b_6\}\}$ and $SS_{r_{13}}=\{\{a_3,a_4\}\}$. Using $T_1=[P_4,P_2,P_6,P_3,P_5]$, $P2P\_DR_{CS}$ determines that $\{a_2,b_6\}$ is the strongest set in $SS_{r_{12}}$, and is also stronger than $\{a_3,a_4\}$ (as P_6 precedes P_3 in T_1). Consequently, it returns a positive answer for a_1 and eventually a positive answer for x_1 as well.

Analytical descriptions of the three latter algorithms, as well as some results on their formal properties are omitted due to space limitations. Briefly, the three algorithms share the same properties regarding termination, number of messages, and the existence of an equivalent unified defeasible theory with $P2P\_DR_{SA}$. The computational complexity of second and third strategy is similar to $P2P\_DR_{SA}$; the fourth strategy imposes a much heavier computational overhead (exponential to the number of literals defined in the system).

4 Prototypical Implementation & Experimental Evaluation

In order to evaluate the four strategies, we implemented the respective versions of *P2P_DR* and a P2P system simulating the Multi-Context framework in Java.

4.1 Implementation

For the network library as well as the peer-to-peer communication library, we used a custom-built library based on the java.network packages. Libraries such as JXTA would be inefficient due to the complexity in configuring such a simple ad-hoc peer-to-peer network. The message exchanging protocol in our custom library is also simple and straightforward. However, one can use any other peer communication libraries, as the system uses an abstract network manager interface.

The system consists of 5 packages: *agencies, logic, knowledge, network, peerlib*. The *agencies* package contains the classes that implement the input file parsers and those that implement the four algorithms. The *logic* package contains the classes the represent (in memory) the literals and rules. The *knowledge* package includes the *KnowledgeBase* class; a Singleton class that stores the local and mapping rules, the preference orders and any other required information. The *network* package includes the mechanism that associates a new socket connection with a new thread, whereas the *peerlib* contains the higher-level classes that operate the communication between two peers (e.g. the *Pipe* class).

4.2 Setup of the Experiments

The goal of the experiments was to compare the four strategies in terms of actual computational time spent by a peer to evaluate the answer to a single query. Using a tool that we built for the needs of the experiments, we created theories that correspond to the worst case that the computation of a single query requires computing the truth value of all literals from all system nodes. The test theories that we created have the following form:

$$r^m{}_1 : a_2, a_3, \ldots, a_n \Rightarrow a_0$$

$$\ldots$$

$$r^m{}_{n/2} : a_1, \ldots a_{n/2-1}, a_{n/2+1} \ldots, a_n \Rightarrow a_0$$

$$r^m{}_{n/2+1} : a_1, \ldots a_{n/2}, a_{n/2+2} \ldots, a_n \Rightarrow \neg a_0$$

$$\ldots$$

$$r^m{}_n : a_1, a_2, \ldots, a_{n-1} \Rightarrow \neg a_0$$

The above mapping rules are defined by P_0 and associate the truth value of a_0 with the truth value of the literals from n other system peers. Half of them support a_0 as their conclusion, while the remaining rules contradict a_0. In case the truth values returned for all foreign literals $a_1, a_2, \ldots, a_n$ are all positive then all mapping rules are applicable and are involved in the computation of the truth value of a_0.

To exclude the communication overhead from the total time spent by P_0 to evaluate the truth value of a_0, we filled a local cache of P_0 with appropriate answers for all the foreign literals. Specifically, for all strategies we used positive truth values for all foreign literals. For the second strategy (*Strength of Answers*), the type of positive answer (*strict* or *weak*) was chosen randomly for each literal, and for the last two strategies we used Supportive Sets that involve all literals.

For each version of the algorithm we tested six experiments with a variant number of system peers (n): 10, 20, 40, 60, 80, and 100. The test machine was an Intel Celeron M at 1.4 GHz with 512 MB of RAM.

4.3 *Results*

Table 1 shows in msec the computation time for each version of *P2P_DR*. In the case of $P2P\_DR_{CS}$, we were able to measure the computation time only for the cases $n = 10, 20, 40$; in the other cases the test machine ran out of memory.

The computation time for the first three strategies is proportional to the square of the number of system peers. The fourth strategy requires much more memory space and computation time (almost exponential to the number of peers), which make it inapplicable in cases of very dense systems. The results also highlight the tradeoff between the computational complexity and the extent of context information that each strategy exploits to evaluate the confidence in the returned answers.

Table 1: Computation time for the four versions of *P2P_DR*

# peers (n)	$P2P\_DR_{SA}$	$P2P\_DR_{SWA}$	$P2P\_DR_{PS}$	$P2P\_DR_{CS}$
10	78	80	1313	2532
20	469	540	1534	4305
40	2422	3102	3466	207828
60	5719	6390	7188	-
80	10437	10302	15484	-
100	16484	15550	27484	-

5 Conclusions and Future Work

In this paper, we proposed a totally distributed approach for reasoning with mutually inconsistent rule theories in Multi-Context Systems. The proposed model uses rule theories to express local context knowledge, defeasible rules for the definition of mappings, and a preference order to express confidence in the imported context information. We also described four strategies that use context and preference information for conflict resolution, and which differ in the extent of context information exchanged between the system contexts, and described how each strategy is implemented in a different version of a distributed algorithm for query evaluation in Multi-Context Systems. Finally, we described the implementation of the four strategies in a simulated peer-to-peer environment, which we used to evaluate the strategies with respect to their computational requirements. The obtained results highlight the tradeoff between the extent of context information exchanged between the contexts to evaluate the quality of the imported context and the computational load of the algorithms that implement the four strategies.

Part of our ongoing work includes: (a) Implementing the algorithms in Logic Programming, using the equivalence with Defeasible Logic [3], and the well-studied translation of defeasible knowledge into logic programs under Well-Founded Semantics [2]; (b) Adding non-monotonic features in the local context theories to express uncertainty in the local knowledge; (c) Extending the model to support overlapping vocabularies, which will enable different contexts to use elements of common vocabularies (e.g. URIs); and (d) Implementing real-world applications of our approach in the Ambient Intelligence and Semantic Web domains. Some initial results regarding the application of our approach in Ambient Intelligence are already available in [4].

References

1. Antoniou G., Billington D., Governatori G., Maher M.J.: Representation results for defeasible logic. ACM Transactions on Computational Logic 2(2):255-287, 2001.
2. Antoniou G., Billington D., Governatori G., Maher M.J.: Embedding defeasible logic into logic programming. Theory and Practice of Logic Programming 6(6):703-735, 2006.
3. Bikakis A., Antoniou G.: Distributed Defeasible Reasoning in Multi-Context Systems. In NMR'08, pp. 200-206, (2008)
4. Bikakis A., Antoniou G.: Distributed Defeasible Contextual Reasoning in Ambient Computing. In AmI'08 European Conference on Ambient Intelligence, pp. 258-375, (2008)
5. Benerecetti M., Bouquet P., Ghidini C.: Contextual reasoning distilled. JETAI 12(3): 279-305, 2000.
6. Brewka G., Roelofsen F., Serafini L.: Contextual Default Reasoning. In: IJCAI, pp. 268-273 (2007)
7. Buvac, S, Mason I.A.: Propositional Logic of Context. In AAAI, pp. 412-419, (1993).
8. Ghidini C., Giunchiglia F.: Local Models Semantics, or contextual reasoning = locality + compatibility. Artificial Intelligence, 127(2):221-259, 2001.
9. Giunchiglia F., Serafini L.: Multilanguage hierarchical logics, or: how we can do without modal logics. Artificial Intelligence, 65(1), 1994.
10. McCarthy J.: Generality in Artificial Intelligence. Communications of the ACM, 30(12):1030-1035, 1987.
11. McCarthy J., Buvac S.: Formalizing Context (Expanded Notes). Aliseda A., van Glabbeek R., Westerstahl D. (eds.) Computing Natural Language, pp. 13-50. CSLI Publications, Stanford (1998)
12. Roelofsen F, Serafini L.: Minimal and Absent Information in Contexts. In IJCAI, pp. 558-563, (2005).
13. Serafini L., Bouquet P.: Comparing formal theories of context in AI. Artificial Intelligence, 155(1-2):41-67, 2004.

Certified Trust Model

[1]Vanderson Botêlho, [1]Fabríco Enembreck, [1]Bráulio C. Ávila, [2]Hilton de Azevedo, [1]Edson E. Scalabrin

[1]PUCPR, Pontifical Catholic University of Paraná

PPGIA, Graduate Program on Applied Computer Science

R. Imaculada Conceição, 1155

Curitiba PR Brazil

{vanderson, fabricio, avila, scalabrin}@ppgia.pucpr.br

[2]UTFPR, Federal Technological University of Paraná

PPGTE, Graduate Program on Technology

Av. 7 de Setembro, 3165

Curitiba, PR, Brazil

hilton@utfpr.edu.br

Abstract This paper presents a certified confidence model which aims to ensure credibility for information exchanged among agents which inhabit an open environment. Generally speaking, the proposed environment shows a supplier agent *b* which delivers service for a customer agent *a*. The agent *a* returns to *b* a cryptographed evaluation *r* on the service delivered. The agent *b* will employ *R* as testimonial when requested to perform the same task for a distinct customer agent. Our hypotheses are: (i) control over testimonials can be distributed as they are locally stored by the assessed agents, i.e., each assessed agent is the owner of its testimonials; and (ii) testimonials, provided by supplier agents on their services, can be considered reliable since they are encapsulated with public key cryptography. This approach reduces the limitations of confidence models based, respectively, on the experience resulted from direct interaction between agents (*direct confidence*) and on the indirect experience obtained from reports of witnesses (*propagated confidence*). Direct confidence is a poor-quality measure for a customer agent *a* hardly has enough opportunities to interact with a supplier agent *b* so as to grow a useful knowledge base. Propagated confidence depends on the willingness of witnesses to share their experiences. The empiric model was tested in a multiagent system applied to the stock market, where supplier agents provide recommendations for buying or selling assets and customer agents then choose suppliers based on their reputations. Results demonstrate that the confidence model proposed enables the agents to more efficiently choose partners.

Please use the following format when citing this chapter:

Botêlho, V., Enembreck, F., Ávila, B.C., de Azevedo, H. and Scalabrin, E.E., 2009, in IFIP International Federation for Information Processing, Volume 296; *Artificial Intelligence Applications and Innovations III*; Eds. Iliadis, L., Vlahavas, I., Bramer, M.; (Boston: Springer), pp. 41–49.

1 Introduction

Nowadays, distributed and flexible approach seems to be a good to complex applications that deal with huge amount of data and services, the main reason being the system necessity of dynamic adaptation to structure and environment changes. Thus, multiagent systems are good candidates for building distributed heterogeneous flexible open architectures that shall ensure a great amount of services in a collective work context with no *a priori* structure. Nevertheless, even if data and control distribution may bring reliability when considering service availability, the lack of a information centralizer adds weakness to the trust relations the clients of a service or product and its service providers or hosts. For Huynh *et al* [2], the basic question is: in an open system how can an agent trust in a stranger?

The way to get the value that represents the level of trust depends on the system architecture, particularly, in how it allows getting and giving feedbacks. For instance, in an eBay like system [6], where transactions are made by people, the delays may attain days. On another hand, in P2P systems [7], where transactions may be concluded in some milliseconds. In this case, scalability becomes a crucial factor, requesting a distributed trusting model to bring more reliability when comparing with centralized models.

Studies were made in order to reduce the interaction risk between agents in open systems. Castelfranchi and Falcone [10] consider the trust relation inside a MAS as a mental state that is essential to allow delegation mechanisms between agents. Other works [11], [12] sustain that trust may be useful for reducing the risk related to interactions among agents. Mui et al. [13] consider trust as a multidisciplinary subject, representing it by the use of ontologies. They divide trust definitions as direct and indirect. REGRET [8] combines the models of direct and propagated trust and defines three agent interaction dimensions (i.e. individual, social and ontological). In the Individual Dimension, trust is obtained by direct interaction. In the Social Dimension, trust is obtained by indirect interaction (i.e. testimonies). In the Ontological Dimension, trust is obtained by the combination of both. Huynh et al. [2] propose a trust model based on *certified reputation*, which combines both direct trust and indirect trust by testimonies.

The trust model based in *certified reputation* [2], where testimonies are store locally by the agents that were assessed, has two advantages: (i) The assessment agent shares its experience only once and, (ii) in order to obtain a trust information it's necessary only two agents. Nevertheless, the set of trust assessments about a service provider agent may be changed by that agent in order to better notify its reputation, i.e. a service provider agent may inform, when asked, only its positive assessments, omitting its bad ones. This arbitrary selection adds distortions when computing the trust and decreases the efficiency of agents when choosing partners. Our proposal is to enhance the model of certified reputation by the use of assessment that has signatures made by asymmetric keys [14], doing so, the assessment content can not be read by the assessed agent.

Section 2 presents our model of certified trust. Section 3 describes a test scenario where, in a multiagent system, provider agents give recommendations about buying and selling assets for client agents. The client agents have the interest in select the best provider agents. Section 4 illustrates how the experiment has being conducted and discusses the results till now.

2 Certified Trust Model

Basically, a trust model takes into account an agent *a* that quantifies the trust it has regarding an agent *b* [2]. For example, agent *a* is the *evaluator* and the agent *b is the target.* A rating is calculated based on the past experiences regarding the quality of a service made by an agent to the other. Every *rating* is represented by a *tuple r=(a,b,i,v,c)*, where *a* and *b* are agents that participate in a interaction *i* and *v* is the assessment made by *a* over *b* about a given term *c*. Every assessment is stored locally by the service agent that was evaluated. So, when asked by a client agent, it can inform about the assessment results it had before. Term *c* brings to the trust model the capability assess every agent in different contexts. For instance, every evaluation is given for a specific time. The notation of the trust from *a* on *b,* about the term *c* is *T(a,b,c)*. Quantifying trust requires a set of relevant assessments. This set is notated as *R(a,b,c)* and is the basis for the certified trust model we propose.

2.1 Model Definition

The certified model follows a typical scenario. An agent *b* provides a service to a client agent *a*. The client agent *a* returns agent *b* an assessment *r* about the service performed. Agent *b* stores *r* locally and will use *r* as a testimony if it is inspected by another client agent to realize the same kind of service. Target agent can not modify assessment contents or inform only about a minimal set of its better assessments. The reason is that assessments are signed by their evaluators. Only evaluators can know about the assessment contents regarding a target agent.

When an interaction *i* ends up, the target agent *b* asks the client agent *a* to assess its performance *v* about a given term *c.* This ends in a rating *r=(a,b,i,v,c)*. Agent *b* stores the rating inside its local repository. When an client agent *a* informs its interest on a term *c,* from a provider *b*, *b* answers informing its more relevant ratings *R*. This approach reduces the problem when an evaluator agent refuses to share its experiences. Another advantage is that the request is made one time and only two agents are concerned by the procedure. The calculus is made by weighed mean (Equation 1) of all ratings returned by the target agent. *Ratings* have a coefficient that decreases as the rating gets older. The calculus of a *rating r* in function of time is named $\omega(r_i)$, with $(\omega(r_i) \geq 0)$. The calculus of trust is defined by:

$$\mathrm{T}(a,b,c)=\frac{\sum_{r_i\in R(a,b,c)}\omega(r_i)\cdot v_i}{\sum_{r_i\in Rc(a,b,c)}\omega(r_i)} \tag{1}$$

Rating coefficients have their values decreased (Equation 2) by a time dependent exponential law; this makes old ratings few significant or irrelevant. This is important because it allows a client agent detect changes in quality of services provided by a provider more quickly, because the recent ratings have more relevance than the other ratings:

$$\omega\,\mathrm{Re}(r_i)=e^{-\frac{\Delta t(r_i)}{\lambda}} \tag{2}$$

Where $\omega\mathrm{Re}(r_i)$ is the value of coefficient r_i related to the time variation $\Delta t(r_i)$, that means the time elapsed between the time at the moment of the request and the moment the rating was created. Finally, λ is the factor that determines the coefficient decreasing speed related to time.

We point that there is no guarantee that the agents are honest on their assessments or that their capabilities to assess service agents are inaccurate or imprecise. Our trust certified model reduces this problem introducing in the process the *credibility* of the evaluator agent as another element in order to determine the relevance of a specific rating inside a trust calculus. This process determines how an evaluator is reliable and can be calculated when customers evaluate their personal interactions in order to compare with the ratings received. The *credibility* of an assessment agent *w* is calculated by another assessment agent *a* and, is named $TRCr(a,w)\in[-1,+1]$, where *RCr.* A rating weight is related to the time $\omega\mathrm{Re}(r_i)$ and the credibility $\omega RCr(r_i)$:

$$\omega c(r_i)=\omega\,\mathrm{Re}(r_i)\cdot\omega RCr(r_i) \tag{3}$$

When $\omega RCr(r_i)$ is negative, the assessment agent has no credibility and its rating is adjusted to zero:

$$\omega RCr(r_i)=\begin{cases}0 & se\quad TRCr(a,w)\le 0\\ TRCr(a,w) & se\quad TRCr(a,w)>0\end{cases} \tag{4}$$

The scenario considers a minimum of three agents: *a, b* and *w*. Considering that *a* assess *b* and *b* stores locally its rating, given by $r_a=(a,b,i_a,c,v_a)$. When agent *a* receives a *rating* of another evaluator agent, at this case agent *w*, *a* calculates w credibility by comparing the performance of agent *b* (i.e. v_a) with the evaluation made by *w* over *b*. The *rating* of *w* related to *b* is given by $r_w=(a,b,i_w,c,v_w)$. The credibility of agent *w* is obtained by the difference between both values (v_a,v_w). It is expressed by v_k, according to equation 5.

$$v_k = \begin{cases} 1-|v_w - v_a| & se \quad |v_w - v_a| < \iota \\ -1 \quad se & |v_w - v_a| > \iota \end{cases} \qquad \text{where: } (0 \le \iota \le 2) \tag{5}$$

So, v_k receives a positive value if the difference between v_w and v_a stays below the limit ι, otherwise, the credibility is negative, i.e. the evaluator agent can not be trusted.

The honesty of provider agents when they envoy their ratings is granted by a digital signature based on asymmetric keys. The signature is composed by both, private and public keys. With this method, a System Administrator agent creates a code key for every kind of service *c*. This key is sent to all agents, it is a public key. Then the System Administrator agent creates a second key that is used only for decoding. This key is sent only for the evaluators agents.

Every time a evaluator/client agent sends a rating to a provider agent, the public key for service *c* is used to encrypt the value of *v*. As *v* can be decrypted only with the private key that belongs to the client agents, no provider agent can know about the value of *v* related to the rating *r*. This avoids that a provider agent selects a subset of relevant ratings *R*. In our experiments we used the Pretty Good Privacy (PGP) algorithm [16] to encrypt and decrypt the values of the ratings.

3 Experiment

We defined four behavior groups for the provider agents: *good providers* (which use a analysis method with gives high level of success to their recommendations), *bad providers* (with low level of success in their recommendations), *ordinary providers* (with a level of recommendations success around the average, i.e. a mobile average) and, *malicious providers* (this provider agents used the same method used by the third group but they order their ratings with the purpose of sending only the better ones and make difficult the differentiation between good and bad service provider agents).

Client agents are organized in four groups: *No_Trust* (the ones that do not have any trust model); *Direct_Trust,* (the ones that implement a direct trust model); *Cr_Trust,* (the ones that implement certified trust model based on certified reputation and; *Cryp_Trust,* (the ones that implement the certified trust model). Client agents interact with different kind of service provider agents and, according to the trust model they have, they select the service provider agent that seems to maximize their interests.

Every client agent starts consulting several service provider agents with whom it performs as many buying/selling orders of actions as necessary. The evaluation of the trust model is made by measuring the performance of every service agent portfolio. Every agent receives the same amount of money to invest. At the end of every working day, the percentage of every service agent portfolio is observed growing. The agents acted over historical real data of Bovespa stock market [15]. To this experiment we considered only one kind of action quoted at Bovespa from January/2nd/2006 to December/18th/2007, totalizing 473 working days. Data regarding 2006 were used for training. At the end of 2006, the portfolios were restarted. Nevertheless, the agents kept the experience acquired during 2006 year. Then, during the year of 2007, every client agent (investor) evaluated the performance of its service provider agents (market expert) by using its trust model.

Every experiment was started by the creation of client and service agents. Service agents had only one strategy to perform financial analysis. Client agents had only one trust model. Client agent's utility gain, named UG, represents the utility gain of the trust model. At the end of every working day, the function of utility of client agents was added according to agent's trust model. The average of those values represented the utility gain of the trust model.

Four scenarios were set in order to evaluate the behavior of the trust model. At the Scenario I has service agents that are honest, despite they select their *ratings*, that selection do not disturbed their real performance because all service provider agents use the same technique of analysis during the all scenario (Table 1 presents the variables used).

Table 1. System variables for a honest environment.

Simulation variable	Symbol	Value
Number of simulation rounds	N	473
Total number of provider agents:	N_P	500
Good providers	N_{PG}	166
Ordinary providers	N_{OP}	168
Bad providers	N_{PB}	166
Malicious providers	N_{MI}	0
Number of consumers in each group	N_C	500

At the scenario II, service provider agents have different performance because their techniques of analysis change during the scenario. By doing so, a service provider agent that was using a very good analysis technique may have its performance decreased because it starts using a worse one, and vice-versa. Parameters defined at Table 2 ensure that scenarios I and II have service provider agents with rational behavior and constant performance due to the absence of agents from the *Malicious service provider* agent group. Here, all service provider agents used a same financial analytical technique.

Table 2. Parameters of the model.

Parameters	Symbol	Value
Speed Factor	λ	$-\frac{5}{\ln(0.5)}$
Maximum number of better ratings	NR	10
Credibility limit	ι	0.5

Figure 1 shows that at Scenario I all agents that use a trust model obtained similar results (+100%). This happened because service agents had completely predictable behaviors. In another hand, agent without trust model had their performance compromised (-23%). Figure 2 shows (Scenario II) that the *cryp_trust* model has the best performance in most of the time. Significant variations happen when a good service provider agent starts to have a bad performance (due to changes in the financial analytical technique). The reason is because the service provider agent sends good ratings, related to a recent past. This deceives the *cr_trust* model and decreases its performance.

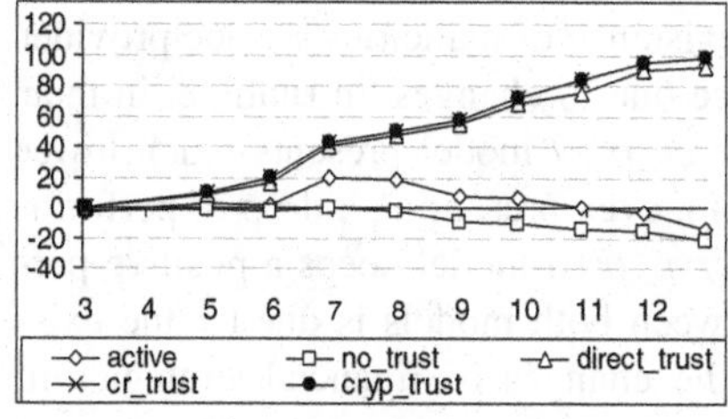

Fig. 1. Honest context without changes.

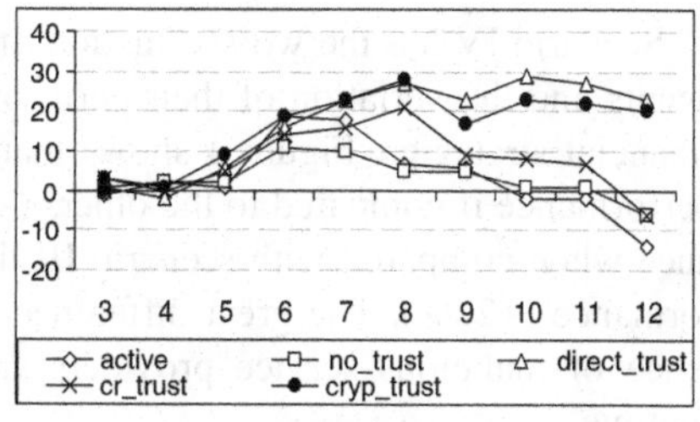

Fig. 2. Honest context with changes.

In scenarios III and IV, we introduce malicious service providers that even select and send their best ratings in order to influence calculus of trust made by the client agents. Similarly to scenarios I and II, at Scenario III service providers agents have a constant performance. At Scenario IV, they have variations in their performance. Table 3 shows the configuration used.

Figure 3 shows a simulation where service provider agents do not make changes in their financial analytical techniques, thus keeping their performance constant. The *cr_trust* model had the worst result (-58%). The reason is that the client agent is deceived by the malicious service agents that send ratings arbitrary selected. On the other hand, the *cryp_trust* model with crypted rating avoid malicious service agent to select their best ratings. As consequence, the *cryp_trust* model performance remains similar to the scenario where there are no malicious agents.

Table 3. System variables for dishonest context.

Simulation variable	Symbol	Value
Number of simulation rounds	N	473
Total number of provider agents:	N_P	500
Good providers	N_{PG}	100
Ordinary providers	N_{OP}	100
Bad providers	N_{PB}	100
Malicious providers	N_{MI}	100
Number of consumers in each group	N_C	500

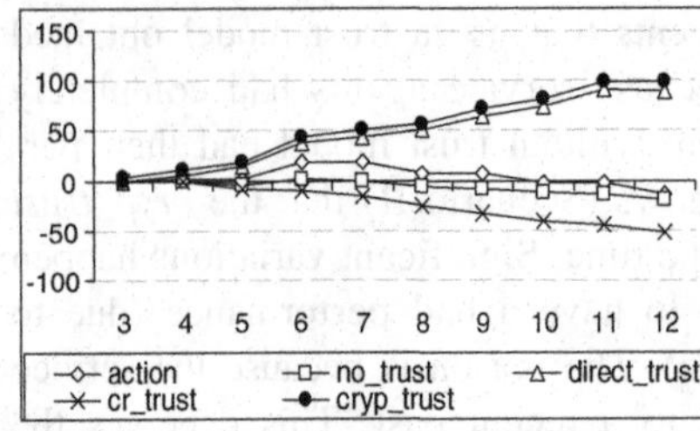

Fig. 3. Dishonest context without changes.

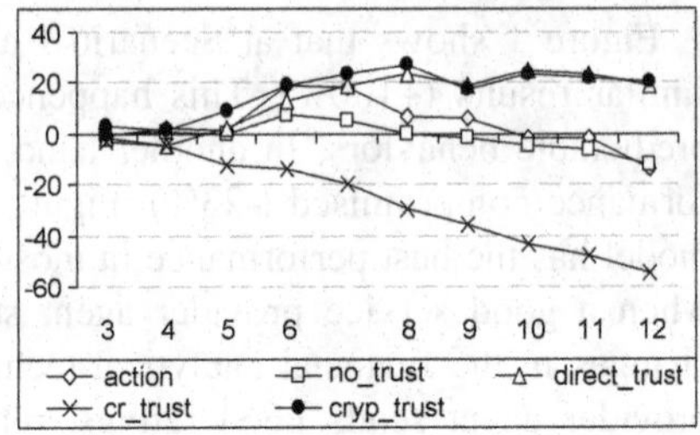

Fig. 4. Dishonest context with changes.

Scenario IV has the worst situation: the existence of malicious service provider agents and the variation of their performance due to changes, in runtime, in their financial strategies. Figure 4 shows that the *cr_trust* model presents much lower performance if compared to the others (-55%), even presenting a drop of performance when compared with scenario III the *cryp_trust* model keeps a positive performance (+20%). The great difference between both models is due to: the existence of malicious service providers and the changes of financial strategies in runtime.

5 Conclusion

We presented a certified trust model applied to multiagent systems (*cryp_trust model)*. The model enhances the concept of reputation from the certified reputation model. Both approaches, certified trust and certified reputation, use the assessment of service providers agents made by client agents. The assessments act as testimonies about their performance. The certified trust model allows increasing the system reability against malicious service provider agents that could try to manipulate the information concerning their performance in order to have some benefits. The results show that our certified trust model is more efficient specially in malicious scenarios. A key point is the use of asymmetric signing keys in order to protect and keep the ratings distributed.

Future works shall focus on online detection of service provider agents and the treatment of malicious agents. Here a hypothesis to improve the *cryp_trust model* may be the use of strategies for tendency change detection.

References

1. Wooldridge, M. and Jennings, N. R.: Pitfalls of agent-oriented development. In: Proceedings 2nd International Conf. on Autonomous Agents, Minnesota, United States (1998)

2. Huynh, T. D., Jennings, N. R., and Shadbolt, N. R: Certified reputation: how an agent can trust a stranger. In: Proceedings 5th international Joint Conference on Autonomous Agents and Multiagent Systems, Hakodate, Japan (2006)
3. Jennings, N. R., Huynh, D., Shadbold, N. R.: Developing an integrated trust and reputation model for open multi-agent systems. In: Proceedings 7th International Workshop on Trust in Agent Societies, New York, United States (2004)
4. Teacy, W. T., Patel, J., Jennings, N. R., and Luck, M: Coping with Inaccurate Reputation Sources: Experimental Analysis of a Probabilistic Trust Model. In: Proceedings 4th Inter. Joint Conf, on Autonomous Agents and Multiagent Systems. The Netherlands (2005)
5. Nguyen, G. H., Chatalic, P., and Rousset, M. C.: A probabilistic trust model for semantic peer to peer systems. In: Proceedings International Workshop on Data Management in Peer-To-Peer Systems, Nantes, France (2008)
6. Ebay Inc. http://www.ebay.com.
7. Aberer, K. and Despotovic, Z.: Managing trust in a peer-2-peer information system. In: Proceedings 10th international Conference on information and Knowledge Management, Atlanta, Georgia, United States (2001)
8. Sabater, J. and Sierra, C.: REGRET: reputation in gregarious societies. In: Proceedings 5th international Conference on Autonomous Agents, Montreal, Quebec, Canada (2001)
9. Ramchurn, S. D., Huynh, D., and Jennings, N. R.: Trust in multi-agent systems. Knowl. Eng. Rev. 19, 1 (Mar. 2004)
10. Castelfranchi, C. and Falcone, R.: Principles of Trust for MAS: Cognitive Anatomy, Social Importance, and Quantification. In: Proceedings 3rd international Conference on Multi Agent Systems. ICMAS, Washington, United States (1998).
11. Griffiths, N.: Task delegation using experience-based multi-dimensional trust. In: Proceedings 4th international Joint Conference on Autonomous Agents and Multiagent Systems, Netherlands (2005)
12. Fullam, K. K., Klos, T. B., Muller, G., Sabater, J., Schlosser, A., Topol, Z., Barber, K. S., Rosenschein, J. S., Vercouter, L., and Voss, M.: A specification of the Agent Reputation and Trust (ART) testbed: experimentation and competition for trust in agent societies. In: Proceedings 4th international Joint Conference on Autonomous Agents and Multiagent Systems, Netherlands, (2005)
13. Mui, L., Mohtashemi, M., and Halberstadt, A.: Notions of reputation in multi-agents systems: a review. In: Proceedings 1st International Joint Conference on Autonomous Agents and Multiagent Systems, Bologna, Italy (2002)
14. Rivest, R. L., Shamir, A., and Adleman, L.: A method for obtaining digital signatures and public-key cryptosystems. Commun. ACM 26, 1 (Jan. 1983)
15. Bovespa: Bolsa de Valores de São Paulo, http://www.bovespa.com.br
16. Branagan, J. Ippolito, K. Musgrave, and Waggenspack W.: Pretty good privacy. In: ACM SIGGRAPH 96 Visual Proceedings: the Art and interdisciplinary Programs of SIGGRAPH '96, New Orleans, United States, (1996)

A Fuzzy Knowledge-based Decision Support System for Tender Call Evaluation

Panos Alexopoulos, Manolis Wallace, Konstantinos Kafentzis, and Aristodimos Thomopoulos

Abstract In the modern business environment, the capability of an enterprise to generate value from its business knowledge influences in an increasingly important way its competitiveness. Towards this direction, knowledge-based systems can be a very effective tool for enhancing the productivity of knowledge workers by providing them with advanced knowledge processing capabilities. In this paper we describe such a system which utilizes organizational and domain knowledge in order to support consultants in the process of evaluating calls for tender.

1 Introduction

In the modern business environment, the capability of an enterprise to generate value from its business knowledge influences in an increasingly important way its competitiveness [2]. In fact, in the knowledge management terminology, the term "knowledge asset" is used for denoting enterprise knowledge that regards markets, products, technologies and organisations and which enables the enterprise's business processes to generate profits and value [4].

The techniques to manage knowledge assets are drawn from two distinct areas: traditional business management and knowledge-based systems. The latter are software applications that are able to emulate the work of experts in specific areas of

Panos Alexopoulos · Konstantinos Kafetzis
IMC Technologies S.A., Fokidos 47, 11527, Athens, Greece,
e-mail: {palexopoulos, kkafentzis}@imc.com.gr

Manolis Wallace
Department of Computer Science and Technology University of Peloponnese, End of Karaiskaki St., 22100, Tripolis, Greece, e-mail: wallace@uop.gr

Aristodimos Thomopoulos
DIADIKASIA S.A., 180 Kifissias Av.,152 31, Halandri, Athens, Greece,
e-mail: athomopoulos@diadikasia.gr

Please use the following format when citing this chapter:

Alexopoulos, P., Wallace, M., Kafentzis, K. and Thomopoulos, A., 2009, in IFIP International Federation for Information Processing, Volume 296; *Artificial Intelligence Applications and Innovations III*; Eds. Iliadis, L., Vlahavas, I., Bramer, M.; (Boston: Springer), pp. 51–59.

knowledge. As such they can be a very effective tool for enhancing the productivity of knowledge workers who are, after all, some of the most important knowledge assets of an enterprise.

In this paper we describe a knowledge-based system that is used by consulting firms for tackling the problem of the evaluation of tender calls. A tender call is an open request made by some organization for a written offer concerning the procurement of goods or services at a specified cost or rate. The evaluation of a (consulting related) tender call by a consulting company refers to the process of deciding whether the company should devote resources for preparing a competitive tender in order to be awarded the bid.

In our approach, we formulate the above problem as a decision making problem in which the decision to be taken is whether the company should write the tender or not. The evaluation criterion is the probability that the company will be assigned the call's project. This is usually estimated by some consultant who takes in mind a number of different (and often conflicting) factors (criteria) that, according to his/her judgement and experience, influence it. These factors can be classified into objective and subjective but, most importantly, the whole process of evaluating and combining all those factors is knowledge-intensive. And that is because the consultant utilizes during this process aspects of the company's organizational knowledge as well as knowledge derived from his/her own expertise.

For that, the key characteristic of our system is that it stores and utilizes all the necessary knowledge that the consultant needs for taking an informed decision and performs reasoning that is very close to the his/her way of thinking. Furthermore, both the reasoning and the underlying knowledge have fuzzy characteristics and that is because many aspects of the knowledge the consultant utilizes for his/her evaluation are inherently imprecise.

The structure of the rest of the paper is as follows: In section 2 we outline some of the key criteria that the consultant uses for evaluating the partial factors that influence the company's chances to win the tender should a proposal be written. For each criterion, we highlight the knowledge that is required for its evaluation. In section 3 we describe the system's knowledge base which consists of a fuzzy domain ontology while in section 4 we present the reasoning mechanism in the form of fuzzy reasoning procedures for each criterion. Finally, in section 5 we provide a representative use case of the system and in section 6 we conclude by addressing issues for future work.

2 Tender Call Evaluation Criteria

The tender call evaluation process that our system implements comprises the evaluation of a number of partial criteria such as the call's budget, the call's coverage by the consulting company's expertise and experience and the potential competition. Due to space limitations, we describe here only two of the above criteria which, nevertheless, are quite representative of our approach. Along with the descriptions, we highlight the kind of knowledge required for the evaluation of each criterion.

2.1 Call's Relevance to the Consulting Company's Expertise

Any consultant or consulting company has expertise in specific business or technology areas and thus calls for tender which address topics outside of these areas are usually not pursued. This happens not only because the chances of winning such a call are significantly slimmer but also because, even if the call is won, the project's cost and failure probability will be very high. Thus, an important evaluation criterion is the degree at which the call's addressed topics are satisfied by the consultant's expertise.

The knowledge the consultant utilizes for the estimation of this degree includes first of all the list of areas at which the company is expert. Furthermore, he/she is able to determine whether two different areas are similar or not. For example, if the call is about a marketing project and the company is expert at sales support projects, then the two areas are quite similar. On the other hand, if the call's project is about developing an ontology-based system and the company does not know how to develop ontologies then there is no point at writing a tender for this call.

In any case, the ability to evaluate and quantify the similarity between two areas is of essential importance in deciding whether an effort should be made to address a tender call. As a consequence, the automated estimation of such degrees of relevance is a central part of this work and of our system.

2.2 Call's Coverage by the Consulting Company's Experience

The experience of a consulting company is usually measured by the number of the projects it has successfully implemented and delivered in the past. A large number of successful projects in some specific business area denotes a high level of experience in this area and conversely. And high level of experience in a tender call's addressed business areas is highly desirable for two reasons: i) it provides proof of the consulting company's ability to successfully handle projects similar to the requested and ii) the know-how gained through this experience makes the implementation of the requested project less costly and less risky.

In order to measure the relevant experience of the company, the consultant needs not only to know of all the projects the company has already implemented, but also and to be able to evaluate and quantify their relevance to the call.

3 System's Knowledge Base

The knowledge base of the system is implemented as a Fuzzy Ontology [1]. A Fuzzy Ontology is a tuple $\mathbf{O}_F = \{\mathbf{E}, \mathbf{R}\}$ where $\mathbf{E}$ is a set of semantic entities (or concepts) and $\mathbf{R}$ is a set of fuzzy binary semantic relations. Each element of $\mathbf{R}$ is a function $R : \mathbf{E}^2 \rightarrow [0,1]$.

In particular, $\mathbf{R} = \mathbf{T} \cup \mathbf{NT}$ where $\mathbf{T}$ is the set of taxonomic relations and $\mathbf{NT}$ is the set of non-taxonomic relations. Fuzziness in a taxonomic relation $R \in \mathbf{T}$ has the following meaning: High values of $R(a,b)$, where $a,b \in E$, imply that b's meaning approaches that of a's while low values suggest that b's meaning becomes "narrower" than that of a's.

On the other hand, a non-taxonomic relation has an ad-hoc meaning defined by the ontology engineer. Fuzziness in this case is needed when such a relation represents a concept for which there is no exact definition. In that case fuzziness reflects the degree at which the relation can be considered as true.

In our case, the structure of the system's ontology is dictated by the knowledge requirements identified in the previous section. Thus, the ontology consists of three groups of concepts, namely **Companies**, **Projects** and **ConsultingAreas**. The relation between different consulting areas is represented by means of a taxonomical relation called *hasSubArea*. The areas at which a company considers itself expert, are captured through the fuzzy non-taxonomical relation *isExpertAt* while the areas a project is relevant to are represented through the fuzzy non-taxonomical relation *isRelevantTo*. Finally, the projects a company has implemented or participated in are denoted by the (non-fuzzy) relation *hasImplemented*. A snapshot of the consulting areas taxonomy is shown in figure 1.

4 Evaluation of Criteria

4.1 Call's Relevance to the Consultant's Expertise

As mentioned in paragraph 2.1, the consultant assesses the call's relevance to the company's expertise by comparing the corresponding consulting areas. Consequently, such a comparison will need to be performed by the decision support system. For that there are three requirements:

1. The system needs to know the company's areas of expertise.
2. The system needs to know the areas covered by the call.
3. The system needs to have an explicit mechanism for determining the degree to which the call's areas are covered by the company's ones.

Requirement 2 is the most interesting one from a research point of view. In this work the automated estimation of the thematic coverage of the call is performed via

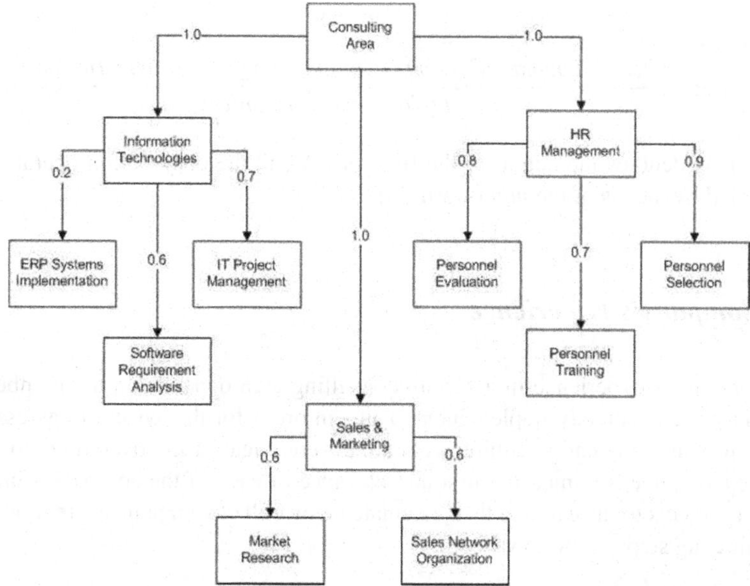

Fig. 1 Consulting Areas Fuzzy Taxonomy

a properly adapted version of the Detection of Thematic Categories (DTC) algorithm [6].

The DTC algorithm processes free text and extracts the fuzzy set of thematic categories that are associated with it via the exploitation of information contained in a fuzzy relational representation. With a small adaptation, the DTC algorithm is used to process the text of a call considering the system's knowledge base as input knowledge, thus generating a fuzzy set that contains the call's consulting areas and their associated degrees.

More specifically, the adapted DTC algorithm identifies in the call's text all terms mentioned in the system's knowledge base and then clusters them using an agglomerative approach; the inter-cluster distance measure used in the agglomeration is based on the notion of context [5], which measures how semantically close two concepts are, based on their distance in the fuzzy relations that comprise the system's knowledge. The thematic content and fuzzy cardinality of the resulting clusters provide the areas and their degrees respectively.

For requirement 1, namely the company's areas of expertise, the system utilizes the fuzzy relation *isExpertAt* from the ontology and retrieves a fuzzy set that contains the consulting areas and their associated degrees. This fuzzy set is then processed by the DTC algorithm and the result is a new fuzzy set that contains the thematic categories of the company's areas of expertise.

Given the above sets, namely the thematic categories of the areas in which the company has expertise and the set of areas relevant to the call, the call's coverage by the consulting company is calculated as follows, thus addressing requirement 3:

$$Coverage = \frac{h(CallThematicContent \cap CompanyExpertiseThematicContent)}{h(CallThematicContent)} \quad (1)$$

where $h(A)$ denotes the height of the fuzzy set A and the conjunction operation is performed by means of the *min* t-norm [3].

4.2 Company's Experience

The company's experience in a certain consulting area depends on the number of relevant projects already implemented. Thus, in order for the system to assess the degree to which the call's requirements are covered against the overall company's experience, it needs to measure first the relevance of each of the company's implemented projects to the call and then calculate an overall coverage measure. For that, the following steps are followed:

1. The call's consulting areas are extracted into a fuzzy set as explained in paragraph 4.1
2. The company's implemented projects are retrieved from the ontology as fuzzy sets.
3. The relevance of each past project to the call is calculated, also as explained in paragraph 4.1
4. Past projects whose relevance is less than a specific threshold (defined by the consultant) are discarded. For the remaining projects we calculate their accumulated relevance to the call.
5. The overall relevance is calculated by applying to the accumulated a fuzzy triangular number of the form $(0, a, \infty)$
6. The parameter a denotes the threshold over which additional past project do not further influence the overall similarity.

4.3 Overall Evaluation

For the overall evaluation of a tender call we use a technique based on the notion of the ordered weighted averaging operator(OWA), first introduced by Yager in [8]. An OWA operator of dimension n is a mapping $F : R^n \rightarrow R$ that has an associated n vector $w = (w_1, w_2, ..., w_n)^T$ such as $w_i \in [0,1], 1 \leq i \leq n$ and $\sum_{j=1}^{n} w_i = 1$. Given this operator the aggregated value of a number of decision criteria ratings is $F(a_1, a_2, ..., a_n) = \sum_{j=1}^{n} w_j b_j$ where b_j is the j-th largest element of the bag $< a_1, a_2, ..., a_n >$.

The fundamental aspect of OWA operators is the fact that an aggregate a_i is not associated with a particular weight w_i but rather a weight is associated with a particular ordered position of the aggregate. This, in our case, is useful as most consultants are not able to define a-priori weights to criteria since, as they say, the low rating of a criterion might be compensated by the high rating of another criterion.

OWA operators can provide any level of criteria compensation lying between the logical *and* and *or*. Full compensation (or) is implemented through the operator $w = (1,0,...,0)^T$ while zero compensation through the operator $w = (0,0,...,1)^T$. In our case the compensation level is somewhat above average. This was determined with the help of domain experts consultants after several trials of the system.

5 Use Case

The testing and evaluation of the effectiveness of our system was conducted by DIADIKASIA S.A., a Greek consulting firm that provides a wide range of specialized services to organizations and companies of both the public and private sector. The whole process comprised two steps, namely the population of the system's ontology with company specific knowledge and the system's usage by the company's consultants for evaluating real tender calls.

For the first step, instances of the relations *isExpertAt* and *hasImplemented* were generated by the consulting company while the population of the relation *isRelevantTo* was performed automatically by applying the DTC algorithm to the company's past projects' descriptions. Thus, considering the areas taxonomy of figure 1, a part of the ontology for DIADIKASIA was as follows:

- *isExpertAt*(DIADIKASIA, Software Requirement Analysis)=0.6
- *isExpertAt*(DIADIKASIA, IT Project Management)=0.8
- *hasImplemented*(DIADIKASIA, EDRASI)
- *isRelevantTo*(EDRASI, Information Technologies) = 0.8

For the second step, the company's consultants used the system for evaluating real tender calls. Figure 2 illustrates an evaluation scenario in which of tender call entitled "Requirement Analysis for the ERP System of company X". As it can be seen in the figure, the system identifies, through the DTC algorithm, the call's area as "Information Technology" at a degree of 0.77 and evaluates the expertise and the experience of the company with scores 77% and 25% respectively. The overall evaluation given these two criteria and through the OWA operator is 60%.

6 Conclusions & Future Work

In this paper we described a knowledge-based decision support system that is used by consulting firms for tackling the problem of the evaluation of tender calls. The key characteristic of our system is that it applies fuzzy reasoning over organizational

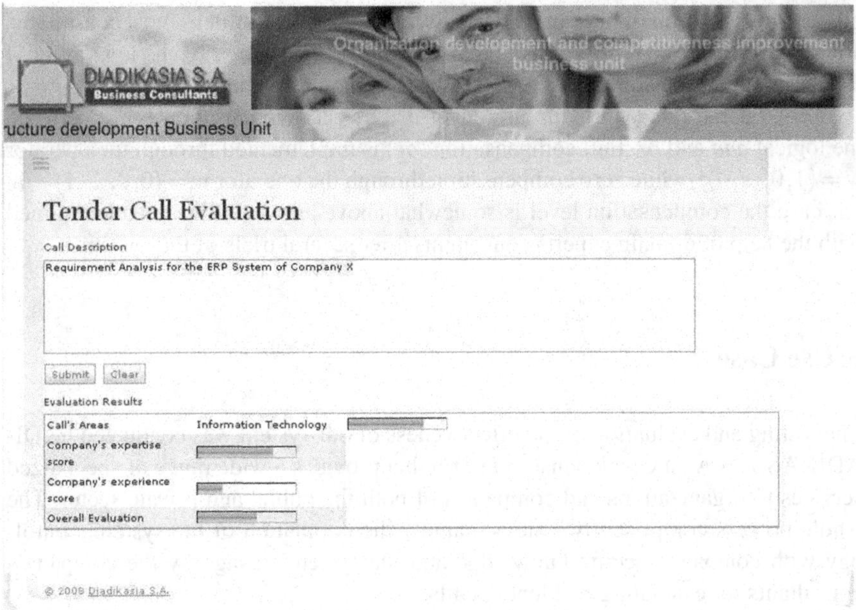

Fig. 2 Evaluation Scenario

and domain specific knowledge in order to model as accurately and as intuitively as possible the consultant's way of thinking.

The work and sub-system presented here in are part of a larger work and integrated system, also comprising the methodology and subsystem to support the consultant in the actual preparation of the proposal text, in the case that the overall evaluation leads to a decision to address the call. This second sub-system is also based mainly on the fuzzy ontology and the DTC algorithm in order to analyze existing texts and estimate which are most relevant and potentially useful inputs in this process. The sub-system supporting the preparation of the proposal, together with the relevant theory and methodologies, fall beyond the scope of the present paper but will be presented in detail in a future work.

References

1. Calegari, S., and Sanchez, E. A Fuzzy Ontology-Approach to improve Semantic Information Retrieval. In Bobillo, F., da Costa, P.C.G., D'Amato, C., Fanizzi, N., Fung, F., Lukasiewicz, T., Martin, T., Nickles, M., Peng, Y., Pool, M., Smrz, P., Vojtas, P., eds.: Proceedings of the Third ISWC Workshop on Uncertainty Reasoning for the Semantic Web - URSW'07. Volume 327 of CEUR Workshop Proceedings., CEUR-WS.org (2007).
2. Drucker, P.F. "The Coming of the New Organization" in Harvard Business Review on Knowledge Management. Harvard Business School Press, 1998. pp. 1-19.

3. Klir, G., Yuan, B. (1995) Fuzzy Sets and Fuzzy Logic, Theory and Applications. Prentice Hall.
4. Mentzas, G., Apostolou, D., Abecker, A., Young, R., 2002, "Knowledge Asset Management: Beyond the Process-centred and Product-centred Approaches", Series: Advanced Information and Knowledge Processing, Springer London.
5. Wallace, M., Avrithis, Y., "Fuzzy Relational Knowledge Representation and Context in the Service of Semantic Information Retrieval", Proceedings of the IEEE International Conference on Fuzzy Systems (FUZZ-IEEE), Budapest, Hungary, July 2004
6. Wallace, M., Mylonas, Ph., Akrivas, G., Avrithis, Y. & Kollias, S., "Automatic thematic categorization of multimedia documents using ontological information and fuzzy algebra", in Ma, Z. (Ed.), Studies in Fuzziness and Soft Computing, Soft Computing in Ontologies and Semantic Web, Springer, Vol. 204, 2006.
7. Yager, R.R. "On ordered weighted averaging aggregation operators in multi-criteria decision making", IEEE Transactions on Systems, Man and Cybernetics 18(1988) 183-190.

3. Klir G., Yuan B. (1995) Fuzzy Sets and Fuzzy Logic, Theory and Applications, Prentice Hall.
4. Mentzas G., Apostolou D., Abecker A., Young R. (2002), Knowledge Asset Management: Beyond the Process-centred and Product-centred Approaches", Series: Advanced Information and Knowledge Processing, Springer-Verlag London.
5. Wallace M., Akrivas G., Avrithis Y., "Fuzzy Relational Knowledge Representation and Context in the Service of Semantic Information Retrieval", Proceedings of the IEEE International Conference on Fuzzy Systems (FUZZ-IEEE), Budapest, Hungary, July 2004.
6. Wallace M., Mylonas P., Akrivas G., Avrithis Y., Kollias S., "Automatic thematic categorization of multimedia documents using ontological information and fuzzy algebra", in Ma Z. (Ed.), Studies in Fuzziness and Soft Computing, Soft Computing in Ontologies and Semantic Web, Springer, Vol. 204, 2006.
7. Yager R. R., "On ordered weighted averaging aggregation operators in multi-criteria decision making", IEEE Transactions on Systems, Man and Cybernetics 18(1) (1988) 183-190.

Extended CNP Framework for the Dynamic Pickup and Delivery Problem Solving

Zoulel Kouki, Besma Fayech Chaar, Mekki Ksouri

National Engineering School of Tunis, Tunis, Belvedère. Tunisia

Email : zoulel.kouki@topnet.tn, {Besma.fayechchaar, Mekki.ksouri}@insat.rnu.tn

Abstract In this paper, we investigate in the applicability of the Contract Net Protocol negotiation (CNP) in the field of the dynamic transportation. We address the optimization of the *Dynamic Pickup and Delivery Problem with Time Windows* also called DPDPTW. This problem is a variant of the Vehicle Routing Problem (VRP) that may be described as the problem of finding the least possible dispatching cost of requests concerning the picking of some quantity of goods from a pick-up to a delivery location while most of the requests continuously occur during the day. The use of contract nets in dynamic and uncertain domains such as ours has been proved to be more fruitful than the use of centralized problem solving [9].We provide a new automated negotiation based on the CNP. Negotiation process is adjusted to deal intelligently with the uncertainty present in the concerned problem.

1 Introduction

In this paper, we deal with the DPDPTW problem which is NP-hard since it is a variant of the well-known NP-hard combinatorial optimization VRP [7]. It is made harder because of the real time requests occurrence and the mandatory precedence between the pick-up and the delivery customer locations [5], [8].

We propose a multi-agent based approach based on the CNP Negotiation. New requests assignment to vehicles will be done according to the rules of the CNP and vehicle agents are responsible for their own routing. Thus, proper pricing strategies are needed to help the system carrying out the minimum transportation and delay costs.

The remainder of the paper is structured as follows: In Section 2, we show a literature review illustrating uses of the CNP in the VRP variants solving. Section 3 gives a detailed description of the DPDPTW. The Extended CNP framework is then globally presented in section 4. Section 5 and section 6 deal with the details of the insertion and optimization processes of the framework. In section 7 we discuss some implementation driven results. Final concluding remarks follow in Section 8.

Please use the following format when citing this chapter:

Kouki, Z., Chaar, B.F. and Ksouri, M., 2009, in IFIP International Federation for Information Processing, Volume 296; *Artificial Intelligence Applications and Innovations III*; Eds. Iliadis, L., Vlahavas, I., Bramer, M.; (Boston: Springer), pp. 61–71.

2 Related Literature

2.1 Dynamic Vehicle Routing Problems

Most techniques and models used in transportation planning, scheduling and routing use centralized approaches. Several techniques and parallel computation methods were also proposed, to solve models using the data that are known at a certain point in time, and to re-optimize as soon as new data become available [3] [7][8][12]. Psaraftis refers to the routing and scheduling in dynamic environments as if the output is not a set of routes, but rather a policy that prescribes how the routes should evolve as a function of those inputs evolving in real-time[7], [8].

2.2 Agent Technology and Agent Based Transportation Planning

Contracts are a powerful coordination mechanism in distributed systems. The CNP has been applied since about 1980. It was first introduced by smith [11] in order to deal with task distribution problems.

Recent researches are investigated in the applicability of multi-agent systems in the field of transportation control. Sandholm [9] applied the Transportation CNP system (TRACONET), a bidding protocol, where dispatch centres of different companies cooperate automatically to provide a least cost vehicle routing. TRACONET extended CNP with bidding and awarding decision processes based on marginal cost calculations. Fischer and al. (1996) developed MARS: a system for cooperative transportation scheduling and a simulation test bed for multi-agent transport planning. The Cooperative Information Agent (CIA) framework introduced the notion of obligations, which was broadened by Contractual Agent Societies to support the fluid organisation of agent societies.

3 Problem Description

3.1 Notations

In the DPDPTW, a set of customers call the dispatch center during the current day before a fixed call for service deadline, asking for the transportation of some load q_v from a pick-up location O_v to a delivery location D_v. These requests occurrence is considered as the single source of the problem's uncertainty. They are denoted by immediate requests and should be scheduled for the same day.

The dispatch center has at its disposal M vehicles moving at a desired fixed velocity and having a maximum capacity Q which should never be exceeded. Each vehicle starts and ends its route R_k at the central depot v_0 respectively at time $\underline{t_k}$ and $\overline{t_k}$. It starts its route with empty load $q_k(t=0)=0$.

Let N be the set of transportation requests of cardinality n and let $N^+ = \underset{i \in N}{\cup} O_i$ and $N^- = \underset{i \in N}{\cup} D_i$ be the sets of the pick-up and delivery locations, respectively. For each location $v \in N = N^+ \cup N^-$, relevant attributes concern mainly: the geographical location (x_v, y_v), the on-site service time $(t_s)_v$ and the time window $[e_v, l_v]$, where e_v and l_v are respectively called release date and service deadline of the location v.

For each location $v \in N = N^+ \cup N^- \cup \{v_0\}$, we consider an arrival time $(t_A)_v$, and departure time $(t_D)_v$, $(t_A)_v$ and $(t_D)_v$ verify $(t_A)_v + (t_s)_v \le (t_D)_v$

For each pair of locations $v_i \in V$ and $v_j \in V$, t_{ij} is the travel cost between v_i and v_j.

3.2 Hypotheses

- The vehicle is not allowed to skip its next service location, once it is travelling towards it [5][3].
- We consider the "Wait First" waiting strategy. Once the pickup or delivery service of some location is finished, the vehicle should wait for its next departure time as long as it is feasible, so that it reaches its next destination after its time window starts [10].

3.3 Constraints

- The service should be made within the time window, and never begin before e_v. A penalty is incurred in the objective whenever l_v is exceeded.
- The precedence constraint between the pick-up and the delivery should be respected.

3.4 Optimization Criterion

The objective is to minimize the transportation costs. The global cost function at time t is denoted by $C_{DPDRTW}(t)$ and can be written as in [5] [3]:

(

$$\sum_{0\le k\le M} T_k + \alpha \sum_{v\in N} \{\max(0, t_v - l_v)\} + \beta \sum_{0\le k\le M} \{\max(0, \overline{t_k} - l_0)\}$$

α and β are the weight parameters and T_k is the travel time of R_k.

$\sum_{0\le k\le M} T_k$ is the total travel time over all vehicles.

$\sum_{v\in N} \max\{0, t_v - l_v\}$ is the penalty, for violating the time window for all the customers of $V \setminus \{v_0\} = N^+ \cup N^-$.

$\sum_{0\le k\le M} \max\{0, \overline{t_k} - l_0\}$ is the sum of the overtime of all vehicles.

4 Extended CNP Framewok for the DPDPTW Solving

4.1 Global Description of our Extended CNP Framework

The main task of our model is to find the best possible solution to the *DPDPTW*. This is done by finding each time the best routing and scheduling of the set of available requests. We define routing as the act of determining an ordered sequence of locations on each vehicle route and scheduling as the act of determining arrival and departure times for each route location.

The dispatch center is represented by the dispatch agent who interacts with the vehicle agents representing the vehicles. Negotiation concerns either the insertion of the new requests or the optimizing of requests insertions into the planned routes.

In fact, the dispatch agent acts uniquely as the manager of new requests insertion negotiations, while vehicle agents may act either as managers of the optimizing negotiations or as participants of both types of negotiations. However, they may certainly not take both roles in the same time.

In the original CNP, several managers may be involved and announcements are allowed to be simultaneous. The available participants evaluate task announcements made by the managers and submit bids on those they think convenient, then managers evaluate the bids and contracts are awarded to the most appropriate bidders [11].

However, our model considers negotiations to be held one by one, because of the complicated nature of the addressed problem. The negotiation process effectively handles the real time events by going through only feasible solutions. Only vehicle agents that are effectively able to carry on the requests without exceeding the vehicles capacities and violating the customers' time windows constraints are involved, and bids are binding so that each vehicle is obliged to honour its awarded tasks. At the end of a negotiation, the task is awarded to the vehicle agent that had submitted the least price bid and who is responsible for improving the routing and scheduling of its not yet served locations.

In order to reduce the uncertainty involved by new requests incurrence, we assume that vehicle agents are completely aware of their environment. All the information about available unassigned requests is accessible to the vehicle agents.

A global description of our multi-agent system (MAS) behaviour is presented in figure2.

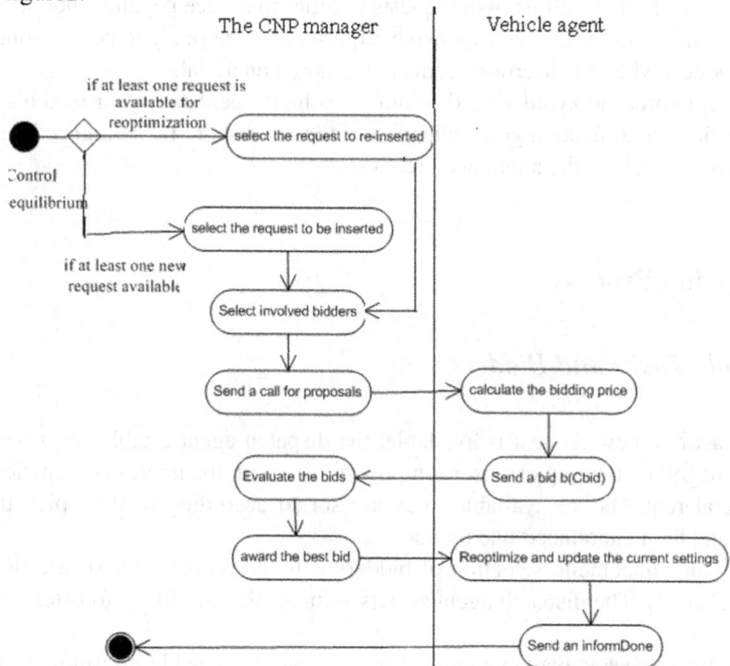

Fig 2. Global description of our DPDPTW- Extended CNP framework.

4.2 Insertion Process

We consider calls for service to arrive one-by-one and to be also announced one by one. The Dispatch agent is the manager of requests insertion tasks. While the set of available requests is not empty, the dispatch agent waits for the system to reach a global equilibrium and then establishes a new negotiation contract dealing with the most impending request. It issues a call for proposals act which specifies the task by giving all the details about the request, as well as the constraints and the conditions placed upon this task execution. Vehicle agents selected as potential participants to the negotiation receive the call for proposals. Their responses, referred to, as bids or submissions indicate the least possible price of inserting the request [2][4].

4.3 Optimizing Process

The second process aims to improve planned routes, it concerns the moving of requests from a first to a second route. This class of negotiations involves only Vehicle agents. Actually, in addition to bidding for new requests, each vehicle agent is also responsible for planning and scheduling its pickup and delivery services. Thus, vehicle agent may sell its own requests in order to reduce penalties put upon its objective function, to remove expensive requests or to be ready to accept some a coming request when its insertion seems to be more beneficial.

Moreover, in order to avoid visited solutions, vehicle agents use their feed back of last negotiations to make a good selection of the requests to be announced and of the vehicles to bid for the announced request.

5 Insertion Process

5.1 Eligible Tasks and Bidders

When at least one new request is available, the dispatch agent establishes a new contract to negotiate the request insertion possibilities with the interested vehicles. When several requests are available, they are sorted according to their pick up deadlines, and then announced one by one.

For each announcement, selection of bidders is based on the request insertion feasibility chances. The dispatch agent selects vehicles that are likely to offer feasible routes.

We assume that, each available request has at least one feasible insertion in the current routes, so that for each announcement, at least one vehicle is eligible for the negotiation. Eligible vehicles are those verifying both constraints of capacity and time window.

- Capacity constraint Check

For each eligible vehicle agent, there exists at least one pair of possible positions i, j in the ordered sequence of service locations of the route R_k such as v^+ may be inserted just next to i and v^- next to j : and that verify :

$$\max_{(t_D)_i \le t \le (t_D)_j} \{q^k(t)\} \le Q - d_v .$$

In fact the insertion of the request v is possible only while (3) is maintained true during the period of time between the departure time $(t_D)_i$ from the i th location of the route towards the pickup location v^+ and the departure time $(t_D)_j$ from the j th location of the route towards to the delivery location v^- .

- Time Window constraint check

Let us divide the vehicle route into two portions: the first portion starts from time $t = 0$ until the current time and the second portion starts from the current time and finishes at the time the vehicle ends its route, only the settings of the second portion of the route may be modified.

We define a possible routing block of a request v in the route R_k as a block that starts at the ith location and ends at the jth location of the route. i.e. v^+ may be inserted just next to i and v^- previous to j: $i < position(v+) < position(v-) < j$

i and j should verify that insertion of v^+ and v^- in the possible routing block bounded by i and j is a feasible insertion that respect v^+ and v^- time windows constraints.

$$e_{v+} + c \geq (t_A)_i + t_{v+,i} \geq e_{v+} - c$$
$$l_{v-} - c \leq (t_A)_j - t_{v-,j} \leq l_{v-} + c$$

c is a parameter specified according to the overall minimum request time window and $t_{v+,j}$ is the travel cost between the pickup location v^+ and the jth location of the route.

5.2 One Contract at a Time

In the original CNP, an agent could have multiple bids concerning different contracts pending concurrently in order to speed up the operation of the system [1], [11]. This was proved to be beneficial when the addressed tasks are independent and the price calculation processes are independent of the agent's assigned tasks and independent of any other tasks being negotiated at the same time.

However, in our model, negotiation concerns tasks that could be more or less inter-related and related with the already assigned tasks.

In fact, at a given time t, for each vehicle agent, because of the capacity constraint, the bidding decision depends conjointly on the vehicle's load which is the sum of its assigned locations loads, and the new request's load.

Besides, considering the problem's precedence and temporal constraints, some requests insertion may be considered to be prior to others. Locations of new and assigned requests may be close in space or in time and this makes their insertion into the same vehicle's route more beneficial. Then new requests pricing and bidding decisions are closely dependent of the earlier awarded requests.

Now, assuming that bids are binding, let us imagine that Vehicle agents may bid on several announcements at a time. In that case, tasks may become awarded to the vehicle while it is still bidding on other tasks. The

Its local settings changes should be considered by the bidder pricing functions.

Otherwise the agent may submit wrong bids that it may be not able to honour and the resulting solution is unfeasible.

Considering all those reasons, we opt for the negotiations over only one contract at a time.

5.3 Bidding and Pricing Mechanism

The key issue to be discussed in this section is how to make pricing of requests insertions as accurate as possible. The pricing mechanism: a quasi-true valuation

We assume that the vehicle agent is bidding its true valuation such that the price of the task does not depend on the value other bidders attach to the task [].

However, because the problem is NP-hard, evaluating the cost of the announced request's insertion depends on the calculation of the truly optimizing function, which requires the search of an optimal routing and the calculation of departure and arrival times for every location included in the route, which is computationally demanding. Thus we consider a fast approximation $C_{add}(v)$ of the announced request v adding cost to the routing solution. The vehicle agent determines first the possible routing block of the request, and while the bidding limit time is not reached it iterates calculating $C_{add}(v)$ for all the feasible pairs of positions i, j included in the possible routing block and selects the best insertion.

$C_{add}(v)$ is the sum of the additional travel cost and the lateness eventually caused to customers expected to be served after the i th position:

- The additional travel cost is given by:

$$\left(c_{add\_travel}(v^+)\right)_k = t_{i,v+} + t_{v+,i+1} - t_{i,i+1}$$

$$\left(c_{add\_travel}(v^-)\right)_k = t_{j,v-} + t_{v-,j+1} - t_{j,j+1}$$

$$\left(c_{add\_travel}(v)\right)_k = \left(c_{add\_travel}(v^+)\right)_k + \left(c_{add\_travel}(v^-)\right)_k$$

-Penalties caused by time windows violations are given by:

$$\left(c_{add\_lateness}(v)\right)_k = \sum_{p>i} \max\left(0, l_p - t_A(p) + \left(c_{add\_travel}(v^+)\right)_k\right) + \sum_{p>j} \max\left(0, l_p - t_A(p) + \left(c_{add\_travel}(v^-)\right)_k\right)$$

5. 4 Near Future Requests are Visible to Bidder Agents

We assume that information about unassigned requests is visible to bidder agents. This information is used to intensify or reduce the agent desire for the acquisition of the negotiated request.

This information about future is useful in situations like the following: Let us consider v_1, v_2 two disjoint requests. v_1 should be negotiated first, and $(c_{add}(v_1))_k$ is the addition cost of v_1 into the route of the vehicle k.

It may exist $k,k',k'' \in \{0,..,M\} / \ k \neq k', k \neq k''$ $(c_{add}(v_1))_k \geq (c_{add}(v_1))_{k'}$

$(c_{add}(v_1))_k + (c_{add}(v_2))_k \leq (c_{add}(v_1))_{k'} + (c_{add}(v_2))_{k''}$

This way, the k'^{th} vehicle agent could be the winner of the request v while, awarding it to the vehicle k' would be more opportunistic.

5.5 *Requests Awarding*

Awarding a contract means assigning the service request to the successful bidder.

Request insertion is performed considering the solution proposed in the bid. Calculation of departure and arrival times of different locations is made immediately once the contract is awarded to the agent, according to the rules of the wait first waiting strategy, except for the possible routing block

The agent then uses its local optimization heuristics to make better the routing and scheduling of its assigned locations. Information about available requests is useful in the management of waiting times, in order to make possible and appropriate the insertion of coming requests.

6 CNP Negotiation for Inter-routes Improvement

Some assigned requests may result in large delays for services of the same vehicle.

Negotiations for post optimization are based on the idea of controlling cycles by avoiding the repetition of visited tours. Some moves or bids or announces or awards could have the status tabu, this helps avoiding the congestion of the negotiation network when an announcement is tabu for a bidder, the bidder is not eligible for this announcement.

In order to avoid infinite negotiation of post-optimization: an initiator could be tabu, in order to let the chance for others to sell their requests.

An agent may not announce a task, just acquired in the last negotiation. At least one change should be performed on its route to become authorized to announce the request.

When the request v is announced, the vehicle that had it in the past in its route and that had announced it in the nth negotiation is eligible for bidding on, only if at least one or more changes are performed into its route or in the current manger's

7 Experimental Results

The purpose of the experiments was to validate the application of the CNP Multi-agent negotiation in dynamic subjected to constraints domains

Our CNP based solution is implemented using the Jadex BDI agent-oriented reasoning engine realised as an extension to the widely used JADE middleware platform [14].

We used the test beds of Mitrovic-Minic [13]. We examined 10 instances of problems with one depot and respectively 100 and 500 requests. The service area is 60 * 60 km^2, and vehicle speed is 60 km/h. In all instances, requests occur during the service period according to a continuous uniform distribution, and no requests are known in advance. The service period is 10 hours. Experiments were performed a simulation speed of 30 which means that one hour of real life operations is simulated in 1/30 hours of computer time.

Preliminary experiments were performed to determine convenient selection and bidding parameter values.

At the end of experiments, we remarked that agents produce improved results. Considering future and past information made solutions to be more accurate. Table 1 provides the average experimental results performed with different initial fleet of vehicles. Tests considers ranging from five to twenty for the 100 requests instances and 20 to 40 for the 500 requests instances. when no near future or past information is considered, when only future information is considered and when both future and past information are considered.

Table 1. Experimental results

	SMinic WF Best values		CNP with no future nor past information		Extended CNP with future information		Extended CNP with past and future information	
	Distance	m	Distance	m	Distance	m	Distance	m
100requests	2453.61	13.76	2449.2	13.96	2462.3	13.42	2462.3	12.56
500requests	5874.11	25.95	5881.3	26.34	5872.4	25.88	5870.45	24.93

The table reports total distance travelled and number of vehicles used (m).

8 CONCLUSION

We proposed a CNP automatic negotiation based approach for the DPDPTW optimization. Negotiation in our system concerned insertion of new requests and optimization of planned routes. It was real time and was adjusted in that way to deal with special features and constraints of the addressed problem. We considered the use of the one by one negotiation in order to carry out precise insertions .We considered also agents to be entirely cooperative since their objectives match that global system objective of reducing the dispatching costs.

We proposed agents to be well informed about their past negotiations and to use their knowledge about the tasks about to be negotiated.

Congestion of the negotiation network was avoided by the use of a thoughtful selection among tasks to be announced and bidders. Experimental results showed that CNP negotiations dealt successfully with dynamic problem of pick-up and delivery.

REFERENCES

1. Demazeau, Y. Multi-agents systems methodology. In Proceedings 4th Brazilian Symposium on Artificial Intelligence SIBA98, Porto Alegre. (1998)
2. FIPA. 1997 Specification. part 2, Agent Communication language, foundation for intelligent physical agents, Geneova, Switzerland. http://www.cselt.stet.it/ufv/leonardo/fipa/index.htm
3. Gendreau, M., Guertin, F., Potvin, J.-Y., and Séguin, R. 2006 GendreauNeighborhood search heuristics for a dynamic vehicle dispatching problem with pick-ups and deliveries. Transportation Research Part C 14, 157-174.
4. Guessoum, Z.. 2003 Modèles et Architectures d'agents et de systèmes Multi-agents adaptifs. Dossier d'habilitation de l'Université de Paris 6, France.
5. Larsen, A. 2001 The Dynamic Vehicle Routing Problem PhD thesis, IMM-Danemark.
6. Lund, K., Oli B. G. M, and Jens M. R. 1996 Vehicle Routing Problems with Varying Degrees of Dynamism. Technical report, IMM, The Department of Mathematical Modelling, Technical University of Denmark.
7. Psaraftis, H. N. 1988 Vehicle Routing: Methods and Studies, chapter Dynamic Vehicle Routing Problems, pages 223{248. Elsevier Science Publishers B.V. (North Holland).
8. Psaraftis, H. N. 1995 Dynamic vehicle routing: Status and prospects. Ann. of Oper. Res., 61:143-164.
9. Sandholm, T. 1993. An Implementation of the Contract Net Protocol Based on Marginal Cost Calculations. In Proceedings 11th National Conference on Artificial Intelligence (AAAI).
10. Mitrovic-Minic, S., G. Laporte. 2004. Waiting strategies for the dynamic pickup and delivery problem with time windows. Transportation Res. B <b>38</b> 635-655.
11. Smith, R.G. 1980. The Contract Net Protocol: High-Level Communication and Control in a Distributed Problem Solver. IEEE Trans. on Computers C-29(12):1104-1113.
12. Thierry, G., Didier, J., Dominique, F., Christian. A, and Élodie, C. Transport à la demande points à points en zone peu dense: Proposition d'une méthode d'optimisation de tournées.
13. http://www.fernunihagen.de/WINF/inhfrm/bench-mark_data.htm
14. http://vsis-www.informatik.unihamburg.de/pro-jects/jadex/

A Logic-Based Approach to Solve the Steiner Tree Problem

Mohamed El Bachir Menai

Abstract Boolean satisfiability (SAT) is a well-studied $\mathcal{NP}$-complete problem for formulating and solving other combinatorial problems like planning and scheduling. The Steiner tree problem (STP) asks to find a minimal cost tree in a graph that spans a set of nodes. STP has been shown to be $\mathcal{NP}$-hard. In this paper, we propose to solve the STP by formulating it as a variation of SAT, and to solve it using a heuristic search method guided by the backbone of the problem. The algorithm is tested on a well known set of benchmark instances. Experimental results demonstrate the applicability of the proposed approach, and show that substantial quality improvement can be obtained compared to other heuristic methods.

1 Introduction

The satisfiability problem in propositional logic (SAT) is the task to decide for a given propositional formula in conjunctive normal form (CNF) whether it has a model. More formally, let $C = \{C_1, C_2, \ldots, C_m\}$ be a set of m clauses that involve n Boolean variables $x_1, x_2, \ldots, x_n$. A literal is either a variable x_i or its negation $\neg x_i$. Each clause C_i is a disjunction of n_i literals, $C_i = \bigvee_{j=1}^{n_i} l_{ij}$. The SAT problem asks to decide whether the propositional formula $\Phi = \bigwedge_{i=1}^{m} C_i$ is satisfiable. SAT is the first problem shown to be $\mathcal{NP}$-complete [2]. The $\mathcal{NP}$-completeness concept deals with the idea of polynomial transformation from a problem P_i to P_j where the essential results are preserved: if P_i returns "yes", then P_j returns "yes" under the same problem input. MAX-SAT (or *unweighted* MAX-SAT) is the optimization variation of SAT. It asks to find a variable assignment that maximizes the number of satisfied clauses. In *weighted* MAX-SAT (or only MAX-SAT), a weight w_i is assigned to each clause C_i (notation: $C_i^{w_i}$), and the objective is to maximize the total weight of

Mohamed El Bachir Menai
Computer Science Department, College of Computer and Information Sciences, King Saud University, PO Box 51178, Riyadh 11543, Kingdom of Saudi Arabia, e-mail: menai@ksu.edu.sa

Please use the following format when citing this chapter:

Menai, M.E.B., 2009, in IFIP International Federation for Information Processing, Volume 296; *Artificial Intelligence Applications and Innovations III*; Eds. Iliadis, L., Vlahavas, I., Bramer, M.; (Boston: Springer), pp. 73–79.

satisfied clauses $\sum_{i=1}^{m} w_i \cdot \Im(C_i)$, where $\Im(C_i)$ is one if and only if C_i is satisfied and otherwise zero. Partial MAX-SAT (PMSAT) involves two weighted CNF formulas f_A and f_B. The objective is to find a variable assignment that satisfies all clauses of f_A (non-relaxable or hard clauses) together with the maximum clauses in f_B (relaxable or soft clauses). SAT has seen many successful applications in various fields such as planning, scheduling, and Electronic Design Automation. Encoding combinatorial problems as SAT problems has been mostly motivated by the simplicity of SAT formulation, and the recent advances in SAT solvers. Indeed, new solvers are capable of solving very large and very hard real world SAT instances. Optimization problems that involve hard and soft constraints can be cast as a PMSAT, e.g. university course scheduling and FPGA routing. In 1995, Jiang *et al.* [6] proposed the first heuristic local search algorithm to solve this problem as a MAX-SAT. In 1997, Cha *et al.* [1] proposed another local search technique to solve the PMSAT problem. In 2005, Menai *et al.* [9] proposed a coevolutionary heuristic search algorithm to solve the PMSAT. In 2006, Fu and Malik [4] proposed two approaches based on a state-of-the-art SAT solver to solve the PMSAT.

The Steiner tree problem (STP) in graphs is a classic combinatorial problem. It can be defined as follows. Given an arbitrary undirected weighted graph $G = (V, E, w)$, where V is the set of nodes, E denotes the set of edges and $w : E \rightarrow \mathbb{R}^+$ is a non-negative weight function associated with its edges. Any tree T in G spanning a given subset $S \subseteq V$ of terminal nodes is called a *Steiner tree*. Note that T may contain non-terminal nodes referred to as *Steiner nodes*. The cost of a tree is defined to be the sum of its edge weights. The STP asks for a minimum-cost Steiner tree. The decision version of STP has been shown to be $\mathcal{NP}$-complete by Karp [8]. STP has found uses across a wide array of applications including network routing [10] and VLSI design [7]. Several implementations of metaheuristics have been proposed for the approximate solution of STP or its variations, such as Simulated Annealing [11], Tabu Search [5], and Genetic Algorithms [3]. In this paper we are interested in solving the STP as a PMSAT problem. We show how to encode the STP into PMSAT and propose a practical approach to solve it based on one of the best known SAT solver WalkSAT [12] with certain extensions. Indeed, the success of WalkSAT and its variations has led to the paradigm of SAT encoding and solving difficult problems from other problem domains. Our approach is based on exploiting problem structural information, backbone in particular, to guide the search algorithm towards promising regions of the search space. We show empirically that this method is effective by comparing our results to those obtained with specialized Steiner heuristic algorithms. The rest of the paper is structured as follows. In the next section, we explain how to encode the STP into PMSAT. In Section 3, we describe a heuristic algorithm for PMSAT using backbone guided search. Computational results are reported in Section 4. Concluding remarks are drawn in the last section.

2 PMSAT Encoding of STP

Jiang *et al.* [6] suggested to encode STP as a weighted MAX-SAT instance and to solve it using a MAX-SAT solver. However, a solution for the MAX-SAT instance may violate some clauses whose satisfiability is required for the feasibility of the STP solution. We propose to encode STP as a PMSAT instance to formulate independently hard and soft constraints and to solve it using a PMSAT solver. Let $G = (V, E, w)$ be a weighted graph of n nodes $v_1, v_2, \ldots, v_n$, and $S \subseteq V$ a set of terminal nodes.

1. For each edge $e_{ij}, 1 \leq i \leq n, 1 \leq j \leq n$, connecting nodes i and j of the graph, introduce a boolean variable x_{ij}. $\mathfrak{I}(x_{ij}) = 1$ if e_{ij} is chosen as part of the Steiner tree.
2. For each variable x_{ij}, construct the clause $c_{ij} = (\neg x_{ij})^{w_{ij}}$ to minimize the cost of including the edge e_{ij} in the tree. $\mathbf{f_B} = \bigwedge \mathbf{c_{ij}}$ are soft clauses.
3. List terminal nodes in an arbitrary order. For some fixed l, generate the possible $k(k \leq l)$ shortest paths between successive pairs of nodes using Dijkstra's algorithm. If no path exists between two terminal nodes, then return no solution. Variables $p^1_{ij}, p^2_{ij}, \ldots, p^k_{ij}$ denote the k shortest paths between terminal nodes i and j. The reduction is an approximation of the original instance, since only the k shortest paths are generated between pairs of nodes.
4. A solution to STP must contain a path between each pair of terminal nodes. Namely, for each $(v_i, v_j) \in S \times S$, construct a clause $(p^1_{ij} \vee p^2_{ij} \vee \cdots \vee p^k_{ij})$. $\mathbf{f_{A_1}} = \bigwedge(\mathbf{p^1_{ij}} \vee \mathbf{p^2_{ij}} \vee \cdots \vee \mathbf{p^k_{ij}})$ are hard clauses.
5. Each path must contain all its edges. Namely, for each path p^k_{ij} containing edges $e_{il}, e_{lm}, \ldots, e_{rj}$, construct clauses $(p^k_{ij} \supset x_{il}) \wedge (p^k_{ij} \supset x_{lm}) \wedge \cdots \wedge (p^k_{ij} \supset x_{rj})$ which are equivalent to $(\neg p^k_{ij} \vee x_{il}) \wedge (\neg p^k_{ij} \vee x_{lm}) \wedge \cdots \wedge (\neg p^k_{ij} \vee x_{rj})$. $\mathbf{f_{A_2}} = \bigwedge((\neg \mathbf{p^k_{ij}} \vee \mathbf{x_{il}}) \wedge (\neg \mathbf{p^k_{ij}} \vee \mathbf{x_{lm}}) \wedge \cdots \wedge (\neg \mathbf{p^k_{ij}} \vee \mathbf{x_{rj}}))$ are hard clauses.
6. Let $\mathbf{f_A} = \mathbf{f_{A_1}} \wedge \mathbf{f_{A_2}}$. $\mathbf{f} = \mathbf{f_A} \wedge \mathbf{f_B}$ is the PMSAT instance yield.

The number of variables is $|E| + k(|S| - 1)$. The total number of clauses is $O(|E| + kL(|S| - 1))$, where L is the maximum number of edges in pre-computed paths. The reduction is linearly dependent on the number of edges. The reduction is sound as any PMSAT solution yields a valid Steiner tree. Since all hard clauses f_A are satisfied, a path exists between each pair of terminal nodes in the obtained set of nodes. The reduction is incomplete, since the PMSAT instance will not yield a solution if there is no Steiner tree using the k paths generated in step 3.

3 Heuristic Search for PMSAT

Backbone variables are a set of literals which are true in every model of a SAT instance. The backbone of a PMSAT instance is the set of assignments of values to variables which are the same in every possible optimal solution. They are proven to influence hardness in optimization and approximation [13]. Heuristic search methods could improve their performance by using backbone information. We propose to solve a PMSAT using a heuristic local search algorithm that takes advantage of a pseudo-backbone sampled using information extracted from local minima. Our method is inspired by a heuristic sampling method for generating assignments for a local search for MAX-SAT [14].

Let Ω be a set of assignments on X, the set of Boolean variables, $A(x_i)$ the value of the variable x_i in the assignment A, and $C(A)$ the contribution of A defined as the total number of satisfied clauses in f_A and f_B: $C(A) = |f_A| \cdot \#sat_{f_A}(A) + \#sat_{f_B}(A)$, where $\#sat_{f_A}(A)$ and $\#sat_{f_B}(A)$ denote the number of satisfied clauses in f_A and f_B, respectively. A multiplier coefficient $|f_A|$ is added to $C(A)$ to underline the priority of satisfying clauses of f_A. A variable frequency p_i of positive occurrences of x_i in all assignments of Ω is defined as $p_i = (\sum_{A \in \Omega} C(A) \cdot A(x_i)) / \sum_{A \in \Omega} C(A)$. $A(x_i) = 1$ with the probability p_i. Let $X(\alpha)$ denote the set of variables which appear in the set of clauses α. The main steps of the algorithm BB_PMSAT are outlined in Figure 1.

procedure BB_PMSAT
input: A formula $F = f_A \wedge f_B$ in CNF containing n variables $x_1, \ldots, x_n$,
`MaxTries1, MaxTries2, MaxSteps.`
output: A solution A for F, or "Not found" if f_A is not satisfiable.
begin
  for $t = 0$ **to** $|\Omega| - 1$ **do**
    $A \leftarrow$ WalkSAT_MAXSAT(F,$X(F)$,`MaxTries=1,MaxSteps`);
    If A satisfies F **then return** A;
    $\Omega[t] \leftarrow A$;
  end for
  $A \leftarrow$ BB_WalkSAT_MAXSAT(F,$X(F)$, Ω, `MaxTries1, MaxSteps`);
  if A satisfies F **then return** A;
  if ($\exists f_{A_{SAT}}, f_{A_{UNSAT}} | f_A = f_{A_{SAT}} \wedge f_{A_{UNSAT}}$) and ($A$ satisfies $f_{A_{SAT}}$)
    and ($X(f_{A_{SAT}}) \cap X(f_{A_{UNSAT}}) = \emptyset$)
  then $f \leftarrow f_{A_{UNSAT}}, X(f) \leftarrow X(f_{A_{UNSAT}})$;
  else $f \leftarrow f_A, X(f) \leftarrow X(f_A)$;
  end if
  $A_f \leftarrow$ BB_WalkSAT(f,$X(f)$, Ω, `MaxTries2, MaxSteps`);
  if A_f satisfies f **then** update A and **return** A;
  return "Not found";
end

Fig. 1 The BB_PMSAT procedure

In a first phase, the PMSAT instance is solved as a MAX-SAT instance using a variation of the procedure WalkSAT [12] for MAX-SAT (WalkSAT_MAXSAT) to initialize the pseudo-backbone Ω with reached local minima. Next, both formulas f_A and f_B are solved together as a MAX-SAT instance using a variation of the procedure BB_WalkSAT for MAX-SAT (BB_WalkSAT_MAXSAT). Figure 2 presents the procedure BB_WalkSAT for SAT. It integrates a pseudo-backbone estimation using variable frequencies p_i to generate initial assignments. The pseudo-backbone Ω is updated at each time a new local minimum is encountered. The second phase of the algorithm is performed if the best assignment found in the previous phase does not satisfy f_A (a PMSAT instance F is satisfied iff f_A is satisfied). In such case, it is recycled to try to satisfy f_A using BB_WalkSAT guided by the information in Ω. If the best assignment found does not satisfy f_A, then it is recycled to a model of f_A using Ω.

```
procedure BB_WalkSAT
input: A formula F in CNF containing n variables x_1,...,x_n,
       Ω, MaxTries, MaxFlips.
output: A satisfying assignment A for F, or "Not found".
begin
       for try = 1 to MaxTries do
         Calculate p_i, (i = 1,n) using Ω;
         A ← best assignment for n variables among t randomly
         created assignments in Ω using p_i;
         for flip = 1 to MaxFlips do
           if A satisfies F then return A;
           c ← an unsatisfied clause chosen at random;
           if there exists a variable x in c with break value = 0
           then
             A ← A with x flipped;
           else
             with probability p
               x ← a variable in c chosen at random;
             with probability (1 − p)
               x ← a variable in c with smallest break value;
             A ← A with x flipped;
           end if
         end for
         if (A ∉ Ω) and (∃Ω[k]|C(Ω[k]) < C(A)) then Ω[k] ← A;
       end for
       return "Not found"
end
```

Fig. 2 The BB_WalkSAT procedure

4 Computational Experience

The computing platform used to perform the experiments is a 3.40 GHz Intel Pentium D Processor with 1 GB of RAM running Linux. Programs are coded in C language. We compared the BB_PMSAT results with the optimal solutions of a test problems' set of the OR-Library (series D and E). Series D consists of 20 problems with 1000 nodes, arcs varying from 1250 to 25000, and terminals from 5 to 500. Series E consists of 20 problems of 2500 nodes, arcs varying from 3250 to 62500, and terminals from 5 to 1250. In order to test the effectiveness of the proposed approach, we compared BB_PMSAT results with those obtained with the Tabu Search method called Full Tabusteiner (F-Tabu) from Gendreau *et al.* [5], which is one of the best heuristic approach for the STP in terms of solution quality. BB_PMSAT was also compared to one of the best Genetic Algorithms (GA-E) that has solved STP, which is due to Esbensen [3].

Table 1 Results for series D of STP.

			WalkSAT		BB_PMSAT	
Instance	GA-E(%)	F-Tabu (%)	(%)	CPU secs	(%)	CPU secs
D1-20	0.58	0.10	4.19	4.50	0.11	3.14
E1-20	0.42	0.31	4.65	10.67	1.19	8.29
Best approach	18/40	28/40	16/40		28/40	

PMSAT and MAX-SAT instances were generated from STP instances using the reduction described in Section 2. The number k of pre-computed paths between each pairs of nodes was fixed to 10. The total number of tries for each run of BB_PMSAT was shared between its two phases. Let r be the first phase length ratio of the total run length and pb the ratio of pseudo-backbone size to the number of variables n. BB_PMSAT was tested using the following parameter settings: $r = 0.6$, $pb = 0.5$ (values of r and pb are recommended in [9]), $MaxFlips = 10^5$, and $MaxTries = 100$ (shared between $MaxTries1$ and $MaxTries2$). WalkSAT was tested using a noise parameter $p = 0.5$ (recommended by the authors [12]) and the same values of $MaxFlips$ and $MaxTries$ used in BB_PMSAT.

Table 1 shows the mean results in terms of solution quality (in error percentage w.r.t. the optimum) for the series D and E of STP and their comparison with the Tabu Search method F-Tabu [5] and the Genetic Algorithm GA-E [3]. The results reported for WalkSAT and BB_PMSAT include average CPU time required over 10 runs. CPU times of the methods GA-E and F-Tabu are omitted because of a difference in the evaluation of the processing times. BB_PMSAT and F-Tabu were the best approaches in 28 times and gave clearly better solutions than GA-E (18 times) and WalkSAT (16 times). In terms of solution quality, the average results given by BB_PMSAT and F-Tabu for series D were comparable. However, for series E, F-Tabu outperformed BB_PMSAT. We expect that greater exploration of the parameters of BB_PMSAT may yield still better results.

Overall, BB_PMSAT found more optimal solutions than WalkSAT on all instances in less average CPU time. Indeed, the average CPU time achieved by BB_PMSAT and WalkSAT on all the problems is 5.71 secs and 7.58 secs, respectively. These positive results can demonstrate the superiority of the PMSAT encoding and the use of BB_PMSAT search procedure in comparison to the MAX-SAT encoding and the use of WalkSAT procedure for STP. BB_PMSAT's overall performance is comparable to the Tabu Search method F-Tabu.

5 Conclusions

In this paper we have examined a logic-based method to solve STP. We have considered MAX-SAT and Partial MAX-SAT encodings of STP. Empirical evaluation has been conducted on these encodings using two heuristic algorithms: BB_PMSAT and WalkSAT. BB_PMSAT relies on a pseudo-backbone sampling to guide the search trajectory through near-optimal solutions. We have reported some computational results showing that BB_PMSAT can solve large instances of STP. It appears that solving STP as a PMSAT using BB_PMSAT is more effective than solving it as a MAX-SAT using WalkSAT. Results are compared to those of specialized STP algorithms (F-Tabu and GA-E). The performance of BB_PMSAT is better than that of GA-E and close to that of F-Tabu in terms of solution quality . We have tested larger STP instances and obtained good results. However, the lack of space prevents us to present them and to discuss the choice of k, the number of precomputed shortest paths. We can conclude that the reduction of STP into PMSAT and the use of BB_PMSAT represent an effective means of solving STP.

References

1. Cha, B., Iwama, K., Kambayashi, Y., Miyazaki, S.: Local search algorithms for Partial MAXSAT. In Proc. AAAI-97, (1997), 263–268
2. Cook, S.A.: The complexity of theorem proving procedures. In Proc. 3rd ACM Symposium of the Theory of Computation, (1971) 263–268
3. Esbensen, H.: Computing near-optimal solutions to the Steiner problem in graphs using a genetic algorithm. Networks 26, (1995) 173–185
4. Fu, Z., Malik, S.: On solving the Partial MAX-SAT problem. In Proc. SAT'06, LNCS 4121, (2006) 252–265
5. Gendreau, M., Larochelle, J.-F., Sansò, B.: A tabu search heuristic for the Steiner tree problem. Networks 34(2), (1999) 162–172
6. Jiang, Y., Kautz, H.A., Selman, B.: Solving problems with hard and soft constraints using a stochastic algorithm for MAX-SAT. In Proc. 1st Inter. Joint Workshop on Artificial Intelligence and Operations Research, (1995)
7. Kahng, A.B., Robins, G.: On optimal interconnections for VLSI. Kluwer Publishers, (1995)
8. Karp, R.M.: Reducibility among combinatorial problems. In E. Miller and J.W. Thatcher, eds, Complexity of Computer Computations, Plenum Press, (1972) 85–103
9. Menaï, M.B., Batouche, M.: A backbone-based co-evolutionary heuristic for Partial MAX-SAT. In Proc. EA-2005, LNCS 3871, (2006) 155–166, Springer-Verlag
10. Nguyen, U.T.: On multicast routing in wireless mesh networks. Computer Communications 31(7), (2008), 1385–1399
11. Osborne, L.J., Gillett, B.E.: A comparison of two simulated annealing algorithms applied to the directed Steiner problem on networks. ORSA Journal on Computing 3, (1991), 213–225
12. Selman, B., Kautz, H.A., Cohen, B.: Noise strategies for improving local search. In Proc. AAAI-94, (1994) 337–343
13. Slaney, J., Walsh, T.: Backbones in optimization and approximation. In Proc. IJCAI-01, (2001) 254–259
14. Telelis, O., Stamatopoulos, P.: Heuristic backbone sampling for maximum satisfiability. In Proc. 2nd Hellenic Conference on AI, (2002) 129–139

An Argumentation Agent Models Evaluative Criteria

John Debenham

Abstract An approach to argumentation attempts to model the partner's evaluative criteria, and by attempting to work with it rather than against it. To this end, the utterances generated aim to influence the partner to believe what we believe to be in his best interests — although it may not be in fact. The utterances aim to convey what is so, and not to point out "where the partner is wrong". This behaviour is intended to lead to the development of lasting relationships between agents.

1 Introduction

This paper is based in rhetorical argumentation [1] and is in the area labelled: *information-based agency* [3]. An information-based agent has an identity, values, needs, plans and strategies all of which are expressed using a fixed ontology in probabilistic logic for internal representation. All of the forgoing is represented in the agent's deliberative machinery. [2] describes a rhetorical argumentation framework that supports argumentative negotiation. It does this by taking into account: the relative information gain of a new utterance and the relative semantic distance between an utterance and the dialogue history. Then [4] considered the effect that argumentative dialogues have on the on-going *relationship* between a pair of negotiating agents.

This paper is written from the point of view of an agent α that is engaged in argumentative interaction with agent β. The history of all argumentative exchanges is the agents' *relationship*. We assume that their utterances, u, can be organised into distinct dialogues, Ψ^t. We assume that α and β are negotiating with the mutual aim of signing a contract, where the contract will be an instantiation of the mutually-understood object $o(\Psi^t)$. An argumentation agent has to perform two key functions: to understand incoming utterances and to generate responses.

John Debenham
University of Technology, Sydney, Australia, e-mail: debenham@it.uts.edu.au

Please use the following format when citing this chapter:

Debenham, J., 2009, in IFIP International Federation for Information Processing, Volume 296; *Artificial Intelligence Applications and Innovations III*; Eds. Iliadis, L., Vlahavas, I., Bramer, M.; (Boston: Springer), pp. 81–86.

2 Assessing a Contract

No matter what interaction strategy an agent uses, and no matter whether the communication language is that of simple bargaining or rich argumentation, a negotiation agent will have to decide whether or not to sign each contract on the table. An agent's preferences may be uncertain. In which case, we ask the question: "how certain am I that $\delta = (\phi, \varphi)$ is a good contract to sign?" — under realistic conditions this may be easy to estimate. $\mathbb{P}^t(\text{sign}(\alpha, \beta, \chi, \delta))$ estimates the certainty, expressed as a probability, that α should sign proposal δ in satisfaction of her need χ, where in (ϕ, φ) ϕ is α's commitment and φ is β's. α will accept δ if: $\mathbb{P}^t(\text{sign}(\alpha, \beta, \chi, \delta)) > c$, for some level of certainty c.

To estimate $\mathbb{P}^t(\text{sign}(\alpha, \beta, \chi, \delta))$, α will be concerned about what will occur if contract δ is signed. If agent α receives a commitment from β, α will be interested in any variation between β's commitment, φ, and what is actually observed, as the enactment, φ'. We denote the relationship between commitment and enactment:

$$\mathbb{P}^t(\text{Observe}(\alpha, \varphi') | \text{Commit}(\beta, \alpha, \varphi))$$

simply as $\mathbb{P}^t(\varphi' | \varphi) \in \mathcal{M}^t$, and now α has to estimate her belief in the acceptability of each possible outcome $\delta' = (\phi', \varphi')$. Let $\mathbb{P}^t(\text{acc}(\alpha, \chi, \delta'))$ denote α's estimate of her belief that the outcome δ' will be acceptable in satisfaction of her need χ, then we have:

$$\mathbb{P}^t(\text{sign}(\alpha, \beta, \chi, \delta)) = f(\mathbb{P}^t(\delta' | \delta), \mathbb{P}^t(\text{acc}(\alpha, \chi, \delta'))) \tag{1}$$

for some function f; if f is the arithmetic product then this expression is mathematical expectation. f may be more sensitive; for example, it may be defined to ensure that no contract is signed if there is a significant probability for a catastrophic outcome.

There is no prescriptive way in which α should define $\mathbb{P}^t(\text{acc}(\alpha, \chi, \delta'))$; the following three components at least will be required. $\mathbb{P}^t(\text{satisfy}(\alpha, \chi, \delta'))$ represents α's belief that enactment δ' will satisfy her need χ. $\mathbb{P}^t(\text{obj}(\delta'))$ represents α's belief that δ' is a fair deal against the open marketplace — it represents α's *objective* valuation. $\mathbb{P}^t(\text{sub}(\alpha, \chi, \delta'))$ represents α's belief that δ' is acceptable in her own terms taking account of her ability to meet her commitment ϕ [2] [3], and any way in which δ' has value to her personally — it represents α's *subjective* valuation. That is:

$$\mathbb{P}^t(\text{acc}(\alpha, \chi, \delta')) = g(\mathbb{P}^t(\text{satisfy}(\alpha, \chi, \delta')), \mathbb{P}^t(\text{obj}(\delta')), \mathbb{P}^t(\text{sub}(\alpha, \chi, \delta'))) \tag{2}$$

for some function g.

Suppose that an agent is able to estimate: $\mathbb{P}^t(\text{satisfy}(\alpha, \chi, \delta'))$, $\mathbb{P}^t(\text{obj}(\delta'))$ and $\mathbb{P}^t(\text{sub}(\alpha, \chi, \delta'))$. The specification of the aggregating g function will then be a strictly subjective decision. A highly cautious agent may choose to define:

$$\mathbb{P}^t(\text{acc}(\alpha,\chi,\delta')) = \begin{cases} 1 & \text{if: } \mathbb{P}^t(\text{satisfy}(\alpha,\chi,\delta')) > \eta_1 \\ & \wedge\, \mathbb{P}^t(\text{obj}(\delta')) > \eta_2 \,\wedge\, \mathbb{P}^t(\text{sub}(\alpha,\chi,\delta')) > \eta_3 \\ 0 & \text{otherwise.} \end{cases}$$

for some threshold constants η_i.

First β must give meaning to $\mathbb{P}^t(\text{satisfy}(\beta,\chi,\delta))$ by defining suitable criteria and the way that the belief should be aggregated across those criteria. Suppose the information acquisition process is managed by a plan π. Let random variable X represent $\mathbb{P}^t(\text{ease-of-use}(\beta,\delta) = e_i)$ where the e_i are values from an evaluation space that could be $\mathscr{E}$ ={fantastic, acceptable, just OK, shocking}. Then given a sequence s that was supposed to achieve task τ, suppose that β's tame human rates s as evidence for ease-of-use as $e \in \mathscr{E}$ with probability z. Suppose that β attaches a weighting $\mathbb{R}^t(\pi,\tau,s)$ to s, $0 < \mathbb{R} < 1$, which is β's estimate of the *significance* of the observation of sequence s within plan π as an indicator of the true value of X. For example, the on the basis of the observation alone β might rate ease-of-use as $e =$ acceptable with probability $z = 0.8$, and separately give a weighting of $\mathbb{R}^t(\pi,\tau,s) = 0.9$ to the sequence s as an indicator of ease-of-use. For an information-based agent each plan π has associated *update functions*, $J_\pi(\cdot)$, such that $J^X_\pi(s)$ is a set of linear constraints on the posterior distribution for X. In this example, the posterior value of 'acceptable' would simply be constrained to 0.8.

Denote the prior distribution $\mathbb{P}^t(X)$ by $\mathbf{p}$, and let $\mathbf{p}_{(s)}$ be the distribution with minimum relative entropy with respect to $\mathbf{p}$: $\mathbf{p}_{(s)} = \arg\min_{\mathbf{r}} \sum_j r_j \log \frac{r_j}{p_j}$ that satisfies the constraints $J^X_s(s)$. Then let $\mathbf{q}_{(s)}$ be the distribution:

$$\mathbf{q}_{(s)} = \mathbb{R}^t(\pi,\tau,s) \times \mathbf{p}_{(s)} + (1 - \mathbb{R}^t(\pi,\tau,s)) \times \mathbf{p} \tag{3}$$

and then let:

$$\mathbb{P}^t(X_{(s)}) = \begin{cases} \mathbf{q}_{(s)} & \text{if } \mathbf{q}_{(s)} \text{ is more interesting than } \mathbf{p} \\ \mathbf{p} & \text{otherwise} \end{cases} \tag{4}$$

A general measure of whether $\mathbf{q}_{(s)}$ is more interesting than $\mathbf{p}$ is: $\mathbb{K}(\mathbf{q}_{(s)} \| \mathbb{D}(X)) > \mathbb{K}(\mathbf{p} \| \mathbb{D}(X))$, where $\mathbb{K}(\mathbf{x}\|\mathbf{y}) = \sum_j x_j \log \frac{x_j}{y_j}$ is the Kullback-Leibler distance between two probability distributions $\mathbf{x}$ and $\mathbf{y}$, and $\mathbb{D}(X)$ is the expected distribution in the absence of any observations — $\mathbb{D}(X)$ could be the maximum entropy distribution. Finally, $\mathbb{P}^{t+1}(X) = \mathbb{P}^t(X_{(s)})$. This procedure deals with integrity decay, and with two probabilities: first, the probability z in the rating of the sequence s that was intended to achieve τ, and second β's weighting $\mathbb{R}^t(\pi,\tau,s)$ of the significance of τ as an indicator of the true value of X. Equation 4 is intended to prevent weak information from decreasing the certainty of $\mathbb{P}^{t+1}(X)$. For example if the current distribution is $(0.1, 0.7, 0.1, 0.1)$, indicating an "acceptable" rating, then weak evidence $\mathbb{P}(X =$ acceptable$) = 0.25$ is discarded.

3 Modelling the Argumentation Partner

In this Section we consider how the agent models its partner's contract acceptance logic in an argumentative context. In Section 2 we discussed modelling contract acceptance, but there is much more to be done.

Estimating β's evaluative criteria. α's world model, $\mathcal{M}^t$, contains probability distributions that model the agent's belief in the world, including the state of β. In particular, for every criterion $c \in \mathcal{C}$ α associates a random variable C with probability mass function $\mathbb{P}^t(C = e_i)$.

The distributions that relate object to criteria may be learned from prior experience. If $\mathbb{P}^t(C = e|O = o)$ is the prior distribution for criteria C over an evaluation space given that the object is o, then given evidence from a completed negotiation with object o we use the standard update procedure described in Section 2. For example, given evidence that α believes with probability p that $C = e_i$ in a negotiation with object o then $\mathbb{P}^{t+1}(C = e|O = o)$ is the result of applying the constraint $\mathbb{P}(C = e_i|O = o) = p$ with minimum relative entropy inference as described previously, where the result of the process is protected by Equation 4 to ensure that weak evidence does not override prior estimates. In the absence of evidence of the form described above, the distributions, $\mathbb{P}^t(C = e|O = o)$, should gradually tend to ignorance. If a decay-limit distribution [2] is known they should tend to it otherwise they should tend to the maximum entropy distribution.

In a multiagent system, this approach can be strengthened in repeated negotiations by including the agent's identity, $\mathbb{P}^t(C = e|(O = o, Agent = \beta))$ and exploiting a similarity measure across the ontology. Two methods for propagating estimates across the world model by exploiting the $\text{Sim}(\cdot)$ measure are described in [2]. An extension of the $\text{Sim}(\cdot)$ measure to sets of concepts is straightforward, we will note it as $\text{Sim}{*}(\cdot)$.

Disposition: shaping the stance. Agent β's *disposition* is the underlying rationale that he has for a dialogue. α will be concerned with the confidence in α's beliefs of β's disposition as this will affect the certainty with which α believes she knows β's key criteria. Gauging disposition in human discourse is not easy, but is certainly not impossible. We form expectations about what will be said next; when those expectations are challenged we may well believe that there is a shift in the rationale.

α's model of β's *disposition* is $D_C = \mathbb{P}^t(C = e|O = o)$ for *every* criterion in the ontology, where o is the object of the negotiation. α's confidence in β's disposition is the confidence he has in these distributions. Given a negotiation object o, confidence will be aggregated from $\mathbb{H}(C = e|O = o)$ for *every* criterion in the ontology.

4 Strategies

This section describes the components of an argumentation strategy starting with tools for valuing information revelation that are used to model the fairness of a negotiation dialogue.

Information Revelation: computing counter proposals. Everything that an agent communicates gives away information. *Illocutionary categories* and an *ontology* together form a framework in which the value of information exchanged can be categorised. The LOGIC framework for argumentative negotiation [4] is based on five illocutionary categories: Legitimacy of the arguments, Options i.e. deals that are acceptable, Goals i.e. motivation for the negotiation, Independence i.e: outside options, and Commitments that the agent has including its assets. In general, α has a set of illocutionary categories $\mathcal{Y}$ and a categorising function $\kappa : \mathcal{L} \rightarrow \mathcal{P}(\mathcal{Y})$. The power set, $\mathcal{P}(\mathcal{Y})$, is required as some utterances belong to multiple categories. For example, in the LOGIC framework the utterance "I will not pay more for a bottle of Beaujolais than the price that John charges" is categorised as both Option (what I will accept) and Independence (what I will do if this negotiation fails).

Then two central concepts describe relationships and dialogues between a pair of agents. These are *intimacy* — degree of closeness, and *balance* — degree of fairness. In this general model, the *intimacy* of α's relationship with β, A^t, measures the amount that α knows about β's private information and is represented as real numeric values over $\mathcal{G} = \mathcal{Y} \times V$.

Suppose α receives utterance u from β and that category $y \in \kappa(u)$. For any concept $x \in V$, define $\Delta(u,x) = \max_{x' \in concepts(u)} \text{Sim}(x',x)$. Denote the value of A^t_i in position (y,x) by $A^t_{(y,x)}$ then:

$$A^t_{(y,x)} = \rho \times A^{t-1}_{(y,x)} + (1-\rho) \times \mathbb{I}(u) \times \Delta(u,x)$$

for any x, where ρ is the discount rate, and $\mathbb{I}(u)$ is the *information*[1] in u. The *balance* of α's relationship with β_i, B^t, is the element by element numeric difference of A^t and α's estimate of β's intimacy on α.

Given the needs model, υ, α's *relationship model* (Relate$(\cdot)$) determines the target *intimacy*, A^{*t}_i, and target *balance*, B^{*t}_i, for each agent i in the known set of agents *Agents*. That is, $\{(A^{*t}_i, B^t_{*i})\}_{i=1}^{|Agents|} = \text{Relate}(\upsilon, \mathbf{X}, \mathbf{Y}, \mathbf{Z})$ where, $\mathbf{X}_i$ is the trust model, $\mathbf{Y}_i$ is the honour model and $\mathbf{Z}_i$ is the reliability model as described in [2]. As noted before, the values for intimacy and balance are not simple numbers but are structured sets of values over $\mathcal{Y} \times V$.

When a need fires α first selects an agent β_i to negotiate with — the social model of trust, honour and reliability provide input to this decision, i.e. $\beta_i = \text{Select}(\chi, \mathbf{X}, \mathbf{Y}, \mathbf{Z})$. We assume that in her social model, α has medium-term intentions for the state of the relationship that she desires with each of the available agents — these intentions are represented as the target intimacy, A^{*t}_i, and target balance, B^{*t}_i, for each agent β_i. These medium-term intentions are then distilled into short-term targets for the intimacy, A^{**t}_i, and balance, B^{**t}_i, to be achieved in the current dialogue Ψ^t, i.e. $(A^{**t}_i, B^{**t}_i) = \text{Set}(\chi, A^{*t}_i, B^{*t}_i)$. In particular, if the balance

[1] Information is measured in the Shannon sense, if at time t, α receives an utterance u that may alter this world model then the (Shannon) *information* in u with respect to the distributions in $\mathcal{M}^t$ is: $\mathbb{I}(u) = \mathbb{H}(\mathcal{M}^t) - \mathbb{H}(\mathcal{M}^{t+1})$.

target, B_i^{**t}, is grossly exceeded by β failing to co-operate then it becomes a trigger for α to terminate the negotiation.

Computing arguments For an information-based agent, an incoming utterance is only of interest if it reduces the uncertainty (entropy) of the world model in some way. Information-based argumentation is particularly interested in the effect that an argumentative utterance has in the world model including β's disposition, and α's estimate of β's assessment of current proposals in terms of its criteria.

If u requests α to perform a task then u may modify β's disposition i.e. the set of conditional estimates of the form: $\mathbb{P}^t(C = e|O = o))$. If β rates and comments on the demonstration of a sequence then this affects α's estimate of β's likelihood to accept a contract as described in Equation 1 (this is concerned with *how* β will apply his criteria).

Suppose that u rates and comments on the performance of a sequence then that sequence will have been demonstrated in response to a request to perform a task. Given a task, τ, and a object, s, α may have estimates for $P^t(C = e|(O = o, \mathcal{T} = \tau))$ — if so then this suggests a link between the task and a set of one or more criteria C_u. The effect that u has on β's criteria (what ever they are) will be conveyed as the rating. We assume that for every criterion and object pair (C, o) α has a supply of positive argumentative statements $\mathcal{L}_{(C,o)}$. Suppose α wishes to counter the negatively rated u with a positively rated u'. Let Ψ_u be the set of all arguments exchanged between α and β prior to u in the dialogue. Let $M_u \subseteq \mathcal{L}_{(C,o)}$ for any $C \in C_\mu$. Let $N_u \subseteq M_u$ such that $\forall x \in N_u$ and $\forall u' \in \Psi_u$, $\text{Sim}*(concepts(x), concepts(u')) > \eta$ for some constant η. So N_u is a set of arguments all of which (a) have a positive effect on at least one criterion associated with the negative u, and (b) are at 'some distance' (determined by r) from arguments already exchanged. Then:

$$u' = \begin{cases} \arg\min_{u' \in N_u} \text{Sim}*(concepts(u), concepts(u')) & \text{if } N_u \neq \emptyset \\ \arg\min_{u' \in M_u} \text{Sim}*(concepts(u), concepts(u')) & \text{otherwise.} \end{cases}$$

So using only 'fresh' arguments, α prefers to choose a counter argument to u that is semantically close to u, and if that is not possible she chooses an argument that has some general positive effect on the criteria and may not have been used previously.

References

1. Rahwan, I., Ramchurn, S., Jennings, N., McBurney, P., Parsons, S., Sonenberg, E.: Argumentation-based negotiation. Knowledge Engineering Review **18**(4), 343–375 (2003)
2. Sierra, C., Debenham, J.: Trust and honour in information-based agency. In: P. Stone, G. Weiss (eds.) Proceedings 5th International Conference on Autonomous Agents and Multi Agent Systems AAMAS-2006, pp. 1225 – 1232. ACM Press, New York, Hakodate, Japan (2006)
3. Sierra, C., Debenham, J.: Information-based agency. In: Proceedings 12th International Joint Conference on Artificial Intelligence IJCAI-07, pp. 1513–1518. Hyderabad, India (2007)
4. Sierra, C., Debenham, J.: The LOGIC Negotiation Model. In: Proceedings 6th International Conference on Autonomous Agents and Multi Agent Systems AAMAS-2007, pp. 1026–1033. Honolulu, Hawai'i (2007)

ASIC Design Project Management Supported by Multi Agent Simulation

Jana Blaschke, Christian Sebeke, Wolfgang Rosenstiel

Abstract The complexity of Application Specific Integrated Circuits (ASICs) is continuously increasing. Consequently chip-design becomes more and more challenging. To handle this complexity for a fast ASIC development, the existing design process has to become more efficient. To achieve this, we used an approach based on a multi-agent simulation. A mutli-agent system is an intuitive way to represent a team of designers, creating an ASIC. Furthermore, MAS are capable of coping with the natural dynamics of the design process, reacting to and modelling unforeseen events. The resulting Model is capable of an extensive analysis of the design process. It can make reliable predictions on design project courses and identify weak spots within the design process. It can provide status-anlysis of ongoing projects and suggestions on how to organize, plan and execute a new project efficiently.

1 Introduction

Because of smaller channel width and design automation in microelectronics, ASICs for electronic devices can realize more functionality and become more and more complex. If Moore's Law [5] persists, the required design effort for ICs exceeds the real possibilities. Therefore a way has to be found to make chip-design more efficient and plannable. This is a difficult task because design processes are complex, non-linear and depend on many human decisions. To make the design process more efficient it is necessary to make it assessable at first.

Existing approaches for design process modelling are static and generalizing. Numetrics Management Systems [2] deals on a commercial basis with design process modelling. They provide a benchmarking service that evaluates the design process of completed projects. This allows only a retrospective analysis of terminated

Jana Blaschke
Robert Bosch GmbH, Tübinger Straße 123, 72762 Tübingen, Germany
e-mail: jana.blaschke@de.bosch.com

Please use the following format when citing this chapter:

Blaschke, J., Sebeke, C. and Rosenstiel, W., 2009, in IFIP International Federation for Information Processing, Volume 296; *Artificial Intelligence Applications and Innovations III*; Eds. Iliadis, L., Vlahavas, I., Bramer, M.; (Boston: Springer), pp. 87–93.

projects is enabled. This neither allows what-if analysis of projects nor a reasonable planning for investments and resources.

To overcome these disadvantages we developed a flexible approach that allows status-analysis and an efficient planning of project courses. The approach was developed within the context of a public enhanced research project called PRODUKTIV+. The objective of PRODUKTIV+ is the development of a comprehensible model and reference system to measure and assess the productivity and performance of design processes [7].

2 The Concept

The approach needs to be able to make predictions for real and suggestions for optimal project courses. It should give status analysis of ongoing and finished projects and has to be flexible enough to handle and compare heterogeneous designs.

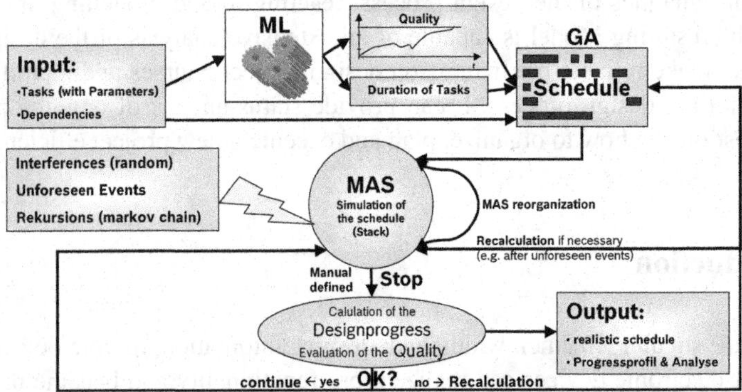

Fig. 1 Our dynamic approach to assess the design process in order to make it analysable and plannable. Inputs into the system are design tasks generated by a machine learning model. The core of the model consists of a multi agent simulation, processing the tasks. The simulation is organized by a scheduling algorithm. An interference module introduces dynamics to the system.

At first we generated a machine learning (ML) model of the design process. We split the design process into four subparts, the analogue and digital frontend and the analogue and digital backend. After detecting influential parameters, we analysed them regarding their impact on the generalization performance of the models. With the most relevant parameters we trained Neural Network, Gauss Process and Support Vector Machine models. None was precise enough to meet our requirements. The best model achieved was a support vector model for the analogue backend. It had a generalization error of 10% and a variance of 3.2. Another problem is that the models are static, neither considering the time course of the design process nor the dynamics of human-dependent processes. However, the ML models can be used for modelling the average duration of basic design tasks.

To overcome the lack of the ML model we developed a time-dependent simulation that is able to handle the natural dynamics immanent to human-lead processes. The model consists of several interacting modules, creating a flexible, dynamic and accurate model of the design process. An overview of the system is given in Fig. 1.

A MA simulation builds the core of the system model. The tasks to be executed are basic design tasks, derived from historical data or generated by a ML model. The simulation is organized by an optimized schedule calculated by an integer linear program (ILP). Dynamics are introduced by an interference module, perturbing the smooth schedule execution. The schedule and the MAS organization are adapted during the simulation if their deviation exceeds a given limit. The tracked agent activity gives a realistic estimate of the design process duration and a suggestion how to organize it. Multiple design-simulation runs give a statistic of average runtimes.

3 The Multi Agent Systems Architecture

We use a Multi Agent System (MAS) to describe the design process. MAS accomplish time-dependent simulations of complex interactions within a group of agents. This is a very important characteristic for our purpose, because it allows an inspection and analysis of the design process at any point of time.

The structure of the MAS depicts the design process of ASICS. Therefore the agents, their interactions and organization has to describe a design team, the design environment and structure. Every agent runs in an independent thread. Basic design tasks that have to be accomplished during the design process, determining the structure of a simulation run. The duration and sector of the tasks as well as its dependencies to other tasks account for a large part of the simulation organisation.

We defined four different agent types. The *designer agent* resembles the human designer. At their initialization characteristics have to be defined that assign working areas and properties to the designer. A designer can access a tool-pool that it can use to accomplish tasks of a specified working sector. The *tool agent* specifies a design tool. Its properties denote the design tasks that can be executed with the tool. The management and alignment of tasks to agents is done by an *administration agent*. Dynamics are introduced to the simulation by an *interference module*. It accounts for a realistic simulation.

The simulation structure is determined by the tasks and the agent interactions. Designers can only execute a task belonging to their working area using an appropriate tool. A designer can accomplish only one task at a time. A tool license can only be used by one designer at a time. If a designer has snatched a free tool license, he sends a task-request to the administration agent. If an executable task matching the designer's capabilities exists, the administration agent will provide it. For implementation we used the agent platform *A*-globe [6].

4 Introducing Dynamics to the MAS: the Interference Module

To obtain a simulation that reflects reality as close as possible, dynamics are introduced to the MAS. This is accomplished by an interference module. We identified four main factors that have a strong influence on the course of the design process.

The first factor is the agent availability restricted by illness and holidays. If an agent is out of office, he is not able to take and process a task. If he is already working on a task, the task duration will be prolonged or the task has to be passed to another agent. The second factor is the occurrence of unforeseen events, say long term resource drop outs or the introduction of new workload. The recursion of tasks depicts a third factor. There can be intense recursions between front- and backend design. The recursion probabilities were extracted from historical data and are inserted into a Markov Chain. As the tasks that are passed from the ML models to the MAS have averaged durations, a fourth factor is the task duration deviation.

5 MAS Scheduling with ILP

The administration agent has to manage the design tasks and to assign them to the designers. A natural way of doing this is to use a task schedule. As the duration and efficiency of the whole design process strongly depends on the tasks arrangement, schedule optimization is very important. This problem is known as the precedence, resource constrained scheduling problem, which is NP-complete [3]. An efficient, heuristical way to address this problem is the formulation of a zero-one ILP [4].

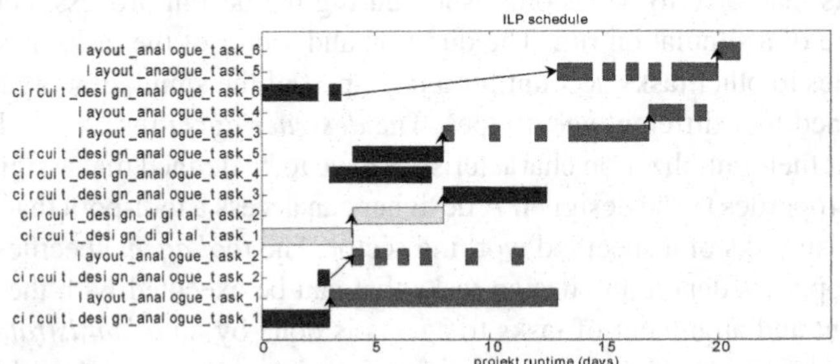

Fig. 2 ILP schedule of a real design subproject. It was optimized in terms of resource and time constraints and data dependencies between tasks. The constraints were formulized for three different regions, the analogue frontend (blue) and backend (red) and the digital frontend (yellow).

The objective of the optimization is to minimize the overall execution time of an ASIC-design project: min T_{design}. The problem is represented by binary variables. x_i^j represents the decision to schedule (1) or not schedule (0) task i at time j. The variables form a $m \times n$ matrix X, representing a design task in every row and a point in time in every column. The last column containing a 1 denotes the overall design execution time T_{design}. As the solution is restricted to some conditions, constraints have to be formulated to generate a valid schedule: The *must-schedule constraint* guarantees that every task is scheduled to one and only one point in time:

$$\sum_{j=1}^{m} x_i^j = 1\,, \tag{1}$$

To ensure that the number of r_{type} resources, here designers or tools, is not exceeded at any point in time, the *issue constraint* is formulated for every resource type:

$$\sum_{i=1}^{n} x_i^j \leq r_{type}\,, \tag{2}$$

The *precedence constraint* makes sure that dependencies between tasks are met, if a task k depends on a task i, i has to be scheduled before k:

$$\sum_{j=1}^{m} j * x_k^j + L_{ki} \leq \sum_{j=1}^{m} j * x_i^j\,, \tag{3}$$

where L_{ki} denotes the latency between x_k^j and x_i^j.

The *time constraint* ensures that deadlines $t_{deadline}$ are met:

$$\sum_{j=1}^{m} j * x_i^j \leq t_{deadline}\,. \tag{4}$$

The ILP was solved with the tool LPSolve [1].

The obtained schedules are used as input to the MAS.

6 First Results: Validation of MAS and Simulation of a Dynamic Design Process

We used part of a real ASIC-design project to evaluate our approach. The design task durations were averaged durations, gained from machine learning models. We initialized a MAS with one designer and one tool licence for digital the frontend, three designers and two tool licenses for the analogue frontend and 1.5 analogue layouter (one is part-time) and two tool licenses. We created a schedule by solving the ILP for these tasks.

At first we switched the interference module off and defined very tight degrees of freedom to obtain a validation of the MAS. Our expectations, that the MAS executes exactly the schedule were met. The ILP schedule, see figure 2, and the result of the simulation run, shown in figure 3(a), exhibit exactly the same project course.

The validation of the MAS was only a sanity check. To get a realistic simulation the interference module was switched on. Several runs gave an estimation for the

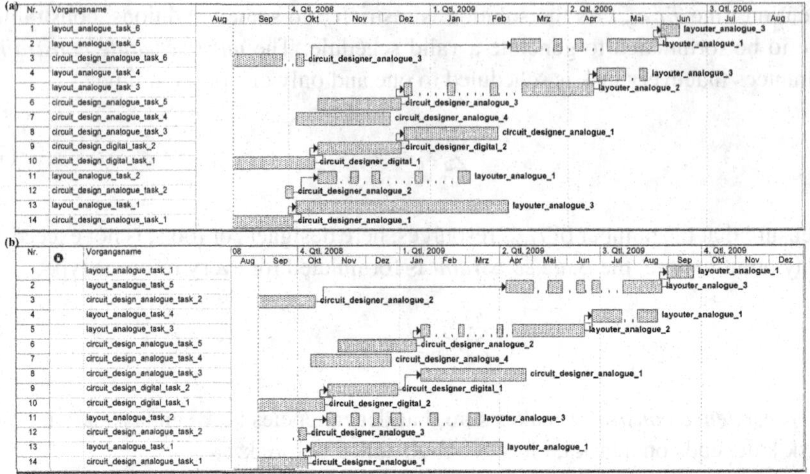

Fig. 3 (a) Simulation of the schedule provided by the ILP. The interference module is turned off. This run gives a simulation of the MAS. (b) Simulation of the schedule provided by the ILP. The interference module is switched on.

average runtime and the deviation of the project. Figure 3(b) shows an average run. The deviation of the runtime is 5 weeks . The simulation results reflect the real course of the project. They give a good picture of reality and allow an analysis of the project as well as suggestions on how to arrange the tasks in a good manner.

7 Conclusions and Future Work

The results of our simulation are quite satisfying. The MAS introduces a good possibility to simulate the complex and dynamic ASIC-design process and to make it assessible. A realistic simulation is achieved by the introduction of an interference module. To guide and improve the simulation, a schedule optimization is accomplished that offers ideal task-arrangements and resource allocations.

Up to 20 tasks (average 5 weeks duration for one task) can be handled efficiently by the ILP. Because of its ploynomial runtime, bigger problems have very long runtimes. Therefore we are working on a scheduling optimization based on genetic algorithms to overcome these limitations.

References

[1] http://sourceforge.net/projects/lpsolve.
[2] http://www.numetrics.com/homepage.jsp.

[3] M. R. Garey and D. S. Johnson. *Computers and Intractability: a Guide to the Theory of NP-Completeness*, Series of Books in the Mathematical Sciences. W. H. Freeman, January 1979.
[4] D. Kastner, M. Langenbach, and Fb Informatik. Integer linear programming vs. graph-based methods in code generation. Technical report, 1998.
[5] G. E.Moore. Crammingmore components onto integrated circuits. *Proceedings of the IEEE*, 86(1):8285, 1998.
[6] David Šišlák, Milan Rollo, and Michal Pěchouček. A-globe: Agent platform with inaccessibility and mobility support. In Matthias Klusch, Sascha Ossowski, Vipul Kashyap, and Rainer Unland, editors, *Cooperative Information Agents VIII*, volume 3191 of Lecture Notes in Computer Science, pages 199 214. Springer, 2004.
[7] J. Alt; A. Voerg. Produktiv+: Referenzsystem zur messung der produktivität beim entwurf nanoelektronischer systeme. *Newsletter edacentrum*, 1, 2006.

On the Combination of Textual and Semantic Descriptions for Automated Semantic Web Service Classification

Ioannis Katakis and Georgios Meditskos and Grigorios Tsoumakas and Nick Bassiliades and Ioannis Vlahavas

Abstract Semantic Web services have emerged as the solution to the need for automating several aspects related to service-oriented architectures, such as service discovery and composition, and they are realized by combining Semantic Web technologies and Web service standards. In the present paper, we tackle the problem of automated classification of Web services according to their application domain taking into account both the textual description and the semantic annotations of OWL-S advertisements. We present results that we obtained by applying machine learning algorithms on textual and semantic descriptions separately and we propose methods for increasing the overall classification accuracy through an extended feature vector and an ensemble of classifiers.

1 Introduction

Semantic Web services (SWSs) aim at making Web services (WSs) machine understandable and use-apparent, utilizing Semantic Web technologies (e.g. OWL-S[1], WSMO[2], SAWSDL [11]) and tools (e.g. Description Logic (DL) reasoners [2]) for service annotation and processing.

The increasing number of available WSs has raised the need for their automated and accurate classification in domain categories that can be beneficial for several tasks related to WSs, such as:

Ioannis Katakis · Georgios Meditskos · Grigorios Tsoumakas · Nick Bassiliades · Ioannis Vlahavas
Department of Informatics, Aristotle University of Thessaloniki, Thessaloniki 54124, Greece,
e-mail: {katak, gmeditsk, greg, nbassili, vlahavas}@csd.auth.gr

[1] http://www.daml.org/services/owl-s/

[2] http://www.wsmo.org/

Please use the following format when citing this chapter:

Katakis, I., Meditskos, G., Tsoumakas, G., Bassiliades, N. and Vlahavas, I., 2009, in IFIP International Federation for Information Processing, Volume 296; *Artificial Intelligence Applications and Innovations III*; Eds. Iliadis, L., Vlahavas, I., Bramer, M.; (Boston: Springer), pp. 95–104.

- *Discovery.* The effectiveness and efficiency of service discovery algorithms can be improved using WS classification by filtering out services that do not belong to the domain of interest.
- *Composition.* The classification of WSs can be used in order to increase the accuracy of WS composition by examining only the domain-relevant services in each step of the service workflow generation process.
- *Management.* The management of large number of WSs in repositories (UDDI[3]) is more effective when services are organized into categories. Furthermore, automated service classification can be utilized during the process of registering WSs in repositories by recommending service categorizations to the users.

This work presents a method for the automatic classification of SWSs based on their OWL-S Profile instances (advertisements). A Profile instance provides descriptive information about the service, such as textual description, as well as semantic annotations of WS's *inputs*, *outputs* (annotated with ontology concepts), *preconditions*, *effects* (expressed using a rule formalism, e.g. SWRL[4]), *non-functional properties*, etc. The definition of complete WS advertisements requires people with elaborate skill on description creation. Such advertisements are seldom encountered in practice. We therefore focus on the minimum piece of information that always exists in WS advertisements: the textual description and the I/O annotation concepts, also called *signatures*.

The main contribution of our work can be summarized in the following points:

1. We study the utility of four representation models for automated WS classification based on textual descriptions and signatures using a set of five different machine learning classifiers.
2. We propose and evaluate three different approaches for combining textual and semantic features. We consider such a combination vital since the textual descriptions are unable by itself to capture service's semantics, and that signatures are sometimes not sufficient to identify the service's application domain. Our experiments have shown that such a combination achieves the best overall accuracy through an ensemble of classifiers.
3. For evaluation purposes we create six different versions of our dataset of WSs that we make available online.

The rest of the paper is structured as follows. In the following section (Section 2) we briefly comment on related work on WS classification. Next (Section 3) we present four different representation methods of WSs for classification and three different approaches for combining them (Section 4). All of these methods are evaluated in Section 5 while Section 6 concludes the paper with plans for future work.

[3] http://www.oasis-open.org/committees/uddi-spec

[4] http://www.w3.org/Submission/SWRL/

2 Related Work

During the last years, a considerable effort was made for developing automatic or semi-automatic methods for classifying WSs into their application domain. In [3], WSDL[5] text descriptions are used in order to perform automatic classification of WSs using Support Vector Machines (SVMs) [21]. Many approaches [7, 13, 18, 6] use structured text elements from various WSDL components (e.g. operations) as input to various classification methods like naive Bayes [7, 13], SVMs [7], decision trees [18] or even ensemble of classifiers [6, 18]. The main disadvantage of such approaches is that no semantic information is taken into account that, as we discuss in this paper, can be considerably beneficial for classification.

In [5], the classification of WSs is based on OWL-S advertisements and it is achieved tby calculating the similarities of I/O annotation concepts between the unclassified WS and a set of preclassified WSs for each class. The predicted class is the one with the greatest overall similarity. The main disadvantage of this approach is that the representation is not flexible enough in order to be used with any machine learning algorithm and that the text of the description is ignored. We provide evaluation results that prove the utility of even short textual descriptions that may appear in the description of the WS advertisement.

A similar task to classification is SWS matchmaking. In this case a query WS description is given in order to find a set of similar WSs [9, 10].

3 Vector-based Representation of OWL-S Advertisements

This section describes a number of approaches for representing the OWL-S advertisement of a WS as a feature vector. Given a collection of labeled WSs, the corresponding feature vectors along with the labels will constitute the training examples for the machine learning algorithm.

3.1 Textual Description

Textual descriptions can be obtained from the `textDescription` property of OWL-S advertisements, from semantically enhanced UDDI registries [14], or even from the WSDL grounding of OWL-S advertisements. We represent an advertisement as a vector $\mathbf{T}_i = \left(t_{(i,1)}, ..., t_{(i,|V|)}\right)$ where $|V_T|$ is the size of the vocabulary V_T (the set of all distinct words in the textual descriptions of all WSs in the collection) and $t_{(i,j)}$ is the weight of the j-th word of the vocabulary for the i-th WS. A popular way to select weight for document classification is to use $t_{(i,j)} = 1$ if the j-th word appears in the document or $t_{(i,j)} = 0$ if not. The intuition behind this representation is

[5] www.w3.org/TR/wsdl

that the human entered textual description will contain words that will discriminate one category from another.

3.2 Ontology Imports

An OWL-S advertisement contains import declarations that denote the ontologies that are used for signature (I/O) annotations. It could be argued that these import declarations can be used in the classification procedure, following the intuition that advertisements with similar import declarations might belong to the same thematic category. To investigate this assumption, we introduce the *OntImp* vector representation of an advertisement. Let V_O be the ontology vocabulary, that is, the set of all distinct ontologies that are imported by the advertisements, taking into consideration import closures. The vector-based representation of an advertisement in the *OntImp* approach is of the form $\mathbf{O}_i = \left(o_{(i,1)}, \ldots, o_{(i,|V_O|)}\right)$, where $o_{(i,j)} = 1$, if the j-th ontology is imported (directly or indirectly) by the advertisement of the i-th WS, or $o_{(i,j)} = 0$, otherwise.

3.3 Syntactic and Semantic Signature

The signature of a WS encapsulates important domain knowledge that can be used in the classification procedure. Users annotate the I/O WS parameters with ontology concepts, defining abstractly the domain of the parameters using formal semantic descriptions. The relationships among the I/O concepts, such as *exact*, *plugin* and *subsume* [15], are determined using an ontology reasoner that computes the subsumption hierarchy of the underlying ontologies. Therefore, if two WS signatures have all or some of their I/O parameters relevant, according to some degree of relaxation, then they can possibly belong to the same category. In order to investigate the impact of the WSs' signatures, we have implemented two versions of signature-based classification; one based on the syntax (*SynSig*), treating the annotation concepts as plain text, and another based on the semantics (*SemSig*) of I/O concept annotations utilizing an OWL DL reasoner.

Syntactic Signature. Let V_C be the vocabulary of the ontology concepts, that is, the set of the distinct concepts that are used as I/O annotations in the advertisements. The representation of an advertisement in the *SynSig* approach is of the form $\mathbf{N}_i = \left(n_{(i,1)}, \ldots, n_{(i,|V_C|)}\right)$, where $n_{(i,j)} = 1$, if the j-th ontology concept is used as an input or output annotation by the advertisement of the i-th WS, or $n_{(i,j)} = 0$, otherwise.

Semantic Signature. The vector-based representation of an advertisement in the *SemSig* approach is of the form $\mathbf{S}_i = \left(s_{(i,1)}, \ldots, s_{(i,|V_C|)}\right)$. The weights are again binary, but they are selected as depicted in Algorithm 1. More specifically, if the j-th concept is referenced directly in the description of the i-th WS (line 4), or there is an annotation concept k in the i-th WS, such that j is equivalent ($j \equiv k$), superclass

($j \sqsupseteq k$) or subclass ($j \sqsubseteq k$) to k (line 8), then $s_{(i,j)} = 1$. Otherwise, if there is not such a concept k or the concepts j and k are disjoint (line 6), then $s_{(i,j)} = 0$.

Algorithm 1: semSigVector

Input: The ontology concept vocabulary V_C, the WS description i and the DL reasoner R
Output: The weighted vector S_i

```
1  Set inouts ← i.inputs ∪ i.outputs;
2  S_i ← [0,..,0];
3  forall j ∈ inouts do
4      S_i[V_C.index(j)] ← 1;
5      forall k ∈ V_C do
6          if R(j ⊓ k ⊑ ⊥) then
7              continue;
8          if R(j ≡ k) ∨ R(j ⊑ k) ∨ R(k ⊑ j) then
9              S_i[V_C.index(k)] ← 1
10 return S_i
```

4 Combining Text and Semantics

The WS classification based only on the semantics of signatures (*SemSig*) is not always sufficient to determine the category, since the semantic information that can be expressed is limited with respect to the details that can be captured. In that way, two WSs with different domains may have the same signature, for example, a car and an apartment rental service. In such cases, the textual descriptions can be used in order to perform a more fine-grained categorization.

On the other hand, the classification of WSs using only the text descriptions (or the *SynSig* approach) is not sufficient enough. Plain text is unable to give a formal and machine-processable semantic specification to the annotated resources that would enable the use of inference engines. Therefore, the semantic descriptions can provide an explicit and shared terminology to describe WSs, offering a more formal representation with an underlying formalization.

We argue that the combination of textual and semantic information can lead to more descriptive representations of WS advertisements. In the following sections, we propose two methods for such a combination.

4.1 Extended Feature Vector

In this case we merge the textual and syntactic / semantic vector into one, expecting from the classifier to learn relationships between textual features, syntactic/semantic features and categories. We denote the vector that represents the combination of the textual description (**T**) and the syntactic signature *TextSynSig* (**N**) as:

$$(\mathbf{TN})_i = (t_{(i,1)}, \ldots, t_{(i,|V_T|)}, n_{(i,1)}, \ldots, n_{(i,|V_C|)}) \tag{1}$$

and the one that represents the combination of the textual description and the semantic signature *TextSemSig* (**S**) as:

$$(\mathbf{TS})_i = \left(t_{(i,1)}, \ldots, t_{(i,|V_T|)}, s_{(i,1)}, \ldots, s_{(i,|V_C|)}\right) \tag{2}$$

4.2 Classifier Ensemble

Many machine learning algorithms can output not only the predicted category for a given instance but also the probability that the instance will belong to each category. Having two classifiers trained, one on textual features $H_T(d,\lambda) \rightarrow [0,1]$ and one on semantic features $H_S(d,\lambda) \rightarrow [0,1]$ that output the probability that the WS d will belong to category λ, we define two different decision schemas. If L is the set of all categories then let $h_T = \arg\max_{\lambda \in L} H_T(d,\lambda)$ and $h_S = \arg\max_{\lambda \in L} H_S(d,\lambda)$ be the decisions of H_T and H_S respectively and h_E the decision of the ensemble. The first schema (E_{max}) just selects the decision of the most confident classifier. In other words, $h_E = h_T$ if $H_T(d,h_T) \geq H_S(d,h_S)$ or $h_E = h_S$ otherwise. The second schema (E_{avg}) averages the probabilities over both classifiers for a given category and then selects the category with the maximum average:

$$h_E = \arg\max_{\lambda \in L} \left(\frac{H_T(d,\lambda) + H_S(d,\lambda)}{2} \right) \tag{3}$$

5 Evaluation

In order to evaluate the aforementioned methodologies and study their advantages and limitations we have applied them into a dataset of pre-classified WSs.

5.1 Experimental Setup

We used the OWLS-TC ver. 2.2 collection[6] that consists of 1007 OWL-S advertisements, without any additional modification. The advertisements define profile instances with simple atomic processes, without pointing to physical WSDL descriptions. Therefore, in our experiments we did not incorporate any WSDL construct. The textual description of each advertisement consists of the service name and a short service description. The WS I/O parameters are annotated with concepts from a set of $23 (= |Vo|)$ ontologies that the collection provides. The advertisements are also preclassified in seven categories, namely *Travel*, *Education*, *Weapon*, *Food*, *Economy*, *Communication*, and *Medical*. Please note that this collection is an artificial one. However, it is the only publicly available collection with a relatively large number of advertisements, and it has been used in many research efforts. After a preprocessing of the collection we obtained $|V_c| = 395$ and $|V_T| = 456$. All different versions of the resulting dataset are available online in Weka format at http://mlkd.csd.auth.gr/ws.html.

In all of experiments we used the 10-fold cross validation evaluation procedure and the Pellet DL reasoner [19] in order to compute the subsumption hierarchies of the imported ontologies. In order to obtain classifier-independent results, we have tested all of the approaches discussed in the previous section with 5 different classifiers: 1) the Naive Bayes (NB) [8] classifier, 2) the Support Vector Machine (SVM) (SMO Implementation [16]), 3) the k Nearest Neighbor (kNN) classifier [1], 4) the RIPPER rule learner [4] and 5) the C4.5 decision tree classifier [17]. We used algorithms from different learning paradigms, in order to cover a variety of real-world application requirements. We used the Weka [22] implementations of all algorithms with their default settings. The kNN algorithm was executed with $k = 3$. E_{max} and E_{avg} are implemented by training two classifiers of the *same* type (one from *Text* and one from *SemSig* representation) and using the combination schemes described in Section 4. It would be interesting to study the combination of models of different type but we consider this study out of the scope of this paper.

5.2 Results and Discussion

Table 1 presents the predictive accuracy for all methods and classifiers. With bold typeface we highlight which method performs best for a specific classifier while we underline the accuracy of the best performing classifier for each method. We first notice the high performance of the SVM which achieves the best predictive accuracy for almost all cases. The second best performance is achieved by C4.5.

Considering the different representation methods we first observe that the accuracy of the *Text* representation reaches high levels (outperforming *SynSig* and *OntImp*) even with this small amount of text from the OWL-S `textDescription`

---

[6] http://projects.semwebcentral.org/projects/owls-tc/

property. This is probably due to the existence of characteristic words for each category. The *OntImp* vector-based representation performs the worst mainly because there are general-purpose ontologies in the collection that are imported by domain unrelated advertisements. Moreover the *SynSig* approach despite its simplicity (without the use of Pellet) achieves a decent performance. However, the better performance of *SemSig* over *SynSig* stretches the importance of the inferencing mechanism. By employing a reasoner, we are able to deduce more semantic relationships among the annotation concepts, beyond simple keyword matches, such as equivalent ($\equiv$) or subsumed ($\sqsubseteq$) concepts.

By studying the results of the enhanced representations *TextSynSig* and *TextSemSig* we observe that both approaches outperform their corresponding basic representations (*Text* and *SynSig* for the former and *Text* and *SemSig* for the latter). This fact is an indication that the classifier successfully takes advantage of both textual and syntactic / semantic features .

Another fact that stretches the importance of combining text and semantics is the accuracy of the two ensemble methods E_{max} and E_{avg} that present the best overall performance. E_{max} and E_{avg} outperform *TextSemSig* probably because they build two experts (one from text and one from semantics) while *TexSemSig* builds one model that learns to combine both set of features.

Method / Classifier	NB	SVM	*k*NN	C4.5	Ripper	AVG
Text	90.37	94.04	91.96	90.17	87.98	90.90
OntImp	60.68	79.64	77.16	80.04	74.98	74.50
SynSig	84.51	94.04	89.37	87.19	86.59	88.34
SemSig	85.80	**96.92**	90.37	93.55	90.86	91.50
TextSynSig	89.97	95.73	92.85	90.57	87.69	91.36
TextSemSig	**91.96**	96.52	93.74	93.15	91.96	93.47
E_{max}	91.76	95.43	94.34	95.63	**92.95**	94.02
E_{avg}	**91.96**	96.23	**94.64**	**95.93**	92.85	94.12
AVG	85.89	93.44	90.55	90.78	88.23	

Table 1 Predictive accuracy of all methods and classifiers

6 Conclusions and Future Work

In this paper we presented an approach for automated WS classification based on OWL-S advertisements. We have presented several ways of representing semantic descriptions as vectors, each one with different semantic capabilities. In general, the exploitation of the semantic signature can lead to better classification accuracy than using the syntactic signature of a WS. Furthermore, we elaborated on two approaches for combining the text- and semantic-oriented vectors in order to exploit the descriptive capabilities of each paradigm, increasing the classification accuracy. Note, that our methodology can be extended to other SWS standards, such as SAWSDL.

Our classification approach can be extended in two directions. Firstly, the *SemSig* representation can be extended in order to incorporate also non-binary vectors, using as weights the similarities that are computed by concept similarity measures [12]. In that way, we will be able to define different degrees of relaxation in the representation. Secondly, it would be interesting to experiment with multilabel classification methods [20] for collections of SWSs that belong to more than one category.

Acknowledgements This work was partially supported by a PENED program (EPAN M.8.3.1, No. 03EΔ73), jointly funded by EU and the General Secretariat of Research and Technology.

References

1. Aha, D., Kibler, D.: Instance-based learning algorithms. Machine Learning **6**, 37–66 (1991)
2. Baader, F., Calvanese, D., McGuinness, D.L., Nardi, D., Patel-Schneider, P.F.: The Description Logic Handbook: Theory, Implementation, and Applications. Cambridge University Press (2003)
3. Bruno, M., Canfora, G., Penta, M.D., Scognamiglio, R.: An approach to support web service classification and annotation. In: Proceedings IEEE International Conference on e-Technology, e-Commerce and e-Service, pp. 138–143. Washington, DC (2005). DOI http://dx.doi.org/10.1109/EEE.2005.31
4. Cohen, W.W.: Fast effective rule induction. In: Proceedings 12th International Conference on Machine Learning, pp. 115–123 (1995)
5. Corella, M., Castells, P.: Semi-automatic semantic-based web service classification. In: J. Eder, S. Dustdar (eds.) Business Process Mangement Workshops, Springer Verlag Lecture Notes in Computer Science, vol. 4103, pp. 459–470. Vienna, Austria (2006)
6. Heß, A., Johnston, E., Kushmerick, N.: ASSAM: A tool for semi-automatically annotating semantic web services. In: Proceedings 3rd International Semantic Web Conference (2004)
7. Hess, A., Kushmerick, N.: Learning to attach semantic metadata to web services. In: Proceedings International Semantic Web Conference (ISWC'03), pp. 258–273 (2003)
8. John, G.H., Langley, P.: Estimating continuous distributions in bayesian classifiers. In: Proceedings 11th Conference on Uncertainty in Artificial Intelligence, pp. 338–345. Morgan Kaufmann, San Mateo (1995)
9. Kiefer, C., Bernstein, A.: The creation and evaluation of isparql strategies for matchmaking. In: M. Hauswirth, M. Koubarakis, S. Bechhofer (eds.) Proceedings 5th European Semantic Web Conference, LNCS. Springer Verlag, Berlin, Heidelberg (2008). URL http://data.semanticweb.org/conference/eswc/2008/papers/133
10. Klusch, M., Kapahnke, P., Fries, B.: Hybrid semantic web service retrieval: A case study with OWLS-MX. In: International Conference on Semantic Computing, pp. 323–330. IEEE Computer Society, Los Alamitos, CA (2008). DOI http://doi.ieeecomputersociety.org/10.1109/ICSC.2008.20
11. Kopecký, J., Vitvar, T., Bournez, C., Farrell, J.: Sawsdl: Semantic annotations for wsdl and xml schema. IEEE Internet Computing **11**(6), 60–67 (2007). DOI http://dx.doi.org/10.1109/MIC.2007.134
12. Meditskos, G., Bassiliades, N.: Object-oriented similarity measures for semantic web service matchmaking. In: Proceedings 5th IEEE European Conference on Web Services (ECOWS'07), pp. 57–66. Halle (Saale), Germany (2007)

13. Oldham, N., Thomas, C., Sheth, A., Verma, K.: Meteor-s web service annotation framework with machine learning classification. In: Proceedings 1st International Workshop on Semantic Web Services and Web Process Composition (SWSWPC'04), pp. 137–146 (2005)
14. Paolucci, M., Kawamura, T., Payne, T.R., Sycara, K.P.: Importing the semantic web in uddi. In: Revised Papers from the International Workshop on Web Services, E-Business, and the Semantic Web (CAiSE'02/WES'02), pp. 225–236. Springer-Verlag, London, UK (2002)
15. Paolucci, M., Kawamura, T., Payne, T.R., Sycara, K.P.: Semantic matching of web services capabilities. In: Proceedings 1st International Semantic Web Conference on The Semantic Web (ISWC'02), pp. 333–347. Springer-Verlag, London, UK (2002)
16. Platt, J.: Machines using sequential minimal optimization. In: B. Schoelkopf, C. Burges, A. Smola (eds.) Advances in Kernel Methods - Support Vector Learning. MIT Press (1998). URL http://research.microsoft.com/jplatt/smo.html
17. Quinlan, R.: C4.5: Programs for Machine Learning. Morgan Kaufmann Publishers, San Mateo, CA (1993)
18. Saha, S., Murthy, C.A., Pal, S.K.: Classification of web services using tensor space model and rough ensemble classifier. In: Proceedings 17th International Symposiumon Foundations of Intelligent Systems (ISMIS'08), pp. 508–513. Toronto, Canada (2008)
19. Sirin, E., Parsia, B., Grau, B.C., Kalyanpur, A., Katz, Y.: Pellet: A practical owl-dl reasoner. Web Semant. **5**(2), 51–53 (2007). DOI http://dx.doi.org/10.1016/j.websem.2007.03.004
20. Tsoumakas, G., Katakis, I.: Multi-label classification: An overview. International Journal of Data Warehousing and Mining **3**(3), 1–13 (2007)
21. Vapnik, V.N.: The nature of statistical learning theory. Springer-Verlag, NY, USA (1995)
22. Witten, I.H., Frank, E.: Data Mining: Practical Machine Learning Tools and Techniques, 2nd Edition. Morgan Kaufmann Publishers Inc., San Francisco, CA (2005)

Revealing Paths of Relevant Information in Web Graphs

Georgios Kouzas[1], Vassileios Kolias[2], Ioannis Anagnostopoulos[1] and Eleftherios Kayafas[2]

[1] University of the Aegean

Department of Financial and Management Engineering

Department of Information and Communications Systems Engineering

{gkouzas, janag}@aegean.gr

[2] National Technical University of Athens

School of Electrical and Computer Engineering

vkolias@medialab.ntua.gr, kayafas@cs.ntua. gr

Abstract In this paper we propose a web search methodology based on the Ant Colony Optimization (ACO) algorithm, which aims to enhance the amount of the relevant information in respect to a user's query. The algorithm aims to trace routes between hyperlinks, which connect two or more relevant information nodes of a web graph, with the minimum possible cost. The methodology uses the Ant-Seeker algorithm, where agents in the web paradigm are considered as ants capable of generating routing paths of relevant information through a web graph. The paper provides the implementation details of the web search methodology proposed, along with its initial assessment, which presents with quite promising results.

1 Introduction

In this paper, a new web search methodology based on the ant colony algorithm, is proposed. In more detail we suggest an ant colony algorithm approach, which is capable of tracing relevant information in Internet. Based on [1][2], Ant Colony algorithm can be applied on a connected graph Gp = (P,L), where P are the nodes, and L the link between the nodes, which represents a problem definition. Every route in this graph represents a solution of the initial problem. ACO converges in an optimal solution tracing routes in the graph. In our approach, we consider the world-wide web as a graph G. Although our methodology maintains most of the

---

Please use the following format when citing this chapter:

Kouzas, G., Kolias, V., Anagnostopoulos, I., and Kayafas, E., 2009, in IFIP International Federation for Information Processing, Volume 296; *Artificial Intelligence Applications and Innovations III*; Eds. Iliadis, L., Vlahavas, I., Bramer, M.; (Boston: Springer), pp. 105–112.

ant colony algorithm characteristics [3][4], its uniqueness lies upon the fact that it applies in an environment, the structure of which is not pre-defined. In addition, some search techniques for locating and evaluating the relevant information are used based on web page similarity [5], [6],[7] as well as web page clustering [8].

2 Basic Concepts Used

The aim of this paper is to propose a methodology that is able to trace routes between hyperlinks, which connect two or more relevant information units (web pages) with the minimum possible cost. Initially we consider a web information unit (web page), which is relevant to the user requests. This web page is considered as the starting point of the search. The search is based on the principle that when some information relevant to the user's request exists on a point-node of the world-wide web, then another point-node in a "close distance" is highly possible to contain similar (and thus relevant) information [9]. We define the hyperlink as the basic distance unit in the web universe. The "distance" between two nodes, is defined as the number of subsequent hops needed in order to be transferred from one node to another and vice versa. The methodology consists of three phases. In the first phase the start point of the search are defined. These could be either user defined web pages, either result of search engines [10][11][12]. In phase two, the suggested search algorithm takes place. The algorithm procedure runs iteratively, and each time that converges to an information unit, it specifies a new starting point. The third and last phase is to group the results according to how relevant their contents are. During the pre-processing of the hypertext documents the textual information is extracted from HTML format. Depending on the tags, we consider three levels of importance (that is High, Medium and Low). Then, the outgoing links are extracted in order to construct the search graph. The final step is the web page similarities calculation according to [13][14], in which the document hyperlink structure is taken into account, while it consists of the pre-process phase and the similarity estimation phase. As document similarity, we consider that sentences and phrases carry also significant information regarding the textual content. According to this, we used a comparison measure based not only on the similarity of individual terms but also on the similarity of sentences and phrases [15]. The similarity between two documents, d_1 and d_2 is computed according to Equation 1. In Equation 1 $g(l_i)$ is a function that marks the length of the common phrase, while s_{j1} and s_{k2} represent the initial length of the d_1 and d_2 document sentences respectively. Function $g(l_i)$ is proportional to the ratio of the common sentence portion length to the total sentence length as defined in Equation 2, while $|ms_i|$ is the matching phrase length and γ indicates a sentence partitioning greater than or equal to 1. Parallel to this procedure, the term-based similarity of the tested web pages takes place using the Vector Space Model (VSM) [16],[17] as defined in Equation 3. However, the inverse document frequency between terms is not taken under consideration, since the estimated similarity value concerns two web pages and not a collection of web pages as required from the VSM. Therefore the final document similarity SIM_i value is given from Equation 4. Result grouping is used for presenting the search results better. The acquired web pages are analyzed and presented in clusters. Each cluster contains a set of high importance information units. The cluster creation is based on the methodology proposed in [13][14] and the similarity histogram analysis. For specifying similarity, the classic vector space model is used [16],[17].

$$S_p(d_1,d_2)=\frac{\sqrt{\sum[g(l_i)\cdot(f_{i1}w_{i1}+f_{i12}w_{i2})]^2}}{\sum|s_{j1}|\cdot w_{j1}+\sum|s_{k2}|\cdot w_{k2}} \quad (1)$$

$$g(l_i)=\left(\frac{|ms_i|}{|s_i|}\right)^{\gamma} \quad (2)$$

$$sim(d_i,d_j)=\frac{d_i\cdot d_j}{|d_i|\times|d_j|}=\frac{\Sigma(w_{k,i}\times w_{k,j})}{\sqrt{\Sigma w_{k,i}^2}\times\sqrt{\Sigma w_{k,j}^2}} \quad (3)$$

$$SIM_i=S(d_1,d_2)=0.5S_p(d_1,d_2)+0.5S_t(d_1,d_2) \quad (4)$$

4 Ant Seeker

In this section we present the proposed search algorithm, which is based on the theoretical model of the ant colony algorithm [1]. The proposed algorithm deals with the world-wide web information search problem. The structure of the world-wide web consists of a set of information units (web pages) and a set of links (hyperlinks) between them. Thus, assuming a graph Gp = (P,L), where P are the nodes, and L the link set between the nodes, we can consider the world-wide web as a graph G with infinite dimensions.

4.1 An Overview of the Proposed Algorithm

The proposed algorithm is a slight modification of the ant colony algorithm [9], [18] and therefore it adopts most of the basic characteristics of the colony algorithms family [1]. However, several modifications were made in order to apply the proposed algorithm in the particular World Wide Web paradigm. Thus:

- Each artificial ant can visit a predefined maximum set of nodes.

- All artificial ants start from the start-node. In addition, when the algorithm starts there is no further information for the graph structure in which search will be applied. In this way, the harvesting procedure of real ants is simulated.
- The process of nodes recognition, which they have relevant content with the initial node, is based on the web page similarity mechanism as described in the previous section.

The search begins from the initial start node which is given by the user and in each step of the algorithm, each ant-agent moves from node i to node j. Assuming that in node j the pheromone value at time t is τj(t), then the ant visits node j through node i according to the pheromone function. The process is repeated until each ant visits the predefined maximum number of nodes. After the creation of the candidate routes, the best route is extracted and the node pheromone values are updated. This process is then repeated, while it ends when a convergence to a specific route is found. The node, which has the route with the maximum similarity value in comparison with the starting node, is assigned as the starting node for the next search. During the initialization phase, three variables are defined: the total ant-agent number NoA, the initial pheromone value IPV is defined in each new node and the number (Nmax) of the maximum nodes an ant can visit.

4.2 Heuristic Function-pheromone Model

For every new node is added, the content similarity to the initial one is checked. Thus, each node is characterized from a similarity value, which implies the quality of a node (Equation 4). In order to specify the quality of a node, apart from its content similarity to the initial node, a second value that defines its ability to leads to a node with high quality content is also specified. Therefore, points (nodes) with low similarity values increase their significance when they lead to points of high frequency. The calculation of a quality value is given by the heuristic function according to Equation 5, where d is the path of an ant-agent where node i is included in $(0 < d < NoA)$, SIM_i is the similarity function of node j as defined in Equation 4, and SIM_j^d stands for the similarity function of node j, which belong to the route d right after its previous visit in the node i $(i < j < N_{\max})$. As mentioned before, in the initial phase, each node inserted in the graph, has a pheromone value IPV. Every time, a complete iteration of algorithm occurs, the pheromone is updated. More specifically, the nodes used as intermediate or final points in the ant routes are updated. This procedure is given from Equations 6 and 7. In Equation 6, h_i is the heuristic function given from Equation 5, while k is the number of ants that used node i for the route creation. According to Equation 7, the nodes that lead to high frequency routes increase their pheromone values substantially over the algorithm iterations. To avoid infinite assignment of pheromone values in certain nodes, the pheromone value is normalized between zero and one as defined by Equation 8, where $\tau_{\max}(t+1)$, is the maximum pheromone value in the current iteration. Each time an ant is in a node *i*, it must choose the next node *j*. The nodes, which are considering to be visited, are the directly connected nodes. This defines the accessibility value of each web page given by Equation 9. In order to avoid endless loops, accessibility excludes the nodes, which contributed in the past in the creation of the route. The algorithm utilizes the classic probability model of the ant colony algorithms given from Equation 10. Whenever an algorithmic iteration occurs, ants make a route, based on the pheromone value and the quality of the nodes in the search graph. The nodes with the highest quality values increase their pheromone values, and thus they have higher probabilities to be chosen. A solution consists of a chosen route (set of nodes) and not a single node. As solution we define the node of the final route, which presents the larger similarity value. This node is then added to the list of solutions.

$$h_i(t+1) = \max(\underset{i<j<N_{MAX}}{SIM_j^d}, SIM_i, h_i(t)) \tag{5}$$

$$\Delta\tau_i = kh_i \tag{6}$$

$$\tau_i(t+1)' = \tau_i(t) + \Delta\tau_i \tag{7}$$

$$\tau_i(t+1) = \frac{\tau_i(t+1)'}{\tau_{\max}(t+1)} \tag{8}$$

$$\eta_{ij} = \begin{cases} 1 & \text{if node j is directly linked from node i} \\ 0 & otherwise \end{cases} \tag{9}$$

$$P_{ij} = \frac{\tau_j \cdot \eta_{ij}}{\sum_{k \in allowed_k} \tau_k \cdot \eta_{ik}} \tag{10}$$

5 Results - Evaluation

This section presents the results of the proposed methodology. The evaluation took place in two experiment phases. In the first we evaluate the performance of the proposed Ant-Seeker algorithm [9], [18] by applying the algorithm in three different queries. In the second phase we evaluate the introduction of some clustering techniques to the methodology for grouping the results. The search procedure was examined by querying different parts of the World Wide Web three times. During this procedure we used only web-pages with English content. In order to apply and evaluate the algorithm, we followed three steps. The first step involves the preprocessing of the WebPages; the second involves the balancing of variables NoA, Nmax and IPV while the third step involves the algorithm execution. For all experiments the variable values where chosen to be NoA=10,

Nmax=3, NC=100 and IPV=0.4. For each search the set of returning results is equal to the number of algorithm iterations. This reduces the result quality, but this is important especially in cases where the algorithm doesn't manage to converge in a relative to the query solution during the initial search stages. The results of clustering to the three algorithm evaluation sets appear in table 6. Applying clustering methods to the returning results, the percentage of related document retrieval is decreasing (between 2% to 5%) but at the same time their quality increases (from 30-50% to 80-90%). This is an expected behavior, because, the nodes-pages used for the search continuation only, are cut off due to the low similarity value with the initial document. However, a small part of the correct results, are not ranked correctly during the clustering. The explanation is that the similarity calculation model during algorithm execution is given by Equation 4 and on the other hand the similarity calculation model, during clustering is the vector space model [17]. We use a different function to calculate the similarity because the final collection of the web pages is unknown during the search, so we use equation 4 that defines similarity between a pair of pages. On the contrary during clustering the total returning results virtually defines the collection. In table 2 the results of applying the methodology for 6 random queries in the world-wide web appear. The proposed algorithm's ability to seek and extract information relative to the query from the world-wide web is outlined in the experimental results. However during the experiments we created a set of constraints.

The most important constraint is the scale of the world-wide web which did not allow applying the algorithm in a wider scale search. The sample size was of value 200.000. The proper evaluation of the algorithm requires full definition of the samples as concerning their informational relativity to the reference node. The classification of all the samples based on similarity gives an estimation of the relation of the documents and therefore a classification measure but still remains a mechanical classification method which cannot replace the human factor. For the evaluation some machine learning techniques could be used as in neural networks [10], [11] but a set of already classified documents is required in order to extract the relative documents.

The second constraint that virtually is a result of the previous constraint is the overlapping between searches. The algorithm includes an overlapping search prevention mechanism in order to avoid creating cyclic search routes. However, in a limited portion of the world-wide web forbidding backtracking would result in a search termination in only a few steps (2 to 5 searches per sample). For this reason, the only constraint assigned for route creation was blocking adding a node, which belongs to the current set of solutions of the algorithm.

6 Conclusion

By evaluating the behavior of the algorithm we observe that it enables search in real time. The ability to choose the direction of the search autonomously, allowing the search of unknown territories at the same time is noteworthy. An important advantage in contrast to other classic search and classification methods is the fact that it does not require covering the whole search space. In the experiments the coverage percentage was at 40%, taking all the constraints under consideration. However the retrieved document percentage is limited to 80% as depicted in table 1. The document structure in which the search takes place doesn't seem to affect the search. In addition as the structure tends to that of a fully linked document the algorithm performance is increasing. In contrast to the most search techniques the ability to use a textual query allows quality searches. Search with queries of type of a set of terms has the advantage of being short as long as the query is accurate. But when the query is inaccurate then the results are confusing. The use of a reference document for the search improves the quality of the returning results. Of course, the documents relative to the informational need, but with low similarity value with the reference document cannot be retrieved. According to the experiment results the covering percentage is about 40% with an average near 90%. Although the download percentage for the specific covering percentage is satisfying, applying the algorithm to large scale searches is prohibitive. Applying the algorithm to the world-wide web for the second set of experiments is quite time-consuming. Additionally, adding solutions unrelated to the query produces low quality results. Adding clustering techniques to the retrieved documents improves the quality of the results, but for each irrelevant to the query document return, an analogical search cost is added. As an alternative method for cutting off bad solutions could be an additional variable to the algorithm solving rule. This value would define a minimum limit value to the similarity of the candidate solution to the reference document.

Table 1 System performance using clustering techniques

Experiment	Relative Pages	Algorithm		Clustering		Download (%)	Accuracy (%)
		Total	Found	Relative	Correct		
1	43	80	37	42	35	81,40	83,33
2	34	85	29	32	26	76,47	81,25
3	72	135	65	70	65	90,28	92,86

Table 2 System Performance for random internet queries

Experiment	Relative Pages	System Relative	Correct	Download (%)	Accuracy (%)
1	32	37	28	87,50	75,68
2	40	56	32	80,00	57,14
3	21	25	19	90,48	76,00
4	10	8	8	80,00	100,00
5	17	17	15	88,24	88,24
6	36	42	33	91,67	78,57

References

1 M. Dorigo and T. St¨utzle. Ant Colony Optimization. The MIT Press, 2004.

2 Dorigo M., and Caro G.D., 1999, "Ant Algorithms Optimization. Artificial Life", 5(3):137-172.

3 Dorigo M., and Maniezzo V., 1996, "The ant system: optimization by a colony of cooperating agents". IEEE Transactions on Systems, Man and Cybernetics, 26(1):1-13.

4 Dorigo M. and Caro G.D., 1999, "The Ant Colony Optimization Meta-heuristic" in New Ideas in Optimization, D. Corne, M. Dorigo, and F. Glover (Eds.), London: McGraw-Hill, pp. 11-32

5 Pokorny J (2004) Web searching and information retrieval. Computing in Science & Engineering. 6(4):43-48.

6 Oyama S, Kokubo T, Ishida T (2004) Domain-specific Web search with keyword spices. IEEE Transactions on Knowledge and Data Engineering. 16(1):17-27.

7 Pokorny J (2004) Web searching and information retrieval. Computing in Science & Engineering. 6(4):43-48.

8 Broder A, Glassman S, Manasse M, Zweig G. Syntactic clustering of the Web. Proceedings 6th International World Wide Web Conference, April 1997; 391-404.

9 G. Kouzas, E. Kayafas, V. Loumos: "Ant Seeker: An algorithm for enhanced web search", Proceedings 3rd IFIP Conference on Artificial Intelligence Applications and Innovations (AIAI) 2006, June 2006, Athens, Greece. IFIP 204 Springer 2006, pp 649-656.

10 I. Anagnostopoulos, C. Anagnostopoulos, G. Kouzas and D. Vergados, "A Generalised Regression algorithm for web page categorisation", Neural Computing & Applications journal, Springer-Verlag, 13(3):229-236, 2004.

11 I. Anagnostopoulos, C. Anagnostopoulos, Vassili Loumos, Eleftherios Kayafas, "Classifying Web Pages employing a Probabilistic Neural Network Classifier", IEE Proceedings – Software, 151(03):139-150, March 2004.

12 Anagnostopoulos I., Psoroulas I., Loumos V. and Kayafas E., "Implementing a customized meta-search interface for user query personalization", Proceedings 24th International Conference on Information Technology Interfaces (ITI'2002), pp. 79-84, June 2002, Cavtat/Dubrovnik, Croatia.

13 K.M. Hammouda, M. S. Kamel,"Phrase-based Document Similarity Based on an Index Graph Model", Proceedings IEEE International Conference on Data Mining (ICDM'2002), December 2002, Maebashi City, Japan. IEEE Computer Society 2002, pp. 203-210.

14 K.M. Hammouda, M. S. Kamel, "Incremental Document Clustering Using Cluster Similarity Histograms", Proceedings WIC International Conference on Web Intelligence (WI 2003), October 2003, Halifax, Canada. IEEE Computer Society 2003, pp. 597-601

15 J. D. Isaacs and J. A. Aslam. "Investigating measures for pairwise document similarity. Technical Report PCS-TR99-357, Dartmouth College, Computer Science, Hanover, NH, June 1999

16 G. Salton, M. E. Lesk. Computer evaluation of indexing and text processing, Journal of the ACM, 15(1):8-36, 1968.

17 G. Salton. The SMART Retrieval System – Experiments in Automatic Document Processing. Prentice Hall Inc., 1971.

18 Kouzas G., E. Kayafas, V. Loumos "Web Similarity Measurements using Ant – Based Search Algorithm", Proceedings XVIII IMEKO WORLD CONGRESS Metrology for a Sustainable Development September 2006, Rio de Janeiro, Brazil.

Preferential Infinitesimals for Information Retrieval

Maria Chowdhury, Alex Thomo, and William W. Wadge

Abstract In this paper, we propose a preference framework for information retrieval in which the user and the system administrator are enabled to express preference annotations on search keywords and document elements, respectively. Our framework is flexible and allows expressing preferences such as "*A* is infinitely more preferred than *B*," which we capture by using *hyperreal numbers*. Due to the widespread of XML as a standard for representing documents, we consider XML documents in this paper and propose a consistent preferential weighting scheme for nested document elements. We show how to naturally incorporate preferences on search keywords and document elements into an IR ranking process using the well-known TF-IDF ranking measure.

1 Introduction

In this paper, we propose a framework for preferential information retrieval by incorporating in the document ranking process preferences given by the user or the system administrator. Namely, in our proposed framework, the user has the option of weighting the search keywords, whereas the system administrator has the option of weighting structural elements of the documents. We address both facets of preferential weighting by using hyperreal numbers, which form a superset of the real numbers, and in our context, serve the purpose of specifying natural preferences of the form "*A* is infinitely more preferred than *B*."

Keyword Preferences. To illustrate preferences on keywords, suppose that a user wants to retrieve documents on research and techniques for "music-information-retrieval." Also, suppose that the user is a fan of Google technology. As such, this user would probably give to a search engine the keywords:

Department of Computer Science, University of Victoria, Canada,
e-mail: {mwchow,thomo,wwadge}@cs.uvic.ca

Please use the following format when citing this chapter:

Chowdhury, M., Thomo, A. and Wadge, W.W., 2009, in IFIP International Federation for Information Processing, Volume 296; *Artificial Intelligence Applications and Innovations III*; Eds. Iliadis, L., Vlahavas, I., Bramer, M.; (Boston: Springer), pp. 113–125.

music-information-retrieval, google-search, google-ranking.

It is interesting to observe that if the user specifies these keywords in Google, then she gets a list of only *three*, low quality, pages. What happens is that the true, highly informative pages about "music-information-retrieval" are lost (or insignificantly ranked) in the quest of trying to serve the "google-search" and "google-ranking" keywords. Unfortunately, in Google and other search engines, the user cannot explicitly specify her real preferences among the specified keywords. In this example, what the user needs is a mechanism for saying that "music-information-retrieval" is of primary importance or *infinitely* more important than "google-search" and "google-ranking," and thus, an informative page about "music-information-retrieval" should be retrieved and highly ranked even if it does not relate to Google technologies.

Structural Preferences. The other facet of using preferential weights is for system administrators to annotate structural parts of the documents in a given corpus. In practice, most of the documents are structured, and often, certain parts of them are more important than others. While our proposed ideas can be applied on any corpus of structured documents, due to the wide spread of XML as a standard for representing documents, we consider in this paper XML documents which conform to a given schema (DTD). In the same spirit as for keyword preferences, we will use hyperreal weights to denote the importance of different elements in the schema and documents.

To illustrate preferences on structural parts of documents, suppose that we have a corpus of documents representing research papers, and a user is searching for a specific keyword. Now, suppose that the keyword occurs in the *title* element of one paper and in the *references* element of another paper. Intuitively, the paper having the keyword in the *title* should be ranked higher than the paper containing the keyword in the *references* element as the title of a paper usually bears more representative and concise information about the paper than the reference entries do. In fact, one could say that terms in the title (and abstract) are *infinitely* more important than terms in the references entries as the latter might be there completely incidental.

While weighting of certain parts of documents has been considered and advocated in the folklore (cf. [5, 8]), to the best of our knowledge there is no work dealing with inferring a consistent weighting scheme for nested XML elements based on the weights that a system administrator gives to DTD elements. As we explain in Section 4, there are tradeoffs to be considered and we present a solution that properly normalizes the element weights producing values which are consistent among sibling elements and never greater than the normalized weight of the parent element, thus respecting the XML hierarchy.

Contributions. Specifically, our contributions in this paper are as follows.

1. We propose using hyperreal numbers (see [6, 7]) to capture both "quantitative" and "qualitative" user preferences on search keywords. The set of hyperreal numbers includes the real numbers which can be used for expressing "quantitative" preferences such as, say "A is twice more preferred than B," as well as *infinites-*

imal numbers, which can be used to express "qualitative" preferences such as, say "*A* is infinitely more preferred than *B*." We argue that without such qualitative preferences there is no guarantee that an IR system would not override user preferences in favor of other measures that the system might use.

2. We extend the ideas of using hyperreal numbers to annotating XML (DTD) schemas. This allows system administrators to preferentially weight structural elements in XML documents of a given corpus. We present a normalization method which produces consistent preferential weights for the elements of any XML document that complies to an annotated DTD schema.
3. We adapt the well-known TF-IDF ranking in IR systems to take into consideration the preferential weights that the search keywords and XML elements can have. Our extensions are based on symbolic computations which can be effectively computed on expressions containing hyperreal numbers.
4. We present (in the appendix) illustrative practical examples which demonstrate the usefulness of our proposed preference framework. Namely, we use a full collection of speeches from the Shakespeare plays, and a diverse XML collection from INEX ([13]). In both these collections, we observed a clear advantage of our preferential ranking over the ranking produced by the classical TF-IDF method. We believe that these results encourage incorporating both quantitative and (especially) qualitative preferences into other ranking methods as well.

Organization. The rest of the paper is organized as follows. In Section 2, we give an overview of hyperreal numbers and their properties. In Section 3, we present hyperreal preferences for annotating search keywords. In Section 4, we propose annotated DTDs for XML documents and address two problems for consistent weighting of document elements. In Section 5, we show how to extend the TF-IDF ranking scheme to take into consideration the hyperreal weights present in the search keywords and document elements. In Appendix, we present experimental results.

2 Hyperreal Numbers

Hyperreal numbers were introduced in calculus to capture "infinitesimal" quantities which are infinitely small and yet not equal to zero. Formally, a number ε is said to be *infinitely small* or *infinitesimal* (cf. [6, 7]) iff $-a < \varepsilon < a$ for every positive *real* number a. Hyperreal numbers contain all the real numbers and also all the infinitesimal numbers. There are principles (or axioms) for hyperreal numbers (cf. [7]) of which we mention:

Extension Principle.

1. The real numbers form a subset of the hyperreal numbers, and the order relation $x < y$ for the real numbers is a subset of the order relation for the hyperreal numbers.
2. There exists a hyperreal number that is greater than zero but less than every positive real number.

3. For every real function f, we are given a corresponding hyperreal function f^* which is called the *natural extension* of f.

Transfer Principle. Every real statement that holds for one or more particular real functions holds for the hyperreal natural extensions of these functions.

In short, the Extension Principle gives the *hyperreal* numbers and the Transfer Principle enables carrying out computation on them. The Extension Principle says that there does exist an infinitesimal number, for example ε. Other examples of hyperreals numbers, created using ε, are: ε^3, $100\varepsilon^2 + 51\varepsilon$, $\varepsilon/300$.

For $a,b,r,s \in \mathbb{R}^+$ and $r < s$, we have $a\varepsilon^r < b\varepsilon^s$, regardless of the relationship between a and b.

If $a\varepsilon^r$ and $b\varepsilon^s$ are used for example to denote two preference weights, then $a\varepsilon^r$ is "infinitely better" than $b\varepsilon^s$ even though a might be much bigger than b, i.e. coefficients a and b are insignificant when the powers of ε are different. On the other hand, when comparing two preferential weights of the same power, as for example $a\varepsilon^r$ and $b\varepsilon^r$, the magnitudes of coefficients a and b become important. Namely, $a\varepsilon^r \leq b\varepsilon^r$ ($a\varepsilon^r > b\varepsilon^r$) iff $a \leq b$ ($a > b$).

3 Keyword Preferences

We propose a framework where the user can preferentially annotate the keywords by *hyperreal numbers*.

Using hyperreal annotations is essential for reasoning in terms of "infinitely more important," which is crucially needed in a scenario with numerous documents. This is because preference specification using only real numbers suffers from the possibility of producing senseless results as those preferences can get easily absorbed by other measures used by search engines. For instance, continuing the example given in the Introduction,

music-information-retrieval, google-search, google-ranking,

suppose that the user, dismayed of the poor result from Google, containing only three low quality pages, changes the query into[1]

music-information-retrieval OR google-search OR google-ranking.

It is interesting to observe that if the user specifies this (modified) query in Google, then what she gets is a list of *many* web-pages (documents)! These pages are ranked by their Google-computed importance which is by far biased toward

[1] This second query style corresponds more closely than the first to what is known in the folklore as the popular "free text query:" a query in which the terms of the query are typed freeform into the search interface (cf. [5, 8]).

general pages about "google-search" and "google-ranking" rather than "music-information-retrieval." The true pages about "music-information-retrieval" are simply buried under tons of other pages about "google-search" and "google-ranking" that are highly ranked, but contain "music-information-retrieval" either incidentally or not at all. Unfortunately, in Google and other search engines, the user cannot explicitly specify her real preferences among the specified keywords. In this example, what the user needs is a mechanism for saying that "music-information-retrieval" is of primary importance or infinitely more important than "google-search" and "google-ranking."

But, let us suppose for a moment that Google would allow users to specify preferences expressed by real numbers. Now, imagine the user who is trying to convey that her "first and foremost" preference is for documents on "music-information-retrieval" rather than general documents about Google technology. For this, the user specifies that *music-information-retrieval* is 100 times more important than *google-search*. After all, "100 times more important" seems quite convincing in colloquial talking! However, what would happen if, according to the score computed by the search engine, general documents about *google-search* were in fact 1000 times more important than documents about *music-information-retrieval*? If the user preference levels were used to simply boost the computed document score by the same factor, then still, documents about *google-search* would be ranked higher than documents about *music-information-retrieval*. What the user would experience in this case is an "indifferent" search engine with respect to her preferences.

The solution we propose is to use hyperreal numbers for expressing preferential weights. In order to always have an effective comparison of documents with respect to a user query, we will fix an infinitesimal number, say ε, and build expressions on it. By the Extension Principle, such a number does exist. Now, we give the following definition.

Definition 1. An *annotated free text query* is simply a set of keywords (terms) with preference weights which are polynomials of ε.

For all our practical purposes it suffices to consider only polynomials with coefficients in $\mathbb{R}^+$. For example, $3+2\varepsilon+4\varepsilon^2$.

By making this restriction we are able to perform symbolic (algorithmic) computations on expressions using ε. All such expressions translate into operations on polynomials with real coefficients for which efficient algorithms are known (we will namely need to perform polynomial additions, multiplications and divisions[2]).

Let us illustrate our annotated queries by continuing the above example. The user can now give

$$\textit{music-information-retrieval, google-search} : \varepsilon,\ \textit{google-ranking} : \varepsilon^2$$

[2] The division is performed by first factoring the highest power of ε. For example, $(6+3\varepsilon+3\varepsilon^2)/(4+2\varepsilon+3\varepsilon^2)$ is first transformed into $(6\varepsilon^{-2}+4\varepsilon^{-1}+3)/(3\varepsilon^{-2}+2\varepsilon^{-1}+4)$, and then we perform the division as we would do for $(6x^2+4x+3)/(3x^2+2x+4)$. Observe that, as ε is infinitely small, ε^{-1} is *infinitely big*.

to express that she wants to find documents on Music Information Retrieval and she is interested in the Google technology for retrieving and ranking music. However, by leaving intact the *music-information-retrieval* and annotating *google-search* by ε and *google-ranking* by ε^2, the user makes her intention explicit that a document on *music-information-retrieval* is infinitely more important than any document on simply *google-search* or *google-ranking*. Furthermore, in accord with the above user expression, documents on *music-information-retrieval* and/or *google-search* are infinitely more important than documents on simply *google-ranking*. Of course, among documents on Music Information Retrieval, those which are relevant to Google search and Google ranking are more important.

We note that our framework also allows the user to specify "soft" preference levels. For example, suppose that the user changes her mind and prefers to have both *google-search* and *google-ranking* in the same "hard" preference level as determined by the power of infinitesimal ε. However, she still prefers, say "twice more," *google-search* over *google-ranking*. In this case, the user gives

$$\textit{music-information-retrieval, google-search} : 2\varepsilon, \textit{google-ranking} : \varepsilon.$$

4 Preferentially Annotated XML Schemas

In this section, we consider the problem of weighting the structural elements of documents in a corpus with the purpose of influencing an information retrieval system to take into account the importance of different elements during the process of document ranking. Due to the wide spread of XML as a standard for representing documents, we consider in this paper XML documents which conform to a given schema (DTD). In the same spirit as in the previous section, we will use hyperreal weights to denote the importance of different elements in the schema and documents.

While the idea of weighting the document elements is old and by now part of the folklore (cf. [8]), to the best of our knowledge, there is no work that systematically studies the problem of weighting XML elements. The problem becomes challenging when elements can possibly be nested inside other elements which can be weighted as well, and one wants to achieve a consistent weight normalization reflecting the true preferences of a system administrator. Another challenging problem, as we explain in Subsection 4.4, is determining the right mapping of weights from the elements of a DTD schema into the elements of XML documents.

4.1 Hyperreal Weights

In our framework, the system administrator is enabled to set the importance of various XML elements/sections in a DTD schema. For example, she can specify that the *keywords* elements of documents in an XML corpus, with "research activities" as the main theme, is more important than than a section, say on *related work*. Intuitively, an occurrence of a search term in the *keywords* section is way more important than an occurrence in the *related work* section as the occurrence in the latter might be completely incidental or only loosely related to the main thrust of the document.

Thus, in our framework, we allow the annotation of XML elements by weights being, as in the previous section, polynomials of a (fixed) infinitesimal ε.

4.2 DTDs

Let Σ be the (finite) tag alphabet of a given XML collection, i.e. each tag is an element of Σ. Then, a DTD D is a pair (d,r) where d is a function mapping Σ-symbols to regular expressions on Σ and r is the root symbol (cf. [2]).

A *valid* XML document complying to a DTD $D = (d,s)$ can be viewed as a tree, whose root is labeled by r and every node labeled, say by a, has a sequence of children whose label concatenation, say $bc\ldots x$, is in $L(d(a))$.

A simple example of a DTD defining the structure of some XML research documents is the following:

$$\begin{aligned}\text{paper} &\rightarrow \text{preamble body}\\ \text{preamble} &\rightarrow \text{title author}^{+}\text{ abstract keywords}\\ \text{body} &\rightarrow \text{introduction section}^{*}\text{ related-work? references}\end{aligned}$$

where '+' implies "one or more," '$*$' implies "zero or more" and '?' implies "zero or one" occurrences of an element.

In essence, a DTD D is an extended context-free grammar, and a valid XML document with respect to D is a parse tree for D.

4.3 Annotated DTDs

To illustrate annotated DTDs, let us suppose that the system administrator wants to express that in the *body* element, the *introduction* is twice more important than a *section*, and both are infinitely more important than *related-work* and *references*, with the latter being infinitely less important than the former, we would annotate the rule for *body* as follows:

$$\text{body} \rightarrow (\text{introduction} : 2)\ (\text{section} : 1)^{*}\ (\text{related-work} : \varepsilon)?\ (\text{references} : \varepsilon^{2}).$$

Further annotations, expressing for example that the *preamble* element is three times more important than the *body* element, and in the *preamble*, the *keywords* element is 5 times more important than *title* and 10 times more important than the rest, would lead to having the following annotated DTD:

$$\begin{aligned}
\text{paper} &\rightarrow (\text{preamble} : 3)\ (\text{body} : 1) \\
\text{preamble} &\rightarrow (\text{title} : 2)\ (\text{author} : 1)^{+}\ (\text{abstract} : 1)\ (\text{keywords} : 10) \\
\text{body} &\rightarrow (\text{introduction} : 2)\ (\text{section} : 1)^{*}\ (\text{related-work} : \varepsilon)?\ (\text{references} : \varepsilon^2).
\end{aligned}$$

Since an annotated element can be nested inside other elements, which can be annotated as well, the natural question that now arises is: How to compute the actual weight of an element in a DTD? One might be tempted to think that the actual weight of an element should obtained by multiplying its (annotation) weight by the weights of all its ancestors. However by doing that, we could get strange results as for example a possibly increasing importance weight as we go deep down in the XML element hierarchy.

What we want here is "an element to never be more important than its parent." For this, we propose normalizing the importance weights assigned to DTD elements. There are two ways for doing this. Either divide the weights of a rule by the sum of the rule's weights, or divide them by the maximum weight of the rule. In the first way, the weight of the parent will be divided among the children. On the other hand, in the second way, the weight of the most important child will be equal to the weight of the parent.

The drawback of the first approach is that the more children there are, the lesser their weight is. Thus, we opt for the second way of weight normalization as it better corresponds to the intuition that nesting in XML documents is for adding structure to text rather than hierarchically dividing the importance of elements.

For example, in the above DTD, for the children of *preamble*, we normalize dividing by the greatest weight of the rule, which is 10. Normalizing in this way the weights of all the rules, we get

$$\begin{aligned}
\text{paper} &\rightarrow (\text{preamble} : 1)\ (\text{body} : 1/3) \\
\text{preamble} &\rightarrow (\text{title} : 1/5)\ (\text{author} : 1/10)^{+}\ (\text{abstract} : 1/10)\ (\text{keywords} : 1) \\
\text{body} &\rightarrow (\text{introduction} : 1)\ (\text{section} : 1/2)^{*}\ (\text{related-work} : \varepsilon/2)?\ (\text{references} : \varepsilon^2/2).
\end{aligned}$$

After such normalization, for determining the actual weight of an element, we multiply its DTD weight by the weights of all its ancestors. For example, the weight of a *section* element is $(1/3) \cdot (1/2)$.

As mentioned earlier, under this weighting scheme, the most important child of a parent has the same importance as the parent itself. Thus, for instance, element *introduction* has the same importance $(1/3)$ as its parent *body*. Note that the weight normalization can of course be automatically done by the system, while we annotate using numbers that are more comfortable to write.

4.4 Weighting Elements of XML Documents

In the previous section, we described how to compute the weight of an element in a DTD. However, the weight of an element in an XML document depends not only on the DTD, but also on the particular structure of the document. This is because the same element might occur differently nested in different valid XML documents. For example, if we had an additional rule, section $\rightarrow$ (title : 1) (text : $1/2$), in our annotated DTD, then, given a valid XML document, the weight of a *title* element depends on the particular nesting of this element. Namely, if the nesting is

$$\langle\text{paper}\rangle\langle\text{preamble}\rangle\langle\text{title}\rangle\ldots\langle/\text{title}\rangle\ldots\langle/\text{preamble}\rangle\ldots\langle/\text{paper}\rangle$$

then the normalized weight of the *title* element is $1/5$. On the other hand, if the nesting is

$$\langle\text{paper}\rangle\ldots\langle\text{body}\rangle\langle\text{section}\rangle\langle\text{title}\rangle\ldots\langle/\text{title}\rangle\ldots\langle/\text{section}\rangle\ldots\langle/\text{body}\rangle\langle/\text{paper}\rangle$$

then the normalized weight of the *title* element is $(1/3)\cdot(1/2)\cdot 1 = 1/6$.

In general, in order to derive the correct weight of an element in an XML document, we need to first build the element tree of the document. This will be a parse tree for the context-free grammar corresponding to the DTD. For each node a of this tree with children $bc\ldots x$, there is a unique rule $a \rightarrow r$ in the DTD such that word $bc\ldots x$ is in $L(r)$.

Naturally, we want to assign weights to a's children b, c, $\ldots$, x based on the weights in annotated expression r. Thus, the question becomes how to map the weights assigned to the symbols of r to the symbols of word $bc\ldots x$.

Since $b, c, \ldots, x$ occur in r, this might seem as a straightforward matter. However, there is subtlety here arising from the possibility of ambiguity in the regular expression. For example, suppose the (annotated) expression r is $(b:1+c:1)^*(b:2)(b:3)^*$, and element a has three children labeled by b. Surely, bbb is in $L(r)$, but what label should we assign to each of b's? There are three different ways of assigning weights to these b's: $(b:1)(b:1)(b:2)$, $(b:1)(b:2)(b:3)$, and $(b:2)(b:3)(b:3)$.

However, according to the SGML standard (cf. [3]), the only allowed regular expressions in the DTD rules are those for which we can uniquely determine the correspondence between the symbols of an input word and the symbols of the regular expression.

These expressions are called "1-unambiguous" in [3].

For such an expression r, given a word $bc\ldots x$ in $L(r)$, there is a unique mapping of word symbols b, c, $\ldots$, x to expression symbols. Thus, when r is annotated with symbol weights, we can uniquely determine the weights for each of the b, c, $\ldots$, x word symbols.

Based on all the above, we can state the following theorem.

Theorem 1. *If T is a valid XML tree with respect to an annotated DTD D, then based on the weight annotations of D, there is a unique weight assignment to each node of T.*

Now, given an XML document, since there is unique path from the root of an XML document to a particular element, we have that

Corollary 1. *Each element of a valid XML document is assigned a unique weight.*

The unique weight of an element is obtained by multiplying its local node weight with the weights of the ancestor nodes on the unique path connecting the element with the document root.[3]

5 Preferential Term Weighting and Document Scoring

Formally, let V (vocabulary) be the set of distinctive terms in a collection C of documents. Denote by m and n the cardinalities of V and C respectively. Let t_i be term in V and d_j a document in C. Suppose that t_i occurs f_{ij} times in d_j. Then, the normalized term frequency of t_i in d_j is

$$tf_{ij} = \frac{f_{ij}}{max\{f_{1j}, \ldots, f_{mj}\}},$$

where the maximum is in fact computed over the terms that appear in document d_j.

Considering now XML documents whose elements are weighted based on annotated DTDs, we have that *not* all occurrences of a term "are created equal." For instance, continuing the example in Section 4, an occurrence of a term t_i in the *keywords* element of a document is 5 times more important than an occurrence (of t_i) in the *title*, and infinitely more important than an occurrence in the *related-work* element.

Hence, we refine the TF measure to take the importance of XML elements into account. When an XML document conforms to an annotated DTD, each element e_k will be accordingly weighted, say by w_k.

Suppose that term t_i occurs f_{ijk} times in element e_k of document d_j. Now, we define the normalized term frequency of t_i in d_j as

$$tf_{ij} = \frac{\sum_k w_k f_{ijk}}{max\{\sum_k w_k f_{1jk}, \ldots, \sum_k w_k f_{mjk}\}}.$$

The other popular measure used in Information Retrieval is the *inverse document frequency* (IDF) which is used jointly with the TF measure. IDF is based on the fraction of documents which contain a query term. The intuition behind IDF is that a query term that occurs in numerous documents is not a good discriminator, or does not bear to much information, and thus, should should be given a smaller weight than other terms occurring in few documents. The weighting scheme known as TF*IDF, which multiplies the TF measure by the IDF measure, has proved to be a powerful heuristic for document ranking, making it the most popular weighting scheme in Information Retrieval (cf. [10, 5, 8]).

Formally, suppose that term t_i occurs n_i times in a collection of n elements. Then, the *inverse document frequency* of t_i is defined to be

---

[3] All weights are considered being normalized.

$$idf_i = \log \frac{n}{n_i}.$$

IDF has a natural explanation from an information theoretic point of view. If we consider a term t_i as a "message" and $p_i = \frac{n_i}{n}$ as the probability of receiving message t_i, then, in Shannon's information theory [9], the information that the message carries is quantified by

$$I_i = -\log p_i,$$

which coincides with the IDF measure. The connection is clear; terms occurring in too many documents do not carry too much information for "discriminating" documents ([1]). On the other hand, terms that occur in few documents carry more information and hence have more discriminative power.

In XML Information Retrieval, considering each XML element that contains text as a mini-document, we can compute multiple IDF scores for a given term. Note that here, we restrict ourselves to *textual* elements only, i.e. those elements that contain terms. For instance, in the above example, *introduction* is a textual element, while *body* is not.

Depending on the importance weight of each textual element, the IDF scores should be appropriately weighted. Intuitively, in the above example, the IDF score of a term with respect to the *related-work* elements is infinitely less important than the IDF score of the term with respect to say *introduction* elements.

Formally, let E be the set of textual element-weight pairs (e_h, w_h) extracted from XML document collection C. This set is finite because C is finite, and for each element in an XML document, there is a unique weight assigned to it (see Corollary 1).

For a textual element-weight pair (e_h, w_h), let n_h be the total number of such elements in the XML documents in collection C. Suppose that a term t_i occurs in n_{hi} of these e_h elements (of weight w_h). Then, we define the IDF of t_i with respect to these elements as

$$idf_{hi} = \log \frac{n_h}{n_{hi}}.$$

Next, we define the IDF score of a term t_i with respect to the whole document collection as

$$idf_i = \frac{\sum_h w_h \cdot idf_{hi}}{\sum_h w_h}.$$

This is the weighted average of IDF scores computed for each textual element-weight pair (e_h, w_h).

Finally, the TF*IDF weighting scheme combines the term frequency and inverse document frequency, producing a composite weight for each term in each document. Namely, the TF*IDF weighting scheme assigns to term t_i a weight in document d_j given by

$$tf\,idf_{ij} = tf_{ij} \times idf_i.$$

In the vector space model, every document is represented by a vector of weights which are the TF*IDF scores of the terms in the document. For the other terms in vocabulary V that do not occur in a document, we have a weight of zero.

Similarly, a query q can be represented as a vector of weights with non-zero weights for the terms appearing in the query. The weights are exactly those hyperreal numbers specified by the user multiplied by the IDF scores of the terms.

Now, we want to rank the documents by computing their similarly score with respect to a query q. The most popular similarity measure is the *cosine similarity*, which for a document d_j with weight vector $\mathbf{w}_j$ and a query q with weight vector $\mathbf{w}_q$ is

$$cosine(\mathbf{w}_j, \mathbf{w}_q) = \frac{\langle \mathbf{w}_j, \mathbf{w}_q \rangle}{||\mathbf{w}_j|| \times ||\mathbf{w}_q||} = \frac{\sum_{i=1}^{m} w_{ij} \times w_{iq}}{\sqrt{\sum_{i=1}^{m} w_{ij}^2} \times \sqrt{\sum_{i=1}^{m} w_{iq}^2}},$$

where m is the cardinality of vocabulary V.

The above formula naturally combines the query preference weights, XML element weights, and Information Retrieval measures. Note that, we can in fact rank documents using instead the square of the cosine similarity. Thus, we only need to compare fractions of polynomial expressions based on the (fixed) infinitesimal ε. As such, these expressions allow for an algorithmic (symbolic) comparison procedure for ranking XML documents.

Finally, the query can be a complete document in its own. Such queries are of the type: Find all the documents which are similar to a given document. We derive weights for the elements of the query document in exactly the same manner as described in Section 4. The vector of weights for the query document is computed as for any other document in the collection. Then, this vector is compared against the vectors of the documents in the collection by computing the cosine similarity as described above.

6 Experiments

We have implemented a system incorporating our proposed framework and compared its ranking effectiveness with that of a system that ranks using the classical TF-IDF measure. The main research question we address is:

Does our preferential IR improve users' search experience compared to a traditional IR?

Through experiments we provide practical evidence that our preferential IR does indeed perform better than a traditional IR.

As described in the previous sections, we annotated XML schema elements and search keywords in order to mark their importance in ranking the documents. We designed our experiments for both document retrieval and element retrieval. We used the following corpora as test-beds.

Corpus I On-line Internet Shakespeare Edition of the English Department ([12]), University of Victoria for element retrieval. This corpus consists of all the Shakespeare plays in XML format. The elements of interest are the speeches which total more than 33,000. For this corpus we consider all the speeches to be of the same importance, and thus, only search keyword preferences are in fact relevant for this corpus in influencing the ranking process.

Corpus II An INEX (INitiative for the Evaluation of XML retrieval) (cf. [13]) corpus. INEX is a collaborative initiative that provides reference collections (corpora). For evaluating our method, we have chosen a collection named "*topic-collection*" with numerous XML documents of moderate size. The topics of documents vary from *climate change* to *space exploration*. We preferentially annotated the DTD of this collection and gave many preferentially annotated search queries.

Due to space constraints, we do not show our results here, but we point the reader to the full version of this paper [4].

References

1. Aizawa N. A. An Information-Theoretic Perspective of TF-IDF measures. *Inf. Process. Manage.* 39(1): 45–65, 2003.
2. Bex J. G., F. Neven, T. Schwentick and K. Tuyls. Inference of Concise DTDs from XML Data. *Proc. VLDB '06*, pp. 115–126.
3. Bruggemann-Klein A. and D. Wood. One-Unambiguous Regular Languages. *Inf. Comput.* 140(2): 229–253, 1998.
4. Chowdhury M., A. Thomo, and W. Wadge. Preferential Infinitesimals for Information Retrieval. *Full version:* http://webhome.cs.uvic.ca/~thomo/papers/aiai09.pdf
5. Liu B. *Web Data Mining: Exploring Hyperlinks, Contents and Usage Data.* Springer, Berlin Heidelberg, 2007.
6. Keisler H. J. *Elementary Calculus: An Approach Using Infinitesimals.* On-line Edition: http://www.math.wisc.edu/~keisler/keislercalc1.pdf 2002.
7. Keisler H. J. *Foundations of Infinitesimal Calculus.* On-line Edition: http://www.math.wisc.edu/~keisler/foundations.pdf 2007.
8. Manning D. C, P. Raghavan and H. Schutze *Introduction to Information Retrieval.* Cambridge University Press. 2008.
9. Shannon C. E. A Mathematical Theory of Communication. *The Bell System Technical Journal* 27: 379-423, 1948.
10. Robertson S. Understanding Inverse Document Frequency: On theoretical arguments for IDF. *J. of Documentation* 60: 503–520, 2004.
11. Rondogiannis P., and W. W. Wadge. Minimum Model Semantics for Logic Programs with Negation-as-Failure. *ACM Trans. Comput. Log.* 6 (2): 441–467, 2005.
12. On-line Internet Shakespeare Edition. English Department, University of Victoria. http://internetshakespeare.uvic.ca/index.html
13. Malik S., A. Trotman, M. Lalmas, N. Fuhr. Overview of INEX 2006. *Proc. 5th Workshop of the INitiative for the Evaluation of XML Retrieval*, pp 1-11, 2007.

OntoLife: an Ontology for Semantically Managing Personal Information

Eleni Kargioti, Efstratios Kontopoulos and Nick Bassiliades

Dept. of Informatics, Aristotle University of Thessaloniki, GR-54124 Thessaloniki, Greece

{elkar, skontopo, nbassili}@csd.auth.gr

Abstract Personal knowledge management has been studied from various angles, one of which is the Semantic Web. Ontologies, the primary knowledge representation tool for the Semantic Web, can play a significant role in semantically managing personal knowledge. The scope of this paper focuses on addressing the issue of effective personal knowledge management, by proposing an ontology for modelling the domain of biographical events. The proposed ontology also undergoes a thorough evaluation, based on specific criteria presented in the literature.

1 Introduction

The latest technological developments and the WWW expose users to a great volume of information. A new perspective in *Knowledge Management* (*KM*) is essential that will filter out irrelevant information and increase knowledge quality, by utilizing the underlying semantic relationships. This requirement is also present in *Personal Knowledge Management* (*PKM*).

The first step towards PKM is to organize personal information. Various tools and applications are used (e.g. task managers, spreadsheet applications), but often comprise isolated solutions, revealing the need for a unified way of managing personal information, so that it becomes knowledge. *Ontologies* can assist towards this direction. They are a key factor towards realizing the *Semantic Web* vision [1], which promises to structure and semantically annotate raw information, to allow its interoperability, reuse and effective search by non-human agents.

This paper focuses on the issue of semantically managing the great volume of personal information by the use of an appropriately defined ontology. More specifically, an ontology called OntoLife is proposed for describing a person's biographical events and personal information. The ontology underwent a thorough evaluation that indicates its suitability for the designated purpose.

The rest of the paper is organized as follows: Section 2 describes related work paradigms, while the next section focuses on the presentation of the proposed on-

---

Please use the following format when citing this chapter:

Kargioti, E., Kontopoulos, E. and Bassiliades, N., 2009, in IFIP International Federation for Information Processing, Volume 296; *Artificial Intelligence Applications and Innovations III*; Eds. Iliadis, L., Vlahavas, I., Bramer, M.; (Boston: Springer), pp. 127–133.

tology, accompanied by its evaluation. The paper concludes with final remarks and directions for future work.

2 Ontologies and the Semantic Web

Ontologies are the primary knowledge representation tool in the Semantic Web [1]. An ontology is a structured representational formalism of a domain, including a set of domain concepts and the relationships between them. The concepts describe classes of objects, while the relationships describe hierarchical dependencies among the concepts.

Regarding the domain of "life", the authors are not aware of an existing appropriate ontology. The *FOAF*[1] ontology is relevant, yet not wide enough for our purposes. *ResumeRDF*[2] is another ontology for representing Curriculum Vitae information about work and academic experience, skills, etc. Finally, another paradigm is *HR-XML*[3], a library of XML schemas that a variety of business processes related to human resource management. Nevertheless, none of the above (or other) ontologies and schemas can cover so broadly all the aspects of a person's biographical events as OntoLife.

3 Proposed Ontology

The scope of the proposed ontology is to model life by describing the person's characteristics, relationships and experiences. Since the domain is broad, an attempt to model it in details would produce a huge and cumbersome ontology. Thus, the domain is modelled in a non-exhaustive yet sufficient way, adopting the definition of generic entities that can easily be extended.

3.1 Description

The backbone of OntoLife is the *Person* entity. The entire ontology is built upon and around a Person, by a set of properties that relate the Person with the rest of the entities, as shown in Fig. 1. At the same time, many auxiliary entities and properties are defined to further describe the domain.

When designing the ontology, the idea of reusing commonly accepted ontologies was always considered. Thus, the Person entity of the FOAF ontology

---

[1] Friend Of A Friend (FOAF) ontology: `http://xmlns.com/foaf/0.1/`

[2] ResumeRDF Ontology: `http://rdfs.org/resume-rdf/`

[3] HR-XML: `http://ns.hr-xml.org/2_5/HR-XML-2_5/SEP/Candidate.xsd`

(foaf:Person) was enriched with new properties. Also, classes from external ontologies were imported, to model specific sub-domains in detail. These are the ISO lists for countries and languages[4] and the *Publication* and *Project* classes[5].

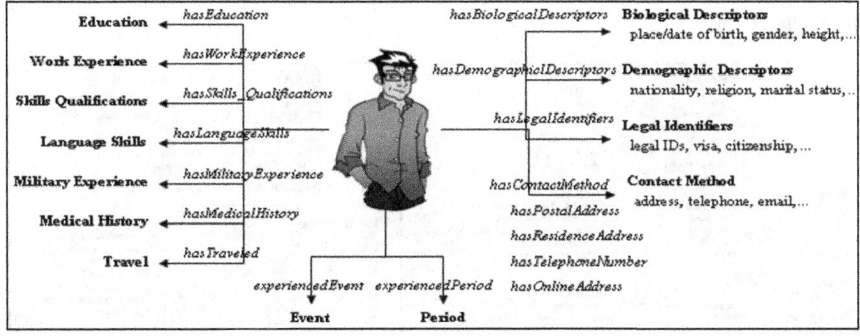

Fig. 1. Object properties with Person as the domain

OntoLife models the Person's demographics, biological and legal descriptors, the various contact methods and online accounts as well as information concerning educational, work and other experiences, qualifications and skills acquired and other CV-related information. Additionally, the link between a person and the periods and events experienced is thoroughly modelled.

Moreover, the Person entity is further extended by various subclasses, defined using external ontologies. Properties defined by the Relationship[6] ontology, which describes the relations between entities of foaf:Person are re-used. Thus, subclasses of Person, such as Friend, Colleague, Tutor, etc, are defined using restrictions on properties. Also, the external ontology Family Tree[7] that describes the domain of Family is imported. This ontology defines subclasses of foaf:Person, such as Child, Parent, Aunt/Uncle etc., using restrictions on related properties.

Two other important entities are *Period* and *Event*. Both are used to organise the biographical experiences in time periods and events and are linked with Person with properties inverse to the properties *experiencedPeriod* and *experiencedEvent* respectively. In further details, a *Period* models a time period and describes the place and dates it occurred, the people and organisations involved, related evaluations and also the events occurred within that period, using the inverse property *relatedEvent* (*duringPeriod*). Direct subclasses are Education, WorkExperience, Travel, MilitaryExperience and MedicalHistory. Similarly, an *Event* models a specific moment in life that can be part of a period or not. The place and date it occurred, the people and organisations involved, related evaluations, weather condi-

[4] Proposed by the Organization for Advancement of Structured Information Standards

[5] Proposed by UMBC eBiquity Research Group of the University Maryland, Baltimore

[6] `http://vocab.org/relationship/`

[7] `http://users.auth.gr/~elkar/thesis/FamilyTree.owl`

tions, scope and possible periodicity are described. Direct subclasses are PurchaseEvent, MedicalExaminationEvent and FamilyEvent. Further properties are defined with domain the subclasses of entities Period and Event and enable a more precise annotation of the related content. Fig. 2 describes in detail these subclasses and properties.

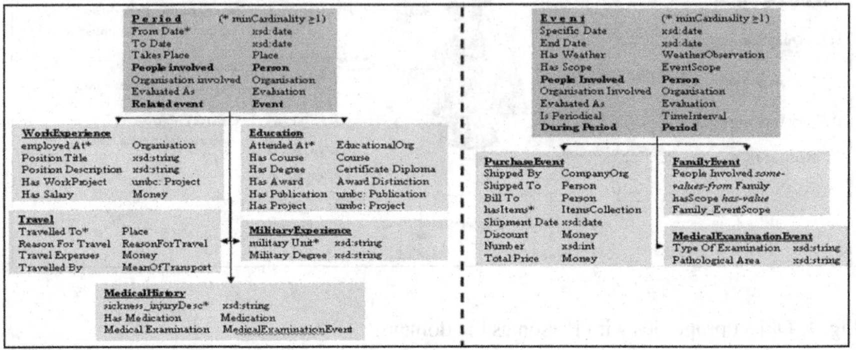

Fig. 2. Properties and subclasses of Period and Event

Finally, the ontology defines a super-class "Resource" which is the domain of four additional properties, *name*, *description*, *is Current*, *mime File* and which purpose is to pass these properties to all other classes, except Person and the Enumeration classes, where these properties are not needed. Resource is disjoint with Person and all auxiliary Enumeration classes.

3.2 Evaluation

The increasing number of ontologies in the web has led research to define methods and measures for evaluation. A popular method, also used in this work, is the *criteria-based evaluation* [3]. Consistency, completeness, expandability, minimal ontological commitment, etc. are some of the criteria listed in literature.

The adopted evaluation methodology includes the definition of specific requirements that the ontology needs to satisfy and the mapping of each requirement to a criterion [4]. Suitable measures are then selected to quantitatively assess each requirement. The main requirement is to be easy and intuitive to annotate content based on the ontology. Towards this, more specific requirements need to be met.

1. The terms used for the class names need to be close to real life terminology.
2. The classes should have a balanced number of subclasses; sufficient enough to facilitate effective annotation, but not too high to confuse the user.
3. The ontology should be rich, concerning attributes and relationships.
4. Cycles and other errors in the ontology structure should be avoided.

The Semantic Quality [5] criterion is mapped to the first requirement and the following measures. *Interpretability*, which is the percentage of class names that have a definition listed in *WordNet*[8] and *Concept Paths* [6], which is the percentage of class hierarchies that are depicted in WordNet through term hyponyms. Expandability/Coverage [7] are the criteria mapped to the second requirement. Related measures are: class tree depth, breath and branching factor. For a broad ontology like OntoLife, a less deep tree with a low branching factor is preferred. The third requirement is mapped to the ontology richness criterion [8], assessed by the attribute and relationship richness. The last requirement is mapped to the Minimal Ontological commitment criterion [9] and ontology validators are used to exclude circularity and other types of errors.

To assess semantic quality, certain assumptions are made. Class names that consist of more than one word written in CamelCase or separated by underscore were considered listed in WordNet, if all included words were listed (e.g. Certificate_Diploma) or a phrase with these words made sense (e.g. ForeignLanguage). Also, class names taken from the HR-XML Candidate specification were considered interpretable. Finally, a concept path (the path from a parent class to a leaf subclass in a class tree) may be fully or partially depicted in WordNet, if all or some subclasses are listed as parent class hyponyms. To measure Interpretability and Concept Paths, a weighted average was calculated (Table 1). To assess ontology expandability/coverage and attribute and relationship richness, the metrics offered by the SWOOP[9] ontology editor were used (Table 2). Finally, to assess the last criterion the *Vowlidator*[10] and *WonderWeb online validator*[11] were used. The ontology was identified as OWL Full compatible, while no errors were indicated.

Table 1. Calculation of measures for the Semantic Quality criterion

Interpretability: (c1 x 0 + c2 x 0.5 + c3 x 1) / c = 66%
c1: no of classes whose sense is not listed in WordNet, *c2: no of classes with a sister/ synonym term* *c3: no of classes with a sense listed in WordNet,* *c: total no of defined classes*
Concept Paths: (p1 x 0 + p2 x 0.5 + p3 x 1) / p = 60%
p1: no of concept paths not depicted by WordNet *p2: no of concept paths partially depicted by WordNet* *p3: no of concept paths depicted by WordNet,* *p: total no of concept paths*

[8] WordNet, a lexical database by the Princeton University Cognitive Science Laboratory

[9] SWOOP: A Hypermedia-based Featherweight OWL Ontology Editor

[10] Vowlidator: `http://projects.semwebcentral.org/projects/vowlidator/`

[11] WonderWeb OWL Validator: `http://www.mygrid.org.uk/OWL/Validator`

The measures show room for improvement in the class name terminology. Nevertheless, 66% and 60% for interpretability and concept paths are satisfactory, especially for such a broad ontology. Also, the number of classes is right based on the measures of the expandability/coverage. For a tree of such breadth, the depth and branching factor are low, resulting in a rather simple class hierarchy. Moreover, the ontology is rich enough concerning attributes and relationships permitting detailed content annotation. Finally, the ontology can be used "safely", since syntactical errors and inconsistencies were excluded.

Table 2. Calculation of measures for the ontology's expandability/coverage criteria and the attributes and relationship richness criterion

Tree Depth
Max. Depth of Class Tree: 4, Min. Depth of Class Tree: 1, Avg. Depth of Class Tree: 1.9
Tree Breadth
Max. Breadth of Class Tree: 33, Min. Breath of Class Tree: 1, Avg. breadth of Class Tree: 25
Tree Branching factor
Max. Branching Factor of Class Tree: 47, Min. Branching Factor of Class Tree: 1 *Avg. Branching Factor of Class Tree: 6.6*
Attribute richness
No. Attributes in all classes / No. classes = 85%
Relationships richness
No. Relations / (No. Subclasses+No. Relations) = 68%

4 Conclusions and Future Work

The paper argued that Personal Knowledge Management is increasingly gaining attention, to facilitate the end-user in handling vast volumes of information. Ontologies and the Semantic Web can support this task, by offering capabilities for semantically managing personal information via properly defined ontologies. Such an ontology is proposed in this work. The ontology, called OntoLife, portrays a person's life, by describing his/her characteristics, his/her relationships with other people and the various events experienced. Since the domain is so broad, the ontology is modelled in a non-exhaustive way, defining generic entities that can easily be extended. OntoLife also underwent a thorough evaluation that indicated its suitability for the designated purpose.

Future research may include a revision of the ontology, which could incorporate the new version of FOAF or of other external ontologies that model a subdomain in detail. Furthermore, it would be interesting to study the combination of the proposed ontology with an appropriate tool for managing ontologies, such as a general-purpose Semantic Wiki. Semantic Wikis enrich standard Wikis with functionalities deriving from the content's semantics and aim at knowledge reuse, adaptive interface and navigation and effective search [10]. The purpose of the study would be on one hand to evaluate how efficiently Semantic Wikis can incorporate and represent the proposed ontology and on the other hand to see how effectively they can support users in order to annotate content, even when with minimal knowledge of the underlying ontology.

References

1. Berners-Lee, T., Hendler, J., Lassila, O.: The Semantic Web. Scientific American, 284(5):34-43, 2001.
2. Staab, S., Studer, R.: Handbook on Ontologies. International Handbooks on Information Systems, Springer Verlag (2004)
3. Gomez-Perez, A.: Evaluation of Ontologies. International Journal of Intelligent Systems, 16(3):391-409, 2001.
4. Yu, J., Thom, A.A., Tam, A.: Ontology Evaluation Using Wikipedia Categories for Browsing. In Proceedings 16th Conference on Information and Knowledge Management (CIKM), pp. 223-232 (2007)
5. Burton-Jones, et al: A Semiotic Metrics Suite for Assessing the Quality of Ontologies. Data Knowledge Engineering, 55(1):84-102, 2005.
6. Sleeman, D., Reul, Q. H.: CleanONTO: Evaluating Taxonomic Relationships in Ontologies. In Proceedings 4th International Workshop on Evaluation of Ontologies for the Web (EON), Edinburgh, Scotland (2006)
7. Gangemi, A. et al: A Theoretical Framework for Ontology Evaluation and Validation. In Proceedings 2nd Italian Semantic Web Workshop (SWAP), Trento, Italy (2005)
8. Tartir, S. et al: OntoQA: Metric-Based Ontology Quality Analysis. IEEE ICDM Workshop on Knowledge Acquisition from Distributed, Autonomous, Semantically Heterogeneous Data and Knowledge Sources, Houston, TX (2005)
9. Yu, J., Thom, A.A., Tam, A.: Evaluating Ontology Criteria for Requirements in a Geographic Travel Domain. In Proceedings International Conference on Ontologies, Databases and Applications of Semantics (2005)
10. Leuf, B., Cunningham, W.: The Wiki Way: Collaboration and Sharing on the Internet. Addison Wesley, Reading, Massachusetts (2001)

AIR_POLLUTION_Onto: an Ontology for Air Pollution Analysis and Control

Mihaela M. Oprea

University Petroleum-Gas of Ploiesti, Department of Informatics,

Bd. Bucuresti nr. 39, Ploiesti, 100680, Romania, mihaela@upg-ploiesti.ro

Abstract The paper describes an ontology for air pollution analysis and control, AIR_POLLUTION_Onto, and presents its use in two case studies, an expert system, and a multiagent system, both dedicated to monitoring and control of air pollution in urban regions.

1 Introduction

The last decade has registered a strong challenge on the improvement of our environment quality under the international research framework of durable and sustainable development of the environment. The main concern of this challenge is to assure a healthy environment (air, water and soil) that allow the protection of ecosystems, and human health. One of the key aspects of this challenge is the air pollution control in urban regions with industrial activity [9]. In this context, more efficient tools has to be developed to solve the current environmental problems. Artificial intelligence provides several techniques that can solve efficiently such problems which have a high degree of uncertainty (see e.g [1] and [11]). The knowledge-based approach and the multi-agent systems (MAS) approach ([17]) offer ones of the best solutions to the environmental problems, as they reduce their complexity by structuring the domain knowledge from different sources in knowledge bases [10]. We have used the solution of expert systems [14], as the main sources of knowledge are given by the human experts as well as by the heuristic rules generated through machine learning techniques. The expert system `DIAGNOZA_MEDIU` was developed for the air pollution state diagnosis and control in urban regions with industrial activity. The solution of MAS was recently adopted by our research group in a postdoctoral research project running at our university. These types of approaches need to use an ontology specific to the expertise domain. Thus, we have developed an ontology dedicated to air pollution analysis and control, `AIR_POLLUTION_Onto`.

Please use the following format when citing this chapter:

Oprea, M.M., 2009, in IFIP International Federation for Information Processing, Volume 296; *Artificial Intelligence Applications and Innovations III*; Eds. Iliadis, L., Vlahavas, I., Bramer, M.; (Boston: Springer), pp. 135–143.

2 Air Pollution Analysis and Control

The main air pollutants are carbone dioxide (CO_2), carbon monoxide (CO), nitrogen dioxide (NO_2) and nitrogen oxides (NO_x), suspended particulates (particulate matters: respirable PM_{10}, and fine $PM_{2.5}$), sulfur dioxide (SO_2), ozone (O_3), lead (Pb), volatile organic compounds (VOC) etc. The concentrations of the air pollutants are measured in specific sites and compared to the standard values, according to national and international reglementations. The air pollutants have different dispersion models, and several mathematical models are used for the description of the relationships between environmental protection and meteorological factors (see e.g. an analysis of NO_2 and PM concentrations contribution to roadside air pollution [7]). Moreover, there are a lot of unpredictable factors that may influence the degree of air pollution, and it is quite difficult to establish with certainty which are the causes of an increase or of a decrease of an air pollutant concentration. The inclusion of most of the factors with their associated uncertainty degree would increase too much the complexity of the mathematical models, thus making them inefficient to solve real-time problems. The solution of a knowledge-based approach is an alternative to the mathematical models, as it allows the integration of multiple sources of knowledge in a knowledge base used by an inference engine that can deal also with uncertainty [12].

Prevention is an important step to air pollution control, and include different measures specific to each type of air pollutant and source of pollution. Some air pollution control strategies includes emission abatement equipment (e.g. wet and dry scrubbers, cyclones, bag filters), a policy of air pollution dispersion and dilution (e.g. a chimney of adequate height so that the pollution returned to ground level it poses no risk to health), change the process technology (e.g. fuel change, combined heat and power plant), change the operating patterns (e.g. alter the time that a process causes peak emissions), relocation (e.g. change the location of the process to have less impact on the urban and rural region).

3 Development of the Ontology `AIR_POLLUTION_Onto`

An ontology is an abstraction about the relevant aspects of the world. According to [4], an ontology is a specification of a conceptualization. The definition of an ontology involves the definition of a vocabulary with different terms for concepts (classes in the ontology), properties of concepts (slots in the ontology), relations between concepts, and instances. Also, a set of axioms must be defined. The axioms include the restrictions on the properties of the concepts (named facets of the slots). During the development of an ontology the following steps must be followed [16]: (1) define classes in the ontologies; (2) arrange the classes in a taxonomic hierarchy; (3) define slots and describe the allowed values for these slots; (4) fill in the values for the slots of the instances. A knowledge base is created by defining individual instances of the classes filling in specific slot value information and additional slot restrictions. The basic types of relations that could appear between concepts are *ISA*, *AKO*, *HAS*, *PART_OF*, *SAME_AS*. They express the relations of membership, inclusion, composition and synonimity. Different names for these relations are *INSTANCE_OF*, *SUBCLASS_OF*, *SAME_AS*, *EQUIVALENT_CLASS*.

An ontology has two parts, the upper level ontology and the lower level ontology. The upper level ontology [5] is a set of general and well-known concepts shared by the most part of the human knowledge. The lower level ontology is a set of domain specific concepts that are shared by the human experts. The development of an ontology could be done by using several public available software. In our work we have used Protégé [15], a Java-based ontology editor.

To develop the air pollution domain ontology `AIR_POLLUTION_Onto`, we have identified the terms specific to the analysis and control of air pollution. The ontology includes general terms (e.g. ENVIRONMENT, INDUSTRY, SOIL, WATER, WIND, WEATHER), and specific terms (e.g. AIR_POLLUTANT, POLLUTION_SOURCE, EMISSION, IMISSION, SO2, PM). After the identification of the general and specific terms, they are defined, characterized by their properties and constraints, and classified in taxonomies or hierarchies of classes. Also, the relationships between concepts are specified. Examples of relations between concepts are given below.

ISA(HUMIDITY, WEATHER_PARAMETER); *ISA*(FACTORY, POINT_SOURCE); *AKO*(AIR_POLLUTANT, POLLUTANT); *HAS*(AIR_POLLUTANT, CONCENTRATION);

The ontology has to include some meteorological terms as they are important for the analysis and control of air pollution. Such meteorological terms are RAINFALL, WIND, TEMPERATURE, RELATIVE HUMIDITY, ATMOSPHERIC PRESSURE. Each meteorological factor has a variability and seasonality.

Figure 1 shows a sequence from the ontology classes hierarchy in Protégé. Figure 2 shows a part from the ontology hierarchy with terms specific to air pollution.

The slots of each term are defined. In Protégé this means to specify for each slot the name, the cardinality (single, multiple), the value type (integer, float, string, symbol, boolean, class, instance, any) and other facets. Figure 3 shows the slots for class PM (term Particulate Matters). These slots are *Concentration level*, *MAC* (maximum admissible concentration for PM), *Network Site* (the site number in the monitoring network), *Period* (the period of concentration level measurement), *Position of the site* (position given on a map, e.g. A3), *Prevention measure*, and *Type of pollution source*.

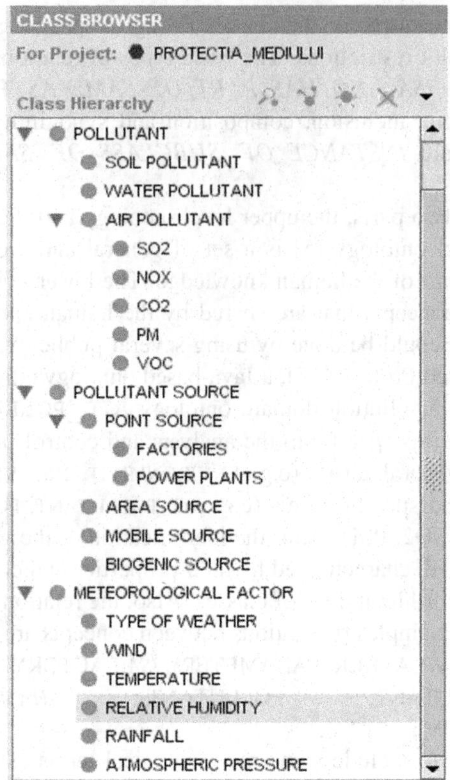

Fig. 1. Ontology hierarchy of classes in Protégé.

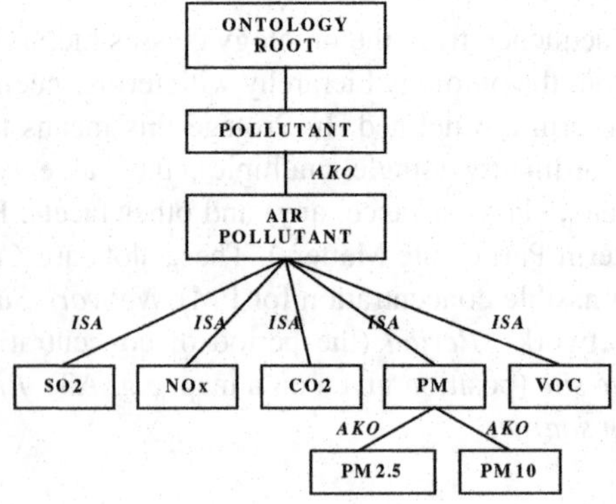

Fig. 2. Hierarchy of air pollution terms.

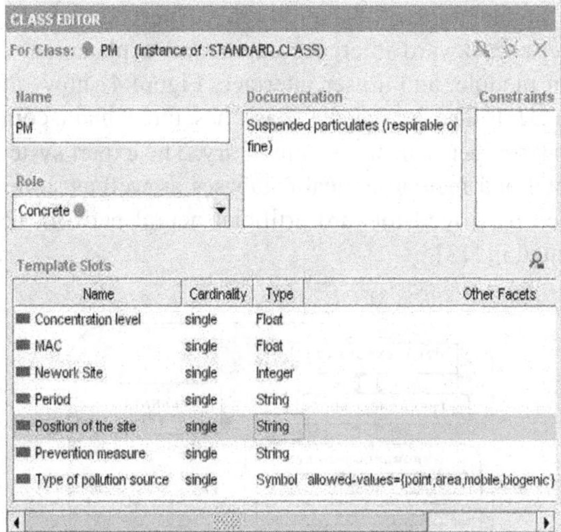

Fig. 3. Slots of PM class (Protégé screenshot).

Restrictions could be applied to the slots of a class. Examples of generic restrictions are given bellow.

Concentration_level <= *MAC* (admissible concentration);

Concentration_level > *MAC* (inadmissible concentration);

Rainfall_level > 1 mm (it rains); *Rainfall_level* < 1 mm (it does not rain)

where *MAC* is the maximum admissible concentration for a specific air pollutant.

`AIR_POLLUTION_Onto` could be extended with new terms to be used by different types of intelligent systems such as expert systems and multiagent systems.

4 Case Studies

We have used `AIR_POLLUTION_Onto` in two systems, `DIAGNOZA_MEDIU`, an expert system for air pollution analysis and control, and `MAS_AirPollution`, a multi-agent system for air pollution monitoring and control, both systems being applied in urban regions.

4.1 DIAGNOZA_MEDIU

The main purpose of `DIAGNOZA_MEDIU` is to provide qualitative information to a decision support system that is used in the environmental protection management. The system was implemented in VP-Expert, a rule-based expert system generator. The architecture of the prototype expert system is composed by a knowledge base, a backward inference engine, an explanation module, a knowledge acquisition module, and a user interface. Figure 4 shows the architecture of DIAGNOZA_MEDIU. The knowledge base has three main components, a rules base and a facts base, permanent and temporary. The expert system uses data from the environmental and meteorological databases as well as some forecasting data that are provided by a feed-forward artificial neural network (previously developed and presented in [13]).

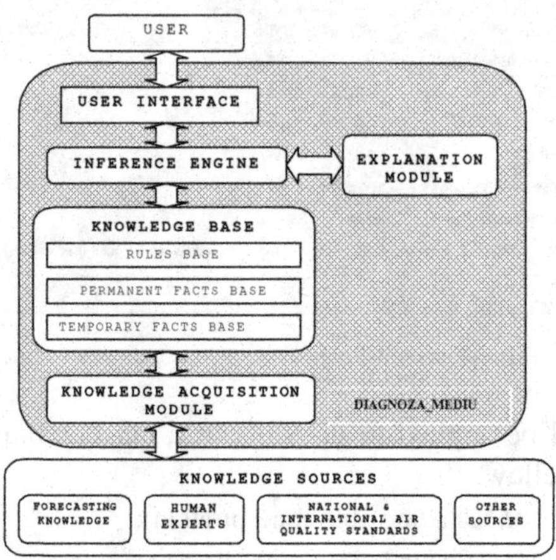

Fig. 4. The architecture of DIAGNOZA_MEDIU.

The knowledge base is generated from the ontology AIR_POLLUTION_Onto. Production rules are used as a knowledge representation method. To express the uncertain knowledge we have used a set of terms with linguistic certainty values that constitutes the verbal scale that the human experts and the users will use to express their degree of confidence in rules and facts. The fuzzy interval (similar with that used in [3]) includes nine ordered values for the goal variable **risk of air pollution**: *impossible*, *almost impossible*, *slightly possible*, *moderately possible*, *possible*, *quite possible*, *very possible*, *almost sure*, and *sure*. The ontology was extended with terms related to all these fuzzy values.

The rules base has mainly three types of rules: behaviour, decision and control. Examples of such rules are given bellow.

RULE BT_15 (*Behaviour rule*)
IF DT >= 7 AND T >= 37 AND MF = not_changed THEN TPRED = much_higher;

RULE CPM_12 (*Control rule*)
IF TPRED = much_higher AND $IP_{PM} \geq MAC_{PM} - 0.005$ THEN
Risk_pollution = quite_possible; Pollution_control =
Control_measure_for_PM_reduction;
// due to higher temperature and very close value of IP to MAC for PM

RULE DPM_7 (*Decision rule*)
IF Risk_pollution = quite_possible AND Air_Pollutant = PM THEN
Warning = "Area with potential air pollution risk – quite possible exceed of PM"
Prevention_measure = "Change the chemical process technology / Change the filter";

where DT is the duration (in days) of air temperatures greater than 37^0C, T is the minimum value of the maximum temperatures measured in the last seven days, MF represents a global parameter that refers to the evolution of the meteorological factors (wind, rainfalls, etc) in the next period of time (i.e. next 2 days minimum), TPRED is the symbolic value of the predicted temperature, IP is the predicted value for an air pollutant indicator (e.g. the concentration level), and MAC is the maximum admissible value for an air pollutant indicator.

The three rules given above are applied to specific sites, and thus the chemical plants, and other air pollution sources are known, and the warning as well as the prevention and counter measures specified in the generic rule DPM_7 are directly related to them. The instances specific to the urban region where `DIAGNOZA_MEDIU` is applied are included in the ontology.

4.2 MAS_AirPollution

`AIR_POLLUTION_Onto` is currently used in `MAS_AirPollution`, a multi-agent system that is under development as a simulation. The goal of the MAS is to monitor and control air pollution in urban regions.

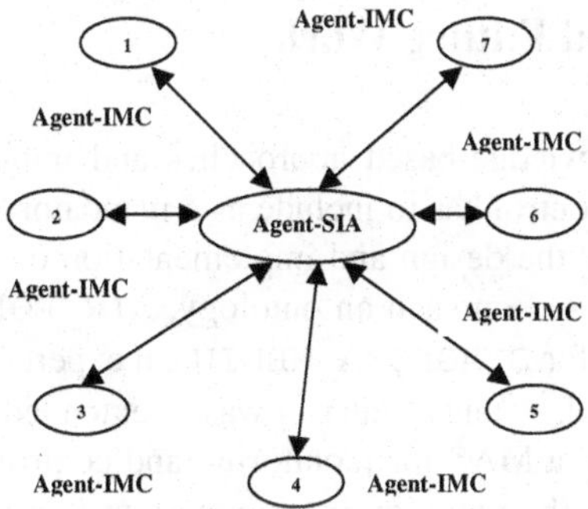

Fig. 5. The architecture of MAS_AirPollution system.

Figure 5 presents its architecture. The system is composed by a set of intelligent monitoring and control agents (Agent_IMC, specific to each site of the monitoring network) and a supervisor intelligent agent (Agent_SIA) in a star like architecture. `AIR_POLLUTION_Onto` is shared by all agents. In case some agents have different ontologies we are using ontology mapping methods (see e.g. [6]). Some of these methods identify maximal similarity between concepts definitions that are terminologically heterogenous, others are using structural methods. As most of the discrepancies of ontologies might be due to different terminology we apply in our simulated MAS a lexicon-based method similar to that given in [8]. Still, in case of real time systems, as it shall be the case of our MAS, a better method is much proper, QOM (Quick Ontology Mapping, [2]).

The agents communicate by using FIPA ACL. Figure 6 shows an example of a FIPA ACL message exchanged between two agents.

```
( inform
      :sender Agent-IMC_3
      :receiver Agent-SIA
      :content
        (warning (increase Temperature)
          (Concentration-level PM 0.14651)
          (meteo_factor wind weak)
        )
      :ontology AIR_POLLUTION_Onto
      :language sl
)
```

Fig. 6. Example of a FIPA ACL message exchanged in the system MAS_AirPollution.

In case one of the agent discovers during conversation that some concepts from the current message are unknown, it will generate a particular feedback message to establish a mapping of its private ontology with that of the sender agent. Usually, only a part of the ontology is mapped.

5 Conclusion and Future Work

The application of knowledge-based approaches and multi-agent systems to air pollution analysis and control has to include as a mandatory step in the system development methodology the design and implementation of a specific ontology. In this paper we have focused on such an ontology, `AIR_POLLUTION_Onto`, that was initially developed for `DIAGNOZA_MEDIU`, an expert system for air pollution analysis and control, and later was extended and applied to `MAS_AirPollution`, a MAS for monitoring and control of air pollution in urban regions. The use of the ontology in an expert system helps the generation of the knowledge base that should be coherent, non-redundant and complete, while in case of a MAS it is an important support for inter-agents communication. In an open multiagent system, it is important to apply ontology mapping to achieve interoperability. As a future work we shall extend `AIR_POLLUTION_Onto` for other applications in the area of environ-mental protection.

Acknowledgement The research reported in this paper was partially funded by the Romanian Education and Research Ministry and the National Council of Academic Research (CNCSIS) under the research grant AT429/2003.

References

1. Buisson, L., Martin-Clonaire, R., Vieu, L., Wybo, J.-L.: Artificial Intelligence and Environmental Protection: A Survey of Selected Applications in France, *Information Processing 92*, vol. II, Elsevier (1992) 635-644.
2. Ehrig, M., Staab, S.: Efficiency of Ontology Mapping Approaches, University of Karlsruhe, research report (2004).
3. Godo, L., Lopez de Mantaras, R., Sierra, C., Verdaquer, A.: MILORD: The architecture and the management of linguistically expressed uncertainty, *International Journal of Intelligent Systems*, 4 (1989) 471-501.
4. Gruber, T.: Towards principles for the design of ontologies used for knowledge sharing, *International Journal of Human-Computer Studies*, 43(5/6) (1995) 907-928.
5. Guarino, N., Giaretta, P.: Ontologies and Knowledge Bases: Towards a Terminological Clarification, in *Towards Very Large Knowledge Bases: Knowledge Building and Knowlede Sharing*, N. Mars (Ed), IOS Press (1995) 25-32.
6. Kalfoglou, Y., Schorlemmer, M.: Ontology mapping: the state of the art, *The Knowledge Engineering Review*, 18(1) (2003) 1-31.
7. Lam, G.C.K., Leung, D.Y.C., Niewiadomski, M., Pang, S.W., Lee, A.W.F., Louie, P.K.K.: Street-level concentrations of nitrogen dioxide and suspended particulate matter in Hong Kong, *Atmospheric Environment*, 33(1) (1999) 1-11.
8. Li, J.: LOM: A Lexicon-based Ontology Mapping Tool, Teknowledge Corporation, research report (2004).
9. Moussiopoulos, N. (Ed): *Air Quality in Cities*, Springer, Berlin (2003).
10. Oprea, M.: A case study of knowledge modelling in an air pollution control decision support system, *AiCommunications*, IOS Press, 18(4) (2005) 293-303.
11. Oprea, M., Sànchez-Marrè, M. (Eds): Proceedings 16th ECAI 2004 Workshop Binding Environmental Sciences and Artificial Intelligence (BESAI-4) (2004).
12. Oprea, M.: Modelling an Environmental Protection System as a Knowledge-Based System, *International Journal of Modelling and Simulation*, ACTA Press, 24(1) (2004) 37-41.
13. Oprea, M.: Some Ecological Phenomena Forecasting by using an Artificial Neural Network, *Proceedings 16th IASTED International Conference on Applied Informatics AI98*, Garmisch-Partenkirchen, ACTA Press (1998) 30-32.
14. Page, B.: An Analysis of Environmental Expert Systems Applications, *Environmental Software*, 5(4) (1990) 177-198.
15. Protégé-2000: http://protégé.stanford.edu
16. Uschold, M., King, M.: Towards a Methodology for Building Ontologies, research report AIAI-TR-183, University of Edinburgh (1995).
17. Wooldridge, M.: *Introduction to Multiagent Systems*, John Wiley and Sons, New York, (2002).

Experimental Evaluation of Multi-Agent Ontology Mapping Framework

Miklos Nagy and Maria Vargas-Vera

Abstract Ontology mapping is a prerequisite for achieving heterogeneous data integration on the Semantic Web. The vision of the Semantic Web implies that a large number of ontologies are present on the Web that needs to be aligned before one can make use of them e.g. question answering on the Semantic Web. During the recent years a number of mapping algorithms, frameworks and tools have been proposed to address the problem of ontology mapping. Unfortunately comparing and evaluating these tools is not a straightforward task as these solutions are mainly designed for different domains. In this paper we introduce our ontology mapping framework called "DSSim" and present an experimental evaluation based on the tracks of the Ontology Alignment Evaluation Initiative (OAEI 2008).

1 Multi Agent Ontology Mapping Framework

As a requirement for the Semantic Web vision to become reality several difficulties have to resolved like ontology mapping, which makes it possible to interpret and align heterogeneous and distributed ontologies in this environment. For ontology mapping in the context of Question Answering over heterogeneous sources we propose a multi agent architecture [2] because as a particular domain becomes larger and more complex, open and distributed, a set of cooperating agents are necessary in order to address the ontology mapping task effectively. In real scenarios, ontology mapping can be carried out on domains with large number of classes and properties. Without the multi agent architecture the response time of the system can increase exponentially when the number of concepts to map increases.

Miklos Nagy
Knowledge Media Institute, The Open University, UK, e-mail: mn2336@student.open.ac.uk

Maria Vargas-Vera
Computing Department,The Open University, UK e-mail: m.vargas-vera@open.ac.uk

Please use the following format when citing this chapter:

Nagy, M. and Vargas-Vera, M., 2009, in IFIP International Federation for Information Processing, Volume 296; *Artificial Intelligence Applications and Innovations III*; Eds. Iliadis, L., Vlahavas, I., Bramer, M.; (Boston: Springer), pp. 145–150.

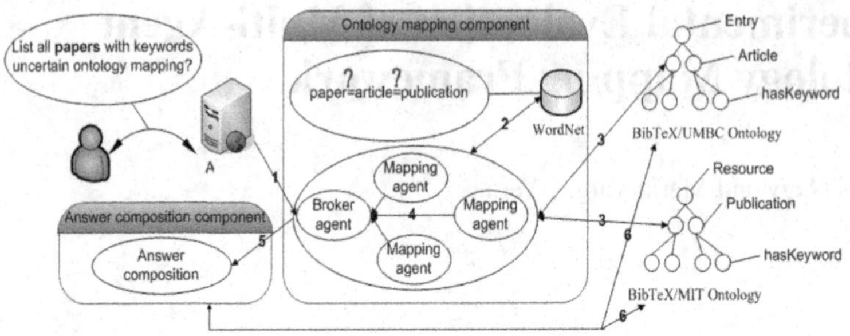

Fig. 1 Overview of the mapping system

An overview of our system is depicted on Fig. 1 The two real word ontologies[1][2] describe BibTeX publications from the University of Maryland, Baltimore County (UMBC) and from the Massachusetts Institute of Technology (MIT) . The AQUA [7] system and the answer composition component are described just to provide the context of our work (our overall framework) but these are not our major target in this paper. The user poses a natural language query to the AQUA system, which converts it into FOL (First Order Logic) terms. The main components and its functions of the system are as follows. First broker agent receives FOL term, decomposes it(in case more than one concepts are in the query) and distributes the sub queries to the mapping agents. Mapping agents retrieve sub query class and property hypernyms from WordNet. and retrieve ontology fragments from the external ontologies, which are candidate mappings to the received sub-queries. Mapping agents use WordNet as background knowledge in order to enhance their beliefs on the possible meaning of the concepts or properties in the particular context. At this point mapping agents build up coherent beliefs by combining all possible beliefs over the similarities of the sub queries and ontology fragments. Mapping agents utilize both syntactic and semantic similarity algorithms build their beliefs over the correctness of the mapping. After this step broker agent passes the possible mappings into the answer composition component for particular sub-query ontology fragment mapping in which the belief function has the highest value. In the last step the answer composition component retrieves the concrete instances from the external ontologies or data sources, which will be included into the answer and creates an answer to the user's question.

The organisation of this paper is as follows. In section 2 we analyse related systems, which have participated in more than 3 OAEI tracks. In section 3 we present our experimental evaluation of the benchmarks, anatomy and library tracks. Finally in section 4 we draw our conclusions of our evaluation.

[1] http://ebiquity.umbc.edu/ontology/publication.owl

[2] http://visus.mit.edu/bibtex/0.01/bibtex.owl

2 System Analysis and Related Work

Several ontology mapping systems have been proposed to address the semantic data integration problem of different domains independently. In this paper we consider only those systems, which have participated in the OAEI competitions and has been participated more than two tracks. There are other proposed systems as well however as the experimental comparison cannot be achieved we do not include them in the scope of our analysis. Lily [8] is an ontology mapping system with different purpose ranging from generic ontology matching to mapping debugging. It uses different syntactic and semantic similarity measures and combines them with the experiential weights. Further it applies similarity propagation matcher with strong propagation condition and the matching algorithm utilises the results of literal matching to produce more alignments. In order to assess when to use similarity propagation Lily uses different strategies, which prevents the algorithm from producing more incorrect alignments. ASMOV [1] has been proposed as a general mapping tool in order to facilitate the integration of heterogeneous systems, using their data source ontologies. It uses different matchers and generates similarity matrices between concepts, properties, and individuals, including mappings from object properties to datatype properties. It does not combine the similarities but uses the best values to create a pre alignment, which are then being semantically validated. Mappings, which pass the semantic validation will be added to the final alignment. ASMOV can use different background knowledge e.g. Wordnet or UMLS Metathesaurus(medical background knowledge) for the assessment of the similarity measures. RiMOM [6] is an automatic ontology mapping system, which models the ontology mapping problem as making decisions over entities with minimal risk. It uses the Bayesian theory to model decision making under uncertainty where observations are all entities in the two ontologies. Further it implements different matching strategies where each defined strategy is based on one kind of ontological information. RiMOM includes different methods for choosing appropriate strategies (or strategy combination) according to the available information in the ontologies. The strategy combination is conducted by a linear-interpolation method. In addition to the different strategies RiMOM uses similarity propagation process to refine the existing alignments and to find new alignments that cannot be found using other strategies. RiMOM is the only system other than DSSim in the OAEI contest that considers the uncertain nature of the mapping process however it models uncertainty differently from DSSim. RiMOM appeared for first time in the OAEI-2007 whilst DSSim appeared in the OAEI-2006.

3 Experimental Analysis

Experimental comparison of ontology mapping systems is not a straightforward task as each system is usually designed to address a particular need from a specific domain. This problem has been acknowledged by the Ontology Mapping community and as a response to this need the Ontology Alignment Evaluation Initiative[3] has been set up in 2004. The evaluation was measured with recall, precision and F-measure, which are useful measures that have a fixed range and meaningful from the mapping point of view. The experiments were carried out to assess the efficiency of the mapping algorithms themselves. The experiments of the question answering (AQUA) using our mappings algorithms are out of the scope of this paper. Our main objective was to compare our system and algorithms to existing approaches on the same basis and to allow drawing constructive conclusions.

3.1 Benchmarks

The OAEI benchmark contains tests, which were systematically generated starting from some reference ontology and discarding a number of information in order to evaluate how the algorithm behave when this information is lacking. The bibliographic reference ontology (different classifications of publications) contained 33 named classes, 24 object properties, 40 data properties. Further each generated ontology was aligned with the reference ontology. The benchmark tests were created and grouped by the following criteria. Group 1xx are simple tests such as comparing the reference ontology with itself, with another irrelevant ontology or the same ontology in its restriction to OWL-Lite. Group 2xx are systematic tests that were obtained by discarding some features from some reference ontology e.g. name of entities replaced by random strings, synonyms, name with different conventions. Group 3xx contain four real-life ontologies of bibliographic references that were found on the web e.g. BibTeX/MIT, BibTeX/UMBC. Figure 2 shows the 6 best performing systems out of 13 participants. We have ordered the systems based on the their the F-Value of the H-means because the H-mean unifies all results for the test and F-Value represents both precision and recall.

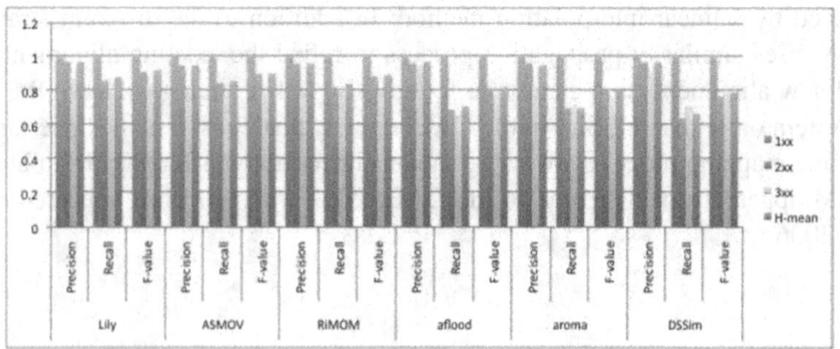

Fig. 2 Best performing systems in the benchmarks track based on H-mean and F-value

[3] http://oaei.ontologymatching.org/

In the benchmark test we have performed in the upper mid range compared to other systems. Depending on the group of tests our system compares differently to other solutions. For the Group 1xx our results are nearly identical to the other systems. In the group 2xx tests where syntactic similarity can determine the mapping outcome our system is comparable to other systems. However where semantic similarity is the only way to provide mappings our systems provides less mappings compared to the other systems in the best six. For the tests in group 3xx considering the F-value only 3 systems SAMBO, RIMOM and Lily performed better than DSSim. The weakness of our system to provide good mappings when only semantic similarity can be exploited is the direct consequence of our mapping architecture. At the moment we are using four mapping agents where 3 carries our syntactic similarity comparisons and only 1 is specialised in semantics. However it is worth to note that our approach seems to be stable compared to our last year's performance as our precision recall values were similar in spite of the fact that more and more difficult tests have been introduced in this year. As our architecture is easily expandable with adding more mapping agents it is possible to enhance our semantic mapping performance in the future.

3.2 Library

The objective of this track was to align two Dutch thesauri used to index books from two collections held by the National Library of the Netherlands. Each collection is described according to its own indexing system and conceptual vocabulary. On the one hand, the Scientific Collection is described using the GTT, a huge vocabulary containing 35,000 general concepts ranging from Wolkenkrabbers (Sky-scrapers) to Verzorging (Care). On the other hand, the books contained in the Deposit Collection are mainly indexed against the Brinkman thesaurus, containing a large set of headings (more than 5,000) that are expected to serve as global subjects of books. Both thesauri have similar coverage (there are more than 2,000 concepts having exactly the same label) but differ in granularity. For each concept, the thesauri provide the usual lexical and semantic information: preferred labels, synonyms and notes, broader and related concepts, etc. The language of both thesauri is Dutch, but a quite substantial part of Brinkman concepts (around 60%) come with English labels. For the purpose of the alignment, the two thesauri have been represented according to the SKOS model, which provides with all these features.

In the library track DSSim has performed the best out of the 3 participating systems. The track is difficult partly because of its relative large size and because of its multilingual representation. However these ontologies contain related and broader terms therefore the mapping can be carried out without consulting multi lingual background knowledge. This year the organisers have provided instances as separate ontology as well however we did not make use of it for creating our final mappings. For further improvements in recall and precision we will need to consider these additional instances in the future.

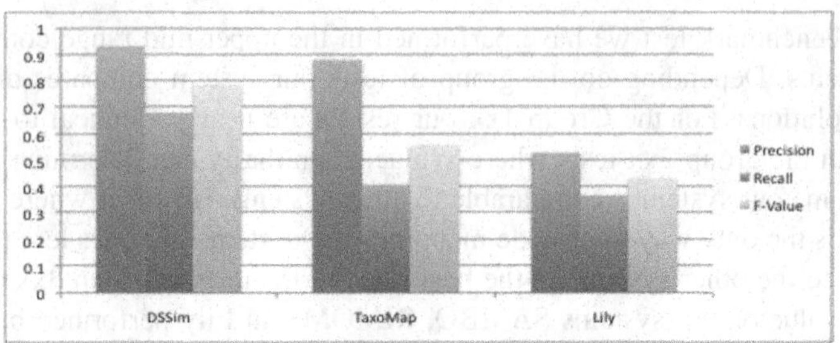

Fig. 3 All participating systems in the library track ordered by F-value

4 Conclusions

In this paper we have analysed two different experimental tests that were carried out in order to evaluate our integrated ontology mapping solution. We have showed that our solution DSSim, which is the core ontology mapping component of our proposed multi agent ontology mapping framework performs really well compared to other solutions. The analysis of other OAEI 2008 tracks in which we have participated are out of the scope of this paper, however, a detailed description of the other tracks can be found in [5]. Nevertheless we continuously evaluate the performance of our system through OAEI competitions [3, 4, 5] that allows us to improve, evaluate and validate our solution compared to other state of the art systems. So far our qualitative results are encouraging therefore we aim to investigate further the belief combination optimisation, compound noun processing and agent communication strategies for uncertain reasoning in the future.

References

1. Yves R. Jean-Mary and Mansur R. Kabuka. Asmov: Ontology alignment with semantic validation. In *Joint SWDB-ODBIS Workshop*, 2007.
2. Miklos Nagy, Maria Vargas-Vera, and Enrico Motta. Multi agent ontology mapping framework in the aqua question answering system. In *MICAI 2005: Advances in Artificial Intelligence, 4th Mexican International Conference on Artificial Intelligence*, pages 70–79, 2005.
3. Miklos Nagy, Maria Vargas-Vera, and Enrico Motta. Dssim-ontology mapping with uncertainty. In *The 1st International Workshop on Ontology Matching*, 2006.
4. Miklos Nagy, Maria Vargas-vera, and Enrico Motta. Dssim - managing uncertainty on the semantic web. In *The 2nd International Workshop on Ontology Matching*, 2007.
5. Miklos Nagy, Maria Vargas-Vera, and Piotr Stolarski. Dssim results for oaei 2008. In *The 3rd International Workshop on Ontology Matching*, 2008.
6. Jie Tang, Juanzi Li, Bangyong Liang, Xiaotong Huang, Yi Li, and Kehong Wang. Using bayesian decision for ontology mapping. *Web Semantics*, 2006.
7. Maria Vargas-Vera and Enrico Motta. Aqua - ontology-based question answering system. In *Third International Mexican Conference on Artificial Intelligence (MICAI-2004)*, 2004.
8. Peng Wang and Baowen Xu. Lily: Ontology alignment results for oaei 2008. In *The 3rd International Workshop on Ontology Matching*, 2008.

Visualizing RDF Documents

Aris Athanassiades[1], Efstratios Kontopoulos[2] and Nick Bassiliades[2]

[1] Dept. of Business Administration, Univ. of Macedonia, GR-54006, Thessaloniki, Greece

mis0620@uom.gr

[2]Dept. of Informatics, Aristotle Univ. of Thessaloniki, GR-54124 Thessaloniki, Greece

{skontopo, nbassili}@csd.auth.gr

Abstract The Semantic Web (SW) is an extension to the current Web, enhancing the available information with semantics. RDF, one of the most prominent standards for representing meaning in the SW, offers a data model for referring to objects and their interrelations. Managing RDF documents, however, is a task that demands experience and expert understanding. Tools have been developed that alleviate this drawback and offer an interactive graphical visualization environment. This paper studies the visualization of RDF documents, a domain that exhibits many applications. The most prominent approaches are presented and a novel graph-based visualization software application is also demonstrated.

1 Introduction

The *Semantic Web* [1] (*SW*) attempts to improve the current Web, by making Web content "*understandable*" not only to humans but to machines as well. One of the fundamental SW technologies is *XML* (*eXtensible Markup Language*) that allows the representation of structured documents via custom-defined vocabulary. However, since XML cannot semantically describe the meaning of information, *RDF* [2] (*Resource Description Framework*), an XML-based statement model, was introduced that captures the semantics of data through metadata representation.

The management of XML-based RDF documents is a task easily handled by machines that can easily process large volumes of structured data. For humans, however, the same objective is highly cumbersome and demands experience and expert understanding [3]. Software tools have been developed that alleviate this drawback, hiding the technical low-level syntactical and structural details and offering a graphical visualization interactive environment. This way, a human-user can easily create new documents or modify their structure and content.

The most substantial requirement for these software tools is the efficient visualization of RDF metadata [4]. The three most prominent RDF visualization ap-

Please use the following format when citing this chapter:

Athanassiades, A., Kontopoulos, E. and Bassiliades, N., 2009, in IFIP International Federation for Information Processing, Volume 296; *Artificial Intelligence Applications and Innovations III*; Eds. Iliadis, L., Vlahavas, I., Bramer, M.; (Boston: Springer), pp. 151–156.

proaches are: *display-at-once*, where the graph representing the document is displayed all at once, *navigational-centric*, where a chosen resource serves as the start-point for the rest of the graph, and *centric-graph-at-once*, a combination of the previous two. This paper studies thoroughly these approaches and demonstrates *RDFViz++*, a novel graph-based visualization software. The tool offers an alternative visualization approach that fulfills the needs unsatisfied by the available tools.

In the rest of the paper, section 2 gives some insight on RDF, followed by a section that focuses on visualizing RDF documents, presenting the three dominant visualization approaches. Section 4 presents RDFViz++, elaborating on its most distinctive features as well as its visualization algorithm. The paper is concluded with the final remarks and directions for future work.

2 RDF – a Common Information Exchange Model in the SW

RDF is a common information data exchange model describing SW resources. It consists of a number of *statements*, each being a *resource-property-value* triple: *resources* are the objects we refer to, *properties* describe attributes of resources or relations between resources and *values* can be either resources or simply literals. An example of a statement is: **<#john> <#age> <26>**, which declares that a specific person (named John) is 26 years old. Here "**#john**" is the resource (or *subject*), "**#age**" is the property (or *predicate*) and the value (or *object*) is "**26**".

In XML, RDF statements can be represented by an **rdf:Description** element. The subject is referred to in the **rdf:about** attribute, the predicate is used as a tag and the object is the tag content. Furthermore, *namespaces* provide a mechanism for resolving name clashes, when more than one document is imported. The element names are defined, using a prefix and a local name that is unique within the base URI. Additionally, external namespaces are expected to be RDF documents defining resources, used by the importing document. This allows reuse of resources, resulting in distributed collections of knowledge.

3 Visualizing RDF Documents

Since RDF is based on XML, human interaction with RDF documents becomes cumbersome, especially in rich, detailed domains with vast numbers of statements. Dedicated software utilities bring the solution: statement visualization through simple, two-dimensional shapes. A graph is usually the final result, where nodes represent resources and arrows represent predicates. Visualizing the whole document, nevertheless, is more complicated, as many resources, properties and values must be combined in one display [5]. Also, each RDF document, demands a different visualization approach, depending on its characteristics. A categorization of the available visualization implementations leads to three main approaches:

- *Display-at-once*: After analyzing the whole RDF document, a graph is produced that includes every single triplet. Resources are represented as rectangular or oval shapes and predicates as arrows directed from subjects towards objects. Resources involved in many statements are drawn only once; thus, multiple connections between the same resources are dealt with extended use of arrows. The greatest advantage of this approach is that it offers a complete aspect of the RDF document. However, as the document size increases, the visual result becomes unsatisfactory, due to the vast number of shapes and multiple crossings. An implementation paradigm that applies display-at-once is the well-known tool *IsaViz* [6]. An interesting feature is the zoom-in/zoom-out function in coalition with the overview map that provides the capability of better utilizing the display panel. The result is quite clear when the RDF document is not very complicated; however, complex graphs quickly become incomprehensible.
- *Navigational-centric* (or *navigational*): It is based on a chosen resource that serves as the centric node. The graph displays all the triplets, for which this node is the subject. The expansion of the rest of the graph can be interactively controlled – every object node that belongs to the already displayed statements can be chosen for further expansion. The navigational approach offers flexibility in RDF graph deployment, since it provides total control on the graph, eliminating the handicap of the display-at-once approach in visualizing "heavy" RDF documents. This is the recommended visualization approach for voluminous, complex documents and for the discovery of a specific knowledge path inside a document. However, it is not possible to have a full graph at once, a need that appears often in small and medium-sized RDF documents. An interesting implementation of this approach is the *HP Node-centric RDF Graph Visualization* [7] utility, where the navigational methodology is extended with special features like *navigation range* and *backward expansion*.
- *Centric-graph-at-once*: It is a combination of the previous two: all statements are displayed at once starting from a central node that is randomly or explicitly chosen. Arrows are designed starting from the central node; each ends at an object node, which also expands if it participates in further statements. Centric-graph-at-once has a major improvement over display-at-once: every resource that occurs in more than one RDF statements is drawn again for every repetition. Thus, contrary to display-at-once, arrow crossings are eliminated and the result is far more legible. The method performs well on small and medium-sized RDF documents; however, as the size of the document increases, more space and processing power is needed. As a result, users can see only a part of the complete graph; the rest is displayed after interacting on the display panel. *Fentwine* [8] is an implementation based on centric-graph-at-once. It allows the user to choose a part of the graph and then zooms out the rest. This assists the user in focusing on the part he is interested in, while the application takes advantage of the rest of the screen to display as many nodes as possible.

4 RDFViz++

The most important factors in visualizing RDF are the document size and complexity. This causes different performances for different documents by the same application – every tool follows a particular non-flexible algorithm that does not adapt to document characteristics. RDFViz++ is an alternative RDF visualization approach that faces this weakness; instead of enforcing one graph style, it combines the three previous visualization techniques, preserving the advantages from each. The software offers various layouts, but even when none of them proves to be efficient enough, a random algorithmic graph layout can be executed as many times as needed, until the final result is acceptable.

The interface consists of the toolbar, the subjects list, the display panel and the status bar. Almost all functions can be executed from the toolbar at the top of the window. The central node of the graph is chosen from the subjects list on the left that contains all the subject resources of the RDF document. The rest of the screen is used for displaying the graph, except from a narrow lane at the bottom, which serves as the status bar. A snapshot of RDFViz++ is shown in Fig. 1.

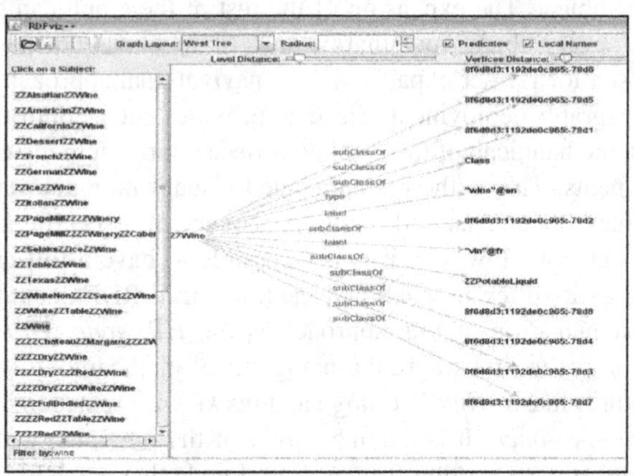

Fig. 1. RDFViz++ user interface

4.1. Visualization Algorithm

RDFViz++ features a recursion-based algorithm for graph construction. The visualization commences by choosing a centric node and continues dynamically, via two user-defined parameters: *Expansion Range* and *Node/Level Distance*. *Expansion Range* defines the expansion depth. *Level distance* is the space between different depths. *Node distance* is the space between each node that resides inside the node group of the same level. Upon choosing the initial node, the first centric graph is constructed around it, according to the parameters above.

The central node resource is passed as a parameter to a procedure that loads all RDF statements, for which this resource is the subject. For each statement, its predicate and object are isolated and drawn as an arrow and a new node, respectively. After visualizing each statement, the system prevents re-expansion of another instance of the same resource. Nevertheless, a resource may be present more than once in a graph by following a strict constraint: it must be displayed only once as a subject and as many times as needed as an object.

The above process accepts a node and draws all adjacent nodes. If the expansion range is set to 1, then a single execution of this process gives the resulting graph. If the range is set to a greater value, then the procedure calls itself recursively. Every object that comes up from expanding the initial node becomes the procedure parameter and another call is performed. If any of the objects that arise has already been expanded as a subject before, then it is just omitted. Finally, if the range is set to 0, recursion occurs until no more objects are able to expand.

Except from the automatic graph generation, RDFViz++ also provides manual expansion via user interaction. When the initial graph is built, any visible object can be expanded, unless it has been already expanded as a subject at previous levels. Also, the RDF statements, where the resource participates as subject, must be available. If these constraints are satisfied, then the selected object is passed as a parameter to the main procedure, which is executed recursively. The number of recursive executions is equal to the number of objects that arise from the levels, which in their turn are defined by expansion range.

4.2. Graph Layouts

Document complexity does not depend only on the number of statements. One of the most significant characteristics is *concentration*, namely, the phenomenon of having only a few specific resources participate repeatedly in a vast number of statements. RDFViz++ provides a variety of graph layouts; the most appropriate can be chosen, according to the document visualization requirements. The layout can even be dynamically modified –the whole graph with the chosen layout is simply redrawn. Thus, experimentation can often lead to the best-suited configuration for each document. The available layouts are:

- *West/East/North/South Tree*: West Tree is one of the most efficient layouts, positioning the central node at the leftmost part and maintaining a left-to-right flow. In East Tree the flow is inversed. North and South Tree layouts have the same arrangement, but start deployment from the top and bottom, respectively.
- *North/West Compact*: Variations of the North and West Tree layouts that improve node placement, aiming at efficiently distributing the available space.
- *Radial Tree*: The initial centric point is the center for all levels, which are drawn as concentric circles with a greater radius than the previous levels.
- *Organic*: Uses a randomized algorithm for calculating positions.

5 Conclusions and Future Work

The paper reported on RDF document visualization, presenting the three most prominent visualization approaches. Each is suitable for specific document types, while no single methodology can handle all documents. This was the primary motivation behind RDFViz++, the RDF visualization tool presented in this work. The software adjusts to the peculiarities of the document to be visualized, offering an adequate array of available layouts and providing the possibility of choosing the most suitable approach each time. Conclusively, the software offers a more inclusive RDF visualization. Expansion range, customized level and node distances and the various graph layouts add up to a flexible interactive application.

As for future work, the software could be enhanced with various controls like zoom-in/zoom-out, inversing the flow of the arrows (from objects to subjects), overview controls etc. Furthermore, it could be enhanced with authoring capabilities; the potential of introducing, modifying or removing statements from an RDF document would transform the tool into an integrated RDF development environment. Finally, the software could also be extended with RDF Schema representation and authoring capabilities, becoming, thus, an RDF Schema *ontology editor*.

References

1. Berners-Lee, T., Hendler, J., Lassila, O.: The Semantic Web. Scientific American, 284(5), pp. 34-43 (2001)
2. Herman, I., Swick, R., Brickley, R.: Resource Description Framework (RDF). http://www.w3.org/RDF/, last accessed: 4 November 2008
3. DeFanti, T. A., Brown, M. D., McCormick, B. H.: Visualization: Expanding Scientific and Engineering Research Opportunities. IEEE Computer, 22 (8), pp. 12-25 (1989)
4. Deligiannidis, L., Kochut, K. J., Sheth, A. P.: RDF Data Exploration and Visualization. Proc. ACM First Workshop on Cyberinfrastructure: Information Management in E-Science (CIMS '07), Lisbon, Portugal, ACM, New York, pp. 39-46 (2007)
5. Frasincar, F., Telea, A., Houben, G. J.: Adapting Graph Visualization Techniques for the Visualization of RDF Data. Visualizing the Semantic Web, pp. 154-171 (2006)
6. Pietriga, E.: IsaViz: A Visual Environment for Browsing and Authoring RDF Models. Proc. 11th World Wide Web Conference (Developer's day), Hawaii, USA (2002)
7. Sayers, C.: Node-Centric RDF Graph Visualization. Technical Report HPL-2004-60, HP Laboratories, Palo Alto (2004)
8. Fallenstein, B.: Fentwine: A Navigational RDF Browser and Editor. Proc. 1st Workshop on Friend of a Friend, Social Networking and the Semantic Web, Galway (2004)

A Knowledge-based System for Translating FOL Formulas into NL Sentences

Aikaterini Mpagouli, Ioannis Hatzilygeroudis

University of Patras, School of Engineering

Department of Computer Engineering & Informatics, 26500 Patras, Hellas

E-mail: {mpagouli, ihatz}@ceid.upatras.gr

Abstract In this paper, we present a system that translates first order logic (FOL) formulas into natural language (NL) sentences. The motivation comes from an intelligent tutoring system teaching logic as a knowledge representation language, where it is used as a means for feedback to the users. FOL to NL conversion is achieved by using a rule-based approach, where we exploit the pattern matching capabilities of rules. So, the system consists of a rule-based component and a lexicon. The rule-based unit implements the conversion process, which is based on a linguistic analysis of a FOL sentence, and the lexicon provides lexical and grammatical information that helps in producing the NL sentences. The whole system is implemented in Jess, a java-based expert system shell. The conversion process currently covers a restricted set of FOL formulas.

1 Introduction

To help teaching the course of "Artificial Intelligence" in our Department a web-based intelligent tutoring system has been created. One of the topics that it deals with is first-order logic (FOL) as a knowledge representation language. One of the issues in the topic is the translation of natural language (NL) sentences into FOL formulas. Given that this is a non-automated process [1, 2], it is difficult to give some hints to the students-users during their effort to translate an "unknown" (to the system) NL sentence into a FOL formula. However, some kind of help could be provided, if the system could translate the proposed by the student FOL formula into a NL sentence. We introduce here a method for converting/translating FOL formulas into NL sentences, called FOLtoNL algorithm. The structure of the paper is as follows. Section 2 deals with related work. Section 3 presents the basic algorithm and Section 4 refers to its implementation and lexicon. Section 5 concludes the paper.

Please use the following format when citing this chapter:

Mpagouli, A. and Hatzilygeroudis, I., 2009, in IFIP International Federation for Information Processing, Volume 296; *Artificial Intelligence Applications and Innovations III*; Eds. Iliadis, L., Vlahavas, I., Bramer, M.; (Boston: Springer), pp. 157–163.

2 Related Work

Our work can be considered as belonging to the field of Natural Language Generation [3], since it generates NL sentences from some source of information, which are FOL formulas. In the existing literature, we couldn't trace any directly similar effort, i.e. an effort to translate FOL sentences into natural language sentences. However, we traced a number of indirectly related efforts, those of translating some kind of natural language expressions into some kind of FOL ones.

In [4] an application of Natural Language Processing (NLP) is presented. It is an educational tool for translating Spanish text of certain types of sentences into FOL implemented in Prolog. This effort gave us a first inspiration about the form of the lexicon we use in our FOLtoNL system.

In [5], ACE (Attempto Controlled English), a structured subset of the English language, is presented. ACE has been designed to substitute for formal symbolisms, like FOL, in the input of some systems to make the input easier to understand and to be written by the users.

Finally, in [6], a Controlled English to Logic Translation system, called CELT, allows users to give sentences of a restricted English grammar as input. The system analyses those sentences and turns them into FOL. What is interesting about it is the use of a PhraseBank, a selection of phrases, to deal with the ambiguities of some frequently used words in English like have, do, make, take, give etc.

3 FOLtoNL Conversion Process

Our FOLtoNL conversion algorithm takes as input FOL formulas [1] of the following form (in a BNF notation, where '[ ]' denotes optional and '< >' non-terminal symbols): [<quant-expr>] [<stmt1> =>] <stmt2>, where <quant-expr> denotes the expression of quantifiers in the formula, '=>' denotes implication and <stmt1> and <stmt2> denote the *antecedent* and the *consequent* statements of the implication. These statements do not contain quantifiers. So, the input formula is in its Prenex Normal Form [1, 2]. Furthermore, <stmt1> and <stmt2> can not contain implications. Hence, the system currently focuses on the translation of simple FOL implications or FOL expressions that do not contain implications at all. For typing convenience, we use the following symbols in our FOL formulas: '~' (negation), '&' (conjunction), 'V' (disjunction), '=>' (implication), 'forall' (universal quantifier), 'exists' (existential quantifier).

The key idea of our conversion method, based on a FOL implication, is that when both the antecedent and the consequent statements exist, the consequent can give us the Basic Structure (BS) of that implication's NL translation. BS may contain variable symbols. In that case, the antecedent of the implication can help us to define the entities represented by those variable symbols. In other words, we can find NL substitutes for those variables and then use them instead of variable symbols in BS to provide the final NL translation of the implication.

If the FOL expression does not contain variables, the translation is simpler: “if <ant-translation> then <con-translation>”, where <ant-translation> and <con-translation> consist of appropriately combined interpretations of atoms and connectives. In case we have only <stmt2>, i.e. an expression without implications, we use the same method with one difference: variable NL substitutes emerge from the expression of quantifiers, since there is no antecedent. Of course, there is a special case in which we choose some atoms of the expression for the estimation of NL substitutes and the rest of them for the BS and we work as if we had an implication.

The basic steps of our algorithm are the following:

1. Scan the user input and determine <quant-expr>, <stmt1> and <stmt2>. Gather information for each variable (symbol, quantifier etc). Each atom represents a statement. Analyze each atom in the three parts of its corresponding statement: subject-part, verb-part and object-part.
2. If <stmt1> $\neq \varnothing$,
   2.1 Find the basic structure (BS) of the final sentence based on <stmt2>.
   2.2 For each variable symbol in BS specify the corresponding NL substitute based on <stmt1>. If there are no variables, then BS is in NL. In that case, find also the Antecedent Translation (AT) based on <stmt1>.
3. If <stmt1> $= \varnothing$,
   3.1 Find BS based on all or some of the atoms of <stmt2>.
   3.2 For each variable symbol in BS specify the corresponding NL substitute based on the information of quantifiers or particular atoms of <stmt2>. If there are no variables, then BS is build via all the atoms of <stmt2> and is in NL.
4. Substitute each variable symbol in BS for the corresponding NL substitute and give the resulting sentence as output. If there are no variables, distinguish two cases: If the initial FOL sentence was an implication then return: “If <AT> then <BS>”. Otherwise, return BS.

In the sequel, we explain steps 2 and 3 of our algorithm, which are quite similar.

3.1 Finding the Basic Structure of the Final Sentence

In this subsection, steps 2.1 and 3.1 are analyzed. First of all, we find the atoms in <stmt2> that can aggregate, i.e. atoms that have the same subject-part and verb-part but different object-parts, or the same subject-part but different verb-parts and object-parts or different subject-parts but the same verb-part and the same object-part. Atoms that can aggregate are combined to form a new sentence which is called a *sub-sentence*. If an atom cannot be aggregated, then it becomes a sub-sentence itself. This process ends up with a set of sub-sentences, which cannot be further aggregated and, when divided by commas, give BS. Let us consider the following input sentences as examples:

(i) (forall x) (exists y) human(x) & human(y) => loves(x,y)
(ii) (exists x) cat(x) & likes(Kate,x)
(iii) (forall x) (exists y) (exists z) dog(x) & master(y,x) & town(z) & lives(y,z) => lives(x,z) & loves(x,y)
(iv) (forall x) bat(x) => loves(x,dampness) & loves(x,darkness) & small(x) & lives(x,caves)
(v) (forall x) bird(x) & big(x) & swims(x) & ~flies(x) => penguin(x)

The basic structures produced for these input sentences are the following (note the aggregation in (iii) and (iv) and the exclusion of the atom 'cat(x)' from BS in (ii)):

(i) x loves y.
(ii) Kate likes x.
(iii) x lives in z and loves y.
(iv) x loves dampness and darkness and x is small and lives in caves.
(v) x is a penguin.

The next stage is the specification of NL substitutes for the variable symbols.

3.2 Finding Natural Language Substitutes for Variable Symbols

Natural language substitutes are specified based on <stmt1>, in case of an implication, or based on quantifiers and maybe some particular single-term atoms of <stmt2>, in case of an implication-less expression. The first step is to determine the primary NL substitutes for all variables. A primary NL substitute contains all the information provided for a variable symbol by single-term atoms. The second step is to enrich each variable's primary NL substitute with information about that variable's relation to other entities, via appropriate two-term atoms. This step is ignored in case of an implication-less expression. We use <name-of-x> to indicate the NL substitute of a variable with symbol x and <refer-x> as a kind of referring expression that we can use instead of <name-of-x> when the latter appears more than once in BS.

For each variable symbol, say x, the algorithm performs the first step as follows:

A-1. If there is only one atom P(x): Depending on the quantifier information we have <quant> = "every"/"some"/"not every"/"no". According to the type of P, the primary name of x is determined as follows: If P is a noun, then <name-of-x>="<quant><P>" and <refer-x>="that <P>". If P is an adjective, then <name-of-x>="<quant> <P> thing" and <refer-x>="that thing". If P is a verb, then <name-of-x>="<quant> thing that <P>" and <refer-x>="that thing".

A-2. If there are more than one atoms, say $P_i(x)$ (i=1,…,k): These atoms are divided into three categories according to the type of their predicate (adjective, noun, verb). We denote by Pa, Pn and Pv predicates of type adjective, noun and verb respectively. The primary name will be of the form: "<quant> [<Pa_1>,<Pa_2>,...and <Pa_n>] thing/<Pn_1>,<Pn_2>,...and <Pn_m> [that <Pv_1>,<Pv_2>,...and <Pv_s>]" and <refer-x> will be of the form "that thing"/"that <Pn_1>, that <Pn_2>,...and that <Pn_m>".

A-3. If there is no atom P(x), then, according to the quantifier, <name-of-x> will be: "everything"/"something"/"not everything"/"nothing".

A-4. Special case: For each variable y, different from x, if there is no atom Pn(y), but there are atoms Pn_i(y, x) and maybe atoms Pa(y) or/and Pv(y), then we treat each of the atoms Pn_i(y, x) as an atom 'has(x,y)', after we have computed the primary name of y, <name-of-y>="a [<Pa_1>, <Pa_2>,...and <Pa_n>] <Pn_1>,<Pn_2>,...and <Pn_m> [that <Pv_1>,<Pv_2>,...and <Pv_s>]" and <refer-y>="that <Pn_1>, that <Pn_2>,...and that <Pn_m>". Hence, <name-of-x> becomes "<name-of-x> that has <name-of-y>".

The primary names of the variables for the example input sentences 1-5 are:

(i) <name-of-x> = "every human", <name-of-y> = "some human" (A-1)

(ii) <name-of-x> = "some cat" (A-1)

(iii) <name-of-x> = "every dog", <name-of-y> = "a master", <name-of-z> = "some town" (A-4)

(iv) <name-of-x> = "every bat" (A-1)

(v) <name-of-x> = "every big bird that swims and does not fly" (A-2)

The second step is the enrichment of primary names via two term atoms, to achieve the final NL substitutes. The enrichment takes place via the recursive call of the function "build-name" which is described below. The enrichment function, each time it is called, uses only the atoms that have not been used in previous calls. For each variable symbol, say x, in BS, following the order of occurrence, the following actions are performed by "build-name":

B-1. If there are no two-term atoms to be used for the enrichment of <name-of-x>: If x has not been referred to in the NL substitute of the previous variable symbol in BS, or x is BS's first variable, then the final NL substitute for x is the primary substitute computed in the previous step.

B-2. If there are two-term atoms for the enrichment of <name-of-x> and x has not been referred to in the NL substitute of the previous variable symbol in BS, he enrichment begins: If x is a subject in BS and appears only as a second term in two-term atoms, the corresponding atoms are transformed appropriately to treat x as a subject-part, either by using passive tense for verb predicates or by analyzing noun predicate atoms Pn(y,x) as "x has y as <Pn>". Then, for each atom having x as a first term we enrich <name-of-x> as follows: <name-of-x>="<name-of-x> [and] that <pred-translation> <build-name(y)>", where <pred-translation>="<Pv>"/ "is the <Pn> of"/ "is <Pa> than>", according to the predicate type.

B-3. If the current variable symbol x has a reference in the NL substitute of the previous one due to recursive calls of "build-name", we do not need to build its NL substitute again. We use, instead, <refer-x> determined earlier.

Via the substitution of variable symbols for NL substitutes, we get the next NL sentences as outputs for the previous five input sentences:

(i) Every human loves some human.
(ii) Kate likes some cat.
(iii) Every dog that has some master that lives in some town lives in that town and loves that master.
(iv) Every bat loves dampness and darkness and every bat is small and lives in caves.
(v) Every big bird that swims and does not fly is a penguin.

4 Implementation Aspects

The FOLtoNL process has been implemented in Jess [7]. Jess is a rule-based expert system shell written in Java, which however offers adequate general programming capabilities, such as definition and use of functions. The system includes two Jess modules, MAIN and LEX. Each Jess module has its own rule base and its own facts and can work independently from the rest of Jess modules. Focus is passed from one module to the other to execute its rules. MAIN is the basic module of the system, whereas LEX is the system's lexicon.

The lexicon consists of a large number of facts concerning words, called word-facts. Each word-fact is an instance of the following template: (word ?type ?gen ?form ?past ?exp ?stem ?lem), where 'word' declares that it is a fact describing the word ?lem and the rest are variables representing the fields that describe the word (part of speech, gender, number, special syntax, stem).

5 Conclusions and Discussion

In this paper, we present an approach for translating FOL formulas into NL sentences, called the FOLtoNL algorithm. The whole system is implemented in Jess and consists of a rule-based system that implements the conversion algorithm and a lexicon. Of course there are some restrictions that are challenges for further work. One problem is the interpretation of sentences which are entirely in the scope of a negation. Yet another constraint is forced upon the use of '=>', which can only occur once in the input sentence. Another restriction is that currently we do not take into consideration the order of quantifiers in the user input. Finally, the lexicon at the moment contains a limited number of words. It should be further extended. All the above problems constitute our next research goals, concerning our algorithm and system.

References

1. Genesereth MR, Nilsson NJ (1988) Logical foundations of AI. Morgan Kaufmann
2. Brachman RJ, Levesque HJ (2004) Knowledge representation and reasoning. Morgan Kaufmann
3. Reiter E, Dale R (2006) Building natural language generation systems. Cambridge University Press
4. Rodríguez Vázquez de Aldana E (1999) An application for translation of Spanish sentences into first order logic implemented in prolog. http://aracne.usal.es/congress/PDF/EmilioRodriguez.pdf
5. Fuchs NE, Schwertel U, Torge S (1999) Controlled natural language can replace first order logic. Proceedings 14th IEEE International Conference on Automated Software Engineering (ASE'99). 295-298. http://www.ifi.unizh.ch/groups/req/ftp/papers/ASE99.pdf
6. Pease A, Fellbaum C (2004) Language to logic translation with PhraseBank. Proceedings 2nd Global Conference (GWC'04). 187-192
7. Friedman Hill E (2003) Jess in action: rule-based systems in Java. Manning Publishing. 2003

Background Extraction in Electron Microscope Images of Artificial Membranes

A. Karathanou, J.-L. Buessler, H. Kihl, J.-P. Urban

MIPS laboratory, University of Haute Alsace, 4 rue des Frères Lumière, F-68093 Mulhouse Cedex, France

Abstract On-line analysis of Transmission Electron Microscope (TEM) images is a field with great interest that opens up new prospects regarding automatic acquisitions. Presently, our work is focused on the automatic identification of artificial membranes derived from 2D protein crystallization experiments. Objects recognition at medium magnification aims to control the microscope in order to acquire interesting membranes at high magnification. A multiresolution segmentation technique has been proposed for the image partition. This paper presents an analysis of this partition to extract the background. To achieve this goal in very noisy images, it is essential to suppress false contours as they split the background into multiple regions. Statistical properties of such regions are not always sufficient for their identification as background. The analysis of these regions contours was therefore considered. In the proposed solution, the elimination of false contours is based on the statistical examination of the perpendicular gradient component along the contour. After this improved segmentation, the background extraction can be easily effectuated since this resulting region appears bright and large.

1 Introduction

2D crystals consist of proteins inserted within bi-lipidic layers in an organized manner. 3D information can be extracted from these artificial crystals; more specifically, it allows membrane proteins structure and function to be assessed. However, optimal conditions need to be established so that crystals formation will be correctly performed. For this purpose, a large quantity of crystallization trials is screened with a Transmission Electron Microscope (TEM). An automatic solution concerning the preparation of these trials and their image analysis is thus essential [1].

As already detailed in previous work [10], automatic assessment of 2D membranes requires the acquisition of a certain number of images at different magnifications. Each magnification step (low, medium, high) is related to two tasks: im-

Please use the following format when citing this chapter:

Karathanou, A., Buessler, J.-L., Kihl, H. and Urban, J.-P., 2009, in IFIP International Federation for Information Processing, Volume 296; *Artificial Intelligence Applications and Innovations III*; Eds. Iliadis, L., Vlahavas, I., Bramer, M.; (Boston: Springer), pp. 165–173.

age acquisition, and on-line image processing. Low and medium magnification image processing aims to globally characterize the sample and determine the regions of interest to be explored. Membranes will be finally examined at high magnification to assess the success of the crystallization. We present here certain aspects of TEM image processing acquired at medium magnification (x5000).

TEM images at medium magnification appear globally within a wide gray level range as they can contain dark objects (protein or membrane aggregates, staining artifacts) within a bright background with gray level fluctuations. However, interesting non-superposed membranes are low contrasted, slightly darker than the background with borders that often mark membrane boundaries. The low contrast of the objects of interest makes image processing all the more difficult as TEM images appear particularly noisy.

The principal objective of our image analysis at medium magnification is to identify interesting membranes to provide certain statistical characteristics (such as quantity, size, shape, etc) and to trigger a new acquisition at high magnification.

This paper deals with the background-foreground objects recognition within medium magnification images. For membrane detection, a multiresolution segmentation approach has been proposed and is briefly discussed in section 2. This segmentation algorithm leads to an image partition, without specifying which regions belong to the foreground objects or the background. A region, by itself, does not have enough characteristics to realize its classification. Membrane object identification therefore requires the background extraction. The segmentation often splits the background into smaller regions. Our approach, described in section 3, eliminates false contours that create the over segmentation. In this way, the background can be regarded as a large and bright region that can be simply extracted based on tthese two hypotheses.

2 TEM Image Segmentation

In this section we will discuss the first part of the membrane identification process: the edge segmentation algorithm applied to membrane detection.

Low contrasted membrane boundaries are not always characterized by a sufficient gradient; their gradient amplitude and/or direction varies along the contour. A multi resolution mechanism was therefore employed. Multi resolution gradient analysis, as proposed in [2], overcomes problems that common edge techniques face in TEM images. This method employs coarser resolutions to enhance edge detection. An automatic, adapted thresholding is embedded to this gradient analysis. The threshold for each resolution is determined automatically based on a histogram analysis that results in a confidence threshold of 2%. In this way, at each resolution, a reasonable amount of noisy gradients is retained.

This analysis results in a set of binary images that are combined to form a *reconstructed gradient like* (RGL) image. The value of each pixel in the RGL image indicates the best scale at which it has been thresholded. RGL image provides a better compromise between edge detection and localization precision. Compared to a gradient image, the RGL image is an edge map almost noise-free and is suitable for the watershed transform.

The watershed transform is then applied on this gradient image which produces the segmented image. This algorithm progressively floods the regions starting from the minima values and marks the merging of two basins with the watershed line [3]. The resulting watershed lines situated along the edge ridges, partition the image into regions formed by 1-pixel-width closed contours; and thus providing a convenient partition of the image.

Results showed that TEM images are segmented satisfactorily. All important low contrasted membrane contours are extracted in various TEM images. We noticed that all membrane regions are detected with an over segmentation disturbing mostly the background of the image.

3 Background Extraction

This section deals with the second part of the membrane recognition process. After having partitioned the image into regions, we need to define the objects that are present in our images. As a straight definition for objects characteristics is difficult to be given, we can consider the recognition problem differently: including gradual steps, beginning from differentiating the background from the foreground objects by extracting it.

The problem of the background extraction is principally raised because of the absence of a simple criterion for the foreground-background separation. Common methods are based on global or local threshold techniques. However, in complex images, such methods cannot be considered. Examples of background extraction can be found in color natural images where the size, the position and the color of the background [9] are used as hypotheses for its extraction. In text document images, background is discriminated from text based on local statistical properties of predefined regions (connected components) [8]. Others refine or adapt segmentation results in order to detect the objects of interest and background [6,7].

3.1 Background Characterization

Region characteristics are not sufficient to classify them into background-foreground regions. The background is generally a large, continuous and bright region that the segmentation algorithm often splits into many unnecessary regions. Fig.1 shows a classical example of such an over segmentation. Four of the segmented regions, where regions 1 and 4 are low-contrasted membranes and 2 and 3 background regions, present similar average intensities. This last does not allow a satisfactory discrimination between membranes and background.

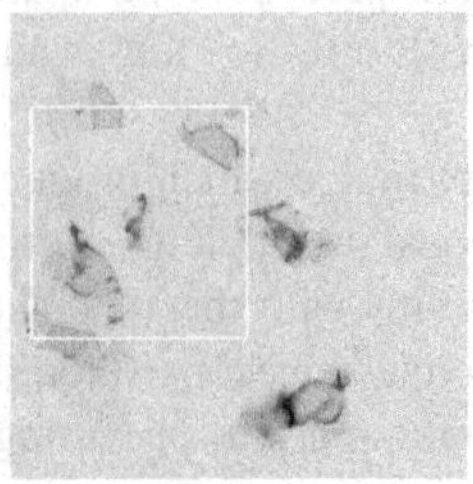

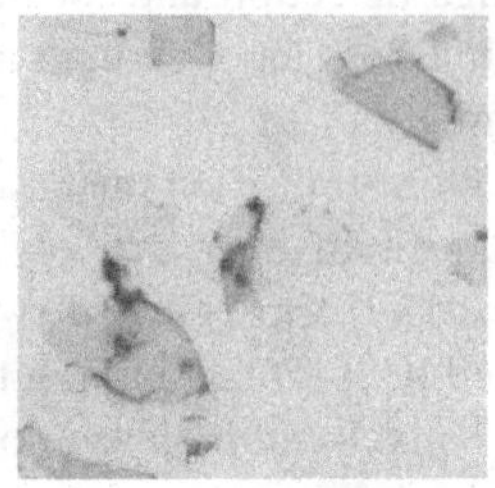

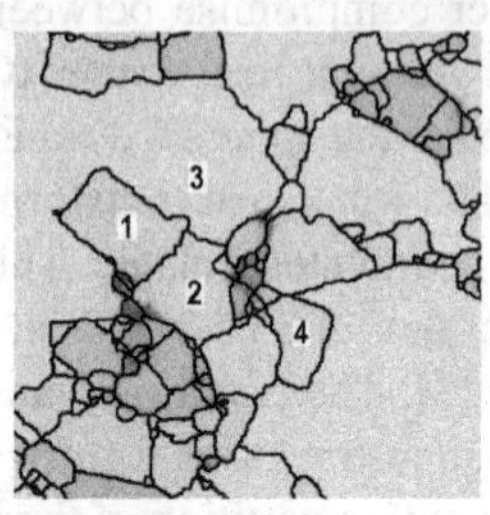

Fig. 1. Left: Initial TEM image, Center: Zoom of the white window of the initial image, Right: Segmentation of the zoomed region where, 1: membrane region with average gray level of 9180, 2: background region with average gray level of 9250, 3: background region with average gray level of 9470, 4: membrane region with average gray level of 9310

We propose a method specific for the treatment of our images. We assume that the background region is characterized by: a) a large and continuous image region with no specific shape, b) a high average gray level, presenting sometimes important local fluctuations in combination with a strong noise, c) almost no structured gradient.

3.2 Contour Validation

Edge detection algorithms are disturbed by statistical fluctuations of the background. False contours appear that can be eliminated with an a posteriori validation method.

The contours, even for a low contrasted membrane, are correlated with a true gradient. This correlation is not verified with false contours, even if they have been induced by a strong gradient. The contrast in the vicinity and along the boundary is therefore clearly an important criterion.

For contour validation, we developed a method based on the gradient perpendicular to the contour [4]. The principle of this method is now described.

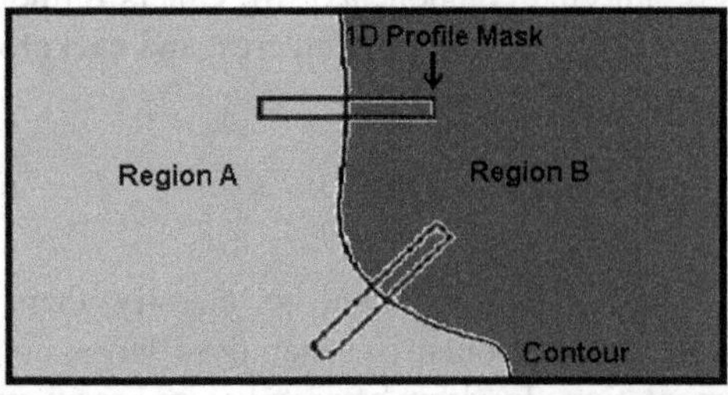

Fig. 2. Perpendicular extraction of profile transitions for a given contour segment separating regions A, B for gradient calculation

The gradient perpendicular to the contour permits to detect and then eliminate the false contours. This gradient measure was computed for each contour pixel by extracting the 1D transition profile perpendicularly, as illustrated in Fig. 2, and then correlating this profile with a gradient reference filter.

The importance of noise and the assumptions concerning its nature, made statistical hypothesis test an essential step. The gradient measure is therefore assessed by means of a hypothesis test. In order to set an optimal threshold for our decision, the average correlation measure was computed for the whole segment; this last is defined as the group of edge pixels that separate two adjacent regions. This measure was reinforced by taking into account the gradient's amplitude and direction along the contour. Finally, a segment is validated if there exists a gradient perpendicular to the contour statistically significant.

However, for false contours elimination, an iterative solution was chosen as in [7]. In order to obtain meaningful regions, we searched for each one the most appropriate fusion. Results showed that this elimination is efficient concerning the background as it is not significantly disturbed by spurious contours, facilitating its extraction.

3.3 Background Extraction Algorithm

After false contours elimination, the background is now considered free from over segmentation. It is no more divided into small regions but appears as a large region. This characteristic is verified in all our images. This background region appears globally bright even though it presents some gray level fluctuations related to the acquisition conditions (non-uniform illumination, etc.).

We propose a background extraction technique that is composed of three steps:

1) For each region R_i whose size is greater than a threshold T_s :

a) Compute average gray level $G(R_i)$ of this region;

b) If $G(R_i)$ is greater than threshold T_i, region R_i is retained as a background region,

We introduce supplementary tests to avoid detecting a large membrane region as background, using the fact that this region neighbors the background.

2) For each background region detected, find all neighbors;

3) If two neighboring regions are selected as background, use the gradient direction of the contour segments validated during the contour validation step (section 3.2) to retain as background only the brightest region.

Thresholds T_s and T_i are set empirically as they are highly image dependent. As an example, T_s is set to 10% of the image size, and T_i to 70% of the maximal region average gray level value. These thresholds were tested for a large number of TEM images providing a satisfactory background selection.

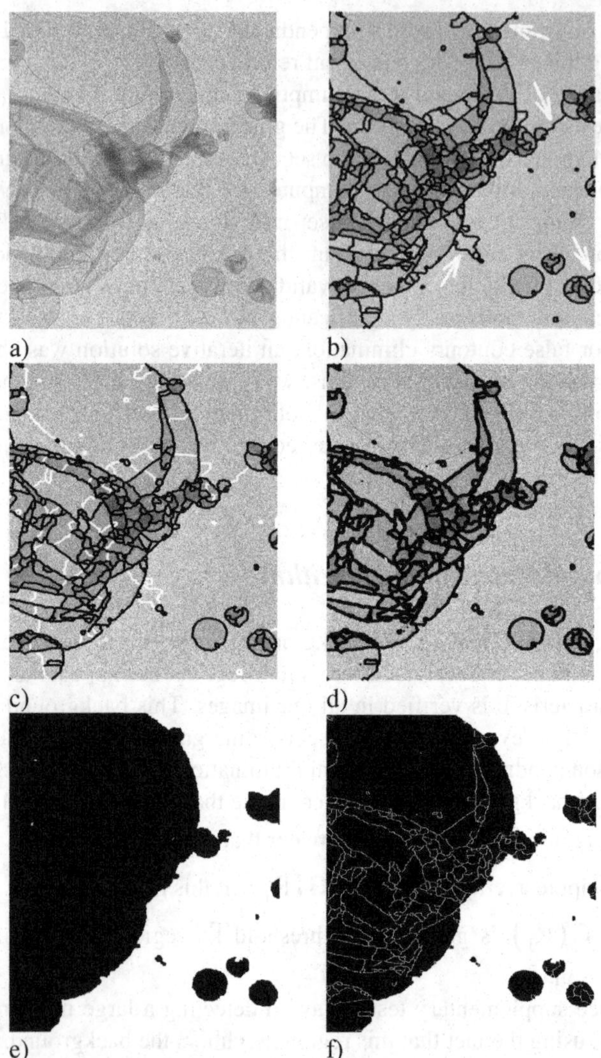

Fig. 3. a) Initial image, b) Initial multiresolution segmentation with the white arrows indicating false contours over segmenting the background, c) False contour detection (in white), d) Final segmentation after elimination of false segments, e) Background extraction (in white), f) Background (in white) with segmented membrane regions (in black)

4 Results

The efficiency of the whole proposed method has been systematically assessed on various series of images acquired with different TEMs taken under standard acquisition conditions of illumination and exposure time. These images contain membranes of different types (such as sheets-like membranes or vesicles) and sizes where our algorithm was able to extract the regions of interest satisfactorily and finally identify the image background.

More specifically, the proposed segmentation and background extraction scheme has been tested on 45 representative TEM images. The quantitative evaluation of Table 1 was established according to an expert's analysis. Our technique extracted and suitably selected the important contours segmenting all foreground objects.

We consider the background well-detected even if small background regions within the image are not identified. They represent less than 4% of the total image size. Table 1 shows that the background in 87% of the images has been well-detected, among them 13% contained small undetected regions (Fig. 4). A background is considered partially detected when a background region of a more important size is not identified (representing 4% to 8% of the total image size). Complementary algorithms are currently implemented to improve the detection of this kind of regions. In the case of a background misclassification, at least 50% of the background surface is not detected.

On the other hand, foreground objects are globally properly classified as such.

Table 1. Quantitative performance measures of the background extraction algorithm for 45 representative images

WELL-DETECTED BACKGROUND INCLUDING 13% OF IMAGES CONTAINING SMALL UNDETECTED REGIONS	**87%**
PARTIALLY DETECTED BACKGROUND	**11%**
BACKGROUND MISCLASSIFICATION	**2%**

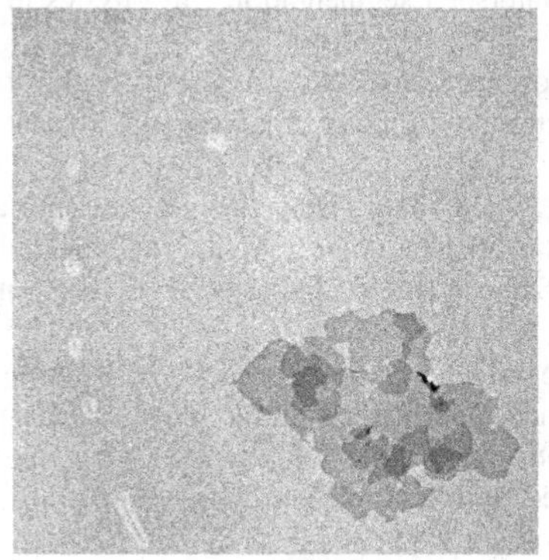
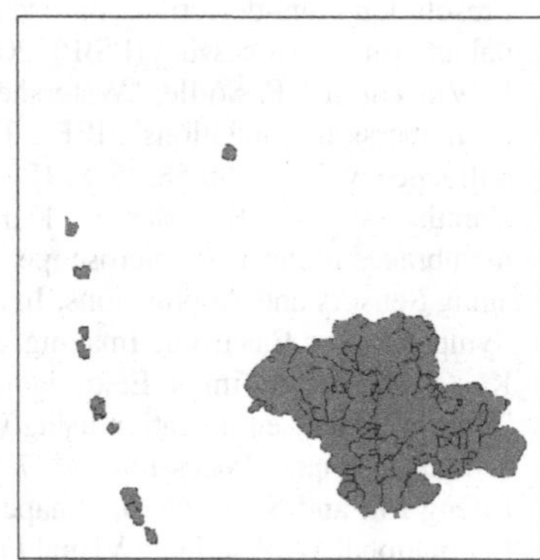

Fig. 4. Left: TEM image, Right: An example of the background extraction (in white)

Fig.3a illustrates an example of a typical TEM image part. In the left hand side of the image, a huge vesicle stack can be observed. Fig.3b shows the initial segmentation of the image where the background over segmentation can be clearly noticed. This last is resolved by the detection and elimination of false contours as shown in the next step of the process (Fig.3c, 3d)). The background is then extracted allowing a clear distinction between the two classes objects-background.

5 Conclusion

We described a chain process for the extraction of the background in gray level TEM images. This process starts with a multiresolution edge extraction technique that segmented low contrasted membrane regions. False contours were then eliminated by means of a statistical validation technique. This last enables a proper false-true edge classification and therefore a correct background-object distinction. Background appears large and bright, characteristics that allow its extraction. This technique is implemented for objects recognition on electron microscope images.

Acknowledgments This work was supported by the EU 6th framework (HT3DEM, LSHG-CT-2005-018811, in collaboration with the Biozentrum of Basel and FEI company who provided the TEM images.

References

1. HT3DEM: High Throughput - Three Dimensional Electron Microscopy, http://www.ht3dem.org/
2. N. Coudray, J.-L. Buessler, H. Kihl, J.-P. Urban "TEM Images of membranes: A multiresolution edge-detection approach for watershed segmentation", in Physics in Signal and Image Processing (PSIP), 2007
3. L. Vincent and P. Soille, "Watersheds in digital spaces: an efficient algorithm based on immersion simulations", IEEE Transactions on Pattern Analysis and Machine Intelligence, vol. 13, pp. 583-598, 1991
4. Karathanou, J.-L. Buessler, H. Kihl, and J.-P. Urban, "Detection of low contrasted membranes in electron microscope images: statistical contour validation", Digital Imaging Sensors and Applications, Imaging Science and Technology/SPIE, 21st Annual Symposium on Electronic Imaging, 2009.
5. Kostas Haris, Serafim N. Efstratiadis, Nicos Maglaveras and Aggelos K. Katsaggelos, "Hybrid image segmentation using watersheds and fast region merging", IEEE Transactions on Image Processing, vol. 7, pp. 1684-1699, 1998
6. Lifeng Liu and Stan Sclaro, "Shape-Guided Split and Merge of Image Regions", 4th International Workshop on Visual Form, vol. 2059, pp. 367-377, 2001
7. Theo Pavlidis and Yuh-Tay Liow, "Integrating region growing and edge detection", IEEE Transactions on Pattern Analysis and Machine Intelligence, vol. 12, pp. 225-233, 1990

8. Utpal Garain, Thierry Paquet, Laurent Heutte, "On foreground – background separation in low quality document images", International Journal on Document Analysis and Recognition, vol. 8, pp. 47-63, 2006
9. Yi Lu and Hong Guo, "Background Removal in Image indexing and Retrieval", 10th International Conference on Image Analysis and Processing, pp. 933, 1999
10. Nicolas Coudray, Jean-Luc Buessler, Hubert Kihl, Jean-Philippe Urban, "Automated image analysis for electron microscopy specimen assessment", 15th EUropean SIgnal Processing COnference (EUSIPCO), pp. 120–124, 2007

8. Utpal Garain, Thierry Paquet, Laurent Heutte: "On foreground - background separation in low quality document images", International Journal on Document Analysis and Recognition, vol.8, pp. 47-63, 2006.
9. Yi Lu and Hong Guo: "Background Removal in Image indexing and Retrieval", 10th International Conference on Image Analysis and Processing, pp. [illegible], 1999.
10. Nicolas Coudray, Jean-Luc Buessler, Hubert Kihl, Jean-Philippe Urban: "Automated image analysis for electron microscopy specimen assessment", 15th European Signal Processing Conference (EUSIPCO), pp. [illegible], 2007.

Confidence Predictions for the Diagnosis of Acute Abdominal Pain

Harris Papadopoulos, Alex Gammerman and Volodya Vovk

Abstract Most current machine learning systems for medical decision support do not produce any indication of how reliable each of their predictions is. However, an indication of this kind is highly desirable especially in the medical field. This paper deals with this problem by applying a recently developed technique for assigning confidence measures to predictions, called *conformal prediction*, to the problem of acute abdominal pain diagnosis. The data used consist of a large number of hospital records of patients who suffered acute abdominal pain. Each record is described by 33 symptoms and is assigned to one of nine diagnostic groups. The proposed method is based on Neural Networks and for each patient it can produce either the most likely diagnosis together with an associated confidence measure, or the set of all possible diagnoses needed to satisfy a given level of confidence.

1 Introduction

Machine learning techniques have been applied successfully to many medical decision support problems [7, 8] and many good results have been achieved. The resulting systems learn to predict the diagnosis of a new patient based on past history of patients with known diagnoses. Most such systems produce as their prediction only the most likely diagnosis of the new patient, without giving any confidence

Harris Papadopoulos
Computer Science and Engineering Department, Frederick University, 7 Y. Frederickou St., Palouriotisa, Nicosia 1036, Cyprus. e-mail: H.Papadopoulos@frederick.ac.cy

Alex Gammerman
Department of Computer Science, Royal Holloway, University of London, Egham Hill, Egham, Surrey TW20 0EX, England. e-mail: Alex@cs.rhul.ac.uk

Volodya Vovk
Department of Computer Science, Royal Holloway, University of London, Egham Hill, Egham, Surrey TW20 0EX, England. e-mail: Vovk@cs.rhul.ac.uk

Please use the following format when citing this chapter:

Papadopoulos, H., Gammerman, A. and Vovk, V., 2009, in IFIP International Federation for Information Processing, Volume 296; *Artificial Intelligence Applications and Innovations III*; Eds. Iliadis, L., Vlahavas, I., Bramer, M.; (Boston: Springer), pp. 175–184.

information in this prediction. This is a major disadvantage, as measures of confidence are of paramount importance in a medical setting [6]. Confidence measures are an indication of how likely each prediction is of being correct. In the ideal case, a confidence of 99% or higher for all examples in a set, means that the percentage of erroneous predictions in that set will not exceed 1%; when this is true we say that the confidence measures are well calibrated.

Conformal prediction (CP) [24] is a recently developed technique, which can be used for obtaining confidence measures. Conformal predictors are built on top of traditional machine learning algorithms, called *underlying algorithms*, and complement the predictions of these algorithms with measures of confidence. Different variants of CPs are described in [11, 15, 16, 17, 18, 21, 22, 23]. The results reported in these papers show that not only the confidence values output by CPs are useful in practice, but also their accuracy is comparable to, and sometimes even better than, that of traditional machine learning algorithms.

Of course other approaches that can be used for deriving some kind of confidence information do exist. One can apply the theory of Probably Approximately Correct learning (PAC theory) to an algorithm in order to obtain upper bounds on the probability of its error with respect to some confidence level. These bounds though, are usually very week [12] and as a result not very useful in practice. Another alternative is the use of Bayesian methods which can give strong confidence bounds. Bayesian methods however, require some a priori assumptions about the distribution generating the data and if these are violated their outputs can become quite misleading [10].

In this paper we apply CP to the problem of acute abdominal pain diagnosis. This is a relatively popular problem in medical decision support, see e.g. [2, 3, 5, 9, 13, 20, 25], due to the poor discrimination between the diseases that cause acute abdominal pain, which results in high diagnostic error rates [25]. Wrong diagnoses may result in unnecessary emergency abdominal operations, or in complications, such as perforation of the appendix.

The CP we use is based on Neural Networks (NNs). NNs have not only been successfully applied to many medical problems [1, 4, 8, 19], but they are also one of the most popular machine learning techniques for almost any type of application. In order to use NNs as the underlying algorithm of a CP, we follow a modified version of the original CP approach called Inductive Conformal Prediction (ICP) [14]. ICP is based on the same general idea as CP but, as its name suggests, it replaces the transductive inference used in the original approach with inductive inference. ICP was first proposed in [16, 17] in an effort to overcome the computational inefficiency problem of CPs. As demonstrated in [18] this computational inefficiency problem renders the original CP approach highly unsuitable for use with NNs; and in extend any other method that requires long training times.

The rest of this paper is structured as follows. In section 2 we summarise the general idea behind CP and its inductive version ICP, while in section 3 we detail the Neural Network ICP method. Section 4 gives an analysis of the data used in this study and section 5 describes our experiments and lists and discusses their results. Finally, section 6 gives our conclusions and the future directions of this work.

2 Conformal Prediction

In this section we give a brief description of the idea behind CP, for more details see [24]. We are given a training set $\{z_1,\ldots,z_l\}$ of examples, where each $z_i \in Z$ is a pair (x_i,y_i); $x_i \in \mathbb{R}^d$ is the vector of attributes for example i and $y_i \in \{Y_1,\ldots,Y_c\}$ is the classification of that example. We are also given a new unclassified example x_{l+1} and our task is to state something about our confidence in each possible classification of x_{l+1}.

CP is based on measuring how likely it is for each extended set of examples

$$\{(x_1,y_1),\ldots,(x_l,y_l),(x_{l+1},Y_j)\} : j = 1,\ldots,c, \tag{1}$$

to have been generated independently from the same probability distribution. First we measure how strange, or non-conforming, each example in (1) is for the rest of the examples in the same set. We use what is called a *non-conformity measure* which is based on a traditional machine learning algorithm, called the *underlying algorithm* of the CP. This measure assigns a numerical score α_i to each example (x_i,y_i) indicating how different it is from all other examples in (1). In effect we train the underlying algorithm using (1) as training set and we measure the degree of disagreement between its prediction for x_i and the actual label y_i; in the case of x_{l+1} we use the assumed label Y_j in the place of y_{l+1}.

The non-conformity score $\alpha_{l+1}^{(Y_j)}$ of (x_{l+1},Y_j) on its own does not really give us any information, it is just a numeric value. However, we can find out how unusual (x_{l+1},Y_j) is according to our non-conformity measure by comparing $\alpha_{l+1}^{(Y_j)}$ with all other non-conformity scores. This comparison can be performed with the function

$$p((x_1,y_1),\ldots,(x_l,y_l),(x_{l+1},Y_j)) = \frac{\#\{i = 1,\ldots,l+1 : \alpha_i \geq \alpha_{l+1}^{(Y_j)}\}}{l+1}. \tag{2}$$

We call the output of this function, which lies between $\frac{1}{l+1}$ and 1, the p-value of Y_j, also denoted as $p(Y_j)$, as that is the only part of (1) we were not given. An important property of (2) is that $\forall\delta \in [0,1]$ and for all probability distributions P on Z,

$$P^{l+1}\{((x_1,y_1),\ldots,(x_{l+1},y_{l+1})) : p(y_{l+1}) \leq \delta\} \leq \delta; \tag{3}$$

for a proof see [12]. As a result, if the p-value of a given label is under some very low threshold, say 0.05, this would mean that this label is highly unlikely as such sequences will only be generated at most 5% of the time by any i.i.d. process.

After calculating the p-value of every possible label Y_j, as described above, we are able to exclude all labels that have a p-value under some very low threshold (or *significance level*) δ and have at most δ chance of being wrong. Consequently, given a confidence level $1-\delta$ a CP outputs the set

$$\{Y_j : p(Y_j) > \delta\}. \tag{4}$$

Alternatively the CP can predict the most likely classification together with a confidence and a credibility measure in this prediction. In this case it predicts the classification with the largest p-value, outputs one minus the second largest p-value as confidence to this prediction and as credibility it outputs the p-value of the predicted classification, i.e. the largest p-value.

2.1 Inductive Conformal Prediction

The original CP technique requires training the underlying algorithm once for each possible classification of every new test example. This means that if our problem has 9 possible classifications and we have to classify 2000 test examples, as is the case in this study, the training process will be repeated $9 \times 2000 = 18000$ times. This makes it very computationally inefficient especially for algorithms that require long training times such as Neural Networks.

Inductive Conformal Predictors (ICPs) are based on the same general idea described above, but follow a different approach which allows them to train their underlying algorithm just once. This is achieved by splitting the training set (of size l) into two smaller sets, the *proper training set* with $m < l$ examples and the *calibration set* with $q := l - m$ examples. The proper training set is used for training the underlying algorithm and only the examples in the calibration set are used for calculating the p-value of each possible classification of the new test example. More specifically, we calculate the p-value of each possible classification Y_j of x_{l+1} as

$$p(Y_j) = \frac{\#\{i = m+1, \ldots, m+q, l+1 : \alpha_i \geq \alpha_{l+1}^{(Y_j)}\}}{q+1}, \tag{5}$$

where $\alpha_{m+1}, \ldots, \alpha_{m+q}$ are the non-conformity scores of the examples in the calibration set and $\alpha_{l+1}^{(Y_j)}$ is the non-conformity score of (x_{l+1}, Y_j).

3 Neural Networks Inductive Conformal Predictor

In this section we analyse the Neural Networks ICP (NN-ICP) algorithm. We first describe the typical output encoding for Neural Networks (NNs) and then, based on this description, we define two non-conformity measures for NNs. Finally, we detail the complete NN-ICP algorithm.

3.1 Non-conformity Measures

Typically the output layer of a classification NN consists of c units, each representing one of the c possible classifications of the problem at hand; thus each label is encoded into c target outputs. To explicitly describe this encoding consider the label, $y_i = Y_u$ of a training example i, where $Y_u \in \{Y_1, \ldots, Y_c\}$. The resulting target outputs for y_i will be

$$t^i_1, \ldots, t^i_c,$$

where

$$t^i_j = \begin{cases} 1, \text{ if } j = u, \\ 0, \text{ otherwise,} \end{cases}$$

for $j = 1, 2, \ldots, c$. In the same manner we will denote the actual outputs of the NN for an example i as

$$o^i_1, \ldots, o^i_c.$$

According to this encoding the higher the output o^i_u (which corresponds to the example's true classification) the more conforming the example, and the higher the other outputs the less conforming the example. In fact, the most important of all other outputs is the one with the maximum value $\max_{j=1,\ldots,c: j \neq u} o^i_j$, since that is the one which might be very near or even higher than o^i_u. So a natural non-conformity measure for an example $z_i = (x_i, y_i)$ where $y_i = Y_u$ would be defined as

$$\alpha_i = \max_{j=1,\ldots,c: j \neq u} o^i_j - o^i_u, \tag{6}$$

or as

$$\alpha_i = \frac{\max_{j=1,\ldots,c: j \neq u} o^i_j}{o^i_u + \gamma}, \tag{7}$$

where the parameter $\gamma \geq 0$ in the second definition enables us to adjust the sensitivity of our measure to small changes of o^i_u depending on the data in question. We added this parameter in order to gain control over which category of outputs will be more important in determining the resulting non-conformity scores; by increasing γ one reduces the importance of o^i_u and consequently increases the importance of all other outputs.

3.2 The Algorithm

We can now use the non-conformity measure (6) or (7) to compute the non-conformity score of each example in the calibration set and each test set pair (x_{l+g}, Y_u). These can then be fed into the p-value function (5), giving us the p-value for each classification Y_u. The exact steps the Neural Networks ICP follows for a training set $\{z_1, \ldots, z_l\}$ and a test set $\{x_{l+1}, \ldots, x_{l+r}\}$ are:

- Split the training set into the *proper training set* with $m < l$ examples and the *calibration set* with $q := l - m$ examples.
- Use the proper training set to train the Neural Network.
- For each example $z_{m+t} = (x_{m+t}, y_{m+t})$, $t = 1, \ldots, q$ in the calibration set:
  - supply the input pattern x_{m+t} to the trained network to obtain the output values $o_1^{m+t}, \ldots, o_c^{m+t}$ and
  - calculate the non-conformity score α_{m+t} of the pair (x_{m+t}, y_{m+t}) by applying (6) or (7) to these values.
- For each test pattern x_{l+g}, $g = 1, \ldots, r$:
  - supply the input pattern x_{l+g} to the trained network to obtain the output values $o_1^{l+g}, \ldots, o_c^{l+g}$,
  - consider each possible classification Y_u, $u = 1, \ldots, c$ and:
    - compute the non-conformity score $\alpha_{l+g} = \alpha_{l+g}^{(Y_u)}$ of the pair (x_{l+g}, Y_u) by applying (6) or (7) to the outputs of the network,
    - calculate the p-value $p(Y_u)$ of the pair (x_{l+g}, Y_u) by applying (5) to the non-conformity scores of the calibration examples and $\alpha_{l+g}^{(Y_u)}$:

$$p(Y_u) = \frac{\#\{i = m+1, \ldots, m+q, l+g : \alpha_i \geq \alpha_{l+g}^{(Y_u)}\}}{q+1},$$

    - predict the classification with the largest p-value (in case of a tie choose the one with the smallest non-conformity score) and output one minus the second largest p-value as confidence to this prediction and the p-value of the output classification as its credibility,
    - or given a confidence level $1 - \delta$ output the prediction set (4).

4 Acute Abdominal Pain Data

The acute abdominal pain database used in this study was originally used in [5], where a more detailed description of the data can be found. The data consist of 6387 records of patients who were admitted to hospital suffering from acute abdominal pain. During the examination of each patient 33 symptoms were recorded, each of which had a number of different discrete values. For example, one of the symptoms is "Progress of Pain" which has the possible values: "Getting Better", "No Change", "Getting Worse". In total there are 135 values describing the 33 symptoms. These values compose the attribute vector for each patient in the form of 135 binary attributes that indicate the absence (0) or presence (1) of the corresponding value. It is worth to mention that there are symptoms which have more than one value or no value at all in many of the records.

There are nine diseases or diagnostic groups in which the patients were allocated according to all information after their initial examination, including the results of

Table 1 Data distribution.

	APP	DIV	PPU	NAP	CHO	INO	PAN	RCO	DYS	Total
Training Set	585	108	88	1941	372	290	65	326	612	4387
Test Set	259	35	42	894	200	127	31	147	265	2000
Total	844	143	130	2835	572	417	96	473	877	6387

surgical operations. These are: Appendicitis (APP), Diverticulitis (DIV), Perforated Peptic Ulcer (PPU), Non-specific Abdominal Pain (NAP), Cholesistitis (CHO), Intestinal Obstruction (INO), Pancreatitis (PAN), Renal Colic (RCO) and Dyspepsia (DYS). NAP is not actually a diagnostic group, it is a residual group in which all patients that did not belong to one of the other groups were placed.

The data are divided into a training set consisting of 4387 examples and a test set consisting of 2000 examples. These are the same training and test sets as in [5]. Table 1 reports the number of examples that belong to each diagnostic group.

5 Experiments and Results

The NN used in our experiments was a 2-layer fully connected feed-forward network, with sigmoid hidden units and softmax output units. It consisted of 135 input, 35 hidden and 9 output units. The number of hidden units was selected by following a cross validation scheme on the training set and trying out the values: 20, 25, 30, 35, 40, 45, 50, 55, 60. More specifically, the training set was split into five parts of almost equal size and five sets of experiments were performed, each time using one of these parts for evaluating the NNs trained on the examples in the other four parts. For each of the five test parts, a further 10-fold cross validation process was performed to divide the examples into training and validation sets, so as to use the validation examples for determining when to stop the training process. Training was performed with the backpropagation algorithm minimizing a cross-entropy loss function.

The results reported here were obtained by following a 10-fold cross validation procedure on the training set in order to divide it into training and validation examples. To create the calibration set of the ICP, 299 examples were removed from the training set before generating the 10 splits. This experiment was repeated 10 times with random permutations of the training examples. Here we report the mean values of all 100 runs.

Table 2 reports the accuracy of the NN-ICP and original NN methods and compares them to that of the Simple Bayes, Proper Bayes and CART methods as reported in [5]. Additionally it compares them to the accuracy of the preliminary diagnoses of the hospital physicians, also reported in [5]. Both the original NN and NN-ICP outperform the other three methods and are almost as accurate as the hos-

Table 2 Predictive Accuracy of NN-ICP Compared to Other Methods.

Method	Correct Diagnoses (%)
Neural Networks ICP	75.74
Original Neural Networks	75.87
Simple Bayes	74
Proper Bayes	65
Classification Tree (CART)	65
Physicians (preliminary diagnoses)	76

pital physicians. As was expected the original NN performs slightly better than the ICP due to the removal of the calibration examples from the training set, however the difference between the two is negligible. This is a very small price to pay considering the advantage of obtaining a confidence measure for each prediction.

Table 3 lists the results of the NN-ICP when producing set predictions for the 99%, 95%, 90% and 80% confidence levels. More specifically it reports the percentage of examples for which the set output by the ICP consisted of only one label, of more than one label or was empty. It also reports in the last column the percentage of errors made by the ICP, i.e. the percentage of sets that did not include the true classification of the example. The values reported here reflect the difficulty in discriminating between the 9 diseases. Nevertheless, the set predictions output by the NN-ICP can be very useful in practice since they pinpoint the cases where more attention must be given and the diagnostic groups that should be considered for each one. Bearing in mind the difficulty of the task and the 76% accuracy of the preliminary diagnoses of physicians, achieving a 95% of accuracy by considering more than one possible diagnosis for only about half the patients is arguably a good result.

Table 3 NN-ICP Set Prediction Results.

Non-conformity Measure	Confidence Level	Only one label (%)	More than one label (%)	No label (%)	Errors (%)
(6)	99%	23.76	76.24	0.00	0.95
	95%	46.62	53.38	0.00	4.10
	90%	62.38	37.62	0.00	8.59
	80%	82.22	17.78	0.00	16.94
(7)	99%	25.80	74.20	0.00	0.95
	95%	47.58	52.42	0.00	3.75
	90%	65.32	34.68	0.00	8.11
	80%	87.32	12.38	0.30	17.23

6 Conclusions and Future Work

We have presented the application of a recently developed technique, called Conformal Prediction, to the problem of acute abdominal pain diagnosis. Unlike most conventional algorithms, our approach produces confidence measures in its predictions which are provably valid under the general i.i.d. assumption. Our experiments demonstrate that the Neural Networks ICP is very successful at this very difficult task, since its predictions are almost as accurate as the preliminary diagnoses of hospital physicians and its confidence measures are well calibrated and practically useful. The set predictions produced by NN-ICP identify the cases that require more attention as well as the most likely diagnoses of these cases.

One undesirable aspect of the data used in this study is the huge difference in the number of examples that belong to each class. For this reason, in the future we plan to repeat our experiments with an artificially balanced version of the training set created by performing random resampling of the training examples. Additionally, our directions for future research include further experimentation with other datasets for acute abdominal pain and with more non-conformity measures based on other popular algorithms such as support vector machines, decision trees and evolutionary techniques.

Acknowledgements This work was supported by the Cyprus Research Promotion Foundation through research contract PLHRO/0506/22 ("Development of New Conformal Prediction Methods with Applications in Medical Diagnosis").

References

1. Anagnostou, T., Remzi, M., Djavan, B.: Artificial neural networks for decision-making in urologic oncology. Review in Urology **5**(1), 15–21 (2003)
2. Anastassopoulos, G.C., Iliadis, L.S.: Ann for prognosis of abdominal pain in childhood: Use of fuzzy modelling for convergence estimation. In: Proceedings 1st International Workshop on Combinations of Intelligent Methods and Applications, pp. 1–5 (2008)
3. Blazadonakis, M., Moustakis, V., Charissis, G.: Deep assessment of machine learning techniques using patient treatment in acute abdominal pain in children. Artificial Intelligence in Medicine **8**(6), 527–542 (1996)
4. Christoyianni, I., Koutras, A., Dermatas, E., Kokkinakis, G.: Computer aided diagnosis of breast cancer in digitized mammograms. Computerized Medical Imaging and Graphics **26**(5), 309–319 (2002)
5. Gammerman, A., Thatcher, A.: Bayesian diagnostic probabilities without assuming independence of symptoms. Methods of Information in Medicine **30**(1), 15–22 (1991)
6. Holst, H., Ohlsson, M., Peterson, C., Edenbrandt, L.: Intelligent computer reporting 'lack of experience': a confidence measure for decision support systems. Clinical Physiology **18**(2), 139–147 (1998)
7. Kononenko, I.: Machine learning for medical diagnosis: History, state of the art and perspective. Artificial Intelligence in Medicine **23**(1), 89–109 (2001)
8. Lisboa, P.: A review of evidence of health benefit from artificial neural networks in medical intervention. Neural Networks **15**(1), 11–39 (2002)

9. Mantzaris, D., Anastassopoulos, G., Adamopoulos, A., Gardikis, S.: A non-symbolic implementation of abdominal pain estimation in childhood. Information Sciences **178**(20), 3860–3866 (2008)
10. Melluish, T., Saunders, C., Nouretdinov, I., Vovk, V.: Comparing the Bayes and Typicalness frameworks. In: Proceedings 12th European Conference on Machine Learning (ECML'01), *Lecture Notes in Computer Science*, vol. 2167, pp. 360–371. Springer (2001)
11. Nouretdinov, I., Melluish, T., Vovk, V.: Ridge regression confidence machine. In: Proceedings 18th International Conference on Machine Learning (ICML'01), pp. 385–392. Morgan Kaufmann, San Francisco, CA (2001)
12. Nouretdinov, I., Vovk, V., Vyugin, M.V., Gammerman, A.: Pattern recognition and density estimation under the general i.i.d. assumption. In: Proceedings 14th Annual Conference on Computational Learning Theory and 5th European Conference on Computational Learning Theory, *Lecture Notes in Computer Science*, vol. 2111, pp. 337–353. Springer (2001)
13. Ohmann, C., Moustakis, V., Yang, Q., Lang, K.: Evaluation of automatic knowledge acquisition techniques in the diagnosis of acute abdominal pain. Artificial Intelligence in Medicine **8**(1), 23–36 (1996)
14. Papadopoulos, H.: Tools in Artificial Intelligence, chap. 18. Inductive Conformal Prediction: Theory and Application to Neural Networks, pp. 315–330. I-Tech, Vienna, Austria (2008). URL http://intechweb.org/downloadpdf.php?id=5294
15. Papadopoulos, H., Gammerman, A., Vovk, V.: Normalized nonconformity measures for regression conformal prediction. In: Proceedings IASTED International Conference on Artificial Intelligence and Applications (AIA 2008), pp. 64–69. ACTA Press (2008)
16. Papadopoulos, H., Proedrou, K., Vovk, V., Gammerman, A.: Inductive confidence machines for regression. In: Proceedings 13th European Conference on Machine Learning (ECML'02), *Lecture Notes in Computer Science*, vol. 2430, pp. 345–356. Springer (2002)
17. Papadopoulos, H., Vovk, V., Gammerman, A.: Qualified predictions for large data sets in the case of pattern recognition. In: Proceedings 2002 International Conference on Machine Learning and Applications (ICMLA'02), pp. 159–163. CSREA Press (2002)
18. Papadopoulos, H., Vovk, V., Gammerman, A.: Conformal prediction with neural networks. In: Proceedings 19th IEEE International Conference on Tools with Artificial Intelligence (ICTAI'07), vol. 2, pp. 388–395. IEEE Computer Society (2007)
19. Pattichis, C., Christodoulou, C., Kyriacou, E., Pattichis, M.: Artificial neural networks in medical imaging systems. In: Proceedings 1st MEDINF International Conference on Medical Informatics and Engineering, pp. 83–91 (2003)
20. Pesonen, E., Eskelinen, M., Juhola, M.: Comparison of different neural network algorithms in the diagnosis of acute appendicitis. International Journal of Bio-Medical Computing **40**(3), 227–233 (1996)
21. Proedrou, K., Nouretdinov, I., Vovk, V., Gammerman, A.: Transductive confidence machines for pattern recognition. In: Proceedings of the 13th European Conference on Machine Learning (ECML'02), *Lecture Notes in Computer Science*, vol. 2430, pp. 381–390. Springer (2002)
22. Saunders, C., Gammerman, A., Vovk, V.: Transduction with confidence and credibility. In: Proceedings of the 16th International Joint Conference on Artificial Intelligence, vol. 2, pp. 722–726. Morgan Kaufmann, Los Altos, CA (1999)
23. Saunders, C., Gammerman, A., Vovk, V.: Computationally efficient transductive machines. In: Proceedings of the Eleventh International Conference on Algorithmic Learning Theory (ALT'00), *Lecture Notes in Artificial Intelligence*, vol. 1968, pp. 325–333. Springer, Berlin (2000)
24. Vovk, V., Gammerman, A., Shafer, G.: Algorithmic Learning in a Random World. Springer, New York (2005)
25. Zorman, M., Eich, H.P., Kokol, P., Ohmann, C.: Comparison of three databases with a decision tree approach in the medical field of acute appendicitis. Studies in Health Technology and Informatics **84**(2), 1414–1418 (2001)

Enhanced Human Body Fall Detection Utilizing Advanced Classification of Video and Motion Perceptual Components

Charalampos Doukas[1], Ilias Maglogiannis[2], Nikos Katsarakis[3], Aristodimos Pneumatikakis[3]

1University of the Aegean

2University of Central Greece

3Athens Information Technology

Abstract The monitoring of human physiological data, in both normal and abnormal situations of activity, is interesting for the purpose of emergency event detection, especially in the case of elderly people living on their own. Several techniques have been proposed for identifying such distress situations using either motion, audio or video data from the monitored subject and the surrounding environment. This paper aims to present an integrated patient fall detection platform that may be used for patient activity recognition and emergency treatment. Both visual data captured from the user's environment and motion data collected from the subject's body are utilized. Visual information is acquired using overhead cameras, while motion data is collected from on-body sensors. Appropriate tracking techniques are applied to the aforementioned visual perceptual component enabling the trajectory tracking of the subjects. Acceleration data from the sensors can indicate a fall incident. Trajectory information and subject's visual location can verify fall and indicate an emergency event. Support Vector Machines (SVM) classification methodology has been evaluated using the latter acceleration and visual trajectory data. The performance of the classifier has been assessed in terms of accuracy and efficiency and results are presented.

1 Introduction

The telemonitoring of human physiological data, in both normal and abnormal situations of activity, is interesting for the purpose of emergency event detection or long term data-storage for later diagnosis or for the purpose of medical exploration. In the case of elderly people living on their own, there is a particular need for monitoring their behavior. The goal of this surveillance is the detection of major

---

Please use the following format when citing this chapter:

Doukas, C., Maglogiannis, I., Katsarakis, N. and Pneumatikakis, A., 2009, in IFIP International Federation for Information Processing, Volume 296; *Artificial Intelligence Applications and Innovations III*; Eds. Iliadis, L., Vlahavas, I., Bramer, M.; (Boston: Springer), pp. 185–193.

incidents such as a fall, or a long period of inactivity in a part of their area. Several techniques have been proposed for identifying such distress situations using either motion, audio or video data from the monitored subject and the surrounding environment. This paper presents a human body fall detection platform based both motion and visual perceptual components. A number of on-body sensors collect the movement data and transmit them wirelessly to the monitoring unit, while overhead cameras track the trajectory and shape of the body and provide information regarding the patient's position and activity. Appropriate classification of the motion data can give an indication of a fall. Combining the latter with unusual change of body' shape followed by inactivity, an alarm can be triggered and more information regarding the severity of the incident can be obtained; in case patient remains still after the fall or moves but the body is detected on the ground then the patient requires immediate assistance.

The rest of the paper is organized as follows; Section 2 discusses related work in the context of patient activity and fall detection. Section 3 describes the proposed system architecture and Sections 4 and 5 describe the acquisition of the patient movement and visual data using sensors and overhead cameras respectively. Section 6 presents the data classification using Support Vector Machines and corresponding evaluation results and finally Section 7 concludes the paper.

2 Related Work

Although the concept of patient activity recognition with focus on fall detection is relatively new, there exists related research work, which may be retrieved from the literature ([1]-[9]). Information regarding the patient movement and activity is frequently acquired through visual tracking of the patient's position. In [5] overhead tracking through cameras provides the movement trajectory of the patient and gives information about user activity on predetermined monitored areas. Unusual inactivity (e.g., continuous tracking of the patient on the floor) is interpreted as a fall. Similarly, in 8 omni-camera images are used to determine the horizontal placement of the patient's silhouettes on the floor (case of fall). Success rate for fall detection is declared at 81% for the latter work. A different approach for collecting patient activity information is the use of sensors that integrate devices like accelerometers, gyroscopes and contact sensors. The latter approach is less depended on the patient and environmental information and can be used for a variety of applications for user activity recognition ([1], [3], [7]). Regarding fall detection, authors in [2], [6], [9] use accelerometers, gyroscopes and tilt sensors for movement tracking. Collected data from the accelerometers (i.e., usually rotation angle or acceleration in the X, Y and Z axis) is used to verify the placement of the patient and time occupation in rooms and detect abrupt movement that could be associated with fall. Detection is performed using predefined thresholds [1], [3], [4], [6] and association between current position, movement and acceleration [2], [9]. To our best knowledge there is no work in the literature that combines both visual and sensor information for a more complete and robust estimation of a patient's fall and can provide some information regarding the severity of the incident (e.g. patient has gotten up right after the fall, patient is inactive, etc.).

3 System Architecture Overview

The presented system follows the architecture illustrated in Fig. 1. Accelerometers data are collected through the sensor attached on the user's chest and belt and are transmitted wirelessly to the monitoring node. Transmission of data is performed through J2ME sockets following the client-server architecture. The monitoring unit acting as movement data receiver serves as the server whereas each node is the client.

At the same time, camera devices record video frames from the user's site and provide feed to the video tracker. The latter tracks the movement of the patient's body and generates body shape features (i.e. coordinates of a bounding box containing the subject's body). The data are properly transformed in a suitable format for the classifier and the classification phase begins. Based on a predefined classification model (i.e. train model), the patient status is detected (i.e. emergency status when fall detected, normal status otherwise).

Apart from the indication of a fall incident, an estimation of the severity of the incident can be provided based on the patient's behavior after the fall as recorded visually; movement indicated by accelerometers but visual inactivity or soft activity suggests that patient has not lost consciousness and is trying to recover from the fall, both sensor and normal visual activity can indicate that patient has recovered from fall, and no activity at all can indicate higher severity of the incident.

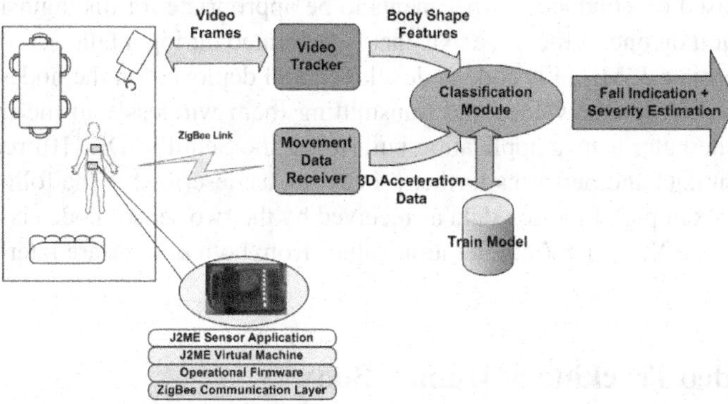

Fig. 1. Platform Architecture and Data interaction between the movement capturing tools and monitoring node.

4 Patient Movement Data Acquisition

This section provides information on the acquisition and pre-processing of the patient movement data. The Sentilla Perk [10] sensor kit has been utilized in our system. The latter contains two 2.4 GHz wireless data transceivers (nodes, see Fig. 2) using the IEEE 802.15.4 (ZigBee) protocol. It also includes a USB port for interface with a personal computer acting as the monitoring unit. Each node has a low-power, low-voltage MCU (MicroController Unit), one 3D Accelerometer for X, Y and Z axis and additional analog and digital input pins for adding more sensors. The Perk nodes are provided in a plastic robust small-sized enclosure (6x3x1.5cm) making them more suitable for placing on patient's body and tolerating falls.

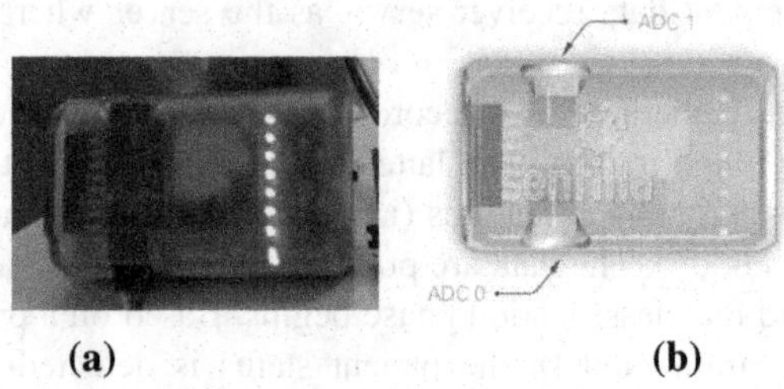

Fig. 2. The Sentilla Perk node containing a 3D accelerometer that can be attached on user and send motion data through the ZigBee wireless protocol. The plastic enclosure can protect the node from falls and makes it more suitable for carrying it on patient's body. A) Actual photo of the node, b) illustration indicating two analog-to-digital converter ports for the addition of alternative sensors.

Two Perk nodes can be placed on patient's body. Preferable positions are close to user's chest and user's belt or lower at user's foot. The latter positions have proven based on conducted experiments to be appropriate for distinguishing rapid acceleration on one of the three axis that is generated during a fall.

Appropriate J2ME [17] code is developed and deployed on the nodes for reading the accelerometer values and transmitting them wirelessly to the monitoring unit. At the latter a Java application built using the Sentilla IDE [10] receives the movement data and performs further processing as described in the following sections. An example of motion data as received by the two sensor nodes is illustrated in Fig. 3. The X, Y and Z acceleration values from both sensors are interlaced.

5 Video Tracking of Human Body

The goal of the developed body video tracker is to provide across time the frame regions occupied by human bodies. The tracker is built around a dynamic foreground segmentation algorithm [12] that utilizes adaptive background modeling. This is based on Stauffer's algorithm [13] to provide the foreground pixels.

Stauffer's algorithm models the different colors every pixel can receive in a video sequence by Gaussian Mixture Models (GMM). One GMM corresponds to every pixel at given coordinates across time. The Gaussians are three-dimensional, corresponding to the red, green and blue components of the pixel color. Their weight is proportional to the time a particular Gaussian models best the color of the pixel. Hence the weight of a given Gaussian is increased as long as the color of the pixel can be described by that Gaussian with higher probability than any other Gaussian in the GMM can, and that probability is above a threshold. As a result, a map can be built in which every pixel is represented by the weight of the Gaussian from its GMM that best describes its current color. This is the Pixel Persistence Map (PPM): Regions of the map with large values correspond to pixels that have colors that appear there for a long time, hence they belong to background. On the contrary, regions with small values correspond to pixels that have colors that appear there for a short time, hence they are foreground. This is true as long as the foreground objects have distinct colors from the background.

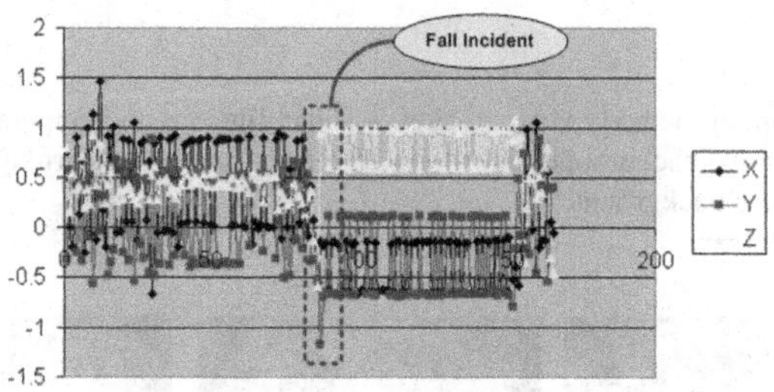

Fig. 3. Illustration of interlaced from both sensors acceleration data in X, Y and Z axis. The Y axis represents the acceleration value (range between -2 and 2) and the X axis the number of samples acquired.

The problem of Stauffer's algorithm is with foreground objects that stop moving. In its original implementation, targets/objects that stop moving are learnt into the background. This happens as the weights of the Gaussians of the GMM of pixels describing the foreground colors and corresponding to immobile foreground objects increase with time. To avoid this, the learning rates of the adaptation that increase the weights of Gaussians are not constant, neither across space, nor across time. Instead, they are spatiotemporally controlled by the states of Kalman filters [11]. Every foreground area corresponds to a target being tracked by a Kalman filter. The foreground pixels are combined into body evidence blobs, used for the measurement update stage of the Kalman filters. The states are used to obtain the position, size and mobility of each target, the latter being a combination of translation and size change. This information is fed back to the adaptive background modeling module to adapt the learning rate in the vicinity of each target: frame regions that at a specific time have a slow-moving target have smaller learning rates. The block diagram of the body tracker is shown in Fig. 4.

With the feedback configuration of the tracker, the learning of the slow moving foreground objects into the background is slowed down long enough for the intended application, i.e. tracking people moving indoors and possibly falling down. The tracker results when applied on the visual feed by an overhead camera are illustrated in Fig. 5.

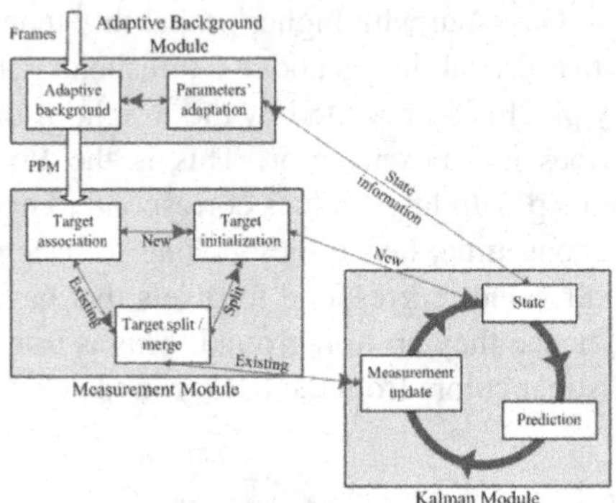

Fig. 4. Block diagram of the body video tracker. Kalman filters spatiotemporally adapt the learning rates of the adaptive background algorithm, effectively avoiding learning of immobile foreground objects into the background.

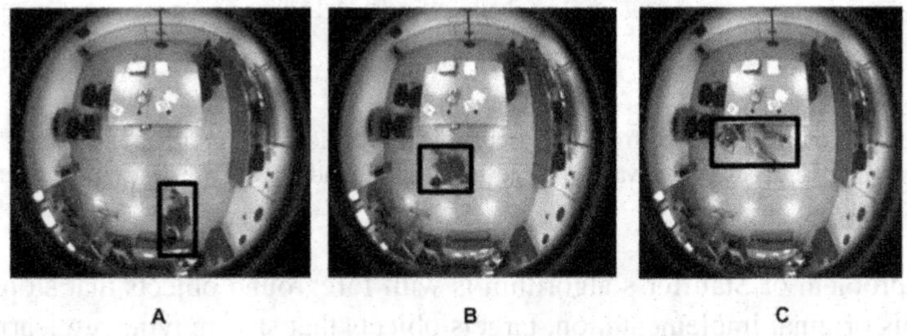

Fig. 5. Visualization of video tracking performance. The tracker detects the movement of the body and correlates it with the movement of a rectangular blob within the visual domain. Upper left X, Y coordinates and respective width and height of the blob are reported for each visual frame. Frame A corresponds to normal walking, Frame B to captured movement during fall and Frame C illustrates detection of body in horizontal position after fall.

Tracking through overhead cameras has been selected due to the fact that it provides a better visual representation of the monitored area and allows the tracker to gain a better estimation of the body shape when subject moves, falls and lays still after fall. The presented tracker creates and tracks a rectangular blob around the detection of the moving body within the frames and reports the upper left corner coordinates and respective width and height of the blog. As indicated in Fig. 5 the size of the blob changes during the fall and after it.

6 The System in Practice: Classification of Motion and Visual Perceptual Components

This Section provides information regarding the classification method used and reports the accuracy of the system in the detection of a patient fall. According to our previous research [14], [15] the SVM (Support Vector Machines) classification method has been proved to obtain high accuracy in the detection of fall incidents based on movement data. More particularly accuracy rates for the distinction of fall against other movement types can reach 98.2%. In previous experiments the train model has been built using only acceleration data whereas in the proposed system the train model contains also visual information as described in Section 5. The WEKA tool [16] has also been used for the development and evaluation the SVM model. Classification data are provided in the following form:

$$Fall\_ID\ X\ \ Y\ \ Z\ \ BBx\ \ BBy\ \ BB_{Width}\ \ BB_{Height}$$

where X, Y and Z are the acceleration data as retrieved from the sensors, BBx and BBy are the upper left coordinates of the bounding box that tracks patient's body and BBwidth and BBheight the width and height of the bounding box respectively. Fall_ID represents the case of fall incident (true or false).

To evaluate the efficiency and accuracy of the presented platform in the context of detecting patient falls, a number of experiments were conducted; a volunteer wearing the sensors devices described in Section 4 was recorded walking and falling in different locations and ways while an overhead camera was capturing visual frames. Motion data and body shape features are utilized for creating classification models. The 10-cross fold validation methodology has been used to verify each model's accuracy and performance.

Apart from the detection of fall the system is also capable of estimating the severity of the incident: When an estimation of a fall has occurred based on the sensor and visual data the standard deviation of accelerometer values and visual bounding box values is calculated for the next 15 seconds. A specific threshold has been determined for each value that can determine the severity of the incident according to the following table:

Table 1. Decision matrix for the severity of a fall incident based on standard deviations of movement data and body bounding box coordinates after a fall has occurred.

Motion STD	Bounding Box (X,Y) STD	Severity
>0.5	> 60	Low. Patient has recovered from fall (gotten up)
>0.5	<60	Medium. Patient is moving but cannot fully recover from fall
<0.5	<60	High. No activity is recorded; patient has probably felt unconscious

Table 2. Accuracy evaluation results of the proposed System. Motion and video tracking data of four fall experiments have been used. Percentage of correctly classified results, Root Mean Squared Error and correctly classified severity of the fall are presented.

Experiment	Correctly Classified Fall (%)	Root Mean Squared Error	Interlaced Motion Data	Correctly Classified Severity
FallA	99.2	0.0112	Yes	Yes
FallB	100.0	0.0072	Yes	Yes
FallC	99.4	0.0082	Yes	Yes
FallD	98.7	0.0121	Yes	Yes
FallA	97.3	0.0242	No	Yes
FallB	98.4	0.0173	No	Yes
FallC	97.1	0.0449	No	Yes
FallD	96.9	0.0534	No	Yes

According to the evaluation results as presented in Table 2, the SVM seem to achieve high accuracy rates in all cases. When the motion data from both on-body sensors are interlaced accuracy proves to be higher than otherwise. Finally, the severity of each fall incident is correctly estimated in all cases based on the motion and video track data after the fall.

7 Conclusions

In this paper an enhanced patient fall detection system has been proposed that combines both motion and visual information. Accelerometer data obtained through wireless sensors in conjunction to body shape features acquired by visual tracking are evaluated through a SVM train model. A detection of a fall incident is then generated. In addition, combining the motion data and movement of the body obtained visually after the fall, the severity of the fall can also be estimated alerting treatment personnel appropriately.

References

1. Noury N., Herve T., Rialle V., Virone G., Mercier E., Morey G., Moro A., Porcheron T., "Monitoring behavior in home using a smart fall sensor and position sensors", In Proc. 1st Annual International Conference on Microtechnologies in Medicine and Biology, pp. 607-610, Oct. 2000.
2. Noury N., "A smart sensor for the remote follow up of activity and fall detection of the elderly", In Proc. 2nd Annual International Conference on Microtechnologies in Medicine and Biology, pp. 314-317, May 2002.
3. Prado M., Reina-Tosina J., Roa L., "Distributed intelligent architecture for falling detection and physical activity analysis in the elderly", In Proc. 24th Annual IEEE EMBS Conference, pp. 1910-1911, Oct. 2002.

4. Fukaya K., "Fall detection sensor for fall protection airbag", In Proc. 41st SICE Annual Conference, pp. 419-420, Aug. 2002.
5. Nait-Charif, H. McKenna, S.J., "Activity summarisation and fall detection in a supportive home environment", In Proc. 17th International Conference on Pattern Recognition ICPR 2004, pp. 323-236, Aug. 2004.
6. Hwang, J.Y. Kang, J.M. Jang, Y.W. Kim, H.C., "Development of novel algorithm and real-time monitoring ambulatory system using Bluetooth module for fall detection in the elderly", In Proc. 26th Annual International Conference of the IEEE Engineering in Medicine and Biology Society, pp. 2204-2207, 2004.
7. Shuangquan Wang, Jie Yang, Ningjiang Chen, Xin Chen, Qinfeng Zhang, "Human activity recognition with user-free accelerometers in the sensor networks", In Proc. International Conference on Neural Networks and Brain, pp. 1212-1217, Oct. 2005.
8. S.-G. Miaou, Pei-Hsu Sung, Chia-Yuan Huang, "A Customized Human Fall Detection System Using Omni-Camera Images and Personal Information", In Proc. 1st Transdisciplinary Conference on Distributed Diagnosis and Home Healthcare, pp.39-42, 2006.
9. Allen, F.R. Ambikairajah, E. Lovell, N.H. Celler, B.G., "An Adapted Gaussian Mixture Model Approach to Accelerometry-Based Movement Classification Using Time-Domain Features", In Proc. 28th Annual International Conference of the IEEE Engineering in Medicine and Biology Society, pp. 3600-3603, Aug. 2006.
10. The Sentilla Perk Pervasive Computing Kit, http://www.sentilla.com/perk.html
11. R. E. Kalman, "A New Approach to Linear Filtering and Prediction Problems", Transactions of the ASME – Journal of Basic Engineering, Vol.82, Series D, pp.35-45, 1960.
12. Pnevmatikakis and L. Polymenakos, "Robust Estimation of Background for Fixed Cameras," International Conference on Computing (CIC2006), Mexico City, Mexico, 2006.
13. Stauffer and W. E. L. Grimson, "Learning patterns of activity using real-time tracking," IEEE Transactions on Pattern Analysis and Machine Intelligence, Vol. 22, No. 8, pp. 747-757, 2000.
14. Charalampos Doukas, Ilias Maglogiannis, Philippos Tragkas, Dimitris Liapis, Gregory Yovanof, "Patient Fall Detection using Support Vector Machines", In Proc. 4th IFIP Conference on Artificial Intelligence Applications & Innovations (AIAI), Sept. 19-21, Athens, Greece.
15. Charalampos Doukas, Ilias Maglogiannis, "Advanced Patient or Elder Fall Detection based on Movement and Sound Data", presented at 2nd International Conference on Pervasive Computing Technologies for Healthcare 2008.
16. Ian H. Witten and Eibe Frank (2005) "Data Mining: Practical machine learning tools and techniques", 2nd Edition, Morgan Kaufmann, San Francisco, 2005.
17. The JAVA ME Platform, http://java.sun.com/javame/index.jspf

An Evolutionary Technique for Medical Diagnostic Risk Factors Selection

Dimitrios Mantzaris[1], **George Anastassopoulos**[1, 2], **Lazaros Iliadis**[2, 3], **Adam Adamopoulos**[2, 4]

[1] Medical Informatics Laboratory, Democritus University of Thrace, GR-68100, Alexandroupolis, Hellas

dmantzar@med.duth.gr anasta@med.duth.gr

[2] Hellenic Open University, GR-26222, Patras, Greece

[3] Department of Forestry & Management of the Environment and Natural Resources, Democritus University of Thrace, GR-68200, Orestiada, Hellas

liliadis@fmenr.duth.gr

[4] Medical Physics Laboratory, Democritus University of Thrace, GR-68100, Alexandroupolis, Hellas

adam@med.duth.gr

Abstract This study proposes an Artificial Neural Network (ANN) and Genetic Algorithm model for diagnostic risk factors selection in medicine. A medical disease prediction may be viewed as a pattern classification problem based on a set of clinical and laboratory parameters. Probabilistic Neural Networks (PNNs) were used to face a medical disease prediction. Genetic Algorithm (GA) was used for pruning the PNN. The implemented GA searched for optimal subset of factors that fed the PNN to minimize the number of neurons in the ANN input layer and the Mean Square Error (MSE) of the trained ANN at the testing phase. Moreover, the available data was processed with Receiver Operating Characteristic (ROC) analysis to assess the contribution of each factor to medical diagnosis prediction. The obtained results of the proposed model are in accordance with the ROC analysis, so a number of diagnostic factors in patient's record can be omitted, without any loss in clinical assessment validity.

1 Introduction

Artificial Intelligence (AI) engineering is a relatively modern scientific field and has been reinforced by computer technology advancement. Artificial Neural Net-

Please use the following format when citing this chapter:

Mantzaris, D., Anastassopoulos, G., Iliadis, L. and Adamopoulos, A., 2009, in IFIP International Federation for Information Processing, Volume 296; *Artificial Intelligence Applications and Innovations III*; Eds. Iliadis, L., Vlahavas, I., Bramer, M.; (Boston: Springer), pp. 195–203.

works (ANNs), Genetic Algorithms (GAs) and Fuzzy Logic are non symbolic approaches of AI.

ANNs have been proved as a powerful tool for solving a variety of problems [1, 2] The problems' categories, where ANNs have been applied, are bioengineering [3], signal processing [4], environmental subjects [5, 6] and other fields.

While the results of medical statistic models are satisfactory, there are non-linear models that may contribute to the enhancement of medical decision support. In particular, ANNs have the ability to correlate input data to corresponding output data. Especially, ANNs have effectively contributed to disease diagnosis [7-14], like oncology [9], pediatrics [10], urology [10, 11], pediatric surgery [12], orthopedics [14], etc.

In an ANN design stage, the implementation of the best ANN architecture to solve a real-world problem is relatively complex. A neural network with few neurons implies inadequate lore, while a big one leads to poor generalization ability, presenting overfitting [15]. Early works for the investigation of appropriate ANN structure is achieved by trial and error method. However, in the last few years, more efficient methods for designing ANN architectures, automatically, have been developed.

This study presents a GA for the ANN pruning and the detection of the essential smallest input data of diagnostic factors for ANN training. The obtained ANN architecture uses diminished number of diagnostic factors and has an evolved structure, without any loss in terms of its performance and functionality ability.

The abdominal pain diagnosis except of the traditional methods (clinical, laboratory, imaging) could also be supported by numerically scoring systems, fuzzy logic techniques, etc [16]. The aim of implemented method was the detection of essential diagnostic factors for construction of PNNs to estimate the abdominal pain in childhood.

The obtained results were compared with the Receiver Operating Characteristic (ROC) analysis outcome. There was a high level of convergence between the two methods and some of the diagnostic factors have proven to be essential for clinical evaluation and prognosis, whereas, some other factors could be excluded during clinical estimation, without any loss in ANNs' prognosis accuracy. From a technical point of view, the detection of essential diagnostic factors gives the ability for the design of an ANN with simpler structure and improved performance, because ANN training is based on smaller data sets.

2 Artificial Neural Network's Pruning With Genetic Algorithm

Both ANNs and GAs are inspired by biological processes. However, ANNs' learning is based on individuals (phenotypic learning), while GAs adapt a population to changing environment (genotypic learning). In recent years, there is a large body of literature in combination of GAs and ANNs to produce evolutionary ANNs, with improved performance and simplified architectures [17].

Trial and error method, which is used for the implementation of ANNs, is computationally complex and does not ensure that the proposed architecture is the best one. These restrictions conduced to the development of more efficient methods which are divided in constructive and pruning (destructive) algorithms [18, 19]. Constructive algorithms start with a minimum number of neurons for ANNs and dynamically add neurons, generating more complex ANNs to achieve a satisfactory ANNs solution. On the other hand, a pruning algorithm starts from maximal ANNs and cuts nodes, layers and synaptic connections during the training based on already collected data.

The constructive and destructive algorithms might investigate restricted topological subsets instead of complete space of ANN's architectures [20]. GAs are another approach to solve the problem of ANN's implementation. GAs are an optimization tool when the search space is of great complexity and large size. The determination of optimal ANN structure that solves a specific problem can be achieved by a GA search [15, 21, 22].

3 Receiver Operating Characteristic

A Receiver Operating Characteristic (ROC) is a graphical plot of the True Positive Rate (or sensitivity) versus False Positive Rate (1 – specificity) for a classifier system as its discrimination threshold is varied.

Sensitivity and specificity are statistical measures of the performance of a binary classification test. The sensitivity measures the proportion of actual positives which are correctly identified as such. The percentage of children with abdominal pain, who need to be operated, is the sensitivity. The mathematical equation of sensitivity or True Positive Rate (TPR) is

$$Sensitivity\,(TPR) = \frac{TP}{TP + FN} \quad (1)$$

where TP is the number of true positive patterns and FN is the number of false negative patterns.

The specificity measures the proportion of negatives which are correctly identified. In particular, the percentage of children having abdominal pain and have not to be operated is the specificity. The mathematical equation of specificity is

$$Specificity\,(SPC) = \frac{TN}{TN + FP} \quad (2)$$

where TN is the number of true negative patterns and the FP is the number of false positive patterns.

The correlation between specificity and False Positive Rate (FPR) is

$$SPC = 1 - FPR \Rightarrow$$
$$FPR = 1 - SPC \quad (3)$$

ROC analysis provides tools to select possibly optimal models and to discard suboptimal ones independently from the cost context or the class distribution. ROC analysis is used for diagnostic decision making in medicine, radiology, psychology and other areas for many decades. Nowadays, it has been introduced in other areas like machine learning and data mining [23].

The essential statistic from ROC is the Area Under Curve (AUC), which is a measure of overall accuracy that is not dependent upon a particular threshold [24]. The mathematical equation of AUC is

$$AUC=\frac{1}{n_{+}n_{-}}\sum_{x\in\{\text{set of all test results}\}}\left(n_{-=j}\times n_{+>j}+\frac{n_{-=j}\times n_{+=j}}{2}\right) \quad (4)$$

where x_+ is each value of a diagnostic factor for cases with positive actual states, x_- is each value of the same diagnostic factor for cases with negative actual states, n_+ is the sample size of data set (D_+) contained cases with positive actual states, and n_- the sample size of data set (D_-) contained cases with negative actual states.

The AUC can be utilized as an estimator of the discriminatory performance of the diagnostic factors of a system. The AUC for a system without resolving power equals to 0.5, while the AUC for a system with perfect discrimination equals to 1. It is clear that the AUC for a system with satisfactory resolving power is between 0.5 and 1. The greater of AUC, the best discrimination ability for the system [24].

4 Data Collection

The abdominal pain data was obtained from the Pediatric Surgery Clinical Information System of Alexandroupolis' University Hospital, Greece. The appendicitis diagnosis is based on 15 clinical and biochemical factors which are sex, age, religion, demographic data, duration of pain, vomitus, diarrhea, anorexia, tenderness, rebound, leucocytosis, neutrophilia, urinalysis, temperature and constipation. The possible diagnosis stages are discharge, observation, no findings, focal appendicitis, phlegmonous or supurative appendicitis, gangrenous appendicitis and peritonitis. These factors and the diagnosis stages are well described in Table 2 and Table 1, correspondingly, in [12]. As presented in [12], the possible stages of abdominal pain examination are seven, whereof four stages demand operative treatment and three are referred for conservative treatment.

The present study is based on a data set consisted of 516 cases, whereof 422 (81.78%) normal and 94 (18.22%) underwent operative treatment. The pruned data set, used in the proposed model, was divided into a set of 400 (77.52%) records for construction of PNNs and another set of 116 (22.48%) records for assessment of PNNs' performance.

5 Evolutionary PNN Architecture

The aim of the present study is the elimination of abdominal pain in childhood diagnostic factors and the determination of essential diagnostic factors for evolved ANN implementation.

A Probabilistic Neural Network (PNN) is the selected ANN architecture among a great variety of ANN topologies that was used in this study. A PNN which is based on Parzen's Probabilistic Density Function (PDF) estimator, is a three-layer feed-forward network, consisting of an input layer, a radial basis and a competitive layer [25].

As it was mentioned in section 4, the number of abdominal pain diagnostic factors equals to 15. The possible combinations of input data subsets are given by following mathematical notation,

$$C = \frac{N!}{k!(N-k)!} \qquad (4)$$

where N is the maximum number of diagnostic factors (in this problem N = 15) and k is an integer for the number of diagnostic factors of each input data subset. The k variable's values are range from 1 to 15.

The chromosome's length of each individual was equal to the total number of diagnostic factors, so that the population of the used GA consisted of binary strings of 15 bits. The GA used is two-objective, thus the GA has to search for diagnostic data sets that at the same time: (a) minimize the number of diagnostic factors used during the training phase and therefore minimize the number of nodes in ANN input and hidden layers, and (b) minimize the Mean Square Error of the testing phase. For this purpose, the following fitness function was used:

$$f = MSE + \frac{I}{N} \qquad (5)$$

where I is the number of ANN input nodes and N is the maximum number of diagnostic factors in the original, full-sized training data set.

To find out the essential diagnostic factors that can be used for evolutionary PNN, different experiments were performed using the scattered crossover, single-point crossover, two-point crossover and uniform crossover, as well as gaussian mutation and uniform mutation binary GA operators.

6 Experimental Results

The aim of the present study is the elimination of abdominal pain diagnostic factors based on GA search for the essential and optimal combination of necessary factors for PNN construction.

Whereas, the PNNs architecture is constrained by the available features of specific problem, the width of the calculated Gaussian curve for each probability density function have to be defined. In the present study, this spread factor varied from 0.1 to 100.

An extensive investigation was performed, to assess the PNNs' performance for training and testing full-sized data set consisted of all the 15 diagnostic factors. The obtained results for best-implemented PNNs are presented in Table 1. The radbas and compet were the transfer functions for hidden and output layers, correspondingly.

The number of neurons for input and hidden layers of PNNs was specified by the number of diagnostic parameters and the cases of training set, correspondingly. The number of neurons for PNNs' output layer is seven and is based on coding of possible diagnosis according to [12]. The values of spread and the MSE for the PNNs with the best performance are recorded, correspondingly, in the 1st and 2nd column of the Table 1.

Table 1. Spread and MSE for the best implemented PNNs with full-sized data set.

Spread	MSE
0.1	0.0025
1.0	0.0025
10.0	0.14
100	0.5375

The obtained results by executing the GA are presented in Table 2. The 2nd column of this table depicts the fitness value of the optimal individual, the 3rd column, the MSE of the optimal individual and the 4th column the independent diagnostic factors that were used as inputs for PNNs construction. It is mentioned that the forenamed values were recorded for the same values of spread as in Table 1.

As it is presented Table 2, the GA managed to converge to PNNs that used 7 up to 8 of the 15 diagnostic factors. At the same time, the MSE of PNNs that were trained with the pruned input data sets is significantly decreased in accordance of MSE of trained PNNs with 15 diagnostic factors. Consequently, the diagnostic ability of evolved PNNs is improved in compare with full-sized trained PNNs.

The decrease in genetically trained PNNs is of the order of 3.15% to 18.9%, depending on the value of spread. The diagnostic factors which are more effective on PNNs training and testing are Demographic Data, Duration of Pain, Leycocytosis, Neutrophilia and Temperature.

7 ROC Curves

The available data set of appendicitis' records was processed by ROC analysis. The aim of this data processing was evaluation of importance role of each diagnostic factor for appendicitis estimation. The obtained results are summarized in Table 3. The diagnostic factors are presented in 2nd column of the Table 3, while the Area Under Curve of ROC for each factor is recorded in the 3rd column of this Table. Each PNN network was evolved genetically using different crossover and mutation operators so the Table 2 records two different results for each spread value.

Table 2. MSE of PNNs trained with pruned sets of diagnostic input factors

Spread	Fitness Value	MSE	Diagnostic Factors
0.1	0.03196126	0.00242131	Demographic data, Vomitus, Rebound, Leucocytosis, Neutrophilia, Temperature, Constipation
	0.03753027	0.00000000	Demographic data, Duration of pain, Anorexia, Tenderness, Leucocytosis, Temperature, Constipation
1.0	0.00823245	0.00242131	Age, Duration of pain, Diarrhea, Anorexia, Tenderness, Leucocytosis, Neutrophilia, Temperature
	0.00435835	0.00000000	Age, Religion, Duration of pain, Tenderness, Lecocytosis, Neutrophilia, Temperature, Constipation
10.0	0.16319613	0.11380145	Age, Demographic data, Duration of pain, Diarrhea, Leucocytosis, Neutrophilia, Temperature
100	1.75484262	0.43583535	Sex, Age, Demographic data, Duration of pain, Tenderness, Leucocytosis, Urinalysis
	1.58002421	0.47457627	Sex, Demographic data, Vomitus, Anorexia, Tenderness, Leucocytosis, Urinalysis

Table 3. Area of Diagnostic factors' curves

Nr	Diagnostic Factors	AUC
1	Sex	0.511
2	Age	0.357
3	Religion	0.560
4	Demographic data	0.572
5	Duration of Pain	0.508
6	Vomitus	0.787
7	Diarrhea	0.535
8	Anorexia	0.690
9	Tenderness	0.947
10	Rebound	0.894
11	Leucocytosis	0.949
12	Neutrophilia	0.977
13	Urinalysis	0.073
14	Temperature	0.929
15	Constipation	0.518

The AUC is an important statistic of ROC analysis. A value of area larger than 0.5, proves the importance role of a diagnostic factor for appendicitis estimation. As it is shown in Table 3, the most important diagnostic factors are Religion, Demographic Data, Vomitus, Anorexia, Tenderness, Rebound, Leucocytosis,

Neutrophilia and Temperature.

The Sex, Duration of Pain, and Constipation are parameters without significant contribution to appendicitis prediction as their values of AUC are equal to 0.5. The Age and Urinalysis are diagnostic factors that have not the ability to discriminate true positive patients as their value are 0.357 and 0.073, correspondingly, which are smaller than 0.5.

The results as obtained by genetically evolved PNNs and ROC analysis were further processed. The aim of this processing is the investigation of the convergence in terms of proposed diagnostic factors for appendicitis estimation. It is concluded that Tenderness, Leucocytosis, Neutrophilia and Temperature are essential factors for appendicitis prediction, so these parameters are strongly recommended have to be recorded for each patient.

8 Discussion

This study presents a specific GA to evolve the subsets of patients' data that are used as inputs for PNN construction and testing. After adequate steps of genetic evolution, the GA converged to diagnostic factors subsets that were consisted from 7 or 8 over a total of 15 diagnostic factors. The evolved PNNs overperformed the full-trained PNNs in terms of the MSE. Consequently, the implementation of PNNs based on specifically selected diagnostic factors, instead of all of them resulted to increase of PNNs' performance and prognostic ability while at the same time the training procedure was speed up. The comparison of genetically evolved PNNs' outcomes with those of ROC analysis concludes that the medical diagnostic factors present a high level of redundancy and overlapping. Therefore, a number of the diagnostic factors for appendicitis estimation may be omitted with no compromise to the fidelity of clinical evaluation.

Acknowledgment We are grateful to the Pediatric Surgeon of the Pediatric Surgery Clinic of the University Hospital of Alexandroupolis, Greece for their valuable contribution.

References

1. Dayhoff J., and DeLeo J., "Artificial Neural Networks Opening the Black Box", CANCER Supplement, 2001, Vol. 91, No. 8, pp. 1615-1635.
2. Huang D., "A Constructive Approach for Finding Arbitrary Roots of Polynomials by Neural Networks", IEEE Transactions on Neural Networks, 2004, Vol. 15, No. 2, pp. 477 - 491.
3. Levano M., and Nowak H., "Application of New Algorithm, Iterative SOM, to the Detection of Gene Expressions", Proceedings 10th International Conference on Engineering Applications of Neural Networks, 2007, Thessaloniki, Greece, pp. 141-147.
4. Zaknick A., "Introduction to the Modified Probabilistic Neural Network for General Signal Processing", IEEE Transactions on Signal Processing, 1998, Vol. 46, No.7, pp. 1980-1990.
5. Iliadis L., "An Intelligent Artificial Neural Network Evaluation System Using Fuzzy Set Hedges: Application in Wood Industry" Proceedings 19th IEEE Annual International Conference on Tools with Artificial Intelligence (ICTA), pp. 366-370.

6. Paschalidou A., Iliadis L., Kassomenos P., and Bezirtzoglou C., "Neural Modelling of the Tropospheric Ozone Concentrations in an Urban Site", Proc. 10th International Conference on Engineering Applications of Neural Networks, 2007 Thessaloniki, Greece, pp. 436-445.
7. Keogan M., Lo J., Freed K., Raptopoulos V., Blake S., Kamel I., Weisinger K., Rosen M., and Nelson R., "Outcome Analysis of Patients with Acute Pancreatitis by Using an Artificial Neural Network", Academic Radiology, 2002, Vol. 9, No. 4, pp. 410-419.
8. Brause R., Hanisch E., Paetz J., and Arlt B., "Neural Networks for Sepsis Prediction - the MEDAN-Project1", Journal für Anästhesie und Intensivbehandlung, 2004, Vol. 11, No. 1, pp. 40-43.
9. Gómez-Ruiz J., Jerez-Aragonés J., Muñoz-Pérez J., and Alba-Conejo E., "A Neural Network Based Model for Prognosis of Early Breast Cancer", Applied Intelligence, 2004, Vol. 20, No. 3, pp. 231-238.
10. Mantzaris D., Anastassopoulos G., Tsalkidis A., and Adamopoulos A., "Intelligent Prediction of Vesicoureteral Reflux Disease", WSEAS Transactions on Systems, 2005, Vol. 4, Issue 9, pp. 1440-1449.
11. Anagnostou T., Remzi M., and Djavan B., "Artificial Neural Networks for Decision-Making in Urologic Oncology", Reviews In Urology, 2003, Vol. 5, No. 1, pp.15-21.
12. Mantzaris D., Anastassopoulos G., Adamopoulos A., and Gardikis S., "A Non-Symbolic Implementation of Abdominal Pain Estimation in Childhood", Information Science, 2008, Vol. 178, pp. 3860-3866.
13. Economou G., Lymperopoulos D., Karavatselou E., and Chassomeris C., "A New Concept Toward Computer-Aided Medical Diagnosis - A Prototype Implementation Addressing Pulmonary Diseases" IEEE Transactions in Information Technology in Biomedicine, 2001 Vol. 5, Issue 1, pp. 55-66.
14. Mantzaris D., Anastassopoulos C., and Lymperopoulos K., "Medical Disease Prediction Using Artificial Neural Networks", Proceedings IEEE International Conference on BioInformatics and BioEngineering, 2008, Athens, Greece
15. Georgopoulos E., Likothanassis S., and Adamopoulos A., "Evolving Artificial Neural Networks Using Genetic Algorithms", Neural Network World, 2000, Vol. 4, pp.565-574
16. Blazadonakis M., Moustakis V., and Charissis G., "Deep Assessment of Machine Learning Techniques Using Patient Treatment in Acute Abdominal Pain in Children", Artificial Intelligence in Medicine, 1996, Vol. 8, pp. 527-542
17. Branke J., "Evolutionary Algorithms for Neural Network Design and Training", Proceedings 1st Nordic Workshop on Genetic Algorithms and its Applications, 1995, Vaasa, Finland.
18. Yao X., "Evolving Artificial Neural Networks", Proceedings of the IEEE, 1999, Vol. 87, No. 9, pp. 1423-1447.
19. Burgess N., "A Constructive Algorithm that Converges for Real-Valued Input Patterns", International Journal on Neural Systems, 1994 Vol. 5, No. 1, pp. 59-66.
20. Angeline P., Sauders G., and Pollack J., "An Evolutionary Algorithm that Constructs Recurrent Neural Networks", IEEE Transaction on Neural Networks, 1994 Vol. 5, pp. 54-65.
21. Adamopoulos A., Georgopoulos E., Manioudakis G., and Likothanassis S., "An Evolutionary Method for System Structure Identification Using Neural Networks", Neural Computation '98, 1998
22. Billings S., and Zheng G., "Radial Basis Function Network Configuration Using Genetic Algorithms", Neural Networks, 1995, Vol. 8, pp. 877-890.
23. Swets J., "Signal Detection Theory and Roc Analysis in Psychology and Diagnostics: Collected Papers", Lawrence Erlbaum Associates, 1996, Mahwah NJ.
24. Streiner D., and Cairney J., "What's Under the ROC? An Introduction to Receiver Operating Characteristics Curves", The Canadian Journal of Psychiatry, 2007, Vol. 52, No. 2, pp. 121-128.
25. Parzen E., "On Estimation of a Probability Density Function and Mode", Annals of Mathematical Statistics, 1962, Vol. 33, No.3, pp. 1065-1076.

Mining Patterns of Lung Infections in Chest Radiographs

Spyros Tsevas[1,*], Dimitris K. Iakovidis[1], and George Papamichalis[2]

1 Technological Educational Institute of Lamia, Dept. of Informatics and Computer Technology, GR-35100 Lamia, Greece

2 Chest Hospital of Athens "Sotiria"

{s.tsevas, dimitris.iakovidis}@ieee.org

Abstract Chest radiography is a reference standard and the initial diagnostic test performed in patients who present with signs and symptoms suggesting a pulmonary infection. The most common radiographic manifestation of bacterial pulmonary infections is foci of consolidation. These are visible as bright shadows interfering with the interior lung intensities. The discovery and the assessment of bacterial infections in chest radiographs is a challenging computational task. It has been limitedly addressed as it is subject to image quality variability, content diversity, and deformability of the depicted anatomic structures. In this paper, we propose a novel approach to the discovery of consolidation patterns in chest radiographs. The proposed approach is based on non-negative matrix factorization (NMF) of statistical intensity signatures characterizing the densities of the depicted anatomic structures. Its experimental evaluation demonstrates its capability to recover semantically meaningful information from chest radiographs of patients with bacterial pulmonary infections. Moreover, the results reveal its comparative advantage over the baseline fuzzy C-means clustering approach.

1 Introduction

Artificial intelligence and data mining applications in medicine are increasingly becoming popular tools as the utilization of digital media meets the everyday clinical practice. Computer-aided diagnosis, intelligent information retrieval and knowledge discovery are some of the associated research directions, which can prove valuable to patient safety and quality of healthcare [1].

Health care–related infections comprise a major threat to patient safety. They are encountered in hospitals or health care facilities and they are usually reported as adverse events associated with medical procedures. Most commonly include pulmonary, urinary tract, skin, and soft tissue infections of bacterial origin [2].

Please use the following format when citing this chapter:

Tsevas, S., Iakovidis, D.K. and Papamichalis, G., 2009, in IFIP International Federation for Information Processing, Volume 296; *Artificial Intelligence Applications and Innovations III*; Eds. Iliadis, L., Vlahavas, I., Bramer, M.; (Boston: Springer), pp. 205–214.

The early detection of such infections as well as the choice of the appropriate antibiotic treatment can be life-saving especially for the critically ill patients. To this end, a computational approach that would be capable of automatically discovering patterns of infections and antibiotic prescription from patients' health records would constitute a valuable tool to the community [3].

Patients' health records may include both structured and unstructured data, digital signals and images. In the case of chest patients, chest radiographs provide substantial indications on the presence of a pulmonary infection. The most common radiographic manifestation of bacterial pulmonary infections is foci of consolidation. These are visible as bright shadows interfering with the interior lung intensities, which include intensities the lung parenchyma and intensities of superimposed structures of the thoracic cavity such as the ribs and the mediastinum. The diversity and the complexity of the visual content of the lung fields as well as the quality variability induced by the variable parameters of the radiation exposure, make its medical interpretation a challenging task. This task has motivated many researchers to develop computational methods for automatic lung field detection and analysis [4][5].

Current lung field analysis methods include size measurements of structures of the thoracic cavity [6], detection of the ribs [7], lung nodule detection [8], whereas fewer methods have been proposed for mining radiographic patterns associated with the presence of pulmonary infections [9]. Mining patterns of pneumonia and severe acute respiratory syndrome (SARS) has also been in the scope of contemporary research. In [10] a supervised approach using intensity-histograms and second-order statistical features has been proposed for mining pneumonia and SARS patterns, whereas most recently, the use of wavelet-based features have been proved useful for the detection radiographic patterns of childhood pneumonia under a supervised classification framework [11].

In contrast to the former methods this paper proposes an unsupervised approach to the discovery of consolidation patterns associated with bacterial pulmonary infections. Such an approach does not take into account any information extracted from previous images, thus avoiding the need for feature normalization between images. We use statistical intensity signatures characterizing the densities of the several anatomic structures depicted in chest radiographs to recover semantically meaningful information regarding the consolidation patterns. This is achieved by a clustering approach based on Non-negative Matrix Factorization (NMF) that involves cluster merging. The results obtained are compared with those obtained with the fuzzy C-means (FCM) clustering approach [12].

The rest of this paper consists of three sections. Section 2 provides a description of the proposed methodology, section 3 presents the results of its experimental application on a set of high-resolution chest radiographs, and section 4 summarizes the conclusions that can be derived from this study.

2 Methodology

Non-negative Matrix Factorization (NMF) was introduced by Paatero and Tapper [13] as a way to find a non-negative reduced representation of non-negative data, but it has gained popularity by the works of Lee and Seung [14, 15]. In contrast to other methods such as Principal Component Analysis (PCA), NMF allows only additive combinations of non-negative data, leading to a representation that is more intuitive and closer to the human perception.

Given a *mxn* non-negative matrix **V** and a reduced rank r $(r < \min(m,n))$, the non-negative matrix factorization problem lies in finding two non-negative factors **W** and **H** of $\overline{\mathbf{V}}$ such that:

$$\mathbf{V} \approx \overline{\mathbf{V}} = \mathbf{W} \times \mathbf{H} \tag{1}$$

where $\mathbf{W} \in \Re^{m \times r}$ and $\mathbf{H} \in \Re^{r \times n}$.

We may think of **W** as the matrix containing the NMF basis and **H** as the matrix containing the non-negative coefficients (or encodings) that exhibit a one-to-one correspondence with the data that consists **V**. To quantify the distance between the data matrix **V** and the model matrix $\overline{\mathbf{V}}$ we used the Frobenius norm:

$$\min_{\mathbf{W,H}} \left\| \mathbf{V} - \mathbf{WH} \right\|_F^2 \ , \ \mathbf{W,H} \geq \mathbf{0} \tag{2a}$$

This optimization problem is solved using the following multiplicative update rules:

$$\mathbf{W}_{ir} \leftarrow \mathbf{W}_{ir} \frac{\left(\mathbf{V} \times \mathbf{W}^{\mathrm{T}}\right)_{ir}}{\left(\mathbf{W} \times \mathbf{H} \times \mathbf{H}^{\mathrm{T}}\right)_{ir}} \tag{2b}$$

$$\mathbf{H}_{rj} \leftarrow \mathbf{H}_{rj} \frac{\left(\mathbf{W}^{\mathrm{T}} \times \mathbf{V}\right)_{rj}}{\left(\mathbf{W}^{\mathrm{T}} \times \mathbf{W} \times \mathbf{H}\right)_{rj}} \tag{2c}$$

NMF can be considered as an alternative clustering technique [16,18-20] since given a normalized solution ($\tilde{\mathbf{W}}$, $\tilde{\mathbf{H}}$) of NMF, $\tilde{\mathbf{H}}^{\mathrm{T}}$ can be interpreted as the cluster posterior and thus $\tilde{\mathbf{H}}_{jr}$ represents the posterior probability that $\mathbf{v}_j$ belongs to the *r*-th cluster [20]. We can express the columns of **W** and $\mathbf{H}^{\mathrm{T}}$ as: $\mathbf{W} = (\mathbf{w}_1,...,\mathbf{w}_r)$, $\mathbf{H}^{\mathrm{T}} = (\mathbf{h}_1,...,\mathbf{h}_r)$ where in clustering terms $\mathbf{w}_r$ can be interpreted as the centroid of the r-th cluster and the $\mathbf{h}_r$ as the posterior probability of the r-th cluster. By normalizing the **W** and $\mathbf{H}^{\mathrm{T}}$ column-wisely we have the normalized columns are $\tilde{\mathbf{W}} = (\tilde{\mathbf{w}}_1,...,\tilde{\mathbf{w}}_r)$ and $\tilde{\mathbf{H}}^{\mathrm{T}} = (\tilde{\mathbf{h}}_1,...,\tilde{\mathbf{h}}_r)$ and the normalization:

$$\mathbf{WH} = \tilde{\mathbf{W}}\mathbf{S}\tilde{\mathbf{H}} \tag{3}$$

where

$$\tilde{\mathbf{W}} = \mathbf{W}\mathbf{D}_W^{-1}, \tag{4a}$$

$$\tilde{\mathbf{H}}^{\mathrm{T}} = \mathbf{H}^{\mathrm{T}}\mathbf{D}_H^{-1} \tag{4b}$$

$$\mathbf{S} = \mathbf{D}_W\mathbf{D}_H \tag{4c}$$

where $\mathbf{D}_W$ and $\mathbf{D}_H$ are diagonal matrices with diagonal elements be in the L_{p}-norm:

$$(\mathbf{D}_C)_{rr} = \|\tilde{\mathbf{c}}_r\|_p, (\mathbf{D}_H)_{rr} = \|\tilde{\mathbf{h}}_r\|_p \tag{5}$$

For the Euclidean distance case (L_2-norm) $\|\tilde{\mathbf{c}}_r\|_2 = 1$, $\|\tilde{\mathbf{h}}_r\|_2 = 1$ and due to the non-negativity of the data, this is just the condition that columns sum to 1. Thus, $\mathbf{D}_W$ contains the column sums of $\mathbf{W}$, and $\mathbf{D}_H$ contains the column sums of $\mathbf{H}^{\mathrm{T}}$.

In this paper, we apply NMF as a clustering technique to extract consolidation patterns from radiographic images. A radiographic image is divided into a set of non-overlapping sub-images which are subsequently clustered into an even number of r clusters. Some of these clusters will correspond to patterns of normal lung parenchyma and the rest will correspond to consolidation patterns. The sub-images are represented by intensity histogram signatures characterizing the densities of the anatomic structures depicted in a chest radiograph [21]. Finally, the r clusters are dyadically merged down to two clusters based on the similarity of their centroids. Considering that the consolidations are dense foci in the lungs which are normally filled with air, we assume that the cluster with the lower intensity centroid corresponds to the patterns of the normal lung field parenchyma, and that the cluster with the higher intensity centroid corresponds to the consolidation patterns.

3 Results and Discussion

For the evaluation of the proposed approach, we used a collection of chest radiographs from twenty patients. The radiographic images were 8-bit grayscale with a size of 2816×2112 pixels. The lung fields were isolated using the methodology proposed in [5] and were divided into 32×32 sub-images. From each sub-image an intensity histogram signature was calculated so as to build the data matrix that was used as input to the NMF. A representative chest radiograph along with the isolated lung fields are illustrated in Fig. 1.

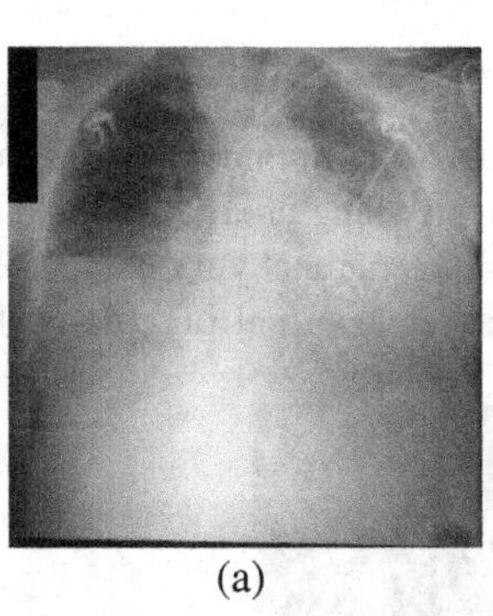

(a)

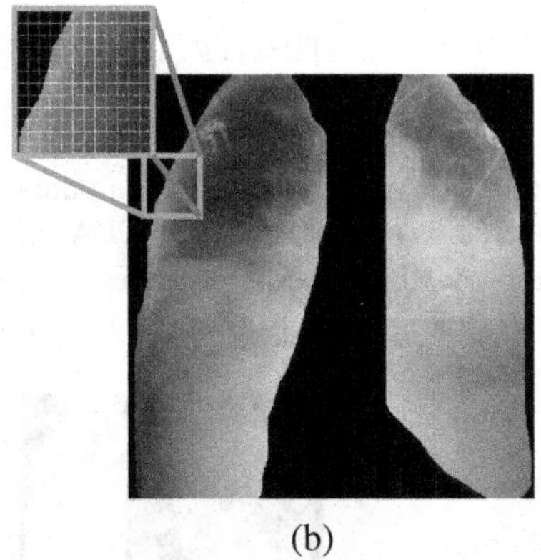

(b)

Fig. 1. (a) A chest radiographic image, (b) the lung fields isolated from (a). The magnified area illustrates the sub-images considered. Consolidation areas are visible as bright shadows within the lung fields.

Each column in the initial data matrix, **V**, corresponds to the histogram information of each window. The resulting non-negative matrices, **W** and **H**, represent the feature bases and their membership probabilities accordingly. Both **W** and **H** were normalized by following the procedure described in the methodology section. Such a normalization allows to easily compare the bases with the initial feature vectors on the one hand, while on the other hand it leads to an easier interpretation of the probability of a signature to belong to a certain cluster or category.

To evaluate the performance of the proposed approach we applied the proposed as well as the conventional NMF-based approach on each radiographic image. Prior to the application of the algorithms, images were annotated by an expert so as to provide us with the necessary ground truth information. The results obtained are compared with the performance obtained with the fuzzy c-means (FCM) algorithm which is considered as a baseline method [12].

The performance measures considered in this study are: sensitivity, specificity and accuracy [23],

$$Sensitivity = \frac{\mathrm{TP}}{\mathrm{TP} + \mathrm{FN}} \tag{6}$$

$$Specificity = \frac{\mathrm{TN}}{\mathrm{TN} + \mathrm{FP}} \tag{7}$$

$$Accuracy = \frac{\mathrm{TP} + \mathrm{TN}}{\mathrm{TP} + \mathrm{FP} + \mathrm{TN} + \mathrm{FN}} \tag{8}$$

where TP (true positive), TN (true negative), FP (false positive) and FN (false negative) are estimated as follows:

$$\begin{aligned} &\text{TP=GTP} \cap \text{PCLA, TN=GTN} \cap \text{NCLA,} \\ &\text{FP=GTN} \cap \text{PCLA, FN=GTP} \cap \text{NCLA} \end{aligned} \quad (9)$$

where PCLA (positive cluster lung area) is the area corresponding to the patterns considered as consolidations, NCLA (negative cluster lung area) is the area corresponding to the patterns considered as normal lung parenchyma, and GTP and GTN are the ground truth areas of consolidations and normal lung parenchyma, respectively.

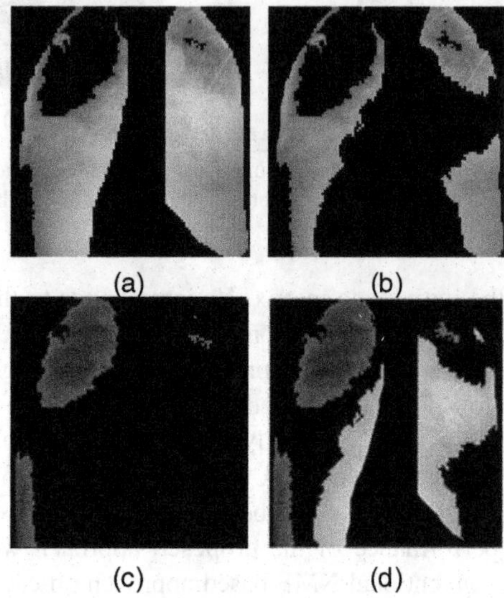

Fig. 2. Mining patterns of infections with the conventional NMF (left) and FCM (right) approaches using two clusters. (a) NMF first cluster, (b) FCM first cluster, (c) NMF second cluster, (d) FCM second cluster.

The formation of the clusters from the dataset derived from the image in Fig.1 is illustrated in Fig.2 for the 2 clusters case and for both NMF (on the left) and FCM (on the right). Figure shows that NMF achieves better separation of the consolidated areas (top left image), in contrast to FCM that fails to separate the consolidated areas from the normal ones. However, the separation of the consolidated from the normal areas is not always feasible using two clusters. An example is provided in Fig. 3 where the clustering of the lung fields in Fig.3(a) in two clusters results in an accuracy that does not exceed 40%. To cope with this problem, clustering in more than two clusters followed by a cluster merging scheme is proposed.

According to this approach the image signatures are initially clustered into an even number of clusters. Considering that the NMF bases actually represent the cluster centroids, the clusters are dyadically merged down to two based on the similarity of their centroids. Since the signatures are intensity histograms the similarity is evaluated by the histogram intersection metric [22].

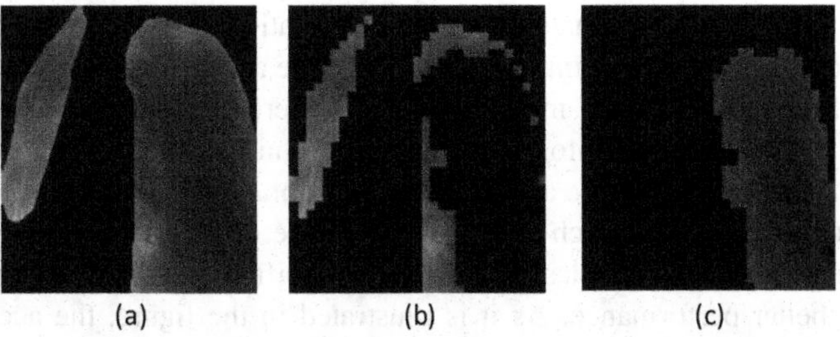

Fig. 3. Mining patterns of infections with the conventional NMF clustering approach using two clusters. (a) The lung fields to be clustered, (b) first cluster (consolidation areas), c) second cluster (normal lung field parenchyma).

An example of the application of this merging procedure is illustrated in Fig.4. The feature vectors (NMF bases) of the four initial clusters are graphically depicted above the upper row of images, which illustrates the image regions assigned to each cluster. The four clusters are subsequently merged down to two clusters, which are visualized in the last row of images in the figure. The consolidated areas are spotted in clusters 1 and 2. It is obvious that the proposed merging scheme achieves a better separation of the consolidation areas in contrast to the conventional clustering in two target clusters, which is quantified to an 87% of accuracy.

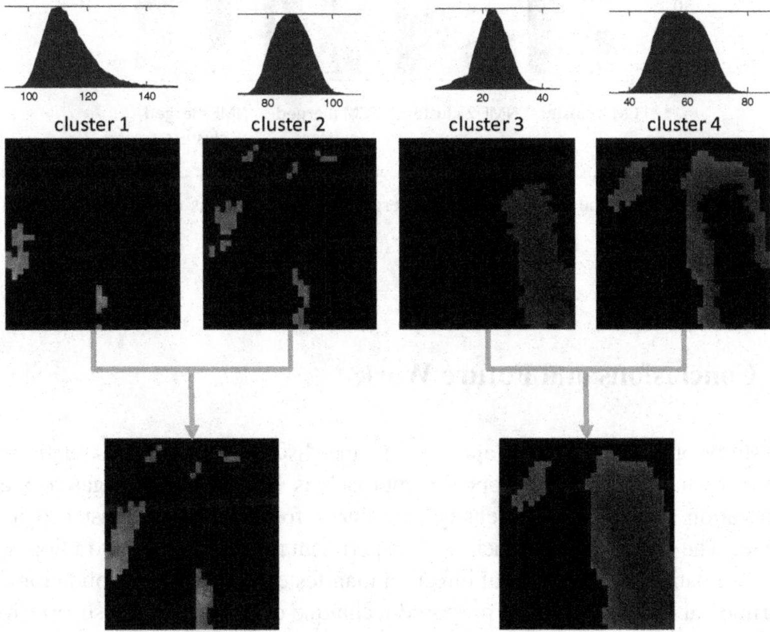

Fig. 4. Mining patterns of infections with the proposed approach. The resulting NMF bases after clustering the dataset derived from Fig.3(a) in 4 clusters (top row), the formation of the 4 clusters (top row) and the resulting merged clusters (bottom row).

The average results estimated from the application of the proposed approach on the whole dataset are summarized in Fig. 5. The average accuracy achieved by the NMF followed by cluster merging is 75%, whereas the accuracy achieved by the direct NMF clustering into two clusters is significantly lower reaching only 35%. It can be noticed that the average accuracy obtained with the FCM is poorer. Though, its sensitivity is much higher than the one obtained with the NMF after cluster merging, NMF provides much higher specificity and accuracy leading to an overall better performance. As it is illustrated in the figure, the accuracy obtained with the FCM is about 29% in the direct clustering case and 61% for the cluster merging case. Comparing the results of the proposed approach with the results of the FCM clustering with and without cluster merging as illustrated in Fig. 5, it becomes evident that the proposed approach is more suitable than the FCM for the particular clustering task.

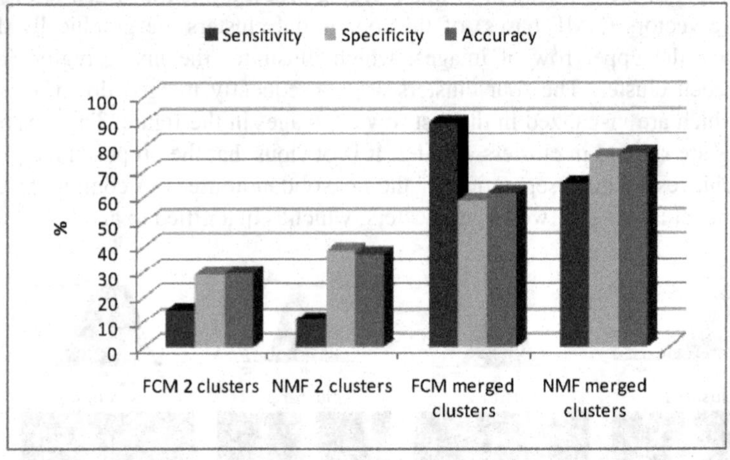

Fig. 5. Performance of the proposed cluster merging method in terms of sensitivity, specificity and accuracy.

4 Conclusions and Future Work

This study presented a novel approach to the discovery of patterns of bacterial pulmonary infections. The proposed approach is based on non-negative matrix factorization of statistical intensity signatures followed by a cluster merging scheme. The proposed approach was experimentally evaluated on radiographic images of patients with bacterial infection manifested as foci of consolidation. The experimental evaluation of the proposed technique demonstrates the superiority of the proposed NMF-based algorithm over the conventional NMF clustering scheme and the standard FCM for non-negative image data.

Currently the improvement of the proposed methodology is considered and our effort is made towards the development of an intelligent system for discovery and assessment of pulmonary infections from radiographic images. Our future work involves further experimentation with the proposed and alternative cluster merging schemes, comparisons with state of the art unsupervised and supervised approaches, and utilization of various image features.

References

1. Irene M. Mullins, Mir S. Siadaty, Jason Lyman, Ken Scully, Carleton T. Garrett, W. Greg Miller, Rudy Muller, Barry Robson, Chid Apte, Sholom Weiss, Isidore Rigoutsos, Daniel Platt, Simona Cohen, William A. Knaus, Data mining and clinical data repositories: Insights from a 667,000 patient data set, Computers in Biology and MedicineVolume 36, Issue 12, , December 2006, Pages 1351-1377
2. D.L. Smith, J. Dushof, E.N. Perencevich, A.D. Harris, S.A. Levin, "Persistent Colonization and the spread of antibiotic resistance in nosocomial pathogens: Resistance is a regional problem," PNAS, vol. 101, no. 10, pp. 3709-3714, Mar. 2004
3. C. Lovis, D. Colaert, V.N. Stroetmann, "DebugIT for Patient Safety - Improving the Treatment with Antibiotics through Multimedia Data Mining of Heterogeneous Clinical Data," Stud Health Technol. Inform., vol. 136, 641-646, 2008
4. B.V. Ginneken, B.T.H. Romeny, and M.A. Viergever, "Computer-Aided Diagnosis in Chest Radiography: A Survey," IEEE Transactions Medical Imaging, vol. 20, no. 12, pp. 1228-1241, Dec. 2001
5. D.K. Iakovidis, and G. Papamichalis, "Automatic Segmentation of the Lung Fields in Portable Chest Radiographs Based on Bézier Interpolation of Salient Control Points," in Proceedings IEEE International Conference on Imaging Systems and Techniques, Chania, Greece, 2008, pp. 82-87
6. I.C. Mehta, Z.J. Khan, and R.R. Khotpa, Volumetric Measurement of Heart Using PA and Lateral View of Chest Radiograph, S. Manandhar et al. (Eds.): AACC 2004, LNCS 3285, pp. 34–40, 2004
7. M. Loog, B.van Ginneken: Segmentation of the posterior ribs in chest radiographs using iterated contextual pixel classification. IEEE Transactions Medical Imaging 25(5): 602-611 (2006)
8. Giuseppe Coppini, Stefano Diciotti, Massimo Falchini, N. Villari, Guido Valli: Neural networks for computer-aided diagnosis: detection of lung nodules in chest radiograms. IEEE Transactions on Information Technology in Biomedicine 7(4): 344-357 (2003)
9. B.V. Ginneken, S. Katsuragawa, B.T.H. Romeny, K. Doi, and M.A. Viergever, "Automatic Detection of Abnormalities in Chest Radiographs Using Local Texture Analysis", IEEE Transactions Medical Imaging, vol. 21, no. 2, pp. 139-149, Feb. 2002
10. X. Xie, X. Li, S. Wan, and Y. Gong, Mining X-Ray Images of SARS Patients, G.J. Williams and S.J. Simoff (Eds.): Data Mining, LNAI 3755, pp. 282–294, 2006
11. L.L.G. Oliveiraa, S. Almeida e Silvaa, L.H. Vilela Ribeirob, R. Maurício de Oliveiraa, C.J. Coelhoc and A.L.S.S. Andrade, "Computer-Aided Diagnosis in Chest Radiography for Detection of Childhood Pneumonia", International Journal of Medical Informatics, vol. 77, no. 8, pp. 555-564, 2007J.

12. C. Bezdek, J. Keller, R. Krisnapuram, and N.R. Pal. Fuzzy Models and Algorithms for Pattern Recognition and Image Processing. Kluwer Academic Publishers, 1999
13. Paatero and U. Tapper. Positive matrix factorization: a nonnegative factor model with optimal utilization of error estimates of data values. Environmetrics, 5(1):111–126, 1994
14. D.D. Lee and H.S. Seung, "Algorithms for non-negative matrix factorization," Advanced Neural Information Processing Systems, 13, 2000, pp. 556–562
15. Chris D, XiaoFeng H, Horst D.S. On the equivalence of nonnegative matrix factorization and spectral clustering, Proceedings SIAM International Conference on Data Mining (SDM'05), 2005: 606–610
16. C. Ding, X. He, H.D. Simon, "On the equivalence of nonnegative matrix factorization and spectral clustering," Proceedings SIAM International Conference on Data Mining, Newport Beach, CA, April 2005, pp. 606–610
17. Xiong H.L, Chen X.W. Kernel-based distance metric learning for microarray data classification, BMC Bioinformatics, 2006, 7
18. Xu W, Liu X, Gong Y. Document clustering based on non-negative matrix factorization, Proceedings ACM Conference Research Development in Information Retrieval, 2003: 267–273
19. Yuan G, George C. Improving molecular cancer class discovery through sparse non-negative matrix factorization, Bioinformatics, 2005, vol 21, no.21:3970–3975
20. Ding, C., Li, T., Peng, W. On the equivalence between Non-negative Matrix Factorization and Probabilistic Latent Semantic Indexing (2008) Computational Statistics and Data Analysis, 52 (8), pp. 3913-3927.
21. Novelline, R.A. (1997) Squires's Fundamentals of Radiology. Cambridge: Harvard University Press
22. M.J. Swain, D.H. Ballard, Color Indexing. Int. J. Computer Vision, Vol. 7, No. 1, pp. 11–32, Nov. 1991
23. Han, J., Kamber, M., 2001. Data Mining: Concepts and Techniques. Morgan Kaufmann Publishers.

Computational Modeling of Visual Selective Attention Based on Correlation and Synchronization of Neural Activity.

Kleanthis C. Neokleous[1], Marios N. Avraamides[2], Christos N. Schizas[1]

[1]Department of Computer Science, [2]Department of Psychology, University of Cyprus, 75 Kallipoleos, 1678, POBox 20537, Nicosia, CYPRUS.

Abstract Within the broad area of computational intelligence, it is of great importance to develop new computational models of human behaviour aspects. In this report we look into the recently suggested theory that neural synchronization of activity in different areas of the brain occurs when people attend to external visual stimuli. Furthermore, it is suspected that this cross-area synchrony may be a general mechanism for regulating information flow through the brain. We investigate the plausibility of this hypothesis by implementing a computational model of visual selective attention that is guided by endogenous and exogenous goals (i.e., what is known as top down and bottom-up attention). The theoretical structure of this model is based on the temporal correlation of neural activity that was initially proposed by Niebur and Koch (1994). While a saliency map is created in the model at the initial stages of processing visual input, at a later stage of processing, neural activity passes through a correlation control system which comprises of coincidence detector neurons. These neurons measure the degree of correlation between endogenous goals and the presented visual stimuli and cause an increase in the synchronization between the brain areas involved in vision and goal maintenance. The model was able to simulate with success behavioural data from the "attentional blink" paradigm (Raymond and Sapiro, 1992). This suggests that the temporal correlation idea represents a plausible hypothesis in the quest for understanding attention.

1 Introduction

Due to the great number of sensory stimulation that a person experiences at any given point of conscious life, it is practically impossible to integrate all information that is available to the senses into a single perceptual event. This implies that a mechanism must be present in the brain to focus selectively its resources on specific information. This mechanism, known as attention, can be described as the

---

Please use the following format when citing this chapter:

Neokleous, K.C., Avraamides, M.N. and Schizas, C.N., 2009, in IFIP International Federation for Information Processing, Volume 296; *Artificial Intelligence Applications and Innovations III*; Eds. Iliadis, L., Vlahavas, I., Bramer, M.; (Boston: Springer), pp. 215–223.

process by which information is passed on to a higher level of processing either through relative amplification of the neural activity that represents the “to be attended” stimuli or by suppression of the distracting stimuli, or both.

Attention can be guided by top-down and bottom-up processing as cognition can be regarded as a balance between internal motivations and external stimulations. Volitional shifts of attention or endogenous attention results from "top-down" signals originating in the prefrontal cortex while exogenous attention is guided by salient stimuli from "bottom-up" signals in the visual cortex (Corbetta and Shulman, 2002).

Previous literature on attention suggests that the attention selection mechanism functions in two hierarchical stages: An early stage of parallel processing across the entire visual field that operates without capacity limitation, and a later limited-capacity stage that deals with selected information in a sequential manner. When items pass from the first to the second stage of processing, they are typically considered as selected. (Treinsman and Gelade 1980).

Previous research suggests that attention is based on two processes. The first is known as “biased competition” (Moran and Desimone, 1985) and it is supported by findings from studies with single-cell recordings. These studies have shown that attention enhances the firing rates of the neurons that represent the attended stimuli and suppresses the firing rates of the neurons that encode the unattended stimuli. The second process, which refers to the synchronization of neural activity during the deployment of attention, is supported by studies showing that neurons selected by attention have enhanced gamma-frequency synchronization (Gruber et al., 1999; Steinmetz et al., 2000; Fries et al., 2001). For example, in a study by Fries et al. (2001) the activity in area V4 of the brain of macaque monkeys was recorded while the macaques attended relevant stimuli. Results showed increased gamma frequency synchronization for attended stimuli compared to the activity elicited by distractors. A recent study by Buelhman and Deco (2008) provided evidence that attention is affected by both biased competition and the synchronization of neural activity.

A computational model for biased competition has been proposed by Deco and Rolls (2005). In this model Deco and Rolls have shown that competition between pools of neurons combined with top-down biasing of this competition gives rise to a process that can be identified with attention. However, it should be pointed out that this model only considered rate effects while gamma synchronization was not addressed.

In the present report, we propose a computational model for endogenous and exogenous visual attention that is based on both the rate and the synchronization of neural activity. The basic functionality of the model relies on the assumption that the incoming visual stimulus will be manipulated by the model based on the rate and temporal coding of its associated neural activity. The rate associated with a visual stimulus is crucial in the case of exogenous attention since this type of attention is mainly affected by the different features of the visual stimuli. Stimuli with more salient features gain an advantage for passing through the second stage of processing and subsequently for accessing working memory. On the other hand, endogenous or top-down attention is mainly affected by the synchronization of incoming stimuli with the goals that guide the execution of a task. These goals are most likely maintained in the prefrontal cortex of the brain. The presence of a closed link between endogenous attention with synchronization is supported by many recent studies (Niebur et al 2002, Gross et al 2004). For example, Saalmann et al (2007) recorded neural activity simultaneously from the posterior parietal cortex as well as an earlier area in the visual pathway of the brain of macaques during the execution of a visual matching task. Findings revealed that there was synchronization of the timing activities in the two regions when the monkeys selectively attended to a location. Thus, it seems that parietal neurons which presumably represent neural activity of the endogenous goals may selectively increase activity in earlier sensory areas. In addition, the adaptive resonance theory by Grossberg (1999) implies that temporal patterning of activities could be ideally suited to achieve matching of top–down predictions with bottom–up inputs, while Engel et al (2001) in their review have noted that "If top–down effects induce a particular pattern of subthreshold fluctuations in dendrites of the target population, these could be 'compared' with temporal patterns arising from peripheral input by virtue of the fact that phase-shifted fluctuations will cancel each other, whereas in-phase signals will summate and amplify in a highly nonlinear way, leading to a salient postsynaptic signal" (p.714). Finally, it should be noted that Hebbian learning suggests that action potentials that arrive synchronously at a neuron summate to evoke larger postsynaptic potentials than do action potentials that arrive asynchronously; thus, synchronous action potentials have a greater effect at the next processing stage than do asynchronous action potentials.

A mechanism for selective attention based on the rate and synchronization of the neural activity for incoming stimuli is thus used in the proposed model. The model has been implemented computationally to simulate the typical data from "the attentional blink" phenomenon (Raymond and Sapiro,1992).

2 The Attentional Blink Phenomenon

The Attentional Blink (AB) is a phenomenon observed with using the rapid serial visual presentation (RSVP) paradigm. In the original experiment by Raymond and Shapiro (1992), participants were requested to identify two letter targets T1 and T2 among digit distractors with each stimulus appearing for about 100ms (Figure 1.a). Results revealed that the correct identification of T1 impaired the identification of T2 when T2 appeared within a brief temporal window of 200-500 ms after T1. When T2 appeared outside this time window it could be identified normally (Figure 1.b series 1.).

Another important finding from the AB task is that when T1 is not followed by a mask/distractor, the AB effect is significantly reduced. That is, if the arrival of the incoming stimulus at t= 200ms (lag 2) and/or lag 3 (t=300ms) are replaced by a blank then the AB curve takes the form shown by series 2 and 3 in Figure 1.

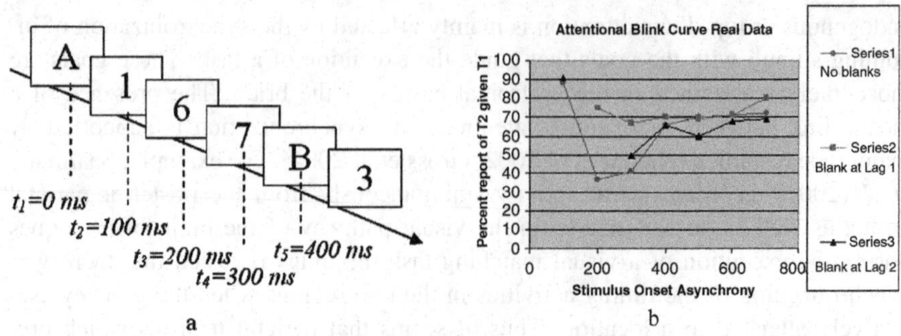

Figure1. Presentation of the RSVP for the "attentional blink" experiment (Figure1.a) and the typical attentional blink curve with no blanks (red series), with blank at lag 1 (green series) and blank at lag 2 (black series) based on the data of Raymond and Sapiro (1992) (Figure1.b).

3 Neural Correlates of the Attentional Blink Phenomenon

Event-related potentials (ERPs) are signals that measure the electrical activity of neuronal firing in the brain relative to events such as the presentation of stimuli. Over the years a number of ERP components related to attention have been identified in the literature.

The first distinguishable physiological signals are observed around 130-150ms post stimulus (P1/N1 signals). Most likely, these signals correspond to the initial processing in the visual cortex and reflect early pre-frontal activation by the incoming visual stimuli. At about 180-240 ms post-stimulus the P2/N2 signals are observed which have become clearer over the last years with the use of MEG (Ioannides and Taylor, 2003). These signals have been proposed as control signals for the movement of attention (Hopf et al., 2000 , Taylor 2002). More specifically, the CODAM model of attention that is proposed by Taylor (2002) follows a control theory approach and uses the N2 signal as the signal from the controller that modulates the direction of the focus of attention. Moreover, in Bowman and Wyble's (2007) Simultaneous Type Serial Token (ST_2) model, when the visual system detects a task-relevant item, a spatially specific Transient Attentional Enhancement (TAE), called the blaster, is triggered. In the ST_2 model the presence of a correlation between the blaster and a component of the P2/N2 signal is also hypothesized. The P300 ERP component which is present at about 350–600 ms post-stimulus is taken to be an index of the availability for report of the attention-amplified input arriving from earlier sensory cortices to the associated working memory sensory buffer site. Thus, access to the working memory sensory site is expected to occur in the specific time window. Finally, the N4 component which is recorded at around 400 ms is related to semantic processing indicating perceptual awareness.

The chronometric analysis of the ERPs occurring during the attentional blink has revealed some important observations. More importantly in the case where the second target was not perceived, the P1/N1 and the N400 components which are considered indices of semantic processing were still obtained even though the N2 and P300 were no longer observed (Sergent et al 2005). Thus, one possible explanation for the classic U-shaped curve of Figure 1.b (series 1) based on the identification of the second target to have a minimum at around 300 ms, is that an early attention processing component of the second target (possibly N2 of T2) is inhibited by a late component of the first target (P300 of T1), (Vogel et al 1998,Fell et al 2001).

4 Proposed Model

The proposed model is a two stage model that, in contrast to other computational models, contains a correlation control module (Figure 3). That is, in the case of endogenous attention tasks, the functioning of the model is based on the synchronization of incoming stimuli with information held in the endogenous goals module which has probably been initialized by information from long –term memory (Engel et al 2001).

In the conducted simulations each stimulus that enters the visual field, is coded by determining the rate of the related neuron spikes (enhanced relatively by the salience filters) as well as the exact timing of the spikes. This means that both of these characteristics are considered in the race between the different visual stimuli to access working memory as initially implemented in a computational model by Niebur and Koch (1994).

As shown in Figure 3, a visual stimulus initially moves from the inputs module into the first stage of parallel processing. In this stage, competition among all stimuli, implemented as lateral inhibition, exerts the first impact on each of the neural responses. Following that, as the neural activity continues up through the visual hierarchy, the information from the visual stimuli passes through the semantic correlation control module. During this stage of process, a coincidence detection mechanism similar to the procedure discussed by Mikula and Niebur (2008) measures the degree of correlation between the visual stimuli and the endogenous goals (in the case of top-down attention).

This procedure provides an advantage (in the case of amplification) to the selected neural activity for accessing working memory. However, the initialization of a signal by the correlation control module (that can be implied to be relevant with the N2pc signal -component of N2/P2), can be represented by the combined firing of a neural network. Thus, it is appropriate to consider a relative refractory period each time the correlation control module "fires" or activates the specific signal for amplification or inhibition. Consequently, the refractory period of the correlation control module combined with the lateral inhibition between the RSVP items causes the attenuation of the attentional blink in the case in which the distractors are replaced by blanks and both these mechanisms are inherited in the proposed model (series 2 and 3 in Figure1.b.).

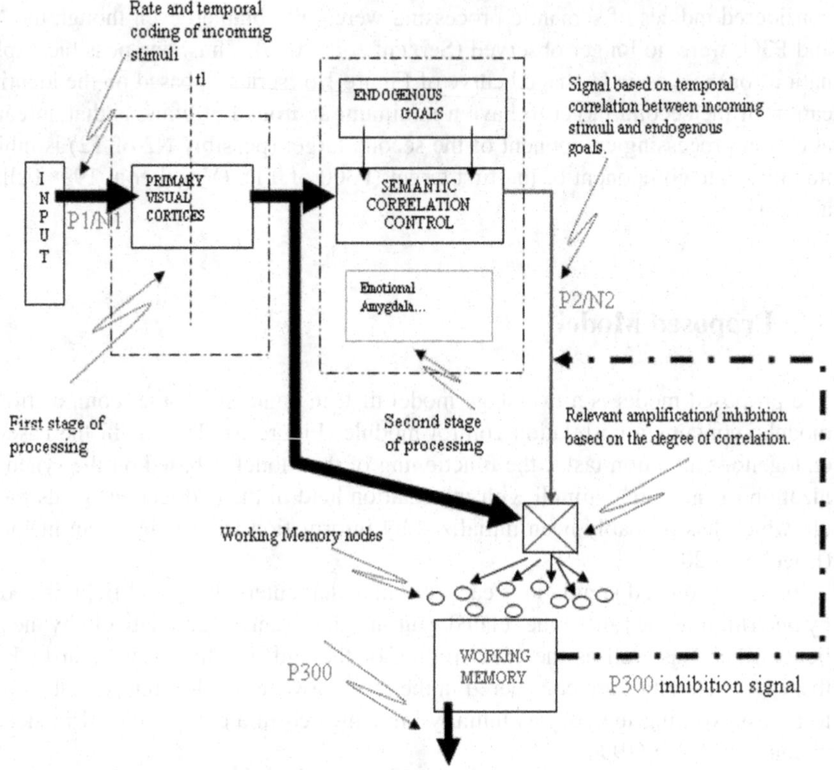

Figure 3. Diagram of the proposed computational model.

Finally, after the handling of the neural activity of each incoming stimulus, a specific working memory node is excited producing inhibition towards the other working memory nodes. After a specific threshold is passed, the working memory node will fire an action potential simulating the initialization of the P300 signal representing perceptual awareness of the specific visual stimuli as well as inhibition of the following signal from the correlation control model (possibly the N2/ P2 signals of the following stimulus) if it appears during that specific timing.

It should be also noted that even stimuli with completely no correlation with the endogenous goals could gain access to working memory sites, provided that their response has been enhanced sufficiently by the salience filters at the first stages of processing. Thus, the model allows for exogenous shifts of attention.

5 Simulations and Results

The computational model has been implemented in the Matlab-Simulink environment. Each of the visual stimuli has been represented by a 10 ms sequence of spikes. As seen in Figure 4, in each ms a value of one (spike) or zero (no-spike) is possible. For coding a target, a specific pattern has been decided so that if the incoming stimulus represents a target, it will have a 0.9 possibility for each time step to have the correct information. On the other hand if the incoming stimulus represents a distractor, it will have a 0.85 possibility of not having the correct information at each time step. Both distractors and targets will have the same rate, which equals to 10 spikes ± a random noise, since both (targets and distractors) have the same effect from the salience filters (same brightness, intensity etc.).

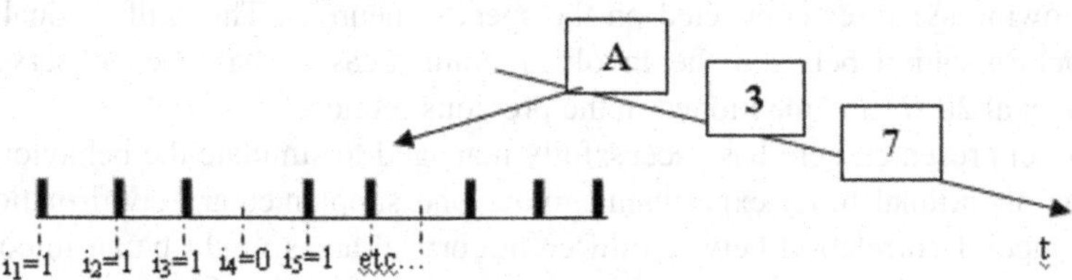

Figure4. Coding of the incoming visual stimuli.

Inside the endogenous goals module, the pattern representing the targets is saved. Therefore, when a visual stimulus enters, a coincidence detector mechanism measures the degree of correlation and fires a relative signal. For the simulations, T1 was always presented at time *t=0* and T2 at each of the following time lags. For each time lag that T2 was presented, the simulations where run for 50 times for the three different cases. That is, when distractors capture all the available positions causing masking to the targets, with blank at lag 1 and with blank at lag 2. The simulation results compared to experimental results can be seen in Figure 5 below.

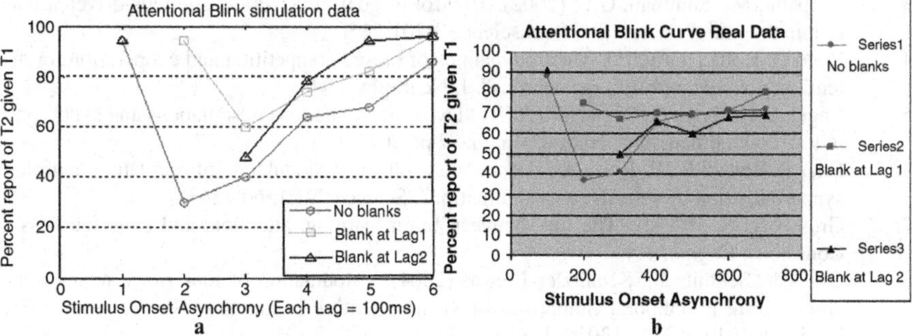

Figure5. Comparison between simulation data (5.a) and experimental data (5.b).

6 Discussion

The model described above has implemented computationally a novel conjecture put forward by Niebur and Koch 1994. Niebur and Koch have suggested that imposing a temporal modulation on attended sensory signals is a plausible mechanism for producing unique percepts within the highly distributed architecture of the cortex.

The coincidence detector mechanism proposed as a basic functionality of the correlation control module between the incoming stimuli and the endogenous goals can cause an increase in the synchronization of the different cortical areas involved in the process. Actually, coincidence detector neurons in the brain are neurons that they fire if they receive synchronous inputs from other neurons. Coincidence of firing between two or more neurons can cause increase in the strength of the following synapses connected on the specific neurons. This will gradually cause synchronization between the involved brain areas as has been observed (Saalmann et al 2007) and mentioned in the previous section.

The model presented here has successfully managed to simulate the behavioral data of the attentional blink experiment giving one supplementary confirmation that the temporal correlation between different cortical areas might be an important mechanism for regulating information through the brain. Furthermore, the coincidence detector neural network model of selective attention can be used to simulate some other important attentional phenomena contributing thus to the formulation of more explicit theories of attention.

References

1. Bowman H.,Wyble S.(2007). "The Simultaneous Type, Serial Token Model of Temporal Attention and Working Memory." Psy. Re., Vol. 114
2. Buehlmann A., Deco G (2008). "The Neuronal Basis of Attention: Rate versus Synchronization Modulation". The Jour. of Neuros. 28(30)
3. Corbetta, M., Shulman, G.L. (2002)."Control of goal-directed and stimulus-driven attention in the brain". Nature R. Neuroscience 3:201-215.
4. Deco G, Rolls ET (2005). "Neurodynamics of biased competition and cooperation for attention: a model with spiking neurons". J. Neurophysi.94
5. Engel A. K., Fries P., Singer W.(2001) "Dynamic predictions: Oscillations and synchrony in top–down processing" Nature, Volume 2 pp.704-716
6. Fries P, Reynolds JH, Rorie AE, Desimone R (2001). "Modulation of oscillatory neuronal synchronization by selective visual attention". Science 291:1560-1563.
7. Grossberg, S. (1999). "The link between brain learning, attention, and consciousness". Conscious. Cogn 8, 1-44
8. Gross J., Schmitz F., Schnitzler I. et al (2004). "Modulation of long-range neural synchrony reflects temporal limitations of visual attention in humans." PNAS August 31, 2004 vol. 101 no. 35 pp13050–13055
9. Gruber T, Muller MM, Keil A, Elbert T (1999). "Selective visual-spatial attention alters induced gamma band responses in the human EEG". Clin Neurophysiol 110:2074-2085.

10. Hopf, J.-M., Luck, S.J., Girelli, M., Hagner, T., Mangun, G.R., Scheich, H., Heinze, H.-J., (2000). "Neural sources of focused attention in visual Search". Cereb. Cortex 10, 1233–1241.
11. Ioannides, A.A., Taylor, J.G., (2003). "Testing models of attention with MEG". In: Proceedings IJCNN'03. pp. 287–297.
12. Mikula S., Niebur E., (2008). "Exact Solutions for Rate and Synchrony in Recurrent Networks of Coincidence Detectors." Neural Computation.20
13. Moran J, Desimone R (1985). "Selective attention gates visual processing in the extrastriate cortex". Science 229:782-784.
14. Niebur E., Hsiao S.S., Johnson K.O., (2002) "Synchrony: a neuronal mechanism for attentional selection?" Cur.Op. in Neurobio., 12:190-194
15. Niebur E, Koch C (1994). "A Model for the Neuronal Implementation of Selective Visual Attention Based on Temporal Correlation Among Neurons". Journal of Computational Neuroseience 1, 141-158.
16. Raymond JE, Shapiro KL, Arnell KM (1992). "Temporary suppression of visual processing in an RSVP task: an attentional blink?". J.of exp. psyc. Human perc, and performance 18 (3): 849–60
17. Saalmann Y.B., Pigarev I.N., et al. (2007). "Neural Mechanisms of Visual Attention: How Top-Down Feedback Highlights Relevant Locations" Science 316 1612
18. Sergent C., Baillet S. & Dehaene S. (2005). "Timing of the brain events underlying access to consiousness during the attentional blink." Nat Neurosci, Volume 8, Number 10, page 1391-1400.
19. Steinmetz PN, Roy A, et al.(2000). "Attention modulates synchronized neuronal firing in primate somatosensory Cortex". Nature 404:187-190.
20. Taylor J.G., Rogers M. (2002). "A control model of the movement of attention". Neural Networks 15:309-326
21. Treisman, A., & Gelade, G. (1980). "A feature-integration theory of attention". Cognitive Psychology, 12, 97-136.
22. Vogel E.K., Luck S.J., Shapiro K.L., (1998). "Electrophysiological evidence for a post-perceptual locus of suppression during the attentional blink." J. Exp. Psychol. Hum. Percept. Perform. 24 pp.1656-1674.

MEDICAL_MAS: an Agent-Based System for Medical Diagnosis

Mihaela Oprea

University Petroleum-Gas of Ploiesti, Department of Informatics,

Bdul Bucuresti Nr. 39, Ploiesti, 100680, Romania

Abstract The paper describes an agent-based system, MEDICAL_MAS, developed for medical diagnosis. The architecture proposed for the system includes mainly two types of agents: personal agents and information searching agents. Each type of personal agent corresponds to the humans involved in the medical diagnosis and treatment process (i.e. the patient, the physician, the nurse). The information searching agents are helping the personal agents to find information from the databases that can be accessed by the system (e.g. patients databases, diseases databases, medication databases etc). A case study is presented in the paper.

1 Introduction

A multi-agent approach is an attempt to solve problems that are inherently (physically or geographically) distributed, where independent processes can be clearly distinguished [1]. Such problems include, for example, decision support systems, networked or distributed control systems (see [2] for a recent review of such applications). The basis of this promising approach is supported by the main characteristics of intelligent agents and/or multi-agent systems, such as autonomy, flexibility, communication, coordination, security and privacy, mobility, adaptability, openness etc. Despite the fact that not all these characteristics are fully implemented at present, their potential application in the area of medicine is important. Due to the fast extension of the Internet and web-based systems in this area too, possible applications that we have identified include: the development of personal agents that assist physicians during their work, the management of a hospital (viewed as a virtual organisation), the patients monitoring and control, wireless applications for ambullance assistance, tutoring systems (e.g. in surgery, or in clinical guideline). At present, there are some agent-based systems or agent-based models for different medical specialities that have been reported in the literature (see e.g. [3], [4], [5], [6]).

Please use the following format when citing this chapter:

Oprea, M., 2009, in IFIP International Federation for Information Processing, Volume 296; *Artificial Intelligence Applications and Innovations III*; Eds. Iliadis, L., Vlahavas, I., Bramer, M.; (Boston: Springer), pp. 225–232.

In this paper, it is presented an application of the multi-agent approach in the medical domain. MEDICAL_MAS is an agent-based system that is under development for medical diagnosis, and whose main purpose is to act as a decision support instrument for physicians during their activity of patients' diagnosis. The paper is organized as follows. Section 2 briefly presents the agent-based approach and some applications in the medical domain. The architecture of the agent-based system MEDICAL_MAS for diagnosis and treatment is described in section 3. A case study in the cardiology area is shown in section 4. The last section concludes the paper and highlights the future work.

2 The Agent-based Approach and its Medical Applications

The agent-based approach can significantly enhances our ability to model, design and build complex (distributed) software systems [7]. An agent can be viewed as a hardware or software entity that has properties such as autonomy and flexibility (social ability, reactivity, pro-activity). From the viewpoint of Artificial Intelligence (AI), an agent is a computer system that apart from the above mentioned properties that must be included in it, it is either conceptualized or implemented by using concepts that are more usually applied to humans (e.g. knowledge, belief, desire, intention, obligation, learning, locality, adaptation, believability, emotion) [8]. Other properties that an agent might have are: mobility, veracity, benevolence, rationality, etc. Also, an important remark is that an agent is embedded in an environment in which lives and interacts with other entities (e.g. agents, legacy software). So, an agent can be viewed as living in a society in which it has to respect the rules of that society. A multi-agent system (MAS) is a particular type of distributed intelligent system in which autonomous agents inhabit a world with no global control or globally consistent knowledge. The characteristics of multi-agent systems include: autonomy, communication, coordination, cooperation, security and privacy, mobility, openness, concurrency, distribution. Most of these characteristics need special approaches when designing and implementing a MAS. Usually, the MAS is based on a multi-agent infrastructure that enables and rules interactions, and acts as a middleware layer that support communication and coordination activities. A major characteristic of the agent technology is the high heterogeneity that means agent model heterogeneity, language heterogeneity, and application heterogeneity. This characteristic has to be manageable by using appropriate models and software toolkits.

Several projects are developing agent-based systems in the medical domain. One type of application is the agent-based modelling of a hospital, viewed as an electronic organization. An example of such framework for modelling a hospital as a virtual multi-agent organization is given in [6]. In some research projects intelligent agents are used for the distribution of human tissues or for the assignment of transplantable organs (see e.g. [6]). A MAS architecture for monitoring medical protocols was developed under the SMASH research project [9]. In [3] it is presented the architecture of a MAS for monitoring medical protocols. Another application that could be modelled by the multi-agent approach is given by the automated clinical guideline in critical care (e.g. an extension of the SmartCare system described in [10], that uses a knowledge-based approach). Other potential applications that we have identified include the development of personal agents that assist physicians during their work, the management of a hospital (viewed as a virtual organisation), the patients monitoring and control, wireless applications for ambullance assistance, tutoring systems (e.g. in surgery). Practically, the main categories of applications are monitoring and control, diagnosis and treatment, planning and scheduling, tutoring. In this paper we shall focus on a multi-agent system dedicated to medical diagnosis and treatment, MEDICAL_MAS, that could act as a decision support instrument for physicians.

3 The Architecture of the System MEDICAL_MAS

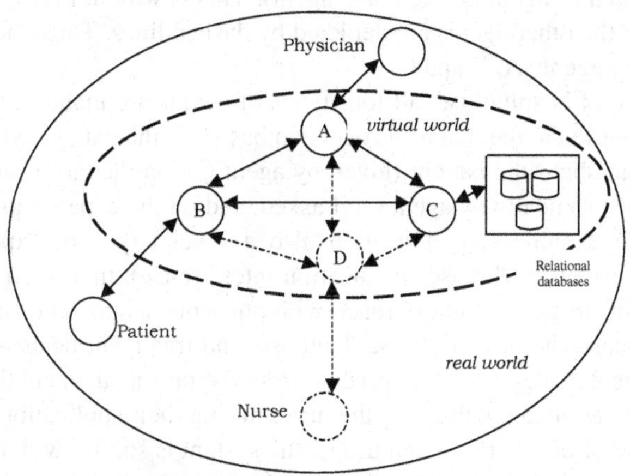

Fig. 1. The architecture of MEDICAL_MAS.

The architecture of the system MEDICAL_MAS is presented in Fig. 1. We have to note that the direct interactions that exist between the humans involved in a diagnosis process are not represented in Fig. 1, as we wanted to focus on the multi-agent system architecture. The agents that compose the system are the virtual correspondences of the humans from the real world, involved in the diagnosis and treatment process, and some auxiliary agents. Thus, there is a physician agent (A), a patient agent (B), a nurse agent (D). All these three types of agents are personal agents that represent the interests of the humans whose representative they are in the virtual world. Other auxiliary agents are used for different purposes, such as for example, the information searching tasks. Agent C is an information searching agent whose task is to find information in the relational databases (patients, diseases, medications etc) that are available to MEDICAL_MAS. The architecture of the physician agent includes a rule-based reasoning mechanism and a knowledge base with decision rules for different diseases diagnosis and treatment. Each rule has associated a degree of confidence in that rule (called confidence factor).

We have designed the system for three possible scenarios of use: e-diagnosis (i.e. distant consultation), hospital use (for patients that are hospitalized), family physician.

In the case of distant consultation (what we've called *e-diagnosis* or *e-consultation*), the system could be used 24 hours from 24 hours. The patients could connect from their homes to the system and give to their personal agents (patient agents B) the description of the symptoms they have and ask for a quick diagnosis and treatment scheme (or at least medical advise) their personal or family physician or guard physician, actually the virtual representative of him, agent A, which is connected on-line (even when the physician is not on-line), and could take a quick decision before a real consultation will take place. We note that such a consultation could be scheduled also via the Internet. Potentially, in this scenario there is no need of agent D (the nurse agent). This is why in Fig. 1 the relations of agent D with the other agents are depicted by dashed lines. Thus, the MAS is composed only by agents A, B and C.

In the case of hospital use, all four types of agents are mandatory, A, B, C and D. Agent A will take the diagnosis decision based on the patient symptoms, on the historical data about the patient (given by agent C), on the lab results (eventually, taken also electronically by agent C) if asked, and on the expert knowledge he has. During this reasoning step it is used also a special type of expert knowledge (drugs' side-effects & diseases medication interference), that referring to possible side-effects of drugs or of interference with other medications taken by the patient for other diseases he has. After the diagnosis and treatment decision made by the physician, the nurse agent D will receive from the physician agent the patient therapy and medication and will guide the nurse during their application.

In the case of family physician usage, the system is similar with that used in the first scenario, with the difference that the physician is always available on-line or at least, can quickly reply after an urgent e-consultation is asked. Basically, there are two possibilities of usage: the patient uses the system from home and has an on-line consultation with his family physician or the patient has a real consultation and during this his family physician uses the system MEDICAL_MAS to take a decision.

Figure 2 describes an interaction diagram. The PatientAgent asks for a consultation. Two situations may arise, either an agreement for the consultation when it is asked (this is the case represented in Fig. 2) or a negotiation for the scheduling of a consultation day and time agreed by both agents (Patient and Physician). During the consultation, the PhysicianAgent will ask the PatientAgent to tell the symptoms he has and also will ask the InfoSearchAgent to tell the historical data on the patient P (which are taken from the PatientsDataBases, PDB). Usually, more information are asked. For example, laboratory tests for the patient P (taken from the LaboratoryDataBases, LDB), more information about some diseases that P might have (taken from the DiseasesDataBases, DDB), and more information on medications and possible side effects and interferences with other medications of the diseases that patient P already has (this last information are taken from the MedicationsDataBases, MDB). All the databases used by the InfoSearchAgent are relational databases. When the PhysicianAgent receives all the asked information, he will use his reasoning mechanism and make a decision regarding the diagnostic (that with the highest confidence factor), the medication and the therapy that should be followed by the patient. In the example shown in Fig. 2, the Patient-Agent is informed on the diagnostic, while the NurseAgent will be informed on the therapy and medication that patient P has to follow. This is the case when MEDICAL_MAS is used in a hospital.

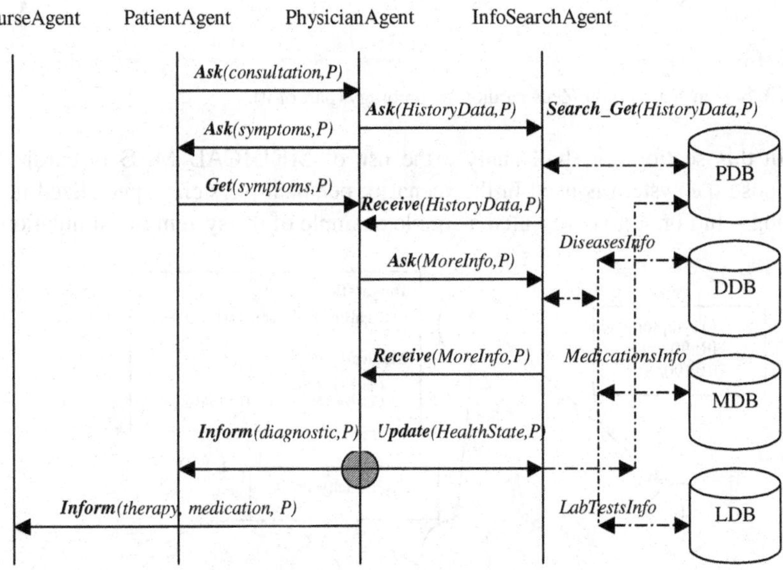

Fig. 2. Example of interaction diagram for the system MEDICAL_MAS.

4 Case Study in Cardiology

The system is developed in Zeus [11], and so far, we have implemented the ontology (Fig. 3 shows a screenshot with a part of the cardiology ontology), and we are currently developing a first version of the multi-agent system.

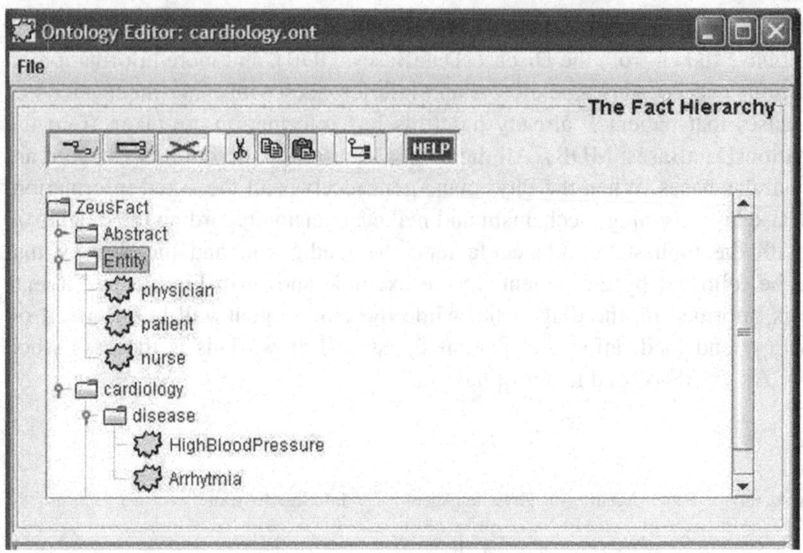

Fig. 3. Screenshot with the Zeus cardiology ontology (part of it).

In this section we shall analyse the use of MEDICAL_MAS in cardiology. Suppose the system is used in the scenario: personal physician specialized in cardiology. In Fig. 4 it is presented a simple example of the system run simulation.

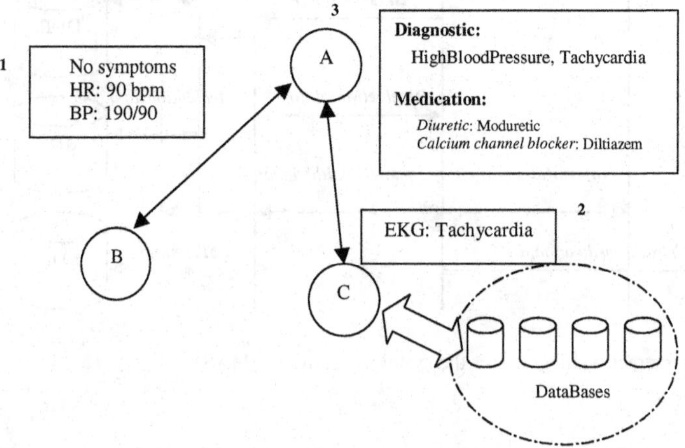

Fig. 4. Example of MEDICAL_MAS use in cardiology.

In the example we have taken the case of a patient that has no symptoms, but has problems with blood pressure. After the examination made by the physician with the use of the sphygmomanometer the collected data are the following:

{ heart rate (HR) = 90 bpm, blood pressure (BP) = 190/90 }

From the InfoSearchAgent (C) the PhysicianAgent (A) receives the result of an EKG Lab Test, which shows the presence of tachycardia. The result of the whole reasoning process of MEDICAL_MAS on the heart health state of patient (represented by agent B) gives the diagnostic of high blood pressure and tachycardia, and prescript a medication with two drugs: Moduretic (chosen so that it has no side effect on the potassium loss), and Diltiazem. As most of the antihypertensives have side-effects, all these interference rules are included in the knowledge base of the PhysicianAgent, A, so that the medication given to the patient will have minimum side-effects.

In the case of cardiology use, MEDICAL_MAS need to have included in the knowledge base of agent A the description of all possible diseases: arrhythmia, high blood pressure, cholesterol, heart attack, peripheral artery disease, congenital heart disease and so on (see e.g. [12]). Also, it should have a description of all categories of drugs. For example, in the case of high blood pressure there are several types of antihypertensives: diuretics, beta-blockers, ACE inhibitors, Angiotensin II receptor blockers, Calcium channel blockers etc. All the side-effects of the drugs need to be included in the knowledge base.

5 Conclusion and Future Work

The agent-based approach is one of the most efficient AI technologies that could be applied with success in the medical field, especially in the case of Internet and web-based applications extension in this area. The paper presented a multi-agent system for medical diagnosis, MEDICAL_MAS, that is under development, and was designed to act as a decision support instrument for physicians. So far, we have realized the analysis, and the design steps of the system development. Also, a first preliminary implementation in Zeus was made, and we have studied the use of the it in different scenarios. As a future work, we will end the implementation phase, and we shall experiment the system use in more different case studies.

The main advantage of using MEDICAL_MAS is given by the possibility of making the best decision regarding the diagnostic for a particular patient as well as giving the best medication in a specific context of the patient health state. We have to note that despite the fact that other artificial intelligence technologies (e.g. expert systems) have offered quite similar benefits in the medical domain, the multi-agent systems technology has the advantages (naming just few of them): of using distributed expertise knowledge (searched and collected on line by the agents), of being pro-active (e.g. taking the initiative to do some search on the web), and of being capable of communication. As time is an important resource for everyone, especially for physicians which are usually work overloaded, MEDICAL_MAS could offer them an efficient decision making instrument that can assist their work.

References

1. Weiss, G. (ed.): Multiagent systems: a modern approach to distributed artificial intelligence, The MIT Press, Cambridge, Massachusetts (1999).
2. Oprea, M.: Applications of multi-agent systems, in: Reis, R. (ed.): Information Technology, Kluwer Academic Publishers, Boston Dordrecht London (2004) 239-270.
3. Alsinet, T., Béjan, R., Fernàndez, C., Manyà, F.: A Multi-Agent System Architecture for Monitoring Medical Protocols, Proceedings 4th International Conference on Autonomous Agents (2000) 499-505.
4. Gatti, N., Amigoni, F.: A Cooperative Negotiation Protocol for Physiological Model Combination, Proceedings 3rd International Joint Conference on Autonomous Agents & Multi Agent Systems AAMAS (2004) 656-663.
5. Vàzquez-Salceda, J., Cortés, U., Padget, J.: Integrating the organ and tissue allocation processes through an agent-mediated electronic institution, Lecture Notes in Artificial Intelligence LNAI 2504, Springer Verlag, Berlin (2002) 309-321.
6. Vàzquez-Salceda, J., Dignum, F.: Modelling Electronic Organizations, in Mařík, V., Müller, J., Pěchouček, M. (eds.): Multi-Agent Systems and Applications III, Lecture Notes in Artificial Intelligence LNAI 2691, Springer Verlag, Berlin (2003) 584-593.
7. Wooldridge, M., Jennings, N.: Intelligent agents: theory and practice, The Knowledge Engineering Review, 10(2) (1995) 115-152.
8. Russel, S., Norvig, P.: Artificial Intelligence: A Modern Approach, Prentice Hall (1995).
9. SMASH project homepage: http://www.iiia.csic.es/Projects/smash/
10. Mersmann, S., Dojat, M.: SmartCare – Automated Clinical Guidelines in Critical Care, Proceedings of ECAI'04, IOS Press (2004) 745-749.
11. Zeus homepage: http://www.labs.bt.com/projects/agents/zeus/
12. http://americanheart.org

Heterogeneous Data Fusion to Type Brain Tumor Biopsies

Vangelis Metsis[1], Heng Huang[1], Fillia Makedon[1], and Aria Tzika[2]

1 University of Texas at Arlington, USA, vangjel.meci@mavs.uta.edu, heng@uta.edu, makedon@uta.edu

2 NMR Surgical Laboratory, Department of Surgery, Harvard Medical School and Massachusetts General Hospital, Boston, USA, tzika@hms.harvard.edu

Abstract Current research in biomedical informatics involves analysis of multiple heterogeneous data sets. This includes patient demographics, clinical and pathology data, treatment history, patient outcomes as well as gene expression, DNA sequences and other information sources such as gene ontology. Analysis of these data sets could lead to better disease diagnosis, prognosis, treatment and drug discovery. In this paper, we use machine learning algorithms to create a novel framework to perform the heterogeneous data fusion on both metabolic and molecular datasets, including state-of-the-art high-resolution magic angle spinning (HRMAS) proton (1H) Magnetic Resonance Spectroscopy and gene transcriptome profiling, to intact brain tumor biopsies and to identify different profiles of brain tumors. Our experimental results show our novel framework outperforms any analysis using individual dataset.

1 Introduction

Brain tumors are the second most common cancer of childhood, and comprise approximately 25% of all pediatric cancers. Over 3,400 children are diagnosed in the U.S. each year; of that, about 2,600 will be under the age of 15. Brain tumors are the leading cause of solid tumor cancer death in children; they are the third leading cause of cancer death in young adults ages 20-39. Many researchers are looking for efficient and reliable ways to early diagnose brain tumor types and detect related biomarkers through different biomedical images or biological data. The machine learning algorithms have been playing the most important role during those heterogamous biomedical/biological datasets analysis to classify different brain tumor types and detect biomarkers.

Magnetic resonance spectroscopic (MRS) studies of brain biomarkers can provide statistically significant biomarkers for tumor grade differentiation and im-

Please use the following format when citing this chapter:

Metsis, V., Huang, H., Makedon, F. and Tzika, A., 2009, in IFIP International Federation for Information Processing, Volume 296; *Artificial Intelligence Applications and Innovations III*; Eds. Iliadis, L., Vlahavas, I., Bramer, M.; (Boston: Springer), pp. 233–240.

proved predictors of cancer patient survival [1]. Instead of selecting biomarkers based on microscopic histology and tumor morphology, the introduction of microarray technology improves the discovery rates of different types of cancers through monitoring thousands of gene expressions in a parallel, in a rapid and efficient manner [23][8]. Because the genes are aberrantly expressed in tumor cells, researchers can use their aberrant expression as biomarkers that correspond to and facilitate precise diagnoses and/or therapy outcomes of malignant transformation.

Different data sources are likely to contain different and partly independent information about the brain tumor. Combining those complementary pieces of information can be expected to enhance the brain tumor diagnosis and biomarkers detection. Recently, several studies have attempted to correlate imaging findings with molecular markers, but no consistent associations have emerged and many of the imaging features that characterize tumors currently lack biological or molecular correlates [7][6]. Much of the information encoded within neuroimaging studies therefore remains unaccounted for and incompletely characterized at the molecular level [4]. This paper presents a computational and machine learning based framework for integrating heterogeneous genome-scale gene expression and MRS data to classify the different brain tumor types and detect biomarkers. We employ wrapper method to integrate the feature selection process of both gene expression and MRS. Three popular feature selection methods, Relief-F (RF), Information Gain (IG) and χ^2-statistic (χ^2), are performed to filter out the redundant features in both datasets. The experimental results show our framework using the combination of two datasets outperforms any individual dataset on sample classification accuracy that is the standard validation criterion in cancer classification and biomarker detection. Our data fusion framework exhibits great potential on heterogeneous data fusion between biomedical image and biological datasets and it could be extended to another cancer diseases study.

2 Methodology

Advancements in the diagnosis and prognosis of brain tumor patients, and thus in their survival and quality of life, can be achieved using biomarkers that facilitate improved tumor typing. In our research, we apply state-of-the-art, high-resolution magic angle spinning (HRMAS) proton (1H) MRS and gene transcriptome profiling to intact brain tumor biopsies, to evaluate the discrimination accuracy for tumor typing of each of the above methods separately and in combination. We used 46 samples of normal (control) and brain tumor biopsies from which we obtained ex vivo HRMAS 1H MRS and gene expression data respectively. The samples came from tissue biopsies taken from 16 different people. Out of the forty-six biopsies that were analyzed, 9 of them were control biopsies from epileptic surgeries and the rest 37 were brain tumor biopsies. The tumor biopsies belonged to 5 different categories: 11 glioblastoma multiforme (GBM); 8 anaplastic astrocytoma (AA); 7 meningioma; 7 schwanoma; and 5 from adenocarcinoma.

HRMAS 1H MRS. Magnetic resonance spectroscopic (MRS) studies of brain biomarkers can provide statistically significant biomarkers for tumor grade differentiation and improved predictors of cancer patient survival [1]. Ex vivo high-resolution magic angle spinning (HRMAS) proton (1H) MRS of unprocessed tissue samples can help interpret in vivo 1H MRS results, to improve the analysis of micro-heterogeneity in high-grade tumors [3]. Furthermore, two-dimensional HRMAS 1H MRS enables more detailed and unequivocal assignments of biologically important metabolites in intact tissue samples [16]. In Fig.1, an ex vivo HRMAS 1H MR spectrum of a 1.9 mg anaplastic ganglioglioma tissue biopsy is shown together with metabolites values that correspond to each frequency of the spectrum. Please see more detailed information in [29].

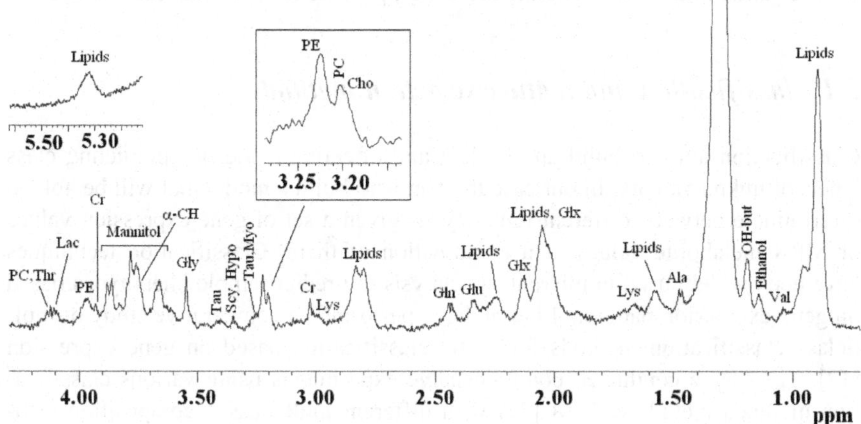

Fig. 1: Ex vivo HRMAS 1H MR spectrum of a 5.8 mg glioblastoma multiforme (GBM) tissue biopsy. Val, Valine; OH-but, OH-butyrate; Lac, Lactate; Ala, Alanine; Lys, Lysine; Glx, □-CH2 of Glutamine and Glutamate; Glu, Glutamate; Gln, Glutamine; Cr, Creatine; Tau, Taurine; Myo, Myo-inositol; Hypo, Hypotaurine; Scy, Scyllo-inositol; Gly, Glycine; □-CH of aliphatic amino-acids; PE, PhosphoEtanolamine; Thr, Threonine; PC, PhoshoCholine; Cho, Choline. The insert shows the choline containing compounds region.

Microscale genomics. A major focus in cancer research is to identify genes, using DNA-microarrays that are aberrantly expressed in tumor cells, and to use their aberrant expression as biomarkers that correspond to and facilitate precise diagnoses and/or therapy outcomes of malignant transformation [17]. In our study, the Affymetrix gene-chip U133Plus® DNA microarray of the complete human genome was used to perform transcriptome profiling on each specimen for two different experimental conditions, minus or plus previous HRMAS NMR analysis. The raw expression data were analyzed for probe intensities using the Affymetrix GeneChip expression analysis manual procedures; and the data were normalized using current R implementations of RMA algorithms [10].

Combining MRS and genomic data. While several studies have utilized MRS data or genomic data to promote cancer classification, to date these two methods have not been combined and cross-validated to analyze the same cancer samples. Herein, we implement a combined quantitative biochemical and molecular approach to identify diagnostic biomarker profiles for tumor fingerprinting that can facilitate the efficient monitoring of anticancer therapies and improve the survival and quality of life of cancer patients. The MRS and genomic data strongly correlate, to further demonstrate the biological relevance of MRS for tumor typing [21]. Also, the levels of specific metabolites, such as choline containing metabolites, are altered in tumor tissue, and these changes correspond to the differential expression of Kennedy cycle genes responsible for the biosynthesis of choline phospholipids (such as phosphatidylcholine) and suggested to be altered with malignant transformation [18]. These data demonstrate the validity of our combined approach to produce and utilize MRS/genomic biomarker profiles to type brain tumor tissue.

2.1 Classification and feature selection methods

Classification aims to build an efficient and effective model for predicting class labels of unknown data. In our case the aim is to build a model that will be able to discriminate between different tumor types given a set of gene expression values or MRS metabolite values or a combination of them. Classification techniques have been widely used in microarray analysis to predict sample phenotypes based on gene expression patterns. Li et al. have performed a comparative study of multiclass classification methods for tissue classification based on gene expression [12]. They have conducted comprehensive experiments using various classification methods including SVM [22] with different multiclass decomposition techniques, Naive Bayes [14], K-nearest neighbor and decision trees [20].

Since the main purpose of this study is not to assess the classification performance of different classification algorithms but to evaluate the potential gain of combining more than one type of data for tumor typing, we only experimented with Naïve Bayes (NB) and Support Vector Machines (SVM) with RBF kernel.

Another related task is *feature selection* that selects a small subset of discriminative features. Feature selection has several advantages, especially for the gene expression data. First, it reduces the risk of over fitting by removing noisy features thereby improving the predictive accuracy. Second, the important features found can potentially reveal that specific chromosomal regions are consistently aberrant for particular cancers. There is biological support that a few key genetic alterations correspond to the malignant transformation of a cell [19]. Determination of these regions from gene expression datasets can allow for high-resolution global gene expression analysis to genes in these regions and thereby can help in focusing investigative efforts for understanding cancer on them.

Existing feature selection methods broadly fall into two categories, wrapper and filter methods. Wrapper methods use the predictive accuracy of predetermined classification algorithms, such as SVM, as the criteria to determine the goodness of a subset of features [9]. Filter methods select features based on discriminant criteria that rely on the characteristics of data, independent of any classification algorithm [5]. Filter methods are limited in scoring the predictive power of combined features, and thus have shown to be less powerful in predictive accuracy as compared to wrapper methods [2]. In our experiments we used feature selection method from both major categories. We experimented with Relief-F (RF), Information Gain (IG), and χ^2-statistic (χ^2), filter methods and we also used wrapper feature selection for each of the two types of classification algorithms.

The basic idea of *Relief-F* [11] is to draw instances at random, compute their nearest neighbors, and adjust a feature weighting vector to give more weight to features that discriminate the instance from neighbors of different classes. Specifically, it tries to find a good estimate of the following probability to assign as the weight for each feature f.

w_f = P(different value of f | different class) - P(different value of f | same class)

Information Gain (IG) [15] measures the number of bits of information obtained for class prediction by knowing the value of a feature. Let $\{c_i\}_{i=1}^{m}$ denote the set of classes. Let V be the set of possible values for feature f. The information gain of a feature f is defined to be:

$$G(f) = -\sum_{i=1}^{m} P(c_i)\log P(c_i) + \sum_{\upsilon\in V}\sum_{i=1}^{m} P(f=\upsilon)P(c_i \mid f=\upsilon)\log P(c_i \mid f=\upsilon)$$

The *χ^2-statistic (χ^2)* [13] measures the lack of independence between f and c. It is defined as follows:

$$\chi^2(f) = \sum_{\upsilon\in V}\sum_{i=1}^{m} \frac{(A_i(f=\upsilon) - E_i(f=\upsilon))^2}{E_i(f=\upsilon)}$$

where V is the set of possible values for feature f, $A_i(f = \upsilon)$ is the number of instances in class c_i with $f = \upsilon$, $E_i(f = \upsilon)$ is the expected value of $A_i(f = \upsilon)$. $E_i(f = \upsilon)$ is computed with $E_i(f = \upsilon) = P(f = \upsilon)P(c_i)N$, where N is the total number of instances.

3 Experimental Results

Initially we aimed at evaluating how well the classifiers would perform when applying them to each of our datasets separately. For that purpose we performed 10-fold cross validation over our 46 samples by using a combination of feature selection and classification methods.

Table 1 shows the classification accuracy of Naïve Bayes (NB) and SVM classifiers when using all 16 *metabolites* and when using a feature selection method. Clearly the wrapper feature selection method gives the better accuracy across all classifiers, followed by the case where we use all metabolites for classification. The SVM classifier using RBF kernel consistently shows the best performance in this type of data. The decision of keeping the top 6 metabolites when using the filter feature selection methods was based on the fact that that was the best number of features that were selected by using the wrapper feature selection method for each classification algorithm.

Table 1: Classification accuracy for the 6-class problem using MRS data only.

	NB	SVM
All metabolites	70.21 %	72.34 %
χ^2 (top 6)	46.81 %	51.06 %
IG (top 6)	46.81 %	51.06 %
RF (top 6)	63.83 %	68.09 %
Wrapper	72.34 %	**78.72 %**

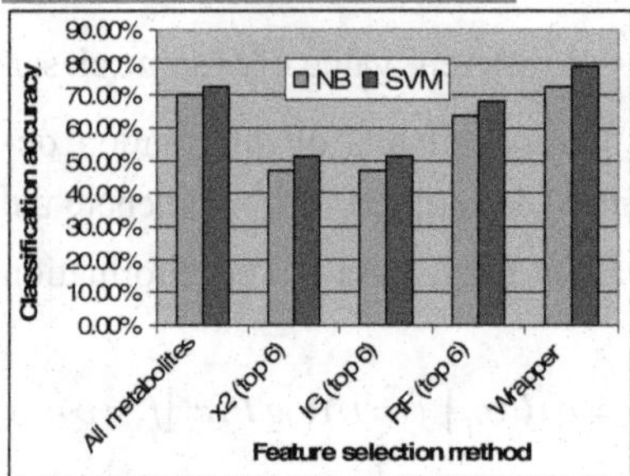

Table 2: Classification accuracy using gene expression data only.

	NB	SVM
χ^2 + wrapper	**82.98 %**	46.81 %
IG + wrapper	80.85 %	61.70 %
RF + wrapper	61.70 %	57.44 %

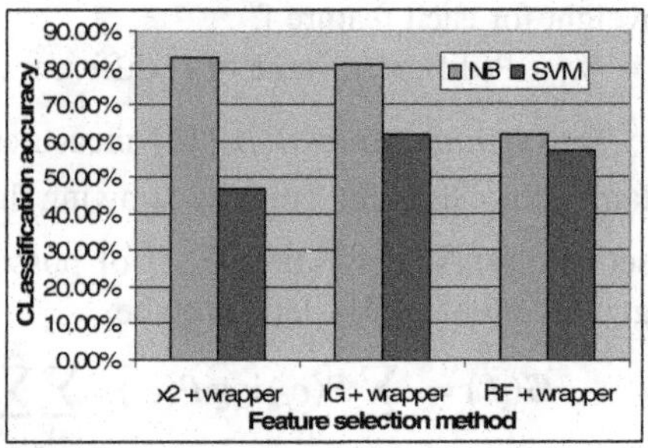

For the problem of the multiclass classification using gene expression data only, we followed a hybrid feature selection method combining filter and wrapper approaches. Using wrapper approach to select a few top genes starting from an initial number of thousands of genes is computationally prohibiting, and using filter approach to select less than 100 genes does not give good classification accuracy because the final set of selected genes contains genes that are highly correlated to each other, thus giving a redundant set of genes. In our approach, first we selected the top 100 genes using filter feature selection and then we used wrapper feature selection to further reduce the number of genes to be used resulting usually in a number between 5 and 15 genes.

The experimental results (Table 2) show that in this type of data the Naïve Bayes was by far the best classification algorithm obtaining a maximum accuracy of 82.98% accuracy when combined with $\chi 2$ and wrapper feature selection.

Finally, we tested the classification accuracy of our methods by using a combination of features from both gene expression and MRS data. For the MRS data we tested the wrapper feature selection method which performed best in our previous experiments. For the gene expression data we used the feature selection method that we described above, i.e. combination of filter and wrapper feature selection. After completing the feature selection stage separately for each of the datasets we combined the selected features by putting them in the same feature vector space and using that space for classification. Table 3 shows the classification accuracy results of our experiments. In most cases, the combination of features sets from the two datasets yield significantly better accuracy than each of them separately.

In general Naïve Bayes gives the best performance with a maximum accuracy of 87.23% when using wrapper feature selection for metabolites and a combination of Information Gain and wrapper feature selection for genes.

Table 3: Classification accuracy using a combination of features from gene expression and MRS datasets.

	NB	SVM
Metabolite selection: wrapper Gene selection: χ^2 + wrapper	85.11%	74.46%
Metabolite selection: wrapper Gene selection: IG + wrapper	**87.23%**	80.85%
Metabolite selection: wrapper Gene selection: RF + wrapper	78.72%	76.59%

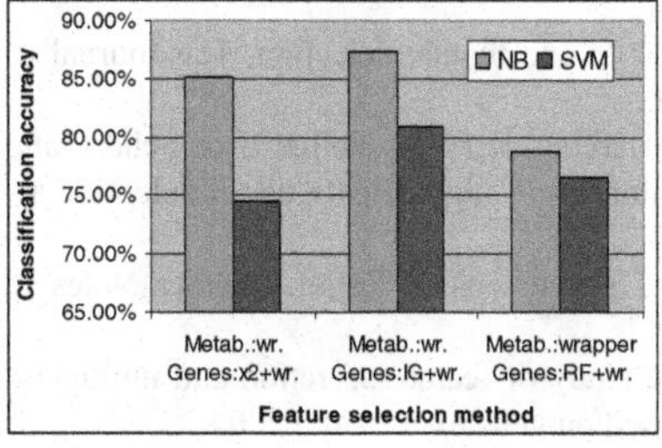

4 Conclusion

In this paper, we propose a machine learning based data fusion framework which integrates heterogeneous data sources to type different brain tumors. Our method employs real biomedical/biological MRS and genomic data and applies a combination of popular feature selection and classification methods to evaluate the tumor type discrimination capabilities of the two datasets separately and together. The feature selection process identifies a number of biomarkers from each dataset which are subsequently used as features for the classification process. The experimental results show that our data fusion framework outperforms each individual dataset in the brain tumor multi-class classification problem. Since our framework is a general method, it can also be applied to any other biomedical and biological data fusion for sample classification and biomarker detection.

References

1. LG Astrakas, D Zurakowski, and AA Tzika et al. Noninvasive magnetic resonance spectroscopic imaging biomarkers to predict the clinical grade of pediatric brain tumors. Clin Cancer Res, 10:8220–8228, 2004.

2. H. Chai and C. Domeniconi. An Evaluation of Gene Selection Methods for Multi-class Microarray Data Classification. ECML/PKDD 2004.
3. L.L. Cheng, D.C. Anthony, A.R. Comite, P.M. Black, A.A. Tzika, and R.G. Gonzalez. Quantification of microheterogeneity in glioblastoma multiforme with ex vivo high-resolution magic-angle spinning (HRMAS) proton magnetic resonance spectroscopy. Neuro-Oncology, 2(2):87–95, 2000.
4. M Diehn, C Nardini, and et al. Identification of noninvasive imaging surrogates for brain tumor gene-expression modules. Proc Natl Acad Sci, 105(13):5213–5218, 2008.
5. C. Ding and H. Peng. Minimum redundancy feature selection from microarray gene expression data. Journal of Bioinformatics and Computational Biology, 3(2):185–205, 2005.
6. Carlson MR et al. Relationship between survival and edema in malignant gliomas: role of vascular endothelial growth factor and neuronal pentraxin. Clin Cancer Res., 13(9):2592–2598, 2007.
7. Hobbs SK et al. Magnetic resonance image-guided proteomics of human glioblastoma multiforme. Magn. Reson. Imaging, 18(5):530–536, 2003.
8. J.N. Rich et al. Gene expression profiling and genetic markers in glioblastoma survival. Cancer Research, 65:4051–4058, 2005.
9. Guyon and A. Elisseeff. An introduction to variable and feature selection. The Journal of Machine Learning Research, 3:1157–1182, 2003.
10. R.A. Irizarry, B. Hobbs, F. Collin, Y.D. Beazer-Barclay, K.J. Antonellis, Uwe Scherf, and T.P. Speed. Exploration, normalization, and summaries of high density oligonucleotide array probe level data. Biostatistics, 4(2):249, 2003.
11. Kononenko. Estimating Attributes: Analysis and Extensions of Relief. Lecture Notes in Computer Science, pages 171–171, 1994.
12. T. Li, C. Zhang, and M. Ogihara. A comparative study of feature selection and multiclass classification methods for tissue classification based on gene expression, 2004.
13. H. Liu and R. Setiono. Chi2: Feature selection and discretization of numeric attributes. In Proceedings 7th International Conference on Tools with Artificial Intelligence, page 88. IEEE Computer Society Washington, DC, 1995.
14. V. Metsis, I. Androutsopoulos, and G. Paliouras. Spam filtering with naive bayes – which naive bayes. In Third Conference on Email and Anti-Spam (CEAS), 2006.
15. T.M. Mitchell. Machine Learning. 1997. Burr Ridge, IL: McGraw Hill.
16. D. Morvan, A. Demidem, J. Papon, M. De Latour, and J.C. Madelmont. Melanoma Tumors Acquire a New Phospholipid Metabolism Phenotype under Cystemustine As Revealed by High-Resolution Magic Angle Spinning Proton Nuclear Magnetic Resonance Spectroscopy of Intact Tumor Samples 1, 2002.
17. C.L. Nutt, DR Mani, R.A. Betensky, P. Tamayo, J.G. Cairncross, C. Ladd, U. Pohl, C. Hartmann, M.E. McLaughlin, T.T. Batchelor, et al. Gene Expression-based Classification of Malignant Gliomas Correlates Better with Survival than Histological Classification 1, 2003.
18. F. Podo. Tumour phospholipid metabolism. NMR in Biomedicine, 12(7):413–439, 1999.
19. MJ Renan. How many mutations are required for tumorigenesis? Implications from human cancer data. Mol Carcinog, 7(3):139–46, 1993.
20. PN Tan, M. Steinbach, and V. Kumar. Introduction to Data Mining. 2005.
21. A.A. Tzika, L. Astrakas, H. Cao, D. Mintzopoulos, O.C. Andronesi, M. Mindrinos, J. Zhang, L.G. Rahme, K.D. Blekas, A.C. Likas, et al. Combination of high-resolution magic angle spinning proton magnetic resonance spectroscopy and microscale genomics to type brain tumor biopsies. International Journal of Molecular Medicine, 20(2):199, 2007.
22. V. Vapnik. Statistical Learning Theory. 1998. NY Wiley.
23. S.J. Watson, F. Meng, R.C. Thompson, and H. Akil. The chip as a specific genetic tool. Biol Psychiatry, 48:1147–1156, 2000.

Automatic Knowledge Discovery and Case Management: an Effective Way to Use Databases to Enhance Health Care Management

[1]Luciana SG Kobus, [2]Fabrício Enembreck, [1,2]Edson Emílio Scalabrin, [1]João da Silva Dias, [1]Sandra Honorato da Silva

Pontifical Catholic University of Paraná - Brazil

[1] Graduate Program on Health Technology
[2] Graduate Program on Applied Informatics

{kobus.l@pucpr.br, fabricio@ppgia.pucpr.br, scalabrin@ppgia.pucpr.br, jdias@voe.com.br, sandra.honorato@pucpr.br}

Abstract This paper presents a methodology based on automatic knowledge discovery that aims to identify and predict the possible causes that makes a patient to be considered of high cost. The experiments were conducted in two directions. The first was the identification of important relationships among variables that describe the health care events using an association rules discovery process. The second was the discovery of precise prediction models of high cost patients, using classification techniques. Results from both methods are discussed to show that the patterns generated could be useful to the development of a high cost patient eligibility protocol, which could contribute to an efficient case management model.

1 Introduction

The public and the supplementary Brazilian health program are strongly based on a health practice focused on curing. This fact leads to a high degree of complexity of procedures, to high costs of health care, to failure of the attendance of the real health clients' needs of health promotion and prevention of diseases, and difficulties on their access to health services. Such contradictory aspects interfere on the management of health organizations.

Case management is an opportunity of improving the population health condition. This model could be improved by the application of precise prediction models to identify a health system user that could become of high risk and high cost. The monitoring of this user could be the foundation to needed health care in the

---

Please use the following format when citing this chapter:

Kobus, L.S.G., Enembreck, F., Scalabrin, E.E., Dias, J.S., da Silva, S.H., 2009, in IFIP International Federation for Information Processing, Volume 296; *Artificial Intelligence Applications and Innovations III*; Eds. Iliadis, L., Vlahavas, I., Bramer, M.; (Boston: Springer), pp. 241–247.

right time, in an efficient way, in an attempt to avoid the development or worsening of a disease.

In this paper, two automatic knowledge discovery techniques were used on patient data. The first aimed to find rules that could show important relationships among variables that describe health care events. The second aimed to find precise prediction models of high risk and high cost patients. To improve the accuracy of the prediction model generated and diminish the negative impact obtained by sampling techniques, ensembles of classifiers were used. The use of these combining techniques was necessary because of the great amount of data. The combining of classifiers generated by samples of a same database could significantly improve the prediction's precision, even when the size of the samples is really small [10, 11]. Results from both methods are discussed, to show that the patterns generated could be useful to the development of a high cost patient eligibility protocol, as well as to the definition of an efficient and particular case management model for the population of the study. This paper is organized as follow. Section 2 shows the particularities of case management. Sections 3 and 4, respectively, show symbolical machine learning theoretical basis and methods. Finally, we present the conclusions from this study in Section 5.

2 Case Management

The case management primary goal is the search for benefits to the health system user and his family, as well for the health care providers and payers. This goals could be achieved by (a) the search for quality health care, in a way that the health care provided be appropriated and beneficial to the population; (b) the inpatient length of stay management; (c) the control of the utilization of support resources by the use of information systems based on protocols and decision support techniques; and (d) health care cost control assuring efficient results [6].

High risk patients correspond to almost 1% of a health care system population. However, this small part of users corresponds to 30% of the available resources utilization ([3, 4, 5]). The users which health care generates high costs to the health systems are those who present the most complex profiles by both clinical and psychosocial points of view. Near 45% of these patients have five or more diagnoses to describe their chronic condition, each one of these diagnostics could be the focus of a specific case management program [4]. However, the precise identification of a high cost patient is not a simple task, mainly if it is done without the help of suitable computational tools. This is why we chose to apply different symbolic machine learning techniques.

3 Symbolic Machine Learning and Meta-Learning

Symbolic learning systems are used in situations where the obtained model assumes a comprehensible shape. The induction of decision trees by ID3 system [7] and the production rules generation by decision trees [8] were important contributions by this field of Knowledge Discovery from Databases. More efficient versions of these algorithms were developed, like C4.5 and C5.0 [9].

Symbolic representation based on *association rules* are a powerful formalism that enables the discovery of items that occur simultaneously and frequently in a database. Each rule has a support. In [1] such support is defined as the relative number of cases in which the rules could be applied. In this study we won't explain how the methods work, because they are very well-known by the literature.

Some combining techniques allow that very precise prediction models could be built by combining classifiers generated by samples of training data sets. Such techniques usually use some heuristics to select examples and partition the dataset. Some studies show that the combining of classifiers generated from many database samples could significantly improve the precision of the prediction, even when the size of these samples is very small ([10, 11]). Two well-known ensemble techniques are *Bagging* e *Boosting*. The reader is invited to consult ([2, 10, 11]) for more details about them.

4 Method

The population of the study was the data from the users of Curitiba Health Institute (ICS), which is responsible for the health care of the Curitiba (Paraná, Brazil) City Hall employees and their families[1]. Initially, data related to the period of 2001 to 2005 were analyzed, in a total of 55.814 users and 1.168.983 entries. Considering that the ICS epidemiological profile is congruent with the one of Curitiba area, and the operational need to decrease the number of entries from the original database, two criteria of data selection were defined: (i) users with age equal or above 40 years old; and (ii) users that had, in their health care entries, at least one registration related to the cardiovascular diseases group of the international code of diseases version 10 (ICD-10).

After we applied the criteria, the initial sample decreased to 401.041 entries, referring to 8.457 users and 1.799 diseases' codes. These two last values will define, respectively, the numbers of lines and columns of the database that will be used ahead for the generation of association rules and prediction models.

The *first phase* aims to discover associations among procedures that generate a pattern which is indicative of high cost and high complexity and learn with this association to detect similar cases in the future. Apriori [1] algorithm was applied to discover such association rules.

1 Data utilization was authorized by both the Institute and the Pontifical Catholic University of Paraná Ethics on Research Committee, register number 924.

The amount of relevant rules after both analysis process (subjective and trust analysis) is of 18. Table 1 shows only 2 of them. The high association of cardiovascular procedures with emergency consultations could be related or to the serious condition of the user's health, or to the poor monitoring of the users with cardiovascular problems, once few procedures or exams are requested in a frequent way to the cardiovascular diagnostic.

The fact of an "emergency consultation" event is associated to a heart procedure shows the importance of establishing a monitoring protocol to users that were submitted to cardiovascular procedures. The outpatient following after heart procedures should be a priority not only for the user's health, but also to the proper management of health care providers and payers.

Table 1: Relevant rules after subjective and trust analysis of the significant events.

ID	Association Rules
R01	10,5% of the users presented in their historic the procedure MYOCARDIC REVASCULARIZATION; among these, 75% have the probability to present association with an EMERGENCY CONSULTATION
R10	11,8% of the users presented in their historic the fact of being from the male sex associated to the procedure of GLYCATED HAEMOGLOBIN; among these, 100% have the probability to present association with referential values of MYOCARDIC REVASCULARIZATION.

The rule R10 was considered relevant because it indicates a relationship between male users, the GLYCATED HAEMOGLOBIN procedure, and the MYOCARDIC REVASCULARIZATION procedure. Accordingly to the same specialists, this is important information to establish educational and preventive programs to users of the male sex. These 18 rules compose the first part of the decision support system to help improve the characterization of a user of the health system that should be managed.

The *second phase*: the training database preparation for obtaining the prediction models uses as entry the same data that were used in the first analysis and the same selection criteria. However, some attributes were removed by a filter process and other attributes were included by derivation (Table 2). Next section shows the application of different machine learning techniques to obtain high cost patients prediction models.

Table 2. Attributes added to training database.

Attribute	Description
procedure	Sequential number indicating the 1st, 2nd, …, nth procedure of a patient.
nprocedure	Number of procedures of a patient.
distance1	Distance, in number of months, between the date of the first procedure, and the date of the nth procedure of a patient.
distance2	Distance, in number of months, between the date of the last event and the date of the first event of a patient.
age	Age, in years, of a patient.
sex	Sex of the patient: {F,M}
class	Each class (CC1, CC2, CC3, CC4, CC5) represents a numeric interval where the values of the class $CC_i < CC_{i+1}$. The class CC_5 represents patients of higher cost. The determination of interval boundaries was done by an expert of the field.

Prediction Models Discovery: Using the prepared database accordingly to the method described in the last section, we considered that an important characteristic would be the comprehensiveness of the models. So, we opted to use as basis an algorithm that generates decision trees like C4.5 and J48 [12].

Samples of different sizes (5% and 10%) were extracted from the database (almost 400.000 entries). The sampling procedure used is the stratification with replacement (similar to that one used in Bagging). Next, the models produced by J48 algorithm, Bagging and AdaBoosting were compared among each other, using the cross validation procedure. Both Bagging and AdaBoosting algorithms implemented in Weka platform used the J48 algorithm as basis, and Bagging was configured to generate 10 classifiers.

Table 3: General Results with Cross Validation.

Algorithm	Sample 5%	Sample 10%
J48	73.78 ±1.02	83.51 ±0.64
Bagging	77.54 ±0.92	87.15 ±0.57
Boosting	81.56 ±0.79	91.30 ±0.59

Results from the Discovered Classification Models: Table 3 illustrates the accuracy of the algorithms. On can notice that the standard deviation is quite small. This shows that the distribution of the samples has a statistical correspondence to the original data. With the results showed in Table 3 we can observe that Bagging and Boosting methods improved the percentage of properly classified examples, and the last one is the best algorithm for the experiments done. From Table 3, we can state with statistical significance that Bagging is better than J48 algorithm and that Boosting is better than Bagging for the present problem. This happens to both samples. It was also possible to observe that as larger the sample is better is the prediction rate. So, we conclude that ensemble of classifiers techniques could be effective in situations where available data correspond only to a small part of the *tuple* space.

Subjective Evaluation of Interesting Patterns: The subjective evaluation of the obtained patterns is part of the quality evaluation of the obtained rules, accordingly to the specialist's points of view. Table 4 presents the first three rules obtained, to make the explanation easier due to the limitations of space in this paper. By now, we can observe that all rules pointed out that a patient considered as of high cost (CC5) is the ones that had a high number of procedures utilization within a period of 30 months.

Table 4. Sample of obtained rules.

R1:	procedure > 47 & distance2 <= 30 & nprocedure > 160: CC5 (3257.0)
R2:	nprocedure > 273 & distance2 > 31 & distance2 <= 32 & age > 40: CC5 (940.0)
R3:	distance2 <= 31 & procedure > 50 & nprocedure > 133 & age > 61: CC5 (530.0/1.0)

Analysis shows coherence with results that arose from the rules. This can be confirmed by the first rule (R1), where the patient of high cost presents a high procedure utilization within a short period of time. In general, we could observe that the frequent utilization of the health care services leads to high cost. This could be easily observed, because the number of procedures was high in all 20 first rules. The lower absolute number of procedures was 78 (R18), which is still a high number. This number is worsened if we consider the short time in which these procedures occur. In the case of rule 18, the period is less than 20 months. This set of rules is the second part of the decision support system to identify the health system user to be managed and it help to predict if a patient will become of high cost or not.

5 Conclusions

It is fundamental that health care providers include intervention protocols and case management in their practice. Then, health care personnel, responsible for the patients' orientation could do their jobs in the most rental manner as possible, focusing on quality aspects of health care for that user already identified with some degree of risk. In this paper, machine learning and data mining techniques were used to help this task. It was observed that ensemble of classifiers could increase the trustiness of the prediction model generated, and decrease the negative impact obtained with the use of sampling techniques, generating a high cost patient's prediction model with accuracy of 90%. This model is very useful for the development of an eligibility protocol of high cost patients, as well for the improvement of an efficient and individualized management model for the population. By the other hand, the discovered associations between procedures and pathologies allow that management protocols could improve health care and direct resources for prevention and education, decreasing the amount of high cost patients in a medium and long period of time.

References

1. Agrawal R, Imielinski T, Swami A, Mining association rules between sets of items in large databases, In Proceedings ACM International Conference on Management of Data (SIGMOD), 1993, pp. 207-216.
2. Breiman L, Bagging Predictors, Machine Learning, n. 2, vol. 24, pp. 123-140, 1996.
3. Crooks P, Managing high-risk, high cost patients: the Southern California Kaiser permanent experience in the Medicare ESRD Demonstration Project, The Permanent Journal. v.9, n.2, 2005.
4. Forman S, Targeting the Highest-Risk Population to Complement Disease Management, Health Management Technology. v. 25, n. 7, Jull, 2004.
5. Knabel T, Louwers J, Intervenability: another measure of health risk, Health Management Technology. v.25, n.7, July, 2004.

6. May CA, Schraeder C, Britt T, Managed care and case management: roles for Professional nursing, Washington: American Nurses Publishing; 1996.
7. Quinlan JR, Induction of decision trees, Machine Learning vol. 1, Kluwer Academic Publishers, pg. 81-106, Netherlands, 1986.
8. Quinlan JR, Generating Production Rules from Decision Trees, In Proceedings International Joint Conference on Artificial Intelligence (IJCAI), pp. 304-307, 1987.
9. Quinlan JR, C4.5: Programs for Machine Learning, Morgan Kaufmann Publishers, 1993.
10. Shapire RE, The Boosting Approach to Machine Learning: An Overview, MSRI Workshop on Nonlinear Estimation and Classification, 2002.
11. Ting KM, Witten IH, Stacking Bagged and Dagged Models, Proceedings International Conference on Machine Learning (ICML), 1997: 367-375.
12. Witten IH, E. Frank, Data Mining, Morgan Kauffman Publishers, San Francisco, USA, 2000.

Combining Gaussian Mixture Models and Support Vector Machines for Relevance Feedback in Content Based Image Retrieval

Apostolos Marakakis[1], Nikolaos Galatsanos[2], Aristidis Likas[3], Andreas Stafylopatis[1]

[1] School of Electrical and Computer Engineering,
National Technical University of Athens, 15780 Athens, Greece
[2] Department of Electrical and Computer Engineering, University of Patras, 26500 Patras, Greece
[3] Department of Computer Science, University of Ioannina, 45110 Ioannina, Greece

amara@central.ntua.gr, galatsanos@cs.uoi.gr, arly@cs.uoi.gr, andreas@cs.ntua.gr

Abstract A relevance feedback (RF) approach for content based image retrieval (CBIR) is proposed, which combines Support Vector Machines (SVMs) with Gaussian Mixture (GM) models. Specifically, it constructs GM models of the image features distribution to describe the image content and trains an SVM classifier to distinguish between the relevant and irrelevant images according to the preferences of the user. The method is based on distance measures between probability density functions (pdfs), which can be computed in closed form for GM models. In particular, these distance measures are used to define a new SVM kernel function expressing the similarity between the corresponding images modeled as GMs. Using this kernel function and the user provided feedback examples, an SVM classifier is trained in each RF round, resulting in an updated ranking of the database images. Numerical experiments are presented that demonstrate the merits of the proposed relevance feedback methodology and the advantages of using GMs for image modeling in the RF framework.

1 Introduction

Content based image retrieval (CBIR) assumes an image description of automatically extracted low-level visual features, such as color, texture and shape. Using this image description, and after a user has submitted one or more query images as examples of his/her preferences, the images of an image database are ranked according to their similarity with the queries and the most similar are returned to the user as the retrieval results, e.g. [1]-[3]. Nevertheless, low-level image features

Please use the following format when citing this chapter:

Marakakis, A., Galatsanos, N., Likas, A. and Stafylopatis, A., 2009, in IFIP International Federation for Information Processing, Volume 296; *Artificial Intelligence Applications and Innovations III*; Eds. Iliadis, L., Vlahavas, I., Bramer, M.; (Boston: Springer), pp. 249–258.

have an intrinsic difficulty in capturing the human perception of image similarity. In other words, it is very difficult to describe the semantic content of an image using only low-level image features. This is the well known in the CBIR community *semantic gap* problem.

In order to alleviate the aforementioned problem, relevance feedback (RF) has been proposed. RF is an interactive process. During a round of RF, users are required to assess the retrieved images as relevant or irrelevant to the initial query. Then, the retrieval system takes into account the user's feedback to update the ranking criterion. In recent years much work has been devoted to the RF problem for CBIR, e.g. [4]-[8], [10], [13]-[15]. The most promising approaches to this problem are based on training a classifier in each RF round, using the user provided feedback examples, e.g. [4], [7], [14], [15]. The most popular learning models used for this classification task are the Support Vector Machines (SVMs) [17].

In the proposed method, before the database images are used for CBIR, they are appropriately modeled using GMs, which are a well-established methodology to model probability density functions (pdfs), e.g. [2], [6], [9], [10], [13], [16]. This methodology is proven to have significant advantages, such as adaptability to the data, modeling flexibility and robustness. The main challenge when using GMs for CBIR is to define a distance measure between GMs which, in addition to quantifying well the difference of GM models, can be computed efficiently. The traditionally used distance measure between pdfs is the Kullback-Leibler (KL) divergence that cannot be computed in closed form for GM models. Thus, one has to resort to time consuming random sampling Monte-Carlo methods to compute this measure for GMs, which makes its use impractical for CBIR. In [18], a new distance measure was introduced, based on the KL divergence, which can be computed in closed form for GMs. Moreover, in [12], the Asymptotic Likelihood Approximation (ALA) was proposed as a measure which, under certain assumptions, approximates the KL divergence and can also be computed in closed form for GMs.

The rest of this paper is organized as follows. In Section 2, we describe GMs in the context of image modeling for CBIR. In Section 3, we present the approximations of the KL divergence which are used in this work. In Section 4, we describe the SVM methodology for binary classification. In Section 5, we present the proposed SVM kernel functions for classification of GMs. In Section 6, we provide the details and the results of the experiments. Finally, in Section 7, we present conclusions and directions for future research.

2 Using GM Models for CBIR

GM models have been used extensively in many data modeling applications. Furthermore, they have already been used in CBIR as probability density models of the features that are used to describe images, e.g. [2], [9], [13]. In this framework, each image is described as a bag of feature vectors which are computed locally (e.g. a feature vector for each pixel or region of the image). This bag of feature vectors is subsequently used to train, in a maximum likelihood manner, a GM that models the probability density of the image features in the feature space. A GM model for the image feature vectors $x \in R^d$ is defined as

$$p(x) = \sum_{j=1}^{K} \pi_j \phi(x \mid \theta_j) \tag{1}$$

$$\theta_j = (\mu_j, \Sigma_j) \tag{2}$$

$$\phi(x \mid \theta_j) = N(x \mid \theta_j) = \frac{1}{\sqrt{(2\pi)^d |\Sigma_j|}} e^{-\frac{1}{2}(x-\mu_j)^{\mathrm{T}} \Sigma_j^{-1} (x-\mu_j)} \tag{3}$$

where K is the number of Gaussian components in the model, $0 \le \pi_j \le 1$ the mixing probabilities with $\sum_{j=1}^{K} \pi_j = 1$, and $\phi(x \mid \theta_j)$ a Gaussian pdf with mean μ_j and covariance Σ_j.

In order to retrieve images from an image database, a distance measure between the image models is needed. The KL divergence cannot be computed analytically for two GMs. Thus, for efficient retrieval using GM models, one has to resort to approximations such as those discussed next.

3 Approximations of the KL Divergence

A distance measure between images represented as GMs, which will be used for CBIR, must have good separation properties and must allow fast computation. This imposes the requirement that the distance can be defined in closed form for the case of GMs, which is not easy to achieve. In this spirit, several distance measures have been proposed, with the aim to address these requirements.

The distance measure introduced in [18] is adapted to the case of mixture models. It is known that the KL divergence between two Gaussian pdfs can be computed in closed form. In particular,

$$KL(\phi(x \mid \theta_1) \parallel \phi(x \mid \theta_2)) = \frac{1}{2}\left(tr(\Sigma_2^{-1}\Sigma_1) - \log\frac{|\Sigma_1|}{|\Sigma_2|} - d \right) + \frac{1}{2}(\mu_1 - \mu_2)^{\mathrm{T}} \Sigma_2^{-1} (\mu_1 - \mu_2) \tag{4}$$

Based on this fact and assuming that we have two GMs $p_1(x)=\sum_{j=1}^{K_1}\pi_{1j}\phi(x\,|\,\theta_{1j})$ and $p_2(x)=\sum_{m=1}^{K_2}\pi_{2m}\phi(x\,|\,\theta_{2m})$, an approximation of the KL divergence between them can be defined using the KL divergence between the Gaussian components of the mixtures:

$$KL_{gkl}(p_1 \,\|\, p_2)=\sum_{j=1}^{K_1}\pi_{1j}\min_{m=1\ldots K_2} KL\big(\phi(x\,|\,\theta_{1j})\,\|\,\phi(x\,|\,\theta_{2m})\big) \quad (5)$$

Using the above definition, we can introduce the symmetric version of this distance measure as

$$SKL_{gkl}(p_1,p_2)=\frac{1}{2}KL_{gkl}(p_1 \,\|\, p_2)+\frac{1}{2}KL_{gkl}(p_2 \,\|\, p_1) \quad (6)$$

In [12], the Asymptotic Likelihood Approximation (ALA) was proposed as a similarity measure for GMs. In particular, for the same GMs $p_1(x)$ and $p_2(x)$ as above, the ALA measure can be computed as

$$ALA(p_1 \,\|\, p_2)=\sum_{j=1}^{K_1}\pi_{1j}\left\{\log\pi_{2\beta(j)}+\left[\log\phi\big(\mu_{1j}\,|\,\theta_{2\beta(j)}\big)-\frac{1}{2}tr\big(\Sigma_{2\beta(j)}^{-1}\Sigma_{1j}\big)\right]\right\} \quad (7)$$

$$\|x-\mu\|_{\Sigma}^{2}=(x-\mu)^{\mathrm{T}}\Sigma^{-1}(x-\mu) \quad (8)$$

$$\beta(j)=k \Leftrightarrow \|\mu_{1j}-\mu_{2k}\|_{\Sigma_{2k}}^{2}-\log\pi_{2\kappa}<\|\mu_{1j}-\mu_{2l}\|_{\Sigma_{2l}}^{2}-\log\pi_{2l},\ \ \forall l\neq k \quad (9)$$

In [12], it is proven that under certain assumptions $ALA(p_1 \,\|\, p_1)-ALA(p_1 \,\|\, p_2)$ approximates $KL(p_1 \,\|\, p_2)$. Thus one can define

$$KL_{ala}(p_1 \,\|\, p_2)=ALA(p_1 \,\|\, p_1)-ALA(p_1 \,\|\, p_2) \quad (10)$$

and

$$SKL_{ala}(p_1,p_2)=\frac{1}{2}KL_{ala}(p_1 \,\|\, p_2)+\frac{1}{2}KL_{ala}(p_2 \,\|\, p_1) \quad (11)$$

as approximations of the KL and the symmetric KL divergence, respectively.

A careful inspection of the measures defined in [18] and [12] (Eq. (5) and Eq. (7)-(9), respectively) shows that they have several similarities. For example, both are based on the computation of a correspondence between the Gaussian components of the two mixtures. Moreover, the final value of these measures for GMs is given by the convex combination (using the mixing weights π_{1j}) of some pairwise measures between Gaussian components.

4 Support Vector Machines

Consider the binary classification problem $\{(x_i, y_i)\}_{i=1}^{N}$ with $y_i \in \{-1,+1\}$ and x_i the labeled patterns based on which we want to train the SVM classifier. The patterns are mapped to a new space, called kernel space, which can be non-linear and of much higher dimension than the initial one, using a transformation $x \quad \phi(x)$. Then a linear decision boundary is computed in the kernel space. The SVM methodology addresses the problem of classification by maximizing the margin, which is defined as the smallest distance in the kernel space between the decision boundary and any of the samples. This can be achieved by solving a quadratic programming problem:

$$\max_{a=(a_1,\ldots,a_N)^{\mathrm{T}}} \sum_{i=1}^{N} a_i - \frac{1}{2}\sum_{i=1}^{N}\sum_{j=1}^{N} a_i a_j y_i y_j k(x_i, x_j) \tag{12}$$

$$s.t.\ 0 \le a_i \le C \text{ and } \sum_{i=1}^{N} a_i y_i = 0 \tag{13}$$

where

$$k(x_i, x_j) = \phi^{\mathrm{T}}(x_i)\phi(x_j) \tag{14}$$

is the kernel function and C is a parameter controlling the trade-off between training error and model complexity. Then, the decision function for a new pattern x is defined by

$$y(x) = \sum_{i=1}^{N} a_i y_i k(x, x_i) + b \tag{15}$$

where b is a bias parameter the value of which can be easily determined after the solution of the optimization problem (see [17]). After training, the value $y(x)$ can be regarded as a measure of confidence about the class of x, with large positive values (small negative values) strongly indicating that x belongs to the class denoted by "+1" ("-1").

It is obvious that the patterns under classification need not be in vectorial form, but they can be any data objects for which an appropriate kernel function expressing their pair-wise similarity can be defined.

5 Combining SVMs with GM Models

In the framework of CBIR with RF, and assuming that we model each image using a GM, in each round of RF we have a number of images, represented as GMs, which correspond to the feedback examples provided by the user until now. Each of these images is labeled by -1 or +1 in case the user considers it as irrelevant or relevant to the initial query, respectively. The initial query is considered to be one of the relevant images and is labeled by +1, of course. The aim of the task is to train an SVM classifier to distinguish between the classes of relevant and irrelevant images.

As mentioned above, the kernel function is defined as the inner product of the patterns in the kernel space (Eq. (14)), namely, it is a similarity measure. The most popular non-linear kernel functions used for SVMs belong to the class of Radial Basis Functions (RBFs). From all RBF functions, now, the most commonly used are the Gaussian, $\exp\left(-\gamma\|x-y\|^2\right)$, and the Laplacian, $\exp\left(-\gamma\|x-y\|\right)$. A straightforward generalization of this concept in the GM framework, is to use as kernel function between GMs a function of the form $\exp(-\gamma d(p,q))$, where p, q are two GMs and $d(p,q)$ is a distance measure between them.

The distances presented in Section 3 fulfill the requirement for effective separation and closed-form computation. Thus, based on the above considerations, we can define the functions

$$k_{gkl}(p,q) = \exp(-\gamma SKL_{gkl}(p,q)) \tag{16}$$

$$k_{ala}(p,q) = \exp(-\gamma SKL_{ala}(p,q)) \tag{17}$$

as kernel functions between GMs p and q.

After the SVM classifier has been trained, each image in the database is presented to the classifier and the value of the decision function (Eq. (15)) is used as the ranking criterion. The higher the value of the decision function for an image, the more relevant this image is considered by the system.

6 Experiments

In order to test the validity of the proposed method, an image set containing 3740 images from the image database in [19] is used. These images are classified in 17 semantic categories. This categorization corresponds to the ground truth.

To model each image, several features are extracted including position, color and texture information. As position features we use the pixel coordinates, as color features we use the 3 color coordinates (L*,a*,b*) in the CIE-Lab color space and as texture features we use the contrast (c), the product of anisotropy with contrast (ac) and the product of polarity with contrast (pc) as described in [9].

Consequently, for each image a set of feature vectors is extracted, which is subsequently used as input to the Greedy EM algorithm [11] to produce a GM model of the image features distribution. For all GM models, 10 Gaussian components are adopted, and each Gaussian component is assumed to have full covariance matrix.

For reasons of comparison, we also applied the SVM-RF approach using the same image feature sets but the standard Gaussian RBF function, which is the most commonly used kernel function for SVMs. This kernel function requires a global vectorial representation of the images. Thus, in this case, we represent each image by the joint position-color and position-texture histogram. The position-color histogram consists of 3x3x4x8x8 (x-y-L*-a*-b*) bins, whereas the position-texture histogram consists of 3x3x4x4x4 (x-y-ac-pc-c) bins.

In order to quantify the performance of the compared methods, we implemented an RF simulation scheme. As a measure of performance we use Precision which is the ratio of relevant images in top N retrieved images. An image is assessed to be relevant or irrelevant according to the ground truth categorization of the image database. In this simulation scheme, 1000 database images are used once as initial queries. For each initial query, we simulated 6 rounds of RF. In each RF round, at most 3 relevant and 3 irrelevant images are selected randomly from the first 100 images of the ranking. These images are used in combination with the examples provided in the previous RF rounds to train a new SVM classifier. Based on this new classifier, the ranking of the database images is updated.

For the experiments presented below, average Precision in scope N = 10, 20, 30 is shown. The values of the SVM parameter C and of the kernel parameter γ are empirically chosen for each method so as to obtain the best performance. As SVM implementation we used the one provided in [20].

In Figures 1-3 we can see that the SVM-RF method based on GMs constantly outperforms the common SVM-RF method which uses histograms and the Gaussian RBF kernel function. Moreover, it can be observed that the method which is based on the distance measure defined in [18] results in slightly superior performance when compared to that obtained by the method which uses the ALA based distance measure.

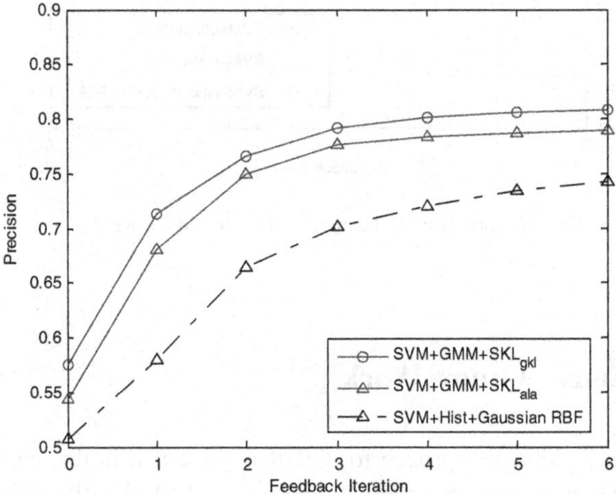

Fig. 1. Average Precision in scope N = 10 during different rounds of RF

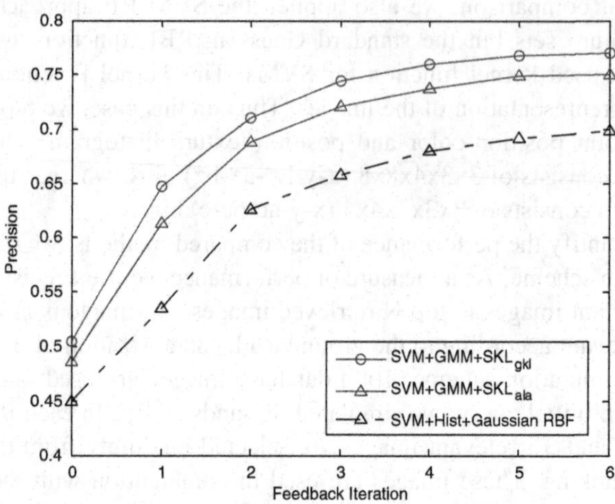

Fig. 2. Average Precision in scope N = 20 during different rounds of RF

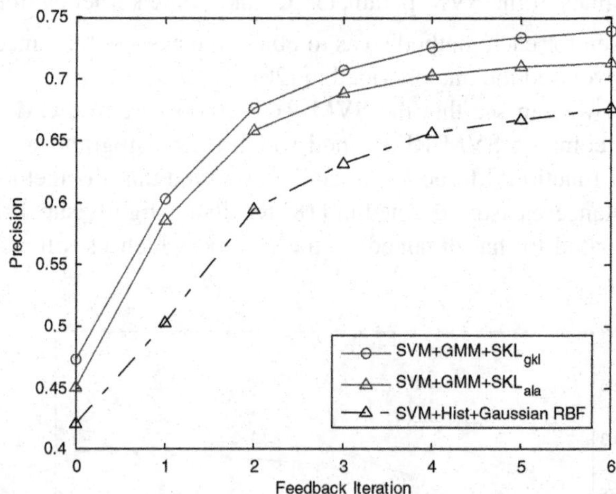

Fig. 3. Average Precision in scope N = 30 during different rounds of RF

7 Conclusions – Future Work

A new relevance feedback approach for CBIR is presented in this paper. This approach uses GMs to model the image content and SVM classifiers to distinguish between the classes of relevant and irrelevant images. To combine these methodologies, a new SVM kernel function is introduced based on distance measures between GMs which can be computed efficiently, i.e. in closed form. The main advantages of the proposed methodology are accuracy as indicated by our experimental results, speed, due to the distance measures used, and flexibility. As indicated by our experiments, very promising results can be obtained using GMs as SVM patterns, even if we are forced to use an approximation and not the exact KL divergence. In particular, for the two KL approximations tested, the performance does not differ significantly. However, the distance measure introduced in [18] gives slightly better results.

In the future, we would like to adapt and test our method using other efficiently computable distance measures for GMs. Moreover, we aim to use more sophisticated image features to represent the image content. In addition, we plan to generalize our RF scheme to support region-based image descriptions. Furthermore, we aim to apply techniques for automatic determination of the appropriate number of components for each GM. Finally, we would like to test the scalability of the proposed method using even larger image databases.

Acknowledgement This work was supported by Public Funds under the PENED 2003 Project co-funded by the European Social Fund (80%) and National Resources (20%) from the Hellenic Ministry of Development - General Secretariat for Research and Technology.

References

1. Y. Ishikawa, R. Subramanya, and C. Faloutsos, "MindReader: Querying databases through multiple examples", *Proceedings International Conference on Very large Data Bases (VLDB)*, 1998.
2. N. Vasconcelos, "Minimum Probability of Error Image Retrieval", *IEEE Transactions on Signal Processing*, vol. 52, no. 8, pp. 2322-2336, Aug. 2004.
3. Ritendra Datta, Jia Li and James Ze Wang, "Content-based image retrieval: approaches and trends of the new age", *Multimedia Information Retrieval*, pp. 253-262, 2005.
4. G. D. Guo, A. K. Jain, W. Y. Ma, and H. J. Zhang, "Learning similarity measure for natural image retrieval with relevance feedback", *IEEE Transactions on Neural Networks.*, vol. 13, no. 4, pp. 811-820, Jul. 2002.
5. C.T. Hsu, and C. Y. Li, "Relevance Feedback Using Generalized Bayesian Framework With Region-Based Optimization Learning", *IEEE Transactions on Image Processing.*, Vol. 14, No. 10, pp. 1617-1631, October 2005.
6. F. Qian, M. Li, L. Zhang, H. J. Zhang, and B. Zhang, "Gaussian mixture model for relevance feedback in image retrieval", *Proceedings IEEE ICME*, Aug. 2002.
7. F. Jing, M. Li, H-J. Zhang, and B. Zhang, "Relevance Feedback in Region-Based Image Retrieval", *IEEE Transactions on Circuits and Systems for Video Technology*, vol. 14, no. 5, pp. 672-681, May 2004.
8. Wei Jiang, Guihua Er, Qionghai Dai and Jinwei Gu, "Similarity-Based Online Feature Selection in Content-Based Image Retrieval", *IEEE Transactions on Image Processing*, vol. 15, no. 3, pp. 702-712, March 2006.

9. C. Carson, S. Belongie, H. Greenspan, and J. Malik, "Blobworld: Image segmentation using expectation-maximization and its application to image querying", *IEEE Transactions on Pattern Analysis and Machine Intelligence*, vol. 24, no. 8, pp. 1026-1038, Aug. 2002.
10. A. Marakakis, N. Galatsanos, A. Likas and A. Stafylopatis, "A Relevance Feedback Approach for Content Based Image Retrieval Using Gaussian Mixture Models", *Proceedings International Conference Artificial Neural Networks* (*ICANN*), Athens, Greece, September 2006.
11. N. Vlassis and A. Likas, "A greedy EM algorithm for Gaussian mixture learning", *Neural Processing Letters*, vol. 15, pp. 77-87, 2002.
12. N. Vasconcelos, "On the Efficient Evaluation of Probabilistic Similarity Functions for Image Retrieval", *IEEE Transactions on Information Theory*, vol. 50, no. 7, pp. 1482-1496, July 2004.
13. N. Vasconcelos and A. Lippman, "Learning from user feedback in image retrieval systems", *Advances in Neural Information Processing Systems*, 1999.
14. S. Tong and E. Chang, "Support vector machine active learning for image retrieval", *ACM Multimedia*, 2001.
15 Dacheng Tao, Xiaoou Tang and Xuelong Li, "Which Components Are Important for Interactive Image Searching?", *IEEE Transactions on Circuits and Systems for Video Technology*, vol. 18, no. 1, pp. 3-11, Jan. 2008.
16. C. M. Bishop, *Neural Networks for Pattern Recognition*, Oxford Univ. Press Inc., New York, 1995.
17. C.M. Bishop, *Pattern Recognition and Machine Learning*, Springer, 2006.
18. Jacob Goldberger and Sam Roweis, "Hierarchical Clustering of a Mixture Model", *Neural Information Processing Systems 17 (NIPS'04)*, pp 505-512, 2004.
19. Microsoft Research Cambridge Object Recognition Image Database, version 1.0. http://research.microsoft.com/research/downloads/Details/b94de342-60dc-45d0-830b-9f6eff91b301/Details.aspx
20. LIBSVM – A Library for Support Vector Machines. http://www.csie.ntu.edu.tw/~cjlin/libsvm

Performance Evaluation of a Speech Interface for Motorcycle Environment

Iosif Mporas, Todor Ganchev, Otilia Kocsis, Nikos Fakotakis

Artificial Intelligence Group, Wire Communications Laboratory,

Dept. of Electrical and Computer Engineering, University of Patras, Rion 26500, Greece

{imporas, , tganchev, okocsis, fakotakis}@upatras.gr

Abstract In the present work we investigate the performance of a number of traditional and recent speech enhancement algorithms in the adverse non-stationary conditions, which are distinctive for motorcycle on the move. The performance of these algorithms is ranked in terms of the improvement they contribute to the speech recognition rate, when compared to the baseline result, i.e. without speech enhancement. The experimentations on the MoveOn motorcycle speech and noise database suggested that there is no equivalence between the ranking of algorithms based on the human perception of speech quality and the speech recognition performance. The Multi-band spectral subtraction method was observed to lead to the highest speech recognition performance.

1 Introduction

Spoken language dialogue systems considerably improve driver's safety and user-friendliness of human-machine interfaces, due to their similarity to the conversational activity with another human, a parallel activity to which the driver is used to and it allows him concentrate on the main activity, the driving itself. Driving quality, stress and strain situations and user acceptance when using speech and manual commands to acquire certain information on the route has previously been studied [1], and the results have shown that, with speech input, the feeling of being distracted from driving is smaller, and road safety is improved, especially in the case of complex tasks. Moreover, assessment of user requirements from multimodal interfaces in a car environment has shown that when the car is moving the system should switch to the "speech-only" interaction mode, as any other safety risks (i.e. driver distraction from the driving task by gesture input or graphical output) must be avoided [2].

The performance of speech-based interfaces, although reliable enough in controlled environments to support speaker and device independence, degrades sub-

Please use the following format when citing this chapter:

Mporas, I., Ganchev, T., Kocsis, O. and Fakotakis, N., 2009, in IFIP International Federation for Information Processing, Volume 296; *Artificial Intelligence Applications and Innovations III*; Eds. Iliadis, L., Vlahavas, I., Bramer, M.; (Boston: Springer), pp. 259–266.

stantially in a mobile environment, when used on the road. There are various types and sources of noise interfering with the speech signal, starting with the acoustic environment (vibrations, road/fan/wind noise, engine noise, traffic, etc.) to changes in the speaker's voice due to task stress, distributed attention, etc. In the integration of speech-based interfaces within vehicle environments the research is conducted in two directions: (i) addition of front-end speech enhancement systems to improve the quality of the recorded signal, and (ii) training the speech models of the recognizer engine on noisy, real-life, speech databases.

In this study, the front-end speech enhancement system for a motorcycle on the move environment is investigated. The speech-based interface, as presented in this study, is part of a multi-modal and multi-sensor interface developed in the context of the MoveOn project. The performance of various speech enhancement algorithms in the non-stationary conditions of motorcycle on the move is assessed. Performance of assessed algorithms is ranked in terms of the improvement they contribute to the speech recognition rate, when compared to the baseline results (i.e. without speech enhancement). Following, a short overview of the MoveOn system, the enhancement methods evaluated, and the experimental setup and results are presented.

2 System Description

The MoveOn project aims at the creation of a multi-modal and multi-sensor, zero-distraction interface for motorcyclists. This interface provides the means for hands-free operation of a command and control system that enables for information support of police officers on the move. The MoveOn information support system is a wearable solution, which constitutes of a purposely designed helmet, waist and gloves. The helmet incorporates microphones, headphones, visual feedback, a miniature camera and some supporting local-processing electronics. It has a USB connection to the waist that provides the power supply and the data and control interfaces. The waist incorporates the main processing power, storage repository, TETRA communication equipment and power capacity of the wearable system, but also a number of sensors, an LCD display, and some vibration feedback actuators. Among the sensors deployed on the waist are acceleration and inclination sensors, and a GPS device, which provide the means for the context awareness of the system. Auxiliary microphone and headphone are integrated in the upper part of the waist, at the front side near the collar, for guaranteeing the spoken interaction and communication capabilities when the helmet is off.

The multimodal user interface developed for the MoveOn application consists of audio and haptic inputs, and audio, visual and vibration feedbacks to the user. Due to the specifics of the MoveOn application, involving hands-busy and eyes-busy motorcyclists, speech is the dominating interaction modality.

The spoken interface consists of multi-sensor speech acquisition equipment, speech pre-processing, speech enhancement, speech recognition, and text-to-speech synthesis components, which are integrated into the multimodal dialogue interaction framework based on Olympus/RavenClaw [3, 4], but extended for the needs of multimodal interaction. Each component in the system is a server on itself, i.e. ASR, TTS, speech preprocessing, speech enhancement, etc are servers, communicating either directly with each other or through a central hub, which provides synchronization.

Since the noisy motorcycle environment constitutes a great challenge to the spoken dialogue interaction, a special effort is required to guarantee high speech recognition performance, as it proved to be the most crucial element for the overall success of interaction.

3 Speech Enhancement Methods

We consider eight speech enhancement techniques, which will be examined in the non-stationary motorcycle environment conditions:

- The spectral subtraction (SPECSUB) algorithm [5], which is a well-known technique will serve as a reference point. It relies on the fact that the power spectra of additive independent signals are also additive. Thus, in the case of stationary noise, to obtain a least squares estimate of the speech power spectrum, it suffices to subtract the mean noise power. Due to its low complexity and good efficiency, the spectral subtraction method is a standard choice for noise suppression at the pre-processing stage of speech recognition systems.
- Spectral subtraction with noise estimation (SPECSUB-NE) [6]. This method tracks spectral minima in each frequency band without any distinction between speech activity and speech pause. Based on the optimally smoothed power spectral density estimate and the analysis of the statistics of spectral minima an unbiased noise estimator is implemented. Due to the last, this algorithm is more appropriate for real world conditions, and outperforms the SPECSUB in non-stationary environments.
- Multi-band spectral subtraction method (M-BAND) [7]. It is based on the SPECSUB algorithm but accounts for the fact that in real world conditions, interferences do not affect the speech signal uniformly over the entire spectrum. The M-BAND method was demonstrated to outperform the standard SPECSUB method resulting in superior speech quality and largely reduced musical noise.
- Speech enhancement using a minimum mean square error log-spectral amplitude estimator [8], which we refer to as (Log-MMSE). This method relies on a short-time spectral amplitude estimator for speech signals, which minimizes the mean-square error of the log-spectra.
- Speech enhancement based on perceptually motivated Bayesian estimators (STSA-WCOSH) of the speech magnitude spectrum [9]. This algorithm utilizes Bayesian estimators of the short-time spectral magnitude of speech based on perceptually motivated cost functions. It was demonstrated that the estimators

which implicitly take into account auditory masking effect perform better in terms of having less residual noise and better speech quality, when compared to the Log-MMSE method.
- Subspace algorithm with embedded pre-whitening (KLT) [10]. It is based on the simultaneous diagonalization of the clean speech and noise covariance matrices. Objective and subjective evaluations suggest that this algorithm offers advantage when the interference is speech-shaped or multi-talker babble noise.
- Perceptually-motivated subspace algorithm (PKLT) [11]. It incorporates a human hearing model in the suppression filter to reduce the residual noise. From a perceptual perspective, the perceptually based eigenfilter introduced here yields a better shaping of the residual noise. This method was reported to outperform the KLT method.
- Wiener algorithm based on wavelet thresholding (WIENER-WT) multi-taper spectra [12]. It uses a low-variance spectral estimators based on wavelet thresholding the multitaper spectra. Listening tests reportedly had shown that this method suppresses the musical noise and yielded better speech quality than the KLT, PKLT and Log-MMSE algorithms.

4 Experiments and Results

The speech front-end described in Section 1.2 was tested with each of the speech enhancement techniques outlined in Section 1.3. Different environmental conditions and configuration settings of the speech recognition engine were evaluated. In the following, we describe the speech data, the speech recognition engine and the experimental protocol utilized in the present evaluation. Finally, we provide the experimental results.

The evaluation of the front-end was carried out on the speech and noise database, created during the MoveOn project [13]. The database consists of approximately 40 hours of annotated recordings, most of which were recorded in three audio channels fed by different sensors, plus one channel for the audio prompts. Thirty professional motorcyclists, members of the operational police force of UK, were recorded when riding their motorcycles. Each participant was asked to repeat a number of domain-specific commands and expressions or to provide a spontaneous answer to questions related to time, current location, speed, etc. Motorcycles and helmets from various vendors were used, and the trace of road differed among sessions. The database includes outdoor recordings (city driving, highway, tunnels, suburbs, etc) as well as indoor (studio) recordings with the same hardware. The database was recorded at 44.1 kHz, with resolution 16 bits. Later on, all recordings were downsampled to 8 kHz for the needs of the present application.

The Julius [14] speech recognition engine was employed for the present evaluation. The decoder of the recognition engine utilizes a general purpose acoustic model and an application-dependent language model. The acoustic model was built from telephone speech recordings of the British SpeechDat(II) database [15], by means of the HTK toolkit [16]. It consists of three-state left-to-right HMMs, without skipping transitions, one for each phone of the British SpeechDat(II) phone set. Each state is modelled by a mixture of eight continuous Gaussian distributions. The state distributions were trained from parametric speech vectors, taken out from speech waveforms after pre-processing and feature extraction. The pre-processing of the speech signals, sampled at 8 kHz, consisted of frame blocking with length and step 25 and 10 milliseconds respectively, and pre-emphasis with coefficient equal to 0.97. The speech parameterization consisted in the computation of twelve Mel frequency cepstral coefficients [17], computed through a filter-bank of 26 channels, and the energy of each frame. The speech feature vector was of dimensionality equal to 39, since the first and second derivatives were appended to the static parameters. All HMMs were trained through the Baum-Welch algorithm [18], with convergence ratio equal to 0.001.

The language models were built by utilizing the CMU Cambridge Statistical Language Modeling (SLM) Toolkit [19]. Specifically, we used the transcriptions of the responses of the MoveOn end-user to the system [20] to build bi-gram and tri-gram word models. Words included in the application dictionary but not in the list of n-grams were assigned as out-of-vocabulary words.

The performance of different enhancement methods, implemented as in [22], was assessed by evaluating their effect on the speech recognition results. Two different experimental setups were considered: (i) indoors and (ii) outdoors conditions. The performance of each enhancement method in the indoors condition was used as a reference, while the outdoors condition is the environment of interest. In contrast to previous work [21], were the performance of enhancement algorithms was investigated on the basis of objective tests on the enhanced signals, here we examine directly the operational functionality of the system by measuring the speech recognition performance. Specifically, the percentage of correctly recognized words (*CRW*) and the word recognition rates (*WRRs*) obtained in the speech recognition process after applying each enhancement method were measured. The *CRW* indicates the ability of the front-end to recognize the uttered message from the end-user, while the *WRR* points out the insertion of non uttered words, together with the word deletions and substitutions that the *CRW* measures. In terms of these performance measures we assess the practical worth of each algorithm and its usefulness with respect to overall system performance. These results are compared against the quality measures obtained in earlier work [21].

We evaluated the speech recognition performance for each speech enhancement method in the indoors and outdoors conditions, with bi-gram and tri-gram language models. Table 1 presents the performance for the indoor experiments, in terms of *WRR* and *CRW* in percentages.

Table 1. Performance (WRR and CRW in percentages) for various speech enhancement techniques for the indoors recordings.

Enhancement Techniques	2-gram LM		3-gram LM	
	WRR	CRW	WRR	CRW
Log-MMSE	76.75	81.41	70.29	81.36
No Enhancement	76.71	81.41	70.25	81.30
M-BAND	75.61	79.87	71.27	80.19
SPECSUB-NE	74.25	81.35	68.53	70.80
PKLT	74.10	80.07	67.85	79.88
WIENER-WT	73.48	80.31	67.15	80.24
KLT	69.69	78.32	63.95	78.09
STSA-WCOSH	66.16	77.30	59.10	77.11
SPECSUB	50.89	77.04	40.35	77.04

As can be seen in Table 1, the best performing method for the case of indoor recordings was the Log-MMSE together with the non-enhanced speech inputs. All remaining methods decreased the speech recognition performance. This is owed to the distortion that these speech enhancement methods introduce into the clean speech signal. Obviously, indoors, i.e. on noise-free speech, the general purpose acoustic model performs better without speech enhancement pre-processing.

As Table 1 presents, the speech recognition performance for the bi-gram language model was better than the one for the tri-gram language model. This is owed to the limited amount of data that were available for training the language models. Obviously the data were sufficient for training the bi-gram model but not enough for the tri-gram model.

In Table 2 we present the speech recognition performance in percentages for the outdoors scenario, in terms of *WRR* and *CRW*, for both the bi-gram and tri-gram language models.

In contrast to the indoors scenario, the speech enhancement in the noisy outdoors scenario (motorcycles on the move) improved the speech recognition per-

Table 2. Performance (WRR and CRW in percentages) for various speech enhancement techniques for the outdoors recordings.

Enhancement Techniques	2-gram LM		3-gram LM	
	WRR	CRW	WRR	CRW
M-BAND	55.16	69.13	49.65	69.63
STSA-WCOSH	49.56	66.00	41.73	65.82
SPECSUB-NE	46.34	67.22	30.87	68.09
PKLT	39.76	58.11	29.40	58.48
Log-MMSE	39.22	64.17	27.83	64.90
KLT	39.20	64.16	27.84	64.92
WIENER-WT	35.64	54.07	29.06	54.59
SPECSUB	26.95	57.49	14.84	57.23
No Enhancement	23.77	54.95	14.29	55.17

formance. Specifically, all speech enhancement methods demonstrated superior performance, when compared to the baseline result, i.e. without speech enhancement. As Table 2 presents, the multi-band speech enhancement technique, M-BAND, outperformed all other methods evaluated here. Similarly to the indoors case, the bi-gram language model provided more accurate recognition results. These results reveal, that the ranking of speech enhancement algorithms based on the human perception of speech quality (please refer to [21]) differs from the ranking in terms of speech recognition performance. Specifically, the M-BAND algorithm, which was among the top-4 performers in terms of perceptual quality, is the best performing algorithm in terms of *CWR* and *WRR*. Moreover, although the spectral subtraction with noise estimation algorithm, SPECSUB-NE, didn't perform well in the perceptual speech quality evaluation, here it has the second best performance in terms of *CRW*.

5 Conclusions

Aiming at successful human-machine interaction in the motorcycle environment we evaluated the recognition performance of a purposely built speech front-end. Various speech enhancement techniques were assessed in an attempt to find the most appropriate pre-processing of the speech signal. The experimental results showed severe degradation of the speech recognition performance in the conditions of the motorcycle environment, compared to the clean-speech recordings conducted with the same hardware setup. The multi-band spectral subtraction method demonstrated the best performance among the eight evaluated techniques, when measured in terms of improvement of the speech recognition rate. Finally, the selection of an appropriate speech enhancement technique, proved to be essential for the successful interaction between the user and the dialogue system.

Acknowledgments This work was supported by the MoveOn project (IST-2005-034753), which is partially funded by the European Commission.

References

1. Gartner, U., Konig, W., Wittig, T. (2001). Evaluation of Manual vs. Speech input when using a driver information system in real traffic. Driving Assessment 2001: 1st International Driving Symposium on Human Factors in Driver Assessment, Training and Vehicle Design, pp. 7-13, CO.
2. Berton, A., Buhler, D., Minker, W. (2006). SmartKom-Mobile Car: User Interaction with Mobile Services in a Car Environment. In SmartKom: Foundations of Multimodal Dialogue Systems, Wolfgang Wahlster (Ed.). pp. 523-537, Springer.
3. Bohus, D., Rudnicky, A.I. (2003). RavenClaw: Dialog Management Using Hierarchical Task Decomposition and an Expectation Agenda. Proceedings European Conference on Speech Communication and Technology (EUROSPEECH):597-600.

4. Bohus, D., Raux, A., Harris, T.K., Eskenazi, M., Rudnicky, A.I. (2007). Olympus: an open-source framework for conversational spoken language interface research, Bridging the Gap: Academic and Industrial Research in Dialog Technology workshop at HLT/NAACL 2007.
5. Berouti, M., Schwartz, R., Makhoul, J. (1979). Enhancement of speech corrupted by acoustic noise. In Proceedings IEEE ICASSP'79:208-211.
6. Martin, R. (2001). Noise power spectral density estimation based on optimal smoothing and minimum statistics. IEEE Transactions on Speech and Audio Processing 9(5):504-512.
7. Kamath, S., Loizou, P. (2002). A multi-band spectral subtraction method for enhancing speech corrupted by colored noise. Proceedings ICASSP'02.
8. Ephraim, Y., Malah, D. (1985). Speech enhancement using a minimum mean square error log-spectral amplitude estimator. IEEE Transactions on Acoustics, Speech, Signal Processing 33:443-445.
9. Loizou, P. (2005). Speech enhancement based on perceptually motivated Bayesian estimators of the speech magnitude spectrum. IEEE Transactions on Speech and Audio Processing 13(5):857-869.
10. Hu ,Y., Loizou, P. (2003). A generalized subspace approach for enhancing speech corrupted by coloured noise. IEEE Transactions on Speech and Audio Processing 11:334-341.
11. Jabloun, F., Champagne, B. (2003). Incorporating the human hearing properties in the signal subspace approach for speech enhancement. IEEE Transactions on Speech and Audio Processing 11(6):700-708.
12. Hu, Y., Loizou, P. (2004). Speech enhancement based on wavelet thresholding the multitaper spectrum. IEEE Transactions on Speech and Audio Processing 12(1):59-67.
13. Winkler, T., Kostoulas, T., Adderley, R., Bonkowski, C., Ganchev, T., Kohler, J., Fakotakis N. (2008). The MoveOn Motorcycle Speech Corpus. Proceedings of LREC'2008.
14. Lee, A., Kawahara, T., Shikano, K. (2001). Julius -- an open source real-time large vocabulary recognition engine. Proceedings European Conference on Speech Communication and Technology (EUROSPEECH):1691-1694.
15. Hoge, H., Draxler, C., Van den Heuvel, H., Johansen, F.T., Sanders, E., Tropf, H.S. (1999). SpeechDat Multilingual Speech Databases for Teleservices: Across the Finish Line. Proceedings 6th European Conference on Speech Communication and Technology (EUROSPEECH):2699-2702.
16. Young, S., Evermann, G., Gales, M., Hain, T., Kershaw, D., Moore, G., Odell, J., Ollason, D., Povey, D., Valtchev, V., Woodland, P. (2005). The HTK Book (for HTK Version 3.3). Cambridge University.
17. Davis, S.B., Mermelstein, P. (1980). Comparison of parametric representations for monosyllabic word recognition in continuously spoken sentences. IEEE Transactions on Acoustics, Speech and Signal Processing 28(4):357-366.
18. Baum, L.E., Petrie, T., Soules, G., Weiss, N. (1970). A maximization technique occurring in the statistical analysis of probabilistic functions of Markov chains. Annals of Mathematical Statistics 41(1):164–171.
19. Clarkson, P.R., Rosenfeld, R. (1997). Statistical Language Modeling Using the CMU-Cambridge Toolkit. Proceedings 5th European Conference on Speech Communication and Technology (EUROSPEECH): 2707-2710.
20. Winkler, T., Ganchev, T., Kostoulas ,T., Mporas, I., Lazaridis, A., Ntalampiras, S., Badii, A., Adderley, R., Bonkowski, C. (2007). MoveOn Deliverable D.5: Report on Audio databases, Noise processing environment, ASR and TTS modules.
21. Ntalampiras, S., Ganchev, T., Potamitis, I., Fakotakis, N. (2008). Objective comparison of speech enhancement algorithms under real world conditions. Proceedings PETRA 2008:34.
22. Loizou P. (2007). Speech Enhancement: Theory and Practice, CRC Press, 2007.

Model Identification in Wavelet Neural Networks Framework

A. Zapranis and A. Alexandridis

Department of Accounting and Finance, University of Macedonia of Economics and Social Studies, 156 Egnatia St., P.O. 54006, Thessaloniki, Greece.

E-mail: zapranis,aalex@uom.gr

Abstract The scope of this study is to present a complete statistical framework for model identification of wavelet neural networks (WN). In each step in WN construction we test various methods already proposed in literature. In the first part we compare four different methods for the initialization and construction of the WN. Next various information criteria as well as sampling techniques proposed in previous works were compared to derive an algorithm for selecting the correct topology of a WN. Finally, in variable significance testing the performance of various sensitivity and model-fitness criteria were examined and an algorithm for selecting the significant explanatory variables is presented.

1 Introduction

This study presents a complete statistical wavelet neural network (WN) model identification framework. Model identification can be separated in two parts, model selection and variable significance testing. Wavelet analysis (WA) has proved to be a valuable tool for analyzing a wide range of time-series and has already been used with success in image processing, signal de-noising, density estimation, signal and image compression and time-scale decomposition.

In [1] have demonstrated that it is possible to construct a theoretical description of feedforward NN in terms of wavelet decompositions. WN were proposed by [2] as an alternative to feedforward NN hoping to elevate the weakness of each method. The WN is a generalization of radial bases function networks (RBFN).WNs are one hidden layer networks that use a wavelet as an activation function instead of the classic sigmoid function. The families of multidimensional wavelets preserve the universal approximation property that characterizes neural networks. In [3] various reasons presented in why wavelets should be used instead of other transfer functions.

Wavelet networks have been used in a variety of applications so far. Wavelet networks were used with great success in short term load forecasting, [4], in time series prediction, [5], signal classification and compression, [6], static, dynamic [1] and nonlinear modeling [7], nonlinear static function approximation, [8]. Fi-

Please use the following format when citing this chapter:

Zapranis, A. and Alexandridis, A., 2009, in IFIP International Federation for Information Processing, Volume 296; *Artificial Intelligence Applications and Innovations III*; Eds. Iliadis, L., Vlahavas, I., Bramer, M.; (Boston: Springer), pp. 267–276.

nally, [9] proposed WN as a multivariate calibration method for simultaneous determination of test samples of copper, iron, and aluminum.

In contrast to sigmoid neural networks, wavelet networks allow constructive procedures that efficiently initialize the parameters of the network. Using wavelet decomposition a wavelet library can be constructed. Each wavelon can be constructed using the best wavelet of the wavelet library. These procedures allow the wavelet network to converge to a global minimum of the cost function. Also starting the network training very close to the solution leads to smaller training times. Finally, wavelet networks provide information of the participation of each wavelon to the approximation and the dynamics of the generating process.

The rest of the paper is organized as follows. In section 2 we present the WN, we describe the structure of a WN and we compare different initialization methods. In section 3 we present a statistical framework in WN model selection and different methods are compared. Various sensitivity criteria of the input variables are presented in section 4 and a variable selection scheme is presented. Finally, in section 5 we conclude.

2 Wavelet Neural Networks for Multivariate Process Modeling

In [10] and [11] we give a concise treatment of wavelet theory. Here the emphasis is in presenting the theory and mathematics of wavelet neural networks. So far in literature various structures of a WN have been proposed [5] [8] [9] [7] [12] [13]. In this study we use a multidimensional wavelet neural network with a linear connection of the wavelons to the output. Moreover for the model to perform well in linear cases we use direct connections from the input layer to the output layer. A network with zero hidden units (HU) is the linear model.

The network output is given by the following expression:

$$y(\mathbf{x}) = w_{\lambda+1}^{[2]} + \sum_{j=1}^{\lambda} w_j^{[2]} \cdot \Psi_j(\mathbf{x}) + \sum_{i=1}^{m} w_i^{[0]} \cdot x_i$$

In that expression, $\Psi_j(\mathbf{x})$ is a multidimensional wavelet which is constructed by the product of m scalar wavelets, $\mathbf{x}$ is the input vector, m is the number of network inputs, λ is the number of hidden units and w stands for a network weight. Following [14] we use as a mother wavelet the Mexican Hat function. The multidimensional wavelets are computed as follows:

$$\Psi_j(\mathbf{x}) = \prod_{i=1}^{m} \psi(z_{ij})$$

where ψ is the mother wavelet and

$$z_{ij} = \frac{x_i - w_{(\xi)ij}^{[1]}}{w_{(\zeta)ij}^{[1]}}$$

In the above expression, $i = 1, \ldots, m$, $j = 1, \ldots, \lambda+1$ and the weights w correspond to the translation ($w_{(\xi)ij}^{[1]}$) and the dilation ($w_{(\zeta)ij}^{[1]}$) factors. The complete vector of the network parameters comprises:

$$w = \left(w_i^{[0]}, w_j^{[2]}, w_{\lambda+1}^{[2]}, w_{(\xi)ij}^{[1]}, w_{(\zeta)ij}^{[1]}\right)$$

There are several approaches to train a WN. In our implementation we have used ordinary back-propagation which is less fast but also less prone to sensitivity to initial conditions than higher order alternatives. The weights $w_i^{[0]}$, $w_j^{[2]}$ and parameters $w_{(\xi)ij}^{[1]}$ and $w_{(\zeta)ij}^{[1]}$ are trained for approximating the target function.

In WN, in contrast to NN that use sigmoid functions, selecting initial values of the dilation and translation parameters randomly may not be suitable, [15]. A wavelet is a waveform of effectively limited duration that has an average value of zero and localized properties hence a random initialization may lead to wavelons with a value of zero. Also random initialization affects the speed of training and may lead to a local minimum of the loss function, [16]. In [2] the wavelons are initialized at the center of the input dimension of each input vector x_i.

The initialization of the direct connections $w_i^{[0]}$ and the weights $w_j^{[2]}$ is less important and they are initialized in small random values between 0 and 1.

The previous heuristic method is simple but not efficient. As it is shown in figure 2 the initial approximation is a bad approximation of the function *f(x)*. The heuristic method does not guarantee that the training will find the global minimum. Moreover this method does not use any information that the wavelet decomposition can provide. In literature more complex initialization methods have been proposed, [17] [14] [18]. All methods can be summed in the following three steps.

1. Construct a library *W* of wavelets
2. Remove the wavelets that their support does not contain any sample points of the training data.
3. Rank the remaining wavelets and select the best regressors.

The wavelet library can be constructed either by an orthogonal wavelet or a wavelet frame. However orthogonal wavelets cannot be expressed in closed form. It is shown that a family of compactly supported non-orthogonal wavelets is more appropriate for function approximation, [19]. The wavelet library may contain a large number of wavelets. In practice it is impossible to count infinite frame or basis terms. However arbitrary truncations may lead to large errors, [20].

In [14] three alternative methods were proposed to reduce and rank the wavelet in the wavelet library namely the Residual Based Selection (RBS) a Stepwise Selection by Orthogonalization (SSO) and a Backward Elimination (BE) algorithm. In [21] the RBS algorithm is used for the synthesis of a WN while in [17] an algorithm similar to SSO is proposed. In [18] an orthogonalized residual based selection (ORBS) algorithm is proposed for the initialization of the WN.

All the above methods are used just for the initialization of the dilation and translation parameters. Then the network is further trained to obtain the vector of the parameters $w = w_0$ which minimizes the cost function.

The heuristic, the SSO, the RBS and the BE methods that constitute the bases for alternative algorithms and can be used with the batch training algorithm will be tested. We test these methods in two examples. The first example where the underlying function *f(x)* is:

$$f(x) = 0.5 + 0.4\sin(2\pi x) + \varepsilon_1(x) \quad x \in [0,1]$$

where x is equally spaced in [0,1] and the noise $\varepsilon_1(x)$ follows a normal distribution with mean zero and a decreasing variance:

$$\sigma_\varepsilon^2(x) = 0.05^2 + 0.1(1 - x^2)$$

Figure 1 show the initialization of all four algorithms for the first example. The network uses 2 hidden units with learning rate 0.1 and momentum 0. The use of a large learning rate or momentum might lead to oscillation between two points. As a result the WN would not be able to find the minimum of the loss function or it will be trapped in a local minimum of the loss function. It is clear that the BE and SSO algorithms starting approximation are very close to the target function *f(x)*. As a result less iterations and training time are needed. To compare the previous methods we use the heuristic method to train 100 networks with different initial conditions of the direct connections $w_i^{[0]}$ and weights $w_j^{[2]}$ to find the global minimum. We find that the smallest mean square error (MSE) is 0.031332. Using the RBS algorithm the MSE is 0.031438 and is found after 717 iterations. The MSE between the underlying function *f(x)* and the network approximation is 0.000676. The SSO needs 4 iterations and the MSE is 0.031332 while the MSE between the underlying function *f(x)* and the network approximation is only 0.000121. The same results achieved by the BE method. Finally, one implementation of the heuristic method needed 1501 iterations.

From the previous examples it seems the SSO and the BE algorithms give the same results and outperform both the heuristic and the RBS algorithm. To have a more clear view we introduce a more complex example where

$$g(x) = 0.5x\sin(x) + \cos^2(x) + \varepsilon_2(x) \quad x \in [-6,6]$$

and $\varepsilon_2(x)$ follows a Cauchy distribution with location 0 and scale 0.05 and x is equally spaced in [-6,6]. While the fist example is very simple the second one proposed by [22] incorporates large outliers in the output space. The sensitive to the presence of outliers of the proposed WN will be tested.

The results for the second example are similar however the BE algorithm is 10% faster than the SSO. Using the RBS, SSO and BE algorithms the MSE is 0.004758, 004392 and 0.04395 and is found after 2763, 1851 and 1597 iterations respectively. The MSE between the underlying function *g(x)* and the network approximation is 0.000609, 0.000073 and 0.000057 respectively.

One can observe in Figure 2 that the WN approximation was not affected by the presence of large outliers in contrast to the findings of [22]. In this study 8 hidden units were used for the network topology proposed by *v-fold* cross-validation while in [22] 10 hidden units were proposed by the FPE criterion. As it is shown in the next section the FPE criterion does not perform as well as sampling techniques and should not be used.

The previous examples indicate that SSO and BE perform similarly whereas BE outperforms SSO in complex problems. On the other hand BE needs the calculation of the inverse of the wavelet matrix which columns might be linear dependent, [14]. In that case the SSO must be used. However since the wavelets come from a wavelet frame this is very rare to happen, [14].

3 Model Selection

In this section we describe the model selection procedure. One of the most crucial steps is to identify the correct topology of the network. A network with less HU than needed is not able to learn the underlying function while selecting more HU than needed will result to an overfitting model. Several criteria exist for model selection, such as Generalized Prediction Error, Akaike's Information Criterion, Final Prediction Error (FPE), Network Information Criterion and Generalized Cross-Validation (GCV). These criteria are based on assumptions that are not necessarily true in the neural network framework. Alternatively we suggest the use of sampling methods such as bootstrap and cross-validation. The only assumption made by sampling methods is that the data are a sequence of independent and identically distributed variables. However, sampling methods are computationally very demanding. In this study we will test the FPE proposed by [14], the GCV proposed by [14], the bootstrap (BS) and the *v-fold* cross-validation (CV) methods proposed by [23] and [24]. These criteria will be tested with and without training of the network.

In both examples BS, FPE and CV propose similar models. In the first example 2 HU were needed to model the underlying function *f(x)*.On the other hand GCV suggests 3 hidden units. The MSE between the underlying function *f(x)* and the approximation of the WN using 3 HU is 0.000271 while using 2 HU is only 0.000121 indicating that the GCV suggested a more complex model than needed. In the second example BS and CV propose the same network topology (8 HU) while using the FPE criterion the prediction risk minimized in 7 HU and using the GCV criterion it is minimized in 14 HU. To compare the performance of each criterion the MSE between the underlying function *g(x)* and the approximation of the WN is calculated. The MSE is 0.000079, 0.000073 and 0.000101 for 7, 8 and 14 HU. Again the BS and CV gave correct results while the FPE performs satisfactorily.

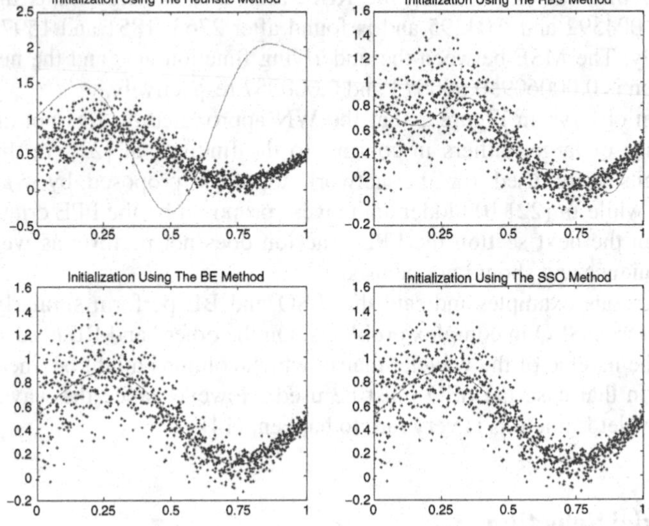

Fig. 1. Four different initialization methods.

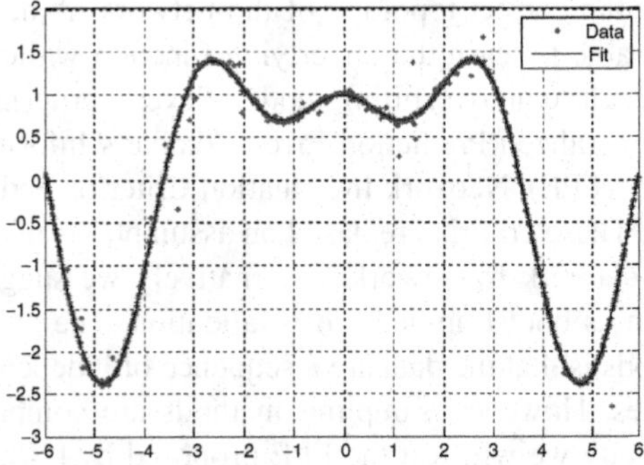

Fig. 2. Data and WN approximation using 8 hidden units.

To significantly reduce the training times [14] propose that since the initialization is very close to the underlying function the prediction risk can be calculated after the initialization. In the first example all information criteria gave the same results as in the previous case. However in the second example in all criteria more than 14 HU were needed proving that early stopping techniques does not perform satisfactory.

Since sampling techniques are very computationally expensive the FPE criterion can be used initially. Then BS or CV can be used in +/-5 HU around the HU proposed by FPE to define the best network topology.

4 Model Fitness and Sensitivity Criteria

In real problems it is important to define correctly the independent variables. In most problems there is a little information about the relationship of any explanatory variable with the dependent variable. As a result unnecessary independent variables included in the model reduce the predictive power of the model. In this section we will present eight different sensitivity criteria and one model fitness sensitivity (MFS) criterion for testing the significance of each explanatory variable.

First we create a second variable X_2 which was randomly drawn from the uniform distribution within the range (0,1). To fit the sample for the first example we use a WN with both X_1 and X_2 as inputs. Using the CV the prediction risk is minimized when 3 HU are used and it is 0.04194. The network approximation converges after 3502 iterations. Comparing the results with the findings in previous section it is clear that including an irrelevant variable to our model increases the training time while the predictive power of the model is reduced. Hence an algorithm that correctly identifies the insignificant variables is needed. For analytical expressions of each criterion we refer to [24].

In linear models the significance of each explanatory variable is determined by the value of the coefficient. In the WN case by observing the weights of the direct connections one concludes that X_2 is more significant than X_1. As expected the listed magnitudes are much larger for the first variable for all nine criteria. However the only information that Table 1 gives is how sensitive is the dependent variable to each independent variable. There is no information if X_2 should be removed from the model. In [24] a novel approach (parametric sampling) is presented to determine if a variable should be removed from the model. In parametric sampling new networks are created by bootstrapping the parameters of the initial network. To reduce training times [24] use local bootstrap. Wavelets are local function and local bootstrapping may cannot be used. Hence we sample from the training patterns. As *v-fold* cross validation performs better than bootstrap [23] we propose an approach where 50 new training samples are created according to *v-fold* cross validation. After the correct topology of the network is determined, the sensitivity criteria are calculated for each sample. Next the *p-values* for each criterion are computed and the variable with the largest *p-value* is removed. The procedure is repeated until all explanatory variables have *p*-value less than 0.1 indicating significant variables.

First the standard deviation and the *p*-values for all sensitivity and model fitness measures for the two variables of the first example are calculated. As it was expected X_1 has a larger impact in the output y. However all eight sensitivity measures consider both variables as significant predictors. As discussed on [24] these criteria are application dependent while MFS criteria are much better suited for testing the significance of the explanatory variables. Indeed the *p*-value for X_2 using the SBP is 0.6019 indicating that this variable must be removed from the model. In the reduced model the *p*-value for X_1 using the SBP is 0 indicating that X_1 is very significant. Next the correctness of removing the X_2 should be tested.

The prediction risk in the reduced model was reduced to 0.0396 from 0.0419 in full model. Moreover the adjusted R^2 increased to 70.8% from 69.7%.

The same analysis is repeated for the second example. In Table 2 the mean, the standard deviation and the *p*-values for all sensitivity and model fitness measures for the two variables of the second example are presented. A network with 10 HU was needed when both variables were included in the model. Only three criteria suggest that X_2 should be removed from the model, the SBP, the MaxDM and MinDM with *p*-values 0.1597, 0.4158 and 0.8433 respectively. However the MinDM wrongly suggests that X_1 should also be removed from the model with *p*-value 0.1795 in the reduced model. On the other hand the p-values for X_1 using the SBP and the MaxDM are 0 indicating a very significant variable in both full and reduced models. The reduced model needed only 8 HU and the prediction risk reduced to 0.0008 from 0.0033 that it was when X_2 was included as an input. Moreover the adjusted R^2 increased to 99.7% from 99.2%. The previous examples show that SBP can be safely used for the identification of irrelevant variables. On the other hand the sensitivity criteria are application dependent and extra care must be taken when used.

5 Conclusions

This study presents a statistical framework for wavelet network model identification. To our knowledge this is the first time that a complete statistical framework for the use of WNs is presented. Several methodologies were tested in wavelet network construction, initialization, model selection and variable significant testing. We propose a multidimensional wavelet neural network with a linear connection of the wavelons to the output and direct connections from the input layer to the output layer. The training is performed by the classic back-propagation algorithm. Next four different methods were tested in wavelet network initialization. Using the BE and SSO the training times were reduced significantly while the network converged to the global minimum of the loss function.

Model selection is a very important step. Four techniques were tested with the sampling techniques to give more stable results than other alternatives. BS and CV found the correct network topology in both examples. Although FPE and GCV are extensively used in the WN framework, due to the linear relation of the wavelets and the original signal, it was proved that both criteria should not be used in complex problems. Moreover using early stopping techniques in complex problems was found to be inappropriate.

A variable selection method was presented. Various sensitivity and model fitness criteria were tested. While sensitivity criteria are application dependent, MFS criteria are much better suited for testing the significance of the explanatory variables. The SBP correctly indentified the insignificant variables while their removal reduced the prediction risk and increased the adjusted R^2 implying the correctness of this decision.

Finally the partial derivatives with respect to the weights of the network, to the dilation and translation parameters as well as the derivative with respect to each input variable are presented. The construction of confidence and prediction intervals as well as a model adequacy testing scheme are left as a future work.

Table 1. Sensitivity measures for the first example.

	$w_i^{[0]}$	MaxD	MinD	MaxDM	MinDM	AvgD	AvgDM	AvgL	AvgLM	SBP
Full model (two variables)										
X_1	0.0161	1.3962	-1.3459	1.3962	0.0005	-0.0529	0.6739	0.2127	1.6323	0.0953
X_2	0.0186	0.4964	-0.7590	0.7590	0.0002	0.0256	0.0915	0.0781	0.1953	0.0001
Reduced model (one variable)										
X_1	0.1296	1.1646	-1.1622	1.1644	0.0014	0.0841	0.7686	0.3165	1.3510	0.0970

MaxD=Maximum Derivative
MinD=Minimum Derivative
MaxDM=Maximum Derivative Magnitude
MinDM=Minimum Derivative Magnitude
AvgD=Average Derivative
AvgDM=Average Derivative Magnitude
AvgL=Average Elasticity
AvgLM=Average Elasticity Magnitude
SBP=Sensitivity Based Pruning

References

1. Pati, Y., Krishnaprasad, P.: Analysis and Synthesis of Feedforward Neural Networks Using Discrete Affine Wavelet Transforms. IEEE Trans. on Neural Networks 4(1), 73-85 (1993)
2. Zhang, Q., Benveniste, A.: Wavelet Networks. IEEE Trans. on Neural Networks 3(6), 889-898 (1992)

3. Bernard, C., Mallat, S., Slotine, J.-J.: Wavelet Interpolation Networks. In Proc. ESANN '98, 47-52 (1998)
4. Benaouda, D., Murtagh, G., Starck, J.-L., Renaud, O.: Wavelet-Based Nonlinear Multiscale Decomposition Model for Electricity Load Forecasting. Neurocomputing 70, 139-154 (2006)
5. Chen, Y., Yang, B., Dong, J.: Time-Series Prediction Using a Local Linear Wavelet Neural Wavelet. Neurocomputing 69, 449-465 (2006)
6. Kadambe, S., Srinivasan, P.: Adaptive Wavelets for Signal Classification and Compression. International Journal of Electronics and Communications 60, 45-55 (2006)
7. Billings, S., Wei, H.-L.: A New Class of Wavelet Networks for Nonlinear System Identification. IEEE Trans. on Neural Networks 16(4), 862-874 (2005)
8. Jiao, L., Pan, J., Fang, Y.: Multiwavelet Neural Network and Its Approximation Properties. IEEE Trans. on Neural Networks 12(5), 1060-1066 (2001)
9. Khayamian, T., Ensafi, A., Tabaraki, R., Esteki, M.: Principal Component-Wavelet Networks as a New Multivariate Calibration Model. Analytical Letters 38(9), 1447-1489 (2005)
10. Zapranis, A., Alexandridis, A.: Modelling Temperature Time Dependent Speed of Mean Reversion in the Context of Weather Derivetive Pricing. Applied Mathematical Finance 15(4), 355 - 386 (2008)
11. Zapranis, A., Alexandridis, A.: Weather Derivatives Pricing: Modelling the Seasonal Residuals Variance of an Ornstein-Uhlenbeck Temperature Process with Neural Networks. Neurocomputing (accepted, to appear) (2007)
12. Becerikli, Y.: On Three Intelligent Systems: Dynamic Neural, Fuzzy and Wavelet Networks for Training Trajectory. Neural Computation and Applications 13, 339-351 (2004)
13. Zhao, J., Chen, B., Shen, J.: Multidimensional Non-Orthogonal Wavelet-Sigmoid Basis Function Neurla Network for Dynamic Process Fault Diagnosis. Computers and Chemical Engineering 23, 83-92 (1998)
14. Zhang, Q.: Using Wavelet Network in Nonparametric Estimation. IEEE Trans. on Neural Networks 8(2), 227-236 (1997)
15. Oussar, Y., Rivals, I., Presonnaz, L., Dreyfus, G.: Trainning Wavelet Networks for Nonlinear Dynamic Input Output Modelling. Neurocomputing 20, 173-188 (1998)
16. Postalcioglu, S., Becerikli, Y.: Wavelet Networks for Nonlinear System Modelling. Neural Computing & Applications 16, 434-441 (2007)
17. Oussar, Y., Dreyfus, G.: Initialization by Selection for Wavelet Network Training. Neurocomputing 34, 131-143 (2000)
18. Xu, J., Ho, D.: A Basis Selection Algorithm for Wavelet Neural Networks. Neurocomputing 48, 681-689 (2002)
19. Gao, R., Tsoukalas, H.: Neural-wavelet Methodology for Load Forecasting. Journal of Intelligent & Robotic Systems 31, 149-157 (2001)
20. Xu, J., Ho, D.: A Constructive Algorithm for Wavelet Neural Networks. Lecture Notes in Computer Science(3610), 730-739 (2005)
21. Kan, K.-C., Wong, K.: Self-construction algorithm for synthesis of wavelet networks. Electronic Letters 34, 1953-1955 (1998)
22. Li, S., Chen, S.-C.: Function Approximation using Robust Wavelet Neural Networks. In Proc. ICTAI '02, 483-488 (2002)
23. Efron, B., Tibshirani, R.: An Introduction to the Bootstrap. Chapman & Hall, USA (1993)
24. Zapranis, A., Refenes, A.: Principles of Neural Model Indentification, Selection and Adequacy: With Applications to Financial Econometrics. Springer-Verlag (1999)

Two Levels Similarity Modelling: a Novel Content Based Image Clustering Concept

Amar Djouak[1] and Hichem Maaref [2]

1 Agriculture high institute (ISA) (computer science and statistics laboratory)- Catholic Lille University. 48, boulevard Vauban. 59000. Lille. France.

E-mail: a.djouak@isa-lille.fr

2 IBISC Laboratory (CNRS FRE 3190) 40 Rue du Pelvoux, 91025 EVRY Cedex. France. Phone: +33169477555, Fax: +33169470306,

E-mail: hmaaref@univ-evry.fr

Abstract In this work, we applied a co-clustering concept in content based image recognition field. In this aim, we introduced a two levels similarity modelling (TLSM) concept. This approach is based on a new images similarity formulation using obtained co-clusters. The obtained results show a real improvement of image recognition accuracy in comparison with obtained accuracy obtained using one of classical co-clustering systems.

1 Introduction

The aim of any unsupervised classification method applied to contend based image retrieval is to gather considered images to be similar. In this case, algorithms treat the data in only one direction: lines or columns, but not both at the same time. Contrary to the one-dimensional clustering, co-clustering (also called biclustering) proposes to process the data tables by taking of account the lines and the columns in a simultaneous way. That implies the consideration of the existing correlation between the data expressed in lines and columns. Thus, co-clustering is a more complete data view since it includes a new concept "the mutual information" which is a bond between the random variables representing the clusters. An optimal coclustering is that which minimize the difference (the loss) of mutual information between the original random variables and mutual information between the clusters random variables. Several co-clustering structures are proposed in the literature [1],[2],[3]. The choice of one of these structures is directly related on the considered application. That is also related to the relational complexity between the lines and the columns elements. Among used co-clustering approaches, in [4], Qiu proposed a new approach dedicated to content based image categorization us-

Please use the following format when citing this chapter:

Djouak, A. and Maaref, H., 2009, in IFIP International Federation for Information Processing, Volume 296; *Artificial Intelligence Applications and Innovations III*; Eds. Iliadis, L., Vlahavas, I., Bramer, M.; (Boston: Springer), pp. 277–282.

ing the bipartite graphs to simultaneously model the images and their features. Indeed, the first bipartite graph set is associated to the images and the second unit is associated to their features. The bonds between the two sets characterize the existing degrees of correspondence between the images and their features. This method is very promising and could open the way for many possibilities to adapt co-clustering techniques to images recognition and retrieval applications. In this work, to propose one of the first coclustering based content based images recognition and search, our images are described by features vectors.

They form a two-dimensional table (lines/columns) such as the lines are the DataBase images and the columns are the features which describe them. Then, we propose in this paper a new co-clustering modelling which introduce a two levels similarity concept. The aim of this method is to improve the image retrieval accuracy and to optimize time processing. In other hand, we use one of classical co-clustering approaches to comparing its performances with those obtained with our method. Moreover, the choice of BIVISU system [5] applied initially to manage gene expression data is justified by its great conceptual simplicity.

This work is organized as follows: section 2 is devoted to the BIVISU co-clustering system. Section 3 introduce the two levels association concept and model the general architecture of the proposed approach. In section 4, different experimental results are presented and commented. Finally, one synthesizes presented work and exposes the future tracks.

2 Used Co-clustering Algorithm: BIVISU

The used co-clustering algorithm (BIVISU system) can detect several co-clusters forms (constant, constant rows, constant columns, additive and multiplicative co-clusters as defined in [5]). Also, this method uses parallel coordinate (PC) plots for visualize high dimensional data in a 2D plane. Besides visualization, it has been exploited to re-formulate the co-clustering problem [5].

To cluster the rows and columns simultaneously, clustering of rows is first performed for each pair of columns in used algorithm. Further columns are then merged to form a big co-cluster. The approach “merge and split”, i.e. merging paired columns and splitting in rows is performed then for obtaining final co-clusters. Actually, the "merge and split" process is repeated for each column-pair. Since there is either no significantly large co-cluster found or the same co-clusters are detected, only the three co-clusters are obtained for our example. This algorithm is based on a clear formalism and provides good quality co-clustering results. In the following paragraph, one extends it with introducing the two levels similarity concept.

3 Two Levels Similarity Model

The difficulty in choosing co-clustering algorithm parameters generates some search errors. To attenuate these errors, one tries to introduce a method which consider the similarity described by the obtained co-clusters in a different way from that usually used..

Initially, the features are extracted from the query image and from all the DataBase images. The extracted features can varying with application context. Two tables are built. One gathers the DataBase images represented by all their features. The other contains the same table with the addition of query image and its features.

The second stage consists in applying – separately- the co-clustering algorithm which allows to obtain a relatively small co-clusters number (a number preliminary chosen $\in[1,20]$). This stage allows to obtain a two-dimensional grouping based on the lines/columns interaction. The choice of a sufficiently small initial co-clusters number has justified by keeping a certain generalization capacity and that by merging the co-clusters wich are sufficiently dependent. After, this number can vary in an iterative way according to desired search quality.

Obtaining a lines/columns grouping generates some associations between these lines and columns. Indeed, co-clustering allows to associate the images to the features according to the obtained co-clusters scheme. In this case, on can obtain two associations sets : a unit to represent the co-clusters relating to the table "DataBase images /features" and another one for the co-clusters relating to the table "DataBase images + query image /features". Each co-cluster is characterized by some associations which one can merge in the columns (images in our case) direction. These associations can be formalized by equation 1.

$$\text{Image x associated to feature y} \tag{1}$$

x vary between 1 and N for the first table (images DataBase before query image introduction, N is the images number in the DataBase) and x vary between 1 and N+1 for the second table (images DataBase after query image introduction,). y vary between 1 and M (M is the features number).

The following stage allows the hierarchical strategy construction which gives the images considered similar to the query image. This strategy is based on a associations combination extracted from the two tables at the same time (before and after query image introduction). In fact, the query image addition generates local lines/columns interactions modifications, which implies a change of the co-clustering diagram obtained before introduction of this new image. The idea is to exploit this variation effect to elaborate a comparative strategy of the interactions between the query image and the DataBase images and also the internal interactions beetwen DataBase images before query image introduction.

Indeed, two similarity levels are proposed: the level relating to associations between the query image and the DataBase images and the level relating to the DataBase images associations between them before query image introduction. That allows after appropriate associations weighting to merge the strongest similarities in the two levels and to exclude the too weak judged bonds progressively and thus consequently to exclude the images considered not sufficiently similar to the query image. For weighting strategy, it is done by calculating the features number relating to each association. Then, a large number implies a strong association and vice versa. Thus, according to user and the application context, a qualitative thresholding is possible by fixing the minimal acceptable associations weights numbers. Figure 1 gives the algorithmic scheme of the two levels association method.

Start_Algorithm

Inputs : *Images DataBase/features table*
Images DataBase+ query image/features table

Co_clustering algorithm application

Co-clusters sets obtention

Direct similarity detection

Indirect similarity detection

Combination of tow similarities into the same set

Outputs : *Similar images appear in the order imposed by the associated features number*

End_Algorithm

Fig. 1. Two levels similarity method algorithm

Finally, one could introduce a precision/recall test which would validate (or not) the obtained result. A result evaluation would be made and that by comparing the obtained precision/recall values with minimal pre fixed thresholds according to application requirements. If the result is judged sufficiently good (stability of obtained error between two successive iterations), the processing operation would stop. If not, one would introduce a co-clusters number gradual increase to obtain a larger precision on the level of the associations development and thus a more precise result. Then, the co-clusters number would be increased in an iterative way until obtaining desired result.

4 Experimental Results

In this section, one experimented two level similarity concept and one compared co-clustering results with those obtained with BIVISU system (initially used for the expression gene data applications).

The tests carried out consist in introducing a features table (26 columns representing 26 features [6] : classical low level features , color histograms features, wavelet transform features and finally rotation translation and scaling invariance by Trace transform) of processed images (200 lines representing the images) and then introducing features vector for each query image and retaining the associations generated by the obtained co-clusters to determine the images subset as being most similar to each query image. Figure 2 shows a sample of the used DataBase images. Thus and for each introduced query image, the initially obtained co-clusters structure is modified, and that modify its local similarity with one or more co-clusters.

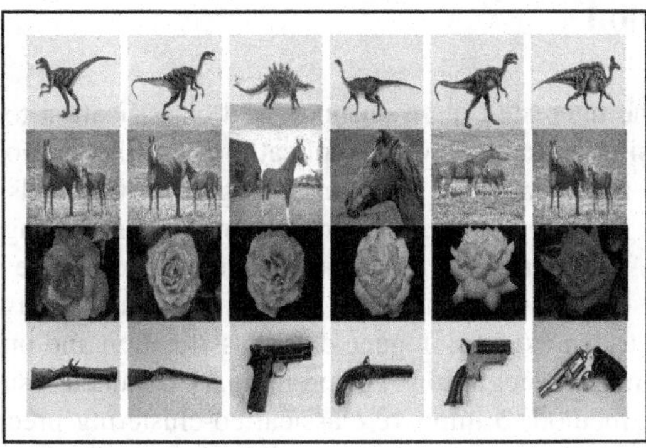

Fig. 2. Used images DataBase sample

Then, the images into the co-clusters associated to query image are turned over in an order which is based on the present features number in each associated co-cluster.

Generally, one notices an acceptable image search quality according to the images heterogeneity and the difficulty in formalizing the BIVISU system parameters adjustments (the maximum lines and columns dimensions per co-cluster...). This difficulty generates some coarse image search errors what leads us to say that an interactive use of this system in the content based image recognition field will be more beneficial in precision term.

Precision/recall diagrams for a sample of 24 images (of figure 2) are given in figure 3 for classical co-clustering method and for TLSM method. We can observe easely the added value and the superiority of our approach for the choosen images.

Finally, one notes that in spite of the first encouraging results, a thorough experimentation will allows to confirm the two levels similarity model potential and thus to give a solid experimental validation of this method.

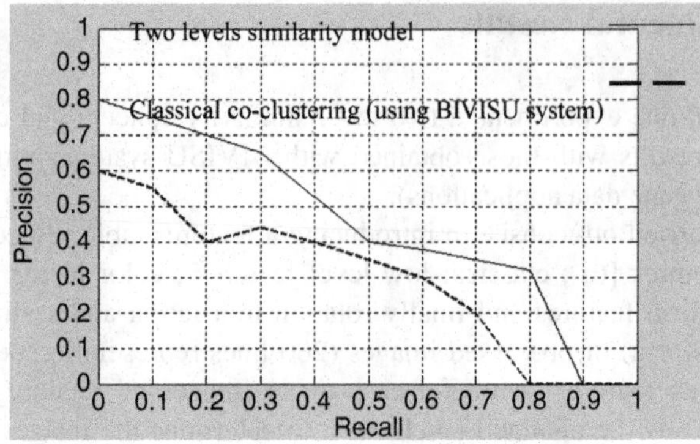

Fig. 3. Pecision/recall diagrams

5 Conclusion

In this work, one interested in an unsupervised classification tool : co-clustering, which is increasingly used in several applications. For this purpose, , one proposed a new co-clustering adaptation by introducing the two levels similarity model (T.L.S.M). This new approach takes into account the query image effect on the initial similarities between used DataBase images. To compare this method with classical co-clustering approaches, one studied a recent co-clustering system initially dedicated to the expression gene data classification and one applied it to the content based images recognition. The preliminary obtained results show the great potential of our method to improve classical co-clustering precision. However, a more solid experimental study allows to validate our method and to generalize its use in various applications.

References

1. I. S. Dhillon, S. Mallela et D. S. Modha: Information theoretic Coclustering, International Conference on Knowledge Discovery and Data Mining (SIGKDD), 2003.
2. A.L. Oliveira, S.C. Madeira : Biclustering algorithms for biological data analysis: a syrvey, EEE/ACM Trans. Computational Biology and Bioinformatics , vol. 1, no. 1, pp. 24-45, 2004.
3. Y. Klugar, R. Basri, J. T. Chang, et M. Gerstein: Spectral biclustering of microarray data: co-clustering genes and conditions. In Genome Research, volume 13, pages 703–716, 2003.
4. G. Qiu : Bipartite graph partitioning and content-based image clustering, CVMP 2004, 1st European Conference on Visual Media Production (CVMP), The IEE, Savoy Place, London, 15-16 March 2004
5. K.O. Cheng, N.F. Law, W.C. Siu, T.H. Lau. : BiVisu: Software Tool for Bicluster Detection and Visualization. Bioinformatics Advance Access published June 22, 2007
6. A.Djouak, K, Djemal and H.Maaref : Modular statistical optimization and VQ method for image recognition – 2nd international workshop on artificial neural networks and intelligent information processing. ANNIP 2006. Portugal. Aout 2006.

Locating an Acoustic Source Using a Mutual Information Beamformer

Osama N. Alrabadi, Fotios Talantzis, and Anthony G. Constantinides

Abstract Beamforming remains one of the most common methods for estimating the Direction Of Arrival (DOA) of an acoustic source. Beamformers operate using at least two sensors that look among a set of geometrical directions for the one that maximizes received signal power. In this paper we consider a two-sensor beamformer that estimates the DOA of a single source by scanning the broadside for the direction that maximizes the mutual information between the two microphones. This alternative approach exhibits robust behavior even under heavily reverberant conditions where traditional power-based systems fail to distinguish between the true DOA and that of a dominant reflection. Performance is demonstrated for both algorithms with sets of simulations and experiments as a function of different environmental variables. The results indicate that the newly proposed beamforming scheme can accurately estimate the DOA of an acoustic source.

1 Introduction

Locating an acoustic source in a reverberant and noisy enclosure using an array of microphones remains an open problem in a class of different applications. Typical examples include smart environments [1] and security systems [2]. Such systems are typically required to identify the location of the active speech source in physical space, from a short time frame on which speech is considered as stationary (typically 10 to 30 ms). Most solutions to the problem require employment of arrays in the enclosure and the use of an Acoustic Source Localization (ASL) system. ASL is based on the asynchrony between the various microphones and the corresponding cross-correlation between their signals. The various methods are based on two approaches: time delay estimation (TDE) [3], and direct methods with the latter shown to be more robust [4].

Please use the following format when citing this chapter:

Alrabadi, O.N., Talantzis, F. and Constantinides, A.G., 2009, in IFIP International Federation for Information Processing, Volume 296; *Artificial Intelligence Applications and Innovations III*; Eds. Iliadis, L., Vlahavas, I., Bramer, M.; (Boston: Springer), pp. 283–291.

The basic component of direct methods is a beamformer that scans a set of candidate directions for the one that exhibits the maximum power [4]. This process is known as estimation of the Direction Of Arrival (DOA). Tuning the beamformer to scan different directions refers to simply delaying the outputs of its microphones by a different amount and then multiplying each of them by a set of appropriate coefficients. In presence of noise and reverberation though the DOA estimate provided could be spurious due to ensuing reflections and noise. Methods to overcome these effects have been presented [5, 6] but still suffer significantly in heavily reverberant environments.

In the present work we present a new criterion for choosing the direction from which the acoustic source emits. We extend the work that was presented in [1] for TDE and use a two-microphone array to look for the DOA that maximizes the marginal Mutual Information (MI) at the output of the beamformer. Information theory concepts in beamforming have been used before [7] but have no mechanisms to deal with reverberation. The approach presented in this paper involves a framework that takes into account the effects of the spreading the information into samples neighboring to the one that maximizes the MI comparing function. Through experiments and extensive simulations we demonstrate that this novel MI based beamformer resolves to a great degree the reverberation problem and generates robust DOA estimations. To verify our mathematical framework we test and compare it with the traditional power-based for a set of different environmental variables.

The rest of the paper is organized as follows. In Section II we formulate the DOA estimation problem under the beamformer constraint and present the typical power-based method which is used at a later stage for comparison purposes. The MI based alternative is presented in Section III. Section IV examines the performance of the two systems under different criteria such as reverberation level, array geometry and other requirements imposed by real-time systems. Section V discusses briefly the conclusions of this study.

2 System Model

A DOA estimation system is typically employed in a reverberant environment and it considers at least two microphones. The sound source that the system attempts to locate and track is assumed to be in the far field of the microphones. Therefore, we can approximate the spherical wavefront emanating from the source as a plane wavefront of sound waves arriving at the microphone pairs in a parallel manner. Let $\mathbf{r}_m, m = 1, 2$ denote the positions of the two microphones with their distance being d meters. The discrete signal recorded at the mth microphone at time k is then:

$$x_m(k) = h_m(k) * s(k) + n_m(k), \tag{1}$$

where $s(k)$ is the source signal, $h_m(k)$ is the room impulse response between the source and m^{th} microphone, $n_m(k)$ is additive white Gaussian noise, and $*$ denotes convolution. The length of $h_m(k)$, and thus the number of reflections, is a function of the reverberation time T_{60} (defined as the time in seconds for the reverberation level to decay to 60 dB below the initial level) of the room and expresses the main problem when attempting to track an acoustic source. Data for DOA estimation is collected over frames of L samples which for the tth frame we denote as $\mathbf{x}_{tm} = [x_{tm}(0)\ldots x_{tm}(L-1)]$ with $x_{tm}(k) = x_m(L(t-1)+k)$.

Estimating the DOA using a traditional beamformer involves scanning a set of geometrical directions and choosing the one that maximizes the beamformer output power. Typically this is performed in the frequency domain. As in the time-domain, processing is performed in frames with the use of an L-point Short Time Fourier Transform (STFT) over a set of discrete frequencies ω. Thus, the output of the beamformer at frame t and frequency ω is:

$$Y_t(\theta,\omega) = \frac{1}{2}\sum_{m=1}^{2} H_{tm}(\theta,\omega)X_{tm}(\omega) \tag{2}$$

where $X_{tm}(\omega)$ is the ωth element of frame $\mathbf{X}_{tm}$ i.e. the STFT of $\mathbf{x}_{tm}$. $H_{tm}(\theta,\omega)$ is the weight applied to the mth microphone when the beamformer is steered toward direction θ. The beamformer weights are calculated as:

$$H_{tm}(\theta,\omega) = e^{-\frac{j\omega d_m}{c}\sin\theta} \tag{3}$$

where d_m is the Euclidean distance of the mth microphone from the origin. Without loss of generality we can consider $\mathbf{r}_1$ as the origin i.e. $d_1 = 0$ and $d_2 = d$. Thus, in the case of the power-based beamforming the estimated direction $\theta_s^{[P]}$ from which the source emits at frame t can be estimated as:

$$\theta_s^{[P]} = \arg\max_{\theta} |\widehat{Y}_t(\theta)|^2 \tag{4}$$

where $|\widehat{Y}_t(\theta)|^2 = \sum_{\omega} W(\omega)|Y_t(\theta,\omega)|^2$ is the average beamformer output power over the L discrete frequencies ω. $W(\omega)$ denotes any frequency weighting that is used. In a reverberant environment though, the true source location is not always the global maximum of the power function and thus the above approach often generates wrong estimates.

3 Mutual Information Beamforming

The MI of two variables is an information theoretical measure that represents the difference between the measured joint entropy of the two variables(in our case these are the microphone signals) and their joint entropy if they were independent. Since the analysis will be independent of the data frame we can drop t to express frames simply as $\mathbf{X}_m$ for any t. So for any set of frames, the MI at the output of the beamformer when steered toward an angle θ is [8]:

$$I_N = -\frac{1}{2} \ln \frac{\mathbf{det}[\mathbf{C}(\theta)]}{\mathbf{det}[\mathbf{C}_{11}]\mathbf{det}[\mathbf{C}_{22}]} \tag{5}$$

the joint covariance matrix $\mathbf{C}(\theta)$ is a concatenation of frames $\mathbf{X}_1$ and $\mathbf{X}_2$ shifted by different amounts in samples:

$$\begin{aligned}
\mathbf{C}(\theta) &\approx \\
&\Re\left\{ \begin{bmatrix} \mathbf{X}_1 \\ \mathcal{D}(\mathbf{X}_1, 1) \\ \vdots \\ \mathcal{D}(\mathbf{X}_1, N) \\ \mathcal{D}(\mathbf{X}_2, \frac{d\sin\theta}{cf_s}) \\ \mathcal{D}(\mathbf{X}_2, \frac{d\sin\theta}{cf_s}+1) \\ \vdots \\ \mathcal{D}(\mathbf{X}_2, \frac{d\sin\theta}{cf_s}+N) \end{bmatrix} \begin{bmatrix} \mathbf{X}_1 \\ \mathcal{D}(\mathbf{X}_1, 1) \\ \vdots \\ \mathcal{D}(\mathbf{X}_1, N) \\ \mathcal{D}(\mathbf{X}_2, \frac{d\sin\theta}{cf_s}) \\ \mathcal{D}(\mathbf{X}_2, \frac{d\sin\theta}{cf_s}+1) \\ \vdots \\ \mathcal{D}(\mathbf{X}_2, \frac{d\sin\theta}{cf_s}+N) \end{bmatrix}^H \right\} \\
&= \begin{bmatrix} \mathbf{C}_{11} & \mathbf{C}_{12}(\theta) \\ \mathbf{C}_{21}(\theta) & \mathbf{C}_{22} \end{bmatrix}
\end{aligned} \tag{6}$$

where the $\Re\{.\}$ operation returns only the real part of its argument. Function $\mathcal{D}(\mathbf{A}, n)$ shifts the frequency components contained in frame $\mathbf{A}$ by n samples. This is typically implemented by using an exponential with an appropriate complex argument.

If N is chosen to be greater than zero the elements of $\mathbf{C}(\theta)$ are themselves matrices. In fact for any value of θ, the size of $\mathbf{C}(\theta)$ is always $2(N+1) \times 2(N+1)$. We call N the *order* of the beamforming system. N is really the parameter that controls the robustness of the beamformer against reverberation. In the above equations and in order to estimate the information between the microphone signals, we actually use the marginal MI that considers jointly N neighboring samples (thus the inclusion of delayed versions of the microphone signals). This way function (5) takes into account the spreading of information due to reverberation and returns more accurate estimates.

The estimated DOA $\theta_s^{[MI]}$ is then obtained as the angle that maximizes (5), i.e.

$$\theta_s^{[MI]} = \arg\max_{\theta} \{I_N\} \tag{7}$$

4 Performance Analysis

In order to demonstrate the improved robustness of the MI based beamformer we conducted DOA estimation experiments and simulations for a single source and a two-microphone system. We used a speech signal of duration 10 sec sampled at

$f_s = 44.1$ kHz which was broken into overlapped frames using a hamming window and an overlap factor of $1/2$. The source was placed at the geometrical angles of $\theta_s = -60^o, -30^o, 0^o, 30^o, 60^o$ (so as to validate the performance under different arrivals), and at a distance $R_o = 2$ m, from the mid-point between the two microphones. The test scenario involves scanning the broadside of the array i.e. from -90° to $+90^o$ in steps of 3° and looking for the values that maximize functions (4) and (7). For each frame of data processed, the beamforming systems return a different DOA estimate. The squared error for frame t is then computed as:

$$\sigma_t = (\theta_s - \widehat{\theta}_t)^2 \tag{8}$$

where θ_s is the actual DOA and $\widehat{\theta}_t$ is either $\theta_s^{[P]}$ or $\theta_s^{[MI]}$, depending on the beamforming system used. The Root Mean Squared Error (RMSE) metric is the performance measure used to evaluate the systems. For a single experiment or simulation this is defined to be the square root of the average value of σ_t over all frames. This is calculated separately for the two beamforming systems. Thus, the lower the average RMSE value, the better the performance of the estimating system.

4.1 Real Experiments

First we look into a set of real experiments performed in a typical reverberant room of size $[5, 3.67, 2.58]$ m equipped with a speaker playing the test signal and a microphone array in which we can change the microphone distances. We repeated the playback of the test signal for 30 random displacements of the overall relative geometry between the source and microphone array inside the room. For each of these displacements we examined the performance of the system for three different inter-microphone distances. The reverberation time of the room was measured to be approximately 0.3 s. In the figures to follow we present the average RMSE over all 30 experiments. It's also worth noting that experiments are conducted in presence of ambient noise from both air-conditioning and personal computers, estimated to be 15 dB.

Fig. 1(a) shows the average RMSE of the beamforming systems for different distances d between the sensors. Effectively, changing the inter-microphone distance changes the resolution of the array. It is evident that the MI based beamformer remains more robust in estimating the correct DOA for all distances. The improvement of performance for both beamforming systems as the spacing decreases can prove misleading since it is caused by the decreased resolution. Safe conclusions were drawn by observing the comparative performance of the two systems for each spacing.

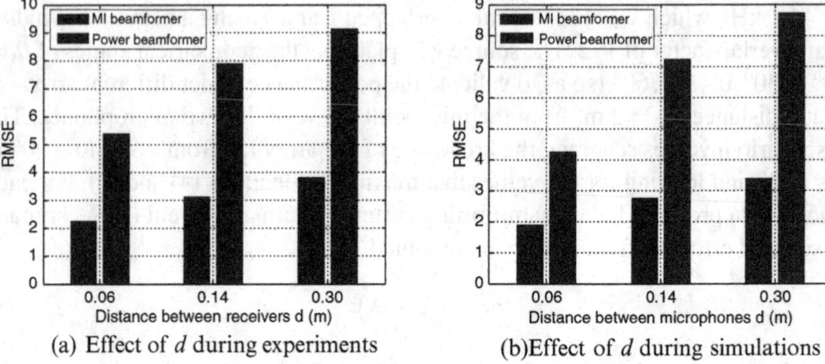

(a) Effect of d during experiments (b)Effect of d during simulations

Fig. 1 Average RMSE for the two beamforming systems during experiments and simulations. Values are shown for three different inter-microphone distances. $L = 0.5 \times T_{60} f_s$ and $N = 4$.

4.2 Simulations

Simulations where performed for three different environments differentiated by their reverberation times T_{60}. For the used sampling rate f_s these result in impulse responses $h(k)$ of different lengths. The impulse responses are generated using the image model [9] modified to allow for non-integer sample delays. The simulated room dimensions are identical to the ones of the room used in the experiments. These where then convolved with the speech signal to create the microphone signals. Moreover, 15dB of additive noise was also introduced to the signals. The process was repeated for 30 random displacements and rotations of the relative geometry between the source and the receivers inside the room.

4.2.1 Effect of system order

Choosing the order N of the MI beamforming system affects performance significantly. Fig. 2 shows the RMSE for varying N for all three environments. L is chosen to be $0.5 \times T_{60} \times f_s$. Since by increasing N we include more information about reverberation, the MI calculations became more accurate and the estimation of the correct DOA becomes more robust. Thus, the effect of N is more evident for higher reverberation times.

4.2.2 Effect of reverberation

The most limiting factor in designing a robust beamformer is the effect of reverberation. As someone might expect, as the room becomes more reverberant the performance of the estimating systems degrades because reflections enforce the power or the MI at a wrong DOA. Fig. 3 summarizes the effect for the case when $L = 0.5 \times T_{60} f_s$, $N = 4$. The MI beamformer exhibits a more robust behavior in all environments when compared to the power-based beamformer of the corresponding order.

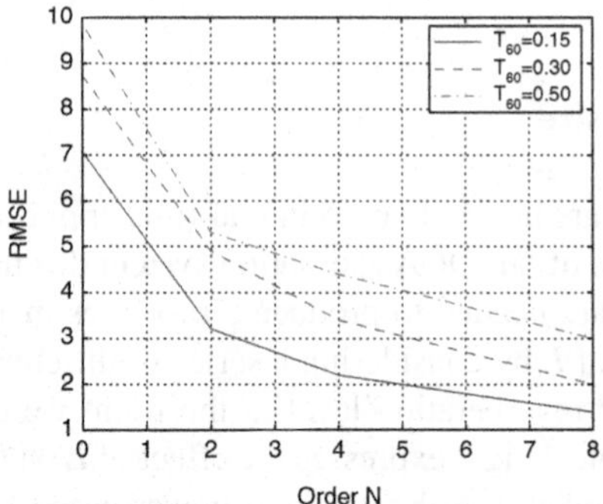

Fig. 2 RMSE of MI system with increasing order N for different values of T_{60}. $L = 0.5 \times T_{60} f_s$. Microphone spacing is 0.30 m.

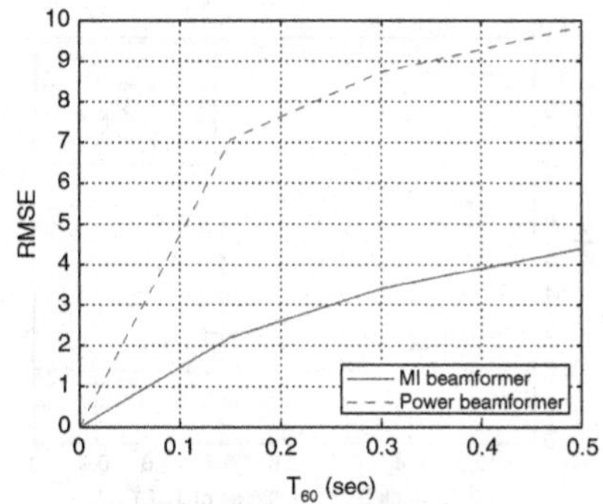

Fig. 3 RMSE of MI and power systems for varying $T60$. $L = 0.5 \times T_{60} f_s$. Shown for microphone spacing of 0.30 m.

4.2.3 Effect of inter-microphone distance

We also investigate the effect of changing the distance between the microphones for $T_{60} = 0.30$ sec, in order to compare the simulation results with those of the experiments in Fig. 1.(a). Fig. 1.(b) shows the resulting RMSE as the distance of the microphones increases. The MI system remains better for any spacing. The values between Fig. 1(b) and Fig.1(a) are not identical but their differences remain small.

These can be explained by noting that the experimental room is far from the idealized version of the simulations. In reality, the experimental environment contains furniture and walls of different texture and materials that a explain to a great degree the differences. Additionally, the image model used in the simulations is subject to a set of assumptions [9].

4.2.4 Effect of frame size

Beamforming systems are normally used in real-time applications so their response time is crucial. In terms of our DOA estimation system this translates into the number of samples L that are needed to produce a robust estimate. Thus, we examine the effect of the value of L by considering a series of different block sizes. To keep these a function of the reverberation level in the room we examine L=[0.25, 0.5, 0.75, 1]$\times T_{60} f_s$ in samples. Fig.4 expresses the effect of L on the performance of the MI beamformer as compared to the classical power-based for $T_{60} = 0.15$ sec and $T_{60} = 0.30$ sec. This shows that, for the chosen parameters, the MI based method is more robust than its counterpart, where $N = 4$ in all cases. In real-time systems where small block sizes are required, the presented system would obviously be preferable since it requires far fewer data to perform satisfactory.

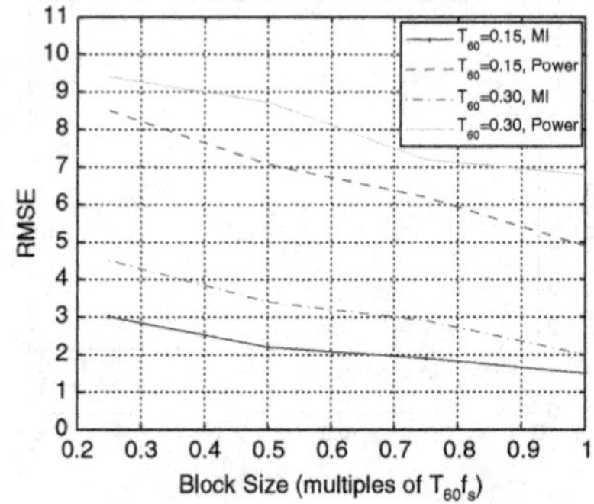

Fig. 4 RMSE of MI and power systems for varying value of L. Shown for $T_{60} = 0.15$ sec and $T_{60} = 0.30$ sec. Microphone spacing is 0.30 m.

5 Conclusions

In this paper a novel beamforming system has been introduced that detects the presence of an acoustic source based on information theory concepts. We demonstrated that such an approach can take into account information about reverberation and thus return DOA estimations those are more robust. This was demonstrated by a set of experiments and simulations under similar conditions. The MI-based beamformer showed improved robustness for all examined scenarios and for any combination of environmental and system variables like reverberation time, inter-microphone spacing and frame size.

Acknowledgment

This work has been partly sponsored by the European Union, under the FP7 project HERMES.

References

1. A. Pnevmatikakis, F. Talantzis, J. Soldatos, L. Polymenakos, "Robust Multimodal Audio-Visual Processing for Advanced Context Awareness in Smart Spaces", *Springer Journal on Personal and Ubiquitous Computing*, DOI: 10.1007/s00779-007-0169-9, April 2007.
2. Y. Wang, E. Chang, K. Cheng, "A Video Analysis Framework for Soft Biometry Security Surveillance", *Proc. ACM Workshop on Video Surveillance and Sensor Networks*, pp. 71-78, Singapore, 2005.
3. C.H. Knapp, G.C. Carter, "The Generalized Correlation Method for Estimation of Time Delay," *IEEE Trans. on Acoust. Speech and Sig. Proc.*, vol. 24, no. 4, pp. 320-327, 1976.
4. E.A. Lehmann and A.M. Johansson, "Particle Filter with Integrated Voice Activity Detection for Acoustic Source Tracking," *EURASIP Journal on Advances in Signal Processing*, vol. 2007, Article ID 50870, 2007.
5. B. Yoon, I. Tashev, A. Acero. "Robust Adaptive Beamforming Algorithm Using Instantaneous Direction of Arrival with Enhanced Noise Suppression Capability", *Proc. ICASSP 2007*, Honolulu, USA, April 2007.
6. M.S. Brandstein, H. Silverman, "A robust method for speech signal time-delay estimation in reverberant rooms", *Proc. ICASSP 1997*, pp. 375-378, 1997.
7. L.C. Parra, C.V. Alvino, "Geometric source separation: Merging convolutive source separation with geometric beamforming," *IEEE Trans. on Speech Proc.*, vol. 10, no. 6, pp. 352-362, 2002.
8. T.M. Cover, J.A. Thomas, "Elements Of Information Theory", *Wiley*, 1991.
9. J.B. Allen, D.A. Berkley, "Image Method for Efficiently Simulating Small-Room Acoustics", *J. Acoust. Soc. Amer.*, vol. 65, no. 4, pp. 943-950, 1979.

Intelligent Modification of Colors in Digitized Paintings for Enhancing the Visual Perception of Color-blind Viewers

Paul Doliotis, George Tsekouras, Christos-Nikolaos Anagnostopoulos, and Vassilis Athitsos

Abstract Color vision deficiency (CVD) is quite common since 8%-12% of the male and 0.5% of the female European population seem to be color-blind to some extent. Therefore there is great research interest regarding the development of methods that modify digital color images in order to enhance the color perception by the impaired viewers. These methods are known as daltonization techniques. This paper describes a novel daltonization method that targets a specific type of color vision deficiency, namely protanopia. First we divide the whole set of pixels into a smaller group of clusters. Subsequently we split the clusters into two main categories: colors that protanopes (persons with protanopia) perceive in a similar way as the general population, and colors that protanopes perceive differently. The color clusters of the latter category are adapted in order to improve perception, while ensuring that the adapted colors do not conflict with colors in the first category. Our experiments include results of the implementation of the proposed method on digitized paintings, demonstrating the effectiveness of our algorithm.

1 Introduction

Color vision deficiency (CVD) is quite common since 8%-12% of the male and 0.5% of the female European population seem to be color-blind to some extent. There is still no known medical treatment for this kind of problem. People suffering from any type of color vision deficiency are not considered to be seriously disabled. However there are certain cases in the daily activities of those people where the different perception of colors could lead to experiences that range from simply an-

Paul Doliotis and Vassilis Athitsos
Computer Science and Engineering Department, University of Texas at Arlington, USA

George Tsekouras and Christos-Nikolaos Anagnostopoulos
Department of Culture, Technology, and Communication, University of the Aegean, Greece

Please use the following format when citing this chapter:

Doliotis, P., Tsekouras, G., Anagnostopoulos, C.-N. and Athitsos, V., 2009, in IFIP International Federation for Information Processing, Volume 296; *Artificial Intelligence Applications and Innovations III*; Eds. Iliadis, L., Vlahavas, I., Bramer, M.; (Boston: Springer), pp. 293–301.

noying (e.g., when viewing artwork or browsing websites) to really dangerous (e.g., traffic signalling).

Several techniques have been proposed that modify digital color images in order to enhance the color perception and reduce the confusion by viewers with CVD. These methods are known as daltonization techniques. In this paper we describe a daltonization technique that targets a specific type of color vision deficiency, namely protanopia. In our method, we first divide the set of image colors into a smaller group of clusters, reducing the amount of distinct colors. Subsequently we split the clusters into two main categories: a category of colors that protanopes can perceive in the same way as the general population, and a category of colors that protanopes perceive differently. The color clusters belonging to the latter category are adapted according to some initial daltonization parameters. Additionally we employ a color checking module to make sure that there will not be any color confusion between the two aforementioned categories. If there is color confusion the daltonization parameters are being iteratively modified until the confusion diminishes.

Many researchers have conducted research for appropriately modeling the visual perception of persons with CVD. In [4], a daltonization technique is presented based on the work published in [11] in order to modify a digital image so that it is more visible to people with CVD. The former work is also compared to the online results that are obtained visiting the Vischeck site [3].

The problem of color adaptation according to the user's perception is also addressed in [9, 12]. In [9], one of the issues addressed was the problem of tailoring visual content within the MPEG-21 Digital Item Adaption (DIA) framework to meet the user's visual perception characteristics. The image retrieval aspect for people with CVD was discussed in [7]. A physiologically motivated human color visual system model which represents visual information with one brightness component and two chromatic components was proposed for testing the color perception of people suffering from CVD [8]. In [1] a method was proposed for automaticly adapting the daltonization parameters for each image, to ensure that there is no loss of image structure due to conflict among colors that were daltonized and colors that remained intact. The method described in this paper builds on top of [1], introducing a color clustering step in order to drastically improve the efficiency of color conflict detection.

2 Image Daltonization

The method is based on the LMS system, which specifies colors in terms of the relative excitations of the longwave sensitive (L), the middlewave sensitive (M), and the shortwave sensitive (S) cones. As dichromats lack one class of cone photopigment, they confuse colors that differ only in the excitation of the missing class of photopigment. In contrast to the case of the trichromatic observer, who perceives three color components, two components are sufficient to specify color for the dichromat. The color perception of dichromats can be modeled using simple color transformations.

As in [3], the transformation from RGB to LMS color is obtained using a matrix T_1, defined as follows:

$$T_1 = \begin{bmatrix} 17.8824 & 43.5161 & 4.1193 \\ 3.4557 & 27.1554 & 3.8671 \\ 0.02996 & 0.18431 & 1.4670 \end{bmatrix} \tag{1}$$

Given matrix T_1, the transformation from RGB to LMS is defined as:

$$[L\ M\ S]^t = T_1[R\ G\ B]^t\ , \tag{2}$$

where X^t denotes the transpose of matrix X.

Protanopes perceive colors in a different way due to the lack of one class of cone photopigment. The different color perception of protanopes can be modeled as a linear transformation, mapping normal cone responses LMS to protanope cone responses $L_pM_pS_p$. This linear mapping is represented by a matrix T_2 defined as:

$$T_2 = \begin{bmatrix} 0 & 2.02344 & -2.52581 \\ 0 & 1 & 0 \\ 0 & 0 & 1 \end{bmatrix} \tag{3}$$

Using T_2, $L_pM_pS_p$ is computed as:

$$[L_p\ M_p\ S_p]^t = T_2[L\ M\ S]^t\ , \tag{4}$$

Finally, the RGB color perception of protanopes is modeled using a matrix $T_3 = T_1^{-1}$ defined as:

$$T_3 = \begin{bmatrix} 0.0809 & -0.1305 & 0.1167 \\ -0.0102 & 0.0540 & -0.1136 \\ -0.0003 & -0.0041 & 0.6935 \end{bmatrix} \tag{5}$$

Given T_3, and given a color described by R, G, B, a protanope perceives that color as R_p, G_p, B_p, defined as follows:

$$[R_p\ G_p\ B_p]^t = T_3[L_p\ M_p\ S_p]^t = T_3T_2T_1[R\ G\ B]^t = T_1^{-1}T_2T_1[R\ G\ B]^t\ , \tag{6}$$

A simulation of the colors perceived by a protanope is highlighted in Figures 1a and 1b. It is evident that reddish tones are confused with black and moreover if those shades are neighbouring they are perceived as one color, thus changing the perception of image structure.

Based on the above definitions, we can define error quantities E_R, E_G, E_B that express the difference between the normal and the protanope perception of a color:

$$E_R = |R - R_p| \tag{7}$$

$$E_G = |G - G_p| \tag{8}$$

$$E_B = |B - B_p| \tag{9}$$

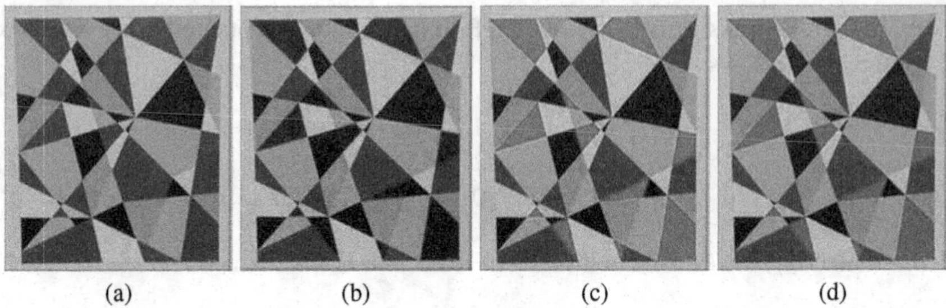

(a) (b) (c) (d)

Fig. 1 (a) Original artwork ("Prism", modern abstract painting in acrylics by Bruce Gray [6]), (b) Simulation of the artwork as perceived by a protanope. Note the confusion of red and black areas in the artwork. www.brucegray.com/images/prism.jpg, (c) original image daltonized with E_{mod}, (d) protanope's perception of (c)

Following [4], these errors are added back to the original image, but in such a way that the error values are redistributed to the blue side of the spectrum, so as to improve the perception of that color by a protanope. In particular, if $E_R(i,j), E_G(i,j), E_B(i,j)$ are the error values at pixel (i,j), these error values are converted to values $E_{R,\mathrm{mod}}(i,j), E_{G,\mathrm{mod}}(i,j), E_{B,\mathrm{mod}}(i,j)$, which represent a shift of color $(E_R(i,j), E_G(i,j), E_B(i,j))$ towards the blue side of the spectrum. This conversion is done using a matrix M defined as follows:

$$M = \begin{bmatrix} 0 & 0 & 0 \\ 0.7 & 1 & 0 \\ 0.7 & 0 & 1 \end{bmatrix} \tag{10}$$

Using M, $E_{R,\mathrm{mod}}(i,j), E_{G,\mathrm{mod}}(i,j), E_{B,\mathrm{mod}}(i,j)$ are obtained as:

$$[E_{R,\mathrm{mod}}(i,j), E_{G,\mathrm{mod}}(i,j), E_{B,\mathrm{mod}}(i,j)]^t = M[E_R(i,j), E_G(i,j), E_B(i,j)]^t \,. \tag{11}$$

Then, the daltonized color is obtained by adding the modified error back to the original color. At position (i,j), given the color $R(i,j), G(i,j), B(i,j)$ of the original image, the color $R_d(i,j), G_d(i,j), B_d(i,j)$ in the daltonized image is defined as follows:

$$\begin{aligned}[R_d(i,j), G_d(i,j), B_d(i,j)] = {} & [R(i,j), G(i,j), B(i,j)] + \\ & [E_{R,\mathrm{mod}}(i,j), E_{G,\mathrm{mod}}(i,j), E_{B,\mathrm{mod}}(i,j)] \,. \end{aligned} \tag{12}$$

Using the above method, good results may be achieved in the majority of color images as shown in Figures 1c and 1d. However, there is still a lot of space for improvements. The most obvious one is the fact that the adaptation parameters of Equation 10 are manually chosen. In addition, there is always the possibility that, in the daltonized image, some of the modified colors may still be confused with other colors in the image by a protanope, as for example in Figure 2. As a result, in addition to loss of color information there can be also loss of information about the image structure. For these important reasons, an intelligent daltonization method is proposed in [1], that uses an automatic iterative technique for the selection of the adaptation parameters. That method also takes into consideration a color checking module, so as to ensure that the modified colors, as perceived by a protanope, do not get confused with other intact colors in the image.

The method described in this paper builds on top of the method proposed in [1]. The key difference between our method and [1] is that, in this paper, a color clustering step is introduced, that drastically improves the efficiency of the color checking module. In the next section we describe the proposed daltonization method.

3 Color Clustering and Selection of Daltonization Parameters

For some colors RGB, the corresponding colors $R_pG_pB_p$ obtained from Equation 6 are very close to the original RGB colors. We define the set C_{correct} to be the set of colors RGB that are present in the image and for which the corresponding $R_pG_pB_p$ is within 1% of RGB. Note that 1% is a threshold which can be changed according to experiments. We define the set $C_{\text{incorrect}}$ to simply be the complement of C_{correct} among all colors appearing in the image. In our daltonization method we want to achieve three goals:

1. Colors in C_{correct} should not be changed.
2. Colors in $C_{\text{incorrect}}$ must be daltonized.
3. No color in $C_{\text{incorrect}}$ should be daltonized to a color that a protanope would perceive as similar to a color from C_{correct}.

Consequently, if the colors that we obtain from Equations 11 and 12 using matrix M violate the third of the above requirements, we use an iterative algorithm, in which M is repeatedly modified, until the third requirement is satisfied.

In order to specify the third requirement in a quantitative way, we define a predicate conflict$(R_1G_1B_1, R_2G_2B_2)$ as follows:

$$\text{conflict}(R_1G_1B_1, R_2G_2B_2) = \begin{cases} \text{true} & \text{if } |R_1 - R_2| < d, |G_1 - G_2| < d, |B_1 - B_2| < d, \\ \text{false} & \text{otherwise.} \end{cases} \tag{13}$$

where d is an appropriately chosen threshold (in our experiments, $d = 10$).

If C_1 and C_2 are sets of colors, we use notation setconflict(C_1, C_2) for the predicate denoting whether there is a conflict between any color in C_1 and a color in C_2:

$$\text{setconflict}(C_1, C_2) = \begin{cases} \text{true} & \text{if } \exists R_1G_1B_1 \in C_1, R_2G_2B_2 \in C_2 | \text{conflict}(R_1G_1B_1, R_2G_2B_2) \\ \text{false} & \text{otherwise.} \end{cases} \tag{14}$$

Given a matrix M and using Equations 11 and 12 we daltonize the colors of $C_{\text{incorrect}}$. We define C_{dalton} to be the set of colors we obtain by daltonizing the colors of $C_{\text{incorrect}}$. Furthermore we define $C_{\text{protanope}}$ to be the set of colors we obtain by applying Equation 6 to the colors of C_{dalton}. Given the above definitions, our goal is to prevent any conflicts between colors in $C_{\text{protanope}}$ and C_{correct}.

However, if the image contains a large number of distinct colors, checking for conflicts can be too time consuming. Thus, we use clustering-based color quantization in order to reduce the number of colors we need to consider, thus obtaining significant speedups in the overall running time. Each color can be regarded as a point in a three dimensional space (e.g., RGB color space). Consequently, an image can be regarded as set (or a "cloud") of points in that space. Our goal is to create groups of points such that:

1. Points belonging to the same group must minimize a given distance function.
2. Points belonging to different groups must maximize a given distance function.

We achieve this clustering by using the Fuzzy-C-means algorithm [13, 5, 2, 10]. An essential parameter for Fuzzy-C-means is parameter C, which is the number of clusters. In our problem, that is the number of colors with which we can describe more efficiently our image. The more colors we use the more accurate the image becomes but at the cost of increased running time. A good value for C in our experiments was defined empirically ($C = 100$).

Next follows our pseudocode:

1. Read an image and run Fuzzy-C-means. We name cluster_centers the matrix containing our clusters' centers.
2. Classify each color from cluster_centers, as belonging to C_{correct} or $C_{\text{incorrect}}$.
3. Apply color daltonization to every color in $C_{\text{incorrect}}$, as described in Equation 12 and name the resulting matrix C_{dalton}.
4. Run protanope simulation on every color in C_{dalton}, as described in Equation 6 and name the resulting matrix $C_{\text{protanope}}$.
5. If setconflict$(C_{\text{correct}}, C_{\text{protanope}})$ is false, go to step 6. Otherwise go back to step 2, after modifying Matrix M appropriately as described in Equation 16.
6. Produce the result image by replacing, in the original image, every color in $C_{\text{incorrect}}$ with the corresponding color in C_{dalton}.

The initial value M_0 given for matrix M of Equation 12 (used in step 3) is defined as follows:

$$M_0 = \begin{bmatrix} m_1 & m_2 & m_3 \\ m_{4,0} & m_5 & m_6 \\ m_{7,0} & m_8 & m_9 \end{bmatrix} = \begin{bmatrix} -1 & 0 & 0 \\ 1 & 1 & 0 \\ 1 & 0 & 1 \end{bmatrix} \tag{15}$$

When we execute step 3 for the first time we use matrix M_0. At the t-th iteration, matrix M_t is obtained from M_{t-1} as follows:

$$M_{t+1} = \begin{bmatrix} m_1 & m_2 & m_3 \\ m_{4,t} & m_5 & m_6 \\ m_{7,t} & m_8 & m_9 \end{bmatrix} = \begin{bmatrix} m_1 & m_2 & m_3 \\ m_{4,t-1} - s & m_5 & m_6 \\ m_{7,t-1} + s & m_8 & m_9 \end{bmatrix} \tag{16}$$

where s is a predefined parameter ($s = 0.05$ in our experiments).

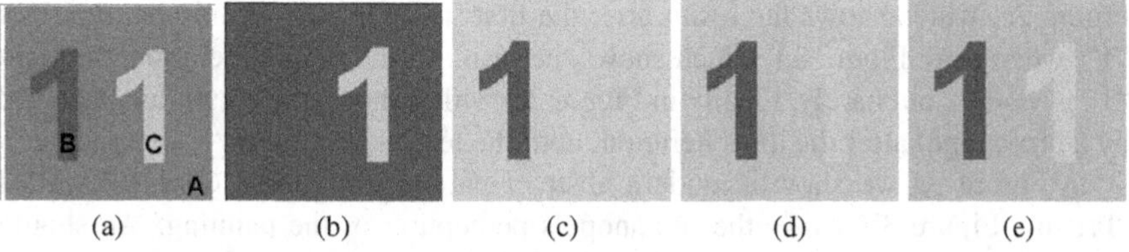

(a) (b) (c) (d) (e)

Fig. 2 (a) Original image, where A(255,51,204), B(73,73,203) and C(193,193,255), (b) protanope perception of (a). Note that left "1" is not visible, (c) First iteration of our algorithm: note that now a protanope can't perceive right "1" , (d) Second iteration: note that the right "1" still isn't clear enough for a protanope, (e) Third iteration: note that now right "1" is visible to the protanope.

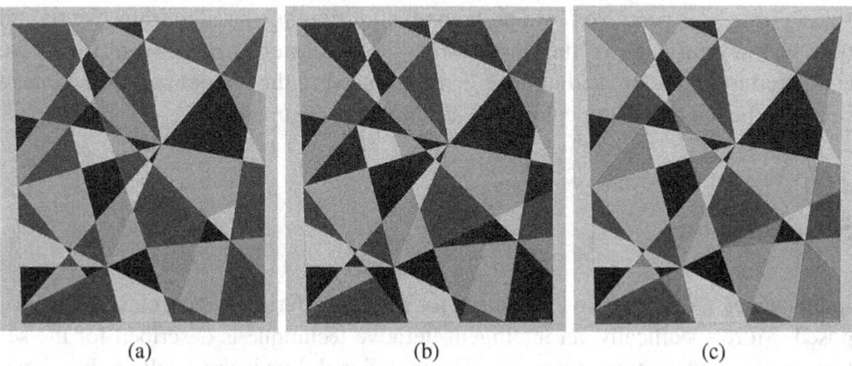

(a) (b) (c)

Fig. 3 (a) Original artwork "Prism", modern abstract painting in acrylics by Bruce Gray [6] , (b) Protanope perception of (a), (c) Protanope perception after running our algorithm.

(a) (b) (c)

Fig. 4 Examples for Paul Gaugin's painting "Market Day" (a) Original image , (b) Protanope vision of (a) , (c) Protanope vision of (a) after running our algorithm

4 Experiments

First we test our algorithm on the image shown in Figure 2a. Note that in 2b, which shows how the image is perceived by a protanope, the left "1" is not visible. In

Figure 2c, which shows the result after the first iteration, we are missing the right "1", whereas in Figure 2d, which shows the result of the second iteration, the right "1" is visible, but barely. Finally in Figure 2e, which shows the result (as perceived by a protanope) after the third iteration, both the left and the right "1" are visible.

In Figure 3a we show a modern abstract painting by Bruce Gray [6], called "Prism". Figure 3b shows the protanope's perception of the painting. We should note that red color is perceived as black, resulting in the protanope perceiving several pairs of adjacent red and black regions as single regions. In Figure 3c we show the result (as perceived by a protanope) after running our algorithm. We can see that the red and black regions that appeared merged in 3b now have distinct colors.

Finally, in Figure 4a we show the painting "Market Day" by Paul Gaugin. Figure 4b shows the protanope's perception of that painting. In Figure 4c we show the resulting image (as perceived by a protanope) after running our algorithm. We should note that several parts of the image structure are easier to perceive in Figure 4c compared to Figure 4b, including, e.g., the contrast in the bottom part of the image between the red and green colors that are shown in Figure 4a.

5 Conclusions

In this paper, a daltonization algorithm for people suffering from protanopia is proposed. More specifically, an intelligent iterative technique is described for the selection of the adaptation parameters. Computational time is drastically reduced due to the use of color quantization. One of our method's main advantages is that with minor modifications, it can be applied to other types of Color Vision Deficiency, such as deuteranopia, widely known as daltonism. An interesting future direction is extending the proposed method to handle video content in addition to static images.

References

1. C. Anagnostopoulos, I. Anagnostopoulos, G. Tsekouras, and C. Kalloniatis. Intelligent modification for the daltonization process of digitized paintings. In *International Conference on Computer Vision Systems*, 2007.
2. J.C. Bezdek and S.K. Pal. Fuzzy models for pattern recognition. methods that search for patterns in data. *IEEE Press*, 11:539, 1992.
3. Bob Dougherty and Alex Wade. Vischeck site. http://www.vischeck.com, last date of access 11/02/08.
4. Onur Fidaner, Poliang Lin, and Nevran Ozguven. http://scien.stanford.edu/class/psych221/projects/05/ofidaner/project_report.pdf, last date of access 11/02/08.
5. Klir G.J. Principles of uncertainty: What are they? why do we. need them? *Fuzzy Sets and Systems*, 74(1):15–31, 1995.
6. Bruce Gray. Bruce Gray site. http://www.brucegray.com, last date of access 11/02/08.
7. V.A. Kovalev. Towards image retrieval for eight percent of color-blind men. In *International Conference on Pattern Recognition*, volume 2, pages 943–946, 2004.

8. Curtis E. Martin, J. O. Keller, Steven K. Rogers, and Matthew Kabrisky. Color blindness and a color human visual system model. *IEEE Transactions on Systems, Man, and Cybernetics, Part A*, 30(4):494–500, 2000.
9. Jeho Nam, Yong Man Ro, Youngsik Huh, and Munchurl Kim. Visual content adaptation according to user perception characteristics. *IEEE Transactions On Multimedia*, 7(3):435–445, 2005.
10. N. R. Pal and J. C. Bezdek. On clustering validity for the fuzzy c-means model. *IEEE Transactions on Fuzzy Systems*, 3:370–379, 1995.
11. F. Vinot, H. Brettel, and J. D. Mollon. Digital video colourmaps for checking the legibility of displays by dichromats. *Color Research and Application*, 24(4):243–252, 1999.
12. Seungji Yang and Yong Man Ro. Visual contents adaptation for color vision deficiency. In *International Conference on Image Processing*, volume 1, pages 453–456, 2003.
13. Lotfi A. Zadeh. Fuzzy sets. *Information and Control*, 8(3):338–353, 1965.

An intelligent Fuzzy Inference System for Risk Estimation Using Matlab Platform: the Case of Forest Fires in Greece

Tsataltzinos T[1], Iliadis L[2], Spartalis S[3]

[1] PhD candidate Democritus University of Thrace, Greece, tsataltzinos@yahoo.gr

[2]Associate Professor Democritus University of Thrace, Greece, liliadis@fmenr.duth.gr

[3] Professor Democritus University of Thrace, Greece, sspart@pme.duth.gr

Abstract This paper aims in the design of an intelligent Fuzzy Inference System that evaluates risk due to natural disasters. Though its basic framework can be easily adjusted to perform in any type of natural hazard, it has been specifically designed to be applied in the case of forest fire risk in the area of the Greek terrain. Its purpose is to create a descending list of the areas under study, according to their degree of risk. This will provide important aid towards the task of distributing properly fire fighting resources. It is designed and implemented in Matlab's integrated Fuzzy Logic Toolbox. It estimates two basic kinds of risk indices, namely the man caused risk and the natural one. The fuzzy membership functions used in this project are the Triangular and the Semi-Triangular.

1 Introduction

Forest fire risk estimation is a major issue. The necessity for more efficient methods of fire fighting resources allocation becomes more and more urgent. This paper aims in the design of a new intelligent decision support system that performs ranking of the areas under consideration according to their forest fire risk. It is designed and implemented in Matlab and it uses fuzzy logic and fuzzy sets. The system assigns a degree of forest fire risk (DFFR) to each area by using Matlab's fuzzy toolbox and its integrated functions. The whole model that has been developed for this purpose consists of three distinct parts.
The first part is related to the determination of the main n risk factors (RF) affecting the specific risk problem. Three fuzzy sets (FS) were formed for each RF:

1. $\tilde{S}_1 = \{(\mu_j(A_j), X_i)$ (forest departments A_j of small risk) $/ j = 1 \ldots N, i = 1 \ldots M\}$
2. $\tilde{S}_2 = \{(\kappa_j(A_j), X_i)$ (forest departments A_j of average risk) $/ j = 1 \ldots N, i = 1 \ldots M\}$

Please use the following format when citing this chapter:

Tsataltzinos, T., Iliadis, L. and Spartalis, S., 2009, in IFIP International Federation for Information Processing, Volume 296; *Artificial Intelligence Applications and Innovations III*; Eds. Iliadis, L., Vlahavas, I., Bramer, M.; (Boston: Springer), pp. 303–310.

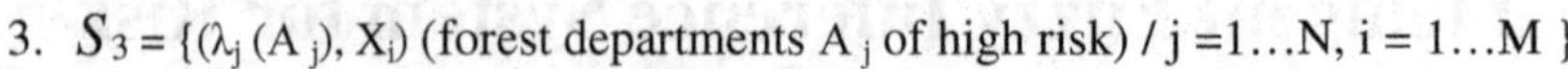

3. $\tilde{S}_3 = \{(\lambda_j (A_j), X_i)$ (forest departments A_j of high risk) / j =1…N, i = 1…M }

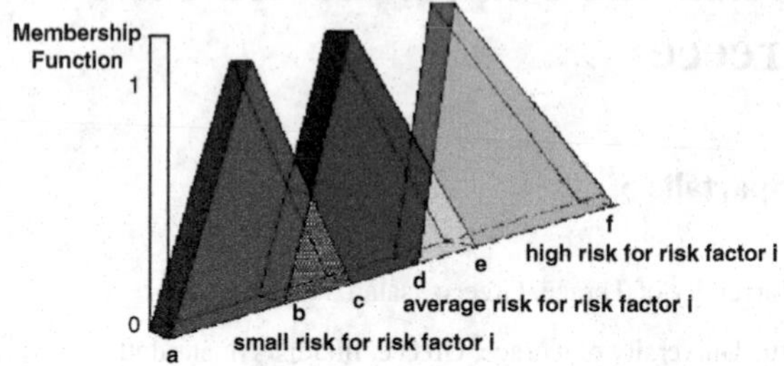

Fig. 1. Degree of fuzzy risk of forest department j for risk factor i

The risk factors are distinguished in two basic categories; Human factors and Natural ones (Kailidis, 1990). Each one of these general risk types consists of several sub-factors that influence in their own way the final risk degree (RD).

The second part was the design of the system's main rule set that would perform the unification of the partial degrees of risk and the output of the unified risk index (URI). These rules are distinct for each risk factor and most of them are specified in bibliography (Kailidis, 1990). The greater the number of factors is, the greater the number of rules required. This is the typical problem of combinatorial explosion in the development of rule based knowledge systems.

To avoid the use of a huge number of rules, so that the project retains its simplicity, the factors were divided into smaller subgroups according to their nature. Decision tables were created and used for each subgroup. In this way the number of rules was minimized significantly.

The third part of the development process was the application of the rule set for the production of the URI. The URI can be produced by applying various types of fuzzy relations to perform fuzzy AND, fuzzy OR operations between the fuzzy sets (and consequently between partial risk indices). The functions for the conjunction are called T-norms and for the union T-conorms or S-norms (Kandel A., 1992).

2 Basic Design Principles of the Intelligent System

The System was developed using Matlab's integrated Fuzzy Logic Toolbox. The row data was input into an MS Access database and extracted into MS Excel datasheets. Next, each column of the data was extracted into a separate Excel file to form an input variable for Matlab. Using the xlsread and xlswrite commands of the fuzzy toolbox, the final results were also extracted into an Excel file. The triangular fuzzy membership function was implemented by the triamf function of the fuzzy toolbox. This Project applied the Matlab's integrated Mamdani Inference method, which operates in a forward chaining mode. The Mamdani inference system comprises of five parts:

1. Fuzzyfication of input with the Triangular membership function (Function 1)
2. Application of fuzzy operators. OR operation is performed by $\mu(x) = \max(x_n)$, while AND operation by using the algebraic product $\mu(x) = x_1 x_2 \quad x_n$
3. Application of the implication method (min) $\mu(x) = \min(x_n)$
4. Aggregation of output values with the use of max function $\mu(x) = \max(x_n)$
5. Defuzzification on the output with the centroid method $\mu(\chi) = \frac{\int_{\chi} x f(x)dx}{\int_{\chi} f(x)dx}$

3 Materials and Methods

3.1 Determination of the risk factors

The problem of forest fire risk estimation can be faced as a daily measured process or as an index indicating the risk of having high volume of forest incidents on an annual basis. Both of these orientations are influenced by a great number of parameters (Kailidis 1990). This project aims in the estimation of the annual forest fire risk due to the lack of daily measurements. To do this, two basic data groups were gathered. Each one of them is consisted of the following factors that can be seen in Table 1.

Table 1. Factor Groups

Human Factors	Natural Factors
Population Density	Average Annual Temperature
Tourism	Average Annual Humidity
Land Value	Average Altitude
Other - User' s estimation	Percentage of Forest Cover
	Average Wind speed

In the case of the human risk factors, the population density and the tourism data was gathered from the General Secretariat of National Statistical Service of Greece. The land value was estimated with the use of the previous two. The bigger the population density of a forest department is and the greater its tourist development the higher its land value. The value is represented in pure numbers from 1 to 10. The fourth factor is input to exploit the experience and the intuition of a forest fire expert on the risk degree of an area.

In the case of natural factors, the Average Annual Temperature, Humidity and Wind Speed were used. For better results, the above three factors' data were separated into seasons or months, because the risk has a seasonal nature. Yet the system is capable of using even daily updates of these data to produce risk analysis on a more frequent basis. The percentage of forest cover does not include the kind of vegetation of each forest department due to the fact that this is a pilot effort. The system also uses the Average Altitude of every data point as a risk factor.

The DSS was applied in all of the Greek territory. Meteorological and morphological data was gathered from Greek public services. Population density data was gathered from General Secretariat of National Statistical Service of Greece. The forest fire data used cover the period between 1983 and 1994, and the population census of 1991. The results were extracted into different MS Excel files. This is a pilot application just to indicate the performance validity of the prototype.

3.2 The fuzzy rule system

Fuzzy Logic (FL) and Fuzzy Sets (FS) can provide aid towards modeling the human knowledge and real world concepts (Leondes, 1998). For example the modeling of the concept "Hot area" in terms of average temperature, is both subjective and imprecise so it can be considered as a fuzzy set (FS). It is clear that real world situations can be described with the use of proper linguistics, each one defined by a corresponding FS. For every FS there exists a degree of membership (DOM) $\mu_s(X)$ that is mapped on [0,1]. For example every forest department belongs to the FS "fire risky forest department" with a different degree of membership (Kandel, 1992). The functions used to define the DOM are called fuzzy membership functions (FMF) and in this project the triangular FMF (TRIAMF) and the semi-triangular FMF (semi-TRIAMF) were applied (Iliadis L. 2005). Functions 1 and 2 below represent the TRIAMF and semi-TRIAMF

Function 1 $$\mu_s(X)=\begin{cases}0 \text{ if } X<a\\ (X-a)/(c-a) \text{ if } X\in[a,c]\\ (b-X)/(b-c) \text{ if } X\in[c,b]\\ 0 \text{ if } X>b\end{cases}$$

Function 2 $$\mu_s(X)=\begin{cases}0 \text{ if } X<a\\ (X-a)/(b-a) \text{ if } X\in[a,b]\end{cases}$$

Singleton functions were used to determine the boundaries of the membership functions. The system assigns each forest department three Partial Risk Indices (PRI), for every one of the nine factors that are taken under consideration, as it is shown below:

1. Low Danger due to each factor
2. Medium Danger due to each factor
3. High Danger due to each factor

Table 2. Values of the Singleton Fuzzy membership functions min and max

Min	Factor	Max
0	Average Temperature	38
0	Average Humidity	80
1	Average Wind speed	3
0	Average Height	1280
0	Average Forest Cover	2
0	Population Density	300000
0	Tourism	10
0	Land Value	10
0	Other - Experts opinion*	10

* depends on the expert. The min and max values are not necessarily those that are shown on this table

For each factor the minimum and maximum boundaries of its fuzzy membership function are shown in table 2 above. This method allows the use of any kind of data and does not need specific metrics for every factor. Due to this fact, there was no need to do any changes in the row data provided by the Greek national services. The above steps resulted in having 27 different PRIs. The more detailed the linguistics become the greater the number of PRIs. Those 27 PRIs are too many and not quite helpful. The next step was to unify them in one Unified Risk Index (URI). To do this, this project had to take into consideration the human experience and to apply the rules that a human expert would use. For example if it is known that an area has great population and tourism (which results in great land value), it is near the sea (which means low altitude) and it has great forest cover, then it definitely is a very dangerous area and needs to have our attention. In this example, four parameters were used.

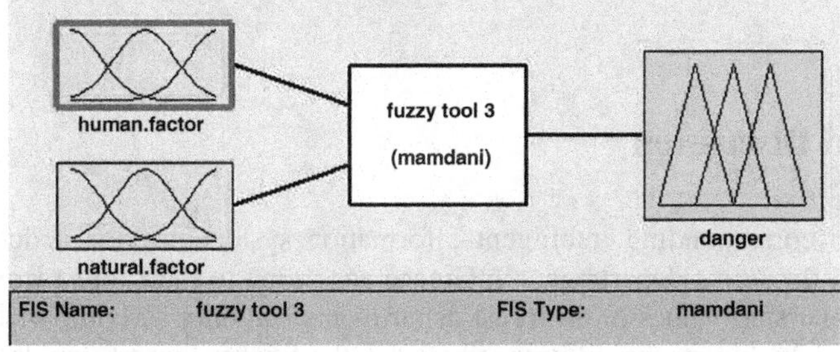

Fig. 2. Fuzzy toolbox sample

If two FSs are used for each factor then the proper number of rules that should be used is 2^4=16. In this project the number of rules that had to be applied was 3^9=19683. To make the number of rules smaller, the factors had to be combined into small subgroups of two or three, as shown in figure 2. This resulted in a much smaller number of rules, much easier to understand and apply. The total amount of rules required was $3^3+6*3^2=81$. For example, to combine the Population Density (Pop) and the Tourism (Tour) factors in one subgroup named "Measurable Human Factors" (MHF) the following 9 rules had to be applied:

1. If **Pop** is low and **Tour** is low then **MHF** is low
2. If **Pop** is average and **Tour** is average then **MHF** is average
3. If **Pop** is high and **Tour** is high then **MHF** is high
4. If **Pop** is low and **Tour** is average then **MHF** is average
5. If **Pop** is low and **Tour** is high then **MHF** is high
6. If **Pop** is average and **Tour** is low then **MHF** is average
7. If **Pop** is average and **Tour** is high then **MHF** is high
8. If **Pop** is high and **Tour** is average then **MHF** is high
9. If **Pop** is high and **Tour** is low then **MHF** is high

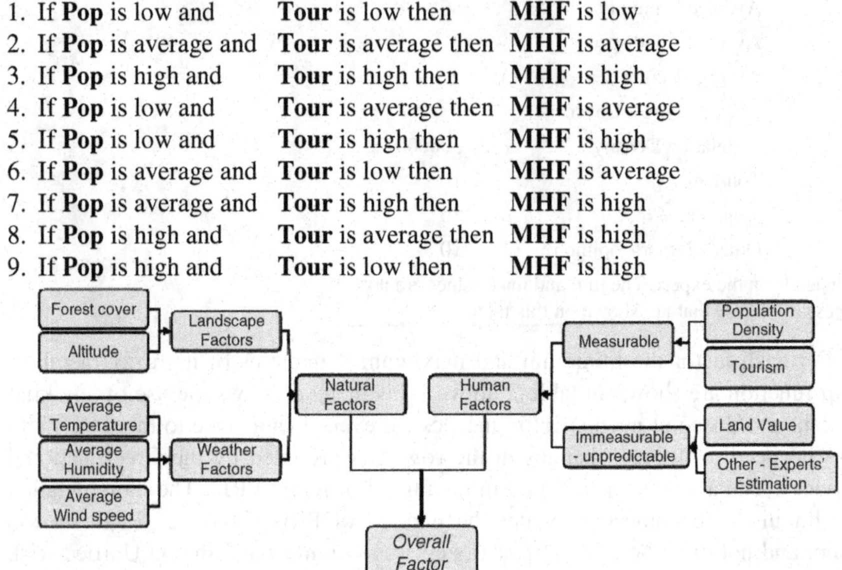

Fig. 3. Categorization of the risk factors

Following the logic of the above structure (Fig. 3) the number of rules was reduced significantly making the operation of the system much simpler. Combined with the proper decision tables (Table 3) the total number of rules was reduced to 73.

5 Results and Discussion

This model and its corresponding intelligent information system provide a descending ranking of the forest departments in Greece according to their forest fire risk. The final membership values of all forest departments can only be compared between each other. The bigger the difference between the final values of two departments is, the bigger the difference in actual risk they have. To check the results validity, each year's data was processed separately. The resulting descending

Table 3. Decision Table sample

Temperature	L	L	L	L	L	L	L	L	L	M	M	M	M	M	M	M	M	M	H	H	H	H	H	H	H	H	H
Wind	L	L	L	M	M	M	H	H	H	L	L	L	M	M	M	H	H	H	L	L	L	M	M	M	H	H	H
Humidity	L	M	H	L	M	H	L	M	H	L	M	H	L	M	H	L	M	H	L	M	H	L	M	H	L	M	H
Low Danger	X	X	X		X	X		X	X																		
Medium Danger				X			X			X	X	X		X	X			X		X	X						
High Danger													X			X	X		X			X	X	X	X	X	X

Final Table	Group 1							Group 2							Group 3				
Temperature	L	L	L	L	L	L	L	M	M	M	M	M	M	M	H	H	H	H	H
Wind	L	M	M	M	H	H	H	L	M	M	M	H	H	H	L	L	L	M	H
Humidity	-	L	M	H	L	M	H	-	L	M	H	L	M	H	L	M	H	-	-
Low Danger	X		X	X		X	X												
Medium Danger		X			X			X		X	X			X		X	X		
High Danger									X			X	X		X			X	X

Legend
L = Low
M = Medium
H = High

list produced from every year's data was compared to the list obtained from the ranking of the departments on their actual annual number of forest fires of the following year. The compatibility of this method to the actual annual forest fire situation varied from 52% to 70% (Table 4). In some cases, forest departments used to mark as "forest fire" agricultural fires (caused on purpose) which makes the actual logic of the Ruleset less efficient. However in a future effort this type of data should be diminished from the fire database.

Table 4. Results.

	83-84	84-85	85-86	86-87	87-88	88-89	89-90	90-91	91-92	92-93
Compatibility with the following year's actual ranking for the risky area fuzzy set	52%	58%	62%	62%	66%	64%	62%	70%	54%	58%

The final ranking of all the forest departments remains almost the same despite the use of other fuzzy membership functions. The system was also tested with the use of Trapezoidal, semi-Trapezoidal and Sigmoid membership functions and the differentiation in the results was not significant. Nevertheless, even if 52% to 70% may not seem an impressively reliable performance from the statistical point of view, it is actually a performance offering a very good practical application. Obviously there would be many governments that would be vary happy if they could know from the previous year 52%-70% of the areas that are threatened seriously by forest fires.

Testing showed that the years that had luck of detailed data for many forest departments resulted in low compatibility, while on the other hand the results were pretty impressive when there was enough data for all the departments. This also was a first attempt to use detailed data for the human factors. The first tests included only the "population density" and "tourism" factors. These tests resulted in a maximum compatibly of 70%.

The more detailed the data becomes on the human factors and with the help of a proper human expert the better the accuracy of the system would become. Forest fires can occur due to a great number of factors. Many of those factors are extremely unpredictable and immeasurable. These facts make the fire estimation a complicated problem that can be studied with the use of fuzzy logic. This system uses an alternative way of thinking and offers a different approach. The fact that it can use any kind of data available and that it can produce results as soon as the data is inserted, makes it a valuable tool for estimating which forest department is in danger. On the other hand, due to the fact that human behavior is pretty unpredictable, the expert's opinion is necessary to enable the production of better results or even to perform various scenarios.

The system has shown that it is quite useful and that it can improve its performance if more data is gathered. It will also be expanded towards the estimation of the daily forest fire risk which can be seen as the problem of having favorable forest fire ignition and acceleration conditions.

References

1. Tsataltzinos T. (2007) "A fuzzy decision support system evaluating qualitative attributes towards forest fire risk estimation", Proceedings 10th International Conference on Engineering Applications of Neural Networks, Thessaloniki, Hellas, August 2007.
2. Iliadis L. (2005) "A decision support system applying an integrated Fuzzy model for long - term forest fire risk estimation" Environmental Modelling and Software, Elsevier Science, Vol.20, No.5, pp.613-621, May 2005.
3. Iliadis L., Maris F., Tsataltzinos T. (2005). "An innovative Decision Support System using Fuzzy Reasoning for the Estimation of Mountainous Watersheds Torrential Risk: The case of Lakes Koroneia and Vovli", Proceedings IUFRO Conference "Sustainable Forestry in theory and practice: recent advances in inventory and monitoring statistics and modeling information and knowledge management and policy science" Pacific Northwest Research Station GTR-PNW-688, University of Edimburgh, UK,
4. Kandel A., 1992, Fuzzy Expert Systems. CRC Press. USA.
5. Kecman V., 2001, Learning and Soft Computing. MIT Press. London England.
6. Leondes C.T., 1998, "Fuzzy Logic and Expert Systems Applications", Academic Press. California USA.
7. Iliadis L., Spartalis S., Maris F., Marinos D. 2004 "A Decision Support System Unifying Trapezoidal Function Membership Values using T-Norms". Proceedings International Conference in Numerical Analysis and Applied Mathematics (ICNAAM), J. Wiley-VCH Verlag GmbH Publishing co., Weinheim Germany.
8. Zhang J.X., Huang C.F., 2005. "Cartographic Representation of the Uncertainty related to natural disaster risk: overview and state of the art", LNAI Vol. 3327, pp. 213-220
9. Nguyen H., Walker E., 2000. "A First Course in Fuzzy Logic", Chapman and Hall, Library of the Congress, USA
10. Cox E., 2005. Fuzzy Modeling and Genetic Algorithms for Data Mining and Exploration, Elsevier Science, USA
11. E A Johnson, Kiyoko Miyanishi, 2001, "Forest Fire: Behavior and Ecological Effects"
12. J Kahlert, H Frank, 1994, "Fuzzy-Logik und Fuzzy-Control"
13. Mamdani, E.H. and S. Assilian, "An experiment in linguistic synthesis with a fuzzy logic controller," International Journal of Man-Machine Studies, Vol. 7, No. 1, pp. 1-13, 1975.
14. Kailidis D. 1990, "Forest Fires"

MSRS: Critique on its Usability via a Path Planning Algorithm Implementation

George Markou and Ioannis Refanidis

Department of Applied Informatics, University of Macedonia
Thessaloniki, Greece
{gmarkou, yrefanid}@uom.gr

Abstract In recent years an expanding number of robotics software platforms have emerged, with Microsoft expressing its interest in the field by releasing its own in 2006. This fact has created a highly competitive environment, as the majority of the products are mostly incompatible to each other, with every platform trying to establish itself as the field's standard. Thus, the question that arises is whether a platform is suited for educational purposes or creating a complete robotics intelligence package. This paper provides a study on the learnability, usability and features of Microsoft Robotics Studio, by creating and integrating into it a version of the Lifelong Planning A* algorithm (LPA*) algorithm.

1 Introduction

In the last few years there has been an increasing interest in the unification of artificial intelligence and robotics platforms. This has led to the creation and use of an expanding number of robotics software platforms, with a significant amount of undergraduate classes making use of the new technologies by creating rather advanced robotics projects within one or two semester courses [1, 23, 26]. In 2006 Microsoft entered the robotics field with its own robotics platform, named Microsoft Robotics Studio, competing against already widespread platforms such as the Player Project.

In this paper we implement a path planning algorithm in a simulated robotics environment, of which will be able to change its topology and the number of obstacles it contains during the agent's movement in it. The robotics platform that will be used is Microsoft's Robotics Studio, due to the fact that its introduction has caused extensive discussion and controversy as to whether or not it is suited for academic research, or educational and industrial purposes [3, 24, 25]. We will address this mixture of skepticism and enthusiasm by giving Microsoft's Robotics

Please use the following format when citing this chapter:

Markou, G. and Refanidis, I., 2009, in IFIP International Federation for Information Processing, Volume 296; *Artificial Intelligence Applications and Innovations III*; Eds. Iliadis, L., Vlahavas, I., Bramer, M.; (Boston: Springer), pp. 311–320.

Studio's features, ease of use and learnability a thorough critique, through the implementation of the aforementioned algorithm.

Due to the nature of the simulated environment in which the agent will move, the path planning algorithm that we will implement will have to be able to create a new plan or adapt an existing one every time the environment's topology changes. Koenig et al. [7] suggested that in systems where an agent has to constantly adapt its plans due to changes in its knowledge of the world, an incremental search method could be very beneficial as it can solve problems potentially faster than solving each search problem from scratch. They combined such a method with a heuristic one, which finds shortest paths for path-planning problems faster than uninformed search methods. This led to the creation of the algorithm we will implement, Lifelong Planning A* (LPA*) [8], which produces a plan, having a quality which remains consistently as good as one achieved by planning from scratch.

The remainder of the paper is organized as follows: In Section 2 we review works related to our own research, while in Section 3 we compare Microsoft's Robotics Studio to other prominent robotics platforms. Section 4 focuses on the theoretical aspects of the LPA* algorithm. In Section 5 we discuss the domain that was created in Robotics Studio, both in regard to the simulated maze and to the robot that was used. Section 6 presents the experiments we implemented, and Section 7 concludes the paper and poses directions for future work.

2 Related Work

For Microsoft Robotics Studio (MSRS) to become the standard robotics development platform, it has to achieve mainly two different goals: First, partnerships within the robotic industry, as well as with the academia. Secondly, the program itself needs to be able to offer advantages in comparison with other platforms. The first goal has been fulfilled to a point, as several companies, universities and research institutes opted to support and use MSRS, such as Kuka, Robosoft, fischertechnik and Parallax, Inc. [13]. Additionally, it is available currently for free download and use to anyone using it for noncommercial purposes.

As to the second goal, in [6] the author concluded that MSRS offers a wide range of technological solutions to problems common in the robotic field, by providing features such as visual programming or its combined system of concurrency control with efficient distributed message passing. However, he admits that there are still evident limitations to the program, like its integration with low level processors. The former opinion is shared by Tsai et al in [23] who used MSRS in an effort to design a service oriented computer course for high schools. They concluded that there are several disadvantages in the structure of the program, mainly that the visual programming language that is used in MSRS requires detailed knowledge of an imperative programming language, and that the loop structures which are used in it are implemented by "Goto", instead of by structure construct.

Also, they pointed out that some of the service oriented features that Microsoft had promised to provide were not available.

Others, however, are far more positive towards MSRS. Workman and Elzer in [26] used the program in an upper-level undergraduate robotics elective to document its usefulness in such an academic environment. They found that MSRS provided a great link between the language syntax already known to students and unfamiliar robotics semantics and highly recommended its use, adding that they were quite satisfied with the available features of the program and the support it provided for different hardware. Tick in [22] goes even further to suggest that the introduction of MSRS in the robotic market shows the future direction for programming for Autonomous Mobile Research Robots and could possibly determine the evolution of these systems as its own features will force other platforms to develop their competitive products so as to offer similar capabilities.

In conclusion, based on the related bibliography up-to-date it still remains unclear whether MSRS will evolve to be the industry's standard, as other Microsoft's programs have achieved in the past. On the other hand, it is quite definitive that it has a lot of useful features to offer, especially in the educational field, as well as that it is already at least a simple starting point for anyone who wants to become involved with a field as complex as robotics.

3 Robotics Platforms Overview

Before we present the domain we created in MSRS we briefly discuss the similarities and differences of it in comparison to some of the most prevalent robotics platforms. Although MSRS is available as a free download for researchers or hobbyists, it is not open source, and it is also not free of charge if intended for commercial use, whereas several platforms like the Player Project are both. Moreover, MSRS is the only platform in our comparison that can only be used in one operating system, while most are compatible with at least two, typically both Windows and Linux operating systems. The Player Project and the Orocos Project do not natively support Windows, but the former can run on Linux, Solaris, Mac OSX and *BSD, whereas the latter is aimed at Linux systems, but has also been ported to Mac OSX. One other major difference of Microsoft's robotics platform in contrast to its antagonists is that it does not provide a complete robotics intelligence system so that the robots it supports can be made autonomous, but relies on the programmers to implement such behaviours.

Its advantages over the competition, however, are also significant. It is one of the few major robotics platforms - along with Gostai's and Cyberbotics' collaborative platform Urbi for Webots - to provide a visual programming environment, and its architecture is based on distributed services, with these services being able to be constructed in reusable blocks. Furthermore, the platform enjoys the financial and technological support of one of the largest corporations in the world. In

Table 1 there is a comparison of some of the available characteristics of six of the most widely used robotics platforms today.

Table 1. Features of several of the most prominent robotics platforms [2, 4, 20].

	MSRS 1.5	MobileRobots	Skilligent	Orocos	Player Project	Urbi/ Webots
Open Source	No	No	No	Yes	Yes	Parts of Urbi
Free of Charge	Express Edition	No	No	Yes	Yes	No
Windows/ Linux	Yes/ No	Yes/ Yes	Yes/ Yes	No/ Yes	No/ Yes	Yes/ Yes
Other OS	No	No	No	No	Yes	Yes
Distributed Services	Yes	No	Yes	No	Limited	Yes
Drag-and-Drop IDE	Yes	No	No	No	No	Yes
Object Recognition	No	No	Yes	No	No	No
Localization	No	Yes	Yes	No	No	No
Learning/ Social Interaction	No	No	Yes	No	No	No
Simulation Environment	Yes	Yes	No	No	Yes	Yes
Reusable Service Blocks	Yes	Yes	Yes	Yes	No	Yes
Real-Time	No	No	No	Yes	No	No

4 Lifelong Planning A*

It is very common for artificial intelligence systems to try and solve path-planning problems in one shot, without considering that the domain in which they operate might change, thus forcing them to adapt the plan that they have already calculated. Solving the new path-planning problem independently might suffice if the domain is sufficiently small and the changes in it are infrequent, but this is not usually the case.

Koenig et al in [8] developed the Lifelong Planning algorithm to be able to repeatedly find a shortest path between two given vertexes faster than executing a complete recalculation of it, in cases where this would be considered a waste of computational resources and time. It combines properties of a heuristic algorithm, namely A* [5], and an incremental one, DynamicSWSF-FP [16]. The first search LPA* executes is identical to a search by a version of A* that breaks ties in favour of vertices with smaller g-values. The rest of its searches, which take place when a change in the domain happens, however, are significantly faster. This is achieved by using techniques which allow the algorithm to recognize the parts of the search tree which remain unchanged in the new one.

Properties of A* are used to focus the search on parts of the tree that are more likely to be part of the shortest path and determine which start distances should not be computed at all, while DynamicSWSF-FP is used to decide whether certain distances remain the same and should not be recomputed. The combination of these techniques can be very efficient in reducing the necessary time to recalculate a new path if the differences between the old and the new domain are not significant, and the changes were close to the goal. Finally, it is noteworthy that our implementation does not follow the original LPA* algorithm. Instead we opted to implement the backwards version presented in [9] which continuously calculates a new shortest path from the goal vertex to the agent's current position, and not, as it originally was, from the start vertex to the goal.

5 Maze Domain

The entire simulation domain was created using Microsoft Robotics Studio 1.5 Refresh, which was the current version of the program when we started working on this paper. Subsequently, as Microsoft released a new version of the platform Microsoft Robotics Developer Studio (MRDS) 2008 we migrated our project to the newest version of the program. The platform allows the creation of new user-defined entities, which can be associated with a mesh, making the entity appear more realistic. As a three-dimensional mesh can be created and imported into the MSRS' simulations environment from most 3D graphical editing programs [15], the resulting simulation can reflect almost any real situation.

Although creating a particularly realistic environment is not suited for a novice user as it can be a very complex procedure, several lifelike environments exist as built-in samples in Microsoft's Visual Simulation Environment in MRDS 2008. They have been developed by SimplySim, a French company that provides professional quality real time 3D simulations, and depict environments ranging from urban sceneries and apartments to a forest [19].

The environment for our experiments is a much simpler one, based on the "MazeSimulator" project, a program which allows users to create labyrinths based on a bitmap image. It was created by Trevor Taylor [21], who in turn used elements from previous work done by Ben Axelrod. The maze environment we simulated is explained in further detail in Section 5.1.

5.1 Simulated Maze

We created a gridworld of size 7×7, containing nodes which can randomly alternate their status between blocked and unblocked. This scenario is an abstraction of the Robocup Rescue Simulator Competition [18], where the roads in a city being hit by an earthquake change their status from free to blocked due to collapsing buildings. The maze is safely explorable, that is the robot can safely reach the goal node from any node of the domain.

To create the obstacles in the maze, and make the environment dynamic, we opted for a solution that removed the obstacles from the simulation, updated their mass appropriately, and then re-inserted them in the Simulation Engine. This implementation, though not the obvious approach, was the simplest possible since the platform does not provide through its libraries a method of dynamically changing the mass of an object. The resulting simulated environment is shown in Fig. 1.

Fig. 1. Initial state of the simulated domain.

5.2 Robot

Microsoft Robotics Studio 1.5 Refresh supported - with built-in services - a wide variety of robots, ranging from simple and affordable hobbyist robots, such as the iRobot Create, to sophisticated humanoid robots capable of performing fighting and acrobatics, like the Kondo KHR-1. The list also includes the Lego Mindstorms NXT, MobileRobots' Pioneer 3DX, the Boe-Bot Robot from Parallax and fischertechnik's ROBO Interface [14]. All the aforementioned robots are also supported in MRDS 2008, with the exception of the Parallax Boe-Bot. The robot used in our experiments was a Pioneer 3DX, with a mounted sick laser range finder on top of it, as at the time it was one of the most widely used in various MSRS' tutorials and projects .

We have defined the movement of the robot to consist of three parts. First, the robot moves in a straight line for a distance equal to the length of a node. Then, it decides, based on the plan created from LPA*, whether or not is required to make a turn, and finally it executes the turn, rotating in angles which are multiple of 90 degrees. Using the laser range finder, the robot builds a tri-color map of the environment, in which white color symbolizes free space that the robot has explored. Black color is drawn on the points on the map that the laser hit an obstacle, and the rest of the map – the part of the environment that the robot has not explored, is shown in grey color. Each time the robot moves through a specific location, the part of the map that corresponds to that region will be overwritten by the new data that the robot collects. In essence, we build a simple occupancy grid map, with each cell of it containing a value that represents the possibility that it is occupied.

6 Experiments

We created three different experiments, all with the same initial maze settings, but each one changing in a different way after the robot had reached a certain node of the domain. In two of the experiments the changes were known beforehand, whereas in the last one they were random. In each one, however, the changes were minimal, blocking / unblocking a maximum of two nodes.

We implemented LPA* in MSRS without having to study the program in great depth or learn a new programming language, since the support for multiple languages gave us the opportunity to work in one related to our previous knowledge, in our case C#. An inexperienced user however, has the option to use a graphical "drag-and-drop" programming language provided by Microsoft, which is designed on a dataflow-based model. Microsoft's Visual Programming Language (VPL) allows users to create their program by simply "orchestrating activities", that is, connecting them to other activity blocks. An activity is a block with inputs and outputs that can be represent pre-built services, data-flow control, a function, or even a composition of multiple activities.

Initially, it was our intention to make use of the visual programming environment that Microsoft developed to implement our project, so as to additionally document the strengths and weakness of the new programming language as well as MSRS. However, the task proved to be extremely difficult, if not impossible, due to obvious deficiencies of VPL: First of all its diagrams tend to become exceedingly large as the program's complexity increases. Moreover, VPL has limited support for arbitrary user-defined data types and does not support a generic object which, naturally, is an important restriction to a programmer's tools. What is more, the only type of control flow and collection of items that have built-in support in VPL are "if statements" and lists respectively; that is, recursion and arrays are not natively supported at the moment.

Thus, expert programmers will likely prefer to write in an imperative programming language, although they can still find VPL useful as a tool, especially if they are not familiar with MSRS' environment, as it can easily be used for creating the skeleton of a basic program by wiring activities to each other and automatically generating the consequent C# code through it. The opinion we formed through our experience though, is that VPL is best suited for novice users who only have a basic understanding of programming concepts such as variables, and might enjoy the easiness of not writing any code.

One element of the platform that is especially helpful to the programming process is the Concurrency and Coordination Runtime (CCR), a programming model that facilitates the development of programs that handle asynchronous behavior. Instead of writing complex multithreaded code to coordinate the available sensors and motors functioning at the same time on a robot, the CCR handles the required messaging and orchestration efficiently as its function is to "manage asynchronous operations, exploit parallel hardware and deal with concurrency and partial failure" [12]. Furthermore, it has been proven to be not only useful as a part of MSRS, but in non-robotics development processes [11, 17].

As aforementioned, we implemented LPA* so that it can work backwards. The reason behind this choice was that in this way we were able to calculate a new shortest path for the part of the maze we were interested in, i.e., from the goal node to the robot. Had we used the original version of LPA*, the algorithm would calculate an entirely new shortest path from the original node to the finish. The algorithm was applied successfully into the rest of the MSRS domain we created and performed as one would expect having read the theoretical properties of LPA* in [7, 8, 9].

The simulation environment was aesthetically appealing and served our functional needs. Based on the robot's interaction with it and in particular while the robot followed the course through the maze depicted in Fig. 2 (b), the laser range finder built the occupancy grid map that is shown in Fig. 2 (a).

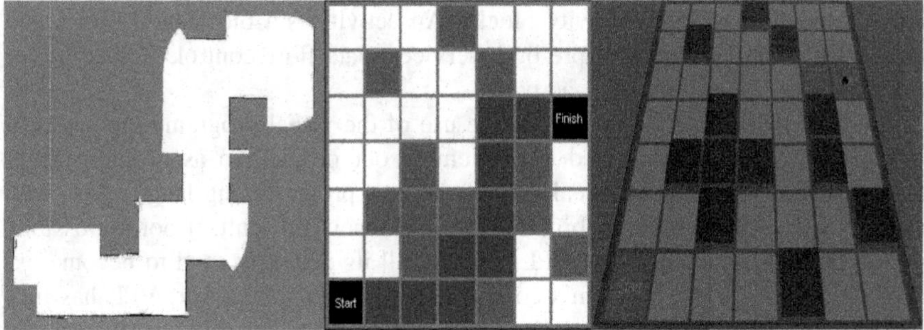

Fig. 2.a (Left) Occupancy grid map of the maze's final state. 2.b (Center) Ground plan of the maze. The robot's course is shown in blue. 2.c (Right) Final state of the simulated domain.

7 Conclusions and Future Work

In this paper we used Microsoft Robotics Studio to implement a realistic environment in which an agent follows a shortest path course from a given node to a goal one using the LPA* algorithm. It was our intention to critique whether or not MSRS is a suitable program for use in academic, educational, or even industrial environments. Our experience indicates that while it may be fairly time-consuming for a person to familiarize himself with the program, the process is made significantly easier by the facts that multiple programming languages are supported and by some of the platform's features, such as the Concurrency and Coordination Runtime. In that sense, our findings are in accordance with those from Workman and Elzer [26] mentioned in Section 2.

Moreover, it is not necessary to delve into all of the aspects of the program to create a simple functional program, especially if the project's basis is formed through orchestrating pre-built services in VPL. Such knowledge may be needed though if more sophisticated programs are to be implemented. Our critique of Microsoft's Visual Language is partly different from that of Tsai et al [23] as we concluded that VPL requires only minimal knowledge of an imperative programming language, is not as strong as one, and if anything its use is greater for a novice programmer than for an expert. Such a programmer will probably find it easier to use one of the multiple imperative programming languages that are supported by the platform.

In general, it was evident that the program has extensive features and capabilities that could potentially establish it as the field's standard, especially considering the vast support a company like Microsoft can provide for it. Initially, while we were implementing our experiments in MSRS 1.5 Refresh we encountered several minor or major difficulties, with the most important being the program's unexpected termination depending on the machine it was executed on. However, in general these problems can be attributed to the relatively small life cycle of the product, as after the migration of our project to MRDS 2008 most of them, including the termination of the program, seemed to have been resolved. Such problems could possibly discourage some researchers or educators from relying solely on MSRS for their needs, and as such it is a matter of utter importance for Microsoft to keep improving the platform as it did with MRDS 2008, so that it can become fully stable and functional.

Future work can focus on inducing more than one changes to the maze domain, and coordinating the MSRS services that are involved in the program so that they communicate with each other every time such a change occurs. Finally, to evaluate the ease of use and learnability of the platform in an academic environment in a more efficient, semi-quantitative way and in greater detail, we could base our assessment on an experiment along the following lines: Develop a structured questionnaire and ask two different groups of students to fill them out after each of them has implemented a similar robotics project in MSRS and another robotic platform such as the ones mentioned in Section 3, to establish the advantages and disadvantages of each one as accurately as possible.

References

1. Blank D, Kumar D, Marshall J & Meeden L (2007) Advanced robotics projects for undergraduate students. AAAI Spring Symposium: Robots and Robot Venues: Resources for AI Education: 10-15
2. Bruyninckx H (2001) Open robot control software: the OROCOS project. Proceedings IEEE International Conference on Robotics and Automation (3): 2523-2528
3. Bruyninckx H (2007) Microsoft Robotics Studio: Expected impact, Challenges & Alternatives. Panel presentation at the IEEE International Conference on Robotics and Automation
4. Gerkey B (2005) The Player Robot Device Interface - Player utilities. http://playerstage.sourceforge.net/doc/Player-2.0.0/player/group__utils.html. Accessed 15 January 2009
5. Hart P E, Nilsson N J, Raphael B (1968) A Formal Basis for the Heuristic Determination of Minimum Cost Paths. IEEE Transactions on Systems Science & Cybernetics, 4(2):100-107

6. Jackson J (2007) Microsoft Robotics Studio: A Technical Introduction. IEEE Robotics & Automation Magazine 14(4):82-87
7. Koenig S, Likhachev M & Furcy D (2004) Lifelong Planning A*. Artificial Intelligence, 155 (1-2):93-146
8. Koenig S, Likhachev M, Liu Y & Furcy D (2004) Incremental Heuristic Search in Artificial Intelligence. AI Magazine, 25(2):99-112
9. Likhachev M & Koenig S (2005) A Generalized Framework for Lifelong Planning A*. Proceedings International Conference on Automated Planning and Scheduling: 99-108
10. Michael N, Fink J & Kumar V (2008) Experimental Testbed for Large Multirobot Teams. IEEE Robots and Automation Magazine, 15(1):53-61
11. Microsoft Corporation (2008) Microsoft CCR and DSS Toolkit 2008: Tyco Case Study. http://go.microsoft.com/fwlink/?LinkId=130995. Accessed 13 January 2009
12. Microsoft Corporation (2008) Microsoft Robotics Developer Studio: CCR Introduction. http://msdn.microsoft.com/en-us/library/bb648752.aspx. Accessed 12 January 2009
13. Microsoft Corporation (2008) Microsoft Robotics Studio Partners. http://msdn.micrsoft.com /en-us/robotics/bb383566.aspx. Accessed 15 October 2008
14. Morgan S (2008) Programming Microsoft Robotics Studio, Microsoft Press
15. Morgan S (2008) Robotics: Simulating the World with Microsoft Robotics Studio. http://msdn.microsoft.com/en-us/magazine/cc546547.aspx. Accessed 13 January 2009
16. Ramalingam G & Reps T (1996) An incremental algorithm for a generalization of the shortest-path problem. Journal of Algorithms, 21:267-305
17. Richter J (2006) Concurrent Affairs: Concurrency and Coordination Runtime. http://msdn. microsoft.com/en-us/magazine/cc163556.aspx. Accessed 13 January 2009
18. RoboCupRescue (2006) Rescue Simulation Leagues. http://www.robocuprescue.org /simleagues.html. Accessed 25 October 2008
19. SimplySim (2008) Generic Environment. http://www.simplysim.net/index.php?scr=scrAccueil&idcategorie=1. Accessed 12 January 2009
20. Somby M (2008) Software Platforms for Service Robotics http://linuxdevices.com /articles/AT9631072539.html. Accessed 18 October 2008
21. Taylor T (2008) MSRS Maze Simulator. http://www.soft-tech.com.au/MSRS/MazeSimulator /MazeSimulator.htm. Accessed 23 September 2008
22. Tick J (2006) Convergence of Programming Development Tools for Autonomous Mobile Research Robots. Proceedings Serbian-Hungarian Joint Symposium on Intelligent Systems: 375-382
23. Tsai W T, Chen Y, Sun X, et al. (2007) Designing a Service-Oriented Computing Course for High Schools. Proceedings IEEE International Conference on e-Business Engineering: 686-693
24. Turner D (2006) Microsoft Moves into Robotics. http://www.technologyreview.com /computing/17419/page2/. Accessed 21 October 2008
25. Ulanoff L (2006) Rivals Skeptical of Microsoft's New Robot Software. http://www.pcmag. com/article2/0,1895,1979617,00.asp. Accessed 21 October 2008
26. Workman K & Elzer S (2009) Utilizing Microsoft robotics studio in undergraduate robotics. Journal of Computing Sciences in Colleges 24(3):65-71

Automated Product Pricing Using Argumentation

Nikolaos Spanoudakis[1,2], Pavlos Moraitis[2]

[1]Department of Sciences - Technical University of Crete,
nikos@science.tuc.gr

[2]Department of Mathematics and Computer Science – Paris Descartes University,
{pavlos, nikolaos.spanoudakis}@mi.parisdescartes.fr

Abstract This paper describes an argumentation-based approach for automating the decision making process of an autonomous agent for pricing products. Product pricing usually involves different decision makers with different - possibly conflicting - points of view. Moreover, when considering firms in the retail business sector, they have hundreds or thousands of products to apply a pricing policy. Our approach allows for applying a price policy to each one of them by taking into account different points of view expressed through different arguments and the dynamic environment of the application. This is done because argumentation is a reasoning mechanism based on the construction and the evaluation of interacting conflicting arguments. We also show how we conceived and developed our agent using the Agent Systems Engineering Methodology (ASEME).

1 Introduction

Automating the product pricing procedure in many different types of enterprises like retail businesses, factories, even firms offering services is an important issue. Product pricing is concerned with deciding on which price each of a firm's products will have in the market. The product pricing agent that we present in this paper allows for the integration of the views of different types of decision makers (like financial, production, marketing officers) and can reach a decision even when these views are conflicting. This is achieved with the use of argumentation.

Argumentation has been used successfully in the last years as a reasoning mechanism for autonomous agents in different situations, as for example for deliberating over the needs of a user with a combination of impairments [8] and for selecting the funds that should be included in an investment portfolio [11]. It is the first time that it is used for decision making in the retail business sector. This paper aims to show that argumentation can be applied successfully in an area that

---

Please use the following format when citing this chapter:

Spanoudakis, N. and Moraitis, P., 2009, in IFIP International Federation for Information Processing, Volume 296; *Artificial Intelligence Applications and Innovations III*; Eds. Iliadis, L., Vlahavas, I., Bramer, M.; (Boston: Springer), pp. 321–330.

sparse works provide solutions, the retail business sector. Argumentation responded well to our requirements, which demanded a system that would have the possibility to apply a pricing policy adjusted to the market context, in the meanwhile reflecting the points of views of diverse decision makers.

This product pricing agent was developed in the context of MARKET-MINER project that was co-funded by the Greek government. After evaluation, its results have been considered to be successful and are expected to have an important impact in the firm's business intelligence software suite in the next four to five years.

In what follows we firstly present the basics of the used argumentation framework in section 2 and then, in section 3, we discuss how we modeled the knowledge of the particular application domain. Subsequently, we present the product pricing agent, including information on how we conceived and modeled the system using the Agent Systems Engineering Methodology (ASEME), in section 4, followed by the presentation of the evaluation results in section 5. Finally, in section 6, we discuss related work and conclude.

2 The Theoretical Framework

Decision makers, be they artificial or human, need to make decisions under complex preference policies that take into account different factors. In general, these policies have a dynamic nature and are influenced by the particular state of the environment in which the agent finds himself. The agent's decision process needs to be able to synthesize together different aspects of his preference policy and to adapt to new input from the current environment. We model the product pricing decision maker as such an agent.

To address requirements like the above, Kakas and Moraitis [5] proposed an argumentation based framework to support an agent's self deliberation process for drawing conclusions under a given policy. The following definitions present the basic elements of this framework:

Definition 1. A **theory** is a pair $(\mathcal{T}, \mathcal{P})$ whose sentences are formulae in the **background monotonic logic** $(\mathcal{L}, \vdash)$ of the form $L \leftarrow L_1,\ldots,L_n$, where $L, L_1, \ldots, L_n$ are positive or negative ground literals. For rules in P the head L refers to an (irreflexive) higher priority relation, i.e. L has the general form $L = h\_p(rule1, rule2)$. The derivability relation, $\vdash$, of the background logic is given by the simple inference rule of modus ponens.

An **argument** for a literal L in a theory $(\mathcal{T}, \mathcal{P})$ is any subset, T, of this theory that derives L, $T \vdash L$, under the background logic. A part of the theory $\mathcal{T}_0 \subset \mathcal{T}$, is the **background theory** that is considered as a non defeasible part (the indisputable facts). An important notion in argumentation is that of **attack**. In the current framework an argument attacks (or is a counter argument of) another when they derive a contrary conclusion. Another notion is that of **admissibility**. An argument (from $\mathcal{T}$) is admissible if it counter-attacks all the attacks it receives. For this it needs to take along priority arguments (from $\mathcal{P}$) and makes itself at least as strong as its counter-arguments

Definition 2. An agent's **argumentative policy theory or theory**, T, is a tuple $T = (\mathcal{T}, \mathcal{P}_R, \mathcal{P}_C)$ where the rules in $\mathcal{T}$ do not refer to h_p, all the rules in $\mathcal{P}_R$ are priority rules with head $h\_p(r_1, r_2)$ s.t. $r_1, r_2 \in \mathcal{T}$ and all rules in $\mathcal{P}_C$ are priority rules with head $h\_p(R_1, R_2)$ s.t. $R_1, R_2 \in \mathcal{P}_R \cup \mathcal{P}_C$.

Thus, in defining the decision maker's theory three levels are used. The first level ($\mathcal{T}$) that defines the rules that refer directly to the subject domain, the second level that define priorities over the first level rules and the third level rules that define priorities over the rules of the previous level.

Gorgias (http://www.cs.ucy.ac.cy/~nkd/gorgias/), a prolog implementation of the framework presented above, defines a specific language for the object level rules and the priorities rules of the second and third levels. A negative literal is a term of the form *neg(L)*. The language for representing the theories is given by rules with the syntax rule(Signature, Head, Body) where Head is a literal, Body is a list of literals and Signature is a compound term composed of the rule name with selected variables from the Head and Body of the rule. The predicate *prefer/2* is used to capture the higher priority relation *(h_p)* defined in the theoretical framework. It should only be used as the head of a rule. Using the previously defined syntax we can write the rule rule(Signature, prefer(Sig1, Sig2), Body)., which means that the rule with signature Sig1 has higher priority than the rule with signature Sig2, provided that the preconditions in the Body hold. If the modeler needs to express that two predicates are conflicting he can express that by using the rule conflict(Sig1,Sig2)., which indicates that the rules with signatures Sig1 and Sig2 are conflicting. A literal's negation is considered by default as conflicting with the literal itself.

3 Domain Knowledge Modeling

Firstly, we gathered the domain knowledge in free text format by questioning the decision makers that participate in the product pricing procedure. They were officers in Financial, Marketing and Production departments of firms in the retail business but also in the manufacture domain. Then, we processed their statements aiming on one hand to discover the domain ontology and on the other hand the decision making rules.

We used the Protégé (http://protege.stanford.edu/) open source ontology editor for defining the domain concepts and their properties and relations. In Figure 1, the *Product* concept and its properties are presented. The reader can see the properties identified previously *hasPrice* and *isAccompaniedBy*. Price is defined as a real number (*Float*) and *isAccompaniedBy* relates the product to multiple other instances of products that accompany it in the consumer's cart. In the figure, we also present the firm strategy concept and its properties that are all *Boolean* and represent the different strategies that the firm can have activated at a given time. For example, the *hitCompetition* property is set to *true* if the firm's strategy is to reduce the sales of its competitors. The property *retail_business* characterizes the firm as one in the retail business sector.

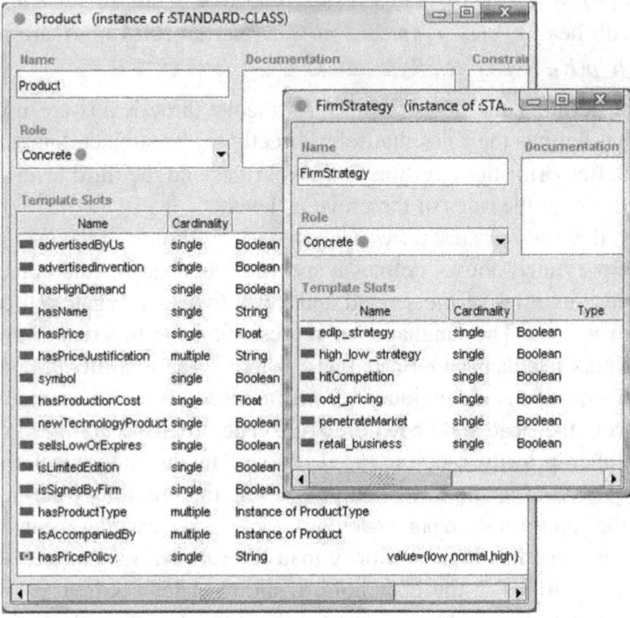

Fig. 1. The Product and FirmStrategy ontology concepts.

For our knowledge base definition we used Prolog. To use the concepts and their properties as they were defined in Protégé we defined that a Boolean property is encoded as a unary predicate, for example the *advertisedByUs* property of the *Product* concept is encoded as *advertisedByUs(ProductInstance)*. A property with a string, numerical, or any concept instance value is encoded as a binary predicate, for example the *hasPrice* property of the *Product* concept is encoded as *hasPrice(ProductInstance, FloatValue)*. A property with a string, numerical, or any concept instance value with multiple cardinality is encoded as a binary predicate. However the encoding of the property to predicate can be done in two ways. The first possibility is for the second term of the predicate to be a list. Thus, the *isAccompaniedBy* property of the *Product* concept is encoded as *isAccompaniedBy(ProductInstance, [ProductInstance1, ProductInstance2, ...])*, where product instances must not refer to the same product. A second possibility is to create multiple predicates for the property. For example the *hasProductType* property of the Product concept is encoded as *hasProductType(ProductInstance, ProductTypeInstance)*. In the case that a product has more than one product types, one such predicate is created for each product type.

Then, we used the Gorgias framework for writing the rules. The goal of the knowledge base would be to decide on whether a product should be priced high, low or normally. Thus it emerged, the *hasPricePolicy* property of the *Product* concept. After this decision we could write the object-level rules each having as head the predicate *hasPricePolicy(Product, Value)* where *Value* can be *low*, *high* or *normal* – the relevant limitation for this predicate is also defined in the ontology (see the *hasPricePolicy* property of the *Product* concept in Figure 1). Then, we defined the different policies as conflicting, thus only one policy was acceptable per product. To resolve conflicts we consulted with the firm (executive) officers and defined priorities over the conflicting object rules. Consider, for example, the following rules (variables start with a capital letter as it is in Prolog):

```
rule(r1_2_2(Product), hasPricePolicy(Product, low), [hitProductTypeCompetition(
        ProductType), hasProductType(Product, ProductType)]).
rule(r2_3(Product), hasPricePolicy(Product, high), [newTechnologyProduct(Product),
        advertisedInvention(Product)]).
rule(pr1_2_6(Product), prefer(r1_2_2(Product), r2_3(Product)), []).
```

Rules *r1_2_2* and *r2_3* are conflicting if they are both activated for the same product. The first states that a product should be priced low if the firm wants to hit the competition for its product type, while the second states that a new technology product that is an advertised invention should be priced high. To resolve the conflict we add the *pr1_2_6* priority rule which states that *r1_2_2* is preferred to *r2_3*.

4 The Product Pricing Agent

In this section we firstly describe the Market-mIner product Pricing Agent (also referred to as MIPA) development process and then we focus in two important aspects of it, the decision making module and human-computer interaction.

We designed our agent using the Agent Systems Engineering Methodology (ASEME) [10]. During the analysis phase we identified the actors and the use cases related to our agent system (see Figure 2). Note that the Agent Modeling Language [9] (AMOLA), which is used by ASEME for modeling the agent-based system, allows for actors to be included in the system box, thus indicating an agent-based system. The system actor is MIPA, while the external actors that participate in the system's environment are the user, external systems of competitors, weather report systems (as the weather forecast influences product demand as in the case of umbrellas) and municipality systems (as local events like concerts, sports, etc, also influence consumer demand). We started by identifying general use cases (like *interact with user*) and then we elaborated them in more specific ones (like *present information to the user* and *update firm policy*) using the <<include>> relation.

Then, we completed the roles model as it is presented in Figure 3(a). This model defines the dynamic aspect of the system, general use cases are transformed to capabilities, while the generic ones are transformed to activities. We used the Gaia operators ([14]) for creating *liveness formulas* that define the dynamic aspect of the agent system, what happens and when it happens. A. B means that activity B is executed after activity A, A^{ω} means that activity A is executed forever (when it finishes it restarts), A | B means that either activity A or activity B is executed and A || B means activity A is executed in parallel with activity B.

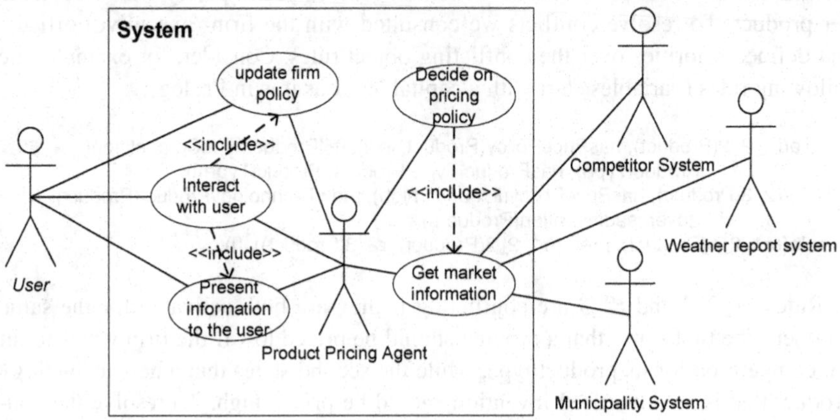

Fig. 2. MIPA Use Case Diagram

The next step was to associate each activity to a functionality, i.e. the technology that will be used for its implementation. In Figure 3(b) the reader can observe the capabilities, the activities that they decompose to and the functionality associated with each activity. The choice of these technologies is greatly influenced by non-functional requirements. For example the system will need to connect on diverse firm databases. Thus, we selected the JDBC technology (http://java.sun.com/javase/technologies/database/) that is database provider independent.

The last step, before implementation, is to extract from the roles model the statechart that resembles the agent. This is achieved by transforming the liveness formula to a statechart in a straightforward process that uses templates to transform activities and Gaia operators to states and transitions (see [9] for more details). The resulting statechart, i.e. the intra-agent control (as it is called in ASEME) is depicted in Figure 7. The statechart can then be easily transformed to a computer program.

The decision making capability includes four activities:

1. *wait for new period* activity: It waits for the next pricing period
2. *get products information* activity: It accesses a corporate database to collect the data needed for inference,
3. *determine pricing policy* activity: It reasons on the price category of each product, and,
4. *fix prices* activity: Based on the previous activity's results, it defines the final product price.

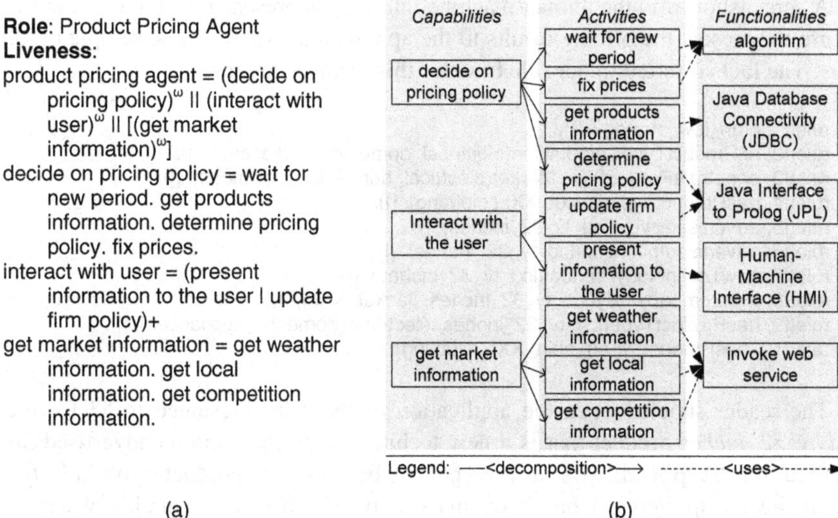

Fig. 3. MIPA Role Model (a) and the relation between Capabilities, Activities and Functionalities (b).

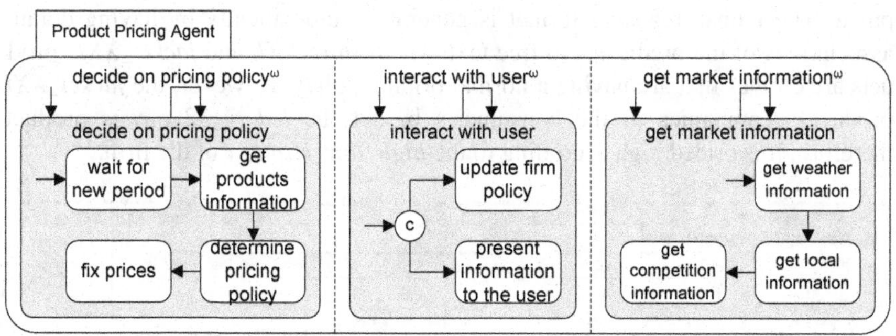

Fig. 4. MIPA Intra-agent Control Model

The *determine pricing policy* activity invokes the prolog rule base presented in §3 that includes 274 rules, 31 of which are the object rules and 243 are the priority rules. The *fix prices* activity's algorithm aims to produce a final price for each product. The algorithm's inputs are a) the procurement/manufacture cost for a product, or its price in the market, b) the outcome of the reasoning process (the price policy for each product), c) the default profit ratio for the firm, d) a step for rising the default profit ratio, e) a step for lowering this ratio, and, f) the lowest profit ratio that the firm would accept for any product. The pricing algorithm also takes into account the number of arguments that are admissible for choosing a specific price policy, strengthening the application of the policy.

A screenshot from the human-machine interface is presented in Figure 5. In the figure we present the pricing results to the application user for some sample products. The facts inserted to our rule base for this instance are the:

```
rule(f1, high_low_strategy, []).
rule(f2, hitProductTypeCompetition(electrical_domestic_appliances), []).
rule(f3, penetrateProductTypeMarket(electrical_domestic_appliances), []).
rule(f4, hasProductType(jacket_XXL, clothing), []).
rule(f5, advertisedByUs(lcd_tv_32_inches), []).
rule(f6, advertisedInvention(lcd_tv_32_inches), []).
rule(f7, newTechnologyProduct(lcd_tv_32_inches), []).
rule(f8, isAccompaniedBy(lcd_tv_32_inches, [jacket_XXL]), []).
rule(f9, hasProductType(lcd_tv_32_inches, electrical_domestic_appliances), []).
rule(f10, hasProductType(t_shirt_XXL, clothing), []).
```

The reader should notice the application of the rules presented in §3 for the *lcd_tv_32_inches* product that is a new technology product and an advertised invention but is priced with a low policy because its product type (*electrical_domestic_appliances*) has been marked by the firm as a market where it should hit competition. Moreover, the firm has also decided that it wants to penetrate the *electrical_domestic_appliances* market, therefore there are two arguments for pricing the *lcd_tv_32_inches* product low. In Figure 5, these reasons are explained to the user in human-readable format and also the final price is computed. The human-readable format is generated automatically by having default associations of the predicates to free text. The *t_shirt_XXL* and *jacket_XXL* products are clothes that are having a normal pricing policy. However, the *jacket_XXL* product accompanies in the consumer's basket the *lcd_tv_32_inches* product, therefore, it is priced high according to the *high_low_strategy* of the firm.

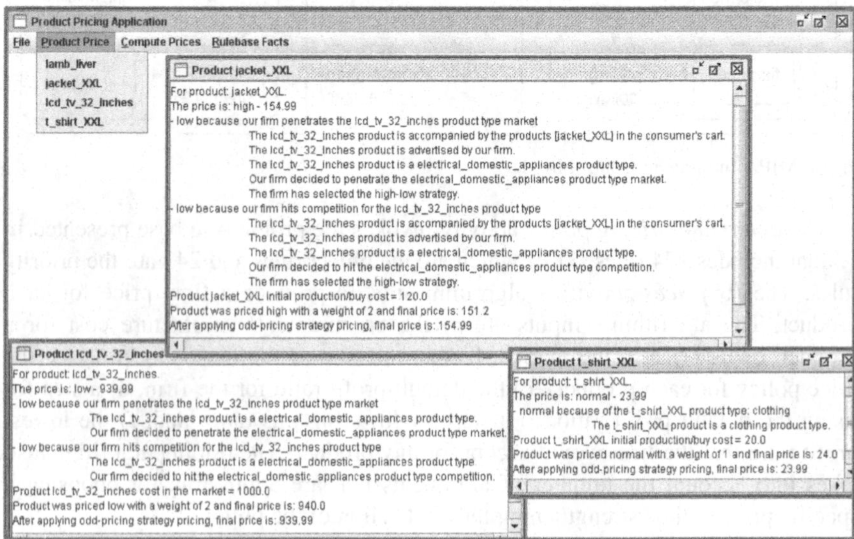

Fig. 5. The Product Pricing Agent Application

5 Evaluation

The product pricing agent application was evaluated by SingularLogic SA, the largest Greek software vendor for SMEs. The MARKET-MINER project included an exploitation plan [12]. The application evaluation goals were to measure the overall satisfaction of its users. In the evaluation report [13] three user categories were identified, System Administrators, Consultants and Data Analysts. The criteria C1) *Performance*, C2) *Usability*, C3) *Interoperability*, and C4) *Security and Trust* were used for measuring user satisfaction. The users expressed their views in a relevant questionnaire and they marked their experience on a scale of one (dissatisfied) to five (completely satisfied) and their evaluation of the importance of the criterion on a scale of one (irrelevant) to five (very important).

The Process of Evaluation of Software Products [2] (MEDE-PROS) was used for our set of criteria. The results of the evaluation are presented in Table 1 and they have been characterized as "very satisfactory" by the SingularLogic research and development software assessment unit. MARKET-MINER has been decreed as worthy for recommendation for commercialization and addition to the Firm's software products suite.

Table 1. MARKET-MINER evaluation results. The rows with white background are those of the consultants, while those with grey background represent the evaluation of the system administrators (see [13] for more details).

Criterion	Criterion performance	Criterion Importance
C1	86%	0,78
C2	83%	0,88
C3	91%	0,88
C4	83%	0,64
C3	86%	0,92
C4	61%	0,92

6 Conclusion and Future Perspectives

This paper presented a novel application of autonomous agents for automating the product pricing process. This issue has never been tackled before in this scale. A patent just provided some guidelines on an architecture for such a system exclusively for super market chains [1]. Earlier works proposed a support of the product pricing process for the retail business sector but did not provide an automated decision mechanism [7]. In this paper we used argumentation that allows for expressing conflicting views on the subject and a mechanism for resolving these conflicts. Moreover, with argumentation it is possible to provide an explanation of the decisions that the agent makes. This is also the main technical difference with existing works in the agent technology literature, where product pricing agents have been referred to as economic agents, as price bots, or, simply, as seller agents (see e.g. [6], [3] and [4]) and their responsibility is to adjust prices automatically on the seller's behalf in response to changing market conditions [6].

All these existing solutions focus on a selected product negotiation rather than bundles of products (as in the retail business sector). The MARKET-MINER product pricing agent borrows interesting features from these works, i.e. resets prices at regular intervals and can employ different strategies for pricing depending on market conditions. The added value of the MARKET-MINER product pricing agent regarding these approaches is the capability to model human knowledge and apply human-generated strategies to automate product pricing with the possibility to provide logical explanations to decision makers, if needed.

The presented application's results were evaluated according to a widely used process (MEDE-PROS [2]) and they were proposed by the SingularLogic research and development department for commercialization by the firm.

References

1. Charles C, Freeny Jr (2000) Automated Synchronous Product Pricing and Advertising. United States Patent 6076071
2. Colombo R, Guerra A (2002) The Evaluation Method for Software Product. In Proc 15th Int Conf on Softw & Syst Eng & Appl, Paris, France, December 3-4
3. Dasgupta P, Das S (2000) Dynamic pricing with limited competitor information in a multi-agent economy. In LNCS 1906, Springer-Verlag: 291-310
4. DiMicco JM, Greenwald A, Maes P (2001) Dynamic pricing strategies under a finite time horizon. In Proc ACM Conf on Electron Commer, October
5. Kakas A, Moraitis P (2003) Argumentation based decision making for autonomous agents. In Proc 2nd Int Conf on Auton Agents and Multi-Agent Syst, Melbourne, Australia, July 14-18
6. Kephart JO, Hanson JE, Greenwald AR (2000) Dynamic pricing by software agents. Comput Netw 36(6):731-752
7. Matsatsinis N, Moraitis P, Psomatakis V et al (2003) An Agent-Based System for Products Penetration Strategy Selection. Appl Artif Intell J 17(10):901-925
8. Moraitis P, Spanoudakis N (2007) Argumentation-based Agent Interaction in an Ambient Intelligence Context. IEEE Intell Syst 22(6):84-93
9. Spanoudakis N, Moraitis P (2008) The Agent Modeling Language (AMOLA). In LNCS 5253, Springer, Varna, Bulgaria
10. Spanoudakis N, Moraitis P (2007) The Agent Systems Methodology (ASEME): A Preliminary Report. In Proc 5th European Workshop on Multi-Agent Systems, Hammamet, Tunisia, December 13 - 14
11. Spanoudakis N, Pendaraki K (2007) A Tool for Portfolio Generation Using an Argumentation Based Decision Making Framework. In Proc Annual IEEE Int Conf on Tools with Artif Intell, Patras, Greece, October 29-31
12. Toulis P, Tzovaras D, Spanoudakis N (2007) MARKET-MINER Project Exploitation Plan. MARKET-MINER Proj Deliv Π6.1 (in Greek language), Singular Logic S.A.
13. Toulis P, Tzovaras D, Pantelopoulos S (2007) MARKET-MINER System Evaluation Report. MARKET-MINER Proj Deliv Π5.1 (in Greek language), Singular Logic S.A.
14. Wooldridge M, Jennings NR, Kinny D (2000) The Gaia Methodology for Agent-Oriented Analysis and Design. J Auton Agents and Multi-Agent Syst 3(3):285-312

User Recommendations based on Tensor Dimensionality Reduction

Panagiotis Symeonidis

Abstract Social Tagging is the process by which many users add metadata in the form of keywords, to annotate and categorize items (songs, pictures, web links, products etc.). Social tagging systems (STSs) can recommend users with common social interest based on common tags on similar items. However, users may have different interests for an item, and items may have multiple facets. In contrast to the current recommendation algorithms, our approach develops a model to capture the three types of entities that exist in a social tagging system: users, items, and tags. These data are represented by a 3-order tensor, on which latent semantic analysis and dimensionality reduction is performed using the Higher Order Singular Value Decomposition (HOSVD) method. We perform experimental comparison of the proposed method against a baseline user recommendation algorithm with a real data set (BibSonomy), attaining significant improvements.

1 Introduction

Social tagging is the process by which many users add metadata in the form of keywords, to annotate and categorize songs, pictures, products, etc. Social tagging is associated to the "Web 2.0" technologies and has already become an important source of information for recommender systems. For example, music recommender systems such as Last.fm and MyStrands allow users to tag artist, songs, or albums. In e-commerce sites such as Amazon, users tag products to easily discover common interests with other users. Moreover, social media sites, such as Flickr and YouTube use tags for annotating their content. All these systems can further exploit these social tags to improve the search mechanisms and personalized recommendations. Social tags carry

Aristotle University, Department of Informatics, Thessaloniki 54124, Greece
e-mail: symeon@csd.auth.gr

Please use the following format when citing this chapter:

Symeonidis, P., 2009, in IFIP International Federation for Information Processing, Volume 296; *Artificial Intelligence Applications and Innovations III*; Eds. Iliadis, L., Vlahavas, I., Bramer, M.; (Boston: Springer), pp. 331–340.

useful information not only about the items they label, but also about the users who tagged. Thus, social tags are a powerful mechanism that reveal 3-dimensional correlations between users, tags, and items.

Several social tagging systems (STSs), e.g., Last.fm, Amazon, etc., recommend *interesting* users to a target user, opting in connecting people with common interests and encouraging people to contribute and share more contents. With the term *interesting* users, we mean those users who have similar profile with the target user. If a set of tags are frequently used by many users, then these users spontaneously form a community of interest, even though they may not have any physical or online connections. The tags represent the commonly interested web contents to this community of common interest. For example, Amazon recommends to a user who used a specific tag, other new users considering them as *interesting* ones. Amazon ranks them based on how frequently they used the specific tag.

In this paper, we develop a model based on the three dimensions, i.e., items, tags, users. The 3-dimensional data are represented by 3-dimensional matricies, which are called *3-order tensors*. We avoid splitting the 3-dimensional correlations and we handle all dimensions equally. To reveal latent semantics, we perform 3-mode analysis, using the Higher Order Singular Value Decomposition (HOSVD) [4]. Our method reveals latent relations among objects of the same type, as well among objects of different types.

The contributions of our approach are summarized as follows:

- We use a 3-order tensor to model the three types of entities (user, item, and tag) that exist in social sites.
- We apply dimensionality reduction (HOSVD) in 3-order tensors, to reveal the latent semantic associations between users, items, and tags.
- For the first time to our knowledge we recommend interesting users to other users.

The rest of this paper is organized as follows. Section 2 summarizes the related work. The proposed approach is described in Section 3. Experimental results are given in Section 4. Finally, Section 5 concludes this paper.

2 Related Work

In the area of discovering shared interests in social networks there are two kinds of existing approaches [5]. One is user-centric, which focuses on detecting social interests based on the on-line connections among users; the other is object-centric, which detects common interests based on the common objects fetched by users in a social community. In the user-centric approach, recently Ali-Hasan and Adamic [1] analyzed user's online connections to discover users with particular interests for a given user. Different from this kind of approaches, we aim to find the people who share the same interest no matter whether they are connected by a social graph or not. In the object-centric approach, recently Guo et al. [6] explored the common interests among users based on the common items they fetched in peer-to-peer networks. However, they cannot differentiate the various social interests on the same items, due to the fact that users may have different interests for an information item and an item may have multiple facets. In contrast, our approach focuses on directly detecting social interests and recommending users by taking advantage of social tagging, by utilizing users' tags.

Differently from existing approaches, our method develops a unified framework to concurrently model the three dimensions. Usage data are represented by a 3-order tensor, on which latent semantic analysis is performed using the Higher Order Singular Value Decomposition (HOSVD), which has been introduced in [4].

HOSVD is a generalization of singular value decomposition and has been successfully applied in several areas. In particular, Wang and Ahuja [8] present a novel multi-linear algebra based approach to reduced dimensionality representation of multidimensional data, such as image ensembles, video sequences and volume data. In the area of Data Clustering, Chen et al. [2] used also a high-order tensor. However, they transform the initial tensor (through Clique Expansion algorithm) into lower dimensional spaces, so that clustering algorithms (such as k-means) can be applied. Finally, in the area of Personalized Web Search, Sun et al. proposed CubeSVD [7] to improve Web Search. They claimed that as the competition of Web Search increases, there is a high demand for personalized Web search. Therefore based on their CubeSVD analysis, Web Search activities can be carried out more efficiently. In the next section, we provide more information on HOSVD.

3 The Tensor Reduction Algorithm

A *tensor* is a multi-dimensional matrix. A N-order tensor $\mathcal{A}$ is denoted as $\mathcal{A} \in R^{I_1 \dots I_N}$, with elements $a_{i_1,\dots,i_N}$. In this paper, for the purposes of our approach, we only use 3-order tensors. In the following, we denote tensors by calligraphic uppercase letters (e.g., $\mathcal{A}$, $\mathcal{B}$), matrices by uppercase letters (e.g., A, B), scalars by lowercase letters (e.g., a, b), and vectors by bold lowercase letters (e.g., $\mathbf{a}$, $\mathbf{b}$).

The high-order singular value decomposition [4] generalizes the SVD computation to multi-dimensional matrices. To apply HOSVD on a 3-order tensor $\mathcal{A}$, three *matrix unfolding* operations are defined as follows [4]:

$$A_1 \in R^{I_1 \times I_2 I_3}, \qquad A_2 \in R^{I_2 \times I_1 I_3}, \qquad A_3 \in R^{I_1 I_2 \times I_3}$$

where A_1, A_2, A_3 are called the 1-mode, 2-mode, 3-mode matrix unfoldings of $\mathcal{A}$, respectively.

Next, we define the n-mode product of an N-order tensor $\mathcal{A} \in R^{I_1 \times \ldots \times I_N}$ by a matrix $U \in R^{J_n \times I_n}$, which is denoted as $\mathcal{A} \times_n U$. The result of the n-mode product is an $(I_1 \times I_2 \times \ldots \times I_{n-1} \times J_n \times I_{n+1} \times \ldots \times I_N)$-tensor, the entries of which are defined as follows:

$$(\mathcal{A} \times_n U)_{i_1 i_2 \ldots i_{n-1} j_n i_{n+1} \ldots i_N} = \sum_{i_n} a_{i_1 i_2 \ldots i_{n-1} i_n i_{n+1} \ldots i_N} u_{j_n i_n} \quad (1)$$

Since we focus on 3-order tensors, $n \in \{1, 2, 3\}$, we use 1-mode, 2-mode, and 3-mode products.

Our Tensor Reduction algorithm initially constructs a tensor, based on usage data triplets $\{u, t, i\}$ of users, tags and items. The motivation is to use all three entities that interact inside a social tagging system. Consequently, we proceed to the unfolding of $\mathcal{A}$, where we build three new matrices. Then, we apply SVD in each new matrix. Finally, we build the core tensor $\mathcal{S}$ and the resulting tensor $\hat{\mathcal{A}}$. All these can be summarized in 5 steps, as follows.

3.1 The initial construction of tensor $\mathcal{A}$

From the usage data triplets (user, tag, item), we construct an initial 3-order tensor $\mathcal{A} \in R^{u \times t \times i}$, where u, t, i are the numbers of users, tags and items, respectively. Each tensor element measures the preference of a (user u, tag t) pair on an item i.

3.2 Matrix unfolding of tensor $\mathcal{A}$

A tensor $\mathcal{A}$ can be matricized i.e., to build matrix representations in which all the column (row) vectors are stacked one after the other. In our approach, the initial tensor $\mathcal{A}$ is matricized in all three modes. Thus, after the unfolding of tensor $\mathcal{A}$ for all three modes, we create 3 new matrices A_1, A_2, A_3.

Then, we apply SVD on the three matrix unfoldings A_1, A_2, A_3. We result to 3 new matrices which contain $U^{(1)}$, $U^{(2)}$, $U^{(3)}$ left-singular vectors of A_1, A_2, A_3 matrices, respectively. After decomposition, we also result to $S^{(1)}$, $S^{(2)}$, $S^{(3)}$ matrices which contain the singular values of A_1, A_2, A_3, respectively(to ease presentation, we omit the corresponding matrices with the right-singular vectors).

3.3 The core tensor $\mathcal{S}$ construction

The core tensor S governs the interactions among user, item and tag entities. From the the initial tensor $\mathcal{A}$ we proceed to the construction of the core tensor S, as follows:

$$\mathcal{S} = \mathcal{A} \times_1 (U_{c_1}^{(1)})^T \times_2 (U_{c_2}^{(2)})^T \times_3 (U_{c_3}^{(3)})^T, \tag{2}$$

where c_1, c_2, and c_3 are parameters chosen by preserving a percentage of information of the original $S^{(1)}$, $S^{(2)}$, $S^{(3)}$ matrices after appropriate tuning.

3.4 The tensor $\hat{\mathcal{A}}$ construction

Finally, tensor $\hat{\mathcal{A}}$ is built by the product of the core tensor $\mathcal{S}$ and the mode products of the three matrices $U_{c_1}^{(1)}$, $U_{c_2}^{(2)}$ and $U_{c_3}^{(3)}$ as follows:

$$\hat{\mathcal{A}} = \mathcal{S} \times_1 U_{c_1}^{(1)} \times_2 U_{c_2}^{(2)} \times_3 U_{c_3}^{(3)} \tag{3}$$

3.5 The generation of the recommendations

The reconstructed tensor $\hat{\mathcal{A}}$ measures the associations among the users, tags and items, so that the elements of $\hat{\mathcal{A}}$ represent a quadruplet $\{u, t, i, p\}$ where p is the likeliness that user u will tag item i with tag t. On this basis, users can be recommended to u according to their weights associated with $\{i, t\}$ pair.

4 Experimental Performance

In this section, in the area of user recommendations, we present experimental results for the performance of our approach against a baseline algorithm (BL). To evaluate the examined algorithms, we have chosen a real data set from BibSonomy which has been used as benchmarks in past works [3]. We used a snapshot of all users, items (both publication references and bookmarks) and tags publicly available at April 30, 2007. The number of users, items and tags is 1,037, 28,648, and 86,563, respectively.

To evaluate the effectiveness of Tensor Reduction and BL algorithms in recommending *interesting* users, we compute the item similarity within the recommended users [5]. This evaluation is based on the fact that users with shared interests are very likely to tag similar items.

A metric to evaluate this characteristic of each Neighborhood N of recommended users is to compute the average cosine similarity of all item pairs inside the Neighborhood of users with common social interest [5]:

$$ACS_N = \frac{\sum_{u,v \in N} \left[\sum_{i \in I(u), j \in I(v)} sim(i,j) \right]}{\sum_{u,v \in N} |I(u)||I(v)|}, \tag{4}$$

where for a user u, $I(u)$ denotes the items tagged by u. ACS_N evaluates the tightness or looseness of each Neighborhood or recommended users.

For each of the algorithms of our evaluation we will now describe briefly the specific settings used to run them:

- **Baseline algorithm (BL):** BL algorithm is quite similar to Amazon.com's method to recommend *interesting* users to a target user. BL logic is as follows: if a user uses a specific tag for item search, then he is recommended (except of recommended items) also *interesting* users, whose profiles are considered similar to him. These recommended users must have used the specific tag and are ranked based on how many times they used it. The basic idea behind this simple algorithm is that a tag corresponds in a topic of common interest. Thus, users that use the same tag could be interested in a common topic, forming a community of common interest.
- **Tensor Reduction algorithm:** Our tensor reduction algorithm is modified appropriately to recommend Neighborhoods of users to a target user. In particular, our tensor represents a quadruplet $\{t, i, u, p\}$ where p is the likeliness that tag t will be used to label item i by the user u. Therefore, new users can be recommended for a tag t, according to their total weight, which results by aggregating all items, which are labelled with the same tag by the target user.

4.1 Results

In this section, we evaluate the effectiveness of Tensor Reduction and BL algorithms in recommending *interesting* users. We compute the item similarity within the recommended neighborhoods of users. Note that as already described, some of the recommended neighborhoods can be consisted of users that are quite related, while others are consisted of users that are less related.

In the BibSonomy data set, users tag web sites. Thus, we crawled for each web site the first page and preprocess it to create a vector of terms. Preprocessing involved the removal of stop words, stemming and TF/IDF. Then, we find correlation between two web sites based on the keyword terms they include. We compute the similarity between two web sites with the inner product, i.e., the cosine similarity of their TF/IDF keyword term vectors [5].

For each user's neighborhood, we compute the Average Cosine Similarity (ACS) of all web site pairs inside the neighborhood, called intra-Neighborhood similarity. We also randomly select 20 neighborhood pairs among the 105 user neighborhoods and compute the average pairwise web site similarity between every two neighborhoods, called inter-Neighborhood similarity. In this figure, x axis is the rank of neighborhoods similarity, sorted by the descending order of their intra-Neighborhood similarities. y-axis shows the intra-Neighborhood similarity of each neighborhood and the corresponding average inter-Neighborhood similarity of this neighborhood with other 20 randomly selected neighborhoods.

Figure 1a, shows the comparison between the intra-Neighborhood and the inter-Neighborhood similarity of our Tensor Reduction Algorithm.

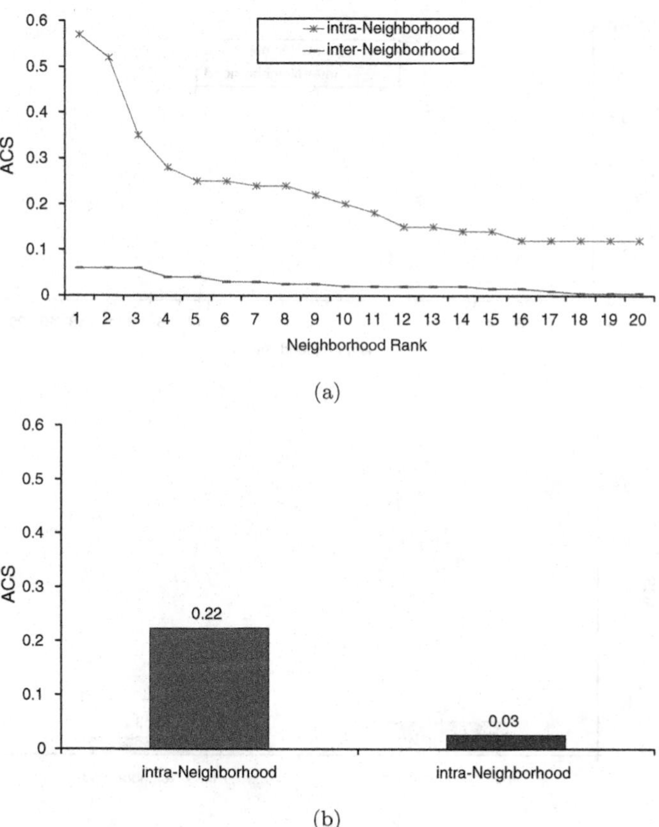

Fig. 1 Comparison of intra-Neighborhood and inter-Neighborhood similarity of Tensor Reduction Algorithm for the BibSonomy data set.

In this figure, x axis is the rank of neighborhoods similarity, sorted by the descending order of their intra-Neighborhood similarities. y-axis shows the intra-Neighborhood similarity of each neighborhood and the corresponding average inter-Neighborhood similarity of this neighborhood with other 20 randomly selected neighborhoods. As we can see, for all users' neighborhoods, the intra-Neighborhood similarity is consistently and significantly higher than the average inter-Neighborhood with others neighborhoods. As also shown in Figure 1b, the average intra-Neighborhood similarity across all neighborhoods is 0.22, while the average of inter-Neighborhood similarities across all neighborhood pairs is only 0.03.

Corresponding to Figures 1a and b, we show for the BL algorithm the comparison of intra- and inter-Neighborhood similarity for each neighborhood, and the average intra- and inter-Neighborhood similarity for all neighborhoods in Figures 2a and b, respectively.

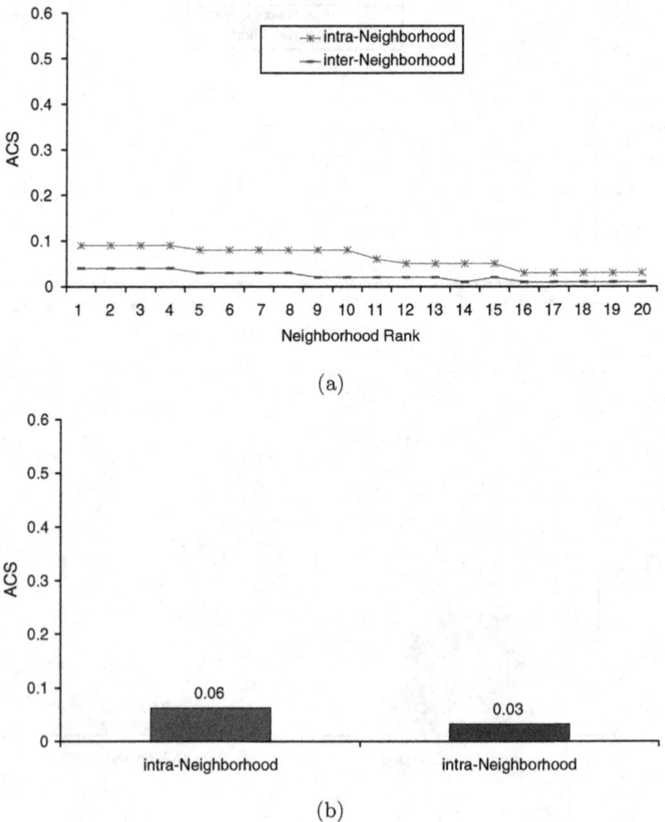

Fig. 2 Comparison of intra-Neighborhood and inter-Neighborhood similarity of BL Algorithm for the BibSonomy data set.

As we can see, BL's intra- and inter-Neighborhood similarity values are very close. This means, that BL fails to recommend coherent and related neighborhoods of users. In addition, our Tensor Reduction algorithm attains at least 3 times higher Average Cosine Similarity (ACS) than BL. That is, our approach recommends neighborhoods of users that are more related, while BL recommends users which are less relevant.

5 Conclusions

STSs provide recommendations to users based on what tags other users have used on items. In this paper, we developed a unified framework to model the three types of entities that exist in a social tagging system: users, items, and tags. We applied dimensionality reduction in a 3-order tensor, to reveal the latent semantic associations between users, items, and tags. The latent semantic analysis and dimensionality reduction is performed using the Higher Order Singular Value Decomposition (HOSVD) method. Our approach improves user recommendations by capturing users multimodal perception of item/tag. Moreover, for the first time to our knowledge, we provide user recommendations. We also performed experimental comparison of the proposed method against a baseline user recommendation algorithm. Our results show significant improvements in terms of effectiveness measured through, intra- and inter-neighborhood similarity.

As future work, we intend to examine the following topics:

- To examine different methods for extending SVD to high-order tensors. Another approach for multi dimensional decompositions is the Parallel factor analysis (Parafac).
- To apply different weighting methods for the initial construction of a tensor. A different weighting policy for the tensor's initial values could improve the overall performance of our approach.
- To adjust our Tensor Reduction framework to be able of handling on-line, the newly emerged objects (new users, new items and new tags), at the time they are inserted in a Social Tagging System. This may result to 4-dimensional tensors, where time represents the additional dimension.

References

1. N. Ali-Hasan and A. Adamic. Expressing social relationships on the blog through links and comments. In *Proceedings ICWSM Conference*, 2007.
2. S. Chen, F. Wang, and C. Zhang. Simultaneous heterogeneous data clustering based on higher order relationships. In *Proceedings Workshop on Mining Graphs and Complex Structures (MGCS'07), in conjunction with ICDM'07*, pages 387–392.

3. A. Hotho, R. Jaschke, C. Schmitz, and G. Stumme. Information retrieval in folksonomies: Search and ranking. In *The Semantic Web: Research and Applications*, pages 411–426, 2006.
4. L. de Lathauwer, B. de Moor, and J. Vandewalle. A multilinear singular value decomposition. *SIAM Journal of Matrix Analysis and Applications*, 21(4):1253–1278, 2000.
5. X. Li, L. Guo, and Y. Zhao. Tag-based social interest discovery. In *Proceedings ACM WWW Conference*, 2008.
6. K. Sripanidkulchai, B. Maggs, and H. Zhang. Efficient content location using interest-based locality in peer-to-peer systems. In *Proceedings INFOCOM Conference*, 2003.
7. J. Sun, D. Shen, H. Zeng, Q. Yang, Y. Lu, and Z. Chen. Cubesvd: a novel approach to personalized web search. In *Proceedings World Wide Web Conference*, pages 382–390, 2005.
8. H. Wang and N. Ahuja. A tensor approximation approach to dimensionality reduction. *International Journal of Computer Vision*, 2007.

A Genetic Algorithm for the Classification of Earthquake Damages in Buildings

Petros-Fotios Alvanitopoulos, Ioannis Andreadis and Anaxagoras Elenas

Faculty of Engineering.

Democritus University of Thrace, Xanthi, Greece.

{palvanit, iandread}@ee.duth.gr, elenas@civil.duth.gr

Abstract In this paper an efficient classification system in the area of earthquake engineering is reported. The proposed method uses a set of artificial accelerograms to examine several types of damages in specific structures. With the use of seismic accelerograms, a set of twenty seismic parameters have been extracted to describe earthquakes. Previous studies based on artificial neural networks and neuro-fuzzy classification systems present satisfactory classification results in different types of earthquake damages. In this approach a genetic algorithm (GA) was used to find the optimal feature subset of the seismic parameters that minimizes the computational cost and maximizes the classification performance. Experimental results indicate that the use of the GA was able to classify the structural damages with classification rates up to 92%.

1 Introduction

Earthquake engineering can be defined as the branch of engineering devoted to mitigate disasters caused by earthquakes. This research area involves designing, constructing and managing earthquake-resistant structures. The main aim of the proposed approach is the automatic approach of the post-seismic status of buildings.

In high potential seismic areas there is an obvious need to have direct knowledge of the damage suffered especially in constructions of special interest (such as schools, bridges, hospitals etc.). This paper examines the structural damages in buildings. It is well known that various damage indicators through nonlinear dynamic equations can represent the damages after severe earthquakes [1, 2].

For the present classification system the proposed algorithm consists of three processing stages. First, a set of artificial accelerograms have been used to describe the earthquake ground motion. Then a set of twenty seismic parameters have been extracted from them to express the damage potential of earthquakes. In

---

Please use the following format when citing this chapter:

Alvanitopoulos, P.-F., Andreadis, I. and Elenas, A., 2009, in IFIP International Federation for Information Processing, Volume 296; *Artificial Intelligence Applications and Innovations III*; Eds. Iliadis, L., Vlahavas, I., Bramer, M.; (Boston: Springer), pp. 341–346.

addition, a satisfactory number of damage indices have been used to estimate the earthquake damages in structures. Previous works prove that there is a correlation between the damage indices and the aforementioned intensity parameters [3, 4].

At the second stage of processing a GA has been used to reduce the number of the seismic parameters and find the subset that maximizes the classification rates. The GA starts the feature extraction process using an initial population of individuals (combination of seismic parameters) and after a specific number of generations produce an optimal single solution.

To select the optimum representation of seismic signals different kinds of classifiers have been used. Previous studies proposed artificial neural networks and artificial neuro-fuzzy inference systems for the classification of earthquake damages [5]. The classification accuracy of these systems has been used to evaluate the fitness value of the individuals.

The last part of the research was the investigation of the classification performance. The classifiers have been trained and simulated using the optimal subset of the intensity parameters. Classification results prove the effectiveness of this method.

2 Genetic Algorithms

A Genetic algorithm is an adaptive search and an optimization model which have been inspired from the principles of natural evolution [6]. GAs were first introduced in the early 1970s by John Holland. They are able to exploit the information from the acceptable solutions and select the optimal one.

The implementation of a GA starts with the generation of the initial population of the candidate solutions. Usually, the selection of the first population is random. GA is an iterative process which modifies the current population by selecting individuals to be parents and uses them to produce the children for the next generation.

GA moves from generation to generation and terminates until a converging criterion is met. The maximum number of generations or a threshold in fitness value, may be used to find the optimal solution.

3 Proposed Method

3.1 Seismic parameters

Accelerograms are records of the acceleration versus time measured during an earthquake ground motion. The seismic accelerograms are a useful tool in earthquake engineering since they are able to provide an explicit description of the seismic excitation. However, due to the random sizes and shapes it is very difficult to exploit their similarities. Therefore, a set of twenty seismic parameters have been used to represent the seismic signals, whose connection to the structural damages is studied through correlation studies in the literature. In our method the GA attempts to produce better classification results.

3.2 Structure of the proposed method

A GA was used to find the optimal feature set to produce the best classification accuracy of the proposed classifiers. First several subsets of seismic parameters have been examined. The classifiers have been trained according to these features. The fitness function of these subsets has been evaluated and the optimal set of seismic parameters have been extracted.

Let $L=20$ (twenty seismic parameters) be the number of feature descriptors. Assume a population of N individuals. In this research a population size of $N=20$ individuals has been used. A chromosome of L genes is an individual which represents the subset of seismic parameters. In the initial population $p = \{x_1, \ldots, x_N\}$ the first sample x_1 has all the genes equal to 1. The genes were allowed to take either values 0 or 1. A value of 1 implied that the corresponding parameter would be included in the feature subset. The seismic parameter would be excluded from the feature subset if its gene value was set to 0. In our method the negative classification accuracy of the classifiers is equal to the fitness function of the subset. We use the negative classification accuracy because the algorithm selects as elitist individuals the subsets which have the lowest fitness value. The GA was allowed to run for a maximum of 100 generations.

The GA creates three types of children to the next generation. The first type of children is the elite children. These are the best individuals in the previous generation which are guaranteed to survive to the next generation. In this approach the elite children parameter was set to 2. Besides elite children, the algorithm creates the crossover and mutation children. The crossover operation recombines genes from different individuals to produce a superior child. After the crossover the mutation step was used to search through a larger search area to find the best solution. In each generation 80% of the individuals in the population excluding the elite children were created through the crossover operation and the remaining 20% were generated through mutation. Using these parameters it is clear that for a population equal to 20 there are 2 elite children from the previous generation, 14 crossover and 4 mutation children.

3.3 ANN as classifier

In the present study an ANN was used for the classification of seismic signals. This network consists of one input layer, a hidden layer of 17 neurons and one output layer. The proposed classifier is a supervised feed-forward ANN with hyperbolic tangent sigmoid activation function. The first layer presents the inputs on the network. The number of the inputs to the first layer is not fixed. All the individuals from the GA are passed through the ANN to estimate the classification accuracy of them and their fitness function. Each time the inputs are equal to the number of genes which their value is set to 1. The number of output units is fixed to four, since four are the categories of possible damages. During the training of the ANN a set of representative vector samples have been used. Then the ANN was simulated using the entire set of seismic signals to evaluate the classification performance. Each time a seismic signal was represented in ANN with the set of seismic parameters according to the individuals of the GA. During the supervised training process whenever a training vector appears, the output of the neuron, which represents the class, where the input belongs, is set to 1 and all the rest outputs are set to 0. The training algorithm for the network is the Levenberg/Marquardt (LM) and is described in [7] in more detail.

3.4 The neuro-fuzzy classifier

The last method for the classification of damages in structures is a neuro-fuzzy approach. This system combines the fuzzy set theory and the ANNs. The neuro-fuzzy system has six layers. The first layer is the input layer where the inputs corespond to the subset of seismic parameters that represent the individual of the GA. The second layer implements the fuzzification process. Each neuron in the second layer represents a membership function. The key point of this step is the fuzzyfication of the inputs using four membership functions for each intensity parameter.

The next layer of the classifier consists of fuzzy rules. Each neuron corresponds to a fuzzy rule. The number of rules is related with the volume of the training samples (training accelerograms). The last three layers comprise an embedded ANN. The inputs of the embedded ANN are the firing strength of rules according to the input seismic sample and the output declares the winning class.

4 Results

After the nonlinear dynamic analysis of the structure, for the entire set of artificial accelerograms, three damage indices (DI), namely, the DI of Park/Ang, of Di-Pasquale/Cakmak and the maximum inter-storey drift ratio (MISDR) have been computed. According to the damage indices, the damages caused by seismic signals, were classified in four to classes. In this experiment a total set of 450 artificial accelerograms have been used. The representation of the artificial accelerograms has been studied using different subsets (individuals) of the twenty intensity parameters. Each individual is a 1x20 bit matrix.

Due to the bit string type of individuals the total number of the possible candidate solution is 2^{20}. A GA with a population of 20 individuals was employed and executed for a maximum number of 100 generations. This means that the GA searches for the optimal feature selection and tests up to 2000 possible solutions. Using only the selection process in the GA without the crossover and mutation step it will create a negative effect on the convergence. On the other hand using mutation alone is similar to a random search. The GA has been used once time for each of the damage indices. Two types of classifiers have been used to estimate the fitness function of the GA. Tables 1 and 2 show the classification rates for the three damage indicators. Fig. 1 presents the total best individuals for the representation of seismic signals using the MISDR and DI of DiPasquale/Cakmak.

Table 1. Classification results using GA and ANN.

	MISDR	DI of DiPasquale/Cakmak	DI of Park/Ang
Number of unknown samples	450	450	450
Number of intensity parameters	13	13	13
Number of well recognized samples	417	410	408
Total % of the recognized vectors	92,60%	91,10%	90,66%

Table 2. Classification results using Neuro-Fuzzy System.

	MISDR	DI of DiPasquale/Cakmak	DI of Park/Ang
Number of unknown samples	450	450	450
Number of intensity parameters	13	13	13
Number of well recognized samples	415	404	410
Total % of the recognized vectors	90,21%	89,70%	91,10%

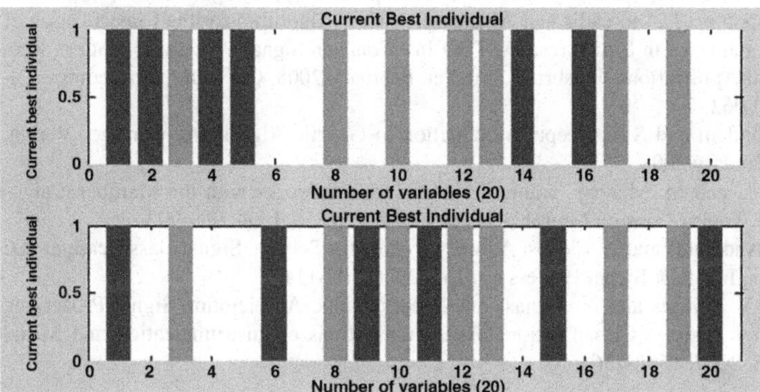

Fig. 1. Seven common Intensity Parameters.

5 Conclusions

GAs are a popular tool in Artificial Intelligence applications. It is well known that GAs can be used for feature extraction. With the use of GAs this approach examined the structural seismic damages in buildings. A training set of 450 artificial accelerograms with known damage effects was used to derive the parameters which are able to describe the seismic intensity. The proposed algorithm was based on a set of seismic parameters. The advantage of this approach is that the proposed algorithm was able to produce high level classification accuracy using a subset of seismic features. The number of intensity parameters was reduced from 20 to 13. The experimental results show that the classification rates are better from previous studies [8, 9]. It was demonstrated, that the algorithm developed herein, presents classification rates up to 92%. The results prove the effectiveness of the proposed algorithm. Until today, survey is performed with on-site examination by expert engineers. With the proposed technique engineers will have an additional tool which can guide them to a faster and more confident estimation of the structural adequacy of constructions.

References

1. E. DiPasquale and A.S. Cakmak, On the relation between local and global damage indices, Technical Report NCEER-89-0034, State University of New York at Buffalo, 1989.
2. Y.J. Park and A.H.S. Ang, Mechanistic seismic damage model for reinforced concrete, Journal of Structural Engineering 111, 1985, 722-739.
3. Elenas and K. Meskouris, Correlation study Between Seismic Acceleration Parameters and Damage Indices of Structures, Engineering Structures 23, 2001, 698-704.
4. Elenas, Correlation between Seismic Acceleration Parameters and Overall Structural Damage Indices of Buildings, Soil Dynamics and Earthquake Engineering, 20, 2000, 93-100.
5. P. Alvanitopoulos, I. Andreadis and A. Elenas, A New Algorithm for the Classification of Earthquake damages in Structures, IASTED Int. Conf. on Signal Processing, Pattern Recognition and Applications, Innsbruck, Austria, February 2008, CD ROM Proceedings, Paper No. 599-062.
6. S.N. Sivanandam and S.N. Deepa, Introduction to Genetic Algorithms, Springer Verlag, Germany, January 2008.
7. Hagan, M.T., and M. Menhaj, Training feed-forward networks with the Marquardt algorithm, IEEE Transactions on Neural Networks, Vol. 5, No. 6, 1994, 989-993.
8. Tsiftzis, I. Andreadis and A. Elenas, A Fuzzy System for Seismic Signal classification, IEE Proc. Vision, Image & Signal Processing, 153, 2006, 109-114.
9. Andreadis, Y. Tsiftzis and A. Elenas, Intelligent Seismic Acceleration Signal Processing for Structural Damage Classification, IEEE Transactions on Instrumentation and Measurement, 56, 2007, 1555-1564.

Mining Retail Transaction Data for Targeting Customers with Headroom - A Case Study

Madhu Shashanka and Michael Giering

Abstract We outline a method to model customer behavior from retail transaction data. In particular, we focus on the problem of recommending relevant products to consumers. Addressing this problem of filling *holes in the baskets* of consumers is a fundamental aspect for the success of targeted promotion programs. Another important aspect is the identification of customers who are most likely to spend significantly and whose potential spending ability is not being fully realized. We discuss how to identify such customers with *headroom* and describe how relevant product categories can be recommended. The data consisted of individual transactions collected over a span of 16 months from a leading retail chain. The method is based on Singular Value Decomposition and can generate significant value for retailers.

1 Introduction

Recommender systems have recently gained a lot of attention both in industry and academia. In this paper, we focus on the applications and utility of recommender systems for brick-and-mortar retailers. We address the problem of identifying shoppers with high potential spending ability and presenting them with relevant offers/promotions that they would most likely participate in. The key to successfully answering this question is a system that, based on a shopper's historical spending behavior and shopping behaviors of others who have a similar shopping profile, can predict the product categories and amounts that the shopper would spend in the future. We present a case study of a project that we completed for a large retail chain. The goal of the project was to mine the transaction data to understand shopping behavior and target customers who exhibit *headroom* - the unmet spending potential of a shopper in a given retailer.

The paper is organized as follows. Section 2 presents an overview of the project and Section 3 provides a mathematical formulation of the problem. After presenting

---

Please use the following format when citing this chapter:

Shashanka, M. and Giering, M., 2009, in IFIP International Federation for Information Processing, Volume 296; *Artificial Intelligence Applications and Innovations III*; Eds. Iliadis, L., Vlahavas, I., Bramer, M.; (Boston: Springer), pp. 347–355.

a brief technical background in Section 4, we present details of the methodology and implementation in Section 5. We end the paper with conclusions in Section 6.

2 Project Overview - Dataset and Project Goals

Data from every transaction from over 350 stores of a large retail chain gathered over a period of 16 months was provided to us. Data is restricted to transactions of regular shoppers who used a "loyalty card" that could track them across multiple purchases. For every transaction completed at the checkout, we had the following information: date and time of sale, the receipt number (*ticket number*), loyalty-card number of the shopper (*shopper number*), the product purchased (given by the *product number*), product quantity and the total amount, and the store (identified by the *store number*) where the transaction took place. A single shopping trip by a customer at a particular store would correspond to several records with the same shopper number, the same store number, and the same ticket number, with each record corresponding to a different product in the shopping cart. There were 1,888,814 distinct shoppers who shopped in all the stores in the period of data collection.

Along with the transaction data, we were also given a *Product Description Hierarchy* (PDH). The PDH is a tree structure with 7 distinct levels. At level 7, each leaf corresponds to an individual product item. Level 0 corresponds to the root-node containing all 296,387 items. The number of categories at the intermediate levels, 1 through 6, were 9, 50, 277, 1137, 3074 and 7528 respectively. All analysis referred to in this paper was performed at level 3 (denoted as L_3 henceforth).

There were two main aspects in the project. The first was to identify those shoppers who were not spending enough to reflect their *spending potential*. These could be shoppers who have significant disposable income and who could be persuaded to spend more or regular shoppers who use the retail chain to fulfill only a part of their shopping needs. In both cases, the customers have *headroom*, i.e. unrealized spending potential.

Once headroom customers have been identified, the next logical step is to find out product categories that would most likely interest them and to target promotions at this group. This is the problem of filling *holes in the baskets*, by motivating them to buy additional products that they are not currently shopping for. In many respects this is similar to a movie recommender problem, where instead of movie watching history and movie ratings of each person, we have the shopping history and spends.

3 Mathematical Formulation

In this section, we introduce mathematical notation and formulate the problem. Let S_{cpm} denote the amount spent by shopper c in the product category p during month m, and n_{cpm} denote the number of items bought in that product category. For the purposes of clarity and simplicity, let us denote the indices $\{c,p,m\}$ by the variable τ. In other words, each different value taken by τ corresponds to a different value of the triplet $\{c,p,m\}$. Let us define the quantity *Spend Per Item* (SPI) as $I_\tau = (S_\tau / n_\tau)$. The above above quantities can be represented as 3-dimensional matrices **S**, **n** and **I** respectively, where the three dimensions correspond to shoppers, product categories and months. These matrices are highly sparse with entries missing for those values of $\tau = \{c,p,m\}$ that correspond to no data in the data set (i.e. items that were not bought by shoppers). Let τ_0 represent the set of values of $\{c,p,m\}$ for which there is no data and let τ_1 represent the set of values of $\{c,p,m\}$ for which data is present, i.e. $\tau = \{\tau_0 \cup \tau_1\}$.

The first problem is to estimate each shopping household's unrealized spending potential in product categories that they haven't bought. This information can then be used for targeting and promotions. Mathematically, the problem is to estimate $\mathbf{S}_{\tau_0}$ given the values in $\mathbf{S}_{\tau_1}$.

The second problem is to identify a set of shoppers who have headroom. Although subjective, the most common usage of this term refers to customers who have additional spending potential or who are not using a retailer to fill shopping needs that could be met there. There are many possible proxy measures of headroom, each focusing on different aspects of shopping behavior. We chose to derive four of these headroom metrics[1] - (a) total actual spend, (b) total actual SPI, (c) residue between model spend and actual spend, and (d) frequency of shopping.

For ease of comparison between the metrics and for the purpose of consolidating them later, we express each metric for all the shoppers in probabilistic terms. Our first three metrics are well suited for representation as *standard z-scores*. The frequency metric requires a mapping to express it as a *standard z-score*. For every metric, we choose a value range and define shoppers with *z*-scores in this range as exhibiting headroom. Section 5 details how the scores are consolidated.

4 Background: Singular Value Decomposition

The Singular Value Decomposition (SVD) factorizes an $M \times N$ matrix **X** into two orthogonal matrices **U**, **V** and a diagonal matrix $\mathbf{S} = diag(\mathbf{s})$ such that

$$\mathbf{USV}^T = \mathbf{X} \quad \text{and} \quad \mathbf{U}^T\mathbf{XV} = \mathbf{S}. \tag{1}$$

The elements of **s** are the *singular values* and the columns of **U**, **V** are the left and right *singular vectors* respectively. The matrices are typically arranged such that the diagonal entries of **S** are non-negative and in decreasing order. The M-dimensional columns of **U**, $\{\mathbf{u}_1, \mathbf{u}_2, \ldots, \mathbf{u}_M\}$, form an orthonormal matrix and correspond to a linear basis for **X**'s columns (span the *column space* of **X**). Also, the N-dimensional

[1] These metrics can be measured separately for each product category if desired. We mention the overall metrics across categories for the sake of simplicity in exposition.

rows of $\mathbf{V}^T$, $\{\mathbf{v}_1, \mathbf{v}_2, \ldots, \mathbf{v}_N\}$, form an orthonormal matrix and correspond to vectors that span the *row space* of $\mathbf{X}$.

Given a data matrix $\mathbf{X}$, a reduced rank SVD decomposition $\mathbf{U}_{M\times R}\mathbf{S}_{R\times R}\mathbf{V}^T_{R\times N} = \mathbf{X}_{M\times N}$, where $R < min(M,N)$ is an approximate reconstruction of the input. This *thin* SVD is also the best rank-R approximation of $\mathbf{X}$ in the least squares sense. The singular values are indicative of the the significance of the corresponding row/column singular vectors in reconstructing the data. The square of each singular value is proportional to the variance explained by each singular vector. This allows one to determine a rank for the desired decomposition to express predetermined percentage of the information (variance) of the data set for approximation. In practice, data is typically centered at the origin to remove centroid bias. In this case, SVD can be interpreted as a Gaussian covariance model.

SVD for Recommendation

Several well-known recommender systems are based on SVD and the related method of Eigenvalue decomposition (eg. [6, 2]). Let the matrix $\mathbf{X}$ represent a matrix of consumer spends over a given period. Each of the N columns represents a different shopper and each of the M rows represents a different product. X_{mn}, the mn-th entry in the matrix, represents how much shopper n spent on product m. Consider the k-rank SVD $\mathbf{U}'\mathbf{S}'\mathbf{V}'^T \approx \mathbf{X}$. The subspace spanned by the columns of $\mathbf{U}'$ can be interpreted as the k most important types of "shopping profiles" and a location can be computed for each shopper in this *shopping profile space*. The relationship between $\mathbf{x}_n$, the n-th column of $\mathbf{X}$ representing the spends of the n-th shopper, and his/her location in the shopping profile space given by a k-dimensional vector $\mathbf{p}_n$ is given by $\mathbf{p}_n = \mathbf{U}'^T\mathbf{x}_n$. It is easy to show that $\mathbf{p}_n$ is given by the n-th row of the matrix $\mathbf{V}'\mathbf{S}'$. This vector $\mathbf{p}_n$ underlies all SVD-based recommender systems, the idea is to estimate $\mathbf{p}_n$ and thus obtain imputed values for missing data in $\mathbf{x}_n$. This also enables one to identify shoppers with similar shopping profiles by measuring the distance between their locations in the *shopping profile space* [6, 7]. Similarly, the *product space* given by columns of $\mathbf{V}'$ show how much each product is liked/disliked by shoppers belonging to the various shopping profiles. These subspaces are very useful for subsequent analysis such as clustering and visualization.

Despite its advantages, the main practical impediment to using a thin SVD with large data sets is the cost of computing it. Most standard implementations are based in Lanczos or Ritz-Raleigh iterations that do not scale well with large data sets. Such methods require multiple passes through the entire data set to converge. Several methods have been proposed to overcome this problem for fast and efficient SVD computations [3, 5]. In this paper, we use the iterative incremental SVD implementation (IISVD) [2, 1] which can handle large data sets with missing values. Details of the implementation are beyond the scope of this paper.

5 Methodology

Data Preprocessing

For our retail sales data, the assumption of log-normal distribution of spend and spend per item on each L_3 product category and for the overall data are very good. There are always issues of customers shopping across stores, customers buying for large communities and other anomalous sales points. We first eliminate these outliers from further analysis. We screen shoppers based on four variables - the total spend amount, the number of shopping trips, the total number of items bought, and the total number of distinct products bought. The log-distribution for each variable showed us that the distributions were close to normal, but containing significant outlier tails corresponding to roughly 5% of the data on either end of the distribution. All the shoppers who fall in the extreme 5% tails are eliminated. This process reduces the number of shoppers from 1,888,814 to 1,291,114.

The remaining data is log-normalized and centered. The relatively small divergence from normality at this point is acceptable for the justification of using the SVD method (which assumes Gaussian data) to model the data.

Clustering

A key to accurate modeling of retail data sets of this size is the ability to break the data into subsegments with differing characteristics. Modeling each segment separately and aggregating the smaller models gives significant gains in accuracy. In previous work [4] we utilized demographic, firmographic and store layout information to aid in segmentation. In this project, we derived our segments solely from shopping behavior profiles.

Shopping behavior profiles are generated by expressing each shopper's cumulative spend for each L_3 product category in percentage terms. The main reason for considering percentage spends is that it masks the effect of the shopper household size on the magnitude of spend and focuses on the relative spend in different L_3 categories. For example, shoppers with large families spend more compared to a shopper who is single and lives alone. We believe that this approach produces information more useful for discriminating between consumer lifestyles.

We begin by creating a 150×1 vector[2] of percent spends per L_3 category. A dense matrix $\mathbf{X}$ containing one column for each shopper is constructed. We generate the SVD decomposition, $\mathbf{X} = \mathbf{USV}^T$, using IISVD.

From experience we know that we can assume a noise content in retail data of more than 15 percent. Using this as a rough threshold, we keep only as many singular vectors whose cumulative variance measures sum to less than 85 percent of the overall data variance. In other words, the rank we choose for the approximation $\mathbf{U'S'V'}^T$ is the minimum value of k such that $(\sum_{i=1}^{k} s_i^2)/(\sum_{i=1}^{150} s_i^2) \geq 0.85$. We

[2] We were asked to analyze only a subset of 150 from among the total 277 categories.

computed the rank to be 26. As we mentioned earlier in Section 4, the rows of matrix $\mathbf{V}'\mathbf{S}'$ correspond to locations of shoppers in this 26-dimensional *shopping profile space*. We segment the shoppers by running K-means clustering on the rows of this matrix. By setting a minimum cluster distance, we limited the number of distinct clusters to 23. Characterizing each cluster to better understand the differentiating customer characteristics unique to each cluster was not carried out. This time intensive process can provide significant efficiencies and be valuable for projects designed to accommodate iterative feedback.

Imputation of Missing Values

Consider $\mathbf{S}$, the 3-D matrix of spends by all shoppers across product categories and across months. We unroll the dimensions along p (product categories) and m (months) into a single dimension of size $|p| \times |m|$.

We now consider each cluster separately. Let $\mathbf{X}$ refer to the resulting sparse 2-D matrix of spends of shoppers within a cluster. Let τ_1 and τ_0 represent indices corresponding to known and unknown values respectively. The non-zero data values of the matrix, $\mathbf{X}_{\tau_1}$, have normal distributions that make SVD very suitable for modeling. Depending on the goal of the analysis, the unknown values $\mathbf{X}_{\tau_0}$ can be viewed as data points with zeros or as missing values.

Treating these as missing values and imputing values using the SVD gives us an estimate that can be interpreted as how much a customer would buy if they chose to meet that shopping need. Again, this is analogous to the approach taken in movie recommender problems. We use IISVD for the imputation and compute full-rank decompositions. Given a sparse matrix $\mathbf{X}$, IISVD begins by reordering the rows and columns of an initial sample of data to form the largest dense matrix possible. SVD is performed on this dense data and is then iteratively "grown" step by step as more rows and columns are added. IISVD provides efficient and accurate algorithms for performing rank-1 modifications to an existing SVD such as updating, downdating, revising and recentering. It also provides efficient ways to compute approximate fixed-rank updates, see [2] for a more detailed treatment. This process is repeated for each of the 23 clusters of shoppers separately and imputed values $\hat{\mathbf{X}}_{\tau_0}$ are obtained. The imputed spends for a shopper are equivalent to a linear mixture of the spends of all shoppers within the cluster, weighted by the correlations between their spends and spends of the current shopper.

Note that if we now use this filled data set and impute the value of a known data point, the imputed values of the missing data have no effect on the solution because they already lie on the SVD regression hyperplane.

Headroom Model

The next step is to measure of how each shopper is over-spending or under-spending in each L_3 subcategory. Overspending corresponds to the degree by which a shopper's spend differs from the expected value given by the SVD imputation of non-zero data.

Using the filled shopper-L_3 spend data $\hat{\mathbf{X}}_{\tau_0}$, we remove 10% of the known data values and impute new values using a thin SVD algorithm [2]. The thin SVD method we use determines the optimal rank for minimizing the error of imputation by way of a cross validation method. Because of this, the reduced rank used to model each cluster and even differing portions of the same cluster can vary. A result of this as shown in [4] is that the error of a model aggregated from these parts has much lower error than modeling all of the data at the same rank. This process is repeated for all known spend values $\mathbf{X}_{\tau_1}$ and model estimates $\hat{\mathbf{X}}_{\tau_1}$ are calculated.

The residues, differences between known spends $\mathbf{X}_{\tau_1}$ and modeled spends $\hat{\mathbf{X}}_{\tau_1}$, are normally distributed and hence can be expressed as Z-scores. Figure 1 illustrates the normality for percent errors in a given cluster. Figure 2 shows the normality plot of the data. The preponderance of points exhibit a normal distribution while the tail extremes diverge from normality.

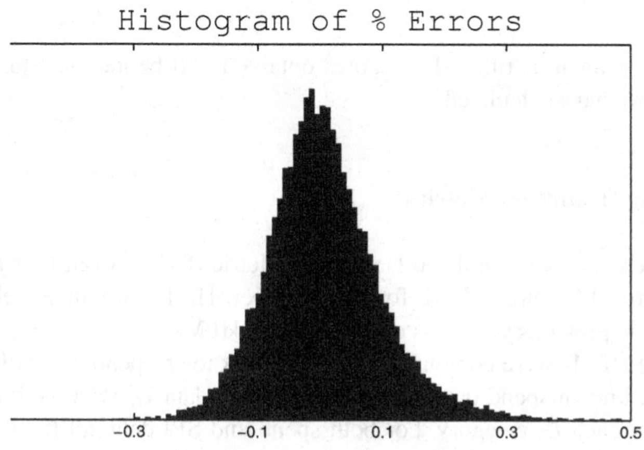

Fig. 1 Histogram of Percent Errors. The difference between the imputed spend values $\hat{\mathbf{S}}_{\tau_1}$ and known spend values $\mathbf{S}_{\tau_1}$ is expressed in terms of percentages. Figure shows that distribution is close to a Gaussian.

Observing the root-mean-squared error of the imputed known values $\hat{\mathbf{X}}_{\tau_1}$ for each L_3 category gives a clear quantification of the relative confidence we can have across L_3 product categories.

The model z-scores generated in this process can be interpreted as a direct probabilistic measure of shopper over-spending/under-spending for each L_3 category. One can do a similar analysis for SPI data and obtain z-scores in the same fashion. How-

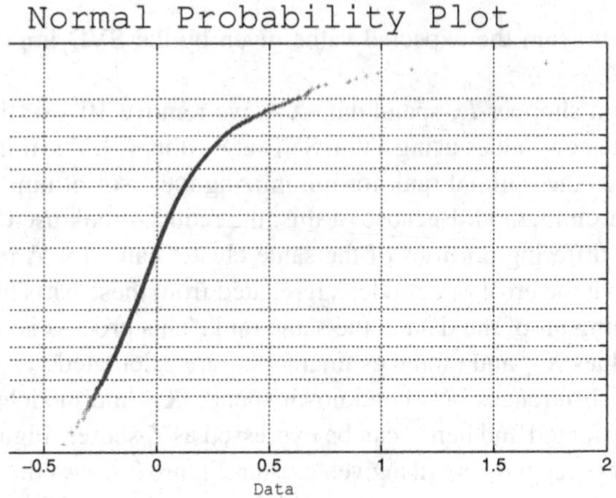

Fig. 2 A normality plot of the percent error data.

ever, it can be shown that the SPI z-scores obtained will be identical to the spend z-scores that we have calculated[3].

Consolidating Headroom Metrics

We chose to create a Consolidated Headroom Metric (CHM) from four individual Headroom Proxy Measures (HPM) for each shopper. The headroom model Z-scores described in the previous section is one of the four HPMs.

Two of the HPMs were computed directly from known spend and SPI data. For each shopper, known spend data $\mathbf{S}_{\tau_1}$ and known SPI data $\mathbf{I}_{\tau_1}$ were both expressed as z-scores for each L_3 category. For both spend and SPI data, all the L_3 z-scores for each shopper were summed, weighted by the percentage spends of the shopper across L_3 categories. The resulting z-scores are the Spend Headroom Metric and the SPI Headroom Metric respectively.

Lastly, we included the shopping frequency of each shopper. Although not a strong proxy for customer headroom, it is of value in identifying which customers with headroom to pursue for targeted marketing and promotions. By determining the probability of shopping frequencies from the frequency probability distribution function, we can map each shopping frequency to a z-score, which then acts as the fourth HPM. This enables us to combine information across all four of our headroom proxy measures.

[3] We model the spend in categories that a customer has shopped in by making a reasonable assumption that the number of items of different products bought will not change. Thus any increase/decrease in total spend is equivalent in percentage terms to the increase/decrease in SPI.

For each of the HPMs, we select the shoppers corresponding to the top 30% of the z-score values. The union of these sets is identified as the screened set of customers with the greatest likelihood of exhibiting headroom.

The Consolidated Headroom Metric for each shopper is created by a weighted sum across each of our four HPMs. In this project, we chose to apply equal weights and computed the CHM as the mean of the four HPMs. However, one could subjectively choose to emphasize different HPMs depending on the analysis goals.

6 Conclusions

In this paper, we presented the case-study of a retail data mining project. The goal of the project was to identify shoppers who exhibit headroom and target them with product categories they would most likely spend on. We described details of the SVD-based recommender system and showed how to identify customers with high potential spending ability. Due to the customers' demand for mass customization in recent years, it has become increasingly critical for retailers to be a step ahead by better understanding consumer needs and by being able to offer promotions/products that would interest them. The system proposed in this paper is a first step in that endeavor. Based on the results of a similar highly successful project that we completed for another retailer previously [4], we believe that with a few iterations of this process and fine tuning based on feedback from sales and promotions performance, it can be developed into a sophisticated and valuable retail tool.

Acknowledgements The authors would like to thank Gil Jeffer for his database expertise and valuable assistance in data exploration.

References

1. M. Brand. Incremental Singular Value Decomposition of Uncertain Data with Missing Values. In *European Conf on Computer Vision*, 2002.
2. M. Brand. Fast Online SVD Revisions for Lightweight Recommender Systems. In *SIAM Intl Conf on Data Mining*, 2003.
3. S. Chandrasekaran, B. Manjunath, Y. Wang, J. Winkeler, and H. Zhang. An Eigenspace Update Algorithm for Image Analysis. *Graphical Models and Image Proc.*, 59(5):321–332, 1997.
4. M. Giering. Retail sales prediction and item recommendations using customer demographics at store level. In *KDD 2008 (submitted)*.
5. M. Gu and S. Eisenstat. A Stable and Fast Algorithm for Updating the Singular Value Decomposition. Technical Report YALEU/DCS/RR-966, Yale University, 1994.
6. D. Gupta and K. Goldberg. Jester 2.0: A linear time collaborative filtering algorithm applied to jokes. In *Proc. of SIGIR*, 1999.
7. B. Sarwar, G. Karypis, J. Konstan, and J. Riedl. Application of dimensionality reduction in recommender system - a case study. In *Web Mining for ECommerce*, 2000.

Adaptive Electronic Institutions for Negotiations

Manolis Sardis, George Vouros

University of the Aegean, Department of Information & Communication Systems Engineering, 83200 Karlovassi, Samos, Greece,

WWW home page: http://www.icsd.aegean.gr

emails: sardis@aegean.gr, georgev@aegean.gr

Abstract The expansion of web technologies pushes human activities over methodologies and software that could ease reactions by means of software transactions. Distribution of human and software agents over the web and their operation under dynamically changing conditions necessitate the need for dynamic intelligent environments. Electronic institutions can play an "umbrella" role for agents' transactions, where institutions' norms could protect and support movements and decisions made through negotiations. However, dynamic information provision may force changes in structures and behaviors, driving electronic institutions' adaptation to changing needs. Viewing negotiation structures as electronic institutions, this paper investigates the impact of a dynamically changing environment to negotiations' electronic institutions.

1 Introduction

The transformation of human transactions into electronic transactions is not an easy task, especially when the rules of the game are not moldable into specific rules and constraints, and when dynamically-appearing information affects these transactions. In this paper we investigate the development of environments for adaptive negotiations, through the incorporation of sources of dynamic information, by utilizing electronic institutions (eIs) [1], [5].

The changes in business conditions most of the times follow the news' speed, which is the main factor for making business negotiations adaptive, as future market situations could be affected from these news: Therefore, during negotiations the involved parties have to be informed online for specific news that could affect their rules of decision, their strategies and their actions. In human transactions, consultation of dynamically-appearing information is out of the negotiation table especially when the involved parties are in the final stage of negotiation, or when

Please use the following format when citing this chapter:

Sardis, M. and Vouros, G., 2009, in IFIP International Federation for Information Processing, Volume 296; *Artificial Intelligence Applications and Innovations III*; Eds. Iliadis, L., Vlahavas, I., Bramer, M.; (Boston: Springer), pp. 357–364.

it cannot be utilized effectively in real time: The dossier of negotiating parties with all the available "movements" and rules almost is fixed. It is the aim of this paper to investigate the incorporation of dynamically provided information and its effects in negotiations' structure and function by means of electronic institutions' constructs.

In our case study we deal with a traditional chartering task, where Shipowners and Cargo owners have to reach, in a best price and under certain conditions and terms, an agreement for a contract for the transferring of cargoes. Let us consider five Shipowners' brokers, which have started negotiating with a specific cargo-owner to conclude in a contract [4]. During the negotiation procedure one Shipowner was informed that its vessel had stopped operating and that could delay its arrival in the cargo port. The remaining Shipowners' brokers continue to negotiate with the cargo owner, when again a market change or a specific exceptional occasion near the cargo destination pushed them to start the whole procedure under the light of the new conditions. Such conditions are affecting the negotiation procedures either by changing participants' strategic decisions and their related actions, or by militate against their scopes. In the worst case a participant could leave the process and search for a new negotiation place. The above generic scenario in the maritime sector is happening many times during negotiations and most of the times the negotiating partners are not in the position to control and filter external info/news that could affect their decisions in real-time. Being motivated by this real-life problem we are investigating the use of a framework that could support solving this type of negotiation problems by means of adaptive environments.

The paper is structured as follows: Section 2 analyzes the electronic negotiations and the missing adaptability. Section 3 proposes eIs as a solution for adaptive negotiations, and according to structure eIs we present the adaptation that can offer. Finally, in Section 4 conclusions and remarks are finalizing the paper structure giving future research topics.

2 Electronic Negotiations

In electronic negotiations, software agents prepare bids for and evaluate offers on behalf of the parties they represent, aiming to obtain the maximum benefit for their owners, following specific negotiation strategies. When building autonomous agents capable of sophisticated and flexible negotiation, the following areas should be considered [4]: (a) negotiation protocol and model to be adopted, (b) issues over which negotiation will take place, (c) events affect the negotiation process and drive adaptability, (d) negotiation strategies employed by agents, under what conditions, and how will be implemented and adapted to changing circumstances. Given the wide variety of possibilities for negotiations, there is no universally best approach or technique for supporting automated negotiations [8]. Protocols, models and strategies need to be set according to the prevailing situations and to adapt accordingly based on new information. The change of negotiation conditions can move the whole negotiation phase in its starting point, maybe causing the adoption of new negotiation protocol/strategies for the involved parties. We consider a generic negotiation environment, covering multi-issue contracts and multi-party situations, where negotiators face strict deadlines: However we deal with a highly dynamic environment, in the sense that its variables, attributes and objectives may change over time. The trigger to this change is the time and the influence on chartering markets of external factors including catastrophes; political crises; environmental disasters; aid programmes. Dynamic changes of variables and conditions that affect negotiations cannot be easily incorporated in human negotiations' transactions. This paper concentrates on the incorporation of these changes in adaptive electronic negotiations in business-to-business (B2B) marketplaces through eIs. The negotiating agents may be divided into *Buyer_Agents*, *Seller_Agents* and *Information_Provision_Agents*. The *Buyer_Agents* (BA) and the *Seller_Agents* (SA) are considered to be self-interested, aiming to maximize their owners' profit. The *Information_Provision_Agents* (IPA) are signaling new events and the changing of conditions (eg. world news, market changes, etc.), that may affect the negotiation procedure or the participation of the negotiation agents.

The proposed infrastructure for using eIs for the modeling of adaptive negotiation structures is depicted in "Fig. 1". Negotiations may adapt as a function of *Time* and *News Information*. Adaptation applies to negotiation areas (NA) and results in a new negotiation area: In the initialization of the negotiation phase (NA 2), negotiation involves five buyer agents (BA) and one seller agent (SA). Some of the BAs are also connected with their information provision agents (IPA): It is not necessary all BA and SA agents to be connected with an IPA agent. Each NA is specified to be an eI. As the conditions are changing, NAs adapt to new structures resulting to a different institution structure: From (NA 2) the negotiating procedures are moved into (NA 2.1) where different eI(i,j,...n) structures control the negotiation conditions and rules.

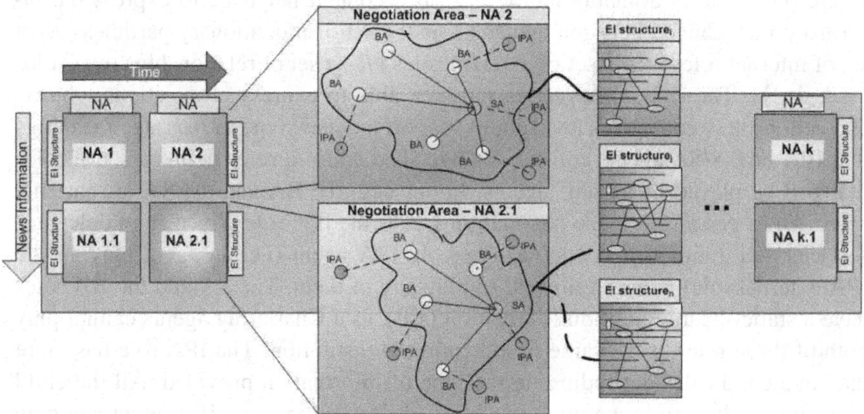

Fig. 1, Adaptive Negotiation Areas in the context of eIs

In the following paragraphs we are analyzing the points of the eIs infrastructure that can be adapted.

3 Adaptive eIs for Negotiations

This section describes how the different constituents of an eI may change due to eI's adaptation to new information provided.

3.1 eIs Roles

The main involved agents' roles in the eI structures are the already presented: BA, SA, and IPA. As in real life conditions, one or more IPA agents may provide information to a BA/SA agent, changing its behavior or strategy during the negotiation. IPA agents are reactive to stimuli from the environment. The BA and SA agents are agents of arbitrary complexity, as they can act autonomously and are able to achieve complex tasks, helping their human peers to achieve their goals and fulfill their commitments. The number of agents participating in the negotiation may change. BA agents may join or leave the negotiation: This may be caused by any condition considered by a BA (for instance a condition that negates its motivation to participate in the negotiation). This is also true for the SA: However its decision to abandon negotiation signals that dissolution of the current negotiation structure. IPA agents may also be dynamically connected or disconnected to BAs or SAs. Also, when the negotiation conditions are not complying with agents' goals, both agents' types (BA/SA) may leave the negotiating area.

3.2 Dialogical Framework Adaptability

The Dialogical Framework [9] for the negotiation area is defined to be

$$DF = <O, L, I, R_I, R_E, R_S>$$

where (O, is the eI domain ontology | L, is a content language to express the information exchanged between agents | I, is the set of illocutionary particles | R_I, a set of internal roles | R_E, a set of external roles | R_S, a set of relationships over roles {ssd, dsd}). The *content language* must be able to express propositions, objects and actions between agents and should support any new type of message meanings that IPA or BA/SA agents could exchange. The *internal* roles define a set of roles that will be played by eI staff agents. In our case the BA and the SA are internal roles. An *external* role in the negotiation area is the IPA role. Since an eI delegates services and duties to the internal roles, an IPA agent (i.e. an agent playing the IPA external role) is never allowed to play any of them. The SA and the BA roles have a static separation of duties relation (ssd), as e-Chartering agents cannot play both of these roles at the same time within the institution. The IPA role has more than one child roles depending on the type of information provided. All the child roles have a dynamic separation of duties (dsd) relation as an IPA agent can play any of these roles. In each negotiating area, at least one eI describes the negotiation structure and function. Each eI is using a dialogical framework to support the involved agents with the type of illocutions exchanged during the negotiation *scenes*. The external information will trigger the eI adaptability, informing agents playing internal roles. This may cause a transformation to a possibly new negotiation structure: This may cause changes in the number of involved agents, and changes in the agents' aims (e.g. utility functions) and negotiation constraints.

3.3 Negotiation Protocol

Although there are many works studying multi-issues negotiations carried out by autonomous agents [3], [6], [11], [12], we consider a generic framework for automated negotiation on multiple issues [8]. During the negotiation process there are several aspects that even though their values are not under negotiation and are not included in the contract parameters, affect the evaluation of the values of the contract issues. These aspects may consider the number of the competitor companies, information affecting the contract parameters, time until the negotiation deadline expires, resources availability and restrictions, and their impact to contract issues, etc. All the above issues are named *Adaptation Issues* (AIs). The values of the AIs may change over time, depending on the e-marketplace conditions and on the Sellers' and Buyers' state. The AIs affect the evaluation of the potential contracts, and they have an impact on the generation of subsequent offers and requests. The values of the AIs (imported by the IPA agents) do not depend on the actions of the negotiating parties, although they may affect one or both negotiators' decisions. AIs values should have a direct influence on the behavior of the negotiating agents, which should be able to evaluate the utility of the contracts under the current circumstances in the e-marketplace and act accordingly. From the above, it is clear that the negotiation protocol which supports and maintains the procedures that agents should follow in each eI, will not be affected in structure but only in time constraints that each agent reacts.

3.4 Scenes

The negotiation procedure comprises phases that can be modeled by scenes in an eI. A scene is a pattern of multi-agent interaction. A scene protocol is specified by a finite state oriented graph, where the nodes represent the different states and oriented arcs are labeled with *illocution schemes* or *timeouts*. Scenes allow agents either to enter or to leave a scene at some particular states of an ongoing conversation and can substantiate a negotiation procedure by splitting it in more than one scene. Its negotiation protocol has a defined scenes structure. The negotiation infrastructure that related agents follow is translated through the eI in a set of defined scenes graph. Scenes are the key points for eI's adaptability, as the AIs conditions affect the structure of the scenes graph.

3.5 Performative Structure

Based on [7], the parameters, upon which the performative structure of each eI in the proposed framework will be based, are as follows: *The negotiation model* (privacy of information, privacy of tactics and strategies, two-sided-uncertainty in negotiation, stochastic negotiation strategy)[2][10]. *Tactics and strategies* (time dependent, resource depended, behaviour depended). *Cost of agreement*, agents have to decide not only which tactic to choose next, but also whether it is worthwhile to go on with the negotiation. An agent under time pressure acts differently than an agent with no time pressure to reach an agreement. *Strategies*, where the decision trees of the agents decisions will be described. All of these parameters can be adjusted according to dynamically provided information, resulting to new performative structures, or to new agents' individual strategies, validation of proposals, and actions.

3.6 Performative Structure and Transitions

The sequence of scenes through a negotiation procedure is based on an eI performative structure. Each eI must include basic negotiation scenes and the rules that trigger the succession of scenes of the negotiation scenario. Scenes and transitions are connected by means of directed *arcs*. The adaptation of the eI is done by means of the scenes' states as well as by means of scenes' dynamic transitions. In "Fig. 2", the negotiation *scene_k*, includes all the agents in the dialogical framework. Concerning this scene as a particular example, in stage *s_0* all the negotiation agents are being involved. In *s_1* we assume that *role_IPA_BA_market* and *role_IPA_SA_market* are providing information to the agents playing the *role_BA* and the *role_SA*. In this case, the *role_BA* can stay or leave *s_1*. If negotiations move to stage *s_2*, the *role_SA* may leave the stage and the whole negotiation procedure will close in stage *s_3*. This result will drive the performative structure to another scene, possibly the *root* scene. The illocutions matching arcs 1 and 3 are bringing new info for *role_BA* and *role_SA*. During stage *s_1*, the arc 3 presents the import of new info that is adapted into the scene by new *role_IPA_BA_market* or *role_IPA_SA_market*. Also new agents by using *role_BA*, could be inserted into the negotiation stage *s_1*.

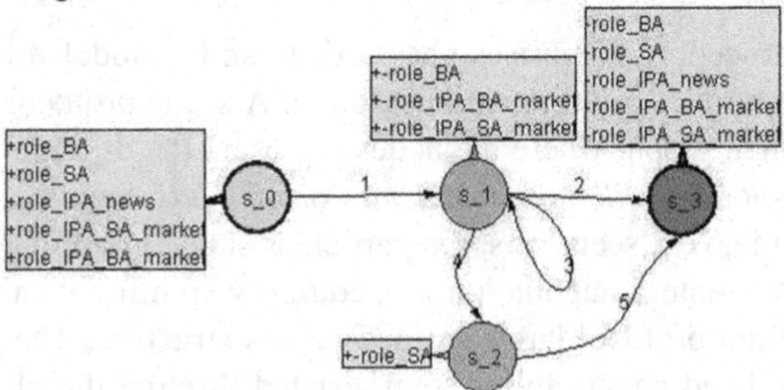

Fig. 2, States of scene_k, using Electronic Institutions Development Environment (EIDE)

Illocutions for arcs 2 and 5 are the transitions for closing negotiation scene. The move from stage *s_1* to stage *s_3* means a positive negotiation result that will be used as an input to a new *scene_l* of the performative structure. The transition arc 4 expresses the attitude of SA agent to leave (*role_SA* live) or stop a negotiation when the conditions from the *role_IPA_SA_market* are not satisfactory and close to its market and profit intentions.

From the above specific example of negotiations through the eIs structure, it is clear that the adaptation could be incorporated during scenes' come round.

3.7 Negotiation Status Snapshots

During the negotiation phases that are involved through the eIs' scenes, the negotiated parties are having the adaptation support of the external IPA agents. The effect of this adaptation could effect the commitment of a contract, with a cancellation or with a new startup using as base the 'snapshot' of the agreements and as a new parameter, the newly added external information. Negotiation status is an information tuple that presents the status of the negotiation phases in a specific time, like a snapshot. During an external event what was previously negotiated and agreed, what were the accepted parts (components and attributes)? This information should be manipulated by the proposed infrastructure giving the opportunity to negotiating parties to restarting with a new session of negotiations following a new possible eI scenario. This snapshot is specified as follows:

Snapshot = <LA, A-P/S, Contract_status >

Snapshot represents a set of agents' commitments. *LA*, represents the list of Agents involved in that contract. *A-P/S*, ties each agent together with the contribution (product or service) that is committed to give. *Contract_status*, presents the agreed attributes of products or services until the time slot, where:

Contract_status=<Pre-cond, Rule-set>, Pre-cond ∈ *{Event, time_slot}*

Event is a specific type of arrived external messages and *time_slot* is a specific point in time that represents current condition.

$Rule\text{-}set = \{<Cond_i, Action_i>\}$

$Cond_i$ is a set of conditions to be checked after *Pre-cond* is true,

$Action_i \in \{Re\_negotiation, Ch\_negotiation\_rules, Cancellation\}$

Re_negotiation, represents the re-negotiation action, *Ch_negotiation_rules* represents the change of the negotiation rules so that the involved parties will follow different eI rules/norms, and *Cancellation_rules*, represents that the external event causes a full abort from the negotiation process, for one or more of the negotiating parties. The above rules are describing the adaptive negotiation phases that the proposed infrastructure should follow to support the adaptability.

4 Concluding Remarks

This paper proposes an infrastructure for adaptive negotiations using the context of eIs. It is analyzing the negotiation aspects and based on a maritime case study tries to analyze all the eI aspects that could support the external information into the negotiation area. In the context of this paper, was investigated the issue of the different eIs structures that should support the negotiation areas. There is a need for a mechanism responsible for the creation of an eI that links different eI structures and negotiation areas. Agents according to their profile characteristics and the negotiation market domain should be forwarded into specific NAs that according to the market constraints will be supported by one or more eI structures. The external info and news adaptability using multi agent systems and through the eIs are an add-on for the electronic negotiations. The design and the creation of a prototype of the proposed infrastructure using technologies that support the adaptability, like Jadex and XML, is our future objective.

References

1. P. Rocha, E. Oliveira, "Electronic Institutions as a framework for Agents' Negotiation and mutual Commitment", Progress in Artificial Intelligence, Springer Berlin / Heidelberg, pp.3-25, (2001)
2. Sierra, P. Faratin, N. R. Jennings, "A Service- Oriented Negotiation Model between Autonomous Agents", In J. Padget (Ed.), Collaboration between Human and Artificial Societies–Coordination and Agent-Based Distributed Computing, LNAI, Vol. 1624, New York, pp. 201-220, (2000)
3. N.C. Karunatillake, N.R. Jennings, I. Rahwan, S.D. Ramchurn, "Managing Social Influences through Argumentation-Based Negotiation", Proceedings 5th International Joint Conference on Autonomous Agents and Multiagent Systems, Hakodate, Japan, pp. 426-428, (2006)
4. M. Sardis, G. Vouros, "Electronic Institutions infrastructure for e-Chartering", Proceedings 8th Annual International Workshop Engineering Societies in the Agents World – ESAW'07, NCSR Demokritos, Greece, (2007)
5. M. Esteva, J. A. Rodriguez, C. Sierra, P. Garcia, and J. L. Arcos, "On the formal specifications of electronic institutions", LNAI Vol. 1991, pp. 126-147, (2001)
6. S.S. Fatima, M.J. Wooldridge, N.R. Jennings, "An agenda-based framework for multi-issue negotiation", Artificial Intelligence 152 (1), pp. 1-45, (2004)
7. F. Teuteberg, K. Kurbel, "Anticipating Agent's Negotiation Strategies in an E-marketplace Using Belief Models", , Proceedings of International Conference on Business Information Systems – BIS'2002, Poznan, Polland, (2002)
8. N.R. Jennings, P. Faratin, A.R. Lomuscio, S. Parsons, M. Sierra, M. Wooldridge, "Automated negotiation: Prospects, methods, and challenges", International Journal of Group Decision and Negotiation 10 (2), pp. 199-215, (2001)
9. J. L. Arcos, M. Esteva, P. Noriega, J. A. Rodriquez-Aguilar, C. Sierra, "Engineering open environments with electronic institutions", In Engineering Applications of Artificial Intelligence 18, Elsevier, pp. 191-204, (2005)
10. K. Kurbel, I. Loutchko, "A Framework for Multiagent Electronic Marketplaces: Analysis and Classification of Existing Systems", Proceedings International ICSC Congress on Information Science Innovations – ISI '2001, American University in Dubai, (2001)
11. Li, G. Tesauro, "A strategic decision model for multi-attribute bilateral negotiation with alternating offers", Proceedings ACM Conference on Electronic Commerce, San Diego, CA, USA, (2003)
12. X. Luo, N.R. Jennings, N. Shadbolt, H. Leung, J.H. Lee, "A fuzzy constraint based model for bilateral multi-issue negotiations in semi-competitive environments", Artificial Intelligence Journal 148 (1-2), pp. 53-102, (2003)

A Multi-agent Task Delivery System for Balancing the Load in Collaborative Grid Environment

Mauricio Paletta[1], and Pilar Herrero[2]

[1] Departamento de Ciencia y Tecnología. Universidad Nacional Experimental de Guayana. Av. Atlántico. Ciudad Guayana. 8050. Venezuela.

mpaletta@uneg.edu.ve

[2] Facultad de Informática. Universidad Politécnica de Madrid. Campus de Montegancedo S/N. 28.660 Boadilla del Monte. Madrid. Spain.

pherrero@fi.upm.es

Abstract This paper focuses on improving load balancing algorithms in grid environments by means of multi-agent systems. The goal is endowing the environment with an efficient scheduling, taking into account not only the computational capabilities of resources but also the task requirements and resource configurations in a given moment. In fact, task delivery makes use of a Collaborative/Cooperative Awareness Management Model (CAM) which provides information of the environment. Next, a Simulated Annealing based method (SAGE) which optimizes the process assignment. Finally, a historic database which stores information about previous cooperation/collaborations in the environment aiming to learn from experience and infer to obtain more suitable future cooperation/collaboration. The integration of these three subjects allows agents define a system to cover all the aspects related with load-balancing problem in collaborations grid environment.

1 Motivation and Related Work

High-performance scheduling is critical to the achievement of application performance on the computational grid [2, 5]. One of its main phases is related to the load balancing problem. An efficient load balancing strategy avoids the situation where some resources are idle while others have multiple jobs queued up. Intensive research has been done in this area and many results have been widely accepted. An interesting reading on the state of the art about this area is given by Fangpeng et al in [4]. Some intelligent agents based approaches for this problem can be found in [3, 7].

However, there are other problems to deal with: 1) the complexity of scheduling problem increases with the size of the grid; 2) the dynamic nature of the grid requires effective and efficient dynamic allocation of available resources tech-

---

Please use the following format when citing this chapter:

Paletta, M. and Herrero, P., 2009, in IFIP International Federation for Information Processing, Volume 296; *Artificial Intelligence Applications and Innovations III*; Eds. Iliadis, L., Vlahavas, I., Bramer, M.; (Boston: Springer), pp. 365–371.

niques [10]; 3) to manage the situation in overloaded conditions. Therefore, a co-operative and dynamic load-balancing strategy becomes highly difficult to solve effectively by taking in consideration these aspects below.

This paper presents a new MAS-based approach to deal with the necessity previously mentioned. The proposal is defined by using some components: 1) awareness management concepts defined in the CAM (Collaborative/ Cooperative Awareness Management) [8] model; 2) a heuristic technique used to optimize the resources-processes assignments needed, named SAGE (Simulated Annealing to cover dynamic load balancing in Grid Environment) [12]; 3) a Radial Based Function Network (RBFN) based learning strategy [11] used to obtain more suitable future collaboration/cooperation based on the experience; and 4) a SOA-based framework to implement Intelligent Agents (IAs) for the grid environments called SOFIA [13].

These components complement each other because CAM manages resources interaction by having information of the environment, SAGE delivers the load dynamically in the environment, SOFIA and the learning strategy will allow the system to have a more suitable cooperation.

The rest of the paper is organized as follows. Section 2 reviewed the technical backgrounds of previous researches. The MAS-based system proposed in this paper is presented in section 3. Section 4 presents some implementation and evaluation aspects. Finally, section 5 exposes the paper conclusions as well as the future work related with this research.

2 Theoretical Background

Details of CAM model and its conceptualization about awareness management can be reviewed in [7, 8]. Given a distributed environment E containing a set of resources R_i ($1 \leq i \leq N$), and a task T which needs to be solved in this environment, CAM objective is to solve T in a collaborative way. T is a set of P tuples (p_j, rq_j) ($1 \leq j \leq P$), where the p_j are the processes needed to solve the task in the system, and rq_j are requirements needed to solve each of these p_j processes. We have:

1) *Focus*(R_i): It can be interpreted as the subset of the space in which the user has focused his attention aiming of interacting with it.

2) *NimbusState*(R_i): The state of R_i in a given time. It could have three possible values: *Null*, *Medium* or *Maximum*.

3) *NimbusSpace*(R_i): The subset of the space where R_i is present. It will determine those machines that could be taken into account in the collaborative process.

4) *TaskResolution*(R_i, T) = {(p_1, s_1), …, (p_P, s_P)}: Determines if there is a service in the resource R_i, being *NimbusState*(R_i) ≠ *Null*, such that could be useful to execute T (or at least a part of it). s_j ($1 \leq j \leq P$) is the "score" to carry out p_j in the resource R_i.

5) *AwareInt*(R_i, R_j): Quantifies the degree, nature or quantity of asynchronous bidirectional interaction between R_i and R_j. It could be Full, Peripheral or Null.

6) *InteractivePool*(R_i): this function returns the set of resources interacting with the resource R_i in a given moment.

On the other hand, SOFIA focuses on the design of a common framework for IAs with the following characteristics: 1) it merges interdisciplinary theories, methods and approaches, 2) it is extensible and open as to be completed with new requirements and necessities, and 3) it highlights the agent´s learning process within the environment. The SOFIA general architecture contains four main components (Fig. 3.1-a):

1) The Embodied Agent (IA-EA) or the "body": It is a FIPA based structure [6] as it has a Service Directory element which provides a location where specific and correspondent services descriptions can be registered. It encloses the set of services related to the abilities of sensing stimuli from the environment and interacting with it.

2) The Rational Agent (IA-RA) or the "brain": This component represents the agent's intelligent part and therefore, it encloses the set of services used for the agent to implement the process associated with these abilities.

3) The Integrative/Facilitator Agent (IA-FA) or the "facilitator": It plays the role of simplifying the inclusion of new services into the system as well as the execution of each of them when it is needed. The basic function of the IA-FA is to coordinate the integration between the IA-SV and the rest of the IA components. This integration is needed when a new service is integrated with the IA and therefore registered into the corresponding Service Directory or even when an existing service is executed.

4) The IA Services or "abilities" (IA-SV): It is a collection of individuals and independent software components integrated to the system (the IA) which implements any specific ability either to the IA-EA or the IA-RA.

Related with SAGE, it is a simulated annealing based method designed to solve the dynamic load-balancing problem in grid environments. The cost function (energy) that measures the quality of each solution, the mechanism of transition of the space of solutions from t to t+1 (dynamic of the model), as well as the parameters that control the rate of cooling, can be reviewed in detail in [12].

Learning cooperation/collaborations in this context means to learn the association between the situation grid environment is in a given moment ($E + T$), and the response given to that specific situation (*TaskResolution*(R_i, T) for each resource R_i). Strategy to achieve this goal, named CoB-ForeSeer (Cooperation Behavior Foreseer), is based on Radial Based Function Network (RBFN). Previous results of this approach can be reviewed in [11]. Basic idea of CoB-ForeSeer is, one, to keep a historic data with all those collaborations that were carried out in the environment. And second, to use this data to train the RBFN model to foresee next collaborations needed. Therefore, the RBFN topology has to be defined so as to receive $E + T$ in the input layer and to produce the corresponding *TaskResolution*(R_i, T).

Next section presents the way in which CAM, SOFIA, SAGE, and CoB-ForeSeer are put together aiming to define a multi-agent task delivery system for balancing the load in collaborative grid environment.

3 Collaborative Dynamic Load Balancing

Our approach integrates SOFIA's framework with the CAM model by adapting the CAM key concepts to the objectives to be achieved as following (see Fig. 3.1-b). In this approach, the IA-SV agent manages *Focus* and *Nimbus* of each resource (as "abilities"). The IA-EA agent ("body") manages the *InteractivePool* of the collaborative grid environment. The load-balancing process is performed by the IA-RA agent ("brain") by using the SAGE method as well as the CoB-ForeSeer strategy (see details below).

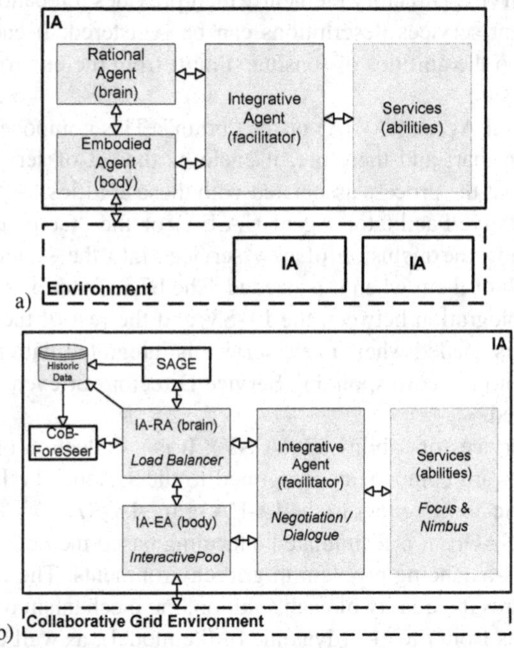

Fig. 3.1. a) The SOFIA general architecture; b) SOFIA-based system for balancing the load in collaborative grid environments.

On the other hand, in overloaded conditions (for example when *AwareInt* is *Peripheral* or *Null*) it is necessary to try to extend the *Focus* or *Nimbus* of one of the nodes so that the *AwareInt* could change to *Full*. This role is also performed by IA-RA through a negotiation process or dialogue that takes place between the IA-RA and the IA-SV. In this regard, the IA-FA agent ("facilitator") is responsible to manage this negotiation process (see details below).

The first thing IA-RA does when a load-balancing process is required in the grid environment is to obtain the corresponding *TaskResolution* "scores" s_j of each p_j by using CoB-ForeSeer. Once the answer is obtained, and depending on how it is, IA-RA takes one of three possible decisions, by using some rules as well as the current information associated with IA-EA (*InteractivePool*) and IA-SV (*Focus* and *Nimbus*):

1) Accept the processes-resources distribution given by CoB-ForeSeer.

2) Decline the answer because it is not keeping with the current situation. One of the reasons why this may happen is because the RBFN in CoB-ForeSeer is not sufficiently trained. In this case, IA-RA uses SAGE to find a better answer.

3) Decline the answer because the grid environment current conditions are overloaded. In this regard IA-RA initiates the negotiation process aiming to change the environment current conditions to obtain a new acceptable answer.

The negotiation process is performed by using a protocol defined as part of this proposal. This protocol is used by IA-RA, IA-FA and IA-SV and consists of the following dialogue:

- REQUEST (IA-RA → IA-FA): The load balancer in IA-RA is aware of an overload in any of the processes-resources assignments and it decides, with this message, to negotiate with any node an option relief.
- REQUEST (IA-FA → IA-SV): Once IA-FA receives the request from IA-RA, and as IA-FA knows what the current "abilities" (*Focus* and *Nimbus*) are, it asks for help aiming to find some node (IA-SV) that could change its abilities.
- CONFIRM (IA-SV → IA-FA): A node is confirming that it has changed its abilities and it is informing its new *Focus* and *Nimbus*.
- DISCONFIRM (IA-SV → IA-FA): A node is confirming that it cannot or it is not interested in changing its abilities.
- INFORM (IA-FA → IA-RA): Once the IA-FA receives the confirmations/disconfirmations from the nodes, and it upgrades all the information related with the *Nimbus* and *Focus* of these nodes, IA-FA sends to IA-RA this updated information.

Next section presents some aspects related with the implementation and evaluation of the model proposed in this paper and previously defined.

4 Implementation and Evaluation

SOFIA was implemented using JADE [1]. JADE behaviour model associated to IA-RA, IA-EA, IA-FA, and IA-SV agents were implemented. Protocol for the negotiation process was implemented using the JADE ACL message class.

The evaluation of the model was carried out by generating different random scenarios in a simulated grid environment and under overload conditions. The tests were mainly focused in the negotiation process aiming to quantify the ability of the model to resolve all these specific situations. In addition, it used different configurations in the grid environment, from 5 nodes to 25 nodes varying in 5 for each test block aiming to evaluate the model capability for managing growth in the grid environment conditions.

The results indicate that the proposed model has 84% success in negotiating the way to resolve overload conditions. In those cases (16%) where the negotiation was not successful any of the nodes (IA-SV) would or could modify its *Fo-*

cus/Nimbus (abilities) based on the current grid environment configurations. Depending on the number of nodes in the system, the negotiation process requires different time periods for execution (from less than 1 second to about 82 seconds), some of which may not be acceptable because the dynamic of the load-balancing process.

5 Conclusions and Ongoing Work

In this paper we present a multi-agent system method to cover dynamic load-balancing problem in collaborative grid environments. This method is defined by using some researches previously developed. The method has been designed aiming to cover the requirements, a cooperative and dynamic load-balancing problem in collaborative grid environments has: effective and efficient dynamic allocation of available resources whatever the size of the grid and the current grid conditions are. The proposal model has the capability to learn from previous collaborations that were carried out in the environment to foresee future scenarios. The model has also the capability to negotiate a new grid configuration in overloaded conditions.

We are working on integrating this method in simulated grid modeling to obtain more accurate results in experiments. We are also working in reducing the time needed for the negotiation process by properly selecting the nodes with which to establish the dialogue and thus reducing the number of nodes to negotiate.

References

1. Bellifemine F., Poggi A., Rimassa G. (1999) JADE – A FIPA-compliant agent framework, Telecom Italia internal technical report, in Proc. International Conference on Practical Applications of Agents and Multi-Agent Systems (PAAM'99), 97–108.
2. Berman F (1999) High-performance schedulers, in The Grid: Blueprint for a New Computing Infrastructure, Ian Foster and Carl Kesselman, (Eds.), Morgan Kaufmann, San Francisco, CA, 279–309.
3. Cao J, Spooner DP, Jarvis SA, Nudd GR (2005) Grid load balancing using intelligent agents, Future Generation Computer Systems, Vol. 21, No. 1, 135–149.
4. Fangpeng D, Selim GA (2006) Scheduling Algorithms for Grid Computing: State of the Art and Open Problems" Technical Report No. 2006-504, Queen's University, Canada, 55 pages, http://www.cs.queensu.ca/TechReports/Reports/2006-504.pdf.
5. Fidanova S, Durchova M (2006) Ant Algorithm for Grid Scheduling Problem, Lecture Notes in Computer Science, VIII Distributed Numerical Methods and Algorithms for Grid Computing, 10.1007/11666806, ISSN: 0302-9743 , ISBN: 978-3-540-31994-8 , Vol. 3743, 405–412.
6. Foundation for Intelligent Physical Agents (2002) FIPA Abstract Architecture Specification, SC00001, Geneva, Switzerland. http://www.fipa.org/specs/fipa00001/index.html.
7. Herrero P, Bosque JL, Pérez MS (2007) An Agents-Based Cooperative Awareness Model to Cover Load Balancing Delivery in Grid Environments, Lecture notes in computer science

2536, On the Move to Meaningful Internet Systems 2007: OTM 2007 Workshops, ISSN: 0302-9743, ISBN: 978-3-540-76887-6, Springer Verlag, Vol. 4805, 64–74.

8. Herrero P, Bosque J L, Pérez MS (2007) Managing Dynamic Virtual Organizations to get Effective Cooperation in Collaborative Grid Environments, Lecture notes in computer science 2536, On the Move to Meaningful Internet Systems 2007: OTM 2007 Workshops, ISBN: 978-3-540-76835-7, Springer Verlag, Vol. 4804, 1435–1452.
9. Jin R., Chen W., Simpson T.W. (2001) Comparative Studies of Metamodelling Techniques under Multiple Modeling Criteria, Struct Multidiscip Optim, Vol. 23, 1–13.
10. McMullan P, McCollum B (2007) Dynamic Job Scheduling on the Grid Environment Using the Great Deluge Algorithm, Lecture Notes in Computer Science, ISSN: 0302-9743, ISBN: 978-3-540-73939-5, Vol. 4671, 10.1007/978-3-540-73940-1, 283–292.
11. Paletta M., Herrero P. (2008) Learning Cooperation in Collaborative Grid Environments to Improve Cover Load Balancing Delivery, in Proc. IEEE/WIC/ACM Joint Conferences on Web Intelligence and Intelligent Agent Technology, IEEE Computer Society E3496, ISBN: 978-0-7695-3496-1, 399–402.
12. Paletta M., Herrero P. (2008) Simulated Annealing Method to Cover Dynamic Load Balancing in Grid Environment, in Proc. International Symposium on Distributed Computing and Artificial Intelligence 2008 (DCAI 08), Advances in Soft Computing, J.M. Corchado et al. (Eds.), Vol. 50/2009, Springer, ISBN: 978-3-540-85862-1, 1–10.
13. Paletta M., Herrero P. (2008) Towards Fraud Detection Support using Grid Technology, accepted for publication in a Special Issue at Multiagent and Grid Systems - An International Journal. (To be published).

[illegible] Nature-Inspired [illegible] (ICONS 2008). Workshop. ISSN 0302-9743 (Print), ISBN 978-3-540-78687 [illegible] Springer Verlag Vol 5055, p 4[illegible]

8. Herrero P, Bosque JL, Pérez MS (2007) Managing Dynamic Virtual Organizations to get Effective Cooperation in Collaborative Grid Environments. Lecture notes in computer science 4804: On the Move to Meaningful Internet Systems 2007: OTM 2007 Federated Conferences, ISBN 978-3-540-76835-7, Springer Verlag, Vol 4804, p 1435–1452

9. Jin R, Chen W, Simpson TW (2001) Comparative Studies of Metamodelling Techniques under Multiple Modelling Criteria. Struct Multidisc Optim, Vol 23, p 1–13

10. McMullan P, McCollum B (2007) Dynamic Job Scheduling on the Grid Environment Using the Great Deluge Algorithm. Lecture Notes in Computer Science, ISSN 0302-9743, ISBN 978-3-540-73939-9, Vol 4671, p 283–292

11. [illegible] (2008) Learning Cooperation in Collaborative Grid Environments to Improve Cover Load Balancing Delivery. In Proc IEEE/WIC/ACM Joint Conferences on Web Intelligence and Intelligent Agent Technology, IEEE Computer Society, [illegible] ISBN 978-0-7695-3496-1, p 399–402

12. [illegible] (2008) A Shared Memory Model to Cover Dynamic Load Balancing in the Grid Environment. In [illegible] International Symposium on Distributed Computing and Artificial Intelligence 2008 (DCAI 2008), Advances in Soft Computing, [illegible] Springer, ISBN 978-3-540-85862-1, p 10–[illegible]

13. [illegible] (2009) Towards [illegible] using Grid Technology [illegible] Systems: An International Journal (to be published)

Backing-up Fuzzy Control of a Truck-trailer Equipped with a Kingpin Sliding Mechanism

G. Siamantas and S. Manesis

Electrical & Computer Engineering Dept., University of Patras, Patras, Greece
gsiama@upatras.gr;stam.manesis@ece.upatras.gr

Abstract For articulated vehicles met in robotics and transportation fields, even for an experienced operator, backing-up leads usually to jack-knifing. This paper presents a fuzzy logic controller for back-driving a truck-trailer vehicle into a pre-defined parking task. The truck-trailer link system is equipped with a kingpin sliding mechanism acting as an anti-jackknife excitation input. By applying fuzzy logic control techniques, precise system model is not required. The developed controller with thirty four rules works well as the presented simulation results demonstrate the avoidance of jack-knife and the accuracy of the backing-up technique.

1 Introduction

Control of the backward movement of a truck and trailer vehicle, called docking task, is known to be a typical nonlinear control problem. The difficulty of the control system design not only causes the dynamics to be nonlinear, but also emphasizes the inherent physical limitations of the system such as the jackknife phenomenon, a mathematical model of which is discussed in (Fossum and Lewis 1981). The control system under investigation is not only nonlinear but also nonholonomic. Backward movement control of computer simulated truck-trailers using various types of intelligent control e.g. fuzzy control, neural control and neurofuzzy or genetic algorithm-based control (Yang et al. 2006, Kiyuma et al. 2004, Riid and Rustern 2001), has been reported. The backing-up control of a truck-trailer is considered in (Park et al. 2007) as a system with time delay. A fuzzy knowledge-based control for backing multi-trailer systems is also considered in (Riid et al. 2007). The kingpin sliding mechanism, used in current work for backward stabilization, has been also used for off-tracking elimination in multi-articulated vehicles (Manesis et al. 2003). In this paper the kingpin sliding mechanism is used mainly as an active anti-jackknife steering mechanism for backward motion. The mathematical model of the considered system is different and more

Please use the following format when citing this chapter:

Siamantas, G. and Manesis, S., 2009, in IFIP International Federation for Information Processing, Volume 296; *Artificial Intelligence Applications and Innovations III*; Eds. Iliadis, L., Vlahavas, I., Bramer, M.; (Boston: Springer), pp. 373–378.

complex from that of a truck-trailer without a kingpin sliding mechanism. The precise mathematical description offers only an initial guidance for writing the fuzzy rules of the controller.

2 System description - Fuzzy Logic Controller Design

The system under consideration is a truck-trailer vehicle with on-axle sliding-able connection. Its geometry along with the directions of all defined angles and axes are shown in Fig. 1. The major difference with a typical truck-trailer system is the use of a sliding kingpin on the rear axle of the tractor.

The nomenclature of the considered model is: (x_0, y_0) coordinates of the truck's rear axle midpoint, (x_1, y_1) coordinates of the trailer's rear axle midpoint, θ_0 angle of the longitudinal axis of the truck w.r.t. the horizontal axis, θ_1 angle of the longitudinal axis of the trailer w.r.t. the horizontal axis, S length of the kingpin slide, l_0 truck's wheelbase length, l_1 length between the trailer's rear axle midpoint and the hinge joint, φ truck's steering wheels turning angle, U_1 truck velocity, $\dot{S}, U_2$ rate of change of the kingpin sliding, α angle between the horizontal axis and the straight line that passes from the axes origin and the (x_1, y_1) point, d distance of the (x_1, y_1) point from the horizontal axis (same as y_1), $\alpha - \theta_1$ angle between the trailer's longitudinal axis and the line that passes from the axes origin and the (x_1, y_1) point, $\theta_0 - \theta_1$ angle between the longitudinal axes of the truck and the trailer. The kinematic equations of the system are the following:

$$
\begin{aligned}
\dot{x}_0 &= U_1 \cos \theta_0 \\
\dot{y}_0 &= U_1 \sin \theta_0 \\
\dot{\theta}_0 &= \frac{U_1}{l_0} \tan \varphi \\
\dot{\theta}_1 &= \frac{1}{l_1}\left(U_1 + S\frac{U_1}{l_0} \tan \varphi \right) \sin(\theta_0 - \theta_1) - \sin^{-1}\left(\frac{\dot{S}}{l_1} \right) \qquad (1) \\
\dot{S} &= U_2 \\
x_1 &= x_0 - l_1 \cos \theta_1 + S \sin \theta_0 \\
y_1 &= y_0 - l_1 \sin \theta_1 - S \cos \theta_0
\end{aligned}
$$

The $-\sin^{-1}(\dot{S}/l_1)$ term was added to take into account the change of angle θ_1 in case where the velocity U_1 is zero and the rate of change of the kingpin sliding

U_2 is not zero. The above system model will be used in the evaluation of the designed fuzzy logic controller performance through simulations.

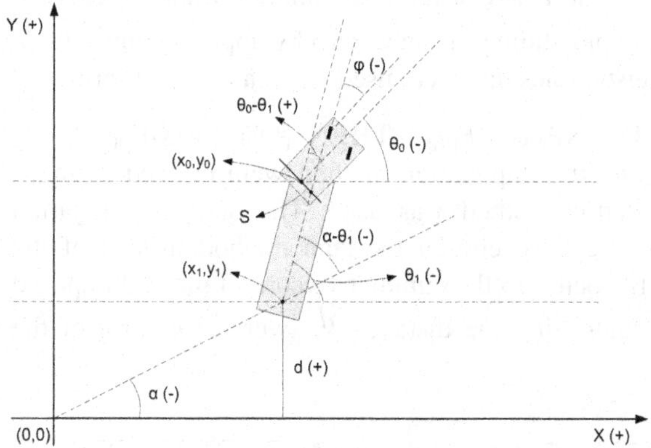

Fig. 1. System geometry

The main objective of this Fuzzy Logic Controller (FLC) is the backward motion control of the truck and trailer system to follow a target line, a procedure similar to parking. In the design of the fuzzy logic controller we used 4 inputs ($\alpha-\theta_1, \theta_0-\theta_1, d$, S) and 2 outputs (φ, S). From the four inputs the first three are needed for achieving the control objective and the fourth one (S) is needed to make S zero when the first two inputs become zero. The input and output variables were defined to have 5 membership functions each: **NL**: Negative Large, **NS**: Negative Small, **ZE**: Zero, **PS:** Positive Small, **PL**: Positive Large. The normalized degree of membership function diagrams for each input or output variable are shown in Fig. 2. For the input variables the NS, ZE, PS membership functions are triangular and the NL, PL are trapezoidal. The output variables have all 5 membership functions triangular.

The fuzzy logic controller has been developed by defining 34 logical rules shown in Fig. 3. These rules are consistent with the following evaluation strategies: (1) the truck's steering wheels must turn in such a way as to make the system move towards the direction that makes the angle $\alpha-\theta_1$ zero, (2) if the angles $\alpha-\theta_1$ and $\theta_0-\theta_1$ belong to the ZE degree, i.e. the truck-trailer system is moving towards the axes origin and the angle between the truck and the trailer is close to zero, then we can turn the truck's steering wheels in such a way as to minimize the distance d from the horizontal axis, (3) if the angle $\theta_0-\theta_1$ is large (NL, PL degrees) and to avoid jackknifing, regardless of the values of all other variables, the steering wheels should be turned in such a way as to minimize the angle $\theta_0-\theta_1$, (4) the kingpin sliding should have a direction opposite to the centrifugal direction and must be proportional to the angle $\theta_0-\theta_1$. This action will provide greater correction margin to the steering wheels to avoid jackknifing, (5) if the angles $\alpha - \theta_1$ and $\theta_0 - \theta_1$ belong to the ZE degree, i.e. the truck-trailer system is moving towards the axes origin and the angle between the truck and the trailer is close to zero, then we can make the kingpin sliding distance zero by applying opposite $\dot{S}$ proportionally to S. The linguistic rules that were used have the general form:

IF [INP$_1$ **is** MF$_{INP1}$] **AND** [INP$_2$ **is** MF$_{INP2}$] **THEN** [OUT$_1$ **is** MF$_{OUT1}$]

The fuzzy operator AND and the implication method were defined as minimum. The centroid defuzzification method was used. The output aggregation method was defined as sum. We have chosen the sum method instead of the maximum method because it fits better to the cumulative control method imposed from strategy no. 2 used in controlling the distance d over the control of the $\alpha - \theta_1$ angle.

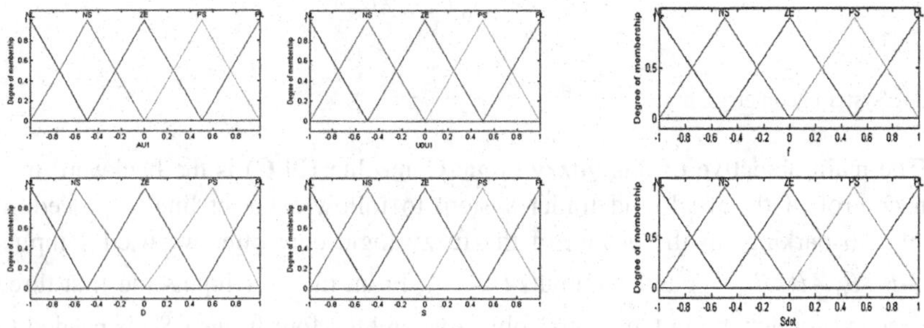

Fig. 2. Normalized degree of membership function diagrams of input-output variables

$\varphi / \dot{S}$		$\theta_0 - \theta_1$				
$\alpha - \theta_1$	d	**NL**	**NS**	**ZE**	**PS**	**PL**
NL		*NL/PL*	*PS/PS*	*PS/ZE*	*PL/NS*	*PL/NL*
NS		*NL/PL*	*ZE/PS*	*PS/ZE*	*PS/NS*	*PL/NL*
	NL			*PL/ZE*		
	NS			*PS/ZE*		
ZE		*NL/PL*	*NS/PS*	*ZE/ZE*	*PS/NS*	*PL/NL*
	PS			*NS/ZE*		
	PL			*NL/ZE*		
PS		*NL/PL*	*NS/PS*	*NS/ZE*	*ZE/NS*	*PL/NL*
PL		*NL/PL*	*NL/PS*	*NS/ZE*	*NS/NS*	*PL/NL*

$\dot{S}$		$\theta_0 - \theta_1$
$\alpha - \theta_1$	S	**ZE**
	NL	*PL*
	NS	*PS*
ZE	**ZE**	*ZE*
	PS	*NS*
	PL	*NL*

Fig. 3. Fuzzy Logic Controller logical rules

3 Simulations, Motion Restrictions, Advantages of Kingpin Sliding

To verify the effectiveness of the proposed fuzzy controller we performed several tests in a simulation environment. The simulation model was based on equations (1) with the following assumptions: U_1 is -1 m/sec, l_0 is 4 m, l_1 is 6 m, φ varies between -50° and 50°, φ varies between -30°/sec and 30°/sec, S varies between -0.6 m and 0.6 m and S varies between -0.1 m/sec and 0.1 m/sec. Because the designed membership function diagrams are normalized we used gains in the inputs and outputs to change their universes of discourse scales.

Several simulation tests were performed, from different system initial positions and directions, with and without kingpin sliding control. In Fig. 4, we see the system response from initial conditions $(x_0, y_0, \theta_0, \theta_1)$ = (60, -10, 45, -45). We see that kingpin sliding control does not have big influence in system response as far as concerning the trajectory of the system. The difference is that we have greater angle margin for the control of a possible jackknife situation in the case where kingpin sliding control is used. This can be shown from simulations and also from the system geometry where we see that with a kingpin sliding along the centripetal direction we gain approximately $\sin^{-1}(S/l_1)$ = 5.74° in $\theta_0 - \theta_1$ angle and by extension to the steering wheel angle φ. The positive effects of this angle gain are demonstrated in Fig. 5 where the initial conditions are (60, 20, 45, -45). In these responses the turn limit of the truck's steering wheels is between -35° and 35°. It is obvious that without kingpin sliding control the system enters a jackknife condition, Fig. 5 (left). The system with kingpin sliding control avoids jackknife, Fig. 5 (right).

It should be noted that when the truck-trailer system is moving backwards the advantages of kingpin sliding control appear during sliding towards the centripetal direction in contrast with the system moving forward where the advantages appear during sliding towards the centrifugal direction.

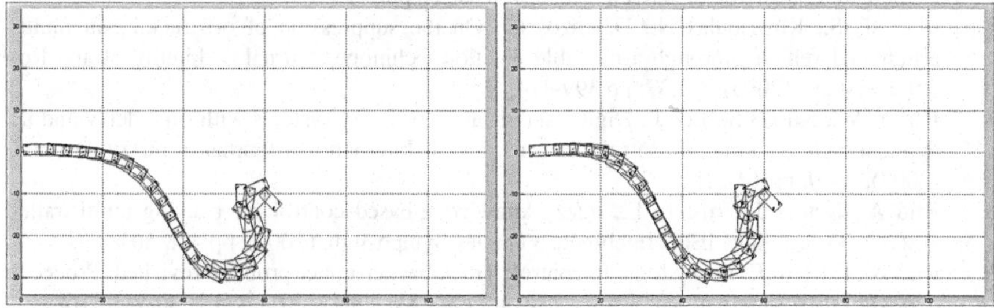

Fig. 4. System response from initial conditions (60, -10, 45, -45). Without sliding control (left), with sliding control (right)

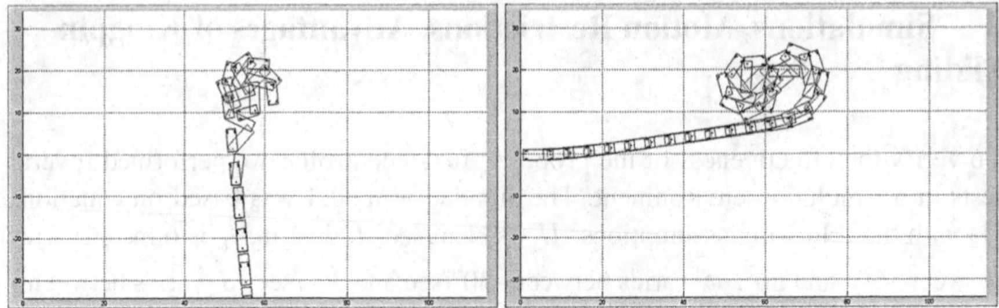

Fig. 5. System response from initial conditions (60, 20, 45, -45) and (-35°, 35°) steering wheel angle limit. Without sliding control (left - jackknife), with sliding control (right)

4 Conclusions

A fuzzy logic controller was designed for the backward motion of a truck-trailer system with on-axle kingpin sliding. Various tests were conducted to test the controller effectiveness. The controller showed good performance with the system starting from various initial conditions. The use of kingpin sliding towards the centripetal direction has no adverse effect in system response while it reduces the maximum turn of the truck's steering wheels when the system is maneuvering backwards. This gives greater steering wheel turn margin for the truck to avoid jackknife.

References

1. Fossum TV., Lewis GN. A mathematical model for trailer-truck jackknife. SIAM Review (1981); vol.23, no.1: 95-99.
2. Kiyuma A., Kinjo H., Nakazono K., Yamamoto T. Backward control of multitrailer systems using neurocontrollers evolved by a genetic algorithm. Proceedings 8th International Symposium on Artificial Life and Robotics (2004); pp.9-13.
3. Manesis S., Koussoulas N., Davrazos G., On the suppression of off-tracking in multi-articulated vehicles through a movable junction technique. Journal of Intelligent and Robotic Systems (2003); vol.37: pp.399-414.
4. Park C.W., Kim B.S., Lee J., Digital stabilization of fuzzy systems with time-delay and its application to backing up control of a truck-trailer. International Journal of Fuzzy Systems, (2007), vol.9, pp.14-21.
5. Riid A., Ketola J., Rustern E., Fuzzy knowledge-based control for backing multi-trailer systems. Proceedings IEEE Intelligent Vehicles Symposium, (2007), pp.498-504.
6. Riid A., Rustern E. Fuzzy logic in control: Track backer-upper problem revisited. Proceedings 10th IEEE International Conference on Fuzzy Systems (2001); vol.1: pp.513-516.
7. Yang X., Yuan J., Yu F. Backing up a truck and trailer using variable universe based fuzzy controller. Proceedings IEEE International Conference on Mechatronics and Automation (2006); pp. 734-739.

Sensing Inertial and Continuously-Changing World Features

Theodore Patkos and Dimitris Plexousakis

Abstract Knowledge and causality play an essential role in the attempt to achieve commonsense reasoning in cognitive robotics. As agents usually operate in dynamic and uncertain environments, they need to acquire information through sensing inertial aspects, such as the state of a door, and continuously changing aspects, such as the location of a moving object. In this paper, we extend an Event Calculus-based knowledge framework with a method for sensing world features of different types in a uniform and transparent to the agent manner. The approach results in the modeling of agents that remember and forget, a cognitive skill particularly suitable for the implementation of real-world applications.

1 Introduction

For decades, research in Artificial Intelligence is concerned with understanding and formalizing the properties of commonsense reasoning. Contemporary progress in cognitive robotics has led to the development of agents with significant reasoning capabilities, demonstrating their applicability in high-level logic-based robot control systems operating in real-life uncertain and highly dynamic environments (i.e., [3, 17, 14]). Formal theories for reasoning about action and change are now widely accepted, building on their expressiveness and the ability to verify the correctness properties of their specifications.

Autonomous agents that act in real-world conditions usually operate with incomplete information about the world they inhabit; therefore they need to acquire information and extend their knowledge base (KB) at execution time. In such settings, the temporal aspects of knowledge plays an essential role. Both ordinary and knowledge-producing (sense) actions need to be performed at specific time instants and information acquired may only be considered valid for limited time periods. The

Theodore Patkos and Dimitris Plexousakis
Institute of Computer Science, FO.R.T.H., Heraklion, Greece e-mail: {patkos,dp}@ics.forth.gr

Please use the following format when citing this chapter:

Patkos, T. and Plexousakis, D., 2009, in IFIP International Federation for Information Processing, Volume 296; *Artificial Intelligence Applications and Innovations III*; Eds. Iliadis, L., Vlahavas, I., Bramer, M.; (Boston: Springer), pp. 379–388.

significance of reasoning about what agents know or do not know about the current world state and how this knowledge evolves over time has been acknowledged as highly critical for real-life implementations [1, 11].

In previous work we have developed a unified formal framework for reasoning about knowledge, action and time within the Event Calculus for dynamic and uncertain environments [9]. The current paper extends the above framework with an account of knowledge-producing actions for both inertial and continuously changing world features in a uniform manner. For instance, a moving robot may be able to sense parameters, such as the state of doors, the number of persons around it or its current position. Knowledge about door states can be preserved in its memory until some relevant event changes it, while knowledge about the other features should be considered invalid after a few moments or even at the next time instant. Still, it is important that the act of sensing can treat the different contingencies in a transparent to the robot fashion.

The contribution of this study is of both theoretical and practical interest. The proposed approach allows sensing of inertial and continuously changing properties of dynamic and uncertain domains in a uniform style, providing a level of abstraction to the design of an agent's cognitive behavior. Moreover, it results in the development of agents that are able not only to remember, but also to forget information, either to preserve consistency between the actual state of the world and the view they maintain in their KB or due to restrictions, such as limited resources, which pose critical constraints when considering real-life scenarios. Finally, the approach is based on a computationally feasible formal framework.

The paper proceeds as follows. We first provide an overview of relevant approaches and background material about the Event Calculus and the knowledge theory. In Section 3 we describe the sensing methodology for inertial relations and in Section 4 we explain how this scheme can also support continuously changing aspects. Section 5 illustrates its application on more complex domains. The paper concludes with remarks in Section 6.

2 Background and Related Work

This study builds on previous work in Knowledge Representation that is concerned with reasoning about actions and causality and has resulted in a family of *action theories* based on variations of the predicate calculus. These theories are formal frameworks for reasoning with action preconditions and effects and have been extended to handle a multitude of commonsense phenomena, such as effect ramifications, non-deterministic actions, qualifications etc. Intense research in the field has been devoted to studying the interaction between action and knowledge, where sensing is treated as a form of action, whose effects do not affect the state of the world but only the agent's mental state. Many of the related studies, though, concentrate on sensing inertial world parameters.

Scherl and Levesque [12] developed a theory of action and sensing within the Situation Calculus, providing a solution to the frame problem by adapting the standard possible worlds specification of epistemic logic to action theories, an approach first proposed by Moore [7]. The significance of an explicit representation of time has been acknowledged in [11], where the formalism has been extended with a treatment of concurrent actions and temporal knowledge. Working on the Fluent Calculus, Thielscher [15] provided a solution to the inferential frame problem for knowledge, along with an elaborate introduction of the notion of *ability* for an agent to achieve a goal. Nevertheless, in both frameworks, once knowledge is acquired it is preserved persistently in memory; it can be modified by relevant actions, but is never lost. The action language $\mathscr{A}_k$ [5] permits information to be retracted from the set of facts known by an agent, as a result of actions that affect the world non-deterministically. Still, sensing continuously changing world aspects is not considered.

Moreover, these frameworks are computationally problematic, due to their dependence on the possible worlds model. Many recent approaches adopt alternative representations of knowledge that permit tractable reasoning in less expressive domains. Petrick and Levesque [10], for instance, define a combined action theory in the Situation Calculus for expressing knowledge of first-order formulae, based on the notion of *knowledge fluents* presented in [2] that treated knowledge change at a syntactical level. To achieve efficient reasoning, knowledge of disjunctions is assumed decomposable into knowledge of the individual components. Still, sensing is again limited to inertial parameters and knowledge is never retracted.

Our approach is based on a knowledge theory that treats knowledge fluents in a style similar to [10], which uses the Event Calculus as the underlying formalism. The Event Calculus is a widely adopted formalism for reasoning about action and change. It is a first-order calculus, which uses *events* to indicate changes in the environment and *fluents* to denote any time-varying property. Time is explicitly represented and reified in the language propositions. The formalism applies the *principle of inertia* to solve the frame problem, which captures the property that things tend to persist over time unless affected by some event; when released from inertia, a fluent may have a fluctuating truth value at each time instant (we further elucidate these concepts in successor sections). It also uses *circumscription* [4] to support nonmonotonic reasoning. The Event Calculus defines predicates for expressing which fluents hold when (*HoldsAt*), what events happen (*Happens*), which their effects are (*Initiates*, *Terminates*, *Releases*) and whether a fluent is subject to the law of inertia or released from it (*ReleasedAt*).

A number of different dialects for the Event Calculus have been proposed summarized in [13] and [6]. For our proposed knowledge theory we have employed and extended the discrete time axiomatization (DEC), thoroughly described in [8]. The knowledge theory can be applied to domains involving incomplete knowledge about the initial state, knowledge-producing actions, actions that cause loss of knowledge and actions with context-dependent effects. The axiomatization is restricted to reasoning about fluent literals, assuming that disjunctive knowledge can be broken apart into the individual components. To simplify the presentation, we assume perfect sensors for the agent, i.e., the result of sensing is always correct.

Knowledge and the Commonsense Law of Inertia

$$ReleasedAt(Knows((\neg)f),t) \quad \text{(KT1)}$$

Knowledge Persistence

$$HoldsAt(KP((\neg)f),t) \Rightarrow HoldsAt(Knows((\neg)f),t) \quad \text{(KT2)}$$

Events with Known Effects

$$\bigwedge_{i=1}^{P}[HoldsAt(Knows((\neg)f_i),t)] \wedge Happens(e,t) \Rightarrow Initiates(e, KP(f_{pos}), t) \quad \text{(KT3.1)}$$

$$\bigwedge_{i=1}^{P}[HoldsAt(Knows((\neg)f_i),t)] \wedge Happens(e,t) \Rightarrow Terminates(e, KP(\neg f_{pos}), t) \quad \text{(KT3.2)}$$

$$\bigwedge_{j=1}^{N}[HoldsAt(Knows((\neg)f_j),t)] \wedge Happens(e,t) \Rightarrow Initiates(e, KP(\neg f_{neg}), t) \quad \text{(KT3.3)}$$

$$\bigwedge_{j=1}^{N}[HoldsAt(Knows((\neg)f_j),t)] \wedge Happens(e,t) \Rightarrow Terminates(e, KP(f_{neg}), t) \quad \text{(KT3.4)}$$

Knowledge-producing (sense) Actions

$$Initiates(sense(f), KPw(f), t) \quad \text{(KT4)}$$

Events with non-deterministic Effects

$$\bigvee_{i=1}^{P}[\neg HoldsAt(Kw(f_i),t)] \wedge \bigwedge_{i=1}^{P}[\neg HoldsAt(Knows(\neg(\neg)f_i),t)] \wedge \neg HoldsAt(Knows(f_{pos}),t) \wedge Happens(e,t) \Rightarrow Terminates(e, KPw(f_{pos}), t) \quad \text{(KT5.1)}$$

$$\bigvee_{j=1}^{N}[\neg HoldsAt(Kw(f_j),t)] \wedge \bigwedge_{j=1}^{N}[\neg HoldsAt(Knows(\neg(\neg)f_j),t)] \wedge \neg HoldsAt(Knows(\neg f_{neg}),t) \wedge Happens(e,t) \Rightarrow Terminates(e, KPw(f_{neg}), t) \quad \text{(KT5.2)}$$

$$\bigwedge_{k=1}^{R}[\neg HoldsAt(Knows(\neg(\neg)f_k),t)] \wedge Happens(e,t) \Rightarrow Terminates(e, KPw(f_{rel}), t) \quad \text{(KT5.3)}$$

State Constraints (Indirect Knowledge)

$HoldsAt(Kw(f),t) \Leftrightarrow$ <There exists some state constraint about f that is known to be triggered> (KT7)

Fig. 1 The DEC Knowledge Theory axiomatization, where e denotes an arbitrary event, f_{pos}, f_{neg}, f_{rel} are positive, negative and non-deterministic effects respectively, and f_i, f_j, f_k are the corresponding effect's preconditions.

Figure 1 summarizes the foundational axioms of the theory. The *KP* fluent ("knows persistently") denotes inertial knowledge as a result of direct action effects. Knowledge can also be inferred indirectly from state constraints. *Kw* ("knows whether") is an abbreviation for $Kw(f) \equiv Knows(f) \vee Knows(\neg f)$, and similarly for *KPw* (for a comprehensive treatment see [9]). Event variables are represented by *e*, fluent variables by f and variables of the timepoint sort by t[1]. The theory assumes the occurrence of an event *e* having direct domain effects captured by positive, negative and release effect axioms of the following form:
$\bigwedge_{i=1}^{P}[(\neg)HoldsAt(f_i,t)] \Rightarrow Initiates(e, f_{pos}, t)$
$\bigwedge_{j=1}^{N}[(\neg)HoldsAt(f_j,t)] \Rightarrow Terminates(e, f_{neg}, t)$
$\bigwedge_{k=1}^{R}[(\neg)HoldsAt(f_k,t)] \Rightarrow Releases(e, f_{rel}, t)$,
Such action occurrences can also cause knowledge effects to the agent's mental state, which are captured by the foundational axioms of our knowledge theory. For instance, axiom (KT3.1) states that whenever an agent knows all preconditions of an occurring event *e* that causes f_{pos} to become true, then it will also *know* the truth value of that effect.

[1] All free variables are implicitly universally quantified.

As a running example for the rest of the paper, we assume a robot named *Rob* either standing or moving with constant velocity v and able to sense the state of doors, the number of persons near him and its current location, represented by fluents $Closed(door)$, $PersonsNear(robot, num)$ and $Position(robot, pos)$, respectively. Initially, Rob is unaware of any relevant information, i.e, $\neg\exists d HoldsAt(Kw(Closed(d)), 0)$, $\neg\exists n HoldsAt(Kw(PersonsNear(Rob, n)), 0)$ and $\neg\exists p HoldsAt(Kw(Position(Rob, p)), 0)$.

3 Inertial Fluents - Remembering and Forgetting

In general, a robot's descriptions of world states involve a large number of components that are assumed stable between action occurrences and preserve their properties for as long as occurring events do not affect them. A door remains open until some $Close(door)$ event happens, while an object's color persists even when someone lifts it and moves it around. This insight is related to the well-known *frame problem* of action theories, which is concerned with specifying the non-effects of actions. In the Event Calculus, the commonsense law of inertia expresses that certain objects tend to stay in the same state, unless an event happens that changes this state. We refer to fluents that are subject to this law as inertial defined as follows:

Definition 1. A fluent is called *inertial* if it tends to maintain its truth value, unless affected by some event.

An inertial fluent, denoted in the Event Calculus by the expression $\neg ReleasedAt(f, t)$, is always subject to inertia. One can easily observe that whenever an agent senses an inertial fluent, the knowledge gained can be stored and preserved in its KB for as long as no event causes its invalidation. Sensing inertial fluents is a well-formalized task in most related epistemic action theories. In order to model real-life agents with limited resources though, the assumption of permanent knowledge preservation is too strong to accept. Apart from issues related to memory storage capacity, the rate of change in dynamic worlds quickly renders information out-of-date, forcing the agent to reconsider its knowledge about the state of certain objects that ideally could have remained unaltered.

In order to represent the "fading" validity of knowledge-producing actions, we introduce a new sense action that extends the one presented in Figure 1. This action is captured by the following axioms:

$$Happens(sense(f), t) \Rightarrow Happens(remember(f), t) \wedge Happens(forget(f), t + T(f)) \quad \text{(KT4.1)}$$

$$Initiates(remember(f), KPw(f), t) \quad \text{(KT4.2)}$$

$$\neg Happens(sense(f), t) \Rightarrow Terminates(forget(f), KPw(f), t) \quad \text{(KT4.3)}$$

where $T(f)$ denotes a function that introduces a time delay dependent on f's properties (certain fluents tend to change more often that others). The axiomatization expresses that whenever an agent senses a fluent, two internal to the agent actions occur that cause knowledge about the state of the fluent to be kept in the memory for a specific time window. The *remember* action produces the traditional sensing effect, while the $forget$ action's effect is canceled if a *sense* action occurs concurrently (axiom (KT4.3) is called *negative canceling effect* axiom for that reason). Notice how the *KP* fluent forces knowledge to become true, according to (KT2).

The above axiomatization provides two alternatives for modeling knowledge-producing actions for inertial fluents. For the purpose of constructing a theoretical framework the desirable side-effect of unlimited memory persistence of fluents is achieved by retracting the instance of the $forget$ action from (KT4.1). In addition, an agent may also be equipped with the mental ability to forget, an essential cognitive skill for practical commonsense reasoning, particularly suited for real-life implementations. Furthermore, one may also use the same axiomatization as a means of sensing continuously changing fluents, as explained below.

4 Non-Inertial and Functional Fluents

Most current logic-based approaches that study the interaction of knowledge and time focus on sensing and obtaining knowledge about inertial fluents. Still, this is hardly the case when reasoning in dynamically changing worlds. Next, we show how the aforementioned approach can also be applied to broader classes of situations. First, we elaborate on the characteristics of such situations.

In addition to inertial fluents there are also fluents that change their truth value in an arbitrary fashion at each time instant. The number of persons entering a building or the mails arriving daily at a mailbox are typical examples. Such fluents are usually applied in order to introduce uncertainty, as they give rise to several possible models, and can be defined as follows:

Definition 2. A fluent is called *non-inertial* if its truth value may change at each timepoint, regardless of occurring events.

A non-inertial fluent is always released from inertia and is represented in the Event Calculus by the predicate $ReleasedAt(f,t)$. A particular use for non-inertial fluents has been proposed by Shanahan [13] as random value generators in problems, such as tossing a coin, rolling a dice etc, naming them *determining fluents*, as they determine non-deterministically the value of other world aspects.

For the purposes of epistemic reasoning, sensing non-inertial fluents provides temporal knowledge that is only valid for one time unit, i.e., it only reflects what is known at the time of sensing, but not what will be known afterwards. Whenever Rob needs to reason about the number of persons around him, it must necessarily perform a new sense action to acquire this information; any previously obtained knowledge may not reflect the current situation. Still, there is a class of non-inertial fluents that is far more interesting, because it expresses continuous change that follows a well-defined pattern. Such fluents are utilized to denote gradual change (or *processes*, according to Thielscher [16]), for instance to represent the height of a falling object, the position of a moving robot, the patience of a waiting person etc. We call this class of fluents functional non-inertial fluents:

Definition 3. A non-inertial fluent is called *functional* if its value changes gradually over time, following a predefined function.

In order to represent gradual change in the Event Calculus, we first need to release the involved fluent from inertia, so that its value is allowed to fluctuate, and then we can apply a state constraint to restrain the fluctuation, so that the fluent can exhibit a functional behavior. For example, to express the change in Rob's location (on a single axis) while moving with constant velocity, we apply the following state constraint concerning the $Position(robot, pos)$ fluent:

$$\begin{aligned} &HoldsAt(Position(Rob,pos),t_1) \wedge t > 0 \Rightarrow \\ &HoldsAt(Position(Rob,pos+(v*t)),t_1+t) \end{aligned} \tag{SC}$$

It is straightforward to observe how axioms (KT4) can accommodate sensing non-inertial fluents (both ordinary and functional). One just needs to set T equal to one time unit. Regarding functional fluents in particular, although the value of the sensed fluent is subject to change, knowledge about future values can still be inferred. The application of an epistemic logic axiom system, such as S5, along with DEC knowledge theory axioms combines the narrative of actions and observations with the agent's cognitive ability. Specifically, the distribution axiom (K) below dictates how the available state constraints can contribute to knowledge inference:

$$\begin{aligned} &HoldsAt(Knows(f_1 \Rightarrow f_2),t) \Rightarrow \\ &(HoldsAt(Knows(f_1),t) \Rightarrow HoldsAt(Knows(f_2),t)) \end{aligned} \tag{K}$$

Example 1 The previous discussion illustrates how the problem of sensing the two non-inertial fluents $PersonsNear(robot, num)$ and $Position(robot, pos)$ can be addressed. Imagine that Rob performs $Happens(sense(PersonsNear(Rob, num)), 0)$ and $Happens(sense(Position(Rob, pos)), 0)$ at timepoint 0. By forming the parallel circumscription of the example's domain theory (no initial knowledge and the two event occurrences) along with Event Calculus, Knowledge Theory and uniqueness-of-names axioms, we can prove several propositions[2]. First, two, internal to the robot, events will be triggered for each fluent; a *remember* event at timepoint 0 and a $forget$ event at timepoint 1. For the $PersonsNear$ fluent it can also be proved that

$$\begin{aligned} &\models \exists x HoldsAt(Knows(PersonsNear(Rob,x)),1) \wedge \\ &\neg \exists x HoldsAt(Kw(PersonsNear(Rob,x)),2) \end{aligned} \tag{4.1}$$

[2] Sample code for the DEC Reasoner tool (http://decreasoner.sourceforge.net/) is available at http://www.csd.uoc.gr/~patkos/deckt.htm

due to (KT4.2) and (KT2) at timepoint 0 and (KT4.3), (KT2) and (KT7) at timepoint 1. The case is different for the robot's position:

$$\models \exists p HoldsAt(Knows(Position(Rob,p)),t) \tag{4.2}$$

for all $t > 0$. This holds true, because, although the $forget$ action results in $\neg HoldsAt(KPw(Position(Rob,pos)),t)$ for $t \geq 1$, axiom (K) transforms (SC) into $HoldsAt(Knows(Position(Rob,pos)),t_1) \wedge t > 0 \Rightarrow$
$HoldsAt(Knows(Position(Rob,pos+(v*t))),t_1+t)$
Consequently, once Rob senses his position at some timepoint, he can infer future positions, without the need to perform further sense actions. The state constraint provides all future derivations, affecting knowledge through (KT7).

5 Context-dependent Inertia

We can now formalize complex domains that capture our commonsense knowledge of changing worlds, where fluents behave in an inertial or non-inertial manner according to context. For instance, a robot's location is regarded as a continuously changing entity only while the robot is moving; when it stands still, the location is subject to inertia. As a result only while the robot *knows* that it is not moving can knowledge about its location be stored persistently in its KB in the style described in Section 3. In general, for any fluent that presents such dual behavior, there usually is some other fluent (or conjunction of fluents) that regulates its compliance to the law of inertia at each time instant. For the $Position(robot,pos)$ fluent, for instance, there can be a $Moving(robot)$ fluent that determines the robot's motion state. Such *regulatory* fluents appear in the body of state constraints to ensure that inconsistency does not arise when inertia is restored. According to their truth state, the fluent that they regulate can either be subject to inertia and maintain its value or released from it in order to be subject to a state constraint. To integrate regulatory fluents in the theory, (KT4.3) must be extended to ensure that the agent does not forget a fluent when it knows that the latter is inertial and should be kept in the KB:

$$\begin{aligned}\neg Happens(sense(f),t) \wedge \neg HoldsAt(Knows(\neg f_{rglr}),t) \Rightarrow \\ Terminates(forget(f),KPw(f),t)\end{aligned} \tag{KT4.3$'$}$$

where f_{rglr} is f's regulatory fluent. Notice that even when the agent is not aware of f's inertia state, i.e., $\neg HoldsAt(Kw(f_{rglr}),t)$, the axiom fires and knowledge about f is lost, to avoid preserving knowledge that does not reflect the actual state.

Example 2 Imagine that Rob's movement is controlled by actions $Start(robot)$ and $Stop(robot)$ with effect axioms:

$$Initiates(Start(robot),Moving(robot),t) \tag{5.1}$$

$$Terminates(Stop(robot), Moving(robot), t) \tag{5.2}$$

While the robot is on the move, its position must no more be subject to inertia:

$$Releases(Start(robot), Position(robot, pos), t) \tag{5.3}$$

$$HoldsAt(Position(robot, pos), t) \Rightarrow Initiates(Stop(robot), Position(robot), t) \tag{5.4}$$

In addition, the state constraint that determines the location as the robot is moving, with the *Moving* fluent playing the regulatory role, is axiomatized as follows:

$$\begin{aligned} &HoldsAt(Moving(robot), t_1) \wedge HoldsAt(Position(robot, pos), t_1) \wedge \\ &\quad t > 0 \wedge \neg\exists t_2 (Happens(Stop(robot), t_2) \wedge t_1 < t_2 < t_1 + t) \Rightarrow \\ &\qquad HoldsAt(Position(robot, pos + (v * t)), t_1 + t) \end{aligned} \tag{5.5}$$

As a result, axiom (KT4.3′) will be instantiated as:

$$\begin{aligned} &\neg Happens(sense(Position(Rob, pos)), t) \wedge \\ &\neg HoldsAt(Knows(\neg Moving(Rob)), t) \Rightarrow \\ &Terminates(forget(Position(Rob, pos)), KPw(Position(Rob, pos)), t) \end{aligned} \tag{5.6}$$

In brief, (5.6) states that the position should be stored if Rob knows that he is not moving. If, on the other hand, the robot does not possess such knowledge (even if he is unaware of his current mobility state, due to a potential malfunction), the information acquired will be retracted one time instant after the sense action. In this case, future knowledge can be inferred only if some state constraint is available.

Moreover, it can be proved that if Rob knows initially *whether* he is moving, a single sense action is sufficient to provide knowledge about all future locations, regardless of any narrative of *Start* and *Stop* actions before or after sensing. And, most importantly, Rob does not need to consider his current state when sensing; the knowledge theory abstracts the reasoning process of determining knowledge evolution, regardless of whether the sensed fluent is inertial or continuously changing.

6 Conclusions

In this paper, we have described a logic-based epistemic framework that addresses a common task in cognitive robotics, namely the way sense actions can update an agent's mental state given world features of different type. Non-logical frameworks, based for instance on probabilistic or qualitative reasoning, have also been proposed leading to computationally more appealing approaches, suffering though from well-known weaknesses concerning openness and correctness verification issues.

The proposed solution extends previous logic-based approaches, as it investigates a broad range of fluent types. It also provides a level of abstraction to the agent's cognitive mechanism, disengaging it from explicitly distinguishing the nature of sensed fluents; whether sensed information should be stored or not is automatically determined by the agent's current knowledge. Different scenarios have been modeled using an offline reasoner. Our intension is to test the efficiency of the framework in more demanding domains and simulate online executions.

Acknowledgements The authors wish to thank Dr. Nick Bassiliades for stimulating comments and interesting discussions.

References

1. Chittaro, L., Montanari, A.: Temporal Representation and Reasoning in Artificial Intelligence: Issues and Approaches. Annals of Mathematics and Artificial Intelligence **28**(1-4), 47–106 (2000)
2. Demolombe, R., Pozos-Parra, M.: A simple and tractable extension of situation calculus to epistemic logic. 12th International Symposium on Methodologies for Intelligent Systems (ISMIS-00) pp. 515–524
3. Fritz, C., Baier, J.A., McIlraith, S.A.: ConGolog, Sin Trans: Compiling ConGolog into Basic Action Theories for Planning and Beyond. In: Proceedings International Conference on Principles of Knowledge Representation and Reasoning (KR), pp. 600–610. Australia (2008)
4. Lifschitz, V.: Circumscription. Handbook of Logic in Artificial Intelligence and Logic Programming **3**, 297–352 (1994)
5. Lobo, J., Mendez, G., Taylor, S.R.: Knowledge and the Action Description Language A. Theory and Practice of Logic Programming (TPLP) **1**(2), 129–184 (2001)
6. Miller, R., Shanahan, M.: Some Alternative Formulations of the Event Calculus. In: Computational Logic: Logic Programming and Beyond, Essays in Honour of Robert A. Kowalski, Part II, pp. 452–490. Springer-Verlag, London, UK (2002)
7. Moore, R.C.: A formal theory of knowledge and action. In: Formal Theories of the Commonsense World, pp. 319–358. J. Hobbs, R. Moore (Eds.) (1985)
8. Mueller, E.: Commonsense Reasoning, 1st edn. Morgan Kaufmann (2006)
9. Patkos, T., Plexousakis, D.: A Theory of Action, Knowledge and Time in the Event Calculus. In: SETN '08: Proceedings 5th Hellenic Conference on Artificial Intelligence, pp. 226–238. Springer-Verlag, Berlin, Heidelberg (2008)
10. Petrick, R.P.A., Levesque, H.J.: Knowledge Equivalence in Combined Action Theories. In: KR, pp. 303–314 (2002)
11. Scherl, R.: Reasoning about the Interaction of Knowledge, Time and Concurrent Actions in the Situation Calculus. In: Proceedings 18th International Conference on Artificial Intelligence (IJCAI), pp. 1091–1098 (2003)
12. Scherl, R.B., Levesque, H.J.: Knowledge, Action, and the Frame Problem. Artificial Intelligence **144**(1-2), 1–39 (2003)
13. Shanahan, M.: The Event Calculus Explained. Artificial Intelligence Today **1600**, 409–430 (1999)
14. Shanahan, M., Witkowski, M.: High-Level Robot Control through Logic. In: ATAL '00: Proceedings 7th International Workshop on Intelligent Agents VII. Agent Theories Architectures and Languages, pp. 104–121. Springer-Verlag, London, UK (2001)
15. Thielscher, M.: Representing the Knowledge of a Robot. In: A. Cohn, F. Giunchiglia, B. Selman (eds.) Proceedings International Conference on Principles of Knowledge Representation and Reasoning (KR), pp. 109–120. Morgan Kaufmann, Breckenridge, CO (2000)
16. Thielscher, M.: The Concurrent, Continuous Fluent Calculus. Studia Logica **67**(3), 315–331 (2001)
17. Thielscher, M.: FLUX: A Logic Programming Method for Reasoning Agents. Theory and Practice of Logic Programming **5**(4–5), 533–565 (2005)

MobiAct: Supporting Personalized Interaction with Mobile Context-aware Applications

Adrian Stoica and Nikolaos Avouris

University of Patras, Department of Electrical and Computer Engineering,
Human Computer Interaction Group,
Eratosthenous Street, 26500 Rio-Patras, Greece
{stoica,avouris}@upatras.gr

Abstract In this paper we present a conceptual framework for interaction with mobile context aware applications. The framework focuses especially on public and semi-public environments. Based on this framework a generic abstract architecture has been designed and several of its parts have been implemented. We discuss the implications and the support that this architecture provides for personalization of interaction. The architecture supports high interoperability and flexibility, with capability of tackling issues like privacy and degree of user control. The framework has been tested in typical spaces: a library and a museum. The paper concludes with a set of examples of use of the defined framework that cover typical situations for intra-space and across spaces usage.

1 Introduction

People need to access information and resources *where* and *when* they are performing their activities to achieve the multitude of daily tasks in a satisfactory manner. Today mobile devices are used widely to provide access to information and services associated with tangible objects through various technologies (RFID tags, two dimensional optical codes, Bluetooth etc.). As a result, an increasing number of context aware applications exist in public environments which provide various services and information to the public *when* and *where* they are needed.

Many institutions that have responsibility for places of public interest (*libraries* [1], *museums* [2], *showrooms* [5], *schools* [4], *supermarkets* [6] etc.) introduce in their environments extensions for mobile applications to harness the new potential technology brings. The physical space owned by these institutions is gradually enriched by and interweaved with a digital information space. Users (visitors, clients, readers etc) need to interact with both spaces to fully benefit of all offered

---

Please use the following format when citing this chapter:

Stoica, A. and Avouris, N., 2009, in IFIP International Federation for Information Processing, Volume 296; *Artificial Intelligence Applications and Innovations III*; Eds. Iliadis, L., Vlahavas, I., Bramer, M.; (Boston: Springer), pp. 389–397.

services to them and inherently they need devices that can link the physical and digital spaces.

Personalization and adaptation of these services to the users are very relevant in this context, however a number of issues mostly related to security and privacy [7] need to be addressed.

Mobile applications can exploit user profiles as valuable information that can dramatically improve their quality and their relevance. User profiles are based on user traces, logs, user selections (small surveys completed, search terms etc), frequency of use of various features. While the information can be used to improve the quality and the efficiency of the services, there is a risk to be used against the user. People are concerned about privacy. They wish to control their own data and they do not like to feel followed. Usually users want the benefits of an adaptive system that gives them relevant feedback but, on the other hand, they do not like that the system gathers data about them.

The system design must take into account that systems and applications must support and facilitate the tasks and the activities of their users. Users must feel that they are in control of the system and they should fully understand the benefits and the trade-offs of using it.

The user profile can be common to more applications using an external user modelling server to allow interoperability [3]. This user profile, which is composed of the traces that the user leaves in the visited places, is enriched and updated according to the security and privacy options selected.

Middleware for context aware applications have been developed to allow fast and consistent deployment of such applications. The existing middleware approaches are tackling issues like context management [8,14,15], privacy and security [11], collaboration and social interaction [10], data sharing [9], service discovery and so on.

For context aware mobile applications to step out from the labs and to be widely used by the general public, it is required to find solutions for consistent management of the service providers and consumers, user profiles and support of heterogeneity of mobile devices' platforms.

2 The MOBIle InterACTion Framework - MobiAct

The key concepts of our **MobiAct** framework are: hybrid space, physical hyperlink, hybrid space interaction device, the context and the dynamic service binding.

Hybrid Space is the space obtained from the fusion of physical and virtual spaces that are interweaved. The need to access the virtual space comes from the actual tasks the users have to perform in a certain physical space. While physical space knowledge can be accessed using perceptual mechanisms, the virtual space needs a mobile device to fetch and present information in a form suitable for human processing.

Almost any physical artefact has associated information/services from different providers. The relevance of the information depends in some extent on the relation that the provider has with the physical space where the artefact is found – e.g. ownership.

The physical world artefacts and the virtual space items are linked together by an unequal correspondence (e.g. a very small physical object can have linked to it many digital objects).

To instantiate the link between the physical and virtual artefacts, we need means of interacting with the real world [12,13]. From the need of this kind of hybrid interactions the concept of physical hyperlink or object hyperlinking emerged.

A **Physical Hyperlink,** as a means to connect a physical artefact with the digital information/ services associated to it that uniquely identifies the physical artefact or a class of equivalent artefacts. A physical hyperlink can be implemented using several modes:

- Human readable visual cue (numbers, letters)
- Machine readable visual cue (2D, 1D barcodes)
- RF tag (RFID, Bluetooth)

The different implementations of physical hyperlinks have various aspects that match characteristics of different mobile devices. Considering this issue, we propose that a standardized multi-modal approach to be adopted for implementing physical hyperlinks. Including a human readable visual cue will ensure mass accessibility provided that many devices support text entry. In figure 1 the book physical hyperlink includes modalities for barcode scanners, camera equipped devices and human visual perception.

Fig. 1. Multimodal physical hyperlink attached to a library book

To access the virtual part of the hybrid space a device is needed. We call this device **Hybrid Space Interaction Device** (typical such devices are a mobile phone or a PDA) and we identified the following requirements:

- Main requirements: Some sort of network connectivity (GPRS, 3G, WiFi), Ability to run third party applications, Basic Input/Output abilities (screen, keyboard, touchscreen, stylus);
- Optional requirements: Camera, RFID reader, Barcode scanner, Other kind of sensors.

Context is very important in mobile interaction because the applications can use it to adapt and filter the relevant information. Context elements are for example: device type and capabilities, user profile, actual task, state of the space, modality of interaction, location.

Another important concept in our proposal is **dynamic service binding**. The dynamic service binding is connecting the physical hyperlinks with the appropriate services and/or information. The choice of services delivered to the user upon selecting a certain physical hyperlink is produced by fusing several elements from the context of use - identity of the user, user preferences or profile, application provider, device used, actual task.

An example of context of use involvement in physical hyperlink selection outcome is the following: in a museum the selection of a physical hyperlink can trigger displaying of textual information or playing audio narrations if in guide mode or could trigger collection of hints, creation of links etc. if in educational game mode.

Services provided for the hybrid space user fall in the following categories: informational, transactional, navigational, control.

3 MobiAct Architecture

Based on the MobiAct framework we have designed an architecture that takes into account among others: roaming among contexts and spaces, personalization, anonymity, privacy and security.

People move every day through a succession of public, semi-public and private spaces according to their goals and their activities. The identity of the people sometimes should be known to grant them access to certain spaces, while some other times, it should be hidden to protect user privacy.

The relevance of accessing mobile services highly depends on user goals and the nature of the tasks she is doing. The utility a mobile service provides to a user depends on users' interests, goals and lifestyle.

The figure 2 depicts the proposed MobiAct architecture. The user is in a hybrid enabled space and she performs a certain task. In the physical space physical artefacts are present which allow user interactions through physical hyperlinks.

The main entities in our architecture are: user, user agency, user agent, physical space administrator/owner, semantics of space service, broker.

The figure 2 focuses on a certain physical space area at a certain moment. The left side presents the physical space, while the right side presents the virtual space elements that are separated by a dashed line for the sake of clarity. The entities "User Agency", "Broker" are represented as single instance for the simplicity of the schema. A different user could use another agency or maybe she could use several agencies. In the same way, there can be more brokers competing between them in the quality of service providing. However, at a certain moment of interaction, the user can be associated with one "User Agency" and she deals with one "Broker".

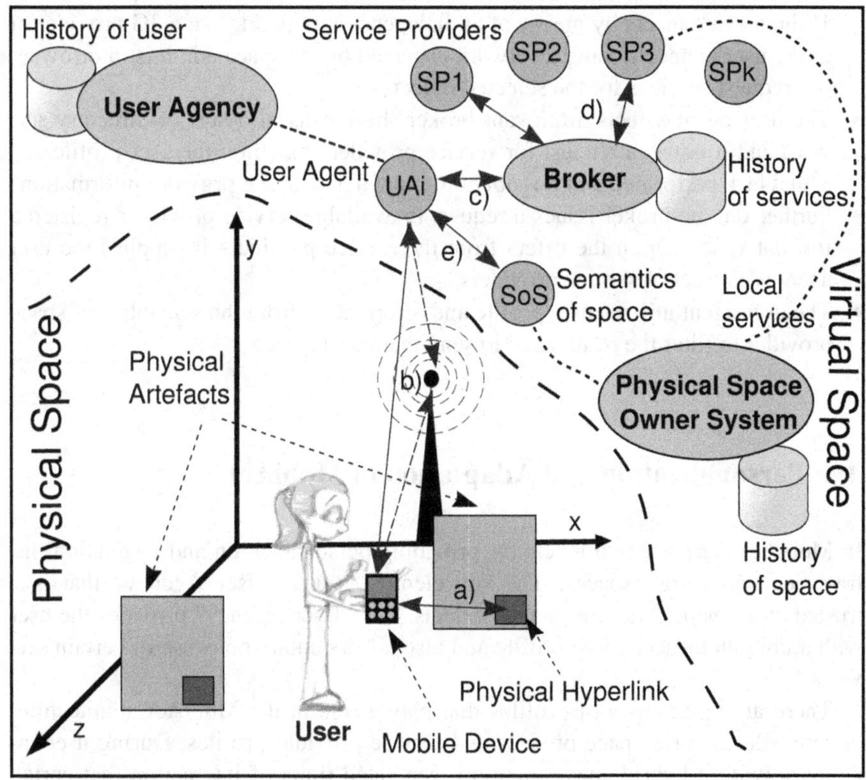

Fig. 2. MobiAct Architecture

The user is represented in the virtual space by "User Agent" that mediates interaction with other entities in the virtual space. The user initiates interaction with an artefact and a typical sequence of actions takes place. Let us examine the scenario of interacting with the hybrid space.

There are several phases of interaction. First there is the initiation phase where the user starts the interaction with an artefact. The user agent has to select a Broker suitable for the space, making use of previous interaction trails from the user to propose a set of available service providers to the user.

After selecting the desired service provider the interaction advances in the second phase of service consuming. During her interaction with one service provider the user might change its goals or she might understand that this service is not what she needed. As a result she might change back to the initiation phase.

We have identified the following typical sequence of events during initial phase of interaction with a hybrid space:

- The user is utilizing her mobile device to interact with the physical hyperlink of an object (physical artefact);
- The device software connects with the user agent – there are two possibilities: 1) the user connects by means of an independent network like a 3G provider or 2) the user connects using a network provided by the space administrator/owner - to request services for the selected object.
- The user agent selects a relevant broker (by means of a sort of directory service) and it issues a request for service providers based on the user profile and actual task performed and possibly on semantics of space provider information.
- Further on, the broker issues a request to available service providers registered for that space. Upon the offers from the service providers it supplies the user agent with a set of service providers.
- The user agent utilizes user profile and information from the semantics of space provider to filter the results and to send them to the user.

4 Personalization and Adaptation in MobiAct

In MobiAct there are two levels for providing personalization and adaptation: intra-space and across spaces. The key element is the "User Agency" that is a trusted entity which the user herself selects. The "User Agency" provides the user with a ubiquitous accessible profile and also allows anonymous use of certain services.

There are three types of profiles that play a role in the MobiAct architecture: user profiles, hybrid space profiles and service provider profiles. During user interaction with a hybrid space there are generated trails of interaction that enrich these profiles. Except interaction trails profiles contain identity, interest ontology, generic user information (e.g. language(s), age, sex etc.) and privacy preferences for the user, rankings for hybrid space, content and service providers

At intra-space level the user experience is improved within a certain hybrid space through filtering and ranking content and service providers according to the user profile, community produced ratings, providers' and content's metadata and collective profile. Both user profile and provider's metadata are being built incrementally.

The relations between the service provider and the physical space the user is immersed in influence the degree of relevance – e.g. In a museum the information provided by the museum service provider (information about exhibits) should be of higher precedence to other service providers

At across spaces level the architecture uses collective profiles and statistical methods to filter and rank content and service providers in new spaces based on trails from other spaces richer in trails and with a more complete profile.

The user agency has access to a multitude of user profiles in a multitude of spaces.

The adaptation of the services for the users is done through the combination of the personal model and the collective model with different weights according to the richness of the personal user model in the specific space.

In figure 3 a structured representation of the information in the user profile database is shown. When a user visits a new space the system can examine the specific context to find popular artefacts, information or activities. Also to match interest across spaces it can examine the interests already depicted in other contexts and to match them against the other users that have also interests defined for our current user new context.

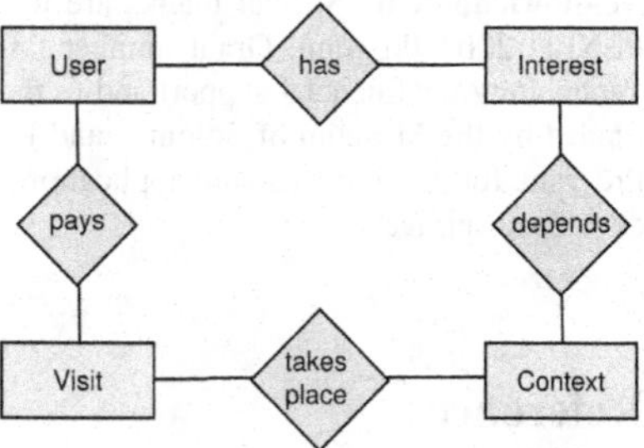

Fig. 3. Simplified ERD of user profile

The sum of trails of interaction over time builds up the history of the user, of the space and of services. Each interaction generates trails on the side of every participating entity. Using historical data each entity can improve its performance.

The visits of the various users in a certain space build up the specific space model. This model has a twofold use: on one hand provides a base for a collective statistical user model for new users and on the other hand provides information for restructuring both the physical and virtual space.

5 Conclusion

The MobiAct framework and the corresponding architecture aim at offering an application independent solution for mobile service providing and consuming. Introducing the User Agency entity the architecture allows not only intra-space but also across spaces personalization and adaptation. It aims at providing readily implemented functionality for the common features of context aware mobile application infrastructure. The benefits of this approach are related to cost and development effort for deployment of mobile services, as well as interoperability and fluidity of user experience across multiple spaces. In this paper the main characteristics of the MobiAct framework and architecture have been outlined together with its uses for personalization and adaptation.

The roadmap for defining this architecture and developing the first prototype involved first gathering of requirement from two quite different semi-public spaces, a large Academic Library and a Cultural Historical Museum. During the requirements gathering phase, which involved stakeholder analysis and focus groups that discussed issues of privacy and service personalization, the two applications have been defined. After we will finalize the evaluation of the framework for intra-space use will follow the across spaces evaluation phase. When the final prototypes are developed, the privacy and trust issues related to the personalization functionality of the architecture will be tested with real users who are going to visit the two sites and experience the effect of different privacy policies on the quality of the service.

Acknowledgments Special thanks are due to the Hybrid Libraries Project, funded under the PENED 2003 Program, Grant number 03ED791 by the General Secretariat of Research and Technology for financial support and to the Project of Supporting visitors of Solomos Museum, funded by the Museum of Solomos and Prominent Zakynthians, under the Information Society Program, for providing us with application requirements for personalization and adaptation of the developed services.

References

1. Aittola M, Ryhänen T & Ojala T (2003) SmartLibrary - Location-aware mobile library service. Proc. 5th International Symposium on Human Computer Interaction with Mobile Devices and Services, Udine, Italy, 411-416.
2. Exploratorium (2005), Electronic Guidebook forum Report, San Francisco, Available at: www.exploratorium.edu/guidebook/eguides_forum2005.pdf Accessed: April 2006
3. Heckmann D., Schwartz T., Brandherm B., Schmitz M., and von Wilamowitz-Moellendorff M., GUMO – The General User Model Ontology, L. Ardissono, P. Brna, and A. Mitrovic (Eds.): UM 2005, LNAI 3538, pp. 428-432, 2005.
4. Liang J.-K., Liu T.-C., Wang H.-Y., Chang B., Deng Y.-C., Yang J.-C., Chouz C.-Y., Ko H.-W., Yang S., & Chan T.-W., A few design perspectives on one-on-one digital classroom environment, Journal of Computer Assisted Learning 21, pp181-189
5. mEXRESS Project Homepage, available at http://mexpress.intranet.gr/index.htm, last accessed October 2006
6. Roussos G., Koukara L., Kourouthanasis P, Tuominen J.O., Seppala O., Giaglis G. and Frissaer J., 2002, "A case study in pervasive retail", ACM MOBICOM WMC02, pp. 90-94.
7. SWAMI Project (2006), Dark scenarios in ambient intelligence: Highlighting risks and vulnerabilities, Deliverable D2, Available: http://swami.jrc.es/pages/documents/SWAMI_D2_scenarios_Final_ESvf_003.pdf Accessed: April 2006
8. Dey, A.K., Salber, D., Abowd, G.: A Conceptual Framework and a Toolkit for Supporting the Rapid Prototyping of Context-Aware Applications. Human-Computer Interaction 16 (2001) 97-166
9. Boulkenafed M, Issarny V, A Middleware Service for Mobile Ad Hoc Data Sharing, Enhancing Data Availability, Middleware 2003 (2003), pp. 493-511.
10. Kern S, Braun P, Rossak W, MobiSoft: An Agent-Based Middleware for Social-Mobile Applications, On the Move to Meaningful Internet Systems 2006: OTM 2006 Workshops (2006), pp. 984-993.

11. Heckmann D, Ubiquitous User Modeling, Vol. 297, Dissertations in Artificial Intelligence, IOS Press, Amsterdam, NL, 2006
12. E. Rukzio, M. Paolucci, T. Finin, P. Wisner, T. Payne (Eds.) , Proceedings Workshop Mobile Interaction with the Real World (MIRW 2006), available at http://www.hcilab.org/events/mirw2006/pdf/mirw2006_proceedings.pdf, retrieved on 11th of April 2008
13. G. Broll, A. De Luca, E. Rukzio, C. Noda, P. Wisner (Eds.) , Proceedings Workshop Mobile Interaction with the Real World (MIRW 2007), available at http://www.medien.ifi.lmu.de/pubdb/publications/pub/broll2007mirwmguidesTR/broll2007mirwmguidesTR.pdf, retrieved on 11th of April 2008
14. Riva O, Contory: A Middleware for the Provisioning of Context Information on Smart Phones, Middleware 2006 (2006), pp. 219-239.
15. Zimmermann A., Specht M. and Lorenz A., Personalization and Context Management, User Modeling and User-Adapted Interaction Special Issue on User Modeling in Ubiquitous Computing, Vol. 15, No. 3-4. (August 2005), pp. 275-302.

Defining a Task's Temporal Domain for Intelligent Calendar Applications

Anastasios Alexiadis and Ioannis Refanidis

Department of Applied Informatics, University of Macedonia
Thessaloniki, Greece

talex@java.uom.gr, yrefanid@uom.gr

Abstract Intelligent calendar assistants have many years ago attracted researchers from the areas of scheduling, machine learning and human computer interaction. However, all efforts have concentrated on automating the meeting scheduling process, leaving personal tasks to be decided manually by the user. Recently, an attempt to automate scheduling personal tasks within an electronic calendar application resulted in the deployment of a system called SELFPLANNER. The system allows the user to define tasks with duration, temporal domain and other attributes, and then automatically accommodates them within her schedule by employing constraint satisfaction algorithms. Both at the design phase and while using the system, it has been made clear that the main bottleneck in its use is the definition of a task's temporal domain. To alleviate this problem, a new approach based on a combination of template application and manual editing has been designed. This paper presents the design choices underlying temporal domain definition in SELFPLANNER and some computational problems that we had to deal with.

1 Introduction

Electronic calendar organizers constitute inseparable companions of almost every busy person, such as managers, professionals, academics, politicians and others. Microsoft Outlook, Google Calendar and Yahoo! Calendar constitute mainstream products of the software industry, with new features being constantly added to them. These products provide convenient ways to help the user organize her tasks as well as to arrange meetings with others (based usually on message exchanging). On the other hand, several researchers in the last decade concentrated on embedding intelligence in electronic organizers, focusing on automating the meeting scheduling process either by exchanging messages between the potential participants or by learning a user's preferences ([1, 4, 7]).

Recently, a research effort attempting to enhance the intelligence of electronic organizers by automating the scheduling of personal task procedure resulted in the deployment of a system called SELFPLANNER [5]. Contrary to other intelligent calendar application efforts that ignore tasks or retain them in task lists without any

Please use the following format when citing this chapter:

Alexiadis, A. and Refanidis, I., 2009, in IFIP International Federation for Information Processing, Volume 296; *Artificial Intelligence Applications and Innovations III*; Eds. Iliadis, L., Vlahavas, I., Bramer, M.; (Boston: Springer), pp. 399–406.

attempt to put them on the user's calendar [2], SELFPLANNER puts them into the user's calendar, taking into account several types of constraints and preferences.

Perhaps the most important attribute of a task is its temporal domain, i.e. when the task can be executed. However, defining a temporal domain is also the most cumbersome part of a task's definition. Having recognized that from the system's design phase, we devised several mechanisms to facilitate domain definition. They are mainly based on a combination of template application and manual editing. So, this paper concentrates on the domain definition issue both from a human-computer interaction and from an algorithmic point of view.

The rest of the paper is structured as follows: Section 2 highlights the key features of the SELFPLANNER application. Section 3 presents the internal representation of task domains in SELFPLANNER, whereas Section 4 discusses the algorithmic issues incurred by the way domains are represented. Finally, Section 5 concludes the paper and poses future research directions.

2 SELFPLANNER Overview

SELFPLANNER is a web-based intelligent calendar application that helps the user to schedule her personal tasks (Fig. 1). With the term 'personal task' we mean any task that has to be performed by the user and requires some of her time. Meetings are considered as milestones, i.e. they cannot be moved by the system. The user can schedule her meetings using alternative tools, such as Google Calendar meeting arrangement facilities.

Each task is characterized by its duration and its temporal domain [6]. A domain consists of a set of intervals, where the task can be scheduled. A task might be interruptible, i.e. it can be executed in parts with the sum of the durations of these parts being equal to the task's duration. Several constraints on the durations of these parts and their temporal distances can be defined. A task can also be periodic, i.e. it has to be performed many times, e.g. daily or weekly. A location or a set of locations is attached to each task; to execute a task or a part of it, the user has to be in one of these locations. Travelling time between pairs of locations are taken into account when the system schedules adjacent tasks.

Ordering constraints and unary preferences are also supported by the system. Unary preferences are monotonic linear or step utility functions over the temporal domain of a task, denoting when the user prefers the task to be scheduled. SELFPLANNER uses an adaptation of the Squeaky Wheel Optimization framework [3] to solve the resulting scheduling problem, while trying to optimize the sum of the various preferences.

SELFPLANNER utilizes Google Calendar for presenting the calendar to the user, and a Google Maps application to define locations and compute the time the user needs to go from one location to another. The system is available for public use at http://selfplanner.uom.gr.

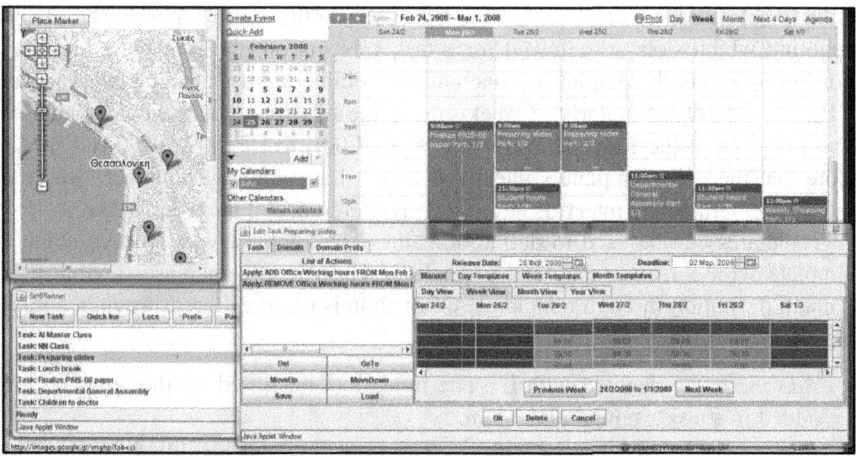

Fig. 1. Overview of the SELFPLANNER intelligent calendar application.

3 Domain Representation

From a theoretical point of view, the temporal domain of a task consists of a set of intervals. For practical reasons we consider only integer domains. In the context of the application, a unit corresponds to the quantum of time that, as in most electronic calendars, is 30 minutes. For reasons of clarity, in the following we will use a notation of the form ⟨DD/MM/YY HH:MM⟩ to denote time points. Depending on the context, several parts of the time stamp will be omitted or altered.

Using intervals to represent domains is however problematic both from a computational and from a user's experience point of view. Suppose for example that a user wants to schedule a task of 2 hours duration and this task has to be performed during office hours next week. Supposing a 5 days working week, this might results in five intervals of the form, say:

[⟨27/10/08 09:00⟩, ⟨27/10/08 17:00⟩] … [⟨31/10/08 09:00⟩, ⟨31/10/08 17:00⟩]

Imagine now what happens if the same task has a deadline after a month or a year: Storing and retrieving the domain of this task would be a time- and space-consuming process. Even worse, having the user to define this domain would be an inhibitory factor to use the system at all. To overcome these deficiencies, we selected to avoid using interval representation for temporal domains.

3.1 Templates and List of Actions

A template is a pattern with specific duration and with no absolute time reference. SELFPLANNER supports three types of templates: Daily, Weekly and Monthly.

Each template consists of a set of intervals covering the entire pattern's period and denoting which slots are allowed for a task's execution (the remaining are not). For example, a daily template of lunch hours would comprise a single interval, say [⟨12:30⟩, ⟨15:00⟩]. Similarly, a weekly template of office hours would comprise five intervals of the form [⟨Mo 09:00⟩, ⟨Mo 17:00⟩] to [⟨Fri 09:00⟩, ⟨Fri 17:00⟩]. Note that the daily template's interval does not have any day reference, whereas the weekly template's intervals have a relative reference of the week's day.

Templates can be used to define domains. The simplest way is to combine a template with a release date and a deadline. However, to increase flexibility in domain definition through templates, we distinguish four different ways in applying a template. These are the following:

- *Add included*, denoted with □ : The time slots identified by the template are added in a task's temporal domain.
- *Remove excluded*, denoted with □ : The time slots not identified by the template are removed from a task's temporal domain.
- *Add excluded*, denoted with □ : The time slots not identified by the template are added in a task's temporal domain.
- *Remove included*, denoted with □ : The time slots identified by the template are removed from a task's temporal domain.

As an example, consider again the daily lunch hours template, named *Lunch*. If we want to include lunch hours to a task's domain we use □ *Lunch*. If we want to say that a task is to be executed only during the lunch hours, we use □ □ *Lunch*. If we want to exclude lunch hours from a task's domain we use □ *Lunch*.

3.2 List of Actions and Temporal Domains

A temporal domain can be defined through a sequence of template applications. For example, one task's domain might consist of office working hours excluding the lunch hours. This could be defined by a list of actions, that initially adds office hours to the temporal domain and then removes lunch hours.

More formally, a *domain action* is defined as a temporally constrained template application. This is denoted by providing an absolute interval with the template, e.g. □ □ *Lunch*@[⟨27/10/08 00:00⟩, ⟨28/10/08 00:00⟩]. Domain actions that are not temporally constrained apply to the whole task's domain.

A *list of domain actions* is an ordered sequence of them. For example, the following list defines office working hours excluding the lunch hours (note that domain actions are not temporally constrained, so they apply to the whole task's domain):

□ □ *OfficeHours,*
□ *Lunch*

Manual editing a domain, i.e. adding or removing a time slot without the use of a template, can be seen as a special case of template application. Suppose we have a daily template named *All*, consisting of the single interval [⟨00:00⟩, ⟨24:00⟩], i.e. the whole day (operators □ and □ are meaningless for this template). So, manually adding (removing) an interval to (from) a task's temporal domain is equivalent to applying □ *All* (□ *All*) temporally constrained over this interval.

Finally, a *temporal domain* is defined as a list of domain actions, accompanied by a release date and deadline. So, the following specifies a task's domain over the week from 27/10/08 to 31/10/2008, including all office hours but the lunch hours:

[⟨27/10/08 00:00⟩, ⟨31/10/08 24:00⟩]
□ □ *OfficeHours*
□ *Lunch*

The semantics of a domain are the following:

1. All time slots before the release date or after the deadline are excluded from the domain.
2. A time slot is included in the domain, if there is a domain action that adds this time slot in the domain, whereas no subsequent domain action removes the time slot.
3. A time slot is excluded from the domain, if there is a domain action that removes this time slot, whereas no subsequent domain action adds the time slot.
4. All unspecified time slots are considered as included in the domain.

4 Computational Issues

Using lists of domain actions to represent temporal domains gives rise to interesting computational problems, such as whether a time slot is included in the domain or not, how to transform the domain into the traditional representation with list of intervals or, finally, how to simplify the list of domain actions. These issues are treated in the following subsections.

4.1 Domain Inclusion

Knowing whether a time slot is included in a task's temporal domain or not is important, among others, when graphically displaying parts of the domain on the screen. The following algorithm answers this question:

Algorithm 1. *GetTimeSlotStatus*

Inputs: A domain represented by a list of domain actions and a time slot *T*.
Output: Either of the *included* or *excluded* values.

1. If *T* is before the release date or after the deadline, return *excluded*.
2. Let *D* be the last domain action. If no such action exists, then *D* is NULL.
3. While *D*≠*NULL*

   a. If *D* adds the *T*, return *included*.
   b. If *D* removes *T*, return *excluded*.
   c. Let *D* be the previous domain action. If no such action exists, *D* is *NULL*.
4. Return *included*.

Algorithm *GetTimeSlotStatus* is very fast. Indeed, suppose that the action list has *N* entries and each template has at most *M* intervals, then the worst case complexity is $O(N \cdot M)$, with *N* and *M* usually taking small values.

4.2 List of Intervals

It is often required to transform a temporal domain represented by a list of domain actions to the traditional list of intervals. For example, most existing schedulers do not support the list of domain actions representation. So, algorithm *GetIntervals* is a generalization of algorithm *GetTimeSlotStatus* and does exactly that:

Algorithm 2. *GetIntervals*

Inputs: A domain represented by a list of domain actions.
Output: A list of intervals.

1. Let **A** be a table of integers, whose size equals the number of time slots between the domain's release date and the deadline. Let *S* this size. Initialize **A** with zeroes. Let C=0.
2. Let *D* be the last domain action. If no such action exists, then *D* is *NULL*.
3. While $D \neq NULL$ and $C<S$.
   a. For each time slot *T* added by *D*
      i. If **A**[*T*] is 0, then set **A**[*T*] to 1 and increase *C* by 1.
   b. For each time slot *T* removed by *D*
      i. If **A**[*T*] is 0, then set **A**[*T*] to -1 and increase *C* by 1.
   c. Let *D* be the previous domain action. If no such action exists, *D* is *NULL*.
4. If $C<S$
   a. For each time slot *T* such that **A**[*T*]=0, set **A**[*T*]=1.
5. Create a list of intervals by joining consecutive time slots having **A**[*T*]$\geq$0.

Algorithm 2 is very fast, however it might have significant memory requirements in case of large domains due to the definition of the temporary variable **A**. However, an alternative design that would directly encode the new domain in intervals would be inefficient, since step 3 would require to traverse the entire list of intervals to decide whether a time slot has already got a status or not.

4.3 Simplifying Domains

There are cases where several domain actions can be removed from the list without any change in the resulting domain. For example, suppose □ □ *OfficeHours* exists in a domain action list. This domain action adds to the domain all the included template's intervals and, at the same time, it removes all excluded template's intervals. Furthermore, this domain action is not temporally constrained, so it covers the entire domain. In this case, any domain action occurring before this one wouldn't have any effect in the domain and thus it could be safely removed.

Detecting domain actions that can be safely removed from the action list requires a simple change in Algorithm 2. In particular, in step 3 we should check, for each domain action D, whether the domain action has increased C or not. In the latter case the domain action does not affect the temporal domain and can be removed. However, from an application point of view, this removal should (and does) not occur without prior confirmation from the user, since the user might intend to remove or modify some of the subsequent domain actions, which could result in ineffective domain actions to become effective.

5 Conclusions and Future Work

This paper presented an alternative way to represent temporal domains of tasks within a deployed intelligent calendar application. This representation can be used both for internal representation and for user interface purposes. We also presented efficient algorithms that answer questions as to whether a specific time-slot is included in the domain or what is the equivalent representation with intervals.

All these features have been implemented in a deployed intelligent calendar assistant application called SELFPLANNER. Fig. 2 shows the task's domain definition dialog box. As we can see, there are four main tabs, labelled as Manual, Day, Week and Month. The first one is for manual editing the domain, whereas the other three are for defining and applying templates. Manual editing allows also the user to view the current domain in various views. What is interesting is that the current list of actions is visible to the user at the left hand side of the dialog box. The user can not only watch it, but she can also change it, by removing domain actions or change their order. Every change in the list of domain actions is immediately displayed on the manual editing tab of the dialog box. She can also save the list of domain actions to retrieve it to define the domain of another task.

As for the future, we are working on allowing the user to link templates with the tasks. Currently, as far as a template is applied to a task's domain, any subsequent change in the template does not affect the task's domain. In other words, a copy of the template is used for each task. However, there are cases where the user might want to change the domains of several tasks that have been defined using a specific template, without the need to redefine all domains (e.g. suppose that the store hours have been changed, so all tasks concerning shopping have to change their domains). The most natural way to do that is to modify the template, but this requires that the template is not embedded but linked with the tasks.

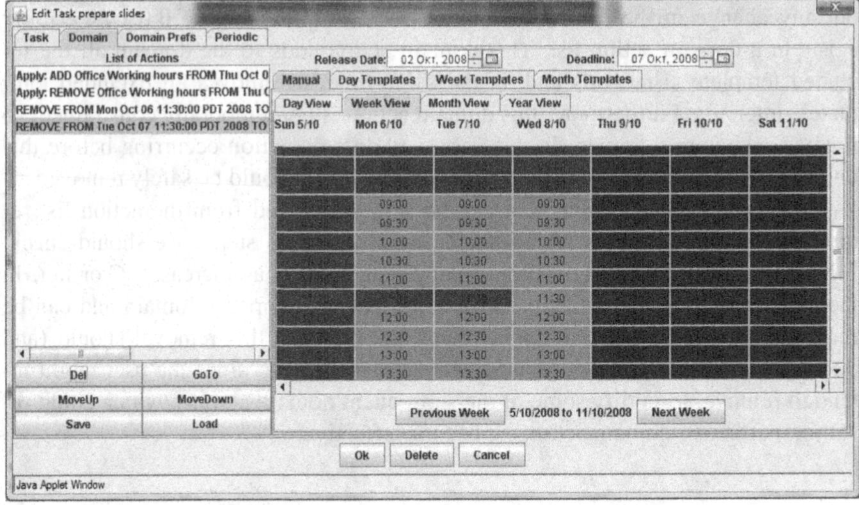

Fig. 2. Overview of the domain definition dialog box.

We are also working on defining and integrating a task ontology, where each class of tasks has its default partially defined temporal domain. To conclude with, we believe that intelligent calendar assistants will play a significant role in organizing our lives in the future but a crucial factor for their adoption is their usability. The work presented in this paper is, we hope, a step towards that direction.

References

1. Berry P, Conley K, Gervasio M, Peintner B, Uribe T & Yorke-Smith N (2006) Deploying a Personalized Time Management Agent. 5th Intl Joint Conf. on Autonomous Agents and Multi Agent Systems, Industrial Track, Hakodate, Japan, pp. 1564-1571.
2. Conley K Carpenter (2007) Towel: Towards an Intelligent To-Do List. AAAI Spring Symposium on Interaction Challenges for Artificial Assistants, Stanford, CA.
3. Joslin D E & Clements D P (1999) "Squeaky Wheel" Optimization. Journal of Artificial Intelligence Research, vol. 10: 375-397.
4. Modi P J, Veloso M, Smith S F & Oh J (2004) CMRadar: A Personal Assistant Agent for Calendar Management. Workshop on Agent Oriented Information Systems.
5. Refanidis I & Alexiadis A (2008) SelfPlanner: Planning your Time! ICAPS 2008 Workshop on Scheduling and Planning Applications, Sydney.
6. Refanidis I (2007) Managing Personal Tasks with Time Constraints and Preferences. 17th Intl. Conf. on Automated Planning and Scheduling Systems, Providence, RI.
7. Singh R (2003) RCal: An Autonomous Agent for Intelligent Distributed Meeting Scheduling. Tech. report CMU-RI-TR-03-46, Robotics Institute, Carnegie Mellon University.

Managing Diagnosis Processes with Interactive Decompositions

Quang-Huy GIAP, Stephane PLOIX, and Jean-Marie FLAUS

Abstract In the scientific literature, it is generally assumed that models can be completely established before the diagnosis analysis. However, in the actual maintenance problems, such models appear difficult to be reached in one step. It is indeed difficult to formalize a whole complex system. Usually, understanding, modelling and diagnosis are interactive processes where systems are partially depicted and some parts are refined step by step. Therefore, a diagnosis analysis that manages different abstraction levels and partly modelled components would be relevant to actual needs. This paper proposes a diagnosis tool managing different modelling abstraction levels and partly depicted systems.

1 Introduction

In the diagnosis community, abstraction has been presented as a promising technique to reduce the computational cost of model-based diagnosis [6, 1, 2, 3]. Abstract procedure tends to aggregate items to describe a system at different levels of abstraction with different levels of details (structural and behavioral). It is called *bottom-up method* because it begins by the most detailed level and stops in the most abstract level. Then, algorithms, which are based on Mozetic's approach, are proposed to solve the problem. Contrary to *bottom-up method*, a *top-down method* is proposed. The important point of our purpose is to use abstraction to fit the actual diagnosis process in the context of human machine cooperation.

In this paper, the term *item* is preferred to *component* because in actual applications different types of elements may be encountered such as functions, operations, components. Moreover, in a multi-abstraction level context, super-functions and a super-components use to appear.

Quang-Huy GIAP · Stephane PLOIX · Jean-Marie FLAUS
Laboratoire G-SCOP, 46, avenue Félix Viallet - 38031 Grenoble Cedex 1 - France,
e-mail: {quang-huy.giap,stephane.ploix,jean-marie.flaus}@g-scop.inpg.fr

Please use the following format when citing this chapter:

Giap, Q.-H., Ploix, S. and Flaus, J.-M., 2009, in IFIP International Federation for Information Processing, Volume 296; *Artificial Intelligence Applications and Innovations III*; Eds. Iliadis, L., Vlahavas, I., Bramer, M.; (Boston: Springer), pp. 407–415.

2 Problem statement

2.1 Behavioural and functional modelling

In a physical system, a phenomenon is a directly observable element of information about the state of a system. It is usually modelled by physical variables. The *behavior* of an item is modelled by constraints characterizing the set of possible values of involved variables. The *behavioral mode* of an item is modelled by one or more constraints. In [5], the model of multiple modes is introduced. Then, each item may have a normal mode *ok* and a set of possible abnormal modes including a complementary unknown fault mode *cfm*. A specific fault mode is denoted by *fm*. Hence, the set of behavioral modes of an item may be written: $Modes(item_i) = \{ok, [fm_1, \ldots, fm_n], cfm\}$

An item is called *non-modelled* if there is no available constraint that represents any of its modes. However, it is convenient to assume the existence of 2 modes *ok* and *cfm* for such an item that can be depicted as a part of another item. It is discussed in the next subsection.

2.2 Formalizing abstraction

Let's consider *behavioral abstraction*. As mentioned before, an item is either a function or a physical resource. The hierarchical decomposition of a system is generally begun by the global function of the system i.e. the most abstract item. Then, this item may be decomposed into child-items that may be child-functions, child-components, ... In other words, an expected behavioral mode of an item is achieved by its child-items. In order to formalize hierarchical relations between items, let's introduce the notion of m-proposition.

Definition 1. (m-proposition) A logical proposition where symbols are modes of items, which can be expressed by a conjunctive normal form, is called a m-proposition. If $\mathscr{P}(mode_1, \ldots, mode_n)$ is a m-proposition, the support $\mathscr{P}$ is defined by $Modes(\mathscr{P}) = \{mode_1, \ldots, mode_n\}$.

For example, $(mode_1 \rightarrow mode_2) \wedge mode_3$, with $\neg mode_1 = mode_4 \vee mode_5$, is a m-proposition because it can be rewritten as: $(mode_4 \vee mode_5 \vee mode_2) \wedge mode_3$.

Definition 2. (monomial of m-proposition) A monomial in a m-proposition is one of the disjunctive proposition appearing in the equivalent conjunctive normal form.

For instance, in the previous example, $mode_4 \vee mode_5 \vee mode_2$ and $mode_3$ are the monomials of the m-proposition.

The concept of partial behavioral abstraction can then be introduced.

Definition 3. (partial behavioral abstraction) Let I be an item and $\mathbb{I} = \{I_1, \ \ldots, \ I_n\}$ a set of items. I is a partial behavioral abstraction of $\mathbb{I}$ if $\forall m_i \in Modes(I)$, it exists a m-proposition $\mathscr{P}_i$ such as: $m_i \rightarrow \mathscr{P}$ with $Modes(\mathscr{P}_i) = \{mode(I_1), \ \ldots, mode(I_n)\}$.

If I is a partial behavioral abstraction of $\mathbb{I} = \{I_1, \ \ldots, \ I_n\}$, I is named *parent-item* of each I_i and each I_i is a child-item of I. Normally, if a parent-item behaves correctly, it is deduced that its child-items are in a normal mode. It is represented by a logical implication $ok(I) \rightarrow ok(I_1) \wedge ok(I_2) \wedge \ldots \wedge ok(I_n)$. In the context of human machine cooperation, partial behavioral abstraction represents the knowledge of expert, who tests the faulty system, about the structure of a system.

Definition 4. (complete behavioral abstraction) Let I be an item and $\mathbb{I} = \{I_1, \ \ldots, \ I_n\}$ a set of items. I is a complete behavioral abstraction of $\mathbb{I}$ if $\forall m_i \in Modes(I)$, it exists a m-proposition $\mathscr{P}_i$ such as: $m_i \leftrightarrow \mathscr{P}$ with $Modes(\mathscr{P}_i) = \{mode(I_1), \ \ldots, mode(I_n)\}$.

A partial behavioral abstraction $\mathbb{I} = \{I_1, \ \ldots, \ I_n\}$ of I can always be transformed into a complete one in introducing a new virtual item that represents the part of item I which is not in $\mathbb{I}$, denoted by *VI* for *virtual item*, with $VI = I \setminus \mathbb{I}$.

2.3 Fault propagation

In actual physical systems, a fault propagation models the fact that a fault (or failure) mode of an item induces fault modes of other items. Fault propagation is usually represented by a logical implication, e.g. $mode(item_i) \rightarrow mode'(item_j)$. To take into account fault propagations, the transformation of logical implications into logical conjunctions is achieved. A logical implication $A \rightarrow B$ is equivalent to $\neg A \vee B$, then $mode(item_i) \rightarrow mode'(item_j)$ is equivalent to $\neg mode(item_i) \vee mode(item_j)$.

2.4 Formulation of a complete diagnostic problem

Let's summarize results that can appears in the statement of a complete diagnostic problem

1. the list of items and possible modes for each item.
2. the partial behavioral abstractions inferred from expert's knowledge.
3. the modes implied in inconsistent tests, modelled by disjunctive m-propositions.
4. the fault propagations, modelled by disjunctive m-propositions.

3 An iterative diagnosis solving process

Let's now detail the diagnosis process based on interactive decompositions (top-down method). It is an interactive process between a diagnosis tool (a machine) and an expert. The diagnosis process begins when a malfunction is detected. Fault isolation usually starts with the tests that check the global function of a system. In each expert's interaction, expert performs tests, collects new data and continues the process. According to the monotony principle, the diagnosis tool provides more and more detailed diagnoses as new results arise. Step by step, it locates the subsystems or components which are in a faulty mode. This diagnosis process is depicted by figure 1.

Note that, the solving process is the same at each interaction. Let's focus now on what happens between two interactions. Diagnosis process between two interactions can be decomposed into two parts. The first one is called *transformation*: it transforms the expert problem with partial behavioral abstractions into a solvable problem. The second one is based on a *MHS-Tree algorithm* which computes and provides diagnoses from the solvable problem.

3.1 Transformation

During the transformation step, the initial knowledge about system (symptoms, decomposition model and fault propagations) can be transformed into a m-proposition by:

1. introducing complementary fault mode for each known item
2. introducing virtual complementary items in order to transform partial behavioral abstractions into complete behavioral abstractions in formalizing all the implications from conjunction of child modes to each parent mode, in order to compute the corresponding equivalent m-propositions.
3. transforming logical implications from fault propagation into disjunctive propositions (see 2.3).
4. replacing the abstract modes by their equivalent m-propositions for points (3) and (4) in section 2.4.
5. developing the m-propositions into a conjunctive normal form and splitting the resulting proposition into a set of monomials.

Finally, after these transformations, the diagnosis problem to be solved may be formulated as m-proposition whose monomials are provided to the solving algorithm to compute diagnoses.

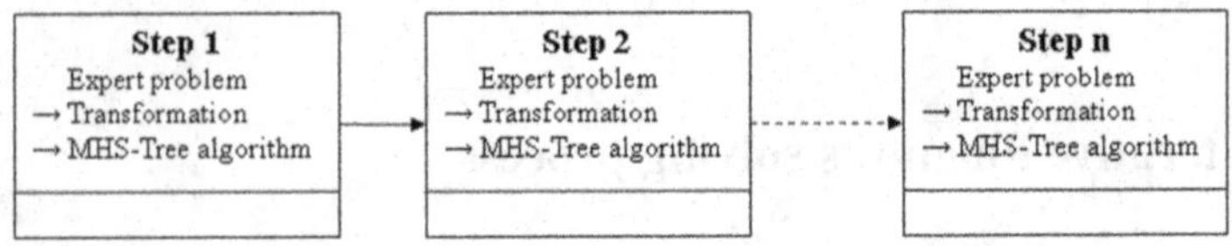

Fig. 1 Diagnosis process

3.2 Solving algorithm

When items contain multiple modes, the standard HS-tree algorithm (a tree whose nodes are hitting sets [8]) may lead to diagnoses that contain several behavioral modes of the same item. However, these diagnoses are impossible because an item may be in only one mode at the same time.

In addition to standard HS-tree approaches, the multi-mode context has to be taken into account. It is not a new problem. In literature, some solving approaches has for instance been proposed in [5, 9]. Based on ATMS [4], the model of faults is integrated in GED+ [9] to analyse whether the faultiness of the components would really explain the observation. In multi-mode context, Sherlock [5] is developed from GDE to compute automatically conflict set and diagnostic hypotheses. It focus reasoning on more probable probabilities firs in attempt to control the combinatorics. Without the constraints propagation technique, HS-Tree based algorithm [8] is preferred in this section to manage multiple-modes. The path from a node to the root node of a HS-Tree show clearly all elements implied in a temporary diagnostic result in the construction of HS-Tree. Then, it is easy to avoid the existence of two or more modes of an Item in a diagnostic result. Moreover, in comparison with original HS-Tree algorithm, which base on a set of conflicts, MHS-Tree is extended to a set of disjunctive propositions to computes hitting set. Each disjunctive proposition can correspond to a test inconsistent or to transformed fault propagation.

In order to keep a sound reasoning, a consistent test is not taken into account to compute diagnoses except if it is fully checked. However, results of normal consistent tests are useful for classification of diagnoses. In [7], an approach based on a distance between theoretical and effective signatures has been proposed. Here, it is extended to multi-mode context.

Let $T = (t_i)$ be an ordered list of tests, and $M = (m_i)$ be a set of faulty modes. the signature of M in T is given by $\sigma_T(M)$:

$$\forall i, \begin{cases} (\sigma_T(M))_i = 1 \leftrightarrow M \bigcap \overline{\prod_{mode}(t_i)} \neq \emptyset \\ (\sigma_T(M))_i = 0 \leftrightarrow M \bigcap \overline{\prod_{mode}(t_i)} = \emptyset \end{cases} \tag{1}$$

where $\prod_{mode}(t_i)$ corresponds to the set of modes implied in the test t_i. And $\overline{\prod_{mode}(t_i)}$ corresponds to the union of complementary modes of each mode implied in the test t_i:

$$\overline{\prod_{mode}(t_i)} = \bigcup_{m(I) \in \prod_{mode}(t_i)} Modes(I) \backslash \{m(I)\}$$

Let $T = (t_i)$ be an ordered list of tests. At an given instant, the effective signature in T, denoted by σ_T^*, is given by:

$$\forall i, \begin{cases} (\sigma_T^*)_i = 1 \leftrightarrow t_i \text{ is inconsistent} \\ (\sigma_T^*)_i = 0 \leftrightarrow t_i \text{ is consistent} \end{cases} \tag{2}$$

The next measurement attempts to measure the similarity between the effective signature and the theoretical signature of a diagnosis [7]. Let $T = (t_i)$ be an ordered list of tests, and $D = d_i$ be a set of diagnoses. The coincidence measurement is given by:

$$\forall d_i \in D, \mu_T^c(d_i) = \frac{|\sigma_T(d_i), \sigma_T^*|_{Hamming}}{dim(T)} \tag{3}$$

Application of this measurement is illustrated in the next example.

4 Application example

In order to illustrate how the proposed approach fits to iterative diagnosis with consecutive decompositions, let's consider a faulty car studied by a car mechanic. Firstly, the car mechanic notes that the car does not start up. At this step, the resulting symptom, which is also a trivial diagnosis, is: *cfm*(car). It is very general and does not direct to the next step: almost every failure is possible. Implicitly, the possible modes for the car are:

$$Modes(car) = \{ok, cfm\} \tag{4}$$

Secondly, because the starting system may be easily checked, the expert implicitly decomposes the car into the electric power resource (*EPR*), the electrical starting system except the starting drive (*ESS*), and the starting drive (*SD*).

The decomposition can be modelled by:

$$ok(car) \to ok(EPR) \wedge ok(ESS) \wedge ok(SD) \tag{5}$$

Then, the expert turns on the key to test whether the starting drive is operating: it corresponds to a new test. Since he hears the starting drive cranking, he infers from *test 1* that:

$$\exists OBS/ok(EPR) \wedge ok(ESS) \wedge ok(SD) \tag{6}$$

The consistency test can be used to sort the diagnoses using the coincidence measurement. The observed symptoms are now:

$$cfm(car) \tag{7}$$

$$\exists OBS/ok(EPR) \wedge ok(ESS) \wedge ok(SD) \tag{8}$$

Expression (8) means that it exists at least an observation such that the test given by (6) is consistent.

The problem is fully defined by (4), (5), (6), (7) and (8). Let's transform this problem into a solvable problem. In order to obtain a complete behavioral abstraction, complementary fault modes and a virtual item are introduced. It is named: $VI_1 = car \setminus \{EPR, ESS, SD\}$.The new transformed set of modes coming from (4) is:

$$\begin{aligned}\{Modes(EPR) = (ok, cfm);\ Modes(ESS) = (ok, cfm);\\ Modes(SD) = (ok, cfm);\ Modes(VI_1) = (ok, cfm)\}\end{aligned} \tag{9}$$

Decomposition can then be written with equivalences:

$$ok(car) \leftrightarrow ok(EPR) \wedge ok(ESS) \wedge ok(SD) \wedge ok(VI_1) \tag{10}$$

$$cfm(car) \leftrightarrow cfm(EPR) \vee cfm(ESS) \vee cfm(SD) \vee cfm(VI_1) \tag{11}$$

Using the MHS-tree algorithm, the diagnosis of the transformed problem can be computed. It leads to:

$$\{cfm(EPR)\}; \{cfm(ESS)\}; \{cfm(SD)\}; \{cfm(VI_1)\} \tag{12}$$

Diagnoses can now be sorted. A signature table (1) can be obtained from (6), (7) and (8):

Table 1 Signature table 1

	ok(EPR)	ok(ESS)	ok(SD)	ok(VI_1)
T_1	1	1	1	0

The theoretical fault signature is: $\sigma_T(cfm(EPR)) = (1)$; $\sigma_T(cfm(ECS)) = (1)$; $\sigma_T(cfm(SM)) = (1)$; $\sigma_T(cfm(VI_1)) = (0)$. Since the test 1 is consistent, the effective signature is $\sigma_T^* = (0)$. From (3), the coincidence measurement is given by: $\mu_T^c(cfm(EPR)) = 1.00$; $\mu_T^c(cfm(ECS)) = 1.00$; $\mu_T^c(cfm(SM)) = 1.00$; $\mu_T^c(cfm(VI_1)) = 0.00$. Because $\mu_T^c(cfm(VI_1)) = 0.00$ is the lowest value, the expert decides to test sub-parts of the virtual item i.e. parts of the car that are not EPR, ESS or SD. He focuses on the ignition system. The expert disconnects the spark plug with its wires from the car engine, holds the end of spark plug with its wire close to a metal surface and gets help to start up the car without using the starting system. Expert does not see any spark coming from spark plugs. These tests are inconsistent. He infers that the electric power resource (*EPR*), the ignition circuit (*IC*) or the spark plugs (SP) are faulty. The virtual item has thus been decomposed into the ignition circuit (*IC*) and the spark plugs (*SP*):

$$ok(VI_1) \rightarrow ok(SP) \wedge ok(IC) \tag{13}$$

The new test leads to:

$$\neg ok(EPR) \vee \neg ok(SP) \vee \neg ok(IC) \tag{14}$$

Consequently, the new set of symptoms is given by (7), (8) and

$$cfm(VI_1) \tag{15}$$

$$\neg ok(EPR) \vee \neg ok(SP) \vee \neg ok(IC) \tag{16}$$

The new problem to be solved is given by: (4), (5), (6), (7), (8), (13), (14), (15), and (16). The problem is transformed by adding an virtual item $VI_2 = VI_1 \setminus \{SP, IC\}$, which is equal to: $car \setminus \{EPR, ESS, SD, SP, IC\}$.

The new transformed set of modes is given by (4), (9)and:

$$\{(SP) = (ok, cfm);\ (IC) = (ok, cfm);\ (VI_2) = (ok, cfm)\} \tag{17}$$

The transformed abstractions are given by (10), (11) and

$$ok(VI_1) \leftrightarrow ok(SP) \wedge ok(IC) \wedge ok(VI_2) \tag{18}$$

$$cfm(VI_1) \leftrightarrow cfm(SP) \vee cfm(IC) \vee cfm(VI_2) \tag{19}$$

Using the MHS-tree algorithm, the diagnosis of the transformed problem can be computed:

$$\{cfm(EPR)\};\ \{cfm(SP)\};\ \{cfm(IC)\} \tag{20}$$

From (6), (7) and (8), a signature table is obtained:

Table 2 Signature table 2

	ok(*EPR*)	ok(*ESS*)	ok(*SD*)	ok(*SP*)	ok(*IC*)	ok(VI_2)
T_1	1	1	1	0	0	0
T_2	1	0	0	1	1	0

The theoretical fault signatures of diagnoses are given by: $\sigma_T(cfm(EPR)) = (1\quad 1)$; $\sigma_T(cfm(ESS)) = (1\quad 0)$; $\sigma_T(cfm(SD)) = (1\quad 0)$; $\sigma_T(cfm(SP)) = (0\quad 1)$; $\sigma_T(cfm(IC)) = (0\quad 1)$; $\sigma_T(cfm(VI_2)) = (0,0)$. And the effective signature is: $\sigma_T^* = (0\quad 1)$.

Then, the coincidence measurement is given by: $\mu_T^c(cfm(EPR)) = 0.50$; $\mu_T^c(cfm(ESS)) = 1.00$; $\mu_T^c(cfm(SD)) = 1.00$; $\mu_T^c(cfm(SP)) = 0.00$; $\mu_T^c(cfm(IC)) = 0.00$; $\mu_T^c(cfm(VI_2)) = 0.50$.

Since $\mu_T^c(cfm(SP)) = 0.00$, $\mu_T^c(cfm(IC)) = 0.00$ are lowest values, in the end of this step, the faulty part is localized at the ignition circuit (*IC*) or at the spark plugs (*SP*).

5 Conclusion

This proposed approach makes it possible to develop human-machine cooperative diagnosis process to tackle diagnosis problems without having an initial complete model of the system. A top-down iterative process has been proposed to handle information step by step thank to hierarchical decomposition. Diagnoses are refined step by step. For this purpose, diagnosis problems inferred from the expert knowledge provided at each iteration, are solved by transformations into a solvable problems composed of the available knowledge (decomposition, inconsistent tests and fault propagation) coming from system modeling. The resulting diagnosis problem can then be solved according to the proposed MHS-tree algorithm. The iterative diagnosis process is illustrated by an example.

References

[1] K. Autio. Abstraction of behaviour and structure in model-based diagnosis. In *the Sixth International Workshop on Principle of Diagnosis (DX95)*, pages 1–7, 1995.

[2] K. Autio and R. Reiter. Structural abstraction in model based diagnosis. In *The 13th European Conference on Artificial Intelligence (ECAI-98)*, pages 269–273. John Wiley and Sons, 1998.

[3] L. Chittaro and R. Ranon. Hierarchical model-based diagnosis based on structural abstraction. *Artificial Intelligence*, 1-2:147–182, 2004.

[4] Johan de Kleer. Problem solving with the atms. *Artif. Intell.*, 28(2):197–224, 1986.

[5] Johan de Kleer and Brian C. Williams. Diagnosis with behavioral modes. *Readings in model-based diagnosis*, pages 124–130, 1992.

[6] I. Mozetic. *Hierarchical model-based diagnosis*, pages 354–372. Morgan Kaufmann Publishers Inc., San Francisco, CA, USA, 1992.

[7] S. Ploix, S. Touaf, and J. M. Flaus. A logical framework for isolation in fault diagnosis. In *SAFEPROCESS'2003*, Washington D.C., U.S.A., 2003.

[8] R. Reiter. A theory of diagnosis from first principles. *Artificial Intelligence*, 32:57–95, 1987.

[9] Peter Struss and Oskar Dressler. "physical negation" integrating fault models into the general diagnostic engine. pages 1318–1323, 1989.

Computer Log Anomaly Detection Using Frequent Episodes

Perttu Halonen, Markus Miettinen, and Kimmo Hätönen

Abstract In this paper, we propose a set of algorithms to automate the detection of *anomalous frequent episodes*. The algorithms make use of the hierarchy and frequency of episodes present in an examined sequence of log data and in a history preceding it. The algorithms identify changes in a set of frequent episodes and their frequencies. We evaluate the algorithms and describe tests made using live computer system log data.

1 Introduction

In security analysis, knowledge-based intrusion detection tools are using pre-defined log entry patterns of known incidents. The patterns cover known vulnerabilities in the system. However, before a pattern can be created, one has to find the vulnerability and identify its traces. Unfortunately, in many cases the vulnerability is found only after it has been exploited.

To identify unknown attacks one should inspect all log entries and their contexts to classify them as a sign of normal operation or a possible intrusion. Due to the huge volume of data, it is impossible to make detailed analyses for everything. However, since an intrusion into a network typically causes chages in event logs, e.g., a missing or changed event in a usual pattern, one can reduce the set of entries requiring thorough inspection by focusing the analysis on only those entries that are anomalous with regard to earlier data. In this paper, we describe *anomaly detection* methods which can be used for this kind of pre-screening of security mon-

Perttu Halonen · Kimmo Hätönen
Nokia Siemens Networks, PL 6, FI-02022, Finland,
e-mail: perttu.halonen@nsn.com, kimmo.hatonen@nsn.com

Markus Miettinen
Nokia Research Center, Itämerenkatu 11–13, FI-00180 Helsinki, Finland,
e-mail: markus.miettinen@nokia.com

Please use the following format when citing this chapter:

Halonen, P., Miettinen, M. and Hätönen, K., 2009, in IFIP International Federation for Information Processing, Volume 296; *Artificial Intelligence Applications and Innovations III*; Eds. Iliadis, L., Vlahavas, I., Bramer, M.; (Boston: Springer), pp. 417–422.

itoring data. Our problem domain is telecommunications network information security monitoring, but the algorithms we present are suitable also for other problem domains.

Related Work Several approaches have been proposed for detecting sudden changes in execution of computer software. Forrest et al. have presented an interesting immunology based approach [3] that imitates the biological immune system. Ko et al. have proposed specification based anomaly detection [4], in which one has to use a formal language to specify which execution traces of computer programs are allowed. Lane and Brodley have proposed to detect anomalous behaviour of a computer system user by monitoring her command history [5].

Organisation of this paper is as follows. Sect. 2 introduces mining of frequent closed episodes and presents our proposal for anomaly detection algorithms. In Sect. 3, we describe the tests we have performed with our algorithms, and in Sect. 4 analyse and discuss the results. Finally, Sect. 5 summarises this paper.

2 Frequent Episode Anomaly Detection Methods

Log sequences consist of *log entries*. A log entry e is a triplet (t, E, s) consisting of a *time* t, an *event type* E and a *source* s. *Frequent episodes* are collections of event types occurring frequently within a given time w in the entries of a log sequence [6].

The concept of frequent episodes is a derivative of *frequent sets* [1]. Frequent sets are sets of items that frequently occur together in the records of a database. The APRIORI algorithm for mining frequent sets [1] can be modified to compute frequent unordered episodes [7]. In this paper, we use unordered episodes.

To mine frequent episodes, we divide the log entry sequence into consecutive non-overlapping time windows of maximal width w. In addition, we require that as soon as a log entry with an event type equal to some event type already included in the window is encountered again, the current window is terminated and a new window started. Thus, each event type can occur only once within each time window.

We use a set of *closed frequent episodes* instead of the set of all frequent episodes. The *closure* of an episode is its largest super-episode that shares the same frequency, and a *closed episode* is a frequent episode that is equal to its closure. The set of all closed episodes effectively encodes information about all freqent episodes and can be used to simplify processing without loosing information about the occurrences of the frequent episodes. Closed frequent episodes are a derivative of so-called closed frequent sets [8, 2].

In the following, we present algorithms that can be used for identifying anomalies in frequent episodes in a set of analysed log data. The aim of the algorithms is to identify new or modified patterns from a set of analysed data.

Let $\mathscr{E}$ be the set $\{E_1, E_2, ..., E_n\}$ of all possible event types E_i that appear in the log data. We denote with C the set of all closed frequent episodes that appear in the analysed log L, i.e. $C = \{f \subseteq \mathscr{E} \mid f \text{ is a closed frequent episode in } L\}$. For each episode $f \in C$ we store as $f.freq$ the frequency of f in L. Frequency denotes here the absolute count of an episode's occurrences.

Finding Changes in Closed Episodes. Algorithm 1 identifies changes in frequent closed episodes by comparing the frequency of an episode $f \in C$ to the frequency of its *specialisations*, i.e., its super-episodes $p \in C$ such that $f \subset p$. If the difference in the frequencies is small, it could be an indication of the fact that a normal event sequence represented by the specialisation has changed. The changed event sequence does not contribute to the frequency of the specialisation, but it does contribute to the frequency of at least some of the subepisodes. A small difference in the episode frequencies can therefore be interpreted as an indication of such a change in an existing episode and can be reported as a potential anomaly.

Algorithm 1 Finding changes in closed episodes

C Set of frequent closed episodes found in the analysed log L and their occurrence frequencies.
Δ_f Threshold specifying maximum difference between the frequencies of compared episodes.
A Set of superepisode-subepisode pairs whose frequencies in L differ at most by Δ_f.

```
for all f ∈ C do
    for all p ∈ C s.t. f ⊂ p do
        if f.freq − p.freq ≤ Δf then
            A ← A ∪ (p,f)
return A
```

The algorithm has one parameter, Δ_f. It is the maximum difference of the frequency of the sub- and super-episodes for them to be considered an anomalous pair. The output of algorithm 1 can be used for analysing the input log and identifying those windows that are anomalous. Algorithm 2 below marks as anomalous those windows of the log data, which match to any of the episode pairs in the set A of anomalous episode pairs.

Algorithm 2 Marking log windows as anomalous

A Set of anomalous superepisode-subepisode pairs
L Log data to be marked
W Set of anomalous windows in the log data

```
repeat
    w ← getFirstWindow(L)
    L ← L \ w
    if ∃(p,f) ∈ A s.t. f ⊂ w ∧ p ⊄ w then
        w.anomaly_body ← f
        w.anomaly_missing ← p \ f
        W ← W ∪ {w}
until L = ∅ return W
```

Finding novel episode patterns. Algorithm 3 searches for new occurrences of frequent closed episodes, which are not present in the preceding history data. We denote with P the episode profile that has been calculated based on a history H of log data. P constitutes the model of normal behaviour and it contains all closed frequent episodes f that appear in H, i.e. $P = \{f \subseteq \mathscr{E} \mid f \text{ is a closed frequent episode in } H\}$.

The algorithm compares the profile episodes in P with the closed frequent episodes C found from the analysed log data L. Such novel frequent episodes are potentially interesting because they may indicate completely new types of activity in the log data.

Algorithm 3 Finding Novel Episode Patterns

P Set of profile episodes extracted from log history database H.
C Set of closed frequent episodes found from the analysed log L.
N Set of new episodes appearing in C but not in the episode profile P.

```
N ← C \ P
for all n ∈ N do
    if ∃p ∈ P s.t. n ⊂ p then
        N ← N \ n
return N
```

3 Tests

We tested the anomaly detection algorithms on several types of logs obtained from a telecommunications network, covering a continuous period of 42 days. The data were divided into data sequences and closed frequent episodes were mined for each data sequence, using a frequency threshold of 5 occurrences and limiting the maximum window length for episodes to 3600 seconds.

We wanted to know, how large a fraction of the input data would be considered anomalous by our methods. We first measured the relation between the log entries marked as anomalous and the total amount of log entries present in the analysed log. For each data sequence, we calculated the number of log entries in windows W covered by the set of anomalous episodes obtained from algorithm 2 which we divided by the total amount of log entries in the sequence.

Figure 1 shows the results of our tests on data from the application log and the system log of the network management system. The fraction of anomalous log entries for the system log varies between ca. 5% and 10%, whereas the fraction of anomalous log entries stays below 2% for the application log. One can see that with the exception of a few observations, the measures maintain the same order of magnitude within the same log type.

The second property we measured is the amount of novel episode patterns detected from the analysed log data. That is, the profile contained the frequent closed episodes that occurred in five days preceeding the analysed data sequence. We executed then algorithm 3 on the analysed data sequence and counted the amount of novel frequent episodes. The counts are show in Figure 2.

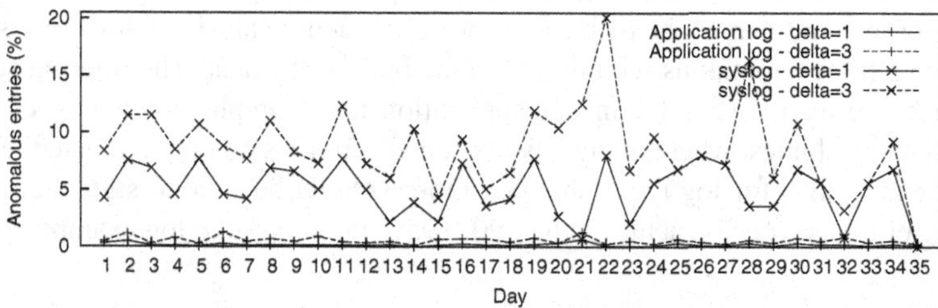

Fig. 1 Fraction of daily log entries marked as anomalous by algorithm 2. The number of daily entries in the application log was between 3284 and 5357 (average 5097). Reported anomalies varied between 0 and 31 (average 9) for $\Delta_f = 1$ and between 6 and 64 (average 28) for $\Delta_f = 3$. The system log contained 223 to 546 entries (average 280), for which 0 to 30 (average 14) anomalies were reported for $\Delta_f = 1$ and 0 to 75 (average 25) anomalies for $\Delta_f = 3$.

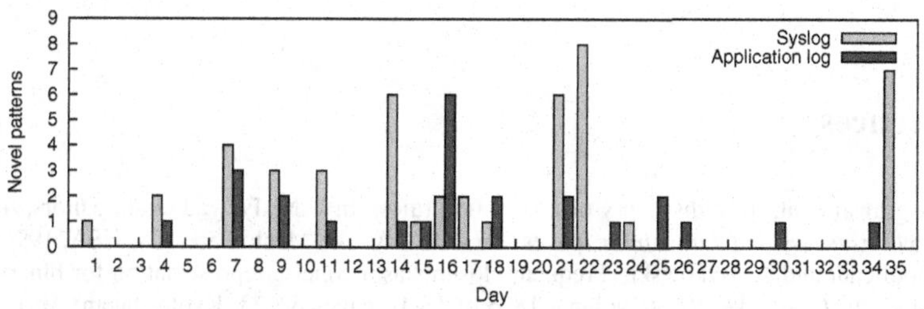

Fig. 2 Daily amounts of new episode patterns in the application and system logs

4 Discussion

Figure 1 shows a clear difference between the analysed log types. The application log contains a large amount of routinely recorded event records. The percentage of anomalous entries remains low due to the large overall record mass of the application log. The system log on the other hand monitors the operation of the basic system components and records any errors and deviations occurring in the system. The amount of log entries is smaller and the relative likelihood of error occurrences higher.

The novel episode pattern measure in Figure 2 shows that the appearance of entirely new episodes is rather exceptional for both shown log types. The number of reported daily novel episodes remains so small that they could be easily inspected on a daily basis by a human monitoring officer.

The results suggest that algorithms 1 and 2 can be used to filter out log entries that deviate from the usual frequent behaviour. Such pre-filtering would enable an expert system or even human analysts to focus the subsequent analysis on log entries that are known to be anomalous with regard to the bulk of the data. The filtering seems to be more effective ($> 98\%$ in our application log example) for log types with higher entry volumes, where obviously abnormal activities do not dominate the data set. However, also for log types showing more volatile behaviour, significant data filtering efficiency can be achieved (ca. $90-95\%$ in our system log example).

5 Summary

In this paper, we have presented algorithms to detect *anomalous frequent episodes*. The algorithms make use of the hierarchy and frequency of episodes present in an examined log data sequence and in a history preceding it. The algorithms identify changes in a set of frequent episodes and their frequencies. We have evaluated the presented algorithms and described tests made using live network log data.

References

1. R. Agrawal et al. Fast discovery of association rules. In U.M. Fayyad et al., editors, *Adv. in knowl. discovery and data mining*, pages 307 – 328. AAAI, Menlo Park, CA, USA, 1996.
2. J. Boulicaut and A. Bykowski. Frequent closures as a concise representation for binary data mining. In *Proc. PAKDD'00*, volume 1805 of *LNAI*, pages 62–73, Kyoto, Japan, April 2000. Springer.
3. S. Forrest et al. Self-nonself discrimination in a computer. In *Proc. of the 1994 IEEE Symp. on Research in Security and Privacy, Los Alamos, CA*, pages 202–212. IEEE Computer Society Press, 1994.
4. C. Ko et al. Execution monitoring of security-critical programs in distributed systems: a specification-based approach. *1997 IEEE Symp. on Security and Privacy*, 00:175–187, 1997.
5. T. Lane and C.E. Brodley. Sequence matching and learning in anomaly detection for computer security. In *AAAI Workshop: AI Approaches to Fraud Detection and Risk Management*, pages 43–49, July 1997.
6. H. Mannila et al. Discovering frequent episodes in sequences. In *Proc. of the First Int. Conf. on Knowledge Discovery and Data Mining (KDD'95)*, pages 210–215, Montreal, Canada, August 1995. AAAI Press.
7. H. Mannila and H. Toivonen. Discovering generalized episodes using minimal occurrences. In E. Simoudis et al., editors, *Proc. of the Second Int. Conf. on Knowledge Discovery and Data Mining (KDD'96)*, pages 146–151, Portland, Oregon, August 1996. AAAI Press.
8. N. Pasquier et al. Discovering frequent closed itemsets for association rules. *LNCS*, 1540:398–416, 1999.

Semi-tacit Adaptation of Intelligent Environments

Tobias Heinroth[1], Achilles Kameas[2], Hani Hagras[3], Yacine Bellik[4]

1The Institute of Information Technology, Ulm University, Ulm, 89081 Germany (phone: 0049-731-50-26265; fax: 0049-731-50-26259; e-mail: tobias.heinroth@uni-ulm.de)

2The Hellenic Open University and DAISy research unit at the Computer Technology Institute, both in Patras, Hellas

3The Computational Intelligence Centre, Department of Computing and Electronic Systems, University of Essex, Wivenhoe Park, Colchester, CO43SQ, UK

4The National Center for Scientific Research (LIMSI-CNRS) BP 133, 91403, Orsay cedex, France and the Paris-South University

Abstract This paper presents a semi-tacit adaptation system for implementing and configuring a new generation of intelligent environments referred to as adaptive ambient ecologies. These are highly distributed systems, which require new ways of communication and collaboration to support the realization of people's tasks. Semi-tacit adaptation is based on a mixed initiative approach in human-system dialogue management and is supported by three types of intelligent agents: Fuzzy Task Agent, Planning Agent and Interaction Agent. These agents use an ontology as a common repository of knowledge and information about the services and state of the ambient ecology.

1 Introduction

In the Ambient Intelligence (AmI) paradigm, intelligent computation will be invisibly embedded into our everyday environments through a pervasive transparent infrastructure (consisting of a multitude of sensors, actuators, processors and networks) which is capable of recognising, responding and adapting to individuals in a seamless and unobtrusive way [1].

We use the *ambient ecology* (AE) metaphor for Intelligent Environments realizing AmI concepts [2]. The vision of AmI aims at supporting people to carry out new tasks, as well as old tasks in new and better ways. People will realize their tasks using the resources offered by the services and devices of the ambient ecology. However, ambient ecologies are highly dynamic structures, the configuration of which may change, for example, because a new device may enter the ecology,

Please use the following format when citing this chapter:

Heinroth, T., Kameas, A., Hagras, H. and Bellik, Y., 2009, in IFIP International Federation for Information Processing, Volume 296; *Artificial Intelligence Applications and Innovations III*; Eds. Iliadis, L., Vlahavas, I., Bramer, M.; (Boston: Springer), pp. 423–429.

or some other may cease functioning. While successful execution of tasks will depend on the quality of interactions among artefacts and among people and artefacts, it is important that task execution will still be possible, despite changes in the ambient ecology. Thus, the realization of mechanisms that achieve adaptation of system to changing context is necessary. In this paper, we present an adaptation mechanism that uses specialized intelligent agents (for task, plan and interaction adaptation) and a common repository of ecology knowledge and information in the form of an ontology, which is formed by matching the meta-data and self-descriptions of the members of the ambient ecology. More specifically, we shall focus on a mixed initiative approach in human-system dialogue management that we call semi-tacit adaptation.

The remainder of this paper is structured as follows. Section 2 presents a scenario illustrating our concepts. Section 3 gives an overview of the basic modelling of an AE and presents the applications necessary to realize semi-tacit adaptation. The paper concludes in Section 4.

2 Life in Intelligent Adaptive Homes

In this section, we shall present a scenario based on the imaginary life of a user (Suki) who just moved to a home that is characterized by being intelligent and adaptive. The scenario will help to illustrate the concepts presented in the paper. To reference the different parts of the scenario in the other sections we use SP1…SPX as text marks.

Suki has been living in this new adaptive home for the past 10 months. Suki's living room has embedded in the walls and ceiling a number of sensors reading inside temperature and brightness; some more sensors of these types are embedded in the outside wall of the house. A touch screen mounted near the room entrance is used as the main control point. Suki uses an air-conditioning as the main heating / cooling device. The windows are equipped with automated blinds, which can be turned to dim or brighten the room. For the same purpose Suki can use the two lamps hanging from the ceiling. Finally, Suki has brought some hi-tech devices in the room: a digital flat screen TV set and a 9.1 sound system.

Suki's goal is to feel comfortable in his living room, no matter what the season or the outside weather conditions are. After careful thinking, he concluded that for him comfort involved the adjustment of temperature and brightness, the selection of his favourite TV channel and the adjustment of volume level, depending on the programme (SP1). Regarding the latter, the smart home system had observed Suki's choices over the past months and has drawn the conclusion that he tends to increase the volume when music or English speaking movies are shown, except when it's late at night; he keeps the volume low when movies have subtitles, or when guests are around (SP2). Nevertheless, the system does not have enough data to deduce Suki's favourite lighting and temperature conditions as the seasons change. Initially, the system will combine information in Suki's personal profile, the environmental conditions, the weather forecast and anything else that may matter, to tacitly adapt to the values that Suki might want. In case of a doubt, it will engage in dialogue with Suki about specific conditions. Of course, Suki can always set directly the values he desires by manipulating the devices that affect them; the system will monitor such activity and tacitly will adjust its rules.

For the past few days, as the weather has grown warmer, Suki has gone into a spring time mood; the system in his smart home has read the changing context and is trying to adapt, by decreasing the time that the heating system is on and by leaving the windows open for longer time intervals, during the sunny days (SP3). Suki still thinks that the living room is too warm and instructs the house to lower the temperature even further (SP4); the system, noticing that the day is sunny (it is early afternoon) and no rain or wind is foreseen for today, asks if Suki would prefer to open the windows, as well. Suki agrees, so the system opens the windows and lowers the thermostat only slightly. At the same time, it decreases slightly the volume of the TV set, as it may disturb the neighbours.

An hour later, Joan, Suki's friend arrives; she and Suki have arranged to go to a concert in the evening. Already the temperature has fallen and Suki asks the system to close the windows and lower the blinds; as a consequence, the system turns on the room lights, but Suki immediately switches it off. The system is puzzled and asks Suki if he wants some light or no light at all (SP5). Suki turns on a floor lamp that he bought only yesterday, but didn't have the chance to use until now (SP6). The system registers the new source of light and then asks Suki if this will be a new permanent brightness level, but Suki declines. After a while, Suki and Joan leave for the concert; the system shuts down all light and sound sources, but maintains the temperature until Suki's return.

3 Modelling and Supporting Semi-tacit Adaptation

An AE offers both physical properties and digital services and acts as a container for "activity spheres" (AS, see Fig. 1) [3]. An AS consists of passive entities (sensors, actuators, users, services, devices, etc.) and active entities namely Fuzzy Task Agent (FTA), Interaction Agent (IA) and Planning Agent (PA). It is intentionally created by an actor (human or agent) to support the realization of a specific goal. The sphere is deployed over an AE and uses its resources (artefacts, networks, services). The goal is described as a set of interrelated tasks; the sphere contains models of these tasks and their interaction. An AS is considered as a distributed yet integrated system that is formed on demand to support people's activities. It is adaptive in the sense that it can be instantiated within different environments and adaptively pursue its goals. An AS is realized as a composition of configurations between the artefacts and the provided services into the AE.

The configuration and the adaptation of a sphere could be realized in three ways, *explicit*, *tacit* and *semi-tacit*. In the former mode, people configure spheres by explicitly composing artefact affordances, based on the visualized descriptions of the artefact properties, capabilities and services [4]. In a highly dynamic system, such as an AS, explicit configuration is useful only for setting up the initial values or to model a default profile of the AS (see Fig. 2), because the huge number of interactions involved would impose a heavy cognitive load to the user, should he became aware of all of them. The tacit mode operates completely transparently to the user and is based on the system observing user's interactions with the sphere and actions within the sphere.

Agents in the intelligent environment can monitor user actions and record, store and process information about them [5], [6]. The sphere can learn user preferences and adapt to them, as it can adapt to the configuration of any new AE that the user enters. Tacit adaptation may achieve the opposite effect than the one it aims for, as people might feel that they have lost control over system's operation, which will appear incomprehensible and untrustworthy.

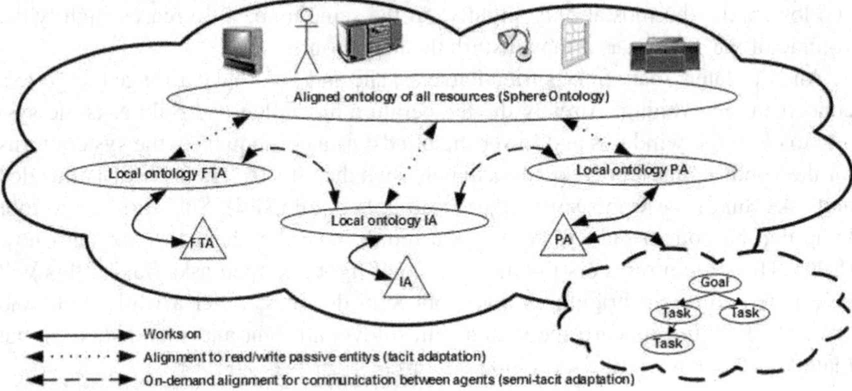

Fig. 1 Architectural overview of an activity sphere.

The semi-tacit mode realizes a third way of configuring and adapting the sphere by combining the explicit and the implicit way. The user interacts with the system, for example, using speech or screen-based dialogues. The user does not have to explicitly indicate resources to be used to program task models but the user can provide only basic information regarding his goals and objectives. The system, at the same time, attempts to tacitly resolve abstract tasks into concrete tasks and realize them, while monitoring user's actions with the resources involved. In case of rules that cannot be resolved, the system pro-actively engages into adaptive dialogue with the user.

The system uses the sphere ontology and three types of Agents: Planning Agent (PA), Fuzzy Task Agent (FTA) and Interaction Agent (IA). Each AS is composed by heterogeneous artefacts, each of which contains local descriptions of its services, which can be regarded as independent ontologies of varying complexity. to achieve efficient communication between the artefacts in the context of a task, we propose the application of ontology matching, to make the ontologies of the interacting artefacts semantically interoperable. Ontology matching is the process of finding relationships or correspondences between entities of different ontologies.

This set of correspondences, is called an alignment [7]. So, by applying alignment algorithms to the local ontologies of the AE members, the user profile and the local agent ontologies, the sphere ontology is formed, which at each given moment, represents the collective knowledge required to realize a given task, as well as the state of the AS that supports this realization. Consequently, any adaptation mechanism needs to access the sphere ontology, not only for obtaining access to the correct AE resources, but also for obtaining the linguistic descriptions of the resources state.

To realize semi-tacit adaptation and thanks to the descriptive power of speech, we assume spoken dialogue interaction fits well to ask the user for further information to enhance planning or, if necessary, to resolve conflicts that may occur by negotiating with the user. One part of the IA is a speech dialogue manager (SDM) that receives problem descriptions from the PA and the FTA whenever semi-tacit adaptation is needed. Thus, the SDM tries to generate dialogues to react adequately.

The PA main task is to find out which tasks must be realized to support the user's activity and how they could be combined with the resources of the AE. During initialisation, the PA can use predefined rules and default domain models described in the task model. This initial information can either be pre-defined explicitly or in a semi-tacit way by utilising the IA to generate a (spoken) dialogue to retrieve general information from the user to personalize, for example, a default profile (see Fig. 2 and SP1). Then the system will form the sphere ontology by aligning the local ontologies of the members of the ecology, the agents and the user profile. But planning must also be done during the lifetime of the AS: The task model can be affected when conflicts arise (Suki behaves contrary to the system's consequences – SP5) or when a new device enters the ecology (SP6). In the first case it is usually not possible for the system to act completely tacitly so it tries to involve the user in a dialogue for conflict resolution. The latter case can normally be handled tacitly, by re-aligning the sphere ontology.

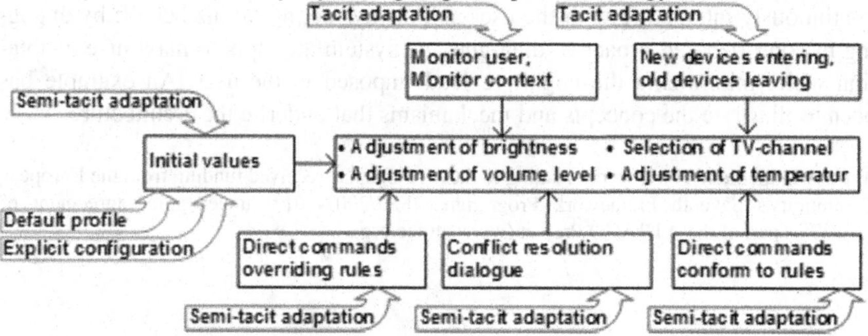

Fig. 2 Modes of configuration in ambient ecologies

The FTA will start to build an initial fuzzy logic based model of Suki's preferences and behaviour to realise the given tasks of maintaining the temperature, light levels and entertainment systems at the desired levels (SP2). To build the initial model, the system will collect timestamped data (i.e. containing the related time and date) of the environment status (given temperature, light levels, user context (which room, activity, etc), the weather forecast, etc.) together with the user actions for such environment status (air-conditioning settings, blind settings, entertainment systems settings, etc). From the collected data, the FTA learns the needed fuzzy logic membership functions and rules needed to build the fuzzy logic model of Suki's preferences to realise the given task. The system then begins to adapt the generated fuzzy models over the short time interval to account for any environment of user behaviour changes. Over the long term, the fuzzy logic system will need to be adapted to Suki's change of preferences associated with seasonal variation (SP3). The FTA will then adapt its fuzzy logic systems rules and membership function to accommodate the faced uncertainties where the FTA will employ type-2 fuzzy logic systems [6]. The FTA acts completely in a tacit way similar to the PA as long as there are no conflicts or situations where the user is not satisfied with the adaptation (SP4).

4 Conclusions

In this paper, we presented a ubiquitous system architecture that achieves task-centred adaptation using intelligent agents and ontologies. A task is modelled as part of a goal and is realized with the set of resources offered by an ambient ecology of smart artefacts and services. We call the combination of task descriptions and actual resources an activity sphere; then, the proposed architecture supports the execution of activity sphere applications. In the proposed architecture, adaptation is achieved with the help of an Interaction Agent, which engages in adaptive interaction with the user who is supported by the activity sphere. The system implements semi-tacit adaptation, in the sense that it achieves a balance between continuously interacting with the user and always acting on his behalf: by engaging in context-based proactive dialogue, the system attempts to maximize adaptation while minimizing the cognitive load imposed to the user. An example has been to illustrate the concepts and mechanisms that underlie the architecture.

Acknowledgement The research leading to these results has received funding from the European Community's Seventh Framework Programme (FP7/2007-2013) under grant agreement n° 216837 as part of the ATRACO Project (www.atraco.org).

References

1. K. Ducatel, M. Bogdanowicz, F. Scapolo, J. Leijten, and J.-C. Burgelman, "Scenarios for ambient intelligence in 2010", IST Advisory Group Final Report, European Commission, February 2001.

2. C. Goumopoulos and A. Kameas, "Ambient ecologies in smart homes", The Computer Journal, August 2008.
3. Zaharakis and A. Kameas, Engineering Emergent Ecologies of Interacting Artifacts, Handbook of Research on User Interface Design and Evaluation for Mobile Technology. 2008.
4. N. Drossos, C. Goumopoulos, and A. Kameas, "A conceptual model and the supporting middleware for composing ubiquitous computing applications", Journal of Ubiquitous Computing and Intelligence, vol. 1.
5. F. Doctor, H. Hagras, and V. Callaghan, "An intelligent fuzzy agent approach for realising ambient intelligence in intelligent inhabited environments", IEEE Transactions on System, Man & Cybernetics, vol. 35.
6. H. Hagras, F. Doctor, A. Lopez, and V. Callaghan, "An incremental adaptive life long learning approach for type-2 fuzzy embedded agents in ambient intelligent environments", IEEE Transactions on Fuzzy Systems, vol. 15.
7. J. Euzenat and P. Schvaiko, Ontology Matching, 2007.

A Formal Fuzzy Framework for Representation and Recognition of Human Activities

Suphot Chunwiphat[†], Patrick Reignier[‡] and Augustin Lux[‡]

[†]Department of Electronic Engineering Technology, College of Industrial Technology

King Mongkut's University of Technology North Bangkok

1518 Pibulsongkram Road, Bangsue, Bangkok 10800, Thailand

[‡]LIG – PRIMA – INRIA Rhône-Alpes,

655 avenue de l'Europe, Montbonnot, 38334 Saint Ismier cedex, France

spcp@kmutnb.ac.th , {Patrick.Reignier, Augustin.Lux}@inrialpes.fr

Abstract This paper focuses on the problem of human activity representation and automatic recognition. We first describe an approach for human activity representation. We define the concepts of roles, relations, situations and temporal graph of situations (the context model). This context model is transformed into a Fuzzy Petri Net which naturally expresses the smooth changes of activity states from one state to another with gradual and continuous membership functions. Afterward, we present an algorithm for recognizing human activities observed in a scene. The recognition algorithm is a hierarchical fusion model based on fuzzy measures and fuzzy integrals. The fusion process nonlinearly combines events, produced by an activity representation model, based on an assumption that all occurred events support the appearance of a modeled scenario. The goal is to determine, from an observed sequence, the confidence factor that each modeled scenario (predefined in a library) is indeed describing this sequence. We have successfully evaluated our approach on the video sequences taken from the European CAVIAR project[1].

1 Introduction

As one of the most active research areas in computer vision, human activity analysis is currently receiving a great interest in computer vision research community. This is due to its promising applications in many areas such as visual surveillance, human machine interaction, content-based image storage and retrieval, video con-

[1] European CAVIAR project/IST 2001 37540: http://homepages.inf.ed.ac.uk/rbf/CAVIAR/

Please use the following format when citing this chapter:

Chunwiphat, S., Reignier, P. and Lux, A., 2009, in IFIP International Federation for Information Processing, Volume 296; *Artificial Intelligence Applications and Innovations III*; Eds. Iliadis, L., Vlahavas, I., Bramer, M.; (Boston: Springer), pp. 431–439.

ferencing, etc. One of the major problems in such systems is how the system can produce the high-level semantic interpretation of human activities from the low-level numerical pixel data.

This paper focuses on the representation and recognition of human activities for a generic human activity interpretation system. We propose formalism for context aware observation to describe and model human activities. Then the activity models will be transformed into a graphical model, a fuzzy Petri net, for analyzing the activities in a mathematical way. Finally, we present a hierarchical fusion model, based on fuzzy measures, for recognizing the human activities.

The rest of this paper is organized as follows. Related work is discussed in Section 2. Section 3 describes architecture for human activity modeling. Section 4 presents our technique for representing human activities. A hierarchical fusion model for activity recognition is proposed in Section 5. Section 6 presents experimental results. Section 7 summarises the paper and discusses future work.

2 Related Work

Madabhushi [6] presented a Bayesian network approach to recognize human activity by making an assumption that the change of position of human head is related with some human action. A more complicated Bayesian network is proposed by [5]. Their framework contains a chained hierarchical representation that describes scenarios from general properties of the moving objects. One practical difficulty in applying Bayesian networks is that they typically require initial knowledge of many probabilities.

Yamato [10] proposed a method based on Hidden Markov Models (HMMs) for recognizing different tennis strokes. Recently, Duong [3] proposed the Switching Hidden Semi-Markov Model (S-HSMM), which is a two-layered extension of HSMM, to recognize human activities of daily living (ADL). However, their work only focused on detecting a more subtle form of abnormalities, which are only abnormalities in the state duration, not in the state order.

Ghanem [4] presented an interactive system for querying events on surveillance video. The Petri nets are provided with primitive events detected from video streams and are used as complex filters to recognize composite events. Although Petri nets provide a nice graphical representation and support the representation of sequentiality, concurrency and synchronization of events. However, the firing process of transitions in Petri nets has a binary characteristic. Moreover, Petri nets themselves lack a mechanism for aggregating values issued by their places.

Shi et al. [8] presented a model, called Propagation Networks (P-Nets), for representing and recognizing partially ordered sequential activities. To recognize activities, they proposed a discrete particle filter based search algorithm, called D-Condensation. However, many activities form a network rather than a sequence and may often exhibit loops. The recognition algorithm is difficult to be adapted for dealing with such activities.

3 A Formalism for Context Aware Observation

The core component of our architecture is a situation model [2]. This framework organizes the observation of interaction using a hierarchy of concepts: scenario (context), situation, role and relation. A *scenario* is a composition of situations that share the same set of roles and relations. A *role* is an agent that performs certain action, while a *relation* describes a connection among objects that play the roles in the situation. Thus, *situations* are a form of state defined over observations.

As an example, we consider a simple video, called "Browsing", from the CAVIAR project. The situation model for this video is described by an occurrence of three situations and the related roles and relations as follows:

Situation 1 (s_1): A person walks toward an information desk.
 Role: *Walker* (anyone walking in the scene)
 Relation: *Toward* (Walker heading toward an information desk)
 Relation: *Close* (small distance between the walker and the information desk)
 Relation: *Slow* (speed)

Situation 2 (s_2): The person stops to read some information at the information desk.
 Role: *Browser* (anyone immobile)
 Relation: *Toward* (direction heading toward an information desk)
 Relation: *Very close* (distance being very close to the information desk)
 Relation: *Very slow* (speed)

Situation 3 (s_3): The immobile person starts to walk away from the information desk.
 Role: *Walker* (anyone walking in the scene)
 Relation: *Away* (direction heading away from the information desk)
 Relation: *Close* (distance being close to the information desk)
 Relation: *Slow* (speed)

The situation network (context model), associated with the scenario is shown in Fig. 1. An arc between two situations is the temporal operator "followed by". The transition between two situations is triggered by an event. The event corresponds to changes of the roles or relations of the corresponding situations.

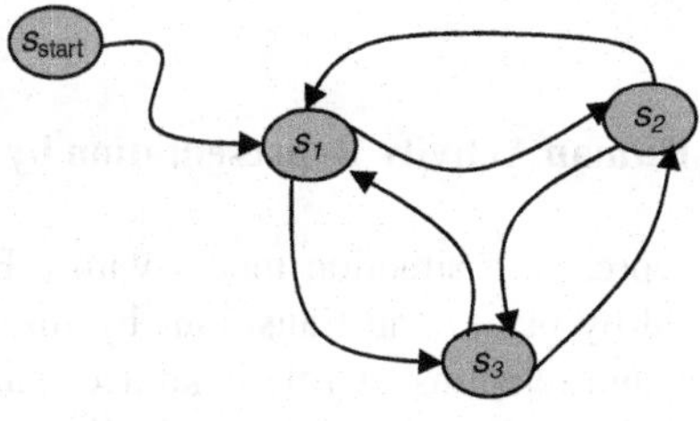

Fig. 1. Situation network of scenario "Browsing".

In the next section, we propose to transform the situation model into a Petri net. As described above, the transition firing in Petri Nets is the instantaneous change from one state to another. However, in real world situations, the change of human activities from one state to another is not binary. In the next section, a method for relaxing this binary character of the transition firing in Petri nets is presented.

4 Fuzzy Petri Nets Representation

4.1 Fuzzy Transition Condition [1]

Let us consider a fuzzy set A in Fig. 2(a). This fuzzy set can be interpreted as a condition, called *fuzzy condition*, used to describe the concept of "the sensor value is close to 7". When the fuzzy condition is assigned to a transition in Petri nets, the transition firing will be defined by duration according to the membership function. The duration of a transition firing can be described by the support of fuzzy set as shown in Fig. 2(a). From Fig. 2(b), the occurrence of an event "x" on the transition t_1 is associated to the fuzzy condition represented by the fuzzy set A. The firing of t_1 will begin as soon as the support of the condition is reached and it terminates when the event has crossed this support completely. During this firing, we will consider that the token is on both input and output place. The functions on the input and output place will proceed simultaneously. The two corresponding situations are simultaneously active.

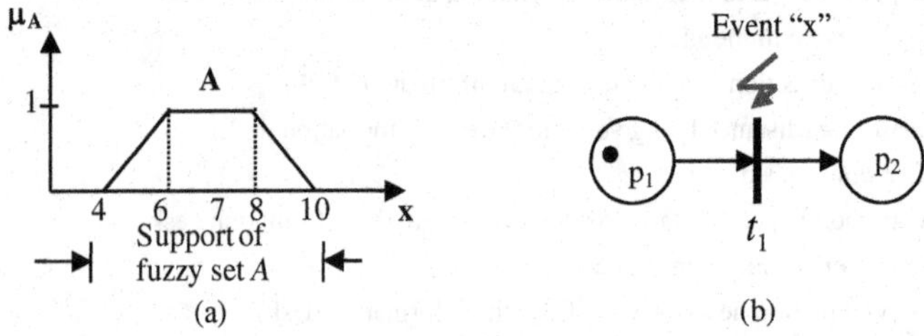

Fig. 2. (a) A Concept "the sensor value is close to 7". (b) An Occurred event "x" at t_1.

4.2 Human Activity Representation by Fuzzy Petri Nets

To represent a situation model with a Fuzzy Petri Net, situations will be represented by places and transitions by fuzzy conditions. Situations are defined with roles and relations. A role is an acceptance test. We have used a Support Vector Machines approach to automatically learn from objects' properties the person's roles (we have used the LIBSVM library from Chang and Lin whose software is available at http://www.csie.nut.edu.tw/~cjlin/libsvm). A relation is a predicate on entities selected by roles.

In Fig. 3, place s_1, s_2 and s_3 represent three situations of scenario "Browsing" (see Sect. 3). The signs → represent the changes of relation truth value from one situation to other. The fuzzy condition function that describes, for example, the change of speed between s_1 and s_2 can be constructed by creating a link between

"Slow" and "Very slow" of the speed relation, and "Close" and "Very close" of the distance relation. The transition occurs when two membership functions are true simultaneously: "Slow" AND "Very slow". The logical connective AND can be implemented by the intersection operator ($\cap$) in fuzzy sets. Examples of membership functions representing the speed relations, "Very slow" and "Slow" in situation s_2 and s_1 are show in Fig. 4(a) and (b). The shaded are shown in Fig. 4(c) represents the transition between "Slow" AND "Very slow".

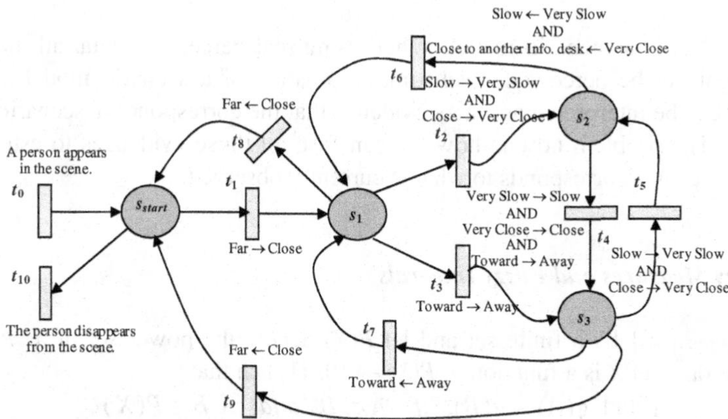

Fig. 3. A fuzzy Petri net model for the scenario "Browsing"

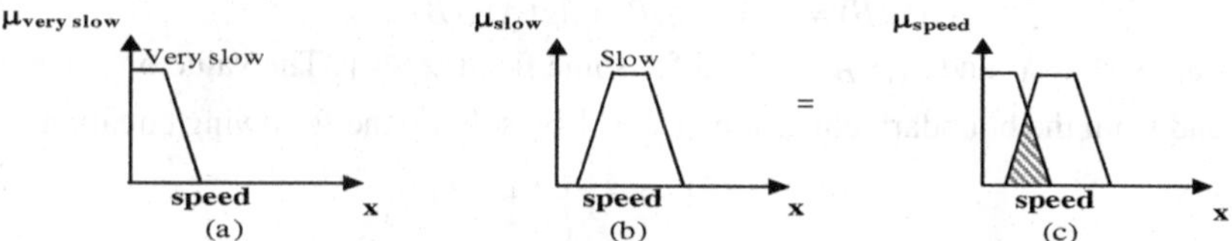

Fig. 4. (a) Fuzzy term "very slow". (b) Fuzzy term "slow". (c) Fuzzy condition attached to t2.

The fuzzy condition describing the transition between "Close" and "Very close" for the distance relation is built using the same approach. Finally, we can show the firing rule attached to transition t_2 in Fig. 3 as follows:

IF [(**Speed** is *Slow*) AND (**Speed** is *Very slow*)] AND
[(**Distance** is *Close*) AND (**Distance** is *Very close*)]
THEN Fire the transition t_2

The complete representation of the scenario "Browsing" by using fuzzy Petri nets shown in Fig. 3, places can be considered as a classifier. Namely when a token is inserted into a place, functions that support roles and relations in the situations will calculate the values of roles and relations for confirming the state of the situation: it is interpreted as the confidence value for the recognition of this situation. A simple sequence of situations as well as their confidence values, obtained by the evolution of a fuzzy Petri net model, can be shown in the forms of $s_1, s_2, \ldots, s_n \Rightarrow h_1, h_2, \ldots, h_n$. Where n is the number of situations in a model. $s_1, s_2, \ldots, s_n$ is a sequence of situations provided by the evolution of a fuzzy Petri model. $h_1, h_2, \ldots, h_n$ is a set of confidence values associated to $s_1, s_2, \ldots, s_n$.

5 Scenario Recognition Algorithms

A Fuzzy Petri Net is a scenario model. When using real perception data, all the situations might not be perceived. Each time a situation of a scenario model is recognized, it can be interpreted as a new evidence that the corresponding scenario is recognized. The problem now is how we can fuse all those evidences to estimate how the scenario corresponds to what is currently observed.

5.1 Fuzzy Measures and Fuzzy Integrals

Let $X = \{x_i, x_2, \ldots, x_n\}$ be a finite set and let $P(X)$ denote the power set of X. A fuzzy measure on a set X is a function $g: P(X) \rightarrow [0, 1]$ such that

$$g(\phi) = 0, g(X) = 1 \text{ and } g(A) \leq g(B), \text{ if } A \subset B \text{ and } A, B \in P(X)$$

Following the definition, Sugeno [9] introduced the so-called g_λ-fuzzy measure satisfying the following additional property

$$g(A \cup B) = g(A) + g(B) + \lambda g(A) g(B) \tag{1}$$

for all $A,\ B \subset X$ and $A \cap B = \phi$, and for some fixed $\lambda > -1$. The value of λ can be found from the boundary condition $g(X) = 1$ by solving the following equation

$$\lambda + 1 = \prod_{i=1}^{n} (1 + \lambda g^i) \tag{2}$$

where g^i is called a fuzzy density value. Let $A_i = \{x_i + x_{i+1}, \ldots, x_n\}$. When g is a g_λ-fuzzy measure, the values of $g(A_i)$ can be computed recursively [9]. Murofushi [7] proposed the so-called Choquet fuzzy integral which can be determined in the following form

$$\int_X h(x) \quad g(\cdot) = \sum_{i=1}^{n} [h(x_i) - h(x_{i+1})] g(A_i), \tag{3}$$

where $h(x_1) \geq h(x_2) \geq \ldots \geq h(x_n)$ and $h(x_{n+1}) = 0$. In this paper, $h(x_i)$ represents the confidence value produced by each situation.

5.2 A Hierarchical Fusion Model for Evidence Combination

Consider a scenario composed of three situation sources, i.e. $S = \{s_1, s_2, s_3\}$ together with density values (degrees of importance of the situations) $g^1 = 0.14$, $g^2 =$

0.45 and $g^3 = 0.12$. The fuzzy measure on the power set of S can be calculated by Eq. (1) and shown in Table 1.

Table 1. Fuzzy measure on the power set of S.

Subset X	$g_{1.953}(X)$
Ø	0
$\{s_1\}$	0.14
$\{s_2\}$	0.45
$\{s_3\}$	0.12
$\{s_1, s_2\}$	0.71
$\{s_1, s_3\}$	0.29
$\{s_2, s_3\}$	0.67
$\{s_1, s_2, s_3\}$	1.0

The power set of S enumerates situations that can occur from a combination of situation sources. From Table 1, we can consider that the fuzzy measure, g(X), is the values for confirming the occurrence of combined situations. Thus, we use these values as density values and determine them to the situations that arise from a combination of situation sources. The hierarchical model for the combination of three situation sources is shown in Fig. 6. The nodes at the middle level will be determined as the degrees of importance of combined situations using the values of fuzzy measure in Table 2. We reduce the degree of importance of the sequence $\{s_1, s_2, s_3\}$ from 1.0 to 0.9 in order to prevent the effect of source that is over confident. To combine the evidence, a sequence of occurred situations, s_i, and its confidence values, h_i, are first separated according to the subset of the power set of S (see Fig. 6). Then the separated group of h_i will be aggregated by using Eq. (3) at the bottom level of the model. Afterward the aggregated values will be conveyed up to the nodes at the middle level and aggregated by Eq. (3) again. Finally, the aggregated value at the middle level will be propagated to the top level for representing the confidence value of the scenario, *e*.

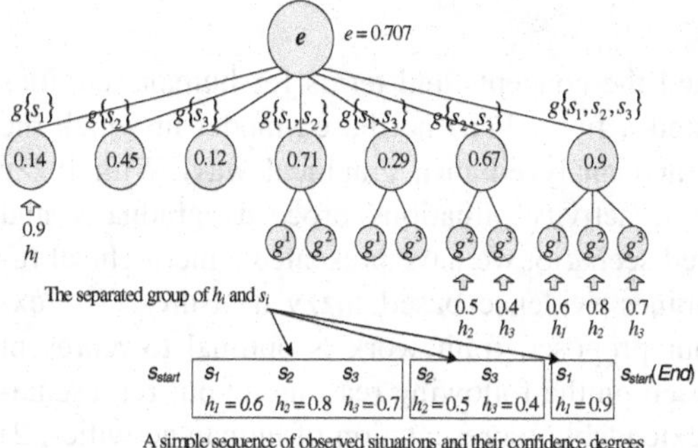

Fig. 6. Hierarchical model for evidence combination.

6 Experimental Results

We have created four different models of activities for the European Caviar project: “Browsing”, “Leaving bag behind”, “Two people fighting” and “People meeting walking together and splitting up". Table 2 only shows the results produced by the "Browsing" model when all sample videos are feed as an input.

The model produces the best confidence value when the most relevant video is presented to the model. We can also classify the videos pertinent to the "Browsing" scenario from the confidence value that the model produces on each video. The overall confidence value is rather high on the video "Person leaving bag but then pick it up again" because the activities contained in these video can also be interpreted as "Browsing" (the person leaves a bag near a desk, stays for a while and then goes away with the bag). Other videos may consist of activities that support the "Browsing" scenario partly.

7 Conclusions and Future Work

In this paper, we have first defined the concepts and terms for human activities modelling. Then, we have presented a fuzzy Petri net based-model in which the human activities are represented and analyzed in a graphical way. With fuzzy transition functions, the change of activity situations proceeds gradually and smoothly. To recognize an observed scenario, we have presented a hierarchical fusion model that nonlinearly combines evidence based fuzzy measures. The experimental results confirm that our proposed framework is optimal to represent and recognize human activities based on the following reasons: 1) our representation model allows a flexible and extendable representation of human activities, 2) the importance of information sources is taken account, which makes the process of evidence combination more consistent with real world situations. In the future, we plan to develop sophisticated temporal constraints in order to build a more generic model for representing scenarios in complicated situations.

Table 2. Confidence values produced by the "Browsing" model.

"Browsing" Model / Input Videos	Sequence of Situations												(e)
	s_1	s_2	s_3	s_1	s_2	s_3	s_1	s_2	s_3	s_1	s_2	s_3	
Person browsing back and forth	0.53	0.88	0.89	0.42	0.71	0.87	-	-	-	-	-	-	**0.6322**
Person browsing and reading for a while	0.68	0.86	0.84	-	-	-	-	-	-	-	-	-	**0.7184**
Person browsing and reading with back turned	0.48	0.71	0.93	-	-	-	-	-	-	-	-	-	**0.5959**
Person leaving bag by wall	0.53	-	0.78	0.65	-	0.94	0.19	-	0.32	-	-	-	**0.14**
Person leaving bag at chairs	0.42	-	0.93	-	-	-	-	-	-	-	-	-	**0.1406**
Person leaving box	0.38	-	0.89	-	-	-	-	-	-	-	-	-	**0.1287**
Two people meet, fight and run away *													
Person's ID 6	0.14	-	0.81	-	-	-	-	-	-	-	-	-	**0.0626**
Person's ID 7	0.42		0.43										**0.1224**
Two other people meet, fight and run away	0.54	-	0.84	-	-	-	-	-	-	-	-	-	**0.1676**
Two people meet, fight and chase each other	0.38	-	0.9	-	-	-	-	-	-	-	-	-	**0.13**
Two people meet, walk together and split*													
Person's ID 1	0.22	-	0.83	-	-	-	-	-	-	-	-	-	**0.085**
Person's ID 3	0.24		0.87										**0.0855**
Two people meet, walk together	0.44	-	0.92	-	-	-	-	-	-	-	-	-	**0.144**
Two other people meet, walk together	0.62	-	0.68	-	-	-	-	-	-	-	-	-	**0.182**
Person leaving bag but then pick it up again	0.16	-	0.93	0.8	0.71	0.89	0.47	0.93	0.91	0.55	-	0.93	**0.702**

*There is more than one person whose actions provoke the evolution of situations in the "Browsing" model.

References

1. D. Andreu, J. C. Pascal, R. Valette, Fuzzy Petri Net-Based Programmable Logic Controller, IEEE Transactions on Systems, Man, and Cybernetics-Part B: Cybernetic, 27(6), 1997, pp. 952-961.
2. J. L. Crowley, J. Coutaz, G. Rey, P. Reignier, Perceptual Components for Context Aware Computing, In Proceedings International Conference on Ubiquitous Computing, 2002, pp. 117-134.
3. T. V. Duong, H. H. Bui, D. Q. Phung, S. Venkatesh, Activity Recognition and Abnormality Detection with the Switching Hidden Semi-markov Model. In Proceedings IEEE Computer Society Conference on Computer Vision and Pattern Recognition, 2005, pp. 838-845.
4. N. M. Ghanem, Petri Net Models for Events Recognition in Surveillance Video, PhD thesis, University of Maryland, USA, 2007.
5. S. Hongeng, F. Bremond, R. Nevatia, Bayesian Framework for Video Surveillance Application, In Proceedings 15th International Conference on Pattern Recognition, 2000, pp. 164-170.
6. A. Madabhushi, J. K. Aggarwal, A Bayesian Approach to Human Activity Recognition, In Proceedings 2nd International Workshop on Visual Surveillance, Fort Collins, 1999, pp. 25-32.
7. T. Murofushi, M. Sugeno, An Interpretation of Fuzzy Measures and the Choquet Integral as an Integral with respect to a Fuzzy Measure, Fuzzy Sets System, 29(2), 1989, pp. 201-227.
8. Y. Shi, D. Huang, Y. Minnen, A. F. Bobick, I. A. Essa, Propagation networks for recognition of partially ordered sequential action, In Proceedings IEEE Computer Society Conference on Computer Vision and Pattern Recognition, 2004, pp. 862-869.
9. M. Sugeno, Fuzzy Measures and Fuzzy Integrals - A Survey, In: M.M. Gupta, G.N. Saridis, B.R. Gaines (Eds.), Fuzzy Automata and Decision Processes, Amsterdam, 1977, pp. 89-102.
10. J. Yamato, J. Ohya, K. Ishii, Recognizing Human Action in Time-Sequential Images using Hidden Markov Model. In Proceedings IEEE Conference on Computer Vision and Pattern Recognition, 1992, pp. 379-385.

Multi-modal System Architecture for Serious Gaming

Otilia Kocsis, Todor Ganchev, Iosif Mporas, George Papadopoulos, Nikos Fakotakis

Artificial Intelligence Group, Wire Communications Laboratory,
Dept. of Electrical and Computer Engineering, University of Patras, Rion 26500, Greece

{okocsis, tganchev, imporas, gpap, fakotaki}@upatras.gr

Abstract Human-computer interaction (HCI), especially in the games domain, targets to mimic as much as possible the natural human-to-human interaction, which is multimodal, involving speech, vision, haptic, etc. Furthermore, the domain of serious games, aiming to value-added games, makes use of additional inputs, such as biosensors, motion tracking equipment, etc. In this context, game development has become complex, expensive and burdened with a long development cycle. This creates barriers to independent game developers and inhibits the introduction of innovative games, or new game genres. In this paper the PlayMancer platform is introduced, a work in progress aiming to overcome such barriers by augmenting existing 3D game engines with innovative modes of interaction. Playmancer integrates open source existing systems, such as a game engine and a spoken dialog management system, extended by newly implemented components, supporting innovative interaction modalities, such as emotion recognition from audio data, motion tracking, etc, and advanced configuration tools.

1 Introduction

HCI has a long history, during which various interfaces were developed and currently aiming to a more natural interaction, involving 3D gesture recognition and speech-based interfaces. Achievement of naturalness involves progress from command or menu-based (system driven) to user-driven dialog management. System intelligence to allow adaptation to environment/context changes and user preferences is considered a must. The games domain has a special position in the area of HCI, holding a leading position in the research of attractive interfaces and interaction modes. Game development has become complex, expensive and burdened with a long development cycle, this creating barriers to independent games

---

Please use the following format when citing this chapter:

Kocsis, O., Ganchev, T., Mporas, I., Papadopoulos, G. and Fakotakis, N., 2009, in IFIP International Federation for Information Processing, Volume 296; *Artificial Intelligence Applications and Innovations III*; Eds. Iliadis, L., Vlahavas, I., Bramer, M.; (Boston: Springer), pp. 441–447.

developer and inhibiting the introduction of innovative games or new game genres, i.e. serious games or games accessible to communities with special needs.

Serious games (SGs) or persuasive games are computer and video games used as educational technology or as a vehicle for presenting or promoting a point of view. They can be similar to education games, but are often intended for an audience outside of primary or secondary education. SGs can be of any genre and many of them can be considered a kind of edutainment, intended to provide and engage self-reinforcing context in which to motivate and educate players towards non-game events or processes.

PlayMancer, a European Commission co-funded project, aims to implement a platform for serious games, which allows: (i) augmenting the gaming experience with innovative modes of interaction between the player and the game world, (ii) shorter and most cost-effective game production chain, (iii) evolvement of Universally Accessible Games principles for application into action based 3D games.

In this in-progress work, the PlayMancer concept and the architectural model of the multimodal platform are presented. The proposed platform architecture integrates a series of existing open source systems, such as a game engine, a spoken dialog management system, spoken interface components (speech recognition, understanding and synthesis). The existing components are augmented to support multimodality, to be adaptable to context changes, to user preferences/needs, and to game tasks. New interaction modes are provided by newly developed components, such as emotion recognition from speech audio data or motion tracking. One of the most important features of the proposed architecture is mixed-initiative dialogue strategy, enabled through dynamic generation of task-related interaction data, by coupling dialog and interactive 3D graphics objects at the design phase. Fast development of new games and adaptation to specific game scenario or user needs is facilitated by a configuration toolbox.

2 The PlayMancer Platform

The general architecture of the PlayMancer platform, illustrated in Fig. 1, has been designed taking into account: (i) functional and technical specifications derived from generic and specific domain user requirements, and (ii) the main technological challenge of the project – the rendering of an open source game engine multimodal. In particular, multi-modality is achieved by developing an enhanced multimodal dialogue interaction platform, based on the RavenClaw/Olympus architecture [1], which is further extended to render other modalities than speech.

The platform relies on a modular architecture, where components processing the data streams from the individual modalities and input sources interact through the central hub of Olympus, which allows synchronous or alternative use of input/output modalities. This way, in addition to traditional inputs/outputs used in games (joystick, keyboard, mouse, display), the PlayMancer architecture integrates also speech, touch, biosensors, and motion-tracking. These additional mo-

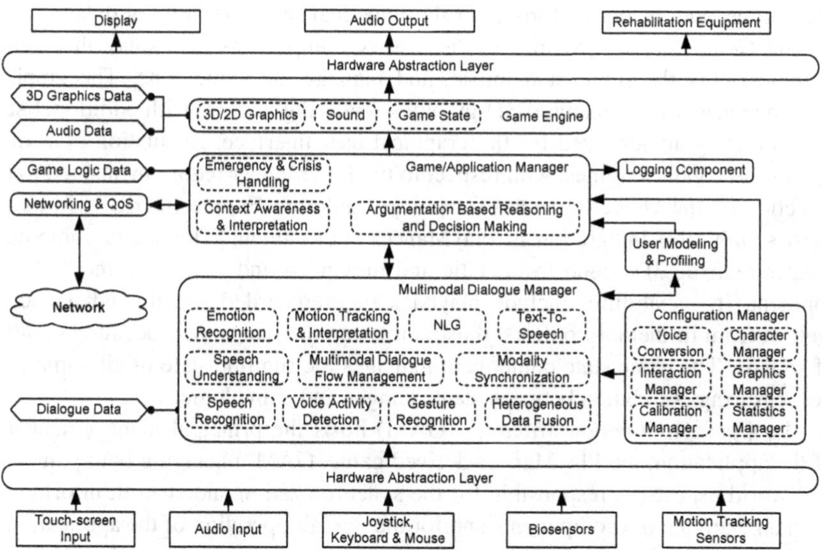

Fig.1 Architectural model of the PlayMancer platform

dalities allow the introduction of new game paradigms for fighting various eating and addiction disorders or for physical rehabilitation purposes, and, at the same time, offering enhanced game experience.

As illustrated in Fig. 1, the PlayMancer platform is composed of three major parts: (i) the Game Engine, (ii) the Game/Application Manager, and (iii) the Multimodal Dialogue Manager, as well as the Hardware Abstraction Layer, providing the interface to the input/output devices, and some auxiliary components. Of the auxiliary components, the Logging Component handles the long-term logging of data, which are processed statistically, and stored in a format convenient for interpretation by the healthcare supervisors (i.e. medical doctors, psychologists, rehabilitation experts, etc). The networking and Quality of Service (QoS) monitoring component provides the means for multiplayer experience over existing global or local area networks. The User Modeling and Profiling component is responsible for personalization and adaptation of interaction to user preferences [2].

The *Configuration Manger* (CM) is an off-line toolbox of utilities and resources (such as Voice Conversion tools and resources, game Character Manager, Graphics Manager, etc), which are not part of the run-time application. Instead, they provide to the developers, the supervisor or the player of the game the tool to create new games, to customize and fine-tune the entire game or specific game level, and to contribute own content. The CM also provides the means for configuration setup of the interaction modes, calibration of the sensors, introducing user-specific game settings, management of the overall game resources, developing new game characters/actors, game levels, etc. For the newly generated playing characters, a Voice Conversion component allows the user to create new voices that will fit to the profile of the new characters. The Statistics Manager allows the healthcare supervisor to configure the necessary health indicators to be monitored, the settings and the output format for the statistical summarization of data.

The *Game Engine* provides the necessary components to display the game's graphics, play the sound and music, and manage the game state. The graphics component is a fully featured 3D graphics rendering engine, with additional support for 2D graphics, used for the graphical user interface. Evaluation of various open source game engines, with respect to the PlayMancer requirements, led to the selection of the Object-Oriented Graphics Rendering Engine (OGRE) [3] as the most suitable for integration in PlayMancer environment. The sound component creates realistic 3D sound from static and moving sound sources in the 3D environment. Its capabilities include playback of prerecorded sounds and music, as well as from in-memory buffers, thus facilitating the real-time procedural creation of sounds. The game state component manages the runtime state of all game entities, ensuring correlation between state changes and game logic.

The *Game/Application Manager* (GAM) hosts the principal management unit of the application, the PlayMancer-derived game. GAM, managing both game and real-world aspects, is responsible for the synchronization and smooth information exchange among the components and for the overall operation of the application.

Through the Context Awareness and Interpretation component, the GAM administers the smooth interaction between the physical and the synthetic world of the game, offering a high-level supervision of the user interaction, experiences and reactions. Emotion arousal, bio-indicators, and game-specific information from the synthetic world, provide context clues that can variously be exploited depending on the particular game. GAM also hosts the Emergency and Crisis Handling component, which enables alteration of the interaction style and the game flow, to prevent danger and harm to the player in case of atypical behaviors or development of emergency situation. Monitoring of context parameters and detection of atypical behaviors is supported by personalized game-specific user profile data, set-up by the supervisor for each player. The Argumentation-Based Reasoning and Decision Making component implements the top-level decision making logic of the system that is responsible for achieving the goals of the application.

The major task of the *Multimodal Dialogue Manager* is to handle user-machine interaction: handle events from different input modalities, interpret inputs, fuse and disambiguate these inputs when necessary, personalize and adapt interaction, etc. The PlayMancer-based interaction has the following features:

- The description of the 3D game interactive objects has been enhanced with information regarding interaction modalities allowed and dialogue data (interaction resources, such as understanding grammars for speech interface) to be used for each modality. This data will be used by the Multimodal Dialogue Manager to select the most suitable modality for interaction and the resources to be used by each input/output modality when interaction is requested.
- The use of modality independent interaction task plan, allowing to synchronize and fuse data from different modalities.
- Interaction ambiguities solving is employed by the Multimodal Dialogue Manager when commands, which apply to more than one interactive object, are issued by the player.

Integration of spoken dialogue interfaces in the game domain is a challenging research issue, especially when the gaming environment is multimodal, where the domain boundary is not always clear. In PlayMancer, we consider a speech interface which incorporates the following components: Voice Activity Detection (VAD), Speech Recognition, Speech Understanding, Text-to-Speech Synthesis (TTS) and Natural Language Generation (NLG) [4-6]. Data stream of the infrared Motion Tracking Sensor array is processed by the OpenTracker framework [7, 8], which in Fig. 1 is designated as Motion Tracking and Interpretation component.

The biosensor input is used to monitor various bio-indicators of the player. The biomedical data are recorded for diagnostic purposes. In addition, the speech and biosensor data streams are fed to the Emotion Recognition (ER) component [9]. The ER component detects the emotional state of the player among a group of emotional categories, such as neutral, angry, happy, panic, fear, boredom, etc. The information of the emotional condition of the player is used as a supplementary parameter for estimating the cognitive load of the player. Depending on the purpose of the game, the emotional state and the cognitive load of the player, the GAM and Game Engine can implement different strategies; change the interaction style; or the level of difficulty at the current scenario.

The data streams from all modalities are time-aligned in the Modality Synchronization component, and then disambiguated and fussed in the Heterogeneous Data Fusion component. The success of multimodal data integration depends on the abstraction level to which data are fused and the method applied to carry out the multi-sensory data fusion. In PlayMancer, various abstraction levels will be considered, depending on the sensor type and task goal.

The complexity of the PlayMancer platform implies modeling of knowledge in relation to the components involved and tasks to be completed. Data that are already handled by the existing components integrated into the platform, such as the 3D Graphics Data (3DGD) and Audio Data handled by the game engine, are related to higher abstraction level data, needed for the multimodal interaction. The 3DGD represents all graphical objects needed to build game environment in the virtual world, including shape, color and textures descriptions. Some of these objects are interactive, allowing different states. Thus a description of their alternative states and behavior when passing from one state to another, game logic data, is also attached to the 3DGD. In PlayMancer, the 3D Graphics Data is coupled to Dialog Data. Dialog Data consists of description of interaction modes that can be used to interact with the virtual object, and modality specific data used for interpretation of input row data to higher abstraction level concepts. This coupling allows dynamic generation of task-related interaction resources and high level of reusability of dialog data for different games or scenes design.

3 Conclusion

Playmancer is built on top of existing open-source software, such as OGRE 3D rendering engine [3] and RavenClaw/Olympus dialog management platform [1], aiming to provide a novel development framework for serious game development. The existing components are augmented to support multimodality, to be adaptable to context changes, to user preferences, and to game task. Game developers are provided with a series of configuration and management components, to shorten the development cycle of games and to enable high level of code re-usability. Architecture design of multimodal systems, especially for virtual reality environments in the games domain, requires addressing several issues related to redundancy of input/output modalities, complementarity, disambiguation, etc [10]. Common approaches for modality integration are frame-, grammar- or agent-based, while the concept of Interactive Cooperative Objects (ICO) is emerging [11]. PlayMancer considers a mixed approach, integrating features of the grammar-based method and ICO formalism for the dynamic modeling of multimodal interaction. Dynamic generation of task-related interaction data is enabled by coupling dialog and interactive 3D graphics objects at the design phase.

Acknowledgment This work was supported by the PlayMancer project (FP7 215839), which is partially funded by the European Commission.

References

1. Bohus, D., Rudnicky, A. (2003). RavenClaw: Dialog management using hierarchical task decomposition and expectation agenda. In: Proceedings Eurospeech 2003, pp.597-600, Geneva.
2. Vildjiounaite, E., Kocsis, O., Kyllonen, V., Kladis, B. (2007) Context-dependent user modeling for smart homes. In: Proceedings 11th International Conference on User Modeling, LNCS, vol. 4511/2007, pp. 345-349, Springer, Heidelberg.
3. Object-Oriented Graphics Rendering Engine, http://ogre3d.org
4. Nuance Recognizer, http://www.nuance.com.
5. The CMU Sphinx Group Open Source Speech Recognition Engines, http://cmusphinx.sourceforge.net/html/cmusphinx.php.
6. FestVox speech synthesizer, http://festvox.org.
7. Reitmayr, G., Schmalstieg, D. (2001). OpenTracker – an open software architecture for reconfigurable tracking based on XML. In: Proceedings IEEE Virtual Reality 2001, pp. 285-286.
8. OpenTracker – An open architecture for reconfigurable tracking based on XML, http://studierstube.icg.tu-graz.ac.at:80/opentracker/

9. Kostoulas, T., Ganchev, T., Mporas, I., Fakotakis, N. (2008). A real world emotional speech corpus for modern Greek. In: Proceedings LREC'2008, Morocco, May 28-30.
10. Bourguet, M.L. (2004). Software design and development of multimodal interaction. In: Proceedings IFIP 2004, pp. 409-414.
11. Navarre, D., Palanque, P., Bastide, R., Schyn, A., Winckler, M., Nedel, L.P., Freitas, C. (2005) A formal description of multimodal interaction techniques for immersive virtual reality applications. In: Proceedings INTERACT'05, LNCS, vol.3585, Springer, pp.170-183.

Reconstruction-based Classification Rule Hiding through Controlled Data Modification

Aliki Katsarou, Aris Gkoulalas-Divanis, and Vassilios S. Verykios

Abstract In this paper, we propose a reconstruction–based approach to classification rule hiding in categorical datasets. The proposed methodology modifies transactions supporting both sensitive and nonsensitive classification rules in the original dataset and then uses the supporting transactions of the nonsensitive rules to produce its sanitized counterpart. To further investigate some interesting properties of this methodology, we explore three variations of the main technique which differ in the way they select and sanitize transactions supporting sensitive rules. Finally, through extensive experimental evaluation, we demonstrate the effectiveness of the proposed algorithms towards effectively shielding the sensitive knowledge.

1 Introduction

Recent advances in information technology has provided the means to cost–efficient data collection and analysis. Nowadays, organizations collect vast amounts of data on a daily basis to effectively conduct their business. The collected data is usually organized and stored in a data warehouse to allow for its efficient retrieval and manipulation, when necessary. Apart from accommodating the everyday needs of the organizations, the stored data is also a valuable source of knowledge. Modern organizations are usually willing to integrate and mine their data collectively with other organizations in order to derive global knowledge patterns. However, the collective mining of data poses a threat to privacy, as sensitive knowledge patterns can be inferred from the data. The disclosure of sensitive patterns (e.g., trade secrets) to

Aliki Katsarou
Department of Management, London School of Economics and Political Science, Houghton Str, London WC2A 2AE, U.K., e-mail: A.Katsarou1@lse.ac.uk

Aris Gkoulalas-Divanis · Vassilios S. Verykios
Department of Computer & Communication Engineering, University of Thessaly, 37 Glavani - 28th October Str, Volos GR–38221, Greece, e-mail: {arisgd,verykios}@inf.uth.gr

Please use the following format when citing this chapter:

Katsarou, A., Gkoulalas-Divanis, A. and Verykios, V.S., 2009, in IFIP International Federation for Information Processing, Volume 296; *Artificial Intelligence Applications and Innovations III*; Eds. Iliadis, L., Vlahavas, I., Bramer, M.; (Boston: Springer), pp. 449–458.

untrusted entities, such as business competitors, can be deemed catastrophical for the data owner. Therefore, privacy preserving data mining approaches are essential to hide the sensitive knowledge prior to the sharing of the data.

In this paper, we propose an efficient approach for the hiding of sensitive classification rules in categorical datasets. Our proposed methodology uses a rule–based classifier to derive the classification rules for the original dataset, among which there exist rules that are considered as sensitive from the owner's perspective. Given the whole set of classification rules, the algorithm identifies the transactions of the dataset that support both sensitive and nonsensitive rules and modifies them in such a way that they no longer support the sensitive rules. The modification is focused on the attribute–value pair of the transaction that causes the least side–effects to the dataset. Finally, the transactions that support the nonsensitive rules are used to generate the sanitized version of the dataset that can be safely shared. The proposed methodology is simple, time efficient and with very satisfying results.

The remainder of this paper is organized as follows. In Sect. 2, we formalize the problem by providing some basic definitions that allow us to introduce the problem statement. Sect. 3 demonstrates the solution methodology that we followed and presents our basic classification rule hiding algorithm, along with three complementary implementations. In Sect. 4, we present the experimental evaluation of the proposed algorithms. Finally, Sect. 5 presents the related work, and Sect. 6 concludes this paper.

2 Problem Formulation

In this section we first provide some basic definitions that are necessary for the understanding of the proposed methodology, and then we introduce the problem statement.

2.1 Basic Definitions

Definition 1. (Dataset) Let a dataset D be a 4–tuple $\{T, A, V, f\}$, where

- T is a nonempty finite set consisting of N transactions.
- A is a nonempty finite set consisting of M attributes, such that any attribute $A_m \in A$ has a domain of supported values V_{A_m}. Among the M attributes, one attribute C is designated as the class for dataset D and consists of a nonempty finite set of class labels.
- V is a nonempty finite set of values for all attributes, s.t. $V_{A_m} \subseteq V$ and $\bigcup_{V_{A_m}} = V$.
- f is a function such that $f : V \times A \longrightarrow V_{A_m}$, i.e. it assigns a value to an attribute of a given record.

Definition 2. (**Classification Rule**) A classification rule $R_i \in R$, extracted from a dataset D, is a sentence of the form $(A_1 = f(A_1)) \wedge (A_2 = f(A_2)) \wedge (A_3 = f(A_3)) \wedge \ldots \wedge (A_m = f(A_m)) \longrightarrow (C = c)$, where $c \in C$ and $A_1, A_2, A_3, \ldots A_m \neq C$.

Having defined the notion of a classification rule, we state that a transaction *supports* a classification rule if all the attribute–value pairs $(A_m = f(A_m))$ of the classification rule (including the class label) appear in the transaction. Furthermore, we define the (supporting) *size* of a classification rule R_i, and denote it as $|R_i|$, to be the number of transactions from D that support the rule. Pertinent to the definition of a classification rule is the definition of a classification problem.

Corollary 1. ***(Classification Problem)*** *A classification problem over dataset D is the task of learning a target function $F : D \longrightarrow C$ that maps each transaction in D to one of the predefined class labels (a.k.a. categories) $c \in C$.*

2.2 Problem Statement

Given a dataset D, a class attribute C, a set of classification rules R over D, as well as a set of sensitive rules $R_S \subset R$, we want to find a dataset D' such that when mining D' for classification rules using the same parameters as those used in the mining of D, only the (nonsensitive) rules in $R - R_S$ can be derived.

3 Solution Methodology

In this section we elaborate on the proposed methodology for classification rule hiding in categorical datasets. First, we present the main reconstruction–based approach[1] that we developed to solve this problem. Then, we introduce three complementary implementations that differ in the way they select and sanitize the transactions supporting sensitive rules.

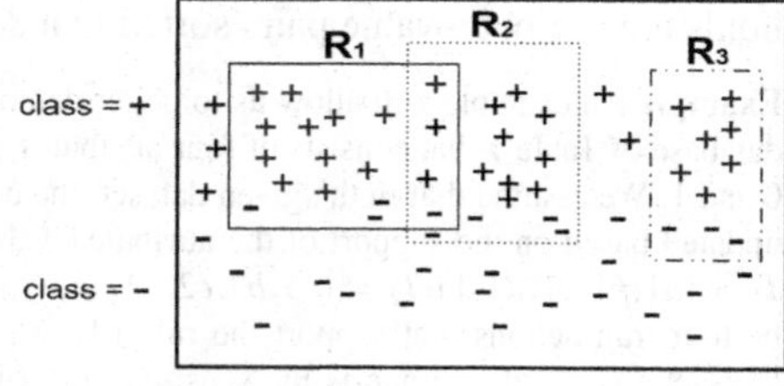

Fig. 1 Rule generation by using a sequential covering algorithm like RIPPER [3]. $\mathbf{R_1}$ and $\mathbf{R_3}$ represent two regions covered by nonsensitive rules, while $\mathbf{R_2}$ is a region covered by a sensitive classification rule.

[1] Reconstruction–based approaches for knowledge hiding, generate the sanitized dataset D' from scratch instead of directly modifying the transactions of the original dataset D.

3.1 The Least Supported Attribute Algorithm

Our proposed methodology, called the Least Supported Attribute (LSA) modification algorithm, uses the nonsensitive rules that are mined from the original database D to reconstruct its sanitized counterpart D'. As a first step, LSA identifies the supporting transactions for each nonsensitive rule $R_i \in R$ in the original dataset. Then, among the supporting transactions for this rule, it selects the ones that are also supporting at least one sensitive rule. Fig. 1 provides an example of such a scenario, generated by a sequential covering algorithm like RIPPER [3] to discriminate between the positive and the negative examples of a two–class classification problem. As one can notice, the rule generation process allows the transactions of the database to support more than one rule, as is the case for rules R_1 and R_2[2].

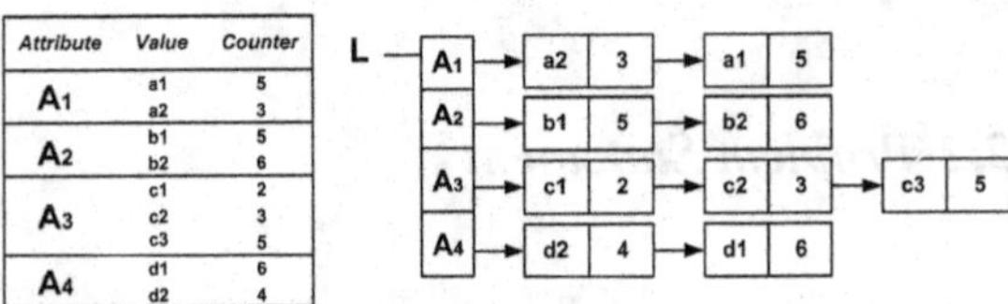

Attribute	Value	Counter
A1	a1	5
	a2	3
A2	b1	5
	b2	6
A3	c1	2
	c2	3
	c3	5
A4	d1	6
	d2	4

Fig. 2 An efficient data structure **L** used by LSA for the selection of the attribute–value pair that will be modified in a transaction to facilitate knowledge hiding.

For each transaction that supports both a nonsensitive and a sensitive classification rule, LSA modifies it appropriately so that it no longer supports the sensitive rule. The proposed modification affects only one attribute–value pair of the transaction, which is selected to be the one having the least support in D, among the attribute–value pairs of the supported sensitive rule. Furthermore, to minimize the side–effects in the sanitized outcome, the new value that will be assigned to the selected attribute will be the one that is supported the least by the transactions of the original dataset (different from the current value in the sensitive rule). By altering the value of the attribute to equal the one that is least supported in D, we manage to moderate the increment of the support of some attribute–value pairs and thus to minimize the probability of producing rules in D' that were nonexistent in D. To make this possible, we employ a data structure that keeps track of the number of times that each attribute–value pair is met in the transactions of D, as shown in Fig. 2. As one can notice, the proposed data structure **L** is a list of lists, the later of which holds the attribute–value pairs sorted in a descending order of support in dataset D.

Example An example will allow us to better demonstrate how this operation works. Consider the database of Table 1 that consists of four attributes A_1,A_2,A_3,A_4 and a class attribute C with labels 0 and 1. We assume that in the given dataset, the counters for the various attribute–value pairs (as updated based on the support of the attributes–values in the dataset) are provided in Table 1. Let $T_1 = (a1,b1,c1,d1,1), T_2 = (a1,b2,c2,d1,1), T_3 = (a1,b1,c2,d1,1)$ and $T_4 = (a1,b2,c3,d1,1)$ be four transactions that support the rule $(A_1 = a1) \wedge (A_4 = d1) \longrightarrow (C = 1)$. Among the four transactions, T_4 also supports the sensitive rule $(A_2 = b2) \wedge (A_3 = c3) \longrightarrow (C = 1)$. In order to modify T_4 in such a way that it no longer supports the sensitive rule, LSA will choose to replace

[2] However, due to the rule ordering scheme that is enforced by the rule generation algorithm, only the first rule in the rule set that is supported by a new transaction is used for its classification.

Table 1 An example of using the data structure L on decision making.

Attribute	Value	Counter
A_1	a1	5
	a2	3
A_2	b1	5
	b2	6
A_3	c1	2
	c2	3
	c3	5
A_4	d1	6
	d2	4

Algorithm 1 The Least Supported Attribute (LSA) algorithm.

Input: Original dataset D, Sensitive rules R_S, Nonsensitive rules $R - R_S$.
Output: Sanitized dataset D'.

$D' \leftarrow \varnothing$, $\mathbf{L} \leftarrow$ all counters initialized to zero.
foreach nonsensitive rule $R_i \in R - R_S$ **do**
  $S \leftarrow$ all transactions in D that support R_i.
  foreach transaction $T_n \in S$ **do**
    foreach attribute $A_m \in T_n$ **do**
      update_list ($\mathbf{L}$, A_m) ▷ Increase the counter of the appropriate value of attribute A_m.
  foreach transaction $T_n \in S$ **do**
    if T_n supports a sensitive rule $R_j \in R_S$ **then**
      select the attribute–value from R_j that has the minimum counter in $\mathbf{L}$ and does not appear in R_i.
      replace the value of this attribute in T_n with the one with the minimum counter in $\mathbf{L}$.
      update_list ($\mathbf{L}$, selected attribute)
  $\mathbf{S} \leftarrow \mathbf{S} \cup (S, |S|)$
foreach pair $(S, |S|) \in \mathbf{S}$ **do**
  Add $|S| \times N / |\mathbf{S}|$ transactions from S to D' in a round–robin fashion.

the value of attribute A_3 in T_4, since $(A_3 = c3)$ is less supported in D than $(A_2 = b2)$. The new value of A_3 in T_4 will be the one from $\mathbf{L}$ that is minimally supported in the dataset; that is $c1$.

The rationale behind the modification of the transactions that support sensitive rules in D is as follows. In LSA (as in most of the currently proposed methodologies for classification rule hiding), we consider that the sanitized dataset D' will consist of the same number of transactions N as the ones of dataset D. However, since the sensitive rules cover a set of transactions that are not covered by the nonsensitive rules, and since D' is formulated only from the transactions supporting the nonsensitive rules, it is reasonable to expect that the transactions that support all the nonsensitive rules in D are less than N. Thus, LSA uses the transactions supporting the nonsensitive rules in a round–robin fashion in order to construct the sanitized outcome. However, we need to mention that LSA ensures that the representation of the nonsensitive rules in D' is proportional to their representation in D. Algorithm 1 provides the details of our implementation.

3.2 Three Complementary Implementations of LSA

To experimentally investigate some of the properties of LSA, we implemented three variations of this algorithm. The first variation, called Naïve LSA (NLSA), differs from LSA in the way it selects the attribute–value pair of a transaction that supports a sensitive rule to facilitate knowledge hiding. Specifically, when a transaction is found to support both a nonsensitive and a sensitive rule, NLSA randomly selects an attribute–value pair of the supported sensitive rule and modifies the value of this attribute based on the counters in **L**.

The second variation, called TR-A (Transaction Removal for All transactions supporting sensitive rules) discards, instead of modifying, all the transactions that support both a nonsensitive and a sensitive rule, while the third variation, called TR-S (Transaction Removal for Selected transactions) is a combination of LSA and TR-A. For every nonsensitive rule, TR-S retrieves its supporting transactions in D. If some of these transactions also support a sensitive rule, then (i) if the number of transactions supporting the nonsensitive rule is greater than the number of instances that have to be generated for this rule in the sanitized dataset D', then any additional transactions from the ones supporting the sensitive rule are removed, and (ii) the remaining transactions that also support the sensitive rule are modified as LSA dictates. Otherwise, the algorithm operates the same way as LSA.

Table 2 The characteristics of the two datasets used for experimentation.

Dataset	# records	# attributes	# rules (prune)	# rules (no prune)
Mushroom	8,124	22	9	8
Vote	435	16	4	10

4 Experimental Evaluation

To experimentally evaluate our proposed algorithms, we implemented the algorithms H(half), H(all), GR and LC, proposed in [5, 6], and then evaluated all the eight methodologies (TR-A, TR-S, NLSA, LSA, H(half), H(all), GR and LC) along two principal dimensions: (i) the number of side–effects (in terms of lost rules, ghost rules and disclosed sensitive rules) caused to the original dataset due to the hiding of the sensitive knowledge, and (ii) the scalability of the approaches under different hiding scenarios. A lost rule is any nonsensitive rule from D that does not appear in D', while a ghost rule is any rule that did not exist in D but is produced for D'. The properties of the categorical datasets that we used to conduct our experiments are shown in Table 2. Both datasets were taken from the UCI machine learning repository (available at http://archive.ics.uci.edu/ml).

Figs. 3–5 present the observed results for the two datasets when a certain number of sensitive rules are hidden. In all cases we tested, both the initial and the final classification rule sets were produced with RIPPER [3], while experiments were conducted with and without rule pruning. As one can notice, LSA and its variations typically achieve better results than their competitors in terms of side–effects caused

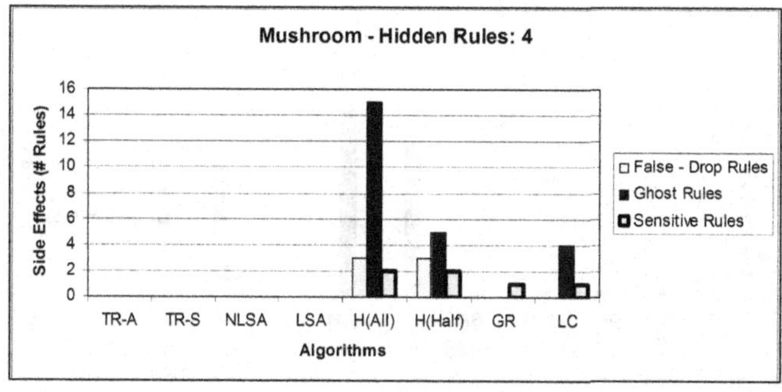

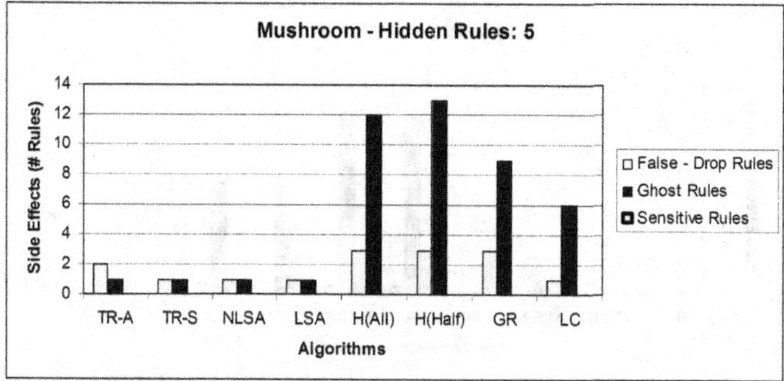

Fig. 3 Experimental results for Mushroom — rules extracted with pruning.

to D' by the sanitization process. Furthermore, the proposed algorithms achieved to appropriately cover–up the sensitive rules in D', in all tested settings.

In terms of scalability, Fig. 6 indicates that the time complexity of the proposed algorithms is kept low, even when the number of rules to be hidden increases. This outcome suggests that the proposed approaches are suitable to facilitate knowledge hiding in very large datasets.

5 Related Work

In the last decade, there has been a lot of active research in the field of privacy preserving data sharing. Vaidya et al. [8] tackle the problem of multiparty data sharing by proposing a distributed privacy preserving version of ID3. The proposed strategy assumes a vertical partitioning of the data where every attribute (including the class) has to be known only by one party. A distributed version of ID3 that is suitable in the case of a horizontal data partitioning scheme, can be found in [9].

Chang and Moskowitz [1] were the first to address the inference problem caused by the downgrading of the data in the context of classification rules. Through a blocking technique, called parsimonious downgrading, the authors block the infer-

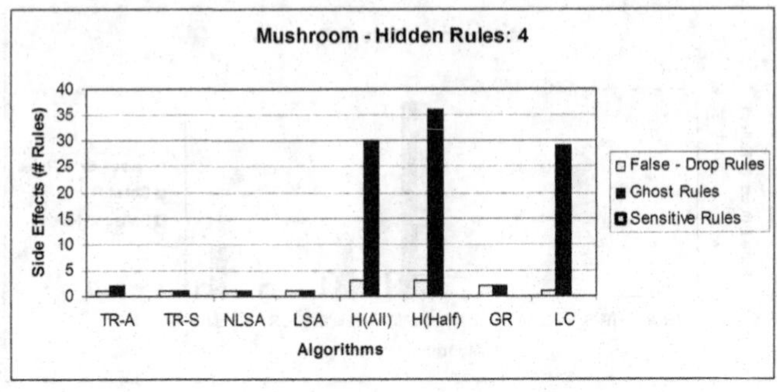

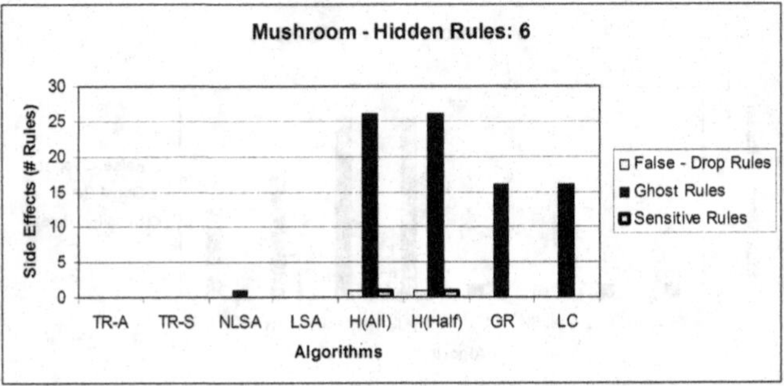

Fig. 4 Experimental results for Mushroom — rules extracted without pruning.

ence channels that lead to the identification of the sensitive rules by selectively sanitizing transactions so that missing values appear in the released dataset. This has as an immediate consequence the lowering of the confidence of an attacker regarding the holding of the sensitive rules.

Chen and Liu [2] present a random rotation perturbation technique to privacy preserving data classification. The proposed methodology preserves the multi–dimensional geometric characteristics of the dataset with respect to task–specific information. As an effect, in the sanitized dataset the sensitive knowledge is protected against disclosure, while the utility of the data is preserved to a large extend.

Natwichai et al. [6] propose a reconstruction algorithm for classification rules hiding. The proposed algorithm uses the nonsensitive rules to build a decision tree from which the sanitized dataset will be generated. To produce the sanitized dataset, the algorithm traverses the paths of the decision tree that correspond to the same rule and repeatedly generates transactions that support this rule in the sanitized outcome. In [6] the decision tree is build based on the gain ratio of the various attributes. An alternative approach that builds the decision tree by using the least common attribute measure is presented in [5]. Finally, in [7] a data reduction approach is proposed, which is suitable for the hiding of a specific type of classification rules, known as canonical associative classification rules.

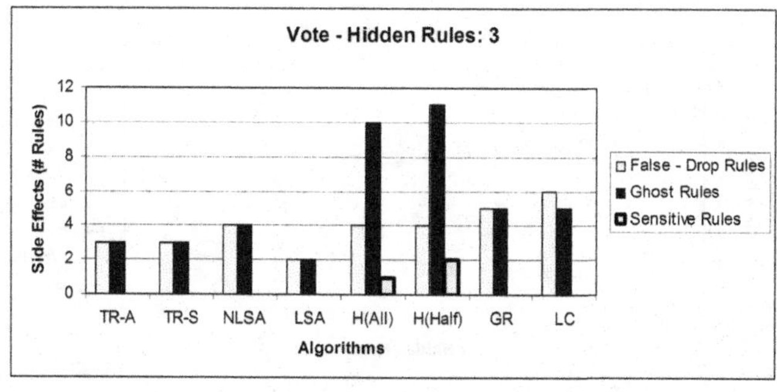

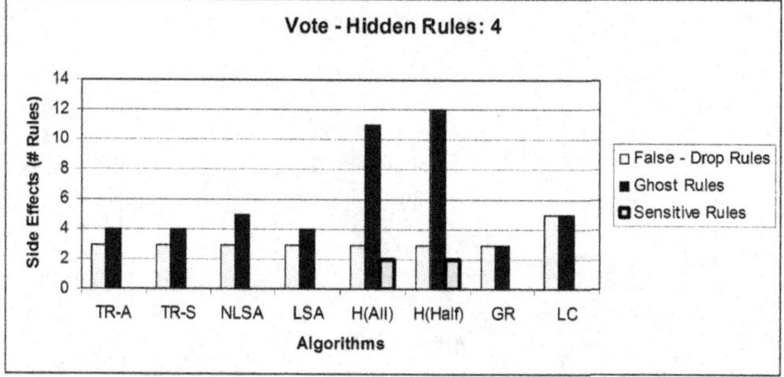

Fig. 5 Experimental results for Vote — rules extracted without pruning.

Finally, Islam and Brankovic [4] present a noise addition framework for the hiding of sensitive classification rules. The suggested framework achieves to protect the sensitive patterns from disclosure, while preserving all the nonsensitive statistical information of the dataset.

6 Conclusions

In this paper, we presented a novel approach to classification rules hiding that guarantees the privacy of the sensitive knowledge, while minimizing the side–effects introduced by the sanitization process. Through a series of experiments, we demonstrated that our approach yields good results in terms of side–effects, while it keeps the computational complexity within reasonable bounds.

Acknowledgements We would like to thank Prof. William W. Cohen from the Carnegie Mellon University for providing us the implementation of the RIPPER algorithm.

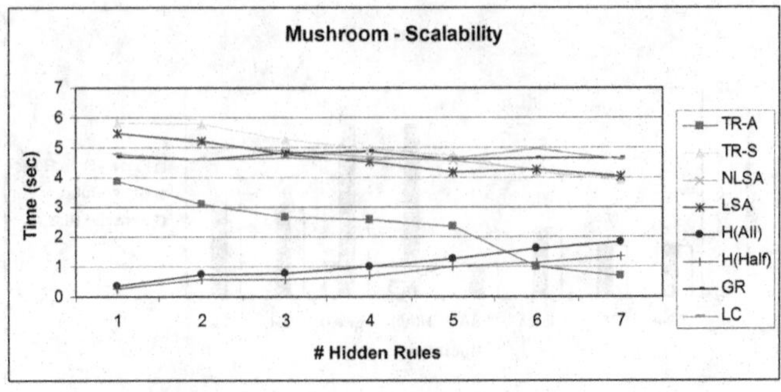

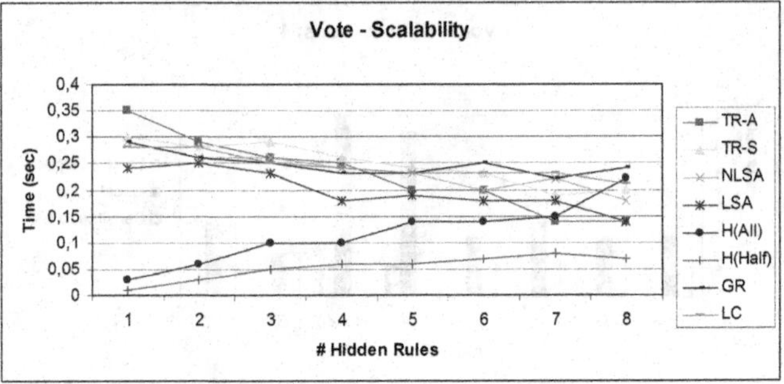

Fig. 6 The scalability of the tested algorithms in the two datasets.

References

1. Chang, L., Moskowitz, I.S.: Parsimonious downgrading and decision trees applied to the inference problem. In: Proceedings 1998 Workshop on New Security Paradigms, pp. 82–89 (1998)
2. Chen, K., Liu, L.: Privacy preserving data classification with rotation perturbation. In: Proceedings 5th IEEE International Conference on Data Mining, pp. 589–592 (2005)
3. Cohen, W.W.: Fast effective rule induction. In: Proceedings 12th International Conference on Machine Learning, pp. 115–123 (1995)
4. Islam, M.Z., Brankovic, L.: A framework for privacy preserving classification in data mining. In: Proceedings 22nd Workshop on Australasian Information Security, Data Mining and Web Intelligence, and Software Internationalisation, pp. 163–168 (2004)
5. Natwichai, J., Li, X., Orlowska, M.: Hiding classification rules for data sharing with privacy preservation. In: Proceedings 7th International Conference on Data Warehousing and Knowledge Discovery, pp. 468–467 (2005)
6. Natwichai, J., Li, X., Orlowska, M.E.: A reconstruction-based algorithm for classification rules hiding. In: Proceedings 17th Australasian Database Conference, pp. 49–58 (2006)
7. Natwichai, J., Sun, X., Li, X.: Data reduction approach for sensitive associative classification rule hiding. In: Proceedings 19th Australian Conference on Databases (2007)
8. Vaidya, J., Clifton, C., Kantarcioglu, M., Patterson, A.S.: Privacy-preserving decision trees over vertically partitioned data. ACM Trans. Knowl. Discov. Data **2**(3) (2008)
9. Xiao, M.J., Huang, L.S., Luo, Y.L., Shen, H.: Privacy preserving ID3 algorithm over horizontally partitioned data. In: Proceedings 6th International Conference on Parallel and Distributed Computing Applications and Technologies, pp. 239–243 (2005)

Learning Rules from User Behaviour

Domenico Corapi, Oliver Ray, Alessandra Russo, Arosha Bandara, and Emil Lupu

Abstract Pervasive computing requires infrastructures that adapt to changes in user behaviour while minimising user interactions. Policy-based approaches have been proposed as a means of providing adaptability but, at present, require policy goals and rules to be explicitly defined by users. This paper presents a novel, logic-based approach for automatically learning and updating models of users from their observed behaviour. We show how this task can be accomplished using a non-monotonic learning system, and we illustrate how the approach can be exploited within a pervasive computing framework.

1 Introduction

Pervasive computing is enabled by the development of increasingly complex devices and software infrastructures that accompany users in everyday life. Such systems must autonomously adapt to changes in user context and behaviour, whilst operating seamlessly with minimal user intervention. They must, therefore, be able to learn from sensory input and user actions. Yet user acceptance requires them to be predictable, capable of explaining their actions, and providing some way for users to understand and amend what has been learnt. This directs us towards techniques that use logical rules for knowledge representation and reasoning. Even though some statistical pre-processing of raw sensor data will inevitably be required, there are considerable advantages in adopting a core logical formalism, such as simple and

Domenico Corapi, Alessandra Russo, Emil Lupu
Imperial College London, Exhibition Road, London UK, email: {d.corapi, a.russo, e.c.lupu}@imperial.ac.uk
Oliver Ray
University of Bristol, Woodland Road, Bristol UK, email: oray@cs.bris.ac.uk
Arosha Bandara
The Open University, Walton Hall Campus, Milton Keynes UK, email: a.k.bandara@open.ac.uk

Please use the following format when citing this chapter:

Corapi, D., Ray, O., Russo, A., Bandara, A. and Lupu, E., 2009, in IFIP International Federation for Information Processing, Volume 296; *Artificial Intelligence Applications and Innovations III*; Eds. Iliadis, L., Vlahavas, I., Bramer, M.; (Boston: Springer), pp. 459–468.

modular enforcement through policy frameworks [1, 18] and principled representations of space and time [23]. Logic programming is an ideal choice for knowledge representation from a computational point of view and it also benefits from Inductive Logic Programming (ILP) [17] tools that permit the learning of logic programs from examples.

Learning rules of user behaviour through inductive reasoning poses several challenges. Learning must be incremental: as examples of user behaviour are continuously added, the system must permit periodic revision of the rules and knowledge learnt. Moreover, the system must cater for temporal aspects, expressing both persistence and change through time, and exceptions to previously learnt rules. For this, the system must be capable of non-monotonic[1] reasoning [13]. The system must reason with partial information whilst providing fine grained control of the reasoning process to satisfy appropriate user-defined language and search biases (such as minimising the changes made to the initial theory).

This paper presents an algorithm for learning and revising models of user behaviour which makes use of a non-monotonic ILP system, called XHAIL (eXtended Hybrid Abductive Inductive Learning) [19], that is capable of learning normal logic programs from a given set of examples and background knowledge. The contribution of this paper is twofold. First a novel algorithm is presented that is able to perform general theory revision by supporting automatic computation of new theories T' that are not necessarily extensions of original theories T, to correctly account for newly acquired examples E. Second, an application of the algorithm to learning rules describing behaviour of mobile phone users is presented by means of a simplified example consisting of learning the circumstances in which users accept, reject or ignore calls. Once learnt, these rules can be periodically reviewed and amended by the user and enacted automatically on the device avoiding user intervention. This work is part of a larger project [2] that seeks to exploit the proposed approach in the context of privacy policies.

The paper is structured as follows. Section 2 summarises relevant background material on ILP. Section 3 describes the main features of the approach by introducing basic concepts, presenting a *learning-based theory revision* algorithm and illustrating its application to the example. Section 4 relates our approach with other existing techniques for theory revision. Section 5 concludes the paper with a summary and some remarks about future work.

2 Background

Inductive Logic Programming (ILP) [17] is concerned with the computation of hypotheses H that generalise a set of (positive and negative) examples E with respect to a prior background knowledge B. In this paper, we consider the case when B and

[1] A logical system is non-monotonic if given a theory (e.g. $\{bird(tweety).\ bird(X) \leftarrow penguin(X).\ fly(X) \leftarrow bird(X), \neg penguin(X).\}$), adding new information ($penguin(tweety)$) may cause some conclusions to be retracted ($fly(tweety)$).

H are normal logic programs [11], E is a set of ground literals (with positive and negative ground literals representing positive and negative examples, respectively) and H satisfies the condition $B \cup H \models E$ under the credulous stable model semantics [9]. As formalised in Definition 1 below, it is usual to further restrict the clauses in H to a set of clauses S called the *hypothesis space*.

Definition 1. Given a normal logic program B, a set of ground literals E, and a set clauses S, the task of ILP is to find a normal logic program $H \subseteq S$, consistent with B such that $B \cup H \models E$. In this case, H is called an *inductive generalisation* of E wrt. B and S.

We use the XHAIL system that, in a three-phase approach [21], constructs and generalises a set of ground hypotheses K, called a *Kernel Set* of B and E. This can be regarded as a non-monotonic multi-clause generalisation of the Bottom Set concept [16] used in several well-known monotonic ILP systems. Like most ILP systems, XHAIL heavily exploits a language bias, specified by a set M of so called *mode declarations* [16], to bound the ILP hypothesis space when constructing and generalising a Kernel Set. A mode declaration $m \in M$ is either a *head declaration* of the form $modeh(s)$ or a *body declaration* of the form $modeb(s)$ where s is a ground literal, called *scheme*, containing *placemarker* terms of the form $+t$, $-t$ and $\#t$ which must be replaced by input variables, output variables, and constants of type t respectively. For example $modeb(in\_group(+contact, \#contact\_list\_group))$ allows rules in H to contain literals with the predicate *in_group*; the first argument of type *contact* must be an input variable (i.e. an input variable in the head or an output variable in some preceding body literal), the second of type *contact_list_group* must be a ground term. The three phases of the XHAIL approach are implemented using a non-monotonic answer set solver. In the first phase, the head declarations are used to abduce a set of ground atoms Δ such that $T \cup \Delta \models E$. Atoms in Δ are the head atoms of the Kernel Set. In the second phase, the body atoms of the Kernel Set are computed as successful instances of queries obtained from the body declarations in M. In the third phase, the hypothesis is computed by searching for a compressive theory H that subsumes the Kernel Set, is consistent with the background knowledge, covers the examples and falls within the hypothesis space.

To represent and reason about dynamic systems, we use the Event Calculus (EC) formalism [23]. EC normal logic programs include core domain-independent rules describing general principles for inferring when properties (i.e. *fluents*) are true (resp. not true) at particular time-points, denoted as $holdsAT(F,T)$ (resp. $notholdsAT(F,T)$), based on which events have previously occurred (denoted as $happens(E,T)$). In addition, the program includes a collection of *domain-dependent* rules, describing the effects of events (using the predicates $initiates(E,F,T)$ and $terminates(E,F,T)$, as well as the time-points at which events occur (using the predicate *happens*).

3 Learning User Behaviour

Pervasive computing requires infrastructures that adapt to changes in user behaviors while minimizing user intervention. For example the user's actions on mobile devices can provide precious information that applications can exploit in order to operate autonomously and/or to improve usability and user acceptance. This can be achieved by complementing applications with policy rules describing user-behaviour. We adopt a *declarative representation* of the knowledge about user behaviour and perform *continuous revision* of this knowledge through learning from instances of user actions. The system we propose *learns* and *revises* a user theory U assumed to be accessible by applications (e.g. for mobile devices) or by policy management systems. U is a normal logic program defining conditions under which user actions are performed. The application (or policy management system) can query U to (autonomously) determine a response to events or requests. For example, on mobile devices, U can be queried to determine if the user would allow access to his/her current location in response to a request:

$$?-do(allow(current\_location, request\_id), time).$$

The answer to this query can be based on various conditions, defined by a *background theory* B about the domain knowledge of the application. These can be, for instance, (a) properties of the request, such as the ID of the requester, the time of the request, proofs of identity, etc., (b) contextual information at the particular *time*, such as the location of the user, the profile active on the mobile phone or the number of nearby devices, (c) logged actions and events and (d) other application-specific knowledge. Learning new user-behavior rules means, in this example, elaborating from instances of allowing and disallowing access to location, general rules that classify when access to location can be allowed. The user may, however, subsequently override policy-based autonomous responses on its own device, thereby generating instances of user actions that are not longer covered by the user theory U. Revising existing user-behavior rules in U means identifying situations of over-generalisation or of lack of coverage in U. This process is *iterative*. Each iteration considers all the new examples which occurred since the last computation and optionally previously computed examples based on a time based sliding window. The computation within a single iteration is captured by Algorithm 3.1.

3.1 The Revision Algorithm

The algorithm consists of three phases: the *pre-processing* phase that "transforms" the rules of the user theory U, into "defeasible" rules with exceptions, the *learning* phase that computes exception rules (if any), and the *post-processing* phase that "re-factors" the defeasible rules into revised non-defeasible rules based on the exceptions rules learnt in the second phase. Informally, exception rules learned by XHAIL are *prescriptions* for changes in the current user theory U in order to cover new examples of user actions. These changes can be addition or deletion of entire rules, and/or addition or deletion of literals in the body of existing rules.

Input: B background theory; U user agent theory; E set of current examples; M mode declarations
Output: U' revised theory according to current examples

```
/*Pre-processing phase */
Ũ = ∅;
foreach rule α_i ← δ_i^1,...,δ_i^n ∈ U do
    S = {δ_i^1,...,δ_i^n};
    α*_i denotes the schema in the modeh declaration referring to α_i;
    Ũ = Ũ ∪ {α_i ← try(i,1,δ_i^1),...,try(i,n,δ_i^n), ¬exception(i,α_i) };
    M = M ∪ {modeh(exception(#int,α*_i))}. ;
    foreach δ_i^j ∈ S do
        Ũ = Ũ ∪ {try(i,j,δ_i^j) ← use(i,j), δ_i^j} ∪ {try(i,j,δ_i^j) ← ¬use(i,j)} ;
    end
end
Ũ = Ũ ∪ {use(I,J) ← ¬del(I,J)} ;
M = M ∪ {modeh(del(#int,#int))} ;
/*Learning phase */
H = XHAIL(B ∪ Ũ, E, M) ;
/*Post-processing phase */
U' = theory_refactoring(U,H);
return U';
```

Algorithm 1: Pseudo code of the algorithm.

The algorithm shows how XHAIL, which would normally be used to learn rules from scratch, can be used to discover a minimal set of revisions to an initial set of rules as well as new rules. The inputs are a set of mode declaration M, a background knowledge B, a user theory U and a set of examples E. The former defines the the atoms that are allowed to be head of new rules and part of the body of the rules. For instance, body literals can be defined as to not contain conditions about GPS location but to refer to higher-level location information (e.g. work, home) thus defining a more appropriate hypothesis space. The background knowledge B, expressed in EC, defines both static and dynamic domain-specific properties of the device and its environment, in addition to the EC domain-independent axioms. The body of these rules includes conditions expressed in terms of *happens* and *holdsAt*. The set E of current examples is a set of *do* ground literals. The output is a revised user theory U' that, together with B, covers the current examples E.

Pre-processing phase: During this phase the given user theory U is rewritten in a normal logic program, $\tilde{U}$, suitable for learning exceptions. This consists of the following two syntactic transformations. First, for every rule in U, every body literal δ^i_j is replaced by the atom $try(i, j, \delta^i_j)$, where i is the index of the rule, j is the index of the body literal in the rule and the third argument is a reified term for the literal δ^i_j. Furthermore, the literal $\neg exception(i, \alpha_i)$ is added to the body of the rule

where i is the index of the rule and α is the reified term for the head of the rule. Intuitively, this transformation lifts the standard ILP process of learning hypotheses about examples up to the (meta-)process of *learning hypothesis about the rules and their exception cases*. Second, for each $try(i, j, \delta_j^i)$ introduced in the program, the rules $try(i, j, \delta_j^i) \leftarrow use(i, j), \delta_j^i$ and $try(i, j, \delta_i{}^j) \leftarrow \neg use(i, j)$ are added to the program together with the definition $use(I,J) \leftarrow \neg del(I,J)$ of the predicate use. Head mode declaration for $exception$ and del are added to M. This sets the learning task to compute exceptions cases for rules in the current user theory U and instances of body literals that need to be deleted.
Learning phase: This phase uses the XHAIL system. In the first phase of XHAIL, a set Δ of ground atoms of the form $exception(i, \alpha_i)$ and $del(i, j)$ are computed so that $B \cup U \cup \Delta \models E$. This set indicates the definitions (*i*) of the predicates α_i that need exceptions, and the literals (with index *j*) in the rules i that need to be deleted for the given set of examples E to be entailed by the user theory U. In the second phase, XHAIL computes the body of the exception rules as instances of body declaration predicates (e.g. *holdsAt*) that are derivable from U. In the third phase, the search for maximally compressed (minimum number of literals in the hypothesis, [15]) hypothesis H such that E is true in a *partial stable model* ([10], [22]) of $B \cup \tilde{U} \cup H$, guarantees minimal induced revisions of U.
Post-processing phase: The *post-processing phase* generates a revised theory U' semantically equivalent to $\tilde{U} \cup H$ (and thus consistent with E). The algorithm is computationally simple. Informally, for each $del(i, j)$ fact in H the corresponding condition j in rule i in U is deleted. For each exception rule in H of the form $exception(i, \alpha_i) \leftarrow c_1, ..., c_n$, the corresponding rule i in U is substituted with n new rules, one for each condition c_h, $1 \leq h \leq n$. Each of these rules (h) will have in the head the predicate α_i and in the body all conditions present in the original rule i in U plus the additional condition $\neg c(h)$. An exception with empty body results in the original rule i to be deleted.

3.2 Example

This section illustrates Algorithm 3.1 with a simple case study where we aim to learn rules that define *the context in which a user accepts incoming calls* on a mobile phone. This is part of a larger test case in which user actions and contextual data are derived from real data on mobile phone usage collected in the Cityware project [4]. We used data collected over three days, running a revision step at the end of each day. Due to space limitations only the outcome of the third day is shown here.
A user theory U is revised up to the end of the second day:

$$U = \{ \begin{array}{l} do(accept\_call(CallId, From), T) \leftarrow T \geq 07{:}30 \wedge in\_group(From, college). \\ do(accept\_call(CallId, From), T) \leftarrow T \geq 07{:}30 \wedge \neg holdsAt(status(location(imperial)), T). \quad \} \end{array} \quad (1)$$

The set of examples collected in the third day is diagrammatically presented in Figure 1.

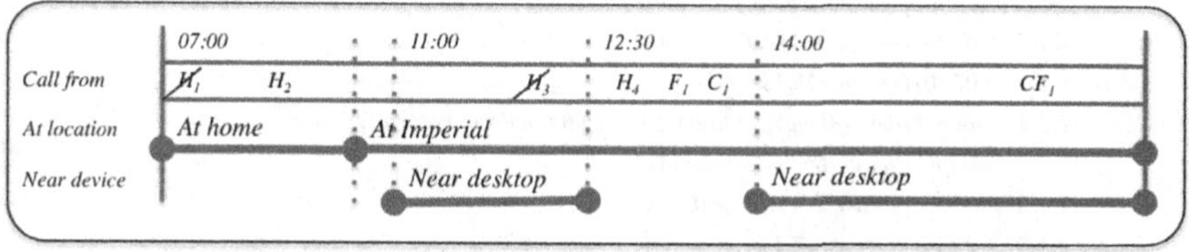

Fig. 1 Example scenario (C, H and F denote incoming calls from the user's college, home, and friends contact lists respectively. Refused calls are marked with a " / ")

Figure 2 displays a subset of the background knowledge *B* used in the scenario.

```
at_location(imperial, W, N) :- W > 95, W < 100, N > 75, N < 82.
...
happens(gps(57, 10), 07:30).
happens(gps(99, 78), 10:30).
...
happens(bluetooth_scan(desktop),  11:00).
happens(bluetooth_scan(daniel_laptop), 11:00).
...
in_group(bob, home).
in_group(alice, friends).
in_group(charles, college).
...
%Event Calculus
holdsAt(F,T+1)   :- holdsAt(F,T), not stopped(F,T).
holdsAt(F,T+1)   :- not holdsAt(F,T), started(F,T).
stopped(F,T)   :- happens(E,T), terminates(E,F,T).
started(F,T)   :- happens(E,T), initiates(E,F,T).
initiates(gps(W,N),status(location(P)) ,T) :- at_location(P, W, N).
initiates(bluetooth_scan(Dev),status(bluetooth_near(Dev)), T).
...
```

Fig. 2 A simplified sample of the background knowledge *B* used in the scenario.

U must be revised, since two calls from contacts not included in the *College* contact list are answered while at Imperial[2]), but no rule in *U* covers this case. The preprocessing phase transforms the user theory *U* into the following theory $\tilde{U}$:

[2] $do(accept\_call(bob), 13{:}00)$ and $do(accept\_call(alice), 13{:}05)$, respectively H_4 and F_1 in Figure 1. The contact lists of *bob* and *alice* are defined in *B* by the following facts: $in\_group(bob, home)$ and $in\_group(alice, friends)$.

$$\begin{aligned}
\tilde{U} = \{ \quad & do(accept_call(CallId, From), T) \leftarrow try(1,1,T \geq 07{:}30) \wedge try(1,2, in_group(From, college)) \wedge \\
& \quad \neg exception(2, do(accept_call(CallId, From), T)). \\
& do(accept_call(CallId, From), T) \leftarrow try(2,1,T \geq 07{:}30) \wedge try(2,2, \neg holdsAt(status(location(imperial)), T)) \wedge \\
& \quad \neg exception(2, do(accept_call(CallId, From), T)). \\
& try(1,1,T \geq 07{:}30)) \leftarrow use(1,1) \wedge T \geq 07{:}30. \\
& try(1,1,T \geq 07{:}30)) \leftarrow \neg use(1,1). \\
& try(1,2, in_group(From, college)) \leftarrow use(1,2) \wedge in_group(From, college). \\
& try(1,2, in_group(From, college)) \leftarrow \neg use(1,2). \\
& try(2,1,T \geq 07{:}30)) \leftarrow use(2,1) \wedge T \geq 07{:}30. \\
& try(2,1,T \geq 07{:}30)) \leftarrow \neg use(2,1). \\
& try(2,2, \neg holdsAt(status(location(imperial)), T)) \leftarrow use(1,1) \wedge T \geq \neg holdsAt(status(location(imperial)), T). \\
& try(2,2, \neg holdsAt(status(location(imperial)), T)) \leftarrow \neg use(1,1). \\
& use(I,J) \leftarrow \neg del(I,J). \quad \}
\end{aligned}$$

Given $\tilde{U}$, it is only possible to prove the examples set E by abducing the predicates $exception$ and del. The former is to be abduced to explain calls rejected or ignored by the user and the latter is to be abduced to explain calls the user accepts (currently not covered by U). Since XHAIL computes a minimal number of $exception$ and del clauses, U will be minimally revised. Thus the learning phase at the end of the third day gives the hypothesis:

$$\begin{aligned}
H = \{ \quad & exception(2, do(accept_call(CallId, From), T)) \leftarrow \\
& \quad holdsAt(status(bluetooth_near(desktop_computer)), T). \\
& del(2,2). \quad \}
\end{aligned}$$

The post-processing phase will then give the following revised user theory

$$\begin{aligned}
U' = \{ \; & do(accept_call(CallId, From), T) \leftarrow \\
& \quad T \geq 07{:}30 \wedge in_group(From, college). \\
& do(accept_call(CallId, From), T) \leftarrow \\
& \quad T \geq 07{:}30 \wedge \neg holdsAt(status(bluetooth_near(desktop_computer)), T). \quad \}
\end{aligned} \tag{2}$$

Note that the choice between learning a new rule or revising an existing one, when both solutions are acceptable, is driven by minimality. In this way, we can preserve much of the knowledge learnt from previous examples. In the above case study, each revision computed by XHAIL took a couple of seconds on a Pentium laptop PC.

4 Discussion and Related Works

Although statistical techniques [6] may be necessary to process, classify and aggregate raw sensor data upstream, the core logical methodology described in this paper is well suited to learning user rules. For the application point of view it enables the computation of declarative rules that can be automatically formulated into structured English description policies which the user can validate, query and amend [3]. At the same time they can be automatically encoded into executable policies to enable dynamic, autonomous adaptation to user behaviour and context change. From a theoretical point of view, the approach proposed here shows that theory revision can be supported by integration of non-monotonic abductive and inductive reasoning. This is made possible by the use of the recently developed non-monotonic ILP system, XHAIL, that has several advantages over other state-of-the-art ILP systems. Among these, Progol5 [16] and Alecto [14], which also employ abduction to learn non-observed predicates, do not have a well-defined semantics for non-monotonic programs and their handling of negation-as-failure is limited. Compared to other first-order theory revision systems, like *INTHELEX* [8], *Audrey II* [25] and *FORTE* [20], the use of XHAIL allows for a more expressive language, more efficient inconsistency detection and exploits existing background knowledge to accurately constrain the computation of possible revisions. None of the above three revision systems can succeed in expressing contextual conditions in dynamic system behavior rules and in constructing compact rules using negated conditions. For example revised rules like (1) and (2) would not be obtained by FORTE as it can only learn Horn clauses (i.e. no negated literals in the body).

5 Conclusions and Future Work

We have proposed an algorithm, based on non-monotonic learning, that supports incremental learning and revision of user behavior rules. Rules are learnt based on past examples, which consist of positive and negative conditions under which the user performs actions. This work is part of a more ambitious effort to learn privacy policies on mobile devices, where the learning task is complemented with statistical learning and classification of raw data, and policy enforcement [18]. Larger scale experiments planned in the project [2], will give us insights on the scalability of the proposed approach.

Further work includes the development of components for efficient access to sensory data, caching and acceleration of the learning process, handling of noisy data and windowing techniques for the examples, mindful of existing solution for concept drift (e.g. [7], [24]). The changing nature of the concepts modelled demands for techniques able to reduce the complexity of the rules after repeated revisions. We are currently investigating probabilistic extensions [5] to address concept drift and two other open issues: establishing a preference criteria to choose the best between a set of minimal solutions and balancing the exploitation of the learned rules with the exploration of revisions. Finally, we are mindful of the complexity of the implementation of such algorithms but we will use valuable lessons and experience acquired through work on policy enforcement and distributed abductive reasoning on mobile devices [12] to improve the scale-down and efficiency of our current implementation.

Acknowledgements This work is funded by the UK EPSRC (EP/F023294/1) and supported by IBM Research as part of their Open Collaborative Research (OCR) initiative and Research Councils UK.

References

1. et al., E.L.: AMUSe: Autonomic Management of Ubiquitous Systems for e-health. J. Conc. and Comp.: Practice and Experience **20**(3), 277–295 (2008)
2. Bandara, A., Nuseibeh, B., Price, B., Rogers, Y., Dulay, N., et al.: Privacy rights management for mobile applications. In: 4th Int. Symposium on Usable Privacy and Security. Pittsburgh (2008)
3. Brodie, C., Karat, C., Karat, J., Feng, J.: Usable security and privacy: a case study of developing privacy management tools. In: SOUPS '05: Proc. of the 2005 symp. on Usable privacy and security, pp. 35–43. ACM, New York, NY, USA (2005)
4. Cityware: Urban design and pervasive systems. http://www.cityware.org.uk/
5. De Raedt, L., Thomas, G., Getoor, L., Kersting, K., Muggleton, S. (eds.): Probabilistic, Logical and Relational Learning - A Further Synthesis, 15.04. - 20.04.2007. IBFI, Schloss Dagstuhl, Germany (2008)
6. Eagle, N., Pentland, A.: Reality mining: sensing complex social systems. Personal and Ubiquitous Computing **10**(4), 255–268 (2006)
7. Esposito, F., Ferilli, S., Fanizzi, N., Basile, T., Di Mauro, N.: Incremental learning and concept drift in inthelex. Intell. Data Anal. **8**(3), 213–237 (2004)
8. Esposito, F., Semeraro, G., Fanizzi, N., Ferilli, S.: Multistrategy theory revision: Induction and Abduction in INTHELEX. Mach. Learn. **38**(1-2), 133–156 (2000)
9. Gelfond, M., Lifschitz, V.: The stable model semantics for logic programming. In: R. Kowalski, K. Bowen (eds.) Logic Programming, pp. 1070–1080. MIT Press (1988)
10. Kakas, A., Kowalski, R., Toni, F.: Abductive logic programming. J. Log. Comput. **2**(6), 719–770 (1992)
11. Lloyd, J.: Foundations of Logic Programming, 2nd Edition. Springer (1987)
12. Ma, J., Russo, A., Broda, K., Clark, K.: DARE: a system for Distributed Abductive REasoning. J. Autonomous Agents and Multi-Agent Systems **16**, 271–297 (2008)
13. Minker, J.: An overview of nonmonotonic reasoning and logic programming. Tech. Rep. UMIACS-TR-91-112, CS-TR-2736, University of Maryland, College Park, Maryland 20742 (August 1991)
14. Moyle, S.: An investigation into theory completion techniques in inductive logic. Ph.D. thesis, University of Oxford (2003)
15. Muggleton, S.: Inverse entailment and Progol. New Generation Comput. J. **13**, 245–286
16. Muggleton, S.: Learning from positive data. In: 6th Int. Workshop on Inductive Logic Programming, pp. 358–376. Springer Verlag, London, U.K. (1996)
17. Muggleton, S., De Raedt, L.: Inductive logic programming: Theory and methods. J. of Logic Programming **19/20**, 629–679 (1994)
18. Ponder2: The ponder2 policy environment. www.ponder2.net
19. Ray, O.: Nonmonotonic abductive inductive learning. In: Journal of Applied Logic. (Elsevier, in press) (2008)
20. Richards, B., Mooney, R.J.: Automated refinement of first-order horn-clause domain theories. Machine Learning **19**(2), 95–131 (1995)
21. Russo, A.: A hybrid abductive inductive proof procedure. Logic J. of the IGPL **12**, 371–397(27)
22. Sacca, D., Zaniolo, C.: Stable models and non-determinism in logic programs with negation
23. Shanahan, M.: The event calculus explained. In: Artificial Intelligence Today, pp. 409–430 (1999)
24. Widmer, G.: Learning in the presence of concept drift and hidden contexts. In: Machine Learning, pp. 69–101 (1996)
25. Wogulis, J., Pazzani, M.: A methodology for evaluating theory revision systems: Results with Audrey II. In: 13th IJCAI, pp. 1128–1134 (1993)

Behaviour Recognition using the Event Calculus

Alexander Artikis and George Paliouras

Abstract We present a system for recognising human behaviour given a symbolic representation of surveillance videos. The input of our system is a set of time-stamped short-term behaviours, that is, behaviours taking place in a short period of time — walking, running, standing still, etc — detected on video frames. The output of our system is a set of recognised long-term behaviours — fighting, meeting, leaving an object, collapsing, walking, etc — which are pre-defined temporal combinations of short-term behaviours. The definition of a long-term behaviour, including the temporal constraints on the short-term behaviours that, if satisfied, lead to the recognition of the long-term behaviour, is expressed in the Event Calculus. We present experimental results concerning videos with several humans and objects, temporally overlapping and repetitive behaviours.

1 Introduction

We address the problem of human behaviour recognition by separating low-level recognition, detecting activities that take place in a short period of time — 'short-term behaviours' — from high-level recognition, recognising 'long-term behaviours', that is, pre-defined temporal combinations of short-term behaviours. In this paper we present our work on high-level recognition. We evaluate our approach using an existing set of short-term behaviours detected on a series of surveillance videos.

To perform high-level recognition we define a set of long-term behaviours of interest — for example, 'leaving an object', 'fighting' and 'meeting' — as temporal combinations of short-term behaviours — for instance, 'walking', 'running', 'inactive' (standing still) and 'active' (body movement in the same position). We employ the Event Calculus (EC) [6], a declarative temporal reasoning formalism, in order

Institute of Informatics and Telecommunications, National Centre for Scientific Research "Demokritos", Athens 15310, Greece
e-mail: {a.artikis,paliourg}@iit.demokritos.gr

Please use the following format when citing this chapter:

Artikis, A. and Paliouras, G., 2009, in IFIP International Federation for Information Processing, Volume 296; *Artificial Intelligence Applications and Innovations III*; Eds. Iliadis, L., Vlahavas, I., Bramer, M.; (Boston: Springer), pp. 469–478.

Table 1 Main Predicates of the Event Calculus.

Predicate	Textual Description
happens(Act, T)	Action Act occurs at time T
initially($F = V$)	The value of fluent F is V at time 0
holdsAt($F = V$, T)	The value of fluent F is V at time T
holdsFor($F = V$, $Intervals$)	The value of fluent F is V during $Intervals$
initiates(Act, $F = V$, T)	The occurrence of action Act at time T initiates a period of time for which the value of fluent F is V
terminates(Act, $F = V$, T)	The occurrence of action Act at time T terminates a period of time for which the value of fluent F is V

to express the definition of a long-term behaviour. More precisely, we employ EC to express the temporal constraints on a set of short-term behaviours that, if satisfied, lead to the recognition of a long-term behaviour.

The remainder of the paper is organised as follows. First, we present the Event Calculus. Second, we describe the dataset of short-term behaviours on which we perform long-term behaviour recognition. Third, we present our knowledge base of long-term behaviour definitions. Fourth, we present our experimental results. Finally, we briefly discuss related work and outline directions for further research.

2 The Event Calculus

Our system for long-term behaviour recognition (LTBR) is a logic programming implementation of an Event Calculus formalisation expressing long-term behaviour definitions. The Event Calculus (EC), introduced by Kowalski and Sergot [6], is a formalism for representing and reasoning about actions or events and their effects. We present here the version of the EC that we employ (for more details see [2]).

EC is based on a many-sorted first-order predicate calculus. For the version used here, the underlying time model is linear and it may include real numbers or integers. Where F is a *fluent* — a property that is allowed to have different values at different points in time — the term $F = V$ denotes that fluent F has value V. Boolean fluents are a special case in which the possible values are true and false. Informally, $F = V$ holds at a particular time-point if $F = V$ has been *initiated* by an action at some earlier time-point, and not *terminated* by another action in the meantime.

An *action description* in EC includes axioms that define, among other things, the action occurrences (with the use of the happens predicate), the effects of actions (with the use of the initiates and terminates predicates), and the values of the fluents (with the use of the initially, holdsAt and holdsFor predicates). Table 1 summarises the main EC predicates. Variables (starting with an upper-case letter) are assumed to be universally quantified unless otherwise indicated. Predicates, function symbols and constants start with a lower-case letter.

The domain-independent definition of the holdsAt predicate is as follows:

$$\begin{aligned}&\mathsf{holdsAt}(\ F{=}V,\ T\ ) \leftarrow \\ &\quad \mathsf{initially}(\ F{=}V\ ), \\ &\quad \mathsf{not\ broken}(\ F{=}V,\ 0,\ T\ )\end{aligned} \tag{1}$$

$$\begin{aligned}&\mathsf{holdsAt}(\ F{=}V,\ T\ ) \leftarrow \\ &\quad \mathsf{happens}(\ Act,\ T'\ ), \\ &\quad T' < T, \\ &\quad \mathsf{initiates}(\ Act,\ F{=}V,\ T'\ ), \\ &\quad \mathsf{not\ broken}(\ F{=}V,\ T',\ T\ )\end{aligned} \tag{2}$$

According to axiom (1) a fluent holds at time T if it held initially (time 0) and has not been 'broken' in the meantime, that is, terminated between times 0 and T. Axiom (2) specifies that a fluent holds at a time T if it was initiated at some earlier time T' and has not been terminated between T' and T. 'not' represents 'negation by failure' [3]. The domain-independent predicate broken is defined as follows:

$$\begin{aligned}&\mathsf{broken}(\ F{=}V,\ T_1,\ T_3\ ) \leftarrow \\ &\quad \mathsf{happens}(\ Act,\ T_2\ ), \\ &\quad T_1 \leq T_2,\ T_2 < T_3, \\ &\quad \mathsf{terminates}(\ Act,\ F{=}V,\ T_2\ )\end{aligned} \tag{3}$$

$F{=}V$ is 'broken' between T_1 and T_3 if an event takes place in that interval that terminates $F{=}V$. A fluent cannot have more than one value at any time. The following domain-independent axiom captures this feature:

$$\begin{aligned}&\mathsf{terminates}(\ Act,\ F{=}V,\ T\ ) \leftarrow \\ &\quad \mathsf{initiates}(\ Act,\ F{=}V',\ T\ ), \\ &\quad V \neq V'\end{aligned} \tag{4}$$

Axiom (4) states that if an action Act initiates $F{=}V'$ then Act also terminates $F{=}V$, for all other possible values V of the fluent F. We do not insist that a fluent must have a value at every time-point. In this version of EC, therefore, there is a difference between initiating a Boolean fluent $F{=}$false and terminating $F{=}$true: the first implies, but is not implied by, the second.

We make the following further comments regarding this version of EC. First, the domain-independent EC axioms (1)–(4) specify that a fluent does not hold at the time that was initiated but holds at the time it was terminated. Second, in addition to the presented domain-independent definitions, the holdsAt and terminates predicates may be defined in a domain-dependent manner. The happens, initially and initiates predicates are defined only in a domain-dependent manner. Third, in addition to axioms (1)–(4), the domain-independent axioms of EC include those defining the holdsFor predicate, that is, the predicate for computing the intervals in which a fluent holds. To save space we do not present here the definition of holdsFor; the interested reader is referred to the source code of the long-term behaviour recognition (LTBR) system, which is available upon request.

3 Short-Term Behaviours: The CAVIAR Dataset

LTBR includes an EC action description expressing long-term behaviour definitions. The input to LTBR is a symbolic representation of short-term behaviours. The output of LTBR is a set of recognised long-term behaviours. In this paper we present experimental results given the short-term behaviours of the first dataset of the CAVIAR project[1]. This dataset includes 28 surveillance videos of a public space. The videos are staged — actors walk around, browse information displays, sit down, meet one another, leave objects behind, fight, and so on. Each video has been manually annotated in order to provide the ground truth for both short-term and long-term behaviours.

For this set of experiments the input to LTBR is: (i) the short-term behaviours walking, running, active and inactive, along with their time-stamps, that is, the frame in which a short-term behaviour took place, (ii) the coordinates of the tracked people and objects as pixel positions at each time-point, and (iii) the first time and the last time a person or object is tracked ('appears'/'disappears'). Given this input, LTBR recognises the following long-term behaviours: a person leaving an object, a person being immobile, people meeting, moving together, or fighting.

Short-term behaviours are represented as EC actions whereas the long-term behaviours that LTBR recognises are represented as EC fluents. In the following section we present example fragments of all long-term behaviour definitions.

4 Long-Term Behaviour Definitions

The long-term behaviour 'leaving an object' is defined as follows:

$$\begin{aligned}
&\mathsf{initiates}(\ \mathit{inactive}(\mathit{Object}),\ \mathit{leaving_object}(\mathit{Person},\ \mathit{Object}) = \mathsf{true},\ T\ ) \leftarrow \\
&\qquad \mathsf{holdsAt}(\ \mathit{appearance}(\mathit{Object}) = \mathit{appear},\ T\ ), \\
&\qquad \mathsf{holdsAt}(\ \mathit{close}(\mathit{Person},\ \mathit{Object},\ 30) = \mathsf{true},\ T\ ), \\
&\qquad \mathsf{holdsAt}(\ \mathit{appearance}(\mathit{Person}) = \mathit{appear},\ T_0\ ), \\
&\qquad T_0 < T
\end{aligned} \tag{5}$$

$$\mathsf{initiates}(\ \mathit{exit}(\mathit{Object}),\ \mathit{leaving\_object}(\mathit{Person},\ \mathit{Object}) = \mathsf{false},\ T\ ) \tag{6}$$

Axiom (5) expresses the conditions in which a 'leaving an object' behaviour is recognised. The fluent recording this behaviour, *leaving_object(Person, Object)*, becomes true at time T if *Object* is inactive at T, *Object* 'appears' at T, there is a

[1] http://groups.inf.ed.ac.uk/vision/CAVIAR/CAVIARDATA1/

Person close to *Object* at T (in a sense to be specified below), and *Person* has appeared at some time earlier than T. The *appearance* fluent records the times in which an object/person 'appears' and 'disappears'. The $close(A,B,D)$ fluent is true when the distance between A and B is at most D. The distance between two tracked objects/people is computed given their coordinates. Based on our empirical analysis the distance between a person leaving an object and the object is at most 30.

An object exhibits only inactive short-term behaviour. Any other type of short-term behaviour would imply that what is tracked is not an object. Therefore, the short-term behaviours active, walking and running do not initiate the *leaving_object* fluent. In the CAVIAR videos an object carried by a person is not tracked — only the person that carries it is tracked. The object will be tracked, that is, 'appear', if and only if the person leaves it somewhere. Consequently, given axiom (5), the *leaving_object* behaviour will be recognised only when a person leaves an object (see the second line of axiom (5)), not when a person carries an object.

Axiom (6) expresses the conditions in which a *leaving_object* behaviour ceases to be recognised. In brief, *leaving_object* is terminated when the object in question is picked up. $exit(A)$ is an event that takes place when $appearance(A) = disappear$. An object that is picked up by someone is no longer tracked — it 'disappears' — triggering an *exit* event which in turn terminates *leaving_object*.

The long-term behaviour *immobile* was defined in order to signify that a person is resting in a chair or on the floor, or has fallen on the floor (fainted, for example). Below is (a simplified version of) an axiom of the *immobile* definition:

$$\begin{aligned}
&\mathsf{initiates}(\ inactive(Person),\ immobile(Person) = \mathsf{true},\ T\ ) \leftarrow \\
&\quad \mathsf{happens}(\ active(Person),\ T_0\ ), \\
&\quad T_0 < T, \\
&\quad duration(\ inactive(Person),\ Intervals\ ), \\
&\quad (T,\ T_1) \in Intervals, \\
&\quad T_1 > T{+}54
\end{aligned} \tag{7}$$

According to axiom (7), the behaviour *immobile(Person)* is recognised if *Person*: (i) has been active some time in the past, and (ii) stays inactive for more than 54 frames (we chose this number of frames given our empirical analysis of the CAVIAR dataset). *duration* is a predicate computing the duration of inactive behaviour, that is, the number of consecutive instantaneous inactive events. The output of *duration* is a set of tuples of the form (s,e) where s is the time in which *inactive(Person)* started and e is the time in which *inactive(Person)* ended. Note that this is not the only way to represent durative events in EC. See [9] for alternative representations.

Axiom (7) has an additional constraint requiring that *Person* is not close to an information display or a shop — if *Person* was close to a shop then she would have to stay inactive much longer than 54 frames before *immobile* could be recognised. In this way we avoid classifying the behaviour of browsing a shop as *immobile*. To simplify the presentation we do not present here the extra constraint of axiom (7).

The definition of *immobile* includes axioms according to which *immobile(Person)* is recognised if *Person*: (i) has been walking some time in the past, and (ii) stays inactive for more than 54 frames. We insist that *Person* in *immobile(Person)* has been active or walking before being inactive in order to distinguish between a left object, which is inactive from the first time it is tracked, from an immobile person.

immobile(Person) is terminated when *Person* starts walking, running or 'disappears' — see axioms (8)–(10) below:

$$\text{initiates}(\ \mathit{walking}(\mathit{Person}),\ \mathit{immobile}(\mathit{Person})=\text{false},\ T\ ) \tag{8}$$

$$\text{initiates}(\ \mathit{running}(\mathit{Person}),\ \mathit{immobile}(\mathit{Person})=\text{false},\ T\ ) \tag{9}$$

$$\text{initiates}(\ \mathit{exit}(\mathit{Person}),\ \mathit{immobile}(\mathit{Person})=\text{false},\ T\ ) \tag{10}$$

The following axioms represent a fragment of the *moving* behaviour definition:

$$\begin{aligned}&\text{initiates}(\ \mathit{walking}(\mathit{Person}),\ \mathit{moving}(\mathit{Person},\ \mathit{Person}_2)=\text{true},\ T\ ) \leftarrow\\ &\quad\text{holdsAt}(\ \mathit{close}(\mathit{Person},\ \mathit{Person}_2, 34)=\text{true},\ T\ ),\\ &\quad\text{happens}(\ \mathit{walking}(\mathit{Person}_2),\ T\ )\end{aligned} \tag{11}$$

$$\begin{aligned}&\text{initiates}(\ \mathit{walking}(\mathit{Person}),\ \mathit{moving}(\mathit{Person},\ \mathit{Person}_2)=\text{false},\ T\ ) \leftarrow\\ &\quad\text{holdsAt}(\ \mathit{close}(\mathit{Person},\ \mathit{Person}_2,\ 34)=\text{false},\ T\ )\end{aligned} \tag{12}$$

$$\begin{aligned}&\text{initiates}(\ \mathit{active}(\mathit{Person}),\ \mathit{moving}(\mathit{Person},\ \mathit{Person}_2)=\text{false},\ T\ ) \leftarrow\\ &\quad\text{happens}(\ \mathit{active}(\ \mathit{Person}_2\ ), T\ )\end{aligned} \tag{13}$$

$$\text{initiates}(\ \mathit{running}(\mathit{Person}),\ \mathit{moving}(\mathit{Person},\ \mathit{Person}_2)=\text{false},\ T\ ) \tag{14}$$

$$\text{initiates}(\ \mathit{exit}(\mathit{Person}),\ \mathit{moving}(\mathit{Person},\ \mathit{Person}_2)=\text{false},\ T\ ) \tag{15}$$

According to axiom (11) *moving* is initiated when two people are walking and are close to each other (their distance is at most 34). *moving* is terminated when the people walk away from each other, that is, their distance becomes greater than 34 (see axiom (12)), when they stop moving, that is, become active (see axiom (13)) or inactive, when one of them starts running (see axiom (14)), or when one of them 'disappears' (see axiom (15)).

The following axioms express the conditions in which *meeting* is recognised:

$$\begin{aligned}&\text{initiates}(\ \mathit{active}(\mathit{Person}),\ \mathit{meeting}(\mathit{Person},\ \mathit{Person}_2)=\text{true},\ T\ ) \leftarrow\\ &\quad\text{holdsAt}(\ \mathit{close}(\mathit{Person},\ \mathit{Person}_2,\ 25)=\text{true},\ T\ ),\\ &\quad\text{not happens}(\ \mathit{running}(\mathit{Person}_2),\ T\ )\end{aligned} \tag{16}$$

$$\begin{aligned}&\text{initiates}(\ \mathit{inactive}(\mathit{Person}),\ \mathit{meeting}(\mathit{Person},\ \mathit{Person}_2)=\text{true},\ T\ ) \leftarrow\\ &\quad\text{holdsAt}(\ \mathit{close}(\mathit{Person},\ \mathit{Person}_2,\ 25)=\text{true},\ T\ ),\\ &\quad\text{not happens}(\ \mathit{running}(\mathit{Person}_2),\ T\ )\end{aligned} \tag{17}$$

meeting is initiated when two people 'interact': at least one of them is active or inactive, the other is not running, and the distance between them is at most 25. This interaction phase can be seen as some form of greeting (for example, a handshake). *meeting* is terminated when the two people walk away from each other, or one of them starts running or 'disappears'. The axioms representing the termination of *meeting* are similar to axioms (12), (14) and (15). Note that *meeting* may overlap with *moving*: two people interact and then start *moving*, that is, walk while being close to each other. In general, however, there is no fixed relationship between *meeting* and *moving*.

The axioms below present the conditions in which *fighting* is initiated:

$$\begin{array}{l}\text{initiates}(\ \mathit{active}(\mathit{Person}),\ \mathit{fighting}(\mathit{Person},\ \mathit{Person2}){=}\text{true},\ T\ ) \leftarrow \\ \quad \text{holdsAt}(\ \mathit{close}(\mathit{Person},\ \mathit{Person2},\ 24){=}\text{true},\ T\ ), \\ \quad \text{not happens}(\ \mathit{inactive}(\mathit{Person2}),\ T\ )\end{array} \tag{18}$$

$$\begin{array}{l}\text{initiates}(\ \mathit{running}(\mathit{Person}),\ \mathit{fighting}(\mathit{Person},\ \mathit{Person2}){=}\text{true},\ T\ ) \leftarrow \\ \quad \text{holdsAt}(\ \mathit{close}(\mathit{Person},\ \mathit{Person2},\ 24){=}\text{true},\ T\ ), \\ \quad \text{not happens}(\ \mathit{inactive}(\mathit{Person2}),\ T\ )\end{array} \tag{19}$$

Two people are assumed to be *fighting* if at least one of them is active or running, the other is not inactive, and the distance between them is at most 24. We have specified that running initiates *fighting* because, in the CAVIAR dataset, moving abruptly, which is what happens during a fight, is often classified as running. *fighting* is terminated when one of the people walks or runs away from the other, or 'disappears' — see axioms (20)–(22) below:

$$\begin{array}{l}\text{initiates}(\ \mathit{walking}(\mathit{Person}),\ \mathit{fighting}(\mathit{Person},\ \mathit{Person2}){=}\text{false},\ T\ ) \leftarrow \\ \quad \text{holdsAt}(\ \mathit{close}(\mathit{Person},\ \mathit{Person2},\ 24){=}\text{false},\ T\ )\end{array} \tag{20}$$

$$\begin{array}{l}\text{initiates}(\ \mathit{running}(\mathit{Person}),\ \mathit{fighting}(\mathit{Person},\ \mathit{Person2}){=}\text{false},\ T\ ) \leftarrow \\ \quad \text{holdsAt}(\ \mathit{close}(\mathit{Person},\ \mathit{Person2},\ 24){=}\text{false},\ T\ )\end{array} \tag{21}$$

$$\text{initiates}(\ \mathit{exit}(\mathit{Person}),\ \mathit{fighting}(\mathit{Person},\ \mathit{Person2}){=}\text{false},\ T\ ) \tag{22}$$

Under certain circumstances LTBR recognises both *fighting* and *meeting* — this happens when two people are active and the distance between them is at most 24. This problem would be resolved if the CAVIAR dataset included a short-term behaviour for abrupt motion, which would be used (instead of the short-term behaviour active) to initiate *fighting*, but would not be used to initiate *meeting*.

5 Experimental Results

We present our experimental results on 28 surveillance videos of the CAVIAR project. These videos contain 26419 frames that have been manually annotated in order to provide the ground truth for short-term and long-term behaviours. Table 2 shows the performance of LTBR — we show, for each long-term behaviour, the number of True Positives (TP), False Positives (FP) and False Negatives (FN), as well as Recall and Precision.

LTBR correctly recognised 4 *leaving_object* behaviours. Moreover, there were no FP. On the other hand, there was 1 FN. This, however, cannot be attributed to LTBR because in the video in question the object was left behind a chair and was not tracked. In other words, the left object never 'appeared', it never exhibited a short-term behaviour.

Table 2 Experimental Results.

Behaviour	True Positive	False Positive	False Negative	Recall	Precision
leaving object	4	0	1	0.8	1
immobile	9	8	0	1	0.52
moving	16	12	1	0.94	0.57
meeting	6	3	3	0.66	0.66
fighting	4	8	2	0.66	0.33

Regarding *immobile* we had 9 TP, 8 FP and no FN. The recognition of *immobile* would be much more accurate if there was a short-term behaviour for the motion of leaning towards the floor or a chair. Due to the absence of such a short-term behaviour, the recognition of *immobile* is primarily based on how long a person is inactive. In the CAVIAR videos a person falling on the floor or resting in a chair stays inactive for at least 54 frames. Consequently LTBR recognises *immobile* if, among other things, a person stays inactive for at least 54 frames (we require that a person stays inactive for a longer time period if she is located close to a shop to avoid FP when a person is staying inactive browsing a shop). There are situations, however, in which a person stays inactive for more than 54 frames and has not fallen on the floor or sat in a chair: people watching a fight, or just staying inactive waiting for someone. It is in those situations that we have the FP concerning *immobile*. We expect that in longer videos recording actual behaviours (as opposed to the staged behaviours of the CAVIAR videos) a person falling on the floor or resting in a chair would be inactive longer than a person staying inactive while standing. In this case we could increase the threshold for the duration of inactive behaviour in the definition of *immobile*, thus potentially reducing the number of FP concerning *immobile*.

LTBR recognised correctly 16 *moving* behaviours. However, it also recognised incorrectly 12 such behaviours. Half of the FP concern people that do move together: walk towards the same direction while being close to each other. According to the manual annotation of the videos, however, these people do not exhibit the *moving* long-term behaviour. The remaining FP fall into two categories. First, people walk close to each other as they move to different directions — in such a case the duration of a FP is very short. We may eliminate these FP by adding a constraint that the duration of *moving* is greater than a specified threshold. Second, the short-term behaviours of people *fighting* are sometimes classified as walking. Consequently, the behaviour of these people is incorrectly recognised by LTBR as *moving* since, according to the manual annotation of the CAVIAR dataset, they are walking while being close to each other (moreover, their coordinates change). Introducing a short-term behaviour for abrupt motion would resolve this issue, as abrupt motion would not initiate *moving*.

LTBR did not recognise 1 *moving* behaviour. This FN was due to the fact that the distance between the people walking together was greater than the threshold we have specified. Increasing this threshold would result in substantially increasing the number of FP. Therefore we chose not to increase it.

LTBR recognised 9 *meeting* behaviours, 6 of which took place and 3 did not take place. 2 FP concerned *fighting* behaviours realised by people being active and close to each other. As mentioned in the previous section, in these cases LTBR recognises both *meeting* and *fighting*. The third FP was due to the fact that two people were active and close to each other, but were not interacting. LTBR did not recognise 3 *meeting* behaviours. 2 FN were due to the fact that the distance between the people in the meeting was greater than the threshold we have specified. If we increased that threshold LTBR would correctly recognise these 2 *meeting* behaviours. However, the number of FP for *meeting* would substantially increase. Therefore we chose not to increase the threshold distance. The third FN was due to the fact that the short-term behaviours of the people interacting — handshaking — were classified as walking (although one of them was actually active). We chose to specify that walking does not initiate a *meeting* in order to avoid incorrectly recognising meetings when people simply walk close to each other.

Regarding *fighting* we had 4 TP, 8 FP and 2 FN. The FP were mainly due to the fact that when a meeting takes place LTBR often recognises the long-term behaviour *fighting* (as well as *meeting*). LTBR did not recognise 2 *fighting* behaviours because in these two cases the short-term behaviours of the people *fighting* were classified as walking (recall the discussion on the recognition of *moving*). We chose to specify that walking does not initiate *fighting*. Allowing walking to initiate *fighting* (provided, of course, that two people are close to each other) would substantially increase the number of FP for *fighting*, because *fighting* would be recognised every time a person walked close to another person.

6 Discussion

We presented our approach to behaviour recognition. As demonstrated by the presented experiments, the use of EC allows for the development of a recognition system capable of dealing with, among other things, durative (short-term and long-term) behaviours, temporally overlapping, repetitive, and 'forbidden' behaviours, that is, behaviours that should not take place within a specified time-period in order to recognise some other behaviour (see [9, 8] for presentations of the expressiveness of EC). Furthermore, the availability of the full power of logic programming, which is one of the main attractions of employing EC as the temporal formalism, allows for the development of behaviour definitions including complex temporal and atemporal constraints. The majority of behaviour recognition systems (see [5, 4, 11, 10, 7] for a few well-known examples) employ less formal and less expressive formalisms to represent the properties of behaviours. For example, the well-known *chronicle recognition system*[2] (a 'chronicle' can be seen as a long-term behaviour) does not support any form of spatial reasoning and thus cannot be directly used for behaviour recognition in video surveillance applications. Our approach for more expressive be-

[2] `http://crs.elibel.tm.fr/`

haviour definitions leads to the recognition of more complex behaviours. Although the practicality of our approach, in terms of real-time recognition, remains to be investigated — this is an area of current research — the presented work can, at the very least, be applied to post-mortem analysis. A thorough comparison of our work with related research is not possible in the available space — such a comparison will be presented elsewhere.

We outline two directions for future research. First, we plan to perform behaviour recognition using datasets exhibiting a finer classification of short-term behaviours — for instance, explicitly representing abrupt motion. Second, we aim to employ inductive logic programming (ILP) techniques for fine-tuning in an automated way behaviour definitions (see, for example, [1] for an application of ILP techniques on EC formalisations).

Acknowledgements We would like to thank Anastasios Skarlatidis for converting the XML representation of the CAVIAR dataset into an Event Calculus representation.

References

1. D. Alrajeh, O. Ray, A. Russo, and S. Uchitel. Extracting requirements from scenarios with ILP. In *Inductive Logic Programming*, volume LNAI 4455. Springer, 2007.
2. A. Artikis, M. Sergot, and J. Pitt. Specifying norm-governed computational societies. *ACM Transactions on Computational Logic*, 10(1), 2009.
3. K. Clark. Negation as failure. In H. Gallaire and J. Minker, editors, *Logic and Databases*, pages 293–322. Plenum Press, 1978.
4. C. Dousson and P. Le Maigat. Chronicle recognition improvement using temporal focusing and hierarchisation. In *Proceedings International Joint Conference on Artificial Intelligence (IJCAI)*, pages 324–329, 2007.
5. M. Ghallab. On chronicles: Representation, on-line recognition and learning. In *Proceedings Conference on Principles of Knowledge Representation and Reasoning*, pages 597–606, 1996.
6. R. Kowalski and M. Sergot. A logic-based calculus of events. *New Generation Computing*, 4(1):67–96, 1986.
7. D. Luckham. *The Power of Events: An Introduction to Complex Event Processing in Distributed Enterprise Systems*. Addison-Wesley, 2002.
8. R. Miller and M. Shanahan. The event calculus in a classical logic — alternative axiomatizations. *Journal of Electronic Transactions on Artificial Intelligence*, 4(16), 2000.
9. M. Shanahan. The event calculus explained. In M. Wooldridge and M. Veloso, editors, *Artificial Intelligence Today*, LNAI 1600, pages 409–430. Springer, 1999.
10. V.-T. Vu. *Temporal Scenarios for Automatic Video Interpretation*. PhD thesis, Université de Nice — Sophia Antipolis, 2004.
11. V.-T. Vu, F. Brémond, and M. Thonnat. Automatic video interpretation: A novel algorithm for temporal scenario recognition. In *Proceedings International Joint Conference on Artificial Intelligence*, pages 1295–1302, 2003.

Multi-Source Causal Analysis: Learning Bayesian Networks from Multiple Datasets

Ioannis Tsamardinos and Asimakis P. Mariglis

Abstract We argue that causality is a useful, if not a necessary concept to allow the integrative analysis of multiple data sources. Specifically, we show that it enables learning causal relations from (a) data obtained over different experimental conditions, (b) data over different variable sets, and (c) data 'over semantically similar variables that nevertheless cannot be pulled together for various technical reasons. The latter case particularly, often occurs in the setting of analyzing multiple gene-expression datasets. For cases (a) and (b) above there already exist preliminary algorithms that address them, albeit with some limitations, while for case (c) we develop and evaluate a new method. Preliminary empirical results provide evidence of increased learning performance of causal relations when multiple sources are combined using our method versus learning from each individual dataset. In the context of the above discussion we introduce the problem of Multi-Source Causal Analysis (MSCA), defined as the problem of inferring and inducing causal knowledge from multiple sources of data and knowledge. The grand vision of MSCA is to enable the automated or semi-automated, large-scale integration of available data to construct causal models involving a significant part of human concepts.

1 Introduction

Unlike humans that continuously and synthetically learn from their observations modern data-analysis fields, for the greatest part, approach learning as single, isolated, and independent tasks. The data analyzed form a relatively

Ioannis Tsamardinos
CSD, University of Crete and BMI, ICS, FORTH, e-mail: tsamard at ics and forth and gr

Asimakis P. Mariglis
BMI, ICS, FORTH, and Physics Dept, University of Crete

Please use the following format when citing this chapter:

Tsamardinos, I. and Mariglis, A.P., 2009, in IFIP International Federation for Information Processing, Volume 296; *Artificial Intelligence Applications and Innovations III*; Eds. Iliadis, L., Vlahavas, I., Bramer, M.; (Boston: Springer), pp. 479–490.

homogenous group of observations in terms of observed quantities (i.e., variables), sampling methodology, experimental conditions, and typically, source: that is, they form a single dataset. The computation and inferences of the analysis of one dataset are rarely used in the analysis of other datasets. Consider the following scenario:

- **Dataset 1**: An experimenter is observing variables $\{A, B, C, D\}$ in an independently and identically distributed (i.i.d.) sample of a population with the intent to learn a predictive or diagnostic model for D based on the remaining variables. For example, the predictors $\{A, B, C\}$ could be medical quantities and D the presence or absence of a specific disease in the general population.
- **Dataset 2**: A randomized clinical trial is performed measuring $\{A, B, C, D\}$ where variable B is randomly set to different values (e.g. a medication is prescribed that directly controls the value of B) and the effect on disease D is observed. These data cannot be merged with Dataset 1 because the joint distributions of the data are different. For example, if B is caused by the disease (e.g., the disease increases the concentration of a protein in the blood) then B will be highly associated with D in Dataset 1; in Dataset 2 where the levels of B exclusively depend on the medication administered, B and D are not associated.
- **Dataset 3**: Variables $\{D, E, F\}$ for prediction of disease F. These data cannot be pulled together with Dataset 1 or 2 because they measure different variables.
- **Dataset 4**: Variables $\{A', B', C, D\}$ are observed in an i.i.d. sampling, where A' , B' are semantically similar but not identical to A, B respectively. These data may not be pulled together with Dataset 1 for a number of reasons. It could be the case for example, that A and B are continuous, while A' , B' are recorded as discrete (e.g., low, medium, high); or they measure the same quantity using different scales and methods with no apparent mapping from one to the other. This is common in psychology where quantities such as psychological improvement or degree of depression of a patient can be measured using several methods, sometimes not fully objective. Particularly, this is a common situation in gene-expression measurements where the gene-expression level A of a specific gene in one study is not directly comparable to the gene-expression level A' of the same gene in a different study due to multiple technology barriers for translating A to A' (see [4] for a more detailed explanation of these limitations).

State-of-the-art machine learning and statistical methods will typically be applied to identify a predictive or diagnostic model from the above datasets. No matter what kind of analysis is performed however, **each dataset is typically analyzed in isolation**. A growing number of datasets such as the above is made public, each developed with a specific hypothesis in mind or to build a specific predictive model. Modern machine-learning methods have yet to fully address, or even focus, on the problem of synthesizing such information.

The current practice is instead for humans to serve as the means of integrating the extracted knowledge. Researchers read the scientific literature and form inside their heads a (causal, arguably) model of the working mechanisms of the entity they study. A conscious effort of manual knowledge synthesis in biology is for example the KEGG PATHWAY database at http://www.genome.jp/kegg/pathway.html defined as "... a collection of manually drawn pathway maps representing our knowledge on the molecular interaction and reaction networks ". Obviously, the manual synthesis of information is severely limited by our mental capacities.

At a first glance, it may seem impossible that the above datasets can be analyzed simultaneously. However, modern theories of causality are gradually making this possible. We argue that the concept of causality is fundamental in achieving an automated, or semi-automated, combined analysis of different data-sources as in the above scenario. This is because causality (a) can model the effects of actions, such as setting different experimental conditions and sampling methodology and (b) it can be inferred by tests of conditional independence that can be performed on different datasets. We introduce the general problem and conceptual framework of **Multi-Source Causal Analysis** (MSCA) defined as *the problem of inferring and inducing causal knowledge from multiple sources of data and knowledge.* We consider as the main components of MSCA (i) a formal representation and modeling of causal knowledge, (ii) algorithms for inducing causality from multiple sources and for making causal inferences, and (iii) the ability to justify and explain the causal inferences to human experts. The vision of MSCA is to enable data and knowledge synthesis on a grand-scale were thousands of studies are simultaneously analyzed to produce causal models involving large parts of human concepts. We now present algorithms that allow the simultaneous inference of causal knowledge from the above datasets.

2 Causal Bayesian Networks as a Language for Causality

We assume the readers' familiarity with the standard Pearl [5] and Spirtes et al. [6] causality framework based on the concept of Causal Bayesian Network and only briefly review it. We consider the standard notions of probabilistic causality for "X is causing Y" and for defining direct causality. Let us consider a set of random variables $\mathbf{V}$. We represent the causal structure among the variables in $\mathbf{V}$ with a directed acyclic graph (DAG) G with the vertexes corresponding to the variables $\mathbf{V}$; an edge $X \to Y$ exists in G if and only if X directly causes Y relatively to $\mathbf{V}$. We define a Causal Bayesian Network (CBN) as the tuple $\langle G, P \rangle$, where G is a causal structure over $\mathbf{V}$ and P is the joint probability distribution of variables $\mathbf{V}$. We assume that for a CNB

$\langle G, P \rangle$ the Causal Markov Condition ($\mathcal{CMC}$) holds: every variable X is probabilistically independent of any subsets of its non-effects (direct or indirect) given its direct causes. A causal graph G is depicted in Figure 1(a).

We denote the independence of X with Y given $\mathbf{Z}$ as $I(X; Y|\mathbf{Z})$. We also denote the d-separation of two nodes X and Y by a subset $\mathbf{Z}$ as $Dsep(X; Y|\mathbf{Z})$ (see [5] for a formal definition). The d-separation criterion is a graphical criterion that determines all the independencies in the distribution P that are entailed by the graph and the $\mathcal{CMC}$: $Dsep(X; Y|\mathbf{Z}) \Rightarrow I(X; Y|\mathbf{Z})$. If $\neg Dsep(X; Y|\mathbf{Z})$ we say that X is d-connected to Y given $\mathbf{Z}$. For a broad class of distributions, called Faithfull distributions, the converse also holds, i.e., $I(X; Y|\mathbf{Z}) \Leftrightarrow Dsep(X; Y|\mathbf{Z})$ named as the Faithfulness Condition ($\mathcal{FC}$). The name faithful stems from the fact that the graph faithfully represents all and only the independencies of the distribution; another equivalent way of expressing faithfulness is that the independencies are a function only of the causal structure and not accidental properties derived by a fine tuning of the distribution parameters. In Pearl's terminology, faithful distributions and corresponding CBNs are called stable: under small perturbations of the distribution, the set of independencies remains the same.

A large class of causal discovery algorithms performs statistical tests in the data to determine whether $I(X; Y|\mathbf{Z})$; subsequently, since in faithful distributions this is equivalent to $Dsep(X; Y|\mathbf{Z})$, the result of the test imposes a constraint on the data-generating graph. By combining and propagating these constraints these algorithms, named *constraint-based*, can determine the causal graphs that exactly encode (are consistent with) the independencies observed in the data distribution.

In practice, there are typically many latent variables. We can think of the variables $\mathbf{V}$ partitioned into observed variables $\mathbf{O}$ and hidden variables $\mathbf{H}$: $\mathbf{V} = \mathbf{O} \cup \mathbf{H}, \mathbf{O} \cap \mathbf{H}$. The data are sampled from the marginal $P_{\mathbf{O}}$ of the observed variables only, i.e., we can only test independencies involving variables in $\mathbf{O}$. A prototypical, constraint-based causal discovery algorithm is the FCI [6]. The output of FCI is what is called a Partial Ancestral Graph (PAG) containing common features of all causal graphs (including ones with hidden variables) that could faithfully capture the marginal data distribution $P_{\mathbf{O}}$. A PAG is shown in Figure 1(b). The edges have the following semantics [1]:

- $A \rightarrow B$ means that A is a direct cause[2] of B relatively to $\mathbf{O}$.
- $A \leftrightarrow B$ means that neither A directly causes B relatively to $\mathbf{O}$ nor vice-versa, but A and B have a common latent cause.

---

[1] Due to space limitations and for clarity of presentation, we do not discuss here the possibility of selection bias in sampling the data that can be addressed with the FCI algorithm.

[2] This is a simplification for purposes of removing some technical details from the presentation, not necessary for conveying the main ideas. The exact semantics of an edge is that there is an inducing path from A into B relative to $\mathbf{O}$, where the concept of inducing path is defined in [6].

- $A \diamond - \diamond B$ with the $\diamond$ denoting the fact that there is at least one causal graph consistent with the data where $\diamond$ is replaced by an arrowhead and at least one graph where there is no arrowhead (e.g., an edge $A \diamond - \diamond B$ means that $A \rightarrow B$, $A \leftarrow B$, and $A \leftrightarrow B$ are all possible).

3 Learning from Data Obtained over Different Experimental Conditions

We now argue that causality could be used to make inductions about the data-generating process of samples obtained under different experimental conditions. *This is because a causal model directly encodes the effects of manipulations of the system.* Assume for example that G represents the causal structure of the system without any intervention. Now assume that in i.i.d. datasets $\{D_i\}$ a set of variables $\mathbf{M}_i$ is being manipulated, i.e., obtains values set by an external agent performing an experiment. Then, the causal graph $G_{\mathbf{M}_i}$ of the system under manipulations $\mathbf{M}_i$ is derived from G by removing all incoming edges into any $V_j \in \mathbf{M}_i$. The intuitive explanation is that the value of V_i now only depends on the external agent and has no other causal influence [5, 6]. Assuming an unmanipulated graph G and known performed manipulations $\{\mathbf{M}_i\}$, graphs $\{G_i\}$ can be constructed; the fitness of each one to the corresponding data D_i can be estimated. This in turn allows us to estimate the overall fitness of the assumed model G to the set of datasets $\{D_i\}$. For example, the algorithm in [3] greedily searches the space of CBNs to find the best-fitting graph G to the set of datasets. The key-point is that unlike causality-based formalisms, correlation-based ones do not allow us to predict the effect of manipulations $\mathbf{M}_i$ in order to fit standard predictive or diagnostic models or even to perform feature selection. The algorithm in [3] could jointly analyze Datasets 1 and 2 of the scenario in the introduction.

4 Learning from Data over Different Variable Sets

Let us consider Dataset 1 of the example scenario measuring variables $\mathbf{V}_1 = \{A, B, C, D\}$ and Dataset 3 measuring $\mathbf{V}_1 = \{D, E, F\}$. Standard statistics and machine learning methods would analyze the datasets in isolation (e.g., build predictive models). Why cannot these methods make any additional inferences? Current state-of-the-art Machine Learning is arguably for the most part correlation-based and aims at identifying the set and type of such correlations. Given this observation, it may come as no surprise the difficulty found in combining knowledge and models; for one thing, correlation transitivity does not hold. If A is correlated with B and B is correlated with C, nothing can be said about the correlation between A and C. There are no further inferences about the joint $P(A, B, C)$ other than the observed correlations. Is there anything more to infer from the above datasets? Unlike pairwise correlations, pairwise causal relations are transitive: if A is causing B and B is causing C, then A is causing C. These and other more complicated inferences allow us in some cases to induce more causal knowledge from the combined data, than from each dataset individually.

We will present an example of such inferences on the structure of the union set of variables $\mathbf{V} = \mathbf{V}_1 \cup \mathbf{V}_2$. The variables of each dataset are by definition latent when we infer structure from the other dataset. Thus, we will use the FCI algorithm. Let us assume that the true (unknown) causal structure is the one shown in Figure 1. From dataset on $\mathbf{V}_1$ we expect to observe the independencies $I(A; B|\emptyset)$, $I(A; D|C)$, $I(A; D|C, B)$, $I(B; D|C)$, $I(B; D|C, A)$ and only (because the graph is assumed faithful) and from the dataset $\mathbf{V}_2$ we will observe $I(D; F|\emptyset)$ and only. Running FCI on each dataset independently (assuming enough sample so that our statistical decisions about conditional independence are correct) will identify these independencies and obtain the two PAGs shown in Figure 1(b) and (c) named G_1 and G_2. The edges with a square in one of their ends-points denote that an arrowhead could or not substitute the end-point. For example, in Figure 1(b) the edge $A\diamond \rightarrow C$ denotes the fact that FCI cannot determine whether the true edge is $A \rightarrow C$ (i.e., A directly causes C) or $A \leftrightarrow C$ (i.e., there is no direct causation between A and C but the observed dependencies and independencies are explained by the existence of at least one common hidden ancestor H, a.k.a. confounder $A \leftarrow H \rightarrow C$).

The models are informally combined as shown in Figure 1(d). An algorithm that formalizes and automates the procedure combining the PAGs stemming from different datasets is presented in [7] independently discovered at the same time our group was designing a version of such an algorithm. Due to space limitations, we only present some key inferences to illustrate our argument. There is nothing we can infer about the causation between E and $\{A, B, C\}$. We have no evidence for or against the existence of such causal relations so the corresponding edges are shown in dashed in the figure. In addition, there are CBNs that are compatible with any possible direction of such edges. Similarly, there is no evidence for or against edges between F and $\{A, B\}$. However, one can rule out the case that $A \rightarrow F$ because then at least one of the paths $D \leftarrow C \leftarrow A \rightarrow F$ or $D \leftarrow C \leftarrow H \rightarrow A \rightarrow F$ (if there is a latent variable H between C and A) would exist in the data-generating DAG. That is, there would be a d-connecting path from F to D given the emptyset, which contradicts the observed independence $I(D, F|\emptyset)$. With a similar reasoning, the possibility $B \rightarrow F$ is ruled out. *Even more impressive is the inference that there is no edge between F and C, a pair of variables that we have never measured together in the available data!* No matter what kind of edge we insert in the graph, it would create a d-connecting path between F and D. For example, if we insert an edge $F \leftrightarrow C$, it would imply the path $F \leftarrow H \rightarrow C \rightarrow D$, which contradicts the

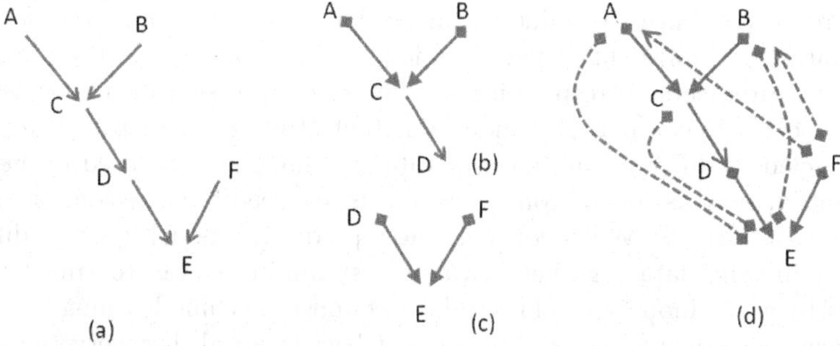

Fig. 1 (a) Presumed true, unknown, causal structure among variables $\{A, B, C, D, E, F\}$. (b)-(c) The causal structure identified by FCI when run on any large-enough dataset over $\{A, B, C, D\}$ and $\{D, E, F\}$ respectively. (d) Informally combining all the causal knowledge together and inferring new knowledge. Edges in dash are possible but have no direct evidence. Particularly notice, F cannot be a cause of A or B and there is no edge between C and F even though they are never measured together; this is because such edges would lead to a contradiction with the observed independencies in the data of (b) and (c).

observed independence $I(F, D|\emptyset)$ in D_2. In general, we can rule out edges or edge directions that create possible d-connecting paths that contradict the observed independencies in any dataset that we have available. *In essence, the $\mathcal{CMC}$ and the $\mathcal{FC}$ entail new constraints on the distribution of the union of the variables in all datasets.*

At this point we cannot help but wonder whether a similar modeling goes on in the brain. How do we know that the bus delays have no correlation with the corn price? Most of us have never measured them together (i.e., measured their correlation) and certainly do not check the corn price before deciding when to run to the bus station. We assume independence since we consider as improbable the cases of bus delays causing changes in corn price, or vice versa, as well as the existence of any common cause. There are probably an astronomical number of such independencies implicitly stored in our brains. We argue that they may be explained by causal inferences and presumptions about the causal structure of the natural world; they are not based on reasoning about correlations alone.

5 Learning from Data Obtained over Semantically Similar Variables

It is often the case that a common set of variables (i.e., variables that semantically correspond to the same quantity) is observed in different datasets, but for technical reasons the data cannot be pulled together in one dataset. For example, the variables may be measured by different equipment and so it may be hard to translate the values from all datasets to a common scale. Such a situation is typical in gene-expression studies: for various technical reasons measurements corresponding to the gene-expression of a specific gene are not directly comparable among different studies [4]. In psychology and social sciences different and incomparable methods may be used to measure a quantity, such as social-economical status, degree of depression, or mental capacity of patients. When constructing a predictive model it seems difficult to combine the data together, without first finding a way to translate the values to a common scale. This rules out most machine-learning methods. However, certain inferences in constraint-based causal discovery (as in the previous sections) are possible using only tests of conditional independence.

We now develop a multi-source test of conditional independence that employs all available data without the need to translate them first. We denote with $T(X;Y|\mathbf{Z})$ the test of conditional independence of X with Y given $\mathbf{Z}$. $T(X;Y|\mathbf{Z})$ returns a p-value assuming the null hypothesis of the independence. Constraint-based algorithms then use a threshold t rejecting the independence if $T(X;Y|\mathbf{Z}) < t$ (i.e., they accept $\neg I(X,Y|\mathbf{Z})$) and accepting the independence $I(X,Y|\mathbf{Z})$ otherwise. Since, we cannot pull all the data together, we perform the test of independence $T(X;Y|\mathbf{Z})$ individually in each available dataset D_i obtaining the p-values $\{p_i\}$. Fisher's Inverse χ^2 test can then be used to compute a combined statistic $S = -2\sum \log p_i$. S follows a χ^2 distribution with $2n$ degrees of freedom, where n is the number of datasets contributing data to the test, from which we can obtain the combined p-value p^* for the test $T(X;Y|\mathbf{Z})$ employing all available data. Other methods to combine p-values exist too [4].

An important detail of the implementation of the test is the following. Constraint-based methods do not perform a test $T(X;Y|\mathbf{Z})$ if there is not enough statistical power. The statistical power is heuristically assumed adequate when there are at least k available samples per parameter to be estimated in the test (typically k equals 5 or 10 [8] in single-source analysis; in our experiments it was set to 15). When combining multiple datasets, each dataset may not have enough sample to perform the test, but their combination could have. So, we implemented a new rule: the test $T(X;Y|\mathbf{Z})$ is performed when the total average samples per parameter exceeds k, i.e., $\sum n_i/m_i \geq k$, where n_i the samples of dataset i and m_i the parameters estimated by the specific test in dataset i (these maybe different if for example a variable takes 3 possible values in one dataset and 4 in another). When all datasets have the same number of parameters for the test, the rule results in testing whether $n/m \geq k$ as in the single-dataset case. *The new multi-source test $T(X;Y|\mathbf{Z})$ can be used in any constraint-based algorithm for combining data from different sources provided: X, Y and $\mathbf{Z}$ are measured simultaneously and the data are sampled under the same causal structure, experimental conditions, and sampling conditions (e.g., case-control data cannot be combined with i.i.d. data using this test).*

As a proof-of-concept we have performed experiments using the ALARM [1] network, the above multi-source test of independence, and our implementation of the PC algorithm [6] (similar to FCI but in addition assuming no latent variables so there are no bidirectional edges output). First, we sample data from the network distribution for n different sources (datasets) and measure the difference of the reconstructed network with the data-generating one using the Structural Hamming Distance (SHD) measure, which corresponds roughly to the sum of missing and extra edges, and wrong orientations [8]. Figure 2 on the left shows the SHD vs. the number n of combined datasets, *assuming each dataset has a fixed number of training samples equal to 500.* Figure 2 on the right shows the SHD vs. the number n of equal-sized datasets, *assuming a fixed total available sample of 5000 cases.* Each point in the graph is the average of 5 different runs of the same experiment. There are two lines in each graph. The blue (bottom) one corresponds to datasets having no difference in the measurement of their variables, i.e., their values could be pulled together in a single dataset. This line serves as a baseline and to test the validity of the method and the implementation. The green (top) line in each graph stems from combining datasets that simulate the effect of measuring the same quantity with different methods or scales. For each dataset, a non-binary variable with probability 10% was binarized by grouping a set of consecutive values together (e.g., values Low and Medium would be grouped to a single value).

In general, the number of errors measured by the SHD is decreasing as the total available sample size is increasing (Figure 2 left) until it flattens out and reaches the limit of the method. In addition, Figure 2 right shows that the number of errors is increasing for a fixed sample size that becomes increasingly fragmented into different datasets. Notice that, the lines corresponding to datasets where the variables are measured in different scales are always above (exhibit more errors) than when the datasets are homogenous. Curiously, the green line in Figure 2 left seems to be increasing again with the number of datasets, which requires further investigation. This artifact seems persistent in other experiments we run and it seems unlikely it is due to statistical fluctuations.

We would also like to note an important detail of the method. The p-values produced by the individual tests $T(X;Y|\mathbf{Z})$ on a single dataset are typically based on the Pearson's χ^2 or the likelihood ratio test that are only asymptotically correct. When the sample size is low the approximations to the p-values are rough and the statistic $S = -2\sum \log p_i$ and corresponding compound p-value severely skewed. Thus, the method as implemented should not be used with small sample sizes. We are currently investigating Bayesian methods, exact independence tests and other techniques based on permutations and ranking [4] to overcome this problem.

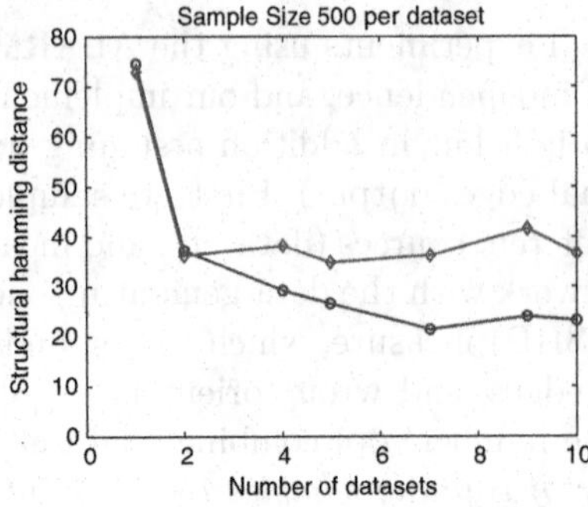

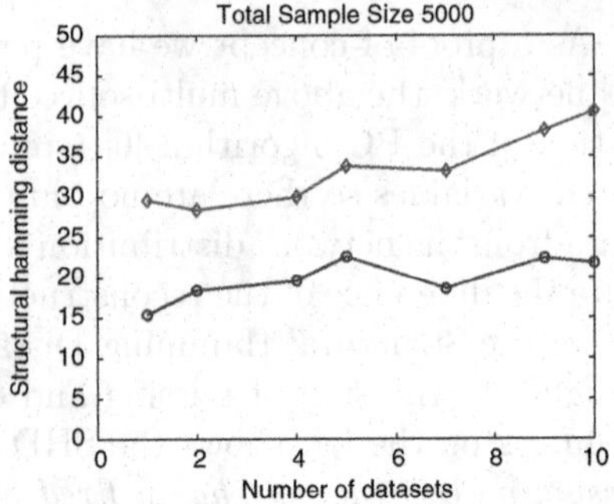

Fig. 2 Left: the Structural Hamming Distance (SHD) versus the number of datasets, when each dataset has 500 sample cases. Right: the SHD versus the number of datasets, assuming a fixed total sample size of 5000. The line with the circles in each graph corresponds to datasets having no difference in the measurement of their variables. The line with the diamonds in each graph stems from combining datasets where some non-binary variables have been binarized by grouping together consecutive values.

6 Discussion and Conclusions

We show that the concept of causality, causal theories, and recently developed algorithms allows one to combine data-sources under different experimental conditions, different variables sets, or semantically-similar variables to infer new knowledge about the causal structure of the domain. Omitted due to space limitations, is a similar discussion about data obtained under different sampling methods (e.g., case-control vs. i.i.d. data) and selection bias (see [6] for a discussion). If one examines closely the basic assumptions of the algorithms mentioned, causal induction as presented is based on the following assumptions: the Causal Markov Condition, the Faithfulness Condition and acyclicity of causal relations. Even though debatable, these assumptions are broad, reasonable, and non-parametric (see [5, 6] for a discussion). In addition, they could be substituted for other sets of assumptions depending on the domain, e.g., if one is willing to accept linearity and multivariate normality, Structural Equation Models can be employed for modeling causality that deal with cyclic (a.k.a. non-recursive) networks.

Other work in data analysis for merging datasets exists. This includes the field of meta-analysis [4] and multi-task learning [2]. The former mainly focuses on identifying correlations and effect sizes. It does not model causation so it can only deal with datasets sampled using the same method over the same experimental conditions and variables. Multi-task learning is limited to building predictive models for different tasks with a shared representation and input space (predictor variables) in order to extract useful common features [2]. It cannot deal with the range of different data sources for which causality provides the potential.

Our contribution in this paper is to draw attention to the various, recent, existing causal algorithms and techniques for merging datasets, to develop a new method for the case of learning networks from datasets over semantically similar variables, and to note some of the current limitations. For example, using the methods presented, Dataset 1 could be analyzed in conjunction with Dataset 2 or Datasets 3 and 4; however, Dataset 2 cannot be analyzed together with the rest because the algorithm in [3] is not constraint-based. In addition, the latter algorithm assumes there are no common hidden confounders (a.k.a. Causal Sufficiency). We are currently working on constraint-based methods for analyzing datasets obtained under different experimental conditions that will allow all the datasets in the scenario to be analyzed together. We also note that the algorithm for merging datasets over different variable sets [7] is impractical because of its time and memory requirements; further improvements are required before it becomes useful to the average researcher. We have named the effort of inducing causal knowledge from multiple data and knowledge sources as Multi-Source Causal Analysis (MSCA), with the vision of enabling the automation of the large-scale, co-analysis of available datasets; essentially MSCA aims in formalizing and automating the scientific process to some degree, since the result of the latter is typically causal knowledge.

References

1. I. Beinlich, G. Suermondt, R. Chavez, and G. Cooper. The ALARM monitoring system: A case study with two probabilistic inference techniques for belief networks. In *Proceedings 2nd European Conference in Artificial Intelligence in Medicine*, pages 247–256, 1989.
2. Richard A. Caruana. Multitask learning: A knowledge-based source of inductive bias. In *Proceedings 10th International Conference on Machine Learning*, pages 41–48. Morgan Kaufmann, 1993.
3. Gregory F. Cooper and Changwon Yoo. Causal discovery from a mixture of experimental and observational data. In *UAI*, pages 116–125. Morgan Kaufmann, 1999.
4. Fangxin Hong and Rainer Breitling. A comparison of meta-analysis methods for detecting differentially expressed genes in microarray experiments. *Bioinformatics*, 24:374–382, 2008.
5. J. Pearl. *Causality, Models, Reasoning, and Inference.* Cambridge University Press, Cambridge, U.K., 2000.
6. P. Spirtes, C. Glymour, and R. Scheines. *Causation, Prediction, and Search.* MIT Press, Cambridge, MA, 2nd edition, 2000.
7. R. E. Tillman, D. Danks, and C. Glymour. Integrating locally learned causal structures with overlapping variables. In *NIPS*, 2008.
8. I. Tsamardinos, L.E. Brown, and C.F. Aliferis. The Max-Min Hill-Climbing Bayesian Network Structure Learning Algorithm. *Machine Learning*, 65(1):31–78, 2006.

A Hybrid Approach for Improving Prediction Coverage of Collaborative Filtering

Manolis G. Vozalis, Angelos I. Markos and Konstantinos G. Margaritis

Abstract In this paper we present a hybrid filtering algorithm that attempts to deal with low prediction Coverage, a problem especially present in sparse datasets. We focus on Item HyCoV, an implementation of the proposed approach that incorporates an additional User-based step to the base Item-based algorithm, in order to take into account the possible contribution of users similar to the active user. A series of experiments were executed, aiming to evaluate the proposed approach in terms of Coverage and Accuracy. The results show that Item HyCov significantly improves both performance measures, requiring no additional data and minimal modification of existing filtering systems.

1 Introduction

Recommendations are generated based on taste information from users with similar interests in common items. Recommender Systems (RS), described as computer-based intelligent techniques which can provide personalized recommendations, were introduced to alleviate the problem of information and product overload.

RSs utilize various types of data and tools in order to achieve their purpose. Collaborative Filtering (CF) is one of the most successful methods among those utilized by RSs. It applies Information Retrieval and Data Mining techniques to extract automated recommendations for a user, based upon the assumption that users who have agreed in the past, tend to agree in the future.

A number of fundamental problems may reduce the quality of the predictions generated by a RS. Among others we have to mention *sparsity*, which refers to the problem of insufficient data, *scalability*, which refers to a performance degradation following a possible increase in the amount of data involved, and *synonymy*, which is

Department of Applied Informatics, University of Macedonia, Thessaloniki, Greece, e-mail: {man,amarkos,kmarg}@uom.gr

Please use the following format when citing this chapter:

Vozalis, M.G., Markos, A.I. and Margaritis, K.G., 2009, in IFIP International Federation for Information Processing, Volume 296; *Artificial Intelligence Applications and Innovations III*; Eds. Iliadis, L., Vlahavas, I., Bramer, M.; (Boston: Springer), pp. 491–498.

caused by the fact that similar items may have different names and cannot be easily associated. Furthermore, a filtering algorithm should be able to generate accurate predictions, as measured by the appropriate metric of choice.

The fraction of items for which predictions can be formed over the total number of rated items, is measured by prediction Coverage [4]. It is a common occurrence that a RS will not be able to provide a prediction for specific users on specific items because of either the sparsity in the data or other parameter restrictions, which are set during the system's execution. Systems with low Coverage are less valuable to users, since they will be limited in the decisions they are able to help with. On the other hand, RSs with high Coverage, combined with a good accuracy measure, will correspond better to user needs.

Hybrid systems [3] combine different filtering techniques in order to produce improved recommendations. Content-Boosted Collaborative Filtering [6] improves on user-based predictions by enhancing the initial matrix of ratings through the application of a content-based predictor. Wang et al. [12] formulate a generative probabilistic framework and merge user-based predictions, item-based predictions and predictions based on data from other but similar users rating other but similar items. Jin et al. [5] propose a Web recommendation system which integrates collaborative and content features under the maximum entropy principle.

In this paper, we present a hybrid approach that increases the percentage of items for which predictions can be generated, while it can potentially improve the system's accuracy. The proposed algorithm combines Item-based and User-based CF implementations in an attempt to effectively deal with the prediction coverage problem. A series of experiments were executed in order to evaluate the performance of the proposed approach.

The rest of this paper is organized as follows: In Section 2 we describe in brief two existing CF algorithms we built our work upon. In Section 3 we sketch the outline of Item HyCov, a hybrid approach. The results of two different sets of experiments that compare the proposed approach with Item-based filtering are discussed in Section 4. Finally, in Section 5 we draw the conclusions from the outcome of our experiments and present the future work.

2 The Base Algorithms

In this section we discuss in brief the two filtering algorithms which will be utilized by the proposed approach, *User-based Collaborative Filtering* (UbCF) and *Item-based Collaborative Filtering* (IbCF).

The inspiration for UbCF methods comes from the fact that people who agreed in their subjective evaluation of past items are likely to agree again in the future [7]. The execution steps of the algorithm are (a) *Data Representation* of the ratings provided by m users on n items, (b) *Neighborhood Formation*, where the application of the selected similarity metric leads to the construction of the active user's neighborhood, and (c) *Prediction Generation*, where, based on this neighborhood, predictions for items rated by the active user are produced.

IbCF is also based on the creation of neighborhoods. Yet, unlike the User-based filtering approach, those neighbors consist of similar items rather than similar users [8].

3 The HyCov Algorithm

In this section, we present a hybrid algorithm that keeps the core implementations of existing recommender systems and enhances them by adding a way to increase the percentage of items for which a filtering algorithm can generate predictions. In the following paragraphs we will describe how this general approach can be applied in the case of Item-based Collaborative Filtering, improving the coverage of their predictions, and, depending on the various parameter settings, leading to more accurate recommendations.

The Item HyCov Implementation

Let **R** be the $m \times n$ user-item ratings matrix, where element r_{ij} denotes the rating that user u_i (row i from matrix **R**) gave to item i_j (column j from matrix **R**).

- *Step 1*: **Item Neighborhood Formation.** The basic idea in that step is to isolate couples of items, i_j and i_k, which have been rated by a common user, and apply an appropriate metric to determine their similarity. We utilized the Adjusted Cosine Similarity approach, which, as shown in previous experiments [8], performs better than Cosine-based Similarity or Correlation-based Similarity.
  The formula for Adjusted Cosine Similarity of items i_j and i_k is the following:

$$sim_{jk} = adjcorr_{jk} = \frac{\sum_{i=1}^{m}(r_{ij}-\bar{r}_i)(r_{ik}-\bar{r}_i)}{\sqrt{\sum_{i=1}^{m}(r_{ij}-\bar{r}_i)^2 \sum_{i=1}^{m}(r_{ik}-\bar{r}_i)^2}} \quad (1)$$

  where r_{ij} and r_{ik} are the ratings that items i_j and i_k have received from user u_i, while $\bar{r}_i$ is the average of user's u_i ratings. The summations over i are calculated only for those of the m users who have expressed their opinions over *both* items. Based on the calculated similarities, we form item neighborhood *IN*, which includes the l items which share the greatest similarity with item i_j. Finally, we require that a possibly high correlation between the active item and a second random item is based on an adequate number of commonly rating users, known as *Common User Threshold*.
- *Step 2*: **User Neighborhood Formation.** User Neighborhood Formation is not part of the base algorithm of IbCF. It is implemented in the proposed approach for reasons that are explained in the following step of the procedure. The main purpose is to create a neighborhood of users most similar to the selected active user, u_a. We achieve that by simply applying *Pearson Correlation Similarity* as follows:

$$sim_{ai} = corr_{ai} = \frac{\sum_{j=1}^{n}(r_{aj} - \bar{r_a})(r_{ij} - \bar{r_i})}{\sqrt{\sum_{j=1}^{n}(r_{aj} - \bar{r_a})^2 \sum_{j=1}^{n}(r_{ij} - \bar{r_i})^2}} \tag{2}$$

where r_{aj} and r_{ij} are the ratings that item i_j has received from users u_a and u_i, while $\bar{r_a}$ and $\bar{r_i}$ are the average ratings of users' u_a and u_i, respectively. The summations over j are calculated only for those of the n items which have been rated by *both* users. Now we can select the p users who appear to have the greatest similarity to the active user, u_a, thus generating his neighborhood, *AN*. Again, we require that a possibly high correlation between the active user and a second random user is based on an adequate number of commonly rated items, known as *Common Item Threshold*.

- *Step 3*: **Prediction Generation.** The most crucial step of the recommendation procedure is Prediction Generation. At this step lies the main contribution of this hybrid approach.
  In the base algorithm of IbCF, a prediction of the active user's, u_a, rating on item i_j is generated by computing the weighted sum of ratings given by u_a on items belonging to the neighborhood of i_j (Equation 3):

$$pr_{aj} = \frac{\sum_{k=1}^{l} sim_{jk} * r_{ak}}{\sum_{k=1}^{l} |sim_{jk}|}, \tag{3}$$

  where sim_{jk} is the Adjusted Cosine Similarity between the active item, i_j, and an item, i_k, from its neighborhood, while r_{ak} is the rating awarded by the active user to i_k.
  However, it is probable, especially when the dataset is sparse, that the active user hasn't rated *any* of the active item's neighbors. When that happens, the base algorithm is unable to generate a prediction for the item in mind.
  The idea behind the Item HyCov algorithm is that, instead of ignoring the specific item, and, consequently, accepting a reduction in the achieved Coverage, we can take into consideration what users similar to the active user, as expressed by belonging to his neighborhood, are thinking about item i_j. The proposed algorithm implements this idea by checking whether one or more neighbors of the active user, as calculated in the *User Neighborhood Formation* step, have expressed their opinion on the neighbor items. After identifying which user neighbors have rated the required items, the Item HyCov algorithm will utilize their ratings and generate a prediction for the active user, u_a, on the active item, i_j, by applying the following equation:

$$pr_{aj} = \frac{\sum_{k=1}^{l}\sum_{i=1}^{p} sim_{jk} * r_{ik}}{\sum_{k=1}^{l}\sum_{i=1}^{p} |sim_{jk}|} \tag{4}$$

  As shown in Equation 4, we generate a prediction for the active user u_a by summing up the ratings of one or more of its p neighbors ($\sum_{i=1}^{p}$) on the l items as taken from the active item's i_j neighborhood ($\sum_{k=1}^{l}$). The summations over l are calculated only for those items which have been rated by at least one of the p

Fig. 1 Item HyCov Pseudo-code (Prediction Generation)

```
PredictItemHyCov( u_a , i_j ,AN, IN)
% u_a , i_j : active user/item % AN, IN: user/item neighborhood
NN ← ∅ %set of neighbor items rated by u_a or its neighbors
Foreach ( i_k , sim_jk ) ∈ IN
    If ∃ r_ak Then next(NN) ← (r_ak , sim_jk)
If NN ≠ ∅ Then Apply Equation (3)
Else
    Foreach ( i_k , sim_jk ) ∈ IN
        Foreach ( u_i , sim_ai ) ∈ AN
            If ∃ r_ik Then next(NN) ← ( r_ik , sim_jk)
    If NN ≠ ∅ Then Apply Equation (4)
```

neighbor users. Of course, users with zero correlation with the active user are excluded. The user ratings are weighted by the corresponding similarity, sim_{jk}, between the active item i_j and the neighbor item i_k, with $k = 1, 2, ..., l$.
The pseudo-code of the prediction step of the Item HyCov is given in Figure 1.

- *Step 4*: **Measures of Performance.** Finally, two evaluation metrics are calculated, Mean Absolute Error and Coverage [9]. Mean Absolute Error (MAE) measures the deviation of predictions generated by the RS from the true rating values, as they were specified by the user. Coverage is computed as the fraction of items for which a prediction was generated over the total number of items that all available users have rated in the initial user-item matrix.

A similar approach could be followed in the case of User-based filtering. The main difference is that when the system cannot provide a prediction for the active item, its neighborhood is formulated through Item-based CF, and the ratings of neighbor users on these items are used for Prediction Generation.

4 Experimental Results

In this section we will evaluate the utility of the HyCov method. We will provide a brief description of the various experiments we executed and then we will present the results of these experiments.

For the execution of the subsequent experiments we utilized MovieLens, the dataset publicly available from the GroupLens research group [1]. The MovieLens dataset, used by several researchers [10, 2], consists of 100.000 ratings which were assigned by 943 users on 1682 movies. Ratings follow the 1(bad)-5(excellent) numerical scale. The sparsity of the data set is high, at a value of 93.7%. Starting from the initial data set, a distinct split of training (80%) and test (20%) data was generated.

At this point, it is necessary to note that while User-based and Item-based CF each had a couple of changing parameters (size of the user/item neighborhood and common item/user threshold, correspondingly), the proposed hybrid approach has four free parameters, all of which can be altered during experiment execution: *user neighborhood size (p)* along with *common item threshold (cit)* in the stage of user neighborhood formation, and *item neighborhood size (l)* along with *common user threshold (cut)* in the stage of item neighborhood formation. Differences in MAEs and Coverages were compared using paired t-tests.

Comparing the Item HyCov approach to Item-based Filtering

The Item HyCov approach can be actually considered to be an enhancement of the plain Item-based filtering algorithm, since it proposes a way to increase the percentage of items for which the base algorithm can generate predictions. To support this claim, we include a couple of experiments that compare the performance of the two approaches.

For the first experiment, and specifically for the Item HyCov algorithm part, we kept the user neighborhood set to 18 users ($p = 18$), which, based on a series of preparatory experiments, displayed the best performing behavior for the combinations of the remaining parameters. The common item and common user thresholds were also fixed ($cit = 20$ and $cut = 10$). As for the base algorithm, *cut* was equal to 10. In both cases, the only changing parameter was the item neighborhood size.

Figure 2 depicts the results from this experiment. Figure 2(b) shows that Item HyCov actually improves on plain IbCF in terms of Coverage, for neighborhoods that include up to 100 items. This improvement is even more evident for small item neighborhoods where, because of the lack of sufficient neighbors, IbCF cannot generate an adequate number of predictions.

One might have expected that the inclusion of additional ratings would affect the prediction accuracy in a negative way. On the contrary, as one can see in Figure 2(a), the hybrid approach is constantly more accurate than plain IbCF, especially for neighborhoods including less than 50 items and for neighborhoods with more than 150 items.

A paired t-test indicated the statistical significance of differences ($p < 0.05$) at 95% confidence level between the base and the Item HyCov approaches (the normality requirement is met). The results suggest that the hybrid approach is significantly better than IbCF, both in terms of MAE (t = 3.469, p = 0.002) and Coverage (t = -2.079, p = 0.049).

For the second experiment, based on the MAE and Coverage results which were presented in the preceding section, we set the item neighborhood to include 50 items ($l = 50$) for both the hybrid and the plain IbCF approach. Specifically for the Item HyCov part of the experiment, the common item and common user thresholds were fixed ($cit = 20$ and $cut = 10$), the only changing parameter being the user neighborhood size. The basic idea behind this experiment was to test how different user neighborhood sizes would affect the overall system's performance. The results from this experiment are shown in Figure 3.

The advantage of Item HyCov in terms of Coverage is clear: it peaked at a value of 93.20% for neighborhoods including more than 8 users, whereas IbCF Coverage was equal to 91.31%. Regarding the observed MAE values, the best accuracy

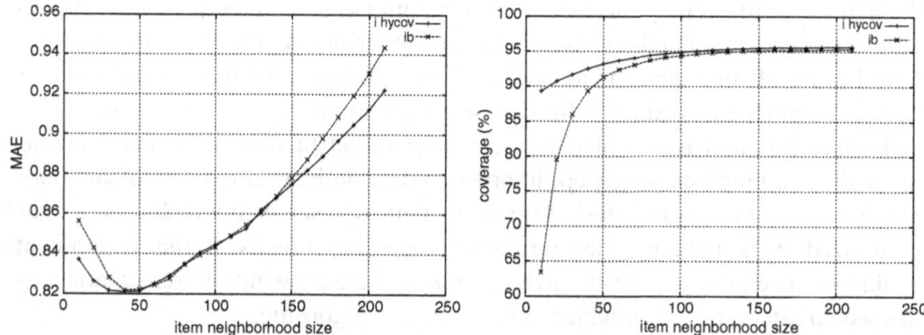

Fig. 2 Comparing Item HyCov to IbCF for varying item neighborhood sizes in terms of (a)MAE and (b)Coverage

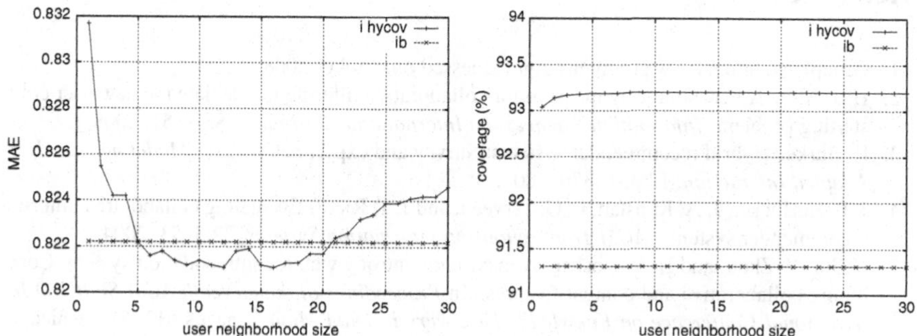

Fig. 3 Comparing Item HyCov to IbCF for varying user neighborhood sizes in terms of (a)MAE and (b)Coverage

achieved by the hybrid approach was equal to 0.8211 for a user neighborhood of 12, while IbCF MAE for the same parameter settings was slightly worse, at 0.8222.

5 Conclusions

This paper presented a filtering algorithm which combines the strengths of two popular CF approaches, IbCF and UbCF, into a feature combination hybrid. Item HyCov attempts to deal with low prediction Coverage, a problem especially present in sparse datasets. The proposed approach was tested using the Movielens dataset and was compared with plain Item-based CF.

The experimental results indicated that the proposed approach significantly increases the prediction Coverage, with a simultaneous significant improvement of accuracy in terms of MAE. Another advantage of the present approach is that it requires no additional data and minimal additional implementation or modification of existing CF recommender systems. However, it must be noted that the application of the hybrid approach may increase the computational cost of the prediction process up to $O(p^2 l)$, for p neighbor users and l neighbor items. This cost may be transferred to an off-line phase if item or user data change infrequently and therefore there is no practical need to perform these computations at prediction time.

Further research issues include the incorporation of dimensionality reduction methods as a preprocessing step, in order to deal with scalability problems (large number of users and/or items). Moreover, item or user demographic data could be utilized in the neighborhood formation stage [11]. Finally, further experiments could be carried out in order to investigate how datasets with different characteristics would affect the performance of the proposed algorithm.

References

1. Grouplens, http://www.grouplens.org/ (accessed on october 2008).
2. H. J. Ahn. A new similarity measure for collaborative filtering to alleviate the new user cold-starting problem. *Information Sciences: an International Journal*, 178:37–51, 2008.
3. R. Burke. Hybrid recommender systems: Survey and experiments. *User Modeling and User-Adapted Interaction*, 12:331–370, 2002.
4. J. L. Herlocker, J. A. Konstan, L. G. Terveen, and J. T. Riedl. Evaluating collaborative filtering recommender systems. *ACM Transactions on Information Systems*, 22:5–53, 2004.
5. X. Jin, Y. Zhou, and B. Mobasher. A maximum entropy web recommendation system: Combining collaborative and content features. In *Proceedings of the eleventh ACM SIGKDD International Conference on Knowledge Discovery in Data Mining*, pages 612–617, Chicago, Illinois, 2005.
6. P. Melville, R. J. Mooney, and R. Nagarajan. Content-boosted collaborative filtering. In *Proceedings of the Eighteenth National Conference on Artificial Intelligence (AAAI-2002)*, pages 187–192, Edmonton, Canada, 2001.
7. P. Resnick, N. Iacovou, M. Sushak, P. Bergstrom, and J. T. Riedl. Grouplens: An open architecture for collaborative filtering of netnews. In *ACM 1994 Conference on Computer Supported Cooperative Work*, pages 175–186, New York, NY, 1994.
8. B. M. Sarwar, G. Karypis, J. A. Konstan, and J. T. Riedl. Item-based collaborative filtering recommendation algorithms. In *10th International World Wide Web Conference (WWW10)*, pages 285–295, Hong Kong, 2001.
9. U. Shardanand and P. Maes. Social information filtering: Algorithms for automating 'word of mouth'. In *Proceedings of Computer Human Interaction*, pages 210–217, 1995.
10. S. Ujjin and P. J. Bentley. Particle swarm optimization recommender system. In *Proceedings of the IEEE Swarm Intelligence Sympoisum 2003*, pages 124–131, Indianapolis, 2003.
11. M. Vozalis and K. G. Margaritis. On the enhancement of collaborative filtering by demographic data. *Web Intelligence and Agent Systems, An International Journal*, 4(2):117–138, 2006.
12. J. Wang, A. P. deVries, and M. J. T. Reinders. Unifying user-based and item-based collaborative filtering approaches by similarity fusion. In *Proceedings of the 29th Annual International ACM SIGIR Conference on Research and Development in Information Retrieval*, pages 501–508, Seattle, Washington, 2006.

Towards Predicate Answer Set Programming via Coinductive Logic Programming

Richard Min, Ajay Bansal, Gopal Gupta

Department of Computer Science

The University of Texas at Dallas, Richardson, Texas, U.S.A.

Abstract Answer Set Programming (ASP) is a powerful paradigm based on logic programming for non-monotonic reasoning. Current ASP implementations are restricted to "grounded range-restricted function-free normal programs" and use an evaluation strategy that is "bottom-up" (i.e., not goal-driven). Recent introduction of coinductive Logic Programming (co-LP) has allowed the development of top-down goal evaluation strategies for ASP. In this paper we present this novel goal-directed, top-down approach to executing predicate answer set programs with co-LP. Our method eliminates the need for grounding, allows functions, and effectively handles a large class of predicate answer set programs including possibly infinite ones.

1 Introduction

Answer Set Programming (ASP) [1,2] is a powerful and elegant way for incorporating non-monotonic reasoning into logic programming (LP). Many powerful and efficient ASP solvers such as Smodels [3,4], DLV, Cmodels, ASSAT, and NoMoRe have been successfully developed. However, these ASP solvers are restricted to "grounded version of a range-restricted function-free normal programs" since they adopt a "bottom-up" evaluation-strategy with heuristics [2]. Before an answer set program containing predicates can be executed, it must be "grounded"; this is usually achieved with the help of a front-end grounding tool such as Lparse [5] which transform a predicate ASP into a grounded (propositional) ASP. Thus, all of the current ASP solvers and their solution-strategies, in essence, work for only propositional programs. These solution strategies are bottom-up (rather than top-down or goal-directed) and employ intelligent heuristics (enumeration, branch-and-bound or tableau) to reduce the search space. It was widely believed that it is not possible to develop a goal-driven, top-down ASP Solver (i.e., similar to a query driven Prolog engine). However, recent techniques such as Coinductive Logic Programming (Co-LP) [6,7] have shown great promise in developing a top-

---

Please use the following format when citing this chapter:

Min, R., Bansal, A. and Gupta, G., 2009, in IFIP International Federation for Information Processing, Volume 296; *Artificial Intelligence Applications and Innovations III*; Eds. Iliadis, L., Vlahavas, I., Bramer, M.; (Boston: Springer), pp. 499–508.

down, goal-directed strategy. In this paper, we present a goal-directed or query-driven approach to computing the stable model of an ASP program that is based on co-LP and coinductive SLDNF resolution [8]. We term this ASP Solver *coinductive ASP solver* (co-ASP Solver). Our method eliminates the need for grounding, allows functions, and effectively handles a large class of (possibly infinite) answer set programs. Note that while the performance of our prototype implementation is not comparable to those of systems such as S-models, our work is a first step towards developing a *complete* method for computing queries for predicate ASP in a top-down, goal driven manner.

The rest of the paper is organized as follows: we first give a brief overview of Answer Set Programming, followed by an overview of coinductive logic programming and co-SLDNF resolution (i.e., SLDNF resolution extended with coinduction). Next we discuss how predicate ASP can be realized using co-SLDNF. Finally, we present some examples and results from our initial implementation.

2 Answer Set Programming (ASP)

Answer Set Programming (ASP) and its stable model semantics [1-4] has been successfully applied to elegantly solving many problems in nonmonotonic reasoning and planning. Answer Set Programming (A-Prolog [1] or AnsProlog [2]) is a declarative logic programming language. Its basic syntax is of the form:

$$L_0 \text{ :- } L_1, \ldots, L_m, \text{not } L_{m+1}, \ldots, \text{not } L_n. \quad (1)$$

where L_i is a literal and $n \geq 0$ and $n \geq m$. This rule states that L_0 holds if $L_1, \ldots, L_m$ all hold and none of $L_{m+1}, \ldots, L_n$ hold. In the *answer set interpretation* [2], these rules are interpreted to be specifying a set *S* of propositions called the answer set. In this interpretation, rule (1) states that L_o must be in the answer set *S* if L_1 through L_m are in *S* and L_{m+1} through L_n are not *S*. If $L_0 = \bot$ (or null), then the rule-head is null (i.e., false) which forces its body to be false (a *constraint rule* [3] or a *headless-rule*). Such a constraint rule is written as follows.

$$\text{:- } L_1, \ldots, L_m, \text{not } L_{m+1}, \ldots, \text{not } L_n. \quad (2)$$

This constraint rule forbids an answer set from simultaneously containing all of the positive literals of the body and not containing any of the negated literals. A constraint can also be expressed in the form:

$$L_o \text{ :- not } L_o, L_1, \ldots, L_m, \text{not } L_{m+1}, \ldots, \text{not } L_n \quad (3)$$

A little thought will reveal that (3) can hold only if L_o is false which is only possible if the conjunction $L_1, \ldots, L_m$, not $L_{m+1}, \ldots$, not L_n is false. Thus, one can observe that (2) and (3) specify the same constraint.

The (stable) models of an answer set program are traditionally computed using the Gelfond-Lifschitz method [1,2]; Smodels, NoMoRe, and DLV are some of the well-known implementations of the Gelfond-Lifschitz method. The main difficulty in the execution of answer set programs is caused by the constraint rules (of the form (2) and (3) above). Such constraint rules force one or more of the literals $L_1, \ldots, L_m$, to be false or one or more literals "$L_{m+1}, \ldots, L_n$" to be true. Note that "not L_o" may be reached indirectly through other calls when the above rule is invoked in response to the call L_o. Such rules are said to contain an *odd-cycle* in the *predicate dependency graph* [9,10]. The predicate dependency graph of an answer set program is a directed graph consisting of the nodes (the predicate symbols) and the signed (positive or negative) edges between nodes, where using clause (1) for illustration, a positive edge is formed from each node corresponding to L_i (where $1 \le i \le m$) in the body of clause (1) to its head node L_0, and a negative edge is formed from each node L_j (where $m+1 \le j \le n$) in the body of clause (1) to its head node L_0. L_i *depends evenly (oddly, resp.) on* L_j if there is a path in the predicate dependency graph from L_i to L_j with an even (odd, resp.) number of negative edges. A predicate ASP program is *call-consistent* if no node depends oddly on itself. The *atom dependency graph* is very similar to the predicate dependency graph except that it uses the ground instance of the program: its nodes are the ground atoms and its positive and negative edges are defined with the ground instances of the program. A predicate ASP program is *order-consistent* if the dependency relations of its atom dependency graph is well-founded (that is, finite and acyclic).

3 Coinductive Logic Programming

Coinduction is a powerful technique for reasoning about unfounded sets, unbounded structures, and interactive computations. Coinduction allows one to reason about infinite objects and infinite processes [11,12]. Coinduction has been recently introduced into logic programming (termed *coinductive logic programming*, or co-LP for brevity) by Simon et al [6] and extended with negation as failure (termed *co-SLDNF* resolution) by Min and Gupta [8]. Practical applications of co-LP include modeling of and reasoning about infinite processes and objects, model checking and verification [6,7,13], and goal-directed execution of answer set programs [7,13]. Co-LP extends traditional logic programming with the *coinductive hypothesis rule* (CHR). The coinductive hypothesis rule states that during execution, if the current resolvent R contains a call C' that unifies with an ancestor call C encountered earlier, then the call C' succeeds; the new resolvent is R'θ where θ = mgu(C, C') and R' is obtained by deleting C' from R. Co-LP allows programmers to manipulate *rational* structures in a decidable manner. Rational structures are: (i) finite structures and (ii) infinite structures consisting of finite number of finite structures interleaved infinite number of times (e.g., a circular list). To achieve this feature of rationality, unification has to be necessarily extended with the "occur-check" removed and bindings such as **X = [1 | X]** (which denotes an infinite list of 1's) allowed [7, 14, 15]. SLD resolution extended with the coinductive hypothesis rule is called co-SLD resolution [6,7]. Co-SLDNF resolution, devised by us, extends co-SLD resolution with negation. Essentially, it augments co-SLD with the *negative coinductive hypothesis rule,* which states that if a negated call not(p) is encountered during resolution, and another call to not(p) has been seen before in the same computation, then not(p) coinductively succeeds. To implement co-SLDNF, the set of positive and negative calls has to be maintained in the *positive hypothesis table* (denoted χ+) and *negative hypothesis table* (denoted χ-) respectively. Note that nt(A) below denotes coinductive "not" of A.

Definition 3.1 Co-SLDNF Resolution: Suppose we are in the state (G, E, χ+, χ-). Consider a subgoal A $\in$ G:

(1) If A occurs in positive context, and A' $\in$ χ+ such that θ = mgu(A,A'), then the next state is (G', Eθ, χ+, χ-), where G' is obtained by replacing A with □.

(2) If A occurs in negative context, and A' $\in$ χ- such that θ = mgu(A,A'), then the next state is (G', Eθ, χ+, χ-), where G' is obtained by replacing A with false.

(3) If A occurs in positive context, and A' $\in$ χ- such that θ = mgu(A,A'), then the next state is (G', E, χ+, χ-), where G' is obtained by replacing A with false.

(4) If A occurs in negative context, and A' $\in$ χ+ such that θ = mgu(A,A'), then the next state is (G', E, χ+, χ-), where G' is obtained by replacing A with □.

(5) If A occurs in positive context and there is no A' $\in$ (χ+ $\cup$ χ-) that unifies with A, then the next state is (G', E', {A} $\cup$ χ+, χ-) where G' is obtained by expanding A in G via normal call expansion using a (nondeterministically chosen) clause C_i (where $1 \le i \le n$) whose head atom is unifiable with A with E' as the new system of equations obtained.

(6) If A occurs in negative context, and there is no A' $\in$ (χ+ $\cup$ χ-) that unifies with A, then the next state is (G', E', χ+, {A} $\cup$ χ-) where G' is obtained by expanding A in G via normal call expansion using a (nondeterministically chosen) clause C_i (where $1 \le i \le n$) whose head atom is unifiable with A and E' is the new system of equations obtained.

(7) If A occurs in positive or negative context and there are no matching clauses for A, and there is no A' $\in$ (χ+ $\cup$ χ-) such that A and A' are unifiable, then the next state is (G', E, χ+, {A} $\cup$ χ-), where G' is obtained by replacing A with false.

(8) (a) nt(..., false, ...) reduces to □, and (b) nt(A, □, B) reduces to nt(A, B) where A and B represent conjunction of subgoals. □

Note (i) that the result of expanding a subgoal with a unit clause in step (5) and (6) is an empty clause (□), and (ii) that when an initial query goal reduces to an empty (□), it denotes a success with the corresponding E as the solution.

Definition 3.2 (Co-SLDNF derivation): Co-SLDNF derivation of the goal G of program P is a sequence of co-SLDNF resolution steps (of Definition 3.1) with a selected subgoal A, consisting of (i) a sequence (G_i, E_i, χ_i+, χ_i-) of state ($i \ge 0$), of (a) a sequence G_0, G_1, ... of goal, (b) a sequence E_0, E_1, ... of mgu's, (c) a sequence

χ_0+, χ_1+, ... of the positive hypothesis table, (d) χ_0-, χ_1-, ... of the negative hypothesis table, where (G_0, E_0, χ_0+, χ_0-) = (G, ∅, ∅, ∅) is the initial state, and (ii) for step (5) or step (6) of Definition 3.1, a sequence C_1, C_2, ... of variants of program clauses of P where G_{i+1} is derived from G_i and C_{i+1} using θ_{i+1} where $E_{i+1} = E_i\theta_{i+1}$ and ($\chi_{i+1}+$, $\chi_{i+1}-$) are the resulting positive and negative hypothesis tables. (iii) If a co-SLDNF derivation from G results in an empty clause, that is, the final state of (□, E_i, χ_i+, χ_i-) is reached, then the co-SLDNF derivation is successful; a co-SLDNF derivation fails if a state is reached in the subgoal-list which is non-empty and no transitions are possible from this state. □

Note that due to non-deterministic choice of a clause in steps (5) and (6) of co-SLDNF resolution (Definition 3.1) there may be many successful derivations for a goal G. Thus a co-SLDNF resolution step may involve expanding with a program clause with the initial goal G = G_0, and the initial state of (G_0, E_0, χ_0+, χ_0-) = (G, ∅, ∅, ∅), and $E_{i+1} = E_i\theta_{i+1}$ (and so on) and may look as follows:

$$(G_0, E_0, \chi_0+, \chi_0-) \xrightarrow{C_1,\theta_1} (G_1, E_1, \chi_1+, \chi_1-) \xrightarrow{C_2,\theta_2} (G_2, E_2, \chi_2+, \chi_2-) \xrightarrow{C_3,\theta_3} \ldots$$

The declarative semantics of negation over the rational Herbrand space is based on the work of Fitting [12] (Kripke-Kleene semantics with 3-valued logic), extended by Fages [9] for stable model with completion of program. Their framework based on maintaining a pair of sets (corresponding to a partial interpretation of success set and failure set, resulting in a partial model) provides a good basis for the declarative semantics of co-SLDNF. An interesting property of co-SLDNF is that a program P coincides with its comp(P) under co-SLDNF.

The implementation of solving ASP programs in a goal-directed (top-down) fashion (just like Prolog) has been discussed in Gupta et al [7] for propositional answer set programs. Here, we show how it can be extended for predicate answer set programs.

4 Coinductive ASP Solver

Our current work is an extension of our previous work discussed in [7] for grounded (propositional) ASP solver to the predicate case. Our approach possesses the following advantages: First, it works with answer set programs containing first order predicates with no restrictions placed on them. Second, it eliminates the preprocessing requirement of grounding, i.e., it directly executes the predicates in the manner of Prolog. Our method constitutes a top-down/goal-directed/query-oriented paradigm for executing answer set programs, a radically different alternative to current ASP solvers. We term ASP solver realized via co-induction as *coinductive ASP Solver* (co-ASP Solver). The co-ASP solver's strategy is first to transform an ASP program into a *coinductive ASP* (co-ASP) program and use the following solution-strategy:

(1) Compute the completion of the program and then execute the query goal using co-SLDNF resolution on the completed program (this may yield a partial model).

(2) Avoid loop-positive solution (e.g., **p** derived coinductively from rules such as { **p :- p.** }) during co-SLDNF resolution: This is achieved during execution by ensuring that coinductive success is allowed while exercising the coinductive hypothesis rule only if there is at least one intervening call to 'not' in between the current call and the matching ancestor call.

(3) Perform an integrity check on the partial model generated to account for the constraints: Given an odd-cycle rule of the form { **p :- body, not p.** }, this integrity check, termed **nmr_check** is crafted as follows: if **p** is in the answer set, then this odd-cycle rule is to be discarded. If **p** is not in the answer set, then **body** must be false. This can be synthesized as the condition: **p** ∨ **not body** must hold true. The integrity check (**nmr_chk**) synthesizes this condition for all odd-cycle rules, and is appended to the query as a preprocessing step.

The solution strategy outlined above has been implemented and preliminary results are reported below. Our current prototype implementation is a first attempt at a top-down predicate ASP solver, and thus is not as efficient as current optimized ASP solvers, SAT solvers, or Constraint Logic Programming in solving practical problems. However, we are confident that further research will result in much greater efficiency; indeed our future research efforts are focused on this aspect. The main contribution of our paper is to demonstrate that top-down execution of predicate ASP is possible with reasonable efficiency.

Theorem 4.1 (Soundness of co-ASP Solver for a program which is call-consistent or order-consistent): Let P be a general ASP program which is call-consistent or order-consistent. If a query Q has a successful co-ASP solution, then Q is a subset of an answer set.

Theorem 4.2 (Completeness of co-ASP Solver for a program with a stable model): If P is a general ASP program with a stable model M in the rational Herbrand base of P, then a query Q consistent with M has a successful co-ASP solution (i.e., the query Q is present in the answer set corresponding to the stable model).

The proofs are straightforward and follow from soundness/completeness results for co-SLDNF [8] (along with Theorem 5.4 in Fages [9] that "an order-consistent logic program has a stable model"). The theorems can also be proved for unrestricted answer set programs, for queries extended with the **nmr_check** integrity constraint.

5 Preliminary Implementation Results

We next illustrate our top-down system via some example programs and queries. Most of the small ASP examples[1] and their queries run very fast, usually under 0.0001 CPU seconds. Our test environment is implemented on top of YAP Prolog[2] running under Linux in a shared environment with dual core AMD Opteron Processor 275, with 2GHz with 8GB memory.

Our first example is "move-win," a program that computes the winning path in a simple game, tested successfully with various test queries (Fig 5.1). Note that in all cases the **nmr_check** integrity constraint is hand-produced.

```
%% A predicate ASP, "move-win" program
%% facts: move
move(a,b). move(b,a). move(a,c). move(c,d). move(d,e).
move(c,f). move(e,f).
%% rule: win
win(X) :- move(X,Y), not win(Y).
%% query: ?- win(a).
```

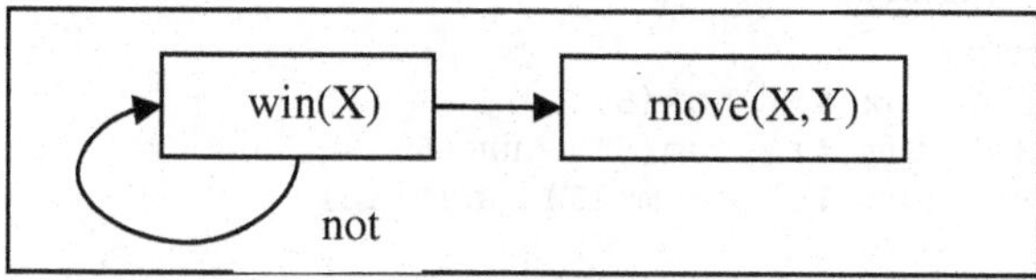

Fig. 5.1 Predicate-dependency graph of Predicate ASP "move-win".

The "move-win" program consists of two parts: (a) facts of move(x,y), to allow a move from x to y) and (2) a rule { win(X) :- move(X,Y), not win(Y). } to infer X to be a winner if there is a move from X to Y, and Y is not a winner. This is a predicate ASP program which is not call-consistent but order-consistent, and has two answer sets: { win(a), win(c), win(e) } and { win(b), win(c), win(e) }. Existing solvers will operate by first grounding the program using the move predicates. However, our system executes the query without grounding (since the program is order consistent, the nmr_check integrity constraint is null). Thus, in response to the query above, we'll get the answer set { win(a), win(c), win(e) }.

The second example is the Schur number problem for NxB (for N numbers with B boxes). The problem is to find a combination of N numbers (consecutive integers from 1 to N) for B boxes (consecutive integers from 1 to B) with one rule and two constraints. The first rule states that a number X should be paired with one and only one box Y. The first constraint states that if a number X is paired with a box B, then double its value, X+X, should not be paired with box B. The second con-

[1] More examples and performance data can be found from our Technical Report, available from: http://www.utdallas.edu/~rkm010300/research/co-ASP.pdf

[2] http://www.dcc.fc.up.pt/~vsc/Yap/

straint states that if two numbers, X and Y, are paired with a box B, then their sum, X+Y, should not be paired with the box B.

```
%% The ASP Schur NxB Program.
box(1). box(2). box(3). box(4). box(5).
num(1). num(2). num(3). num(4). num(5). num(6).
num(7). num(8). num(9). num(10). num(11). num(12).

%% rules
in(X,B) :- num(X), box(B), not not_in(X,B).
not_in(X,B) :- num(X),box(B),box(BB),B ≠ BB,in(X,BB).

%% constraint rules
:- num(X), box(B), in(X,B), in(X+X,B).
:- num(X), num(Y), box(B), in(X,B), in(Y,B), in(X+Y,B).
```

The ASP program is then transformed to a co-ASP program (with its completed definitions added for execution efficiency); the headless rules are transformed to craft the **nmr_check**.

```
%% co-ASP Schur 12x5 Program.
%% facts: box(b). num(n).
box(1). box(2). box(3). box(4). box(5).
num(1). num(2). num(3). num(4). num(5). num(6).
num(7). num(8). num(9). num(10). num(11). num(12).

%% rules
in(X,B) :- num(X), box(B), not not_in(X,B).
nt(in(X,B)) :- num(X), box(B), not_in(X,B).
not_in(X,B) :- num(X),box(B),box(BB),B\==BB, in(X,BB).
nt(not_in(X,B)) :- num(X), box(B), in(X,B).
%% constraints
nmr_chk :- not nmr_chk1, not nmr_chk2.
nmr_chk1 :- num(X),box(B),in(X,B),(Y is X+X),num(Y),in(Y,B).
nmr_chk2 :- num(X),num(Y),box(B),in(X,B),in(Y,B),
            (Z is X+Y), num(Z), in(Z,B).
%% query template
answer :- in(1,B1), in(2,B2), in(3,B3), in(4,B4),
      in(5,B5), in(6,B6), in(7,B7), in(8,B8), in(9,B9),
      in(10,B10), in(11,B11), in(12,B12).
%% Sample query: ?- answer, nmr_chk.
```

First, Schur 12x5 is tested with various queries which include partial solutions of various lengths I (Fig. 5.1; Table 5.1). That is, if I = 12, then the query is a test: all 12 numbers have been placed in the 5 boxes and we are merely checking that the constraints are met. If I = 0, then the co-ASP Solver searches for solutions from scratch (i.e., it will *guess* the placement of all 12 numbers in the 5 boxes provided subject to constraints). The second case (Fig 5.2; Table 5.2) is the general Schur NxB problems with I=0 where N ranges from 10 to 18 with B=5.

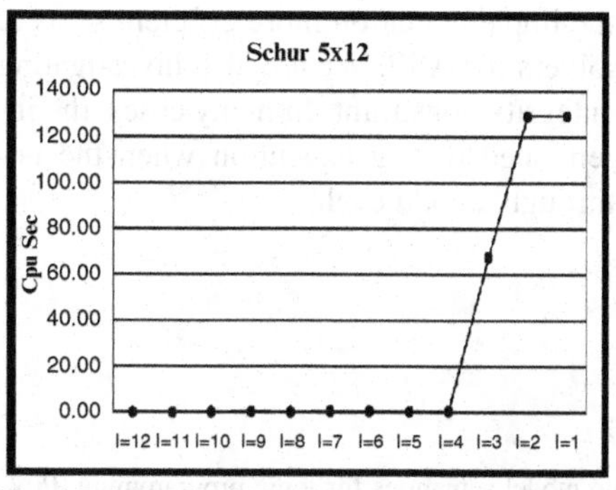

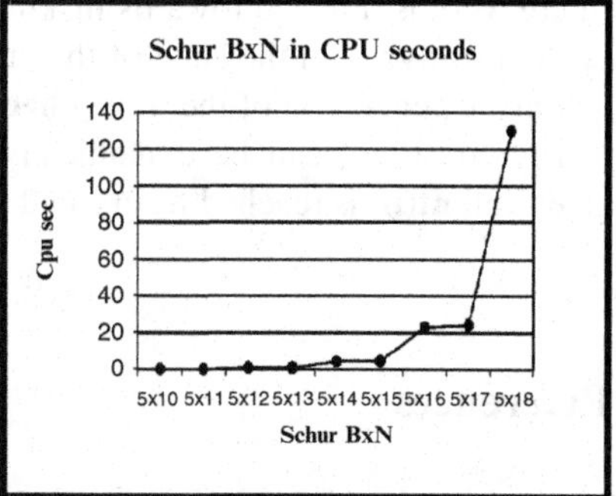

Fig. 5.2 Schur 5x12 (I=Size of the query). Fig. 5.3 Schur BxN (Query size=0).

Table 5.1 Schur 5x12 problem (box=1..5, N=1..12). I=Query size

Schur 5x12	I=12	I=11	I=10	I=9	I=8	I=7	I=6	I=5	I=4
CPU sec.	0.01	0.01	0.19	0.23	0.17	0.44	0.43	0.41	0.43

Table 5.2 Schur BxN problem (B=box, N=number). Query size=0, with a minor tuning.

Schur BxN	5x10	5x11	5x12	5x13	5x14	5x15	5x16	5x17	5x18
CPU sec.	0.13	0.14	0.75	0.80	0.48	4.38	23.17	24.31	130

The performance data of the current prototype system is promising but still in need of improvement if we compare it with performance on other existing solvers (even after taking the cost of grounding the program into account). Our main strategy for improving the performance of our current co-ASP solver is to interleave the execution of candidate answer set generation and nmr_check. Given the query **?- goal, nmr_check**, the call to **goal** will act as the generator of candidate answer sets while **nmr_check** will act as a tester of legitimacy of the answer set. This generation and testing has to be interleaved in the manner of constraint logic programming to reduce the search space. Additional improvements can also be made by improving the representation and look-up of positive and negative hypothesis tables during co-SLDNF (e.g., using a hash table, or a trie data-structure).

6 Conclusion and Future Work

In this paper we presented an execution strategy for answer set programming extended with predicates. Our execution strategy is goal-directed, in that it starts with a query goal G and computes the (partial) answer set containing G in a manner similar to SLD resolution. Our strategy is based on the recent discovery of coinductive logic programming extended with negation as failure. We also presented results from a preliminary implementation of our top-down scheme. Our future work is directed towards making the implementation more efficient so as to be competitive with the state-of-the-art solvers for ASP. We are also investigating automatic generation of the **nmr_check** integrity constraint. In many cases, the integrity constraint can be dynamically generated during execution when the negated call **nt(p)** is reached from a call **p** through an odd cycle.

References

1. Gelfond M, Lifschitz V (1988). The stable model semantics for logic programming. Proc. of International Logic Programming Conference and Symposium. 1070-1080.
2. Baral C (2003). Knowledge Representation, Reasoning and Declarative Problem Solving. Cambridge University Press.
3. Niemelä I, Simons, P (1996). Efficient implementation of the well-founded and stable model semantics. Proc. JICSLP. 289-303. The MIT Press.
4. Simons P, Niemelä I, Soininen, T (2002). Extending and implementing the stable model semantics. Artificial Intelligence 138(1-2):181-234.
5. Simons P, Syrjanen, T (2003). SMODELS (version 2.27) and LPARSE (version 1.0.13). http://www.tcs.hut.fi/Software/smodels/
6. Simon L, Mallya A, Bansal A, Gupta G (2006). Coinductive Logic Programming. ICLP'06. Springer Verlag.
7. Gupta G, Bansal A, Min R et al (2007). Coinductive logic programming and its applications. Proc. ICLP'07. Springer Verlag.
8. Min R, Gupta G (2008). Negation in Coinductive Logic Programming. Technical Report. Department of Computer Science. University of Texas at Dallas. http://www.utdallas.edu/~rkm010300/research/co-SLDNF.pdf
9. Fages F (1994). Consistency of Clark's completion and existence of stable models. Journal of Methods of Logic in Computer Science 1:51-60.
10. Sato, T (1990). Completed logic programs and their consistency. J Logic Prog 9:33-44.
11. Kripke S (1985). Outline of a Theory of Truth. Journal of Philosophy 72:690-716.
12. Fitting, M (1985). A Kripke-Kleene semantics for logic programs. Journal of Logic Programming 2:295-312.
13. Simon L, Bansal A, Mallya A et al (2007). Co-Logic Programming. ICALP'07.
14. Colmerauer A (1978). Prolog and Infinite Trees. In: Clark KL, Tarnlund S-A (eds) Logic Programming. Prenum Press, New York.
15. Maher, MJ (1988). Complete Axiomatizations of the Algebras of Finite, Rational and Infinite Trees. Proc. 3rd Logic in Computer Science Conference. Edinburgh, UK.

An Adaptive Resource Allocating Neuro-Fuzzy Inference System with Sensitivity Analysis Resource Control

Minas Pertselakis, Natali Raouzaiou and Andreas Stafylopatis

National Technical University of Athens

School of Electrical and Computer Engineering

9, Iroon Polytechneiou Str., Zografou, 157 80, Athens, Greece

Abstract Adaptability in non-stationary contexts is a very important property and a constant desire for modern intelligent systems and is usually associated with dynamic system behaviors. In this framework, we present a novel methodology of dynamic resource control and optimization for neurofuzzy inference systems. Our approach involves a neurofuzzy model with structural learning capabilities that adds rule nodes when necessary during the training phase. Sensitivity analysis is then applied to the trained network so as to evaluate the network rules and control their usage in a dynamic manner based on a confidence threshold. Therefore, on one hand, we result in a well-balanced structure with an improved adaptive behavior and, on the other hand, we propose a way to control and restrict the "curse of dimensionality". The experimental results on a number of classification problems prove clearly the strengths and benefits of this approach.

1 Introduction

The guiding principle of soft computing is to exploit the tolerance for imprecision by devising methods of computation that lead to an acceptable solution at low cost [1]. The presented paper, following the same philosophy, proposes a methodology that aims to reduce complexity as well as computational cost by applying a novel resource control-via-evaluation technique. This technique leads to a dynamic and robust network structure that abides by the demands of real time operation in non-stationary environments and by modern requirements concerning energy saving.

Structure identification in neurofuzzy modeling is a relatively underestimated field, in contrast to system parameters adjustment [2]. In most system design approaches, the structure, which usually implies the number of input and rule nodes, is presumed and only parameter identification is performed to obtain the coeffi-

---

Please use the following format when citing this chapter:

Pertselakis, M., Raouzaiou, N. and Stafylopatis, A., 2009, in IFIP International Federation for Information Processing, Volume 296; *Artificial Intelligence Applications and Innovations III*; Eds. Iliadis, L., Vlahavas, I., Bramer, M.; (Boston: Springer), pp. 509–516.

cients (e.g. weights) of the functional system. Even though the literature offers some heuristic but practical and systematic methodologies, the problem of structure determination in fuzzy modeling is yet to be solved [3]. There are many issues in practice that remain to be addressed; the "curse of dimensionality", which leads to high computational cost, and finding the optimum number of rules being the most significant.

A common approach which addresses these problems is node pruning. Node pruning aims to simplify a network by keeping only those nodes that contribute the most to the general solution of the problem at hand. Various such methods have been proposed in literature based on genetic algorithms, reinforcement learning or other soft computing techniques [4-5]. However, more often than not, most of these concepts eliminate the less desired nodes from the network (either input or rule nodes). This action usually leads to reduced computational cost but, on the other hand, it sacrifices bits of information that can affect performance [6].

Our methodology attempts to tackle the problem from a different perspective. On one hand, we propose an updated version of a resource allocating neurofuzzy system [7], which expands its rule base dynamically during training to accommodate more rules to capture the given problem efficiently. On the other hand, we apply a novel sensitivity analysis technique which aims to control and restrict rule usage in real-time. Therefore, we combine efficiently two techniques with opposing philosophies to exploit their advantages and eliminate their individual drawbacks through a hybrid product. The outcome is a well-balanced and possibly optimal rule structure. Experiments on various benchmark classification tasks show that this dynamic and robust approach offers almost the same accuracy as a complete rule base, but with significantly lower amount of computations and less execution time.

The paper is divided in the following sections: Section 2 summarizes the architecture and functionality of the resource allocating subsethood-product neurofuzzy model we employ, whereas in Section 3 we present our proposed methodology of rule base usage control, which relies on the statistical tool of sensitivity analysis. Experimental results can be found in Section 4, while useful deductions and plans for future research conclude the paper in Section 5.

2 Adaptive Resource Allocating Neuro-Fuzzy Inference System

Resource Allocating Network (RAN) architectures [8], were found to be suitable for online modeling of non-stationary processes. The original resource allocating system involved a sequential learning method where the network initially contained no hidden nodes. On incoming training examples, based on certain criteria, the RAN either grew to accommodate more nodes or the existing network parameters were adjusted using a least-mean-square gradient descent learning method.

In our case, a modified RAN methodology is combined with a modern fuzzy neural inference system, named ASuPFuNIS, which has been proven to be a universal approximator [9]. The produced hybrid, ARANFIS, maintains the original functional advantages of its predecessor, while, at the same time, exhibits data-driven knowledge extraction and online adaptation with a resource allocating architecture. During the sequential learning procedure, more hidden nodes can be added in case the few initial ones cannot represent the numerical data.

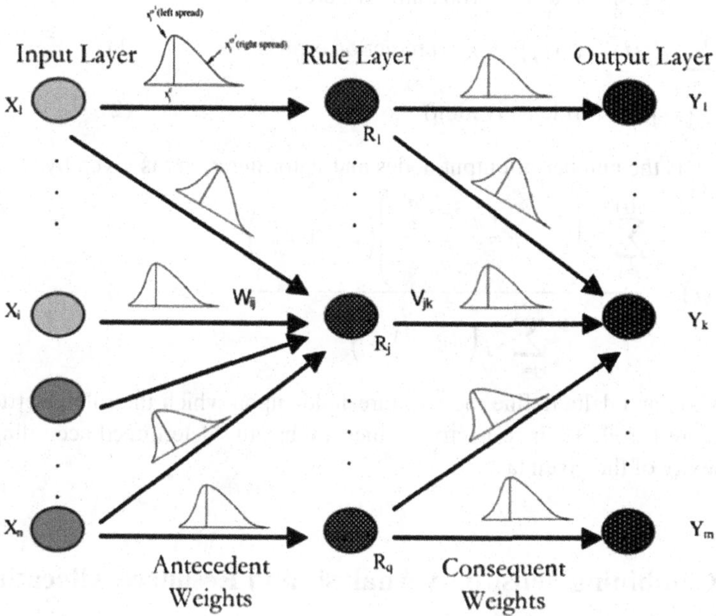

Fig. 1. ARANFIS architecture

ARANFIS architecture, with n input nodes, q hidden nodes and m output nodes, is shown in Fig. 1. Fuzzy antecedent weights are modeled by the center, left spread and right spread of an asymmetric Gaussian fuzzy set, and are denoted by $w_{ij} = (w_{ij}^{c}, w_{ij}^{\sigma^l}, w_{ij}^{\sigma^r})$. In a similar fashion, consequent fuzzy weights from rule node j to output node k are denoted by $v_{jk} = (v_{jk}^{c}, v_{jk}^{\sigma^l}, v_{jk}^{\sigma^r})$. The net activation (or rule strength) zj of rule node j is a product of all mutual subsethoods that fan-in to node j. The mutual subsethood E(A,B) measures the degree to which a fuzzy set A equals a fuzzy set B.

For more details concerning the evaluation and calculation of operational and learning parameters of the system, the reader is referred to [9] since they remain unchanged. The main novelty lies on the way ARANFIS allocates new rules during the learning procedure. Learning is incorporated into ARANFIS using the gradient descent method. Training data are supplied to ARANFIS in the form of pairs

($\underline{x}(t)$, $\underline{d}(t)$) of input and target vectors. If a new input $\underline{x}(t)$ does not significantly activate any rule and the prediction error is significantly large (eq. 1-2), a new hidden node is created, increasing the total number of rules and setting the crisp values of $\underline{x}(t)$ as the new weight centers of the antecedent part. The weight centers of the consequent connections are set as the difference between the desired and the defuzzified output. The respective weight spreads are initialized with random values in the interval (0,1], which will be fine-tuned as training evolves. The mathematical expressions for the two conditions are:

$$\frac{1}{m}\sum_{k=1}^{m}\left(d_k(t)-y_k(t)\right)^2 > \varepsilon \text{, (prediction error)} \quad (1)$$

$$\max_j\{z_j\} < \delta \text{, (rule activation)} \quad (2)$$

where m is the number of output nodes and y_k for iteration t is given by:

$$y_k(t) = \frac{\sum_{j=1}^{q(t)} z_j \left(v_{jk}^{c} + \frac{v_{jk}^{\sigma^r} - v_{jk}^{\sigma^l}}{\sqrt{\pi}} \right)\left(v_{jk}^{\sigma^l} + v_{jk}^{\sigma^r} \right)}{\sum_{j=1}^{q(t)} z_j \left(v_{jk}^{\sigma^l} + v_{jk}^{\sigma^r} \right)} \quad (3)$$

Epsilon and delta define the two thresholds upon which the rule insertion conditions are based. Their respective values are usually determined according to the complexity of the given task.

3 Combining Sensitivity Analysis and Resource Allocating Networks

Sensitivity analysis is a statistical tool that provides us with a way to estimate the influence of a slight change in value of one variable X towards another variable Y. In the field of neural networks it has been widely used as a method to extract the cause and effect relationship between the inputs and outputs of a trained network [10-12]. The input nodes that produce low sensitivity values can be regarded as insignificant and can be pruned from the system.

Obtaining the Jacobian matrix by the calculation of the partial derivatives of the output y_k with respect to the input x_i, that is $\partial y_k/\partial x_i$, constitutes the analytical version of sensitivity analysis [10]. Nevertheless, this method assumes that all input variables are numeric and continuous. When the input variables are discrete or symbolic, which is not rare in systems involving fuzzy attributes, the partial derivative cannot be deemed of practical significance.

Our methodology suggests the use of the activation strength z_j of rule j as our indicator of sensitivity towards the output variable y_k of the output node k. We opt to do this for two main reasons: First, the evaluation of the system rules is as important as the input features evaluation and secondly, the activation strength of a rule is a quantitative and differentiable variable for most modern neurofuzzy systems and thus, we can apply sensitivity analysis on a wide variety of algorithms, regardless of the data set and the nature of the input features. In this paper, we apply this concept on a trained ARANFIS network model with its fully grown rule base.

We define Rule Sensitivity RS_{kj} over a trained rule-output pair p as:

$$RS_{kj}^{(p)} = \frac{\partial y_k}{\partial z_j} \tag{4}$$

Using equation (3), Rule Sensitivity for ARANFIS becomes:

$$RS_{kj}^{(p)} = \frac{\left(v_{jk}^{\sigma^l} + v_{jk}^{\sigma^r}\right)\left(\left(v_{jk}^{c} + \frac{v_{jk}^{\sigma^r} - v_{jk}^{\sigma^l}}{\sqrt{\pi}}\right) - y_k\right)}{\sum_{j=1}^{q(t)} z_j \left(v_{jk}^{\sigma^l} + v_{jk}^{\sigma^r}\right)} \tag{5}$$

Since each training pair p produces a different sensitivity matrix, we evaluate RS over the entire training set and obtain the average matrix:

$$RS_{kj,avg} = \sqrt{\frac{\sum_{p=1}^{N} [RS_{kj}^{(p)}]^2}{N}} \tag{6}$$

where N is the total number of patterns of the given data set. To allow accurate comparison among the variables, it is necessary to scale activation values and outputs to the same range using:

$$RS_{kj,avg} = \frac{(\max_{p=1,\dots,N}\{z_j^{(p)}\} - \min_{p=1,\dots,N}\{z_j^{(p)}\})}{(\max_{p=1,\dots,N}\{y_k^{(p)}\} - \min_{p=1,\dots,N}\{y_k^{(p)}\})} \tag{7}$$

The RSavg matrix of the trained network shows, ultimately, the relation of each rule towards each output node. However, we need the relation of each rule towards the general outcome and so we define the significance Φ_j of rule z_j over all outputs as:

$$\Phi_j = \max_{k=1,\dots,K}\{RS_{kj,avg}\} \tag{8}$$

Our dynamic rule evaluation uses the significance Φ_j as a measure to classify the rules into two subsets based on a rather heuristic approach: If the significance Φ_j of a rule is larger or equal to 1 ($\Phi_j \geq 1$), this rule belongs to the main set of rules. Otherwise, if the significance Φ_j of a rule is less than 1 ($\Phi_j < 1$), this rule belongs to the secondary subset of rules. During real-time operation the system first employs the main rule set which carries the most information. If the output activation is below a confidence threshold, we add the rules of the second set, thus expanding our pool of knowledge as shown in figure 2.

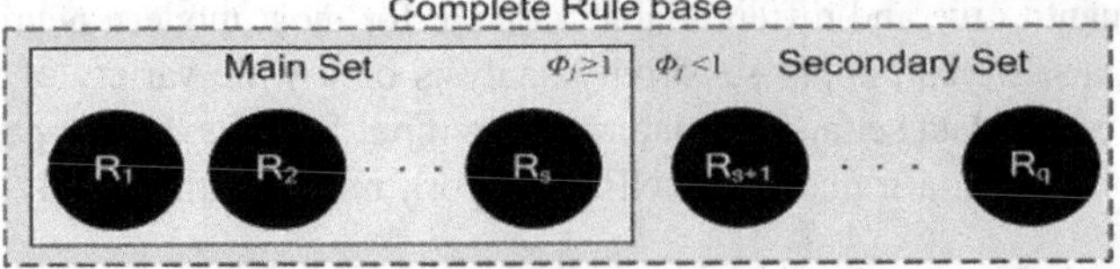

Fig. 2. The rule base split into two subsets.

The selected Confidence measure *Cf* is an extension of the method suggested in [13], where the reliability criterion for a classifier is the difference between the two greatest output values. In our approach, the confidence measure is slightly modified to accommodate more information:

$$Cf = (Ywin1 - Ywin2)*Ywin1 < CfT,$$

where Y_{win1} is the numerical value of the output node having the greatest value and Y_{win2} is the numerical output of the node having the second greatest value. If the confidence measure is below a certain threshold *CfT*, then the system considers the current rule-set insufficient and requests more rules to improve its results.

4 Experimental Results

To solidify our proposed method, a number of experiments were performed using five different datasets with various numbers of attributes as summarized in Table 1.

Table 1.Summarized dataset properties

Dataset	#of Patterns	#of Attributes	#of Classes
Pima Indians	768	8	2
Breast Cancer	699	9	2
Image Segmentation	2310	19	7
Ionosphere	351	34	2
Sonar	208	60	2

We split each dataset in a training set and a testing set on an approximate 60%-40% ratio. We then train our network for 100 epochs, using 0.001 as learning rate. The initialization of weights is random and the initial number of hidden nodes is set equal to 2. Comparisons were made based on the average of ten experiments performed for each dataset. It is worth noting that we compared not only network performance, but execution time values as well, and the percentage of patterns in which only the main subset of rules was employed, in contrast to the number of times the whole rule base was utilized. The careful observation of these factors shows the usefulness of our concept with respect to the computational cost of the network.

Table 2. Comparing properties and test performance for ARANFIS with and without Sensitivity Analysis Resource Control (SARC)

Dataset	Pima Indians	Breast Cancer	Image Segmentation	Ionosphere	Sonar
Epsilon, delta, CfT	0.5,0.1,0.7	0.5,0.1,0.8	0.4,0.1,0.6	0.4,0.1,0.8	0.4,0.1,0.7
Initial Rule number	2	2	2	2	2
Final Rule number (avg.)	8.5	14.5	12.8	48.3	36.4
Number of Main Rules ($\Phi_j \geq 1$)	2.6	4.1	7.7	14.3	21.4
ARANFIS Performance (%)	80.11	98.23	88.33	91.23	72.43
ARANFIS+SARC Performance (%)	**77.67**	**95.92**	**85.42**	**87.80**	**67.78**
ARANFIS Exec. Time (msec)	3.2	14.2	43.5	545.2	942.0
ARANFIS+SARC Exec. Time (msec)	**1.7**	**7.6**	**28.4**	**251.9**	**738.8**
Main rule set usage (%)	58.6	53.7	44.8	61.9	31.2

According to the results shown in table 2, system performance with sensitivity analysis resource control, is barely lower in average than the one without the rule usage restrictions. This may not seem beneficial, but if we take into account the flexibility, the lower overall cost and execution times of our proposed system, we can conclude that this network can be much more efficient and useful in practice.

5 Conclusions

In this paper we prove the efficiency that can be produced when one combines two different techniques of opposing philosophies. A novel neurofuzzy system which relies on a well-balanced and possibly optimal network structure is proposed. Our system is able to control its resource (rule) usage dynamically, through a confidence measure, which leads to lower computational cost and a flexible structure. The experimental study showed an improvement in resource usage of more than 30% with a minimal loss in network performance. It should also be noted that the number of main rules, selected by our method, could be an efficient indicator concerning the optimum number of hidden nodes required for a network and for a given task.

Nevertheless, our approach in its current form can be applied only on classification tasks due to its confidence measure. Thus, the need for an alternative criterion to address regression problems is an important issue under consideration. An interesting research topic of structure identification would also be the parallel evaluation of input and rule nodes with an analogous dynamic control mechanism, but this attempt certainly hides significant risks.

References

1. Zadeh L A (1994) Fuzzy logic, neural networks, and soft computing. Communications of the ACM 37:77-84
2. Jang JS R, Sun C-T, Mizutani E (1997) Neuro-Fuzzy and Soft Computing: a computational approach to learning and machine intelligence. Prentice-Hall Inc., NJ
3. Jang JS R (1994) Structure determination in fuzzy modeling: a fuzzy CART approach. Proceedings IEEE 3rd International Conf on Fuzzy Systems 1:480-485
4. Pal T, Pal NR (2003) SOGARG: A Self-Organized Genetic Algorithm-based Rule Generation Scheme for Fuzzy Controllers. IEEE Transactions on Evolutionary Computation, 7(4):397-415
5. Mitra S, Hayashi Y (2000) Neuro-Fuzzy Rule Generation: Survey in Soft Computing Framework. IEEE Transactions on Neural Networks 11:748-768
6. Nurnberger A, Klose A, Kruse R (2000) Effects of Antecedent Pruning in Fuzzy Classification Systems. Proceedings 4th International Conference on Knowledge-Based Intelligent Engineering Systems and Allied Technologies 1:154-157
7. Pertselakis M, Tsapatsoulis N, Kollias S, Stafylopatis A (2003) An adaptive resource allocating neural fuzzy inference system. Proceedings IEEE 12th Intelligent Systems Application to Power Systems (electronic proceedings)
8. Platt J (1991) A resource-allocating network for function interpolation. Neural Computing 3(2):213-225
9. Velayutham CS, Kumar S (2005) Asymmetric Subsethood-Product Fuzzy Neural Inference System (ASuPFuNIS). IEEE Transactions on Neural Networks 16(1):160-174
10. Engelbrecht P, Cloete I, Zurada JM (1995) Determining the significance of input parameters using sensitivity analysis. In: Miral J, Sandoval F (eds) From Natural to Artificial Neural Computing, LNCS, 930:382-388
11. Zurada JM, Malinowski A, Cloete I (1994) Sensitivity Analysis for Minimization of Input Data Dimension for Feedforward Neural Network. Proceedings IEEE Symposium on Circuits and Systems, 447-450
12. Howes P, Crook N (1999) Using Input Parameter Influences to Support the Decisions of Feedforward Neural Networks. Neurocomputing 24(1-3):191-206
13. Cordella LP, Foggia P, Sansone C, Tortorella F, Vento M (1999) Reliability Parameters to Improve Combination Strategies in Multi-Expert Systems. Pattern Analysis and Application 2:205-214

A Lazy Approach for Machine Learning Algorithms

Inés M. Galván, José M. Valls, Nicolas Lecomte and Pedro Isasi

Abstract Most machine learning algorithms are eager methods in the sense that a model is generated with the complete training data set and, afterwards, this model is used to generalize the new test instances. In this work we study the performance of different machine learning algorithms when they are learned using a lazy approach. The idea is to build a classification model once the test instance is received and this model will only learn a selection of training patterns, the most relevant for the test instance. The method presented here incorporates a dynamic selection of training patterns using a weighting function. The lazy approach is applied to machine learning algorithms based on different paradigms and is validated in different classification domains.

1 Introduction

Lazy learning methods [1, 2, 9] defer the decision of how to generalize or classify until a new query is encountered. When the query instance is received, a set of similar related patterns is retrieved from the available training patterns set and it is used to classify the new instance. To select these similar patterns, a distance measure is used having nearby points higher relevance. Lazy methods generally work by selecting the k nearest input patterns to the query points, in terms of the Euclidean

Inés M. Galván
Universidad Carlos III, Leganés (Madrid) e-mail: igalvan@inf.uc3m.es

José M. Valls
Universidad Carlos III, Leganés (Madrid), e-mail: jvalls@inf.uc3m.es

Nicolas Lecomte
Universidad Carlos III, Leganés (Madrid) e-mail: nicolasm.lecomte@laposte.net

Pedro Isasi
Universidad Carlos III, Leganés (Madrid) e-mail: isasi@ia.uc3m.es

Please use the following format when citing this chapter:

Galván, I.M., Valls, J.M., Lecomte, N. and Isasi, P., 2009, in IFIP International Federation for Information Processing, Volume 296; *Artificial Intelligence Applications and Innovations III*; Eds. Iliadis, L., Vlahavas, I., Bramer, M.; (Boston: Springer), pp. 517–522.

distance. Afterwards, the classification or prediction of the new instances is based on the selected patterns. The most popular lazy algorithm is the k-nearest neighbor method [3]. In this case, the classification of the new sample is just the most common class among the k selected examples. A variant of this methods is the weighted k-nearest neighbor [3], which consists of weighting the contribution of each of the k neighbors. Other strategy is the locally weighted linear regression [2] that constructs a linear approximation over a region around the new query instance. The regression coefficients are based on the k nearest input patterns.

Most of the machine learning algorithms (MLA) -based on trees, rules, neural networks, etc.- are eager learning methods, in the sense that the generalization is carried out beyond the training data before observing the new instance. This is, first a model is built up using the complete training data set and, afterwards, this model is used to classify the test instances. Some times, eager approximations could lead to poor generalization properties because training data are not evenly distributed in the input space. In [4, 5] the authors show that the generalization capability of artificial neural networks is improved when a lazy approach is used. Instead of using the complete training data to train the neural networks, they are trained when a new instance is received using a selection of training samples, which helps to improve the performance of the neural networks.

In this work, we propose to build up classification models using a lazy strategy instead of an eager approach, as usual. The lazy learning approach basically consists on recognizing from the whole training data set the most similar samples to each new query to be predicted. Once a subset of training patterns is selected, the classification model is learned with that subset and used to classify the new query. The subset of relevant patterns is obtained using a weighting function, the inverse function, that assigns high weights to the closest training examples to the new query instance received. The lazy approach studied in this work can be applied to any MLA. In this work, it is applied to classification algorithms based on different paradigms, specifically C4.5, PART, Support Vector Machine and NaiveBayes algorithms. Different classification domains are used to validate the method and the results show that the lazy approach can reach better generalization properties.

2 Lazy Approach for Machine Learning Algorithms

The general idea consists of learning a classification model for each query instance using only a selection of training patterns. A key issue of this method is to weight the examples in relation to their distance to the query instance in such a way that the closest examples have the highest weight. The selected examples are included one or more times in the resulting training subset.

Next, we describe the steps of the lazy approach. Let us consider $\mathbf{q}$ an arbitrary testing pattern described by a n-dimensional vector. Let $X = \{(\mathbf{x_k}, y_k), k = 1, ..., N\}$ be the whole available training data set, where $\mathbf{x_k}$ are the input attributes and y_k the corresponding class. For each new pattern $\mathbf{q}$, the steps are the following:

1. The standard Euclidean distances d_k from the pattern **q** to each input training pattern are calculated.
2. In order to make the method independent on the distances magnitude, relative distances must be used. Thus, a relative distance d_{rk} is calculated for each training pattern: $d_{rk} = d_k / d_{max}$, where d_{max} is the distance from the novel input pattern to the furthest training pattern.
3. A weighting function or kernel function is used to calculate a weight for each training pattern from its distance to the test pattern. This function is the inverse of the relative distance d_{rk}:
$$K(x_k) = \frac{1}{d_{rk}};\ k = 1 \ldots N \tag{1}$$
4. These values $K(x_k)$ are normalized in such a way that the sum of them equals the number of training patterns in X, this is:
$$K_N(x_k) = \frac{N}{\sum_{k=1}^{N} K(x_k)} \cdot K(x_k) \tag{2}$$
5. Both the relative distance d_{rk} and the normalized weights $K_N(x_k)$ are used to decide whether the $k-th$ training pattern is selected and -in that case- how many times is included in the training subset. They are used to generate a natural number, n_k, following the next rule:
$$\begin{array}{ll} \text{if} \quad d_{rk} < r & \text{then} \\ \quad n_k = int(K_N(x_k)) + 1 & \\ \text{else } n_k = 0 & \end{array} \tag{3}$$
where $int(K_N(x_k))$ is the largest integer lower than $K_N(x_k)$. r is a parameter of the method and it means the radius of a n-dimensional sphere centered at the test pattern. The idea is to select only those patterns placed into this sphere.
6. A new training subset associated to the testing pattern **q**, named X_q, is built up. The $k-th$ training pattern from the original training set X is included in the new subset if it is in the sphere centered at test pattern **q** and radius r, this is $d_{rk} < r$. In addition, the $k-th$ pattern is placed n_k times randomly in the training subset X_q.
7. Finally, the MLA is trained using the new subset X_q. Thus, a local model will be built in order to predict the testing pattern class.

3 Experimental Results

In this paper we have applied the lazy proposed method to five domains from the UCI Machine Learning Repository [1]: Bupa, Diabetes, Glass, Vehicle and, Balance.

[1] http://archive.ics.uci.edu/ml/

All of them are classification domains with numerical attributes, although discrete attributes could also be used with the appropriate distance. Also, different MLAs have been chosen as the base algorithm. Although the lazy method can be applied to any MLA, in this work we have used an algorithm based on trees, C4.5 [7]; an algorithm based on rules, PART [7]; an algorithm based on functions approximations, Support Vector Machines [8]; and an algorithm based on probabilities, NaiveBayes [6].

The experiments were performed using the WEKA software package [10] that includes implementations of the classifiers mentioned before: J48 (a variant of C4.5), PART, SMO (an implementation of SVM) and NaiveBayes algorithm. The results for eager or traditional versions of MLAs are obtained directly with WEKA using for each classifier the default parameters provided by the tool.

The lazy method studied in this paper is implemented and incorporated in the WEKA Software. Thus, the comparison of eager and lazy versions is possible because the implementation and parameters of the base algorithms are identical in both eager and lazy approaches.

In all the experiments the attributes values have been normalized to the $[0,1]$ interval. For every domain and every MLA we performed 10 runs using 10-fold cross-validation, which involves a total of 100 runs. The success rate on validation data is averaged over the total number of runs.

When the lazy approach is applied, the relative radius is set as a parameter. In the cases where no training patterns are selected, due to the specific characteristics of the data space and the value of the radius, the lazy approach used the complete training data.

Table 1 displays the average success rate on validation data of the classifiers using the traditional or eager way and the lazy approach studied in this work for the different classification domains, respectively. In most domains and with most MLAs, the lazy approach is better that the eager version of the algorithms. Only, in few cases the performance of the lazy approach is similar to those provided by the eager version, but it is never worse. For instance, in Diabetes domain the performance of the lazy approach is equal than the eager one for all the classification algorithms. This also happens for some classifier in the other domains (Glass domain using J48, Vehicle Domain using Part, Balance using NaiveBayes). However, in most cases, the lazy approach provides a very important improvement.

When the performance of the MLA is poor, the lazy approach reaches more than 10% of improvement. For instance, this can be observed for the lazy version of SVM and NaiveBayes in Bupa and Glass domains, or for the lazy version of J48 in Balance domain.

Comparing both the eager and the lazy versions of all the algorithms, it is interesting to note that the best result in Bupa, Glass and Vehicle domains, is obtained by the lazy approach of one of the algorithms. In Table 1 the best classification rate for each domain is marked in bold. For the Bupa domain the best result is 68.90 %, for the Glass domain 74.20%, for Vehicle 77.78 %, all of them obtained by the lazy version of one of the algorithms. For the Diabetes and Balance domains, the results obtained by both the eager and the lazy approaches are the same.

Table 1 Classification rate: eager and lazy version of different MLAs

Domain	Algorithm	Eager Version	Lazy Version
Bupa	J48	65.84	67.43 (r=0.05)
	PART	65.25	66.81 (r=0.05)
	SVM	58.01	**68.90** (r=0.2)
	NaiveBayes	55.29	66.03 (r=0.2)
Diabetes	J48	74.68	74.68 (r=0.02)
	PART	73.05	73.05 (r=0.02)
	SVM	**76.93**	**76.97** (r=0.02)
	NaiveBayes	75.70	75.70 (r=0.02)
Glass	J48	73.61	73.79 (r=0.2)
	PART	73.32	**74.20** (r=0.2)
	SVM	57.81	70.17 (r=0.2)
	NaiveBayes	46.23	69.69 (r=0.2)
Vehicle	J48	73.61	73.79 (r=0.2)
	PART	73.32	**74.20** (r=0.2)
	SVM	57.81	70.17 (r=0.2)
	NaiveBayes	46.23	69.69 (r=0.2)
Balance	J48	77.82	85.10 (r=0.2)
	PART	83.17	85.36 (r=0.2)
	SVM	87.62	87.70 (r=0.1)
	NaiveBayes	**90.53**	**90.53** (r=0.1)

For the lazy version of MLAs we have made experiments with different radius values for each domain and each classification algorithm. The classification rates displayed in the second column of tables 1 correspond to the radius value that provided the best performance. We have observed that each domain could need a different radius value, because it depends on how the data are distributed in the input space. We have also observed that in some domains (Diabetes, Glass and Vehicle) the most appropriate radius value is the same, independently of the MLA used as base algorithm. However, in the Bupa domain for J48 and PART the most appropriate radius is 0.05 whereas for SVM and NaiveBayes is 0.2. This also happens in the Balance domain where the best result obtained by the lazy version of J48 and PART corresponds to a radius value of 0.2; conversely, SVM and NaiveBayes algorithms need a value of 0.1 to obtain the best rate. Certainly, the radius value is a parameter of the method. Each MLA might require a different number of training examples (which implies a different radius value) due to the different paradigms these methods are based on.

4 Conclusions

Most MLAs are eager learning methods because they build a model using the whole training data set and then this model is used to classify all the new query instances. The built model is completely independent of the new query instances. Lazy methods work in a different way: when a new query instance needs to be classified, a set of similar patterns from the available patterns set is selected. The selected patterns are used to classify the new instance. Sometimes, eager approximations could lead to poor generalization properties because training data are not evenly distributed in the input space and a lazy approach could improve the generalization results.

In this paper, we present a lazy method that can be applied to any MLA. In order to validate the method, we have applied it to some well-known UCI domains (Bupa, Diabetes,Glass, Vehicle and Balance Scale) using classification algorithms based on different paradigms, specifically C4.5, PART, Support Vector Machine and NaiveBayes algorithms. The results show that a lazy approach can reach better generalization properties. It is interesting to note that the lazy approaches are never outperformed by the eager versions of the algorithms. In Bupa, Glass and Vehicle domains the best results are obtained by the lazy version of any of the algorithms. In Diabetes and Balance domains the best results are obtained by both the eager and the lazy version of a specific algorithm. In some cases, when the eager versions of the algorithms have a poor performance, the lazy versions obtain a significant improvement.

Acknowledgements This article has been financed by the Spanish founded research MEC projects OPLINK:UC3M Ref:TIN2005-08818-C04-02 and MSTAR:UC3M Ref:TIN2008-06491-C04-03.

References

1. Aha D.W., Kibler D., Albert M.: Instanced-based learning algorithms. *Machine Learning*, 6:37–66 (1991).
2. Atkeson C.G., Moore A.W., Schaal S.: Locally weighted learning. *Artificial Intelligence Review*, 11:11–73 (1997).
3. Dasarathy, B.: Nearest neighbour(NN) norms: NN pattern classification techniques. *IEEE Computer Society Press* (1991).
4. Galvan I.M., Isasi P. , Aler R., Valls, J.M.: A selective learning method to improve the generalization of multilayer feedforward neural networks. *International Journal of Neural Systems*, 11:167–157 (2001).
5. Valls J.M., Galvan I.M., Isasi P.: Lrbnn: A lazy radial basis neural network model. *Journal AI Communications*, 20(2):71–86 (2007).
6. Langley P., Iba W., Thompson, K.: An analysis of bayesian classifiers. In *National Conference on Artificial Intelligence* (1992).
7. Quinlan R.: *C4.5: Programs for Machine Learning*. Morgan Kaufmann, San Mateo (1993).
8. Vapnik V.: *Statistical Learning Theory*. John Wiley and Sons (1998).
9. Wettschereck D., Aha D.W., Mohri T.: A review and empirical evaluation of feature weighting methods for a class of lazy learning algorithms. *Artificial Intelligence Review*, 11:273–314 (1997).
10. Witten I., Frank E.: *Data Mining: Practical Machine Learning Tools and Techniques*. Morgan Kaufmann (2005)

TELIOS: A Tool for the Automatic Generation of Logic Programming Machines

Alexandros C. Dimopoulos and Christos Pavlatos and George Papakonstantinou

Abstract In this paper the tool TELIOS is presented, for the automatic generation of a hardware machine, corresponding to a given logic program. The machine is implemented using an FPGA, where a corresponding inference machine, in application specific hardware, is created on the FPGA, based on a BNF parser, to carry out the inference mechanism. The unification mechanism is based on actions embedded between the non-terminal symbols and implemented using special modules on the FPGA.

1 Introduction

Knowledge engineering approaches have extensively been used in many application domains such as medicine, scheduling and planning, control, artificial intelligence [12] etc. The low power requirements, small dimensions, and real-time limitations, which are usually specified in such applications, impose the need of designing specialized embedded systems for their implementation [13]. Therefore, the possibility of exploiting knowledge engineering approaches in embedded systems, is of crucial importance.

The first machine introduced for the implementation of logic programs (PROLOG) was the Warren Abstract Machine (WAM) [2]. The 5th generation computing era was targeted towards this direction [1]. The cost for the implementation of such systems, along with their size, prevented their use in small scale applications in embedded system environments [13].

The effort of designing hardware capable of supporting the declarative programming model, for logic derivations, can now lead to intelligent embedded designs

Alexandros C. Dimopoulos · Christos Pavlatos · George Papakonstantinou
National Technical University of Athens, School of Electrical and Computer Engineering, Iroon Polytechneiou, Zografou 15773, Athens, Greece,
e-mail: {alexdem,pavlatos,papakon}@cslab.ece.ntua.gr

Please use the following format when citing this chapter:

Dimopoulos, A.C., Pavlatos, C. and Papakonstantinou, G., 2009, in IFIP International Federation for Information Processing, Volume 296; *Artificial Intelligence Applications and Innovations III*; Eds. Iliadis, L., Vlahavas, I., Bramer, M.; (Boston: Springer), pp. 523–528.

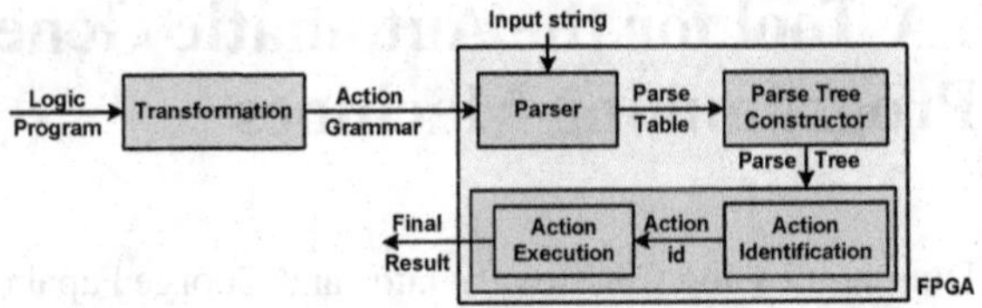

Fig. 1 Overview of our approach

which are considerably more efficient compared to the traditional ones. Some efforts have been done in the past, towards this direction [4], [11], [6] . In [4] a hardware parser was presented based on the CYK parsing algorithm. In [11] another hardware parser was presented based on the Earley's parallel algorithm [7]. Both parsers have been implemented using FPGAs. In [6] a similar approach to the one proposed here was presented. Nevertheless, the unification mechanism was implemented using softcore general purpose on chip processors, hence reducing drastically the speed up obtained by using the hardware parser.

In this paper the tool TELIOS (Tool for the automatic gEneration of LogIc prOgramming machineS) is presented. The user describes his logic program in a subset of PROLOG and the systems generates the necessary code to be downloaded to an FPGA (Field Programmable Gate Array). This FPGA is the machine for this specific logic program. The proposed implementation follows the architecture shown in Fig. 1. The given logic program can be transformed to an equivalent grammar, which feeds the proposed architecture, in order the different components to be constructed. The contribution of this paper is:

1. The modification of the hardware parser of [11], in order to be used for logic programming applications. It is noted that the parser of [11] is two orders of magnitude faster than the one used in [6].
2. The (automatic) mapping of the unification mechanism, to actions, easily implementable in FPGAs. To the best of the authors knowledge, this is the first effort to implement logic programs on FPGAs, without the use of an external real processor or a softcore one on the same chip.

2 Theoretical Background

Attribute Grammars (AG) [8] have been extensively used for logic programming applications [10], [5], [9]. The basic concepts for transforming a logic program to an equivalent AG are the following: Every inference rule in the initial logic program can be transformed to an equivalent syntax rule consisting solely of non-terminal symbols. Obviously, parsing is degenerate since there are no terminal symbols. For every variable existing in the initial predicates, two attributes are attached to the corresponding node of the syntax tree, one synthesized and one inherited. Those attributes assist in the unification process of the inference engine. For more details the user is referred to [10], [9]. The computing power required for the transformation of logic programs to AGs is the one of L-attributed AGs [8]. In these grammars the attributes can be evaluated traversing the parse tree from left to right in one pass.

In this paper it is shown that L-attributed AGs are equivalent to "action" grammars, which are introduced in this paper, due to their easy implementation in hardware. Hence, we can transform a logic program to an equivalent action grammar.

The Action Grammars, are defined in this paper as BNF grammars, augmented with "actions". Actions are routines which are executed before and after the recognition of an input substring corresponding to a non-terminal. In the rule: $< NT >::= \ldots [A_i] < NT_i > \ldots \quad < NT_j > [A_j]$, the actions to be taken are the execution of the routine A_i before recognizing the non-terminal NT_i and the execution of the routine A_j after the recognition of the non-terminal NT_j. The execution of A_i and A_j takes place after the generation of all possible parse trees. In the case of Earley's algorithm this is done in parallel, so that at the end of the parsing process all possible parse trees are available.

As it was stated before, it will be shown here that action grammars are equivalent to L-attributed grammars. For this purpose, some rules must be applied: 1) For each attribute (synthesized or inherited) a stack is defined, having the same name as the attribute. 2) At the end of each rule, unstacking of the synthesized attributes, of the descendant (children nodes) of the non-terminal at the left hand side of the rule (parent node), is done. These synthesized attributes are at the top of the stack. The synthesized attribute of the parent node is calculated according to the corresponding semantic rule and is pushed to the appropriate stack as shown in Fig. 2a. In this way, it is sure that at the top of the stack, the synthesized attributes of the children nodes of the parent (up to the corresponding child) are placed in sequence. 3) Regarding the inherited attributes: a) A push is done at the corresponding stack of the inherited attribute, the first time it is evaluated (produced). A pop is done at the time the inherited attribute is needed (consumed) as in Fig. 2b. b) If in a rule an inherited attribute is used in more than one children non-terminals (as in Fig. 2b), then the same number of pushes of that attribute should be done. c) If a value transfer semantic rule (for the same attribute) is needed in the AG, then no action is required for inherited and synthesized attributes (as in Fig. 2b). In Fig. 2, i is an inherited attribute, s a synthesized, x_i auxiliary (temporary) variables and the arrows indicate attribute dependencies.

The rules described above, will be further clarified with an example which follows.

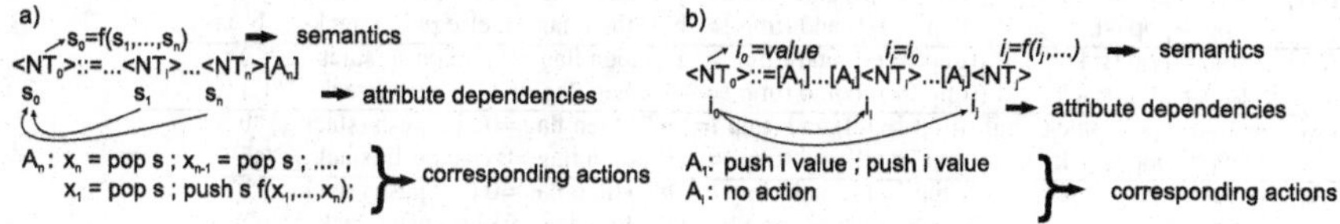

Fig. 2 a) Synthesized attribute example b) Inherited attribute example

3 An Illustrative Example

In order to clarify the aforementioned transformation, we demonstrate a toy-scale example of a logic program which is transformed to its action grammar equivalent one. Consider that we have the knowledge base (logic program) illustrated in Table 1 (First Column) and we want to ask the question "p is successor of whom?" i.e. $Successor(p,?)$. The syntax rules, which form the equivalent action grammar evaluator, are illustrated in Table 1 (Second Column) along with the definition of the actions. The equivalent action grammar does not contain any terminal symbols, therefore every fact P(x,y) is transformed to a syntactic rule of the form P $\rightarrow$ d, where d is a dummy symbol that is also used for the representation of the empty input string. The meta-variable *flag* arises from the transformation of the logic program to the equivalent AG. Its value is used by the attribute evaluator to discard useless subtrees, when it is equal to zero.

It is noted that we have four attributes, two for the two parameters of each predicate, and two (one inherited and one synthesized) for each parameter, denoted by P_{qr}. P_{qr} stands for parameter q of the predicates ($q \in \{1,2\}$ in our example) and r $\in$ {i,s} where i means inherited and s synthesized attribute. Hence, in our example we have the attributes P_{1i}, P_{2i}, P_{1s} and P_{2s}. For each attribute a stack is kept i.e. $stack_{1i}$, $stack_{2i}$, $stack_{1s}$ and $stack_{2s}$, respectively.

The question asked has two solutions, which are "j" and "b". The corresponding parse tree, decorated with the actions are illustrated in Fig. 3. A tracing of the execution of the actions (A_0, A_1, A_3, A_{11}, A_4, A_6, A_8, A_7, A_5, A_2 and A_0, A_1, A_6, A_{11},

Table 1 An AG equivalent representation of the knowledge based of the "successor problem"

Informal Definition of the Knowledge Base	Equivalent Action Grammar
1. Goal(X,Y) ← Successor(X,Y)	< *Goal* > ::= [A_1] < *successor* > [A_2]$
2. Successor(X,Y) ← Parent(Z,X) and Successor(Z,Y)	< *successor* > ::= [A_3] < *parent* > [A_4] < *successor* >[A_5]$
3. Successor(X,Y) ← Parent(Y,X)	< *successor* > ::= [A_6] < *parent* > [A_7] $
4. Parent(j,b)	< *parent* >::= d [A_8] $
5. Parent(j,l)	< *parent* >::= d [A_9] $
6. Parent (b,a)	< *parent* >::= d [A_{10}] $
7. Parent (b,p)	< *parent* >::= d [A_{11}] $
[A_1]→ no action	
[A_2]→ no action	
[A_3] → tmp_1 = pop ($stack_{1i}$);push($stack_{2i}$,tmp_1);push ($stack_{1i}$,nil)	
[A_4] → tmp_1 = pop ($stack_{1s}$);push($stack_{1i}$,tmp_1);	
[A_5]→ tmp_1=pop($stack_{2s}$); tmp_2=pop($stack_{2s}$);tmp_3=pop($stack_{1s}$);push($stack_{2s}$,tmp_1); push($stack_{1s}$,tmp_2);	
[A_6] → tmp_1 = pop ($stack_{2i}$); tmp_2 = pop ($stack_{1i}$); push ($stack_{1i}$, tmp_1); push ($stack_{2i}$, tmp_2);	
[A_7] → tmp_1 = pop ($stack_{2s}$); tmp_2 = pop ($stack_{1s}$); push ($stack_{1s}$, tmp_1); push ($stack_{2s}$, tmp_2);	
[A_8] → tmp = pop ($stack_{1i}$); if ((tmp != nil) and (tmp != "j")) then flag =0 else push ($stack_{1s}$, "j"); tmp = pop ($stack_{2i}$); if ((tmp != nil) and (tmp != "b")) then flag =0 else push ($stack_{2s}$, "b") ;	
[A_9] → tmp = pop ($stack_{1i}$); if ((tmp != nil) and (tmp != "j")) then flag =0 else push ($stack_{1s}$, "j") ; tmp = pop ($stack_{2i}$); if ((tmp != nil) and (tmp != "l")) then flag =0 else push ($stack_{2s}$, "l") ;	
[A_{10}] → tmp = pop ($stack_{1i}$); if ((tmp != nil) and (tmp != "b")) then flag =0 else push ($stack_{1s}$, "b") ; tmp = pop ($stack_{2i}$); if ((tmp != nil) and (tmp != "a")) then flag =0 else push ($stack_{2s}$, "a") ;	
[A_{11}] → tmp = pop ($stack_{1i}$); if ((tmp != nil) and (tmp != "b")) then flag =0 else push ($stack_{1s}$, "b") ; tmp = pop ($stack_{2i}$); if ((tmp != nil) and (tmp != "p")) then flag =0 else push ($stack_{2s}$, "p") ;	
Goal (p,x)	< *Goal* > ::= [A_0] $
[A_0] → push ($stack_{1i}$, p);push ($stack_{2i}$, nil);	

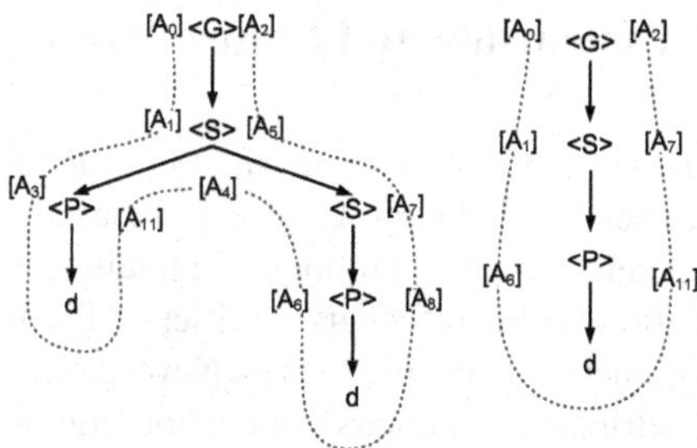

Fig. 3 Parse trees for the "successor" example leading to solutions (Note that tree traversal is top-bottom, left to right)

A_7, A_2 for the two parse trees) will leave at the top of the stack $stack_{2s}$ the values "j", "b" respectively. The predicate names have been abbreviated.

4 Implementation

Chiang & Fu [3] parallelized Early's parsing algorithm [7], introducing a new operator $\otimes$ and proposed a new architecture which requires $\frac{n*(n+1)}{2}$ processing elements (PEs) for computing the parse table. A new combination circuit was proposed in [11] for the implementation of the $\otimes$ operator. In this paper a modification of the parsing algorithm of [11] has been done in order to compute the elements of the parse table PT by the use of only n processing elements that each one handled the cells belonging to the same column of the PT.

It is obvious that since parsing is top-down, when recursion occurs and no input string is used (the empty string is the input string), we may have infinite creation of dotted recursion rule in the boxes. Hence, we have to predefine the maximum recursion depth as well as the maximum number of the input characters (d characters) in the input string, as installation parameters. The unification mechanism has been implemented through actions. The parse trees are constructed from the information provided by the parser. Actions are identified in the Action Identification module and executed in the Action Execution module (Fig. 1).

The system TELIOS has been implemented in synthesizable Verilog in the XILINX ISE 8.2[1] environment while the generated source has been simulated for validation, synthesized and tested on a Xilinx SPARTAN 3E FPGA. Furthermore, it has been tested with hardware examples we could find in the bibliography and in all cases our system runs faster. In the case of the well-documented "Wumpus World Game" and of finding paths in a directed acyclic graph [6], our system was two orders of magnitude faster than the one of [6] required.

[1] Xilinx Official WebSite, http://www.xilinx.com

5 Conclusion and Future Work

The system is very useful in cases where rapid development of small scale intelligent embedded hardware has to be used in special purpose applications, locally in dangerous areas, in robotics, in intelligent networks of sensors e.t.c.. The system in its present form accepts a subset of PROLOG e.g. only variables and constants as parameters of the predicates. Nevertheless, since we have shown the equivalence of L-attributed grammars with action grammars and L-attributed grammars can cover many other characteristics of PROLOG [9] (e.g. functors), it is straightforward to extend our system. Future work aims at: 1) Combining the modules of parsing and action execution in one module so that parsing will be completely semantically driven. This will solve the recursion problem in a more efficient way. 2) Extending the power of the grammar from L-attributed to many passes ones. 3) Applying the tool in medical applications. 4) Extending the PROLOG subset used in this paper.

Acknowledgements This work has been funded by the project PENED 2003. This project is part of the OPERATIONAL PROGRAMME "COMPETITIVENESS" and is co-funded by the European Social Fund (80%) and National Resources (20%).

References

1. *Communications of the ACM*, 26(9), 1983.
2. Hassan Ait-Kaci. *Warren's abstract machine : a tutorial reconstruction*. MIT Press, 1991.
3. Y T Chiang and King-Sun Fu. Parallel parsing algorithms and VLSI implementations for syntactic pattern recognition. *IEEE Trans. on PAMI*, 6:302–314, 1984.
4. C. Ciressan, E. Sanchez, M. Rajman, and J.C. Chappelier. An fpga-based coprocessor for the parsing of context-free grammars. In *FCCM '00: Proceedings of the 2000 IEEE Symposium on Field-Programmable Custom Computing Machines*, page 236, Washington, DC, USA, 2000.
5. Pierre Deransart, Bernard Lorho, and Jan Maluszynski, editors. *Proceedings of the 1st International Workshop on Programming Language Implementation and Logic Programming, PLILP'88, Orléans, France, May 16-18, 1988*. Springer, 1989.
6. A. Dimopoulos, C. Pavlatos, I. Panagopoulos, and G. Papakonstantinou. An efficient hardware implementation for AI applications. *Lecture Notes in Computer Science*, 3955:35–45, April 2006.
7. Jay Earley. An efficient context-free parsing algorithm. *Commun. ACM*, 13(2):94–102, 1970.
8. Jukka Paakki. Attribute grammar paradigms a high-level methodology in language implementation. *ACM Comput. Surv.*, 27(2):196–255, 1995.
9. T. Panayiotopoulos, G. Papakonstantinou, and G. Stamatopoulos. Ai-debot paper. *Angewandte Informatik*, 88(5), 1988.
10. G Papakonstantinou, C Moraitis, and T Panayiotopoulos. An attribute grammar interpreter as a knowledge engineering tool. *Angew. Inf.*, 28(9):382–388, 1986.
11. C. Pavlatos, A. C. Dimopoulos, A. Koulouris, T. Andronikos, I. Panagopoulos, and G. Papakonstantinou. Efficient reconfigurable embedded parsers. *Computer Languages, Systems & Structures*, 35(2):196 – 215, 2009.
12. Stuart Russell and Peter Norvig. *Artificial Intelligence: A Modern Approach*. Prentice-Hall, Englewood Cliffs, NJ, 2nd edition edition, 2003.
13. Frank Vahid and Tony Givargis. *Embedded System Design: A Unified Hardware/Software Introduction*. WILEY, 2002.

GF-Miner: a Genetic Fuzzy Classifier for Numerical Data

Vicky Tsikolidaki, Nikos Pelekis, Yannis Theodoridis

Dept of Informatics, Univ of Piraeus, 80 Karaoli-Dimitriou St, GR-18534 Piraeus, Greece
URL: http://infolab.cs.unipi.gr
E-mail: {vtsikol, npelekis, ytheod}@unipi.gr

Abstract Fuzzy logic and genetic algorithms are well-established computational techniques that have been employed to deal with the problem of classification as this is presented in the context of data mining. Based on *Fuzzy Miner* which is a recently proposed state-of-the-art fuzzy rule based system for numerical data, in this paper we propose *GF-Miner* which is a genetic fuzzy classifier that improves *Fuzzy Miner* firstly by adopting a clustering method for succeeding a more natural fuzzy partitioning of the input space, and secondly by optimizing the resulting fuzzy if-then rules with the use of genetic algorithms. More specifically, the membership functions of the fuzzy partitioning are extracted in an unsupervised way by using the fuzzy c- means clustering algorithm, while the extracted rules are optimized in terms of the volume of the rulebase and the size of each rule, using two appropriately designed genetic algorithms. The efficiency of our approach is demonstrated through an extensive experimental evaluation using the IRIS benchmark dataset.

1 Introduction

Computational Intelligence techniques such as fuzzy logic, artificial neural networks, and Genetic Algorithms (GA) are popular research domains, since they are able to confront intricate engineering problems. Gas are search algorithms, based on natural genetics that offer strong search capabilities in complex spaces. The basic idea is to preserve a population of chromosomes that evolves through a process of competition and controlled variation [1]. On the other hand, fuzzy rules are a collection of linguistic statements that describe how a fuzzy inference system should make a decision regarding classifying an input. They combine two or more input fuzzy sets and associate with them an output. Many researchers have used GA to optimize Fuzzy Rule-Based Systems (FRBS), which are known as Genetic Fuzzy Rule Based System (GFRBS), as in approaches [2, 3] where GA are used

Please use the following format when citing this chapter:

Tsikolidaki, V., Pelekis, N. and Theodoridis, Y., 2009, in IFIP International Federation for Information Processing, Volume 296; *Artificial Intelligence Applications and Innovations III*; Eds. Iliadis, L., Vlahavas, I., Bramer, M.; (Boston: Springer), pp. 529–534.

for the automatic production of the knowledge base of a FRBS, which encodes the expert knowledge in the form of fuzzy rules.

In this paper we propose *GF-Miner* which is a genetic fuzzy classifier that is based on a fuzzy rule based system for numerical data, namely *Fuzzy Miner* [4]. *Fuzzy Miner* implements a heuristic fuzzy method for the classification of numerical data. *GF-Miner* adopts an improved unsupervised clustering method for succeeding a more natural fuzzy partitioning of the input space. Furthermore, a genetic process is devised that gets rid of needless rules from the initial set of rules and at the same time refines the rulebase by eliminating unnecessary terms from the fuzzy if-then rules. As such, *GF-Miner* optimizes not only the number of the produced rules but also their size constructing small rules of different sizes which are more comprehensible by the user and obtain higher classification accuracy.

Two are the most related works to the proposed approach. In [2] the authors create a rule base and optimize it by using two GA. The first GA constructs a rulebase of definite user-defined size. The number of fuzzy sets is static for every variable. The second GA reduces the fuzzy rule base by using the following fitness function: $FitnessFunction(C_i) = NPC(C_i) * (L - NR(C_i))$ where L is the number of rules generated in the previous stage, $NPC(C_i)$ is the number of Patterns Correctly Classified, and $NR(C_i)$ is the number of active rules.

In [3] the authors propose the construction of chromosome from already made fuzzy rules. The variables are separated also in a predefined number of fuzzy sets. The genetic algorithm codes the weights of attributes in the fuzzy rules. Every chromosome consists of real numbers that is the weights of the attributes in the fuzzy rules. The fitness function is the *Classification Accuracy Rate*.

In contradiction to the above approaches our work differs in three major points. First, *GF-Miner* allows the analyst to specify different number of fuzzy sets per input variable. Second, the number of generated rules is optimized by the GA and it is not predetermined by the user. Third, a more efficient fitness function is adopted, which as shown in the experiments, it obtains better results in terms of classification accuracy, while this is succeeded by maintaining a smaller rulebase.

Outlining the major issues that will be addressed in this paper, our main contributions are: a) *Fuzzy Miner* [4] is improved by proposing a new fuzzy partitioning method of the input space utilizing the Fuzzy C-Means (FCM) clustering algorithm [5], b) a genetic algorithm (i.e. GA_{SR}) is appropriately devised for the reduction of the size of the rules that are produced by the improved *Fuzzy Miner*, c) the number of the rules in the rulebase is reduced by the use of a second genetic algorithm (i.e. GA_{NR}) and d) the efficiency of our approach is demonstrated through an extensive experimental evaluation using the IRIS benchmark dataset.

The rest of the paper is structured as follows. Section 2 introduces the *GF-Miner,* describes its architectural aspects and the proposed fuzzy partitioning method. The proposed genetic process is described in Section 3, while Section 4 presents the results of our experimental study and evaluates our system. Finally, Section 5 provides the conclusions of the paper and some interesting research directions.

2 GF-Miner as an Extension of Fuzzy Miner

GF-Miner is based on *Fuzzy Miner* [4]. More specifically, it extends *Fuzzy Miner* by incorporating a more flexible and unsupervised way to partition the input space into fuzzy sets and improves it by optimizing its output with the use of GA.
Fuzzy Miner is composed of four principal components: a *fuzzification interface*, a *knowledge base*, a *decision-making logic* and a *defuzzification interface*. In *GF-Miner* we adapt the fuzzy partition in the database, and we optimize the rulebase of *Fuzzy Miner* (i.e. 1st level rulebase) in two different ways (i.e. 2nd and 3rd level rulebase). The architecture of *GF-Miner* is shown in Figure 1, while we elaborate on each of the components in the current and the following section.

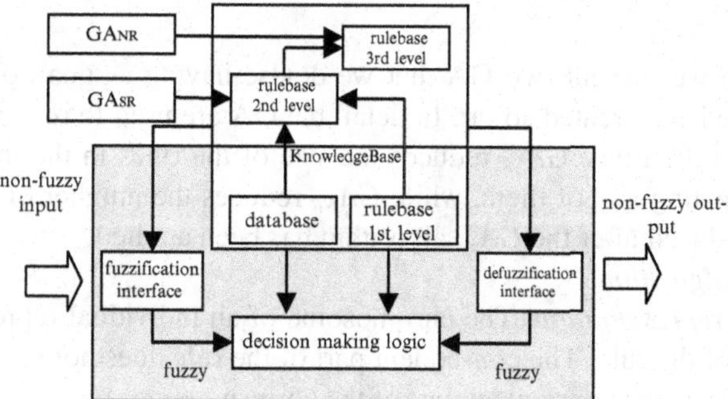

Fig. 1. GF-Miner architecture

The fuzzification interface performs a mapping that converts crisp values of input variables into fuzzy singletons. On the other end, the defuzzification interface performs a mapping from the fuzzy output of a FRBS to a crisp output.

Knowledge base: The knowledge base consists of a *database* and a *rulebase*.

Database - There are two factors that determine a database, i.e., a fuzzy partition of the input space and the membership functions of antecedent fuzzy sets. *GF-Miner* supports two types of membership functions, i.e. triangular and trapezoidal. The *Fuzzy Partition* partitions the input and output spaces to a sequence of fuzzy sets. In *GF-Miner* we use an unsupervised way to define the membership function by using the FCM clustering algorithm [5]. In Table 1 we show how we use the cluster centroids $V_i = \{V_1, V_2, \ldots V_{K_i}\}$, where K_i is the number of fuzzy sets for the *i*-th input variable x_i, to determine the parameters for every fuzzy set:

Table 1: Parameters for membership functions.

	Triangular	Trapezoidal
First fuzzy set:	$-\infty, x_{imin}, V_2$	$-\infty, -\infty, x_{imin}, V_2$
The next fuzzy sets: For j=1 to K_i -2:	V_j, V_{j+1}, V_{j+2}	$V_j, V_{j+1}-(V_{j+1}-V_j)/3, V_{j+1}+(V_{j+2}-V_{j+1})/3, V_{j+2}$
Last fuzzy set:	$V_{K_i-1}, x_{imax}, +\infty$	$V_{K_i-1}, x_{imax}, +\infty, +\infty$

Figure 2 depicts schematically the above fuzzy partition for a single variable.

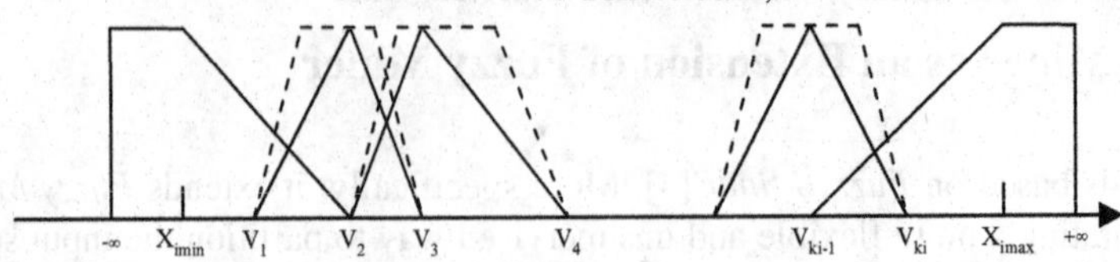

Fig. 2. Membership Function for Triangular and Trapezoidal

The rule base and the decision making logic are the same as in Fuzzy Miner [4].

3 The Genetic Process in GF-Miner

In this section we present two GA that we devise having as goal to optimize the rules that have been created so far. In detail the GA are used to reduce the number and the size of the rules. GA_{SR} reduces the size of the rules in the initial rulebase without eliminating any of them, while GA_{NR} reduces the number of the rules that have been produced after the GA_{SR} algorithm has been applied.

The GA_{SR} algorithm

Individual representation: The chromosome of an individual represents the antecedent part of the rule. The consequent part of the rule does not need to be coded and is the same as the consequent part of the corresponding rule.

Let *k* be the number of rules generated in the previous stage. Then a chromosome is composed of *k* genes, where each gene corresponds to a rule. Each *i* gene is partitioned into *n* binary fields where *n* is the number of input variables. We use 0 when the specific input variable is not important for the rule.

The GA_{SR} proceeds as follows:

Initial Population: It is generated randomly and we additionally introduce a chromosome that represents all rules, that is all genes will receive value 1.

Fitness Function: It is the number of the patterns correctly classified by the fuzzy rule base coded in the corresponding chromosome C_i: $FitnessFunction(C_i) = NPC(C_i)$, where $NPC(C_i)$ is the number of Patterns Correctly Classified.

Genetic Operators: For *selection* we use tournament selector and nonoverlapping populations. Furthermore, we use uniform *crossover* because this crossover operation does not take into account the position of every gene and the changes are randomly made. The *mutation* is done randomly according to the mutation probability and transforms 0 to 1 or 1 to 0. *As Stopping Condition* we used a maximum number of generations *m*. The new rule base is represented by the best chromosome with the best fitness value in the last generation.

Consequently, this GA reduces the number of rule conditions that are not important, thus their absence not affecting the number of Patterns Correctly Classified.

The GA_{NR} algorithm

As soon as the fuzzy rule base that has been created contains possibly redundant and/or unnecessary rules, and the aim of GA_{NR} is to eliminate some of them, having in mind that besides compactness the final rule base should continue giving high classification rates. In this genetic algorithm each individual encodes a set of prediction rules. The chromosomes are coded as a sequence of binary digits with the same length as the number of rules generated in the previous stage. Each gene is associated with one rule. If the binary digit is 1 the rule is active and the rule associated with this gene will be in the final rule base; otherwise will not. The crossover, mutation and stopping condition are the same we used in GA_{SR}. We use tournament selection and overlapping populations to reassure that the result will be the best, as in this case the best chromosomes of every generation are carried over to the next generation. As fitness function we use the following: $FitnessFunction(C_i) = CR(C_i)^2 * (L - NR(C_i) + 1)$, where $CR(C_i)$ is the Classification Rate, L is the number of rules generated in the previous stage and $NR(C_i)$ is the number of active rules. As a result we make sure that we keep a high Classification Rate and we decrease the number of active rules.

4 Evaluation of GF-MINER

We implemented the proposed method using C++ of Microsoft Visual Studio 6.0. The GA where implemented using the *GAlib* which is an object-oriented library of GA components [6]. The aim of our evaluation is twofold: on the one hand, we compare the classification accuracy of *GF-Miner* with the one of the initial FRBS *Fuzzy Miner* [4], while on the other hand, we compare it with two state-of-the-art genetically optimized approaches, namely [2] and [3], which are the most related to our approach. We used the IRIS dataset obtained from UCI repository of machine learning databases [7], which consists of 50 samples from each of 3 species of Iris flowers (*setosa, virginica* and *versicolor*) and 4 features were measured from each sample: the length and the width of sepal and petal.

The data set was partitioned randomly into training and test subset in two ways: *Partition A (70%)*: 105 instances for training and 45 instances for test.

Partition B (50%): 75 instances for training and 75 instances for test.

We used three fuzzy sets for every variable with triangular membership function to be compared with [3] and [2] where the writers use both triangular membership functions with three fuzzy sets. The classification rate and the number of rules are calculated as the average after 10 runs. We also show the minimum and the maximum values achieved by each partition.

The experimental results shown in table 2 prove that our approach presents better results than the other approaches as we can achieve a higher classification rate and still generate few rules. We observe that Fuzzy Miner has high classification rate but constructs many rules. As an improvement we see that GF-Miner increases the classification rate and at the same time reduces dramatically the number of the rules.

Table 2. Experimental Results

Partition	Approach	Classification Rate	#Rules
A	GF-Miner	Avg: 97,56 Max: 97,78Min: 95,56	Avg: 4,9 Max: 7 Min: 3
	Fuzzy Miner	95,56	15
	[2]	96,9	4
B	GF-Miner	Avg: 97,87 Max: 98,67 Min: 97,33	Avg: 4,6 Max: 6 Min: 4
	Fuzzy Miner	93,33	14
	[3]	96,33	3

5 Conclusions and Future Work

In this paper we propose *GF-Miner* which is a genetic fuzzy classifier that improves *Fuzzy Miner* [4] which is a recently proposed state-of-the-art FRBS for numerical data. More specifically, we used the FCM clustering algorithm to succeed a more natural definition of the membership functions of the fuzzy partition, while the extracted rules are optimized as far as the volume of the rulebase and the size of each rule is concerned, using two appropriately designed genetic algorithms. As future work we plan to evaluate *GF-Miner* using high dimensional datasets. Another direction will be to further improve the genetic algorithms to minimize their computational cost.

References

1. Cordón O, Gomide F, Herrera F, Hoffmann F, Magdalena L (2004) Ten years of genetic fuzzy systems: Current framework and new trends, Fuzzy Sets and Systems 41:5-31
2. Castro P, Camargo H (2005) Improving the genetic optimization of fuzzy rule base by imposing a constraint condition on the number of rules, V Artificial Intelligence National Meeting (ENIA), São Leopoldo, Rio Grande de Sul 972-981
3. Chen SM, Lin HL (2006) Generating weighted fuzzy rules from training instances using genetic algorithms to handle the Iris data classification problem. Journal of Information Science and Engineering 22: 175-188
4. Pelekis N, Theodoulidis B, Kopanakis I, Theodoridis Y (2005) Fuzzy Miner: Extracting Fuzzy Rules from Numerical Patterns. International Journal of Data Warehousing and Mining 57-81
5. Bezdek JC (1981) Pattern Recognition with Fuzzy Objective Function Algorithms. Plenum Press, New York
6. Wall M (1996) GAlib: A C++ Library of Genetic Algorithm Components, version 2.4, Documentation Revision B, Massachusetts Institute of Technology. http://lancet.mit.edu/ga/. Accessed January 19 2009
7. Blake CL, Merz CJ, (1998) UCI Repository of machine learning databases, Irvine, University of California, Department of Information and Computer Science. http://www.ics.uci.edu/~mlearn/MLRepository.html. Accessed January 19 2009

Fuzzy Dependencies between Preparedness and Learning Outcome

S. Encheva[1], S. Tumin[2]

[1]Stord/Haugesund University College

Bjørnsonsg. 45, 5528 Haugesund

Norway, sbe@hsh.no

[2]IT Dept., University of Bergen

PO Box 7800, 5020 Bergen

Norway, edpst@it.uib.no

Abstract There is a large number of learning management systems as well as intelligent tutoring systems supporting today's educational process. Some of these systems relay heavily on use and reuse of learning objects. A lot of work has been done on creating, storing, classifying and filtering learning objects with respect to a specific subject. Considerable amount of research focuses on facilitating the process of reusing already available learning objects. This work is devoted to a study of a decision making process related to recommending the most appropriate learning objects to each particular student.

1 Introduction

Learning objects are the core concept in an approach to learning content in which content is broken down into "bite size" chunks. These chunks can be reused, independently created and maintained, and pulled apart and stuck together like so many legos, [25].

Learning technology systems and interoperability standards providing reuse of learning objects and interoperability of content across delivery are developed by [21], [22], and [23].

SCORM [22] provides technical standards that enable web-based learning systems to find, import, share, reuse, and export learning content in a standardized way. However, SCORM is written for toolmakers who know what they need to do to their products to conform with SCORM technically.

Please use the following format when citing this chapter:

Encheva, S. and Tumin, S., 2009, in IFIP International Federation for Information Processing, Volume 296; *Artificial Intelligence Applications and Innovations III*; Eds. Iliadis, L., Vlahavas, I., Bramer, M.; (Boston: Springer), pp. 535–540.

IEEE Learning Object Metadata [21] defines a set of resource description framework constructs that facilitates introduction of educational metadata into the semantic web.

HarvestRoad Hive [23] is an independent, federated digital repository system. It enables the collection, management, discovery, sharing and reuse of LOs used in the delivery of online courses within higher education.

A lot of work has been done on creating, storing, classifying and filtering learning objects with respect to a specific subject. Considerable amount of research focuses on facilitating the process of reusing already available learning objects. This work is devoted to a study of a decision making process related to recommending the most appropriate learning objects to a particular student.

2 The Model

2.1 Conceptual modeling

A level-based instruction model is proposed in [11]. A model for student knowledge diagnosis through adaptive testing is presented in [3]. An approach for integrating intelligent agents, user models, and automatic content categorization in a virtual environment is presented in [6].

A learning style is the general, habitual mode of processing information; it is a predisposition on the part of some students to adopt a particular learning strategy regardless of the specific demands of the learning task: that is, individuals' learning styles are simply the cognitive styles that they evidence when confronted with a learning task [15]. According to the Kolb's model [8] there are four learners types - concrete, reflective, abstract, reflective, abstract, active, and concrete, active.

The three learning preferences are auditory (learning by hearing), visual (learning by seeing), and kinesthetic (learning by doing), [2].

Student learning orientations [9] are critical for individualizing the instructional process. The four learning orientations are transforming learners, performing learners, conforming learners, and resistant learners.

2.2 Concept lattices

A *concept* is considered by its *extent* and its *intent*: the *extent* consists of all objects belonging to the concept while the *intent* is the collection of all attributes shared by the objects [19]. A *context* is a triple (G, M, I) where G and M are sets and $I \subset G \times M$. The elements of G and M are called *objects* and *attributes* respectively. The set of all concepts of the context *(G, M, I)* is a complete lattice and it is known as the *concept lattice* of the context *(G, M, I)*.

2.3 Fuzzy membership

Fuzzy reasoning methods [20] are often applied in intelligent systems, decision making and fuzzy control.

A prediction method in [4] applies formal concept analysis and fuzzy inference. In particular it shows how to calculate the value of a membership function of an object if the object belongs to a particular concept. The *sum-of-1-criterion* states that $\Sigma_{i \in Mi} \mu_i(x) = 1, \forall x \in \chi$, where M_i, $i = 1, ..., k$ denotes all possible membership terms $\{m_i, i = 1, ..., k\}$ of a fuzzy variable in some universe of discourse χ.

An affiliation value to a concept represents the relative extent to which an object belongs to this concept or an attribute is common to all objects in the concept. The threshold for membership values is regarded as significant. This is obtained by computing the arithmetic mean of all entries within a column and take it as a threshold.

2.4 Multi criteria decision making methods

An extensive bibliography review on multi criteria decision making methods are summarised in [5] and [16]. Further interesting discussions may be found in [1], [7], [10] and [12].

Most human beings highly appreciate assistance in a form of well structured technique while working with complex decisions. The Analytic Hierarchy Process (AHP) developed by T. Saaty in 1980 [13] is one of those techniques and it has been applied in a number of different areas like government, business, industry, healthcare, and education. AHP involves mathematical programming, quality function deployment, meta-heuristics, strengths, weaknesses, opportunities and threats analysis and data envelopment analysis, [17] and [18]. The underlying concepts of AHP are structuring the complex decision problem as a hierarchy of goal, criteria and alternatives, pair-wise comparison of elements at each level of the hierarchy with respect to each criterion on the preceding level, and finally vertically synthesizing the judgments over the different levels of the hierarchy.

The analytic hierarchy process is a multi criteria decision making method [14] for working with multi attribute problems. A complex problem is broken down into smaller parts, further organized into levels. Then a hierarchical structure is generated. The goal is to determine the impact of a lower level on an upper level by paired comparisons done by a decision maker.

AHP facilitates estimation of the impact of each alternative on the overall objective of the hierarchy it is used as a consistency test to filter out inconsistent judgements.

2.5 The scenario

In this scenario all students, within a particular subject, are suggested to take a web based test at the beginning of a semester. Test results indicate lack of knowledge and skills, lack of understanding of certain concepts or misconceptions, that are prerequisites for studying that subject. Based on the test results students are placed in different groups. Suitable learning objects are later on suggested to each student based on her group membership.

At the initial stage group types are formed based on previous teaching experience. If such experience is missing the groups can be formed according to a lecture assumption. Group types are further tuned when more experience is obtained.

The theory of concept lattices is applied in establishing relationships among groups of learners and the subject content. The process of assigning a student to a particular group is based on fuzzy functions. Such functions allow partial group membership, i.e. a particular individual may belong to some extend to more than one group. This in contrast to classical set theory where an element is either within a set or does not belong to that set, [24]. This makes the approach much more dynamic, flexible and easy to adapt to the individual needs of each student.

Learning objects are first collected in a database. Metadata is attached to each learning object, describing content, size, purpose and recommended educational level. AHP methods are applied for assigning a learning object to a group and consequently to a student.

3 System

The system prototype is build as a Web-based application using *Apache* HTTP server, *mod_python* module and *SQLite* database. The *mod_python* module provides programmable runtime support to the HTTP server using Python programming language. The whole application components:

- Web-based users interface,
- application logic, and
- database interaction were written in Python.

The system implementation has Web application server architecture:

the presentation layer is handled by an Apache Web server,
the logic layer is written in Python, and
the data layer is implemented using SQLite database engine.

Python provides a programming environment for implementing script-based handler for dynamic content, data integration and users' software agents. The back end SQLite databases are used to store both static and dynamic data. Apache is a modular Web server that can incorporate a high level scripting language as a module such as f. ex. mod_python. Using mod_python, python interpreter becomes a part of the Web server. SQLite is a small footprint, zero-administration and serverless databasesystem. SQLite stores persistence data into files. SQLite thus provides a database platform for multiple databases.

4 Conclusion

While most efforts aim at providing a technology to access and share existing learning objects, much less is known about how to assign the most suitable learning objects for a student.

The proposed method can be used to determine the learning effect of using learning objects in a subject as well as qualities of a single learning object. Learning styles and learning preferences can be further employed in the process of choosing the most appropriate learning object for each student. In addition the applications of fuzzy functions allow partial group membership, i.e. a particular individual may belong to several groups. This makes the approach much more dynamic, flexible and easy to adapt to the individual needs of each student.

References

1. B. Cillo and T. Saaty, The Encyclicon, Volume 2: A Dictionary of Complex Decisions using the Analytic Network Process, 2008
2. R.Dunn, K.Dunn and G.Price, Manual: Learning style inventory, Lawrence, KS: Price Systems, 1985
3. E. Guzman, and R. Conejo, A model for student knowledge diagnosis through adaptive testing, Lecture Notes in Computer Science, vol. 3220, Springer-Verlag, Berlin Heidelberg New York, 2004, pp. 12-21
4. C. S. Herrmann, S. Holldobler, A. Strohmaier, Fuzzy conceptual knowledge processing, ACM Symposium on Applied Computing, 1996, pp. 628-632
5. W. Ho, Integrated analytic hierarchy process and its applications - a literature review. European Journal of Operational Research, vol. 186(1), pp. 211-228
6. D. Huffman, F. Goldberg, and M. Michlin, Using computers to create constructivist environments: impact on pedagogy and achievement, Journal of Computers in Mathematics and Science Teaching, vol. 22(2), 2003, pp. 151-168
7. K. P. Kearns and T. Saaty, Analytical Planning: The Organization of Systems, Pergamon, 1985
8. D. A. Kolb, Experiential Learning: Experience as the Source of Learning and Development, Englewood Cliffs, NJ: Prentice-Hall, 1984
9. M. Martinez and C. V. Bunderson, Building interactive Web learning environments to match and support individual learning differences, Journal of Interactive Learning Research, vol. 11(2), 2000, pp. 163-195.
10. M. S. Özdemir and T. Saaty, The Encyclicon, A Dictionary of Decisions with Dependence and Feedback based on the Analytic Network Process, with Müjgan S. Özdemir, 2005
11. C. Park, and M. Kim, Development of a Level-Based Instruction Model in Web-Based Education, Lecture Notes in Artificial Intelligence, vol. 3190, Springer-Verlag, Berlin Heidelberg New York, 2003, pp. 215-221

12. K. Peniwati and T. Saaty, Group Decision Making: Drawing Out and Reconciling Differences, 2007
13. T. Saaty, The Analytic Hierarchy Process: Planning, Priority Setting, Resource Allocation, McGraw-Hill, 1980
14. T. Saaty, Theory and Applications of the Analytic Network Process: Decision Making with Benefits, Opportunities, Costs and Risks, ISBN 1-888603-06-2, 2005
15. R.Schmeck, Learning Strategies and Learning Styles. New York: Plenum Press, 1988
16. R. E. Steuer, and P. Na, Multiple Criteria Decision Making Combined with Finance: A Categorized Bibliography, European Journal of Operational Research, vol. 150(3), 2003, pp. 496-515.
17. O.S.Vaidya and S.Kumar, Analytic hierarchy process: An overview of applications. European Journal of Operational Research, vol. 169(1), February 2006, pp. 1-29.
18. L.G. Vargas and T.Saaty, Decision Making with the Analytic Network Process: Economic, Political, Social and Technological Applications with Benefits, Opportunities, Costs and Risks, Springer, 2006
19. R. Wille, Concept lattices and conceptual knowledge systems, Computers Math. Applications, vol. 23(6-9), 1992, pp. 493-515
20. L.A.Zadeh, The concept of linguistic variable and its applications to approximate reasoning, Parts I, II, III, Information Sciences, 8(1975) pp. 199-251; 8(1975) pp. 301-357; 9(1975) pp. 43-80.
21. http://www.harvestroad.com/
22. http://www.adlnet.org/index.cfm?fuseaction=scormabt
23. http://kmr.nada.kth.se/el/ims/md-lomrdf.html
24. http://www.engsc.ac.uk/journal/index.php/ee/article/ view/
25. http://www.eduworks.com/LOTT/Tutorial/

Author Index